P9-DBM-911

FOOD & WINE

annual cookbook 2009

an entire year of recipes

FOOD & WINE ANNUAL COOKBOOK 2009

EDITOR **Kate Heddings**
DESIGNER **James Maikowski**
SENIOR EDITOR **Janice Huang**
ASSOCIATE FOOD EDITOR **Melissa Rubel**
COPY EDITOR **Lisa Leventer**
COPY FITTER **Zoe Singer**
EDITORIAL ASSISTANT **Emily Carrus**
PRODUCTION MANAGER **Matt Carson**
DEPUTY PHOTO EDITOR **Anthony LaSala**

FRONT COVER

Chile-Lime Crab Salad with Tomato & Avocado, P. 204
PHOTOGRAPH Quentin Bacon
FOOD STYLING Alison Attenborough
PROP STYLING Jessica Romm

BACK COVER

PHOTOGRAPH (SOUP) Earl Carter
PHOTOGRAPH (BISON) Cedric Angeles
FOOD STYLING (SOUP, BISON) Jee Levin
PHOTOGRAPH (COOKIES) Con Poulos
FOOD STYLING (COOKIES) Alison Attenborough

FLAP PHOTOGRAPHS

PORTRAITS Andrew French

AMERICAN EXPRESS PUBLISHING CORPORATION

PRESIDENT/C.E.O. **Ed Kelly**
S.V.P./CHIEF MARKETING OFFICER **Mark V. Stanich**
C.F.O./S.V.P./CORPORATE DEVELOPMENT & OPERATIONS **Paul B. Francis**
V.P./GENERAL MANAGER **Frank Bland, Keith Strohmeier**

V.P., BOOKS & PRODUCTS/PUBLISHER **Marshall Corey**
DIRECTOR, BOOK PROGRAMS **Bruce Spanier**
DIRECTOR, CUSTOMER RETENTION & LOYALTY **Greg D'Anca**
SENIOR MARKETING MANAGER, BRANDED BOOKS **Eric Lucie**
ASSISTANT MARKETING MANAGER **Lizabeth Clark**
DIRECTOR OF FULFILLMENT & PREMIUM VALUE **Phil Black**
MANAGER OF CUSTOMER EXPERIENCE &
PRODUCT DEVELOPMENT **Charles Graver**
DIRECTOR OF FINANCE **Thomas Noonan**
ASSOCIATE BUSINESS MANAGER **Desiree Bernardez**
PRODUCTION DIRECTOR **Rosalie Abatemarco Samat**
CORPORATE PRODUCTION MANAGER **Stuart Handelman**

ISBN 978-1-60320-054-7
ISSN 1097-1564

Published by American Express Publishing Corporation
1120 Avenue of the Americas, New York, New York 10036

Manufactured in the United States of America

FOOD & WINE MAGAZINE

S.V.P./EDITOR IN CHIEF **Dana Cowin**
CREATIVE DIRECTOR **Stephen Scoble**
MANAGING EDITOR **Mary Ellen Ward**
EXECUTIVE EDITOR **Pamela Kaufman**
EXECUTIVE FOOD EDITOR **Tina Ujlaki**
EXECUTIVE WINE EDITOR **Lettie Teague**

FEATURES

FEATURES EDITOR **Michelle Shih**
RESTAURANT EDITOR **Kate Krader**
SENIOR EDITOR **Christine Quinlan**
TRAVEL EDITOR **Jen Murphy**
STYLE EDITOR **Jessica Romm**
ASSOCIATE EDITOR **Ratha Tep**
EDITORIAL ASSISTANT **Alessandra Bulow**

FOOD

SENIOR EDITOR **Kate Heddings**
ASSOCIATE EDITORS **Kristin Donnelly, Emily Kaiser**
TEST KITCHEN SUPERVISOR **Marcia Kiesel**
SENIOR RECIPE DEVELOPER **Grace Parisi**
SENIOR ASSOCIATE RECIPE DEVELOPER **Melissa Rubel**

WINE

DEPUTY WINE EDITOR **Ray Isle**
ASSISTANT EDITOR **Megan Krigbaum**

ART

ART DIRECTOR **Courtney Waddell Eckersley**
SENIOR DESIGNER **Michael Patti**
DESIGNER **James Maikowski**

PHOTO

DIRECTOR OF PHOTOGRAPHY **Fredrika Stjärne**
DEPUTY PHOTO EDITOR **Anthony LaSala**
ASSISTANT PHOTO EDITOR **Nicole Schilit**
PHOTO ASSISTANT **Rebecca Stepler**

PRODUCTION

PRODUCTION MANAGER **Matt Carson**
DESIGN/PRODUCTION ASSISTANT **Carl Hesler**

COPY & RESEARCH

COPY CHIEF **Michele Berkover Petry**
SENIOR COPY EDITOR **Ann Lien**
ASSISTANT RESEARCH EDITORS **John Mantia, Emily McKenna, Kelly Snowden**

EDITORIAL BUSINESS COORDINATOR **Kerianne Hansen**

FOOD&WINE

annual cookbook
an entire year of recipes
2009

American Express Publishing Corporation, New York

FOOD&WINE
BOOKS

contents

foreword

Over the years, the recipes in FOOD & WINE Magazine have gotten simpler and more accessible, but after reviewing our latest collection, we were amazed at how truly streamlined they've become. Credit today's emphasis on using the best and freshest local ingredients (a mantra of the year): They're so delicious, they need little embellishment. This minimalist approach also reflects the reality of how people want to cook today—including the staff here at FOOD & WINE. Because the recipes are shorter, we can publish more of them in each issue of the magazine. This cookbook includes more than 700 recipes, an increase of over 100 from last year.

While chefs are still masters of the complex recipe, even they have started to accept that when it comes to translating their dishes for home cooks, simple is the way to go. Take a look at the recipes from F&W's 2008 Best New Chefs, among them the playful Greek Grilled Scallop Sandwiches from New York City's Michael Psilakis (p. 24) and the refreshing Chile-Lime Crab Salad with Tomato and Avocado (our cover) from New Orleans chef Sue Zemanick (p. 204). Each requires only 30 minutes to make yet is impressive enough for a dinner party.

In F&W's own Test Kitchen, where the mandate has always been to keep it simple, our cooks are creating ever-more innovative, ever-more doable recipes. One great example is Grace Parisi's incredible Green Jalapeño Hot Wings (p. 99), roasted (not fried), then tossed with hot sauce and pickled jalapeños. Another amazing dish: Melissa Rubel's Asian Chicken Salad with Wasabi Dressing (p. 104)— cleverly garnished with crunchy wasabi peas.

We hope this recipe collection leaves you feeling more efficient in the kitchen and more delighted in the dining room.

Dana Cowin
Editor in Chief
FOOD & WINE Magazine

Editor
FOOD & WINE Cookbooks

HONEY-TOMATO BRUSCHETTA
WITH RICOTTA (P. 13)

starters

66 Ricotta is so cool to make, and you don't have to be a rocket scientist to do it. . . . Have no fear. 99

—**MARIA HELM SINSKEY,** CULINARY DIRECTOR,
ROBERT SINSKEY VINEYARDS, NAPA

CLASSIC CHEESE FONDUE

BROILED RICOTTA WITH OLIVES AND SUN-DRIED-TOMATO RELISH

Grilled Mortadella and Robiola Packets

 TOTAL: 30 MIN
6 SERVINGS

Überchef Mario Batali advises seeking out Italian mortadella (cured sausage made from ground pork with a smooth, delicate flavor) for these wraps; American-made mortadella, he says, is no better than bologna. He also recommends exquisitely milky, creamy fresh robiola cheese, but says that fresh goat cheese or even ricotta would be acceptable stand-ins.

- 12 thin slices of mortadella
- 12 ounces fresh robiola or
      goat cheese
- 12 basil leaves
- 3 cups packed baby arugula leaves
- 2 tablespoons extra-virgin
      olive oil
- 1 tablespoon red wine vinegar

Salt

1. On a work surface, lay out 4 slices of the mortadella. Spoon some robiola in the center of each slice of mortadella and top the cheese with a basil leaf. Fold the mortadella over the cheese, fold in the sides to form a neat packet and secure it with toothpicks. Repeat with the remaining mortadella, robiola and basil.

2. Light a grill or preheat a grill pan. Grill the cheese and mortadella packets over high heat for about 1 minute per side, until the mortadella is lightly charred and the cheese has melted. Remove and discard the toothpicks.

3. In a bowl, toss the arugula with the olive oil and vinegar and season with salt. Transfer to a platter. Arrange the packets around the arugula and serve right away.
—*Mario Batali*

MAKE AHEAD The packets can be refrigerated for up to 4 hours. Bring to room temperature before grilling.

Kentucky Beer Cheese on Toast

 TOTAL: 25 MIN
6 SERVINGS

- 1 pound extra-sharp cheddar,
      cut into 1-inch cubes
- ¾ cup dark beer
- 2 medium garlic cloves, very
      finely chopped
- 1 tablespoon Dijon mustard
- ½ teaspoon cayenne

Salt

Toasted baguette slices from
2 baguettes

Sliced tomatoes

1. In a food processor, combine the cheddar with the beer, garlic, mustard and cayenne and blend until smooth. Season the beer cheese with salt.

2. Preheat the broiler. Spread the toasts with the beer cheese and arrange them on a rimmed baking sheet. Broil the cheese-topped toasts 6 inches from the heat for about 2 minutes, rotating the pan, until the cheese is bubbling and browned around the edges. Top with tomato slices and serve. —*Amber Huffman*

Classic Cheese Fondue

TOTAL: 20 MIN
10 SERVINGS ● ●

Chef Ryan Hardy of the Little Nell hotel in Aspen, Colorado, makes his luxurious fondue with two kinds of Swiss cheese (Emmentaler and Gruyère) and two kinds of spirits (white wine and kirsch), all traditional ingredients. Some of Hardy's dipping items are less conventional: He serves slices of house-cured salami and other hearty charcuterie alongside the classic cubes of crusty bread and pickles. All are wonderful with the winey, cheesy fondue.

- 1 pound Gruyère cheese, coarsely shredded
- 8 ounces Emmentaler cheese, coarsely shredded
- 1½ tablespoons cornstarch
- 1 garlic clove
- 1 cup dry white wine
- 1 tablespoon kirsch

Salt and freshly ground white pepper
Crusty bread cubes, hard salami and small dill pickles, for serving

In a bowl, toss the Gruyère and Emmentaler with the cornstarch. Rub the inside of a cheese fondue pot or medium enameled cast-iron casserole with the garlic clove, then add the wine and bring to a simmer. Add the cheese mixture all at once. Using a wooden spoon, stir over moderately low heat just until the cheese is melted and smooth, about 5 minutes. Stir in the kirsch and season with salt and pepper. Serve with the bread, salami and pickles. —*Ryan Hardy*

MAKE AHEAD The fondue can be refrigerated overnight and reheated in a microwave oven, or on the stove over low heat.

Broiled Ricotta with Olives and Sun-Dried-Tomato Relish

ACTIVE: 45 MIN; TOTAL: 1 HR 10 MIN
4 SERVINGS ●

Broiling ricotta intensifies its creaminess: It's ideal with both sweet and savory toppings. Here, Maria Helm Sinskey (an F&W Best New Chef 1996) serves it on garlic toasts garnished with olives and a tangy sun-dried-tomato relish.

- ½ cup drained oil-packed sun-dried tomatoes, thinly sliced
- 2 teaspoons very finely chopped shallot
- 2 teaspoons very finely chopped flat-leaf parsley
- 1 teaspoon chopped fresh oregano
- 1 teaspoon red wine vinegar
- ½ teaspoon finely grated lemon zest
- ¼ teaspoon crushed red pepper
- 2 tablespoons extra-virgin olive oil, plus more for brushing and drizzling

Salt

- 12 slices of peasant or ciabatta bread, about ½ inch thick
- 1 garlic clove
- 2 cups Creamy Ricotta (recipe follows)
- ¼ cup pitted oil-cured Italian black olives, coarsely chopped

1. Preheat the oven to 400°. In a small bowl, combine the sun-dried tomatoes with the shallot, parsley, oregano, vinegar, lemon zest, crushed red pepper and the 2 tablespoons of oil. Season with salt.
2. Brush the bread on both sides with oil and bake for about 10 minutes, until golden and crisp. Rub lightly with the garlic clove.
3. Preheat the broiler and position a rack 6 inches from the heat. Spread the ricotta in a shallow medium gratin dish in a ¾-inch-thick layer. Drizzle with oil and broil for about 10 minutes, turning the dish

occasionally, until the ricotta is bubbling and golden. Spoon the relish and olives on top. Serve with the garlic toasts. —*Maria Helm Sinskey*

CREAMY RICOTTA

ACTIVE: 20 MIN; TOTAL: 3 HR
MAKES ABOUT 1¾ POUNDS (3½ CUPS) ● ●

"I first tasted fresh ricotta when I was five," says Maria Helm Sinskey. "My great grandmother, who was straight from Italy, made it at her house." Fluffier, creamier and sweeter than even the best store-bought version, this ricotta is also incredibly easy to prepare.

- 2 quarts whole milk, preferably organic
- 1 cup heavy cream, preferably organic
- 3 tablespoons white vinegar
- ½ teaspoon kosher salt

1. In a medium pot, warm the milk and cream over moderately high heat until the surface becomes foamy and steamy and an instant-read thermometer inserted in the milk registers 185°; don't let the milk boil. Remove the pot from the heat. Add the vinegar and stir gently for 30 seconds; the mixture will curdle almost immediately. Add the salt and stir for 30 seconds longer. Cover the pot with a clean towel and let stand at room temperature for 2 hours.
2. Line a large colander with several layers of cheesecloth, allowing several inches of overhang. Set the colander in a large bowl. Using a slotted spoon, transfer the curds to the colander. Carefully gather the corners of the cheesecloth and close with a rubber band. Let the ricotta stand for 30 minutes, gently pressing and squeezing the cheesecloth occasionally to drain off the whey. Transfer the ricotta to a bowl and use at once, or cover and refrigerate. —*MHS*

MAKE AHEAD The fresh ricotta can be refrigerated for up to 4 days.

Crostini with Creamy Ricotta and Chorizo

TOTAL: 40 MIN PLUS OVERNIGHT DRAINING

6 SERVINGS

- 8 ounces fresh ricotta cheese
- 3 tablespoons extra-virgin olive oil, plus more for brushing
- Salt and freshly ground pepper
- Six ½-inch-thick slices of Italian peasant bread
- 2 small garlic cloves, 1 minced
- ¼ small red onion, thinly sliced
- 6 tablespoons balsamic vinegar
- 1 small dry chorizo (about 3 ounces), thinly sliced
- 1 tablespoon chopped tarragon
- 1 tablespoon chopped parsley
- 1 small head of frisée, tender white and light green leaves only

1. Put the ricotta in a fine sieve set over a bowl. Cover with plastic wrap and refrigerate overnight. Discard the liquid in the bowl. Wipe out the bowl, add the thickened ricotta and stir in 1 tablespoon of the olive oil and season with salt and pepper.

2. Preheat a grill pan. Lightly brush both sides of the bread slices with oil and grill, turning once, until toasted, about 3 minutes. Transfer the toasts to a platter and rub them with the whole garlic clove.

3. In a small bowl, toss the red onion with 2 tablespoons of the balsamic vinegar and let stand for 10 minutes; drain the onion, discarding the vinegar. Meanwhile, in a small saucepan, boil the remaining ¼ cup of balsamic vinegar until reduced to 1 tablespoon, about 5 minutes.

4. In a medium skillet, combine the remaining 2 tablespoons of oil with the minced garlic, chorizo, tarragon and parsley. Cook over low heat, stirring occasionally, just until warmed through, about 5 minutes.

5. Spread the ricotta on the toasts and top with the chorizo. Garnish with the frisée and pickled onion. Drizzle with the reduced balsamic and serve. —*Shea Gallante*

Chicken Liver Crostini

ACTIVE: 1 HR; TOTAL: 1 HR 30 MIN

MAKES 24 CROSTINI ● ●

New York City chef Peter Hoffman's beautifully silky chicken liver puree is accented with sweet sautéed apples, smoky bacon and a splash of brandy, then served on crunchy toasts. For a healthier version, omit the 4 tablespoons of butter in Step 4.

- 6 tablespoons unsalted butter, chilled
- 2 tablespoons extra-virgin olive oil
- 1 pound chicken livers, trimmed and patted dry
- 2 ounces thickly sliced bacon, cut into 1-by-¼-inch pieces
- 1 medium onion, finely diced
- 1 Golden Delicious apple—peeled, cored and cut into ¼-inch dice
- ¼ cup brandy
- Salt and freshly ground pepper
- 24 baguette slices, toasted
- Small sage leaves, for garnish

1. In a large skillet, melt 2 tablespoons of the butter in the olive oil until foaming. Add the chicken livers and cook over high heat, turning once or twice, until browned all over, about 3 minutes. Transfer the livers to a small bowl.

2. Add the bacon to the skillet and cook over moderate heat, stirring, until browned and crisp, about 5 minutes. Using a slotted spoon, transfer the bacon to a paper towel–lined plate to drain.

3. Add the onion to the skillet and cook over moderate heat, stirring frequently, until softened and lightly browned, about 10 minutes. Add the apple, reduce the heat to low and cook, stirring, until very soft and just beginning to break down, about 10 minutes longer. Add the brandy to the skillet and carefully ignite with a long match; let the alcohol burn off.

4. Add ¼ cup of the apple mixture to the bacon. Add the remaining apple mixture to a blender along with the chicken livers and blend until smooth. With the machine on, add the remaining 4 tablespoons of butter and puree until creamy. Pass the chicken liver mousse through a fine strainer into a bowl (omit this step for a chunkier mousse). Season with salt and pepper and refrigerate until firm, at least 30 minutes.

5. Spread the chicken liver mousse on the baguette toasts. Garnish with a little of the bacon-apple mixture and the sage leaves and serve at once. —*Peter Hoffman*

MAKE AHEAD The mousse and apple-bacon garnish can be refrigerated separately for up to 2 days. Return to room temperature before serving.

Broccoli Rabe Pesto Bruschetta

TOTAL: 30 MIN

12 SERVINGS ● ● ●

- 1 cup raw, shelled pistachios (5 ounces)
- 1 pound broccoli rabe, thick stems discarded
- 2 garlic cloves
- 2 cups flat-leaf parsley leaves
- ¾ cup extra-virgin olive oil
- 1 cup freshly grated Pecorino Romano cheese
- Kosher salt and freshly ground pepper

1. Preheat the oven to 350°. Spread the pistachios in a pie plate and toast for about 10 minutes, until fragrant and golden. Let cool to room temperature.

2. Meanwhile, bring a large saucepan of salted water to a boil. Add the broccoli rabe and cook until crisp-tender, 2 minutes. Rinse under cold water. Squeeze dry, then transfer to a cutting board and coarsely chop.

3. In a food processor, pulse the pistachios with the garlic until coarsely chopped. Add the parsley and broccoli rabe and pulse until finely chopped. Add the olive oil and process until incorporated. Stir in the pecorino, season with salt and pepper and serve. —*Gabe Thompson*

SERVE WITH Ciabatta toasts.

Roasted Root Vegetable Crostini with Basil Pesto

ACTIVE: 30 MIN; TOTAL: 1 HR 15 MIN
10 SERVINGS ●

- ¼ cup plus 2 tablespoons pine nuts
- ¼ cup freshly grated Parmigiano-Reggiano cheese
- 3 tablespoons freshly grated Pecorino Romano cheese
- 1 garlic clove, smashed, plus 1 head garlic halved crosswise
- 1 cup extra-virgin olive oil
- 4 cups basil leaves
- Salt and freshly ground pepper
- ¾ pound Jerusalem artichokes, peeled and cut into ½-inch dice
- ¾ pound parsnips, peeled and cut into ½-inch dice (2 cups)
- 2 thyme sprigs
- 2 tablespoons aged balsamic vinegar
- Ten ½-inch-thick slices of rustic white bread
- ¼ cup sliced almonds
- ½ pound imported Fontina cheese, thinly sliced

1. Preheat the oven to 400°. In a food processor, combine the pine nuts with the Parmigiano-Reggiano, Pecorino Romano, smashed garlic clove and ¾ cup of the olive oil and pulse until smooth. Add the basil and pulse until finely chopped. Season the pesto with salt and pepper.
2. In a roasting pan, toss the Jerusalem artichokes with the parsnips, thyme sprigs, garlic head and the remaining ¼ cup of olive oil. Season with salt and pepper. Roast the vegetables for 45 minutes, stirring occasionally, until tender and golden. Discard the garlic and thyme; stir in the vinegar.
3. Meanwhile, arrange the bread slices on a large baking sheet and toast in the oven until lightly browned, about 8 minutes. Spread the almonds in a pie plate and toast until golden, about 5 minutes.
4. Preheat the broiler and position a rack 6 inches from the heat. Spread each toast with a rounded tablespoon of the pesto.

Top with the roasted vegetables and Fontina. Broil for about 1 minute, until the cheese is just melted. Sprinkle with the toasted almonds and serve right away. —*Fabio Trabocchi*

Grilled Marrow Bones with Rosemary-Lemon Bruschetta

ACTIVE: 20 MIN; TOTAL: 40 MIN PLUS OVERNIGHT MARINATING
10 SERVINGS ●

Chef Chris Cosentino of San Francisco's Incanto restaurant uses the phrase "God's butter" to describe rich, decadent bone marrow. Here he serves it alongside grilled toasts rubbed with rosemary and lemon. For a more potent herbal flavor, singe the rosemary sprigs on the grill for a few moments before rubbing the toasts.

- ¼ cup rosemary leaves, plus 2 rosemary sprigs
- ¼ cup extra-virgin olive oil, plus more for brushing
- Twenty 2-inch center-cut beef or veal marrow bones
- Salt and freshly ground pepper
- 10 thick slices of country bread
- 1 small lemon, halved

1. In a mortar, gently pound the rosemary leaves with the ¼ cup of olive oil to flavor the oil. Transfer the oil to a large bowl. Add the marrow bones and toss to coat. Season with salt and pepper, cover with plastic wrap and refrigerate overnight.
2. Light a grill. When the coals are hot, rake them to one side. Wrap the marrow bones in foil in packets of 2 and arrange them on the grill opposite the coals. Cover and grill for about 20 minutes, until the marrow is warmed throughout and starting to sizzle. Carefully remove the bones from the foil and arrange them on a platter.
3. Brush the bread on both sides with oil and grill, turning once, until toasted, 3 minutes. Rub with the rosemary sprigs and cut lemon halves. Arrange around the marrow bones and serve. —*Chris Cosentino*

Honey-Tomato Bruschetta with Ricotta

ACTIVE: 20 MIN; TOTAL: 1 HR 45 MIN
6 SERVINGS ● ● ●

In this amazing appetizer, two types of honey serve two distinct purposes: Mellow, slightly spicy clover honey intensifies the sweetness of the tangy tomatoes as they slowly roast. After the bruschetta is assembled, a drizzle of robust buckwheat honey balances the creamy ricotta cheese.

- 2 pints cherry or grape tomatoes, halved lengthwise
- 1½ tablespoons extra-virgin olive oil
- 2 tablespoons clover honey
- 2 teaspoons thyme leaves
- 1 teaspoon kosher salt
- ⅛ teaspoon freshly ground pepper
- 12 baguette slices, cut ½ inch thick on the bias
- 8 ounces fresh ricotta cheese
- 1 tablespoon buckwheat or chestnut honey
- 6 basil leaves, thinly sliced or torn

1. Preheat the oven to 300°. Line a large rimmed baking sheet with parchment paper. In a large bowl, toss the tomatoes with the olive oil, clover honey, thyme leaves, salt and pepper. Scrape the tomatoes onto the prepared baking sheet and turn them cut side up. Bake the tomatoes for about 1 hour and 25 minutes, until they begin to shrivel and brown. Let cool.
2. Preheat the broiler. Spread out the baguette slices on a baking sheet. Broil for about 30 seconds on each side, until the edges are golden brown.
3. Spread the ricotta over the baguette slices and top with the slow-roasted tomatoes. Lightly drizzle the tomatoes with the buckwheat honey, sprinkle with the sliced basil and serve with additional buckwheat honey on the side. —*Susan Spungen*
MAKE AHEAD The roasted tomatoes can be refrigerated for up to 2 days. Bring to room temperature before serving.

starters

Lemony Chickpea Bruschetta

ACTIVE: 30 MIN; **TOTAL:** 2 HR 30 MIN
PLUS OVERNIGHT SOAKING
8 SERVINGS ● ● ○

Chef Gabe Thompson of Dell'anima restaurant in New York City tops bruschetta with pureed chickpeas flavored with preserved lemon (typically sold at specialty food stores).

- 2 cups dried chickpeas, soaked in cold water overnight and drained
- 1 small carrot
- 1 celery rib
- 1 small onion, halved
- 1 small fennel bulb, halved
- 5 garlic cloves
- 3 thyme sprigs
- 1 bay leaf
- ½ cup extra-virgin olive oil
- Kosher salt and freshly ground black pepper
- ½ cup chopped flat-leaf parsley
- 1 preserved lemon, pulp discarded and peel finely chopped
- 2 tablespoons fresh lemon juice

1. In a saucepan, cover the soaked and drained chickpeas with water. Add the carrot, celery, onion, fennel, garlic, thyme, bay leaf and ¼ cup of the olive oil. Bring to a simmer, cover and cook over low heat until the chickpeas are tender, about 1 hour. Let the chickpeas cool in the cooking liquid to room temperature, then drain, reserving ¾ cup of the cooking liquid. Remove and discard the vegetables and herbs.

2. Set aside ½ cup of the chickpeas. In a food processor, puree the remaining chickpeas with the reserved ¾ cup of cooking liquid and the remaining ¼ cup of oil. Season with salt and pepper. Scrape the puree into a large bowl, stir in the parsley, preserved lemon peel, lemon juice and the reserved ½ cup of chickpeas and serve.
—*Gabe Thompson*
SERVE WITH Ciabatta toasts.

Corn-and-Chanterelle Crostini

 TOTAL: 40 MIN
MAKES 40 CROSTINI ● ○

For this fast, flavorful appetizer, Paul Virant combines two of his favorite childhood memories about food. "During the summer, especially around the Fourth of July, we would pick chanterelles that grew around our property," he says. "And my grandmother made this amazing creamed corn. It turns out corn and chanterelles go very well together."

- 1 baguette, cut crosswise into forty ¼-inch-thick slices
- Extra-virgin olive oil, for brushing
- 2 tablespoons unsalted butter
- 1 large shallot, very finely chopped
- 6 ounces chanterelles, coarsely chopped
- 3 ears of corn, kernels cut from the cobs (2 cups)
- 1½ teaspoons chopped tarragon
- Salt and freshly ground black pepper

1. Preheat the oven to 400°. Arrange the baguette slices on 2 large cookie sheets and brush with olive oil. Bake for about 10 minutes, until crisp.

2. Meanwhile, in a large skillet, melt the butter. Add the chopped shallot and cook over moderate heat, stirring occasionally, until softened, about 2 minutes. Add the chopped chanterelles, cover and cook over moderate heat until the musrooms release their liquid, about 4 minutes. Add the corn kernels, cover and cook until the kernels are crisp-tender, about 5 minutes. Stir in the chopped tarragon and season with salt and pepper.

3. Spoon the chanterelle and corn mixture onto the crostini, arrange on a platter and serve the crostini immediately.
—*Paul Virant*
MAKE AHEAD The baguette toasts can be kept overnight in an airtight container.

Beet-and-Burrata Crostini

ACTIVE: 25 MIN; **TOTAL:** 1 HR 35 MIN
MAKES 40 CROSTINI ● ○

Beets are often thought of as a cold-weather vegetable, but Paul Virant (an F&W Best New Chef 2007) loves the sweet varieties, such as Chioggia, available from the late spring through the fall. For this crostini, Virant stacks roasted beets on top of buttery burrata (cream-filled mozzarella) that he buys from California's Caseificio Gioia, which makes a variety of traditional fresh Italian cheeses.

- 1 pound medium beets, preferably Chioggia
- 1 baguette, cut crosswise into forty ¼-inch-thick slices
- 1 tablespoon extra-virgin olive oil, plus more for brushing
- Salt and freshly ground pepper
- 9 ounces burrata, cut into 40 pieces
- Snipped chives, for garnish

1. Preheat the oven to 350°. Place the beets in a small roasting pan and add ¼ inch of water. Cover the pan with foil and bake for about 1 hour, until the beets are tender. Let cool completely.

2. Increase the oven temperature to 400°. Arrange the baguette slices on 2 large cookie sheets and brush with extra-virgin olive oil. Bake for about 10 minutes, until the bread is crisp.

3. Slip the beets out of their peels and halve them lengthwise, then cut the halves crosswise into ⅛-inch slices. Transfer the sliced beets to a bowl. Drizzle in the 1 tablespoon of olive oil, season the beets with salt and pepper and toss to coat.

4. Top each crostini with a piece of burrata and some beet slices. Garnish each beet-and-burrata bruschetta with a sprinkling of the snipped chives and serve immediately.
—*Paul Virant*
MAKE AHEAD The roasted beets can be refrigerated overnight. Slice and serve at room temperature.

CORN-AND-CHANTERELLE
CROSTINI AND BEET-AND-
BURRATA CROSTINI

ISRAELI HUMMUS WITH PAPRIKA AND WHOLE CHICKPEAS

SMOKED BLUEFISH PÂTÉ

Israeli Hummus with Paprika and Whole Chickpeas

ACTIVE: 30 MIN; TOTAL: 1 HR 15 MIN
PLUS OVERNIGHT SOAKING

MAKES 4 CUPS ● ● ○ ○

Before opening Zahav restaurant in Philadelphia, chef Michael Solomonov visited hummus parlors all over Israel trying to find the best recipe. "Hummus is the hardest thing to get right," he says. "It has to be rich, creamy and mildly nutty." To make his hummus supersmooth, he soaks the chickpeas overnight with baking soda to soften them. While Americans now flavor hummus with everything from pureed red peppers to fresh herbs, Solomonov says that among the fanciest garnishes you can find in Israel are whole chickpeas, paprika and lemon-spiked tahini, used for *hummus masabacha.*

- ½ pound dried chickpeas
- 1 tablespoon baking soda
- 7 large garlic cloves, unpeeled
- ½ cup extra-virgin olive oil, plus more for drizzling
- ¼ teaspoon ground cumin, plus more for garnish
- ½ cup tahini, at room temperature (see Note)
- ¼ cup plus 1 tablespoon fresh lemon juice

Salt

Paprika, for garnish

- ¼ cup chopped parsley

Pita bread, for serving

1. In a medium bowl, cover the dried chickpeas with 2 inches of water and stir in the baking soda. Refrigerate the chickpeas overnight. Drain the chickpeas and rinse them under cold water.

2. In a medium saucepan, cover the chickpeas with 2 inches of fresh water. Add the garlic cloves and bring to a boil. Simmer over moderately low heat until the chickpeas are tender, about 40 minutes. Drain, reserving 6 tablespoons of the cooking water and 2 tablespoons of the chickpeas. Rinse the chickpeas under cold water. Peel the garlic cloves.

3. In a food processor, puree the chickpeas with ¼ cup of the reserved cooking water, ¼ cup of the olive oil and 6 of the garlic cloves. Add the cumin along with ¼ cup each of the tahini and lemon juice and process until creamy. Season the hummus with salt and transfer to a serving bowl.

4. Wipe out the food processor. Add the remaining ¼ cup of tahini, ¼ cup of olive oil, 2 tablespoons of reserved cooking water, 1 tablespoon of lemon juice and garlic clove and puree.

5. Using a ladle, make an indent in the center of the hummus. Spoon in the tahini-lemon mixture. Sprinkle the hummus with cumin and paprika. Garnish with the reserved whole chickpeas and the parsley, and serve with pita bread.
—Michael Solomonov

NOTE Tahini has a tendency to separate, so be sure to stir the sesame paste thoroughly before measuring.

MAKE AHEAD The hummus, tahini-lemon mixture and cooked chickpeas can be refrigerated separately for up to 2 days.

Smoked Bluefish Pâté

TOTAL: 15 MIN
12 SERVINGS ● ●

This bluefish pâté from Amanda Lydon (an F&W Best New Chef 2000) and Gabriel Frasca, chefs at Nantucket's Straight Wharf Restaurant, has a rich, smoky flavor.

- **8** ounces cream cheese, softened
- **1** tablespoon Worcestershire sauce
- **1** tablespoon fresh lemon juice
- **1** tablespoon chopped parsley
- **½** medium red onion, very finely chopped
- **4 to 6** dashes of hot sauce
- **¼** cup minced chives
- **½** pound skinless, boneless smoked bluefish fillets, flaked

Toasts or crackers, for serving

In a bowl, blend the cream cheese with the Worcestershire sauce, lemon juice, parsley, onion, hot sauce and half of the chives. Fold in the smoked bluefish. Sprinkle the remaining chives on top and serve with toasts.
—Gabriel Frasca and Amanda Lydon

MAKE AHEAD The pâté can be refrigerated for up to 3 days.

Goat Cheese–Edamame Dip with Spiced Pepitas

TOTAL: 40 MIN PLUS 1 HR CHILLING
MAKES 4 CUPS ● ○ ◐

Canned chipotles in adobo sauce, sold at Latin markets and many supermarkets, give this clever, creamy dip an enticing heat and smokiness. The spiced *pepitas* (roasted and salted pumpkin seeds) scattered on top are addictive and great as a snack on their own.

DIP

- **1½** pounds shelled edamame
- **1** cup sour cream
- **5** ounces fresh goat cheese, crumbled
- **3** chipotles in adobo, chopped, plus 2 tablespoons of adobo sauce from the can
- **¼** cup fresh lemon juice
- **1** small garlic clove, chopped
- **2** teaspoons kosher salt
- **1** tablespoon chopped fresh oregano

PEPITAS

- **½** cup raw pumpkin seeds
- **1** teaspoon extra-virgin olive oil
- **½** teaspoon salt
- **¼** teaspoon ground coriander
- **¼** teaspoon crushed red pepper
- **1** teaspoon finely grated lemon zest
- **1** teaspoon chopped fresh oregano

1. MAKE THE DIP: In a medium pot of boiling salted water, simmer the edamame until tender, about 8 minutes. Drain well and transfer to a food processor. Add the

sour cream, goat cheese, chipotles, adobo sauce, lemon juice, garlic and salt and puree until smooth, scraping down the side of the bowl. Stir in the oregano and transfer the dip to a serving bowl. Cover with plastic wrap and refrigerate for at least 1 hour or overnight.

2. MAKE THE PEPITAS: Preheat the oven to 375°. On a rimmed baking sheet, toss the pumpkin seeds with the olive oil, salt, coriander and crushed red pepper. Bake for 7 minutes, until the seeds begin to brown. Transfer the *pepitas* to a bowl and toss with the lemon zest and oregano.

3. Serve the dip at room temperature, topped with the spiced *pepitas*.
—Rachel Soszynski

SERVE WITH Pita crisps.

MAKE AHEAD The dip can be refrigerated overnight; bring to room temperature before serving. The spiced *pepitas* can be kept in an airtight container for up to 3 days.

Sunflower Seed Dip with Dill

TOTAL: 10 MIN
6 SERVINGS ● ●

This is more than just a dip—you can also eat it wrapped in a piece of lettuce, or scooped on top of a salad with a drizzle of olive oil.

- **2** cups unsalted shelled raw sunflower seeds (10 ounces)
- **¾** cup dill sprigs
- **2** tablespoons fresh lemon juice
- **2** garlic cloves
- **½** cup plus 2 tablespoons water

Kosher salt and freshly ground pepper
Crudités, such as raw carrots, endives, radishes and peppers, for serving

In a food processor, combine the sunflower seeds with the dill sprigs, lemon juice, garlic and water and process until smooth and creamy. Season with salt and pepper and serve with the crudités. *—Ani Phyo*

MAKE AHEAD The dip can be refrigerated in an airtight container for up to 3 days.

GUACAMOLE WITH CHARRED
JALAPEÑO AND SCALLIONS

reinventing guacamole

*F&W's **Grace Parisi** creates a smoky guacamole, then presents three ingenious ways to use it: in a soup, an hors d'oeuvre and a salad dressing.*

Guacamole with Charred Jalapeño and Scallions

TOTAL: 20 MIN

MAKES 2 CUPS ● ●

- 3 medium scallions, white and tender green parts only
- 2 medium garlic cloves, unpeeled
- 1 jalapeño, seeded and quartered lengthwise
- 1 tablespoon vegetable oil
- 3 Hass avocados, halved and pitted
- ¼ cup finely chopped cilantro leaves
- 2 tablespoons fresh lime juice

Salt and freshly ground pepper

1. Preheat a grill pan. In a small bowl, toss the scallions, garlic and jalapeño with the vegetable oil. Grill over moderately high heat, turning occasionally, until charred all over, 5 to 6 minutes. Transfer to a work surface and let cool.

2. Finely chop the scallions and jalapeño and transfer them to a medium bowl. Peel the garlic cloves, mash them to a paste and add them to the bowl. Scoop the avocado flesh into the bowl and coarsely mash with a fork. Fold the chopped cilantro and lime juice into the guacamole, season with salt and pepper and serve right away.

VARIATION For a brighter, crunchier guacamole, finely chop the scallions, garlic and jalapeño and stir them in raw.

Three Great Ways to Use Guacamole

1 **Chilled Avocado Soup Topped with Crab**

In a blender, puree 1 cup of the guacamole with 1 cup cold buttermilk, ¾ cup bottled clam juice, ½ cup ice water and 1 tablespoon fresh lime juice. Season the soup with salt and pepper. Pour the soup into 4 bowls and top with jumbo lump crabmeat. Garnish each bowl of soup with crème fraîche, fried tortilla strips and finely chopped chives.

2 **Smoked Salmon Involtini**

Fold 1 cup of the guacamole with 8 ounces cream cheese and 1 teaspoon jalapeño hot sauce; season with salt and pepper. Overlap 1 pound smoked salmon slices in pairs. Trim each pair to a 4-by-6-inch rectangle. Pipe the guacamole–cream cheese mixture along one of the short sides. Roll into cylinders, transfer to a tray and freeze for 15 minutes. Cut into 4 pieces; serve on mini toasts.

3 **Iceberg Wedges with Guacamole Dressing**

In a blender, puree 1 cup of the guacamole with ⅓ cup fresh lime juice and ¼ cup water. With the machine on, gradually add ½ cup vegetable oil. Season with salt and pepper. Quarter 1 head iceberg lettuce and spoon the dressing on top. Garnish with crumbled bacon, sliced radishes, shredded pepper Jack cheese and diced tomato.

Chunky Guacamole with Cumin

TOTAL: 20 MIN
6 TO 8 SERVINGS ● ● ●

This take on everyone's favorite dip has subtle tartness, balanced heat and a creamy-chunky texture.

- ½ teaspoon cumin seeds
- 5 large Hass avocados
- 3 tablespoons fresh lemon juice
- 2 tablespoons chopped cilantro
- 1 small onion, minced
- 1 large garlic clove, minced
- 1 jalapeño with some seeds, minced
- Salt

1. In a small skillet, toast the cumin seeds over moderately high heat until fragrant, about 30 seconds. Transfer the seeds to a mortar to cool, then finely grind them.

2. Scoop half of the avocados into a large bowl and coarsely mash with a fork. Stir in the lemon juice, cilantro, onion, garlic, jalapeño and ground cumin. Scoop the remaining avocados into the bowl in chunks; stir lightly. Season with salt and serve at room temperature or lightly chilled.
—*Marcia Kiesel*

Warm Piquillo-Crab Dip

TOTAL: 25 MIN
4 SERVINGS ● ●

Philadelphia chef Jose Garces reimagines his smoky piquillo peppers stuffed with creamy crab as a warm dip.

- 1 pound lump crab, picked over
- ¼ cup mayonnaise
- ¼ cup crème fraîche
- 2 tablespoons chopped parsley
- 2 tablespoons snipped chives
- 1 tablespoon Dijon mustard
- 2 teaspoons fresh lemon juice
- ¼ pound Manchego cheese, shredded (1 cup)
- One 9-ounce jar piquillo peppers, drained and cut into strips

Preheat the broiler. In a bowl, combine the crab, mayonnaise, crème fraîche, parsley, chives, mustard, lemon juice and ¾ cup of the Manchego. Spread the crab mixture in an 8-by-11-inch baking dish. Top with the piquillos and sprinkle with the remaining Manchego. Broil about 7 inches from the heat until the cheese is melted and the dip is warmed through. Serve at once.
—*Jose Garces*

SERVE WITH Crusty bread or crostini.

Lump Crab Salsa

ACTIVE: 20 MIN; TOTAL: 1 HR 40 MIN
10 SERVINGS ● ●

Most crab dips are full of mayonnaise, but chef Michael Symon's lighter version is more like a salsa since it's prepared without mayo and laced with shallot, cilantro, jalapeño and red bell pepper. "Although I love mayo," he says, "I'm not a fan of it with crab, since it tends to muddle the flavor. If I'm spending big bucks on crab, I want it to be the star."

- 3 tablespoons chopped cilantro
- 2 medium shallots, minced
- 1 red bell pepper, finely diced
- 1 jalapeño, seeded and finely diced
- Finely grated zest and juice of 1 lime
- 1 medium garlic clove, minced
- ¼ cup extra-virgin olive oil
- 2 pounds lump crabmeat, picked over
- Salt and freshly ground pepper
- ½ cup salted roasted almonds, coarsely chopped
- Thick-cut potato chips, for serving

In a large bowl, combine the cilantro, shallots, bell pepper, jalapeño, lime zest, lime juice, garlic and olive oil. Fold in the crab and season with salt and pepper. Refrigerate for 1 hour. Let the salsa come to room temperature, then fold in the almonds. Serve with potato chips.
—*Michael Symon*

MAKE AHEAD The crab salsa can be refrigerated for up to 4 hours. Fold in the almonds just before serving.

Tomato and Garlic Dip

ACTIVE: 30 MIN; TOTAL: 1 HR
6 SERVINGS ● ●

The iconic Andalucian *salmorejo* is essentially a superthick gazpacho, made with plenty of ripe tomatoes, garlic and olive oil. It's invariably topped with chopped hard-boiled eggs and ham and served with fried eggplant or toasted country bread.

- Ten ½-inch-thick slices of white peasant bread
- 1 pound tomatoes, chopped
- 1 medium garlic clove, very thinly sliced
- 2 teaspoons sherry vinegar
- ¼ cup extra-virgin olive oil, plus more for brushing
- Salt and freshly ground black pepper
- 1 hard-cooked egg, coarsely chopped
- 2 ounces thickly sliced serrano ham, finely diced

1. Preheat the oven to 350°. On a baking sheet, toast 4 slices of the peasant bread for 8 minutes, or until lightly dried out. Cut off and discard the crusts; cut the toasts into ½-inch cubes.

2. In a blender, puree the chopped tomatoes with the sliced garlic, sherry vinegar and the ¼ cup of olive oil until smooth. Add the toasted bread cubes to the blender and puree until the mixture is thick and creamy. Season with salt and pepper. Transfer the *salmorejo* to a bowl, cover and refrigerate until it is lightly chilled, about 30 minutes.

3. Preheat a grill pan. Brush the remaining 6 slices of peasant bread with olive oil; grill over high heat, turning, until the slices are toasted. Transfer the grilled bread to shallow bowls and ladle the *salmorejo* on top. Garnish with the chopped egg and ham and serve the *salmorejo*-topped toasts immediately. —*Mario Batali*

MAKE AHEAD The *salmorejo* can be refrigerated overnight.

TOMATO AND GARLIC DIP

CHORIZO-FILLED DATES WRAPPED IN BACON

Chorizo-Filled Dates Wrapped in Bacon

 **TOTAL: 20 MIN**
MAKES 24 PIECES ● ●

This timeless tapa from Spanish cookbook author Penelope Casas has everything going for it—it's sweet, smoky and savory, all in one bite.

- 1 small dry chorizo sausage (about 2 ounces), casing removed
- 24 Medjool dates, pitted
- 12 slices of bacon, halved crosswise

1. Slice the chorizo crosswise in thirds. Halve each piece lengthwise, then cut each half into 4 lengthwise strips to make a total of 24 small sticks.

2. Tuck a chorizo stick into each date and pinch the dates closed. Wrap a strip of bacon around each stuffed date; secure with a toothpick.

3. Place the wrapped dates in a large skillet, seam side down, and sauté, turning, until the bacon is browned on all sides, about 10 minutes. Drain on paper towels and serve hot. —*Penelope Casas*

Roasted Red Pepper Involtini

ACTIVE: 20 MIN; TOTAL: 1 HR 45 MIN
8 SERVINGS ● ● ○

This simple recipe for *involtini* (little Italian rolls) is all about the deeply flavored, slow-roasted red bell peppers, which get wrapped around fresh ricotta cheese and plum tomatoes.

- 4 large red bell peppers
- 8 ounces fresh ricotta cheese (1 cup)
- 2 tablespoons snipped chives

Salt and freshly ground pepper

- 1 plum tomato—peeled, seeded and finely diced

1. Preheat the oven to 450°. Arrange the peppers on a baking sheet and roast for 1 hour, turning occasionally, until tender and charred in spots. Transfer the peppers to a paper bag, close and let cool.

2. Peel, core and seed the peppers, keeping them intact. Cut each pepper in half lengthwise and pat dry with paper towels.

3. Working over a bowl, press the ricotta through a sieve. Add the snipped chives, season with salt and pepper and stir the tomato into the filling.

4. Arrange the roasted peppers on a work surface, skinned side down. Divide the filling evenly among the halves and roll up into thick cylinders. Refrigerate for at least 15 minutes. Cut the cylinders into ¾-inch-thick slices, transfer to a platter, cut side up, and serve. —*Maurizio Quaranta*

MAKE AHEAD The *involtini* can be refrigerated overnight. Return to room temperature before serving.

● HEALTHY ● MAKE AHEAD ○ VEGETARIAN ● STAFF FAVORITE

starters

Grilled Eggplant Involtini

ACTIVE: 15 MIN; TOTAL: 45 MIN
8 SERVINGS ● ● ○

- 1 eggplant (about 1¼ pounds), sliced lengthwise ¼ inch thick

Salt

Extra-virgin olive oil, for brushing

- 8 ounces fresh ricotta cheese
- 2 tablespoons snipped chives, plus 16 whole chives

Freshly ground pepper

- 1 plum tomato—peeled, seeded and finely diced

1. Lightly sprinkle the eggplant slices with salt and let stand for 15 minutes.

2. Preheat a grill pan. Blot the eggplant slices dry with paper towels and brush with olive oil. Grill the eggplant over moderate heat, turning once, until tender and lightly charred, about 6 minutes. Transfer the eggplant to a platter and let cool.

3. Working over a bowl, press the ricotta through a sieve. Add the snipped chives and season with salt and pepper. Stir the diced tomato into the filling.

4. Blanch the whole chives in boiling water for 10 seconds. Drain and pat dry.

5. Spread the ricotta filling over the eggplant slices and cut each in half crosswise. Roll the halves lengthwise into small cylinders and tie with the blanched chives. Refrigerate for 15 minutes, then serve.
—*Maurizio Quaranta*

Stuffed Grape Leaves with Pork and Fregola

ACTIVE: 1 HR; TOTAL: 3 HR 30 MIN
MAKES 3 DOZEN PIECES ●

- ½ cup *fregola* (see Note)
- 3 cups hot water
- 1 pound ground pork
- ¼ cup minced shallots
- 2 teaspoons kosher salt
- ½ teaspoon freshly ground pepper
- 1 teaspoon finely chopped fresh marjoram or oregano plus 4 marjoram or oregano sprigs

Pinch of cinnamon (optional)

- 40 brined grape leaves, drained (from one 16-ounce jar)
- ½ cup fresh lemon juice
- 2 tablespoons extra-virgin olive oil

1. In a large bowl, cover the *fregola* with the hot water and soak for 15 minutes. Drain, shaking out the excess water.

2. Return the *fregola* to the bowl. Add the pork, shallots, salt, pepper, chopped marjoram and cinnamon and knead until combined. Transfer the meat mixture to a baking sheet and pat into a 6-by-12-inch rectangle. Cut the rectangle lengthwise into three 2-inch-wide strips and cut each strip into 12 logs.

3. Snip off the stems at the base of the grape leaves. Smooth out a few leaves on a work surface. Set a log of the filling at the stem end. Roll up the stem end of each leaf once to enclose the filling, then fold in the sides. Tightly roll up the leaves to form cylinders. Repeat with the remaining grape leaves and filling.

4. Arrange the stuffed grape leaves in a large, deep skillet in a single layer and scatter the marjoram sprigs on top. Drizzle with the lemon juice and olive oil; pour enough water in the skillet to cover the grape leaves by ½ inch. Top with any remaining unfilled grape leaves and a plate to keep the stuffed leaves submerged. Bring the liquid to a boil and cover the skillet. Simmer over low heat until the filling is cooked through and the grape leaves are tender, about 1 hour and 30 minutes. Let the stuffed grape leaves cool in the cooking liquid.

5. Drain the stuffed grape leaves, discarding the unstuffed leaves, and transfer to a paper towel–lined plate. Let stand for 30 minutes, then serve them warm or at room temperature. —*David Page*

NOTE *Fregola*, a toasted, coarser version of couscous, is available at specialty shops or from cybercucina.com.

MAKE AHEAD The stuffed grape leaves can be refrigerated for up to 5 days.

Glazed Japanese Beef-and-Scallion Rolls

ACTIVE: 20 MIN; TOTAL: 45 MIN
6 SERVINGS ●

- 6 thin asparagus spears
- 6 large scallions

Salt

About 1 teaspoon Asian sesame oil, for coating

- 6 thin slices of beef tenderloin (about 2 ounces each), very lightly pounded to a ⅛-inch thickness

Freshly ground pepper

- 2 tablespoons red miso
- 2 tablespoons soy sauce
- 2 tablespoons mirin
- 2 tablespoons sugar
- 1 tablespoon finely grated fresh ginger

Vegetable oil, for brushing

1. Blanch the asparagus in boiling water until bright green, 1 minute. Transfer to a plate and pat dry. Blanch the scallions until bright green, 45 seconds; transfer to the plate and pat dry. Lightly season the vegetables with salt and sesame oil.

2. Set a slice of beef on a work surface and season with salt and pepper. Arrange an asparagus spear and a scallion lengthwise on the meat; trim them flush with the meat. Roll up the meat around the asparagus and scallion and secure with a toothpick. Repeat with the remaining slices of beef, asparagus and scallions.

3. Mix the miso with the soy sauce, mirin, sugar and ginger. Put the beef rolls in a shallow dish and coat generously with the miso mixture. Let stand for 20 minutes.

4. Heat a grill pan over high heat. Lightly brush the pan with vegetable oil. Add the beef-and-scallion rolls and cook over high heat until nicely charred all over, about 1 minute per side. Transfer to a cutting board and remove the toothpicks. Slice each roll on the diagonal 1½ inches thick. Arrange the slices on a platter, cut side up, and serve. —*Anya von Bremzen*

STUFFED GRAPE LEAVES
WITH PORK AND FREGOLA

Pancetta-Wrapped Peaches with Basil and Aged Balsamic

TOTAL: 30 MIN
4 SERVINGS ●

Stuart Brioza (an F&W Best New Chef 2003) rolls wedges of sweet summer peaches and fresh basil leaves in thin slices of salty pancetta, then sears them for a crispy, juicy hors d'oeuvre. These peaches would also be a delightful and unexpected addition to a crisp green salad made with frisée or baby escarole.

luxe party snacks

Warm Olives and Fennel Heat 2 cups assorted olives with ½ cup olive oil and 1 chopped Anaheim chile for 5 minutes. Transfer to a bowl and toss with 1 shaved fennel bulb and 1 teaspoon finely grated orange zest.

Marinated Feta Whisk ¾ cup olive oil with ¼ cup lemon juice; season with pepper. Add 1¼ pounds Greek feta cheese cut into ¾-inch cubes and ¼ cup torn mint and toss gently. Serve with bread.

Sweet-and-Smoky Pecans Toss 4 cups pecans with ¼ cup honey and 1 teaspoon each of ground chipotle and kosher salt. Spread on a parchment-lined baking sheet and toast at 375° for 12 minutes, until fragrant.

Truffled Popcorn Pop 1 cup popping corn. In a bowl, toss with 4 tablespoons melted unsalted butter, ⅓ cup freshly grated pecorino cheese and 1½ teaspoons each of truffle salt and minced rosemary.

16 thin slices of pancetta
2 medium freestone peaches—halved, pitted and cut into 8 wedges each
Salt and freshly ground pepper
16 basil leaves
1 tablespoon olive oil
Aged balsamic vinegar, for drizzling

1. Lay the pancetta slices out on a work surface. Set a peach wedge at the edge of each slice, season with salt and pepper and top with a basil leaf. Roll up the pancetta to enclose the peaches.
2. In a medium skillet, heat the olive oil. Add half of the wrapped peaches and cook over moderate heat, turning occasionally, until the pancetta is browned and crisp, about 4 minutes. Transfer to a platter and repeat with the remaining peaches.
3. Lightly drizzle the peaches with aged balsamic vinegar and serve.
—*Stuart Brioza*

Greek Grilled Scallop Sandwiches

TOTAL: 30 MIN
4 SERVINGS ●

New York City chef Michael Psilakis (an F&W Best New Chef 2008) uses a grilled, sliced scallop as the "bread" in his playful version of a finger sandwich, which is filled with black plums, prosciutto and pea tendrils and topped with Greek yogurt. He says, "It's English high tea meets crazy Greek chef."

¼ cup Greek-style whole-milk yogurt
Pinch of saffron threads, crumbled
1½ teaspoons rice vinegar
Sea salt and freshly ground pepper
1 small black plum, pitted and thinly sliced
Extra-virgin olive oil
12 large sea scallops (1¼ pounds)
2 thin slices of prosciutto, cut into thin strips
36 pea tendrils (1 cup)

1. Light a grill. In a bowl, combine the yogurt, saffron and vinegar and season with salt and pepper.
2. Brush the plum slices with oil and grill over high heat until lightly charred, 30 seconds per side. Brush the scallops with oil, season with salt and pepper and grill them over high heat until charred and just cooked through, about 1½ minutes per side.
3. Cut each scallop in half crosswise. Place a plum slice on the bottom half of each scallop. Lay the prosciutto strips over the plums, then top each one with 2 pea tendrils; cover with the scallop tops. Secure with toothpicks and put 3 on each plate. Top each scallop sandwich with 1 teaspoon of the yogurt sauce and garnish with the remaining pea tendrils. Drizzle with olive oil, sprinkle with salt and serve.
—*Michael Psilakis*

Seafood Pan Roast

TOTAL: 45 MIN
6 SERVINGS

With this mixed seafood roast, F&W's Grace Parisi proves that a dish can be both luxurious and simple. "As a kid, I thought shrimp scampi was the height of sophistication," she says. "I've taken it several steps higher by adding lobster, oysters and scallops."

¼ cup plus 2 tablespoons fresh lemon juice
¼ cup minced shallot
¼ cup crème fraîche
½ cup plus 1 tablespoon extra-virgin olive oil
Salt and freshly ground black pepper
½ fennel bulb, very finely diced
2 tablespoons finely chopped fennel fronds
6 jumbo shrimp, butterflied in their shells
Three 8-ounce frozen raw South African lobster tails, thawed and halved lengthwise

6 oysters, shucked and
   both shells reserved
6 large sea scallops,
   2 to 3 ounces each
Garlic toast, for serving

1. In a medium bowl, whisk the lemon juice with the shallot and crème fraîche. Gradually whisk in the olive oil and season with salt and pepper. Whisk in the diced fennel and chopped fennel fronds.

2. Preheat the broiler and position a rack 6 inches from the heat. Arrange the shrimp, lobster tails and oyster shell halves in a roasting pan in a single layer. Place the scallops in the 6 flattest oyster shells. Place the oysters in the remaining shells. Spoon ¾ cup of the vinaigrette over the seafood, being sure to coat them completely. Season with pepper and broil until lightly browned, about 7 minutes. Transfer the seafood to plates and drizzle with some of the vinaigrette, passing the toast and any remaining vinaigrette at the table. —*Grace Parisi*

Red Snapper Ceviche

TOTAL: 55 MIN

4 SERVINGS ●

For ceviches, Allen Susser of Chef Allen's in Aventura, Florida, prefers to use firm white-fleshed fish like red snapper and grouper, as well as conch and rock shrimp, because they keep their shape well.

1 pound skinless red snapper
   fillets
¾ cup fresh lime juice
¼ cup fresh lemon juice
1 jalapeño, seeded and minced
½ cup each of finely diced red and
   yellow bell peppers
½ small red onion, thinly sliced
1 small garlic clove, minced
Pinch of ground cumin
Pinch of crushed red pepper
Salt
1 tablespoon minced cilantro
1 tablespoon extra-virgin olive oil

Cut the red snapper fillets into ¼-inch dice. In a large bowl, toss the diced fish with the lime and lemon juices, jalapeño, bell peppers, red onion, garlic, cumin and crushed red pepper; season with salt. Refrigerate the snapper ceviche for 30 minutes. Stir in the minced cilantro and olive oil and serve. —*Allen Susser*

Salmon Sashimi with Ginger and Hot Sesame Oil

 TOTAL: 20 MIN

4 SERVINGS ● ●

Boston chef Tim Cushman, an F&W Best New Chef 2008, is a master at preparing raw fish. Here he tops salmon with fresh ginger and chives before bathing it in a hot sesame oil mixture. The heated oil cooks the salmon slightly, creating a lovely texture and fragrance.

¼ cup plus 2 tablespoons
   low-sodium soy sauce
1 teaspoon fresh lime juice
1 teaspoon fresh orange juice
Twelve ⅛-inch-thick slices
   of salmon, cut into 2-inch
   squares (¼ pound)
One ¼-inch piece of fresh ginger,
   sliced paper-thin and
   cut into thin matchsticks
   (about 24 pieces)
1 tablespoon snipped chives
2 tablespoons grapeseed oil
1 teaspoon Asian sesame oil
1½ teaspoons roasted
   sesame seeds
2 tablespoons cilantro leaves

1. In a small bowl, mix 2 tablespoons of the soy sauce with the lime and orange juices. In a medium bowl, toss the salmon with the remaining ¼ cup of soy sauce and let stand for 1 minute, then drain. Arrange 3 slices of salmon on each plate and top the fish with the ginger matchsticks and snipped chives.

2. In a saucepan, heat the grapeseed and sesame oils over moderately high heat until

smoking, about 2 minutes. Drizzle over the salmon. Spoon the soy-citrus sauce on top, sprinkle with the sesame seeds and cilantro and serve. —*Tim Cushman*

Tequila-Flamed Shrimp Tostadas

 TOTAL: 30 MIN

6 SERVINGS ●

1 Hass avocado, mashed
¼ cup finely diced fresh pineapple
½ cup drained canned black beans
2 scallions, finely chopped
3 tablespoons fresh lime juice
Salt and freshly ground pepper
2 tablespoons vegetable oil
¾ pound medium shrimp—
   shelled, deveined and
   cut into ½-inch pieces
2 large garlic cloves, minced
2 tablespoons silver tequila
½ canned chipotle in adobo sauce,
   seeded and minced
1 tablespoon unsalted butter, cubed
24 large round tortilla chips

1. In a bowl, mash the avocado, pineapple, beans, scallions and 1 tablespoon of the lime juice. Season with salt and pepper.

2. Heat a large skillet until very hot. Add the oil and heat until shimmering. Season the shrimp with salt and pepper; add to the skillet along with the garlic and cook, shaking the pan frequently, until the shrimp are almost cooked through, about 2 minutes.

3. Off the heat, add the tequila. Tilt the pan slightly over the burner to ignite the tequila and cook until the flames subside. (Or remove the pan from the heat and ignite with a match.) Stir in the chipotle, butter and the remaining 2 tablespoons of lime juice, swirling until the butter is melted and the liquid is slightly reduced, about 2 minutes longer. Season with salt and pepper.

4. Spoon the avocado mixture onto the chips and top with the shrimp. Drizzle some of the tequila sauce on top and serve right away. —*Sue Torres*

SMOKED SALMON CRISPS

SMOKY SEAFOOD COCKTAIL

Smoked Salmon Crisps

TOTAL: 45 MIN

MAKES 3 DOZEN CRISPS

The original recipe for chef Thomas Keller's salmon cornets, which appears in *The French Laundry Cookbook* (Artisan), requires quickly shaping tuiles into cones with a cornet mold, a sometimes tricky technique. This recipe simplifies the preparation by leaving the tuiles flat, like crackers. Topped with store-bought smoked salmon and crème fraîche, these crisps are surprisingly fast and elegant.

4½ tablespoons all-purpose
    flour
  2 teaspoons sugar
  ½ teaspoon kosher salt
  1 chilled large egg white
  4 tablespoons unsalted butter,
    at room temperature
  1 tablespoon black
    sesame seeds (see Note)
  4 ounces sliced smoked
    salmon, finely chopped
1½ teaspoons very finely
    chopped shallot
1½ teaspoons very finely
    chopped chives, plus a few
    snipped for garnish
  ¼ teaspoon finely grated
    lemon zest
Freshly ground white pepper
  ½ cup crème fraîche

1. Preheat the oven to 400°. Line 2 baking sheets with parchment paper. In a medium bowl, whisk the flour with the sugar and salt. Add the egg white and whisk until smooth. Whisk in the butter until smooth and creamy.

2. Spoon level teaspoons of the batter at least 3 inches apart on the prepared baking sheets and use the back of a spoon to spread the tuiles to 2-inch rounds. Sprinkle the tops of the tuiles with the black sesame seeds and bake in the upper and middle thirds of the oven for about 15 minutes, shifting the pans from top to bottom and front to back, until the tuiles are golden and fragrant. Let cool.

3. In a medium bowl, combine the chopped smoked salmon with the chopped shallot, chopped chives, grated lemon zest and a pinch of white pepper and gently fold the ingredients together. Spoon some of the salmon mixture onto each of the cooled sesame tuiles, then top with a dollop of crème fraîche and a couple of snipped chives. Serve the salmon crisps right away.
—*Thomas Keller*

NOTE Black sesame seeds taste similar to white sesame seeds, but they make a more striking appearance in dishes such as this one. They're available at Asian markets.

MAKE AHEAD The sesame tuiles can be stored in an airtight container at room temperature for up to 2 days.

Smoky Seafood Cocktail

TOTAL: 30 MIN PLUS 4 HR CHILLING
12 SERVINGS ● ●

F&W's Grace Parisi revamps the classic shrimp cocktail recipe by including sea scallops and stone crab claws; she then tweaks the traditional cocktail sauce by replacing ketchup with chile sauce and seasoning it with hot smoked paprika (Spanish pimentón de la Vera) and prepared horseradish.

4 garlic cloves, smashed with
the side of a knife
1 tablespoon coriander seeds
1 tablespoon fennel seeds
½ teaspoon crushed
red pepper
1 tablespoon kosher salt
8 cups water
1 lemon, plus 2 tablespoons
fresh lemon juice
1¾ pounds shelled and deveined
large shrimp
1½ pounds jumbo sea scallops,
halved horizontally
1 cup bottled chile sauce
1 tablespoon prepared
horseradish
1½ teaspoons hot pimentón
de la Vera (smoked paprika;
see Note)
24 stone crab claws, cracked
and chilled (see Note)

1. In a large pot, combine the smashed garlic cloves with the coriander and fennel seeds, crushed red pepper, kosher salt and water. Using a vegetable peeler, remove the zest from the lemon in strips and add them to the pot. Halve the lemon, squeeze the juice into the pot and add the squeezed lemon halves to the pot. Bring the liquid to a boil and then simmer over low heat for about 15 minutes. Add the shelled and deveined shrimp and halved scallops; simmer just until they are white throughout, about 5 minutes. Drain the cooked shrimp and scallops well and transfer them to a large plate. Leave the aromatics on the seafood to flavor it. Cover and refrigerate the scallops and shrimp until they are thoroughly chilled, at least 4 hours or overnight.

2. In a small bowl, whisk the chile sauce with the prepared horseradish, smoked paprika and the 2 tablespoons of lemon juice. Spoon the smoky cocktail sauce into a small serving bowl.

3. Pick any aromatics off the shrimp and scallops and arrange the chilled seafood on a platter or in individual glasses with the crab claws. Serve the seafood with the smoky cocktail sauce for dipping.

—*Grace Parisi*

NOTE Smoked Spanish paprika is available at specialty food stores, or you can order it online at latienda.com. If you can't find precracked stone crab claws, you will need to crack them yourself. Working with one crab claw at a time, wrap it in a kitchen towel. Working carefully, lightly crack the crab claw with the back of a knife or a mallet to expose as much of the meat as possible, leaving the pincers attached so that the crabmeat can be easily pulled from the shell.

MAKE AHEAD The smoky cocktail sauce and cooked shrimp and scallops can be covered and refrigerated separately overnight. The cracked crab claws can be covered and refrigerated overnight.

Fritto Misto with Fennel and Lemons

 TOTAL: 45 MIN
6 SERVINGS

For her supercrispy seafood starter, F&W's Melissa Rubel uses only a thin coating of batter—somewhere between a beer batter and tempura—so the flavor of the fish doesn't get lost.

Vegetable oil, for frying
2½ cups all-purpose flour
½ cup cornstarch
½ teaspoon baking powder
Kosher salt and freshly ground
black pepper
2 cups club soda
12 large shrimp, shelled
and deveined
¾ pound skinless cod fillet,
cut into 12 chunks
½ pound squid, tentacles
halved and bodies sliced
into ½-inch rings
1 small fennel bulb, sliced
lengthwise ⅛ inch thick
1 lemon, very thinly sliced,
plus lemon wedges for
serving
¼ cup coarsely chopped flat-leaf
parsley leaves

1. In a large pot fitted with a deep-frying thermometer (or in a deep fryer), heat 3 inches of vegetable oil over moderately high heat to 350°. In a medium bowl, whisk 1 cup of the flour with the cornstarch, baking powder, 1 teaspoon of kosher salt and a pinch of black pepper. Slowly whisk in the club soda to make a smooth, thin batter. Let the batter stand at room temperature for 5 minutes.

2. Place the remaining 1½ cups of flour in a wide, shallow bowl. Season the shelled shrimp, cod chunks, sliced squid and fennel and lemon slices with salt and black pepper. Toss them, a few at a time, in the flour until they are lightly dusted. Dip the flour-dusted seafood, fennel and lemon slices in the seasoned batter in batches, scraping some of the excess against the side of the bowl, and fry them in batches in the hot oil until they are lightly golden and crisp, about 4 minutes. Use a slotted spoon or long-handled mesh strainer to transfer the fritto misto to paper towel–lined plates to drain. Sprinkle the fritto misto with salt while very hot. Transfer to a large plate, sprinkle with the chopped parsley and serve the fritto misto right away, with lemon wedges.

—*Melissa Rubel*

● HEALTHY ● MAKE AHEAD ● VEGETARIAN ● STAFF FAVORITE

Potato Crisps with Chive–Sour Cream Dip

TOTAL: 40 MIN
4 SERVINGS ● ●

This recipe makes brilliant use of throw-away potato peels: They're deep-fried until crispy, then sprinkled with Parmesan cheese and served with a creamy dip.

- 3 cups canola oil
- Thick peelings from 3 pounds of Yukon Gold or russet potatoes (roughly 1-by-3-inch strips)
- Kosher salt
- 2 tablespoons freshly grated Parmigiano-Reggiano cheese
- ½ cup low-fat sour cream
- 2 tablespoons snipped chives
- Freshly ground pepper

1. Preheat the oven to 350°. In a large saucepan over moderately high heat, heat the canola oil to 360°. Fry the potato skins in batches, stirring them occasionally, until they are browned and crisp, 2 to 3 minutes per batch. Using a slotted spoon, transfer each batch of potato strips to paper towels to drain, then sprinkle with salt immediately.

2. Transfer the fried potato strips to a baking sheet and sprinkle them with the grated Parmigiano-Reggiano. Bake for about 3 to 4 minutes, just until the cheese is melted. Let the crisps cool, then transfer them to a bowl.

3. In a blender or processor, puree the sour cream with the chives and a pinch of salt and pepper until the chives are finely chopped. Transfer the chive–sour cream dip to a small serving bowl and serve it alongside the potato crisps.
—*Grace Parisi*

MAKE AHEAD The chive–sour cream dip can be refrigerated overnight.

Aged Gouda Biscotti with Walnuts

ACTIVE: 45 MIN; TOTAL: 3 HR 30 MIN
MAKES ABOUT 6 DOZEN BISCOTTI
● ● ●

These crunchy biscotti from master cook Terrance Brennan are surprisingly rich-tasting thanks to aged Gouda and chopped walnuts. Try other hard cheeses, too, like aged Prima Donna, a lighter Gouda-style cheese from the Netherlands.

- 1 envelope active dry yeast (2¼ teaspoons)
- ¾ cup plus 2 tablespoons warm water
- 1 tablespoon sugar
- 2¾ cups all-purpose flour, plus more for dusting
- 8 ounces aged Gouda (preferably 4 years), shredded (2 cups)
- ½ cup walnuts, very finely chopped
- 1 teaspoon kosher salt
- 6 tablespoons unsalted butter, softened

1. In a medium bowl, combine the yeast with ½ cup of the warm water and let stand until foamy, about 5 minutes. Stir in the sugar and ¾ cup of the flour to form a sponge; cover and let stand until billowy, about 30 minutes.

2. In a large bowl, combine the remaining 2 cups of flour with the shredded Gouda, chopped walnuts and salt. Make a well in the center and add the yeast mixture and the remaining ¼ cup plus 2 tablespoons warm water; add the softened butter and stir until a dough is formed.

3. Line a baking sheet with parchment paper. Scrape the dough onto a lightly floured work surface and knead until smooth, about 5 minutes; divide into thirds. Roll each piece of dough into a 12-inch log about 1½ inches thick. Arrange the logs on the parchment-lined baking sheet 2 inches apart. Loosely cover with lightly moistened paper towels and plastic wrap. Let stand for about 45 minutes, until the dough has risen.

4. Preheat the oven to 350°. Remove the plastic wrap and paper towels from the biscotti dough and bake the logs for about 35 minutes, until they are golden and puffed and an instant-read thermometer inserted in the center of one registers 205°. Let the logs cool on the baking sheet for about 20 minutes.

cooking with cheese

Here are a few strategies for cooking with cheese from F&W Best New Chef 1995 **Terrance Brennan.**

Fresh When gently heated, fresh cheeses like goat cheese, ricotta and mascarpone make lovely cream sauces for pastas; they're also wonderful in frittatas and root-vegetable gratins.

Washed-Rind Washed-rind cheeses like Reblochon and Taleggio turn runny and soft baked on pizzas and in casseroles; you can trim the rind before cooking, but it's not necessary.

Semihard Firm but still-moist cheeses like cheddar and the Spanish goat's-milk Garrotxa are perfect for grilled cheese sandwiches; they also add nutty flavors to soufflés and gougères.

Hard Aged Gouda, Parmigiano-Reggiano and other dry, salty cheeses season dishes like spaghetti, soups and quiches. They form a great crust when they cool after melting.

5. Reduce the oven temperature to 300° and position 2 racks in the lower and upper thirds of the oven. Transfer the logs to a work surface. Using a serrated knife, slice the logs crosswise ⅓ inch thick. Arrange the slices cut side up on 2 baking sheets and bake for 45 minutes to 1 hour, until golden and crisp; flip the biscotti halfway through and shift the baking sheets from top to bottom and front to back. Transfer the gouda biscotti to a rack and let cool completely before serving.
—*Terrance Brennan*

Butternut Squash Turnovers

ACTIVE: 40 MIN; TOTAL: 1 HR 40 MIN

12 SERVINGS ● ● ●

- ¼ cup extra-virgin olive oil, plus more for brushing
- 3 large leeks, white parts only, cut into 1-inch dice (2 cups)
- ½ pound shiitake mushrooms, stems discarded and caps sliced ¼ inch thick
- 2 garlic cloves, chopped
- 2 tablespoons thyme leaves

Salt and freshly ground black pepper

One 2-pound butternut squash— peeled, seeded and cut into ½-inch dice

- 14 ounces all-butter puff pastry, thawed if frozen
- 12 ounces fresh goat cheese (1½ cups)
- 1 large egg, lightly beaten

1. Preheat the oven to 375°. In a large skillet, heat 2 tablespoons of the olive oil. Add the diced leeks and cook over moderate heat, stirring occasionally, until softened, about 5 minutes. Add the shiitake and cook, stirring often, until their liquid has evaporated, about 5 minutes. Stir in the garlic and the thyme and cook for 2 minutes. Season the vegetables with salt and pepper and transfer to a large bowl.

POTATO CRISPS WITH CHIVE—SOUR CREAM DIP

AGED GOUDA BISCOTTI WITH WALNUTS

2. Line a large rimmed baking sheet with parchment paper and lightly brush the parchment with olive oil. In another large bowl, toss the diced butternut squash with the remaining 2 tablespoons of olive oil and season with salt and black pepper. Spread the seasoned squash on the parchment-lined baking sheet and bake for about 25 minutes, until the cooked squash is softened and starting to brown. Add the squash to the bowl with the cooked leeks and mushrooms and toss the vegetables to combine.

3. Line a large rimmed baking sheet with parchment paper. On a lightly floured work surface, gently roll out the puff pastry to a 12-by-16-inch rectangle about ¼ inch thick. Cut the pastry into twelve 4-inch squares. Spoon 2 tablespoons of the squash mixture onto each square and top with 2 tablespoons of the goat cheese. Lightly brush the edges of the squares with some of the beaten egg. Fold the squares over to form triangles and crimp the edges decoratively with a fork.

4. Arrange the butternut squash turnovers on the parchment paper–lined baking sheet about ½ inch apart. Brush the tops of the turnovers with the remaining beaten egg. Bake the turnovers for about 25 minutes, until the pastry is golden brown. Serve them warm or at room temperature.

—*Jeremy Sommer*

green olive tapenade

For a quick spread (or to use in the antipasto salad recipe on this page), pulse 1½ cups pitted green olives, ¼ cup olive oil, 1 tablespoon capers, 3 garlic cloves, 3 anchovy fillets and 1 tablespoon lemon juice in a food processor until chunky.

Reblochon Tarts with Bacon and Fingerling Potatoes

ACTIVE: 40 MIN; TOTAL: 1 HR 30 MIN
4 SERVINGS

With a golden layer of puff pastry topped by caramelized onions, soft potatoes, bacon and tangy Reblochon cheese, this tart is lighter than the sum of its parts, making for a satisfying fall dish that's great any time of day. The Reblochon, a washed-rind cheese from France, can be replaced with a robust Taleggio from northern Italy or the smooth French soft-ripened cow's-milk cheese Saint-André.

- 2 **medium fingerling potatoes**
- 4 **slices of bacon**
- 1½ **tablespoons extra-virgin olive oil**
- 1 **medium onion, thinly sliced**

Salt and freshly ground pepper
All-purpose flour, for rolling

- 8 **ounces cold all-butter puff pastry**
- 4 **ounces Reblochon cheese, rind removed and cheese thinly sliced**

1. In a small saucepan, cover the potatoes with cold water and bring to a boil. Cook over high heat until tender when pierced with a knife, about 15 minutes. Drain, then peel and thinly slice crosswise.

2. Meanwhile, in a medium skillet, cook the bacon over moderately high heat until crisp, about 5 minutes; transfer to paper towels. Cut the slices in thirds.

3. Preheat the oven to 375°. Pour off the bacon fat in the skillet and add the oil. Add the onion and cook over moderate heat, stirring frequently, until softened and browned, about 15 minutes; add water as necessary, 1 tablespoon at a time, to prevent scorching. Transfer the onion to a bowl; season with salt and pepper.

4. Line a baking sheet with parchment paper. On a lightly floured work surface, roll out the puff pastry to an 11-inch square. Using a plate as your guide, cut out four 5-inch rounds. Transfer the rounds to the prepared baking sheet and prick them all over with a fork.

5. Bake the rounds in the center of the oven for about 8 minutes, until puffed and lightly golden. Using the back of a fork, deflate the rounds and bake for about 4 minutes longer, until the pastry is just set.

6. Top the pastry rounds with the onion, potato slices, bacon and cheese. Bake for about 10 minutes, until the cheese is melted and the pastry is browned. Transfer the tarts to plates; serve hot or warm.

—*Terrance Brennan*

MAKE AHEAD The baked pastry rounds can be prepared through Step 5 and kept at room temperature for up to 6 hours before proceeding.

Antipasto Salad with Green Olive Tapenade

TOTAL: 30 MIN
8 SERVINGS ●

This salad from Nancy Silverton (an F&W Best New Chef 1990), inspired by the antipasto in Italian-American restaurants, is a delicious toss of iceberg lettuce, mozzarella, salami and olives in an herby dressing.

- 3 **tablespoons green olive tapenade, from a jar or homemade (see recipe below left)**
- ¼ **cup peperoncini—stemmed, seeded and finely chopped**
- ½ **cup extra-virgin olive oil**
- 9 **ounces** *bocconcini*
- 1 **tablespoon plus 1 teaspoon fresh lemon juice**
- 1 **tablespoon plus 1 teaspoon red wine vinegar**
- 1 **tablespoon plus 1 teaspoon minced garlic**
- 1 **teaspoon dried oregano**

Salt and freshly ground pepper

- 1 **small head of iceberg lettuce— halved, cored and finely shredded**
- 6 **ounces thinly sliced Genoa salami, cut into thin strips**
- 6 **small basil leaves**
- ½ **cup green olives, such as Lucques or Picholine**

REBLOCHON TARTS WITH BACON AND FINGERLING POTATOES

ANTIPASTO SALAD WITH GREEN OLIVE TAPENADE

1. In a medium bowl, mix the green olive tapenade with the chopped peperoncini and ¼ cup of the olive oil. Add the *bocconcini* and toss.

2. In a small bowl, whisk the lemon juice with the red wine vinegar, minced garlic and dried oregano. Whisk in the remaining ¼ cup of olive oil and season the dressing with salt and pepper.

3. In a large bowl, toss the shredded iceberg lettuce with the strips of salami. Add the marinated *bocconcini* and half of the dressing and toss well. Transfer the antipasto salad to a large serving platter. Top with the basil leaves and green olives. Drizzle the remaining dressing around the salad and serve right away.
—*Nancy Silverton*

MAKE AHEAD The *bocconcini* can be tossed with their marinade and refrigerated overnight. The dressing can be covered and refrigerated overnight.

Sun-Dried Tomato Flans with Arugula Salad

ACTIVE: 20 MIN; TOTAL: 1 HR

4 SERVINGS ●

- 1 cup heavy cream
- ¼ cup sun-dried tomato paste (one 3-ounce tube)

Salt and freshly ground white pepper

- 2 large eggs
- 1 large egg yolk
- 1 tablespoon fresh lemon juice
- 3 tablespoons extra-virgin olive oil
- 4 ounces baby arugula
- ½ cup pitted kalamata olives, halved
- ¼ cup marcona almonds

1. Preheat the oven to 325°. Butter four 3-ounce ramekins. In a small saucepan, heat the cream with the sun-dried tomato paste until simmering. Season with salt and white pepper. In a medium bowl, whisk the eggs with the egg yolk. Gradually whisk in the hot cream.

2. Strain the custard through a fine-mesh sieve and pour it carefully into the prepared ramekins. Set the ramekins in a small baking pan. Add enough hot water to the baking pan to reach halfway up the sides of the ramekins. Bake the flans on the center rack of the oven for about 30 minutes, until they are set. Remove the ramekins from the water bath and let them cool slightly.

3. Meanwhile, in a medium bowl, whisk the lemon juice with the olive oil. Add the baby arugula, kalamata olives and marcona almonds, season with salt and white pepper and toss.

4. Run the tip of a small knife around each flan. Invert a small plate over each flan and, using pot holders, invert again. Gently tap the ramekins to release the flans. Mound the arugula salad alongside the sun-dried tomato flans and serve right away.
—*Maria Hines*

SUMMER RADISHES WITH CHÈVRE,
NORI AND SMOKED SALT

Summer Radishes with Chèvre, Nori and Smoked Salt

TOTAL: 30 MIN PLUS 2 HR SOAKING

4 SERVINGS ● ●

In this very simple appetizer, Jeremy Fox (an F&W Best New Chef 2008) of Napa's Ubuntu restaurant combines slivers of nori with bits of goat cheese—a tantalizing mix of salty and creamy—then serves the dish with radishes and a sprinkle of smoked salt.

28 assorted radishes, greens attached
 4 ounces fresh goat cheese (½ cup), softened
 1 sheet of nori, cut into ½-inch pieces with scissors
 1 tablespoon extra-virgin olive oil
 1 tablespoon Banyuls or other red wine vinegar
 2 teaspoons Dijon mustard
 2 tablespoons vegetable oil
Smoked sea salt, for sprinkling

1. Trim the greens from half of the radishes and reserve for another use. Using a mandoline, slice the trimmed radishes into ⅛-inch-thick rounds. Put the radish rounds in a medium bowl of ice water and refrigerate until the radish slices are curled, about 2 hours.

2. In a small bowl, mix the softened goat cheese with the nori pieces and olive oil. In another small bowl, whisk the Banyuls vinegar and Dijon mustard with the vegetable oil until combined.

3. Spoon a scant tablespoon of the mustard dressing onto each of 4 plates and dollop the goat cheese mixture over the dressing. Drain the sliced radishes and pat dry with paper towels. Arrange the whole and sliced radishes around each plate, sprinkle with smoked salt and serve. —*Jeremy Fox*

MAKE AHEAD The nori–goat cheese mixture can be covered and refrigerated for up to 2 hours; bring to room temperature before serving.

Goat Cheese–Stuffed Mushrooms with Bread Crumbs

ACTIVE: 25 MIN; TOTAL: 1 HR 5 MIN

8 SERVINGS ● ●

24 large cremini mushrooms (1½ pounds), stems discarded
 ¼ cup plus 2 tablespoons extra-virgin olive oil
 1 teaspoon rosemary leaves, plus one 3-inch rosemary sprig
Kosher salt and freshly ground black pepper
 3 tablespoons fine bread crumbs
 6 ounces fresh goat cheese, cut into 24 pieces

1. Preheat the oven to 400°. In a bowl, toss the cremini mushrooms with 3 tablespoons of the olive oil and the rosemary leaves and season with salt and black pepper. Transfer the seasoned mushrooms to a baking sheet, rounded side up. Roast for about 30 minutes, until the mushrooms are tender and browned around the edges. Let the mushrooms cool to room temperature, about 15 minutes.

2. In a skillet, heat the remaining 3 tablespoons of olive oil. Add the rosemary sprig and cook over moderately high heat until the leaves are crisp, about 30 seconds. Drain the fried rosemary sprig on paper towels, then strip off the leaves. Pour off all but 1 teaspoon of the rosemary oil and reserve it for another use.

3. Add the bread crumbs to the skillet and toast over moderate heat until golden and crisp, 2 minutes. Stir in the fried rosemary leaves and season with salt and pepper.

4. Gently press a piece of goat cheese in the center of each mushroom, sprinkle with the bread crumbs and serve. —*Gabe Thompson*

MAKE AHEAD The goat cheese–filled mushrooms can be refrigerated for up to 1 day. Bring them to room temperature and sprinkle with the bread crumbs just before serving.

Red Wine Bagna Cauda with Crudités

 ACTIVE: 15 MIN; TOTAL: 45 MIN

MAKES ABOUT 3 CUPS ● ●

This garnet sauce is San Francisco chef Chris Cosentino's take on the classic Piedmontese anchovy-and-olive-oil dip, enriched here with red wine. Italian for "hot bath," bagna cauda is traditionally served warm with crudités. Cosentino's version, with both oil-packed and marinated anchovies, doubles as a terrific sauce for grilled meat.

One 750-milliliter bottle dry red wine, such as Nebbiolo
 ¼ cup marinated white anchovy fillets, drained and chopped
 4 oil-packed anchovy fillets, drained and chopped
 3 garlic cloves, chopped
Finely grated zest and juice of 1 lemon
1½ cups extra-virgin olive oil
Salt and freshly ground black pepper
Assorted crudités, such as baby carrots, radishes, fennel and bell peppers, for serving

1. In a large saucepan, bring the red wine to a boil and cook over high heat until the wine is reduced to 1 cup, about 20 minutes. Let cool to room temperature.

2. In a blender, combine the reduced wine with the white anchovies and oil-packed anchovies, garlic, lemon zest and lemon juice and blend until smooth. With the machine on, add the olive oil in a thin stream. Season with salt and pepper.

3. Transfer the bagna cauda to a medium saucepan and rewarm over low heat. Pour into a serving bowl and serve with the crudités alongside. —*Chris Cosentino*

MAKE AHEAD The bagna cauda can be prepared through Step 2 and refrigerated overnight. Reheat gently.

Wine Bar Nut Mix

ACTIVE: 10 MIN; TOTAL: 30 MIN
MAKES 6 CUPS ● ● ●

This fantastic sweet-and-savory mix of pecans, almonds and walnuts from *The Casual Vineyard Table* (Ten Speed Press), by Carolyn Wente and Kimball Jones, makes a great gift.

- 2 cups pecans
- 2 cups almonds
- 2 cups walnuts
- ¼ cup pure maple syrup
- 2 tablespoons extra-virgin olive oil
- 2 tablespoons finely chopped mixed fresh rosemary, sage, savory and thyme
- ¼ teaspoon cayenne pepper

Salt and freshly ground pepper

Preheat the oven to 350°. In a bowl, toss the nuts with the maple syrup, olive oil, herbs and cayenne. Spread the nuts on a rimmed baking sheet and bake for 15 minutes, stirring occasionally, until browned. Season the nuts with salt and pepper and toss frequently until cooled.
—*Kimball Jones and Carolyn Wente*

MAKE AHEAD The nut mix can be stored in an airtight container at room temperature for up to 2 weeks.

Tiki Snack Mix

ACTIVE: 20 MIN; TOTAL: 1 HR 15 MIN
MAKES 4½ CUPS ● ●

This irresistible mix is the perfect complement to tiki cocktails (see the recipes on pages 386 and 387) because you get delicious pupu-platter flavors—sweet and salty bacon and chewy glazed pineapple—in every bite.

- 8 thick slices of meaty bacon, (10 ounces)
- 3 cups salted roasted peanuts (15 ounces)
- 4 candied pineapple rings, cut into ⅓-inch triangles
- 2 tablespoons sesame seeds
- 1 tablespoon low-sodium soy sauce
- 1 tablespoon honey
- ¼ teaspoon cayenne pepper

Kosher salt

1. Preheat the oven to 350°. Arrange the bacon slices in a single layer on a rack set over a large rimmed baking sheet. Bake for about 30 minutes, until the bacon is crisp and lightly golden. Drain the bacon on paper towels until cool. Transfer to a board and cut the slices crosswise into ½-inch strips.
2. In a large bowl, toss the peanuts with the bacon, pineapple, sesame seeds, soy sauce, honey and cayenne. Spread the mixture on a rimmed baking sheet and bake for about 20 minutes, stirring halfway through, until the peanuts are fragrant and the bacon is browned. Season with salt and stir occasionally until cool. Transfer to a bowl and serve. —*Melissa Rubel*

Crispy Seeded Pita Chips

TOTAL: 25 MIN
4 SERVINGS ● ● ●

Cookbook author Pam Anderson serves her healthy seed-studded pita chips with soup or by themselves as a "predinner bite," a snack to keep her energy up and her appetite under control. "Dinner is when a lot of people overdo it, but it's one meal when you shouldn't—because you won't burn off the calories," she says.

- 1 teaspoon yellow mustard seeds
- 1 teaspoon caraway seeds
- 1 teaspoon sesame seeds
- ½ teaspoon freshly ground pepper
- ¼ teaspoon kosher salt

Two 6-inch whole wheat pitas, split into 2 rounds and each round cut into 4 triangles

- 1 tablespoon plus 1 teaspoon vegetable oil

Preheat the oven to 350°. In a small bowl, toss the mustard, caraway and sesame seeds with the pepper and salt. Arrange the pita triangles on a large cookie sheet, smooth side down. Brush the pita with the oil and sprinkle the seed mixture on top. Bake until crisp and golden brown, about 10 minutes. Let cool. —*Pam Anderson*

MAKE AHEAD The pita chips can be stored in an airtight container overnight.

Plantain and Goat Cheese Gorditas

ACTIVE: 30 MIN; TOTAL: 1 HR
MAKES 12 GORDITAS ●

Chef Sue Torres serves these crispy, goat cheese–stuffed bites at her downtown Manhattan restaurant, Sueños. "You can stuff the mashed plantains with lots of fun things, like chorizo, beans or shrimp," she says. The key to their success is finding ultraripe plantains, "so black and soft and sweet that you think you should throw them out." As with bananas, underripe plantains ripen more quickly when placed in a paper bag.

imported nuts

Australian Macadamias
Brookfarm's roasted nuts—tossed with sea salt, chiles and native herbs like lemon myrtle—are vacuum-packed to stay superfresh (*$10 for 3.5 oz; igourmet.com*).

Indonesian Cashews Two sisters make garlicky, spicy honey-sesame cashews from a family recipe and pack them in handcrafted bags and boxes made from native materials like banana-tree bark (*from $3.50; nutsplusnuts.com*).

Sicilian Almonds Mastri di San Basilio's varietal almonds are so sweet and creamy, they almost taste like marzipan (*$25 for 1 lb; cheftools.com*).

4 very ripe (almost black),
   unpeeled soft plantains,
   rinsed (2¼ pounds)
2 tablespoons dry bread crumbs
1 teaspoon kosher salt
¼ cup crumbled goat cheese
1 quart vegetable oil,
   for frying
Spicy Tomato Sauce (p. 376),
   Pickled Red Onions (p. 376) and
   sour cream, for serving

1. Bring a large pot of water to a boil. Add the plantains and cook over moderately high heat until the skins split and the plantains are very tender when pierced with a knife, about 15 minutes. Transfer to a plate and let cool slightly. Peel the plantains. Transfer them to a bowl and mash well. Stir in the bread crumbs and salt and let cool.
2. Line a platter with plastic wrap. Form the plantain dough into 12 portions and roll into balls. Poke a hole in the center of each ball and fill it with 1 teaspoon of the goat cheese. Seal the holes and reroll the dough into balls. Set the gorditas on the platter.
3. In a large saucepan, heat the vegetable oil to 350°. Add the gorditas and fry until browned all over, about 5 minutes. Drain on a paper towel–lined plate. Serve the gorditas with the Spicy Tomato Sauce, Pickled Red Onions and sour cream.
—*Sue Torres*

MAKE AHEAD The gorditas can be prepared through Step 2, covered and then refrigerated overnight. Return to room temperature before frying.

Gargantuan Gougères

ACTIVE: 25 MIN; TOTAL: 1 HR 45 MIN
MAKES 30 GOUGÈRES ● ○ ○
Guests at Manhattan's Bar Boulud are greeted with these golden French cheese puffs made with grated Gruyère cheese and the mild Basque pepper piment d'Espelette. Almost twice the size of ordinary gougères, they're a bit like crispy, cheesy, slightly spicy popovers.

1 cup milk
1 cup water
6 tablespoons unsalted butter,
   cut into tablespoons
¾ teaspoon salt
1½ cups plus 1 tablespoon
   all-purpose flour
½ teaspoon piment d'Espelette
4 large eggs
2 cups shredded Gruyère cheese
Fleur de sel and cracked
   black pepper

1. Preheat the oven to 400°. Line 2 baking sheets with parchment paper. In a large saucepan, combine the milk with the water, butter and salt; bring to a boil over moderately high heat. Add the flour all at once with the piment d'Espelette and beat vigorously with a wooden spoon until the flour is thoroughly incorporated. Reduce the heat to low, return the saucepan to the burner and cook the gougère dough, stirring constantly, until it pulls away from the side of the pan, about 8 minutes.
2. Remove the saucepan from the heat and let stand at room temperature, stirring occasionally, until the dough cools slightly, about 5 minutes. Add the eggs one at a time, stirring briskly between additions to thoroughly incorporate each egg.
3. Drop 3-tablespoon mounds of dough onto the baking sheets 2 inches apart. Top each round with 1 tablespoon of cheese; sprinkle with fleur de sel and pepper.
4. Bake the gougères for 15 minutes. Reduce the oven temperature to 350° and bake for 30 minutes longer, switching the baking sheets halfway through, until puffed and browned. Turn off the oven and prop the door ajar with a wooden spoon. Let rest in the oven for about 30 minutes longer, until crisp on the outside but still steamy within. Serve warm or at room temperature. —*Daniel Boulud*

MAKE AHEAD The gougères can be frozen for up to 1 month. Defrost in a 350° oven for about 8 minutes.

Spicy Sriracha Chicken Wings

ACTIVE: 1 HR; TOTAL: 1 HR 30 MIN
PLUS 4 HR MARINATING
10 SERVINGS
These crispy chicken wings get their heat from Sriracha, the Thai hot sauce that Michael Symon (an F&W Best New Chef 1998) says is his favorite in the world. "We always have a couple of extra bottles at home, because my stepson blows right through the stuff."

10 pounds chicken wings, split
¼ cup coriander seeds, crushed
1 teaspoon cumin seeds, crushed
1 teaspoon cinnamon
2 tablespoons kosher salt
¼ cup extra-virgin olive oil
¾ cup Sriracha chile sauce
1½ sticks (12 tablespoons)
   unsalted butter, melted
½ cup chopped cilantro
Finely grated zest and juice of
   3 limes
3 quarts vegetable oil, for frying

1. In a very large bowl, toss the chicken wings with the coriander and cumin seeds, cinnamon, kosher salt and olive oil. Cover the bowl with plastic wrap and refrigerate for at least 4 hours or overnight.
2. Preheat the oven to 375°. Spread the wings on 3 large rimmed baking sheets and roast for about 30 minutes, until firm but not cooked through. (At this point, if you don't want to fry the wings, you can roast them for 1 hour longer, until crispy and golden.) Wash out the bowl. Add the Sriracha, butter, cilantro, lime zest and lime juice.
3. In a deep fryer or a very large saucepan, heat the vegetable oil to 375°. Fry the wings in 4 or 5 batches until golden and crisp, about 5 minutes per batch; drain, shaking off the excess oil. As each batch is finished, add the wings to the sauce and toss well. Transfer the wings to a platter, leaving the sauce in the bowl for the remaining batches. Serve the wings hot.
—*Michael Symon*

ROASTED FINGERLING POTATO AND PRESSED CAVIAR CANAPÉS

TWISTS, PINWHEELS AND SQUARES

Roasted Fingerling Potato and Pressed Caviar Canapés

 TOTAL: 35 MIN
4 SERVINGS

For this easy, impressive hors d'oeuvre, chef Jacques Pépin tops roasted fingerling potatoes with sour cream and slender diamonds of pressed caviar, the dense, salty paste made from fish eggs that break during the packing of traditional caviar. Boiled, sliced red potatoes also work in place of the fingerlings.

10 fingerling potatoes, scrubbed
and halved lengthwise
1 tablespoon extra-virgin olive oil
Salt and freshly ground pepper
2 tablespoons pressed caviar
(2 ounces; see Note)
½ cup sour cream
Chives cut into twenty 1-inch
lengths, for garnish

1. Preheat the oven to 400°. On a large rimmed baking sheet, toss the potatoes with the olive oil; season with salt and pepper. Arrange the potatoes cut side down; bake for 25 minutes, until they are tender and browned on the bottom. Let cool to warm.
2. Meanwhile, roll out the pressed caviar between 2 sheets of plastic wrap to a 5-by-6-inch rectangle about ⅛ inch thick. Cut the caviar into 20 diamonds or rectangles.
3. Transfer the potatoes to a platter, cut side up, and dollop sour cream on each. Top with the caviar and garnish with the chives.
—*Jacques Pépin*

NOTE Pressed caviar is available from californiacaviar.com.

Salmon Trout Tartare with Pressed Caviar and Tomatoes

 TOTAL: 25 MIN
4 SERVINGS ●

Salmon trout has a mild, delicate taste, but regular salmon is also delicious in this bright-flavored tartare; just be sure to use the freshest fish you can find. The chopped pressed caviar adds a lovely saltiness.

2 tablespoons minced sweet onion

2 tablespoons minced scallions

1 tablespoon minced chives

1½ teaspoons fresh lime juice

1 teaspoon Asian sesame oil

1 tablespoon extra-virgin olive oil, plus more for drizzling

2 tablespoons pressed caviar (2 ounces; see Note on p. 36)

½ pound skinless salmon trout or salmon fillet, cut into ¼-inch dice

Salt and freshly ground pepper

12 cherry tomatoes, halved

12 small, tender herb sprigs, such as tarragon, parsley or chervil

1. Rinse the onion and scallions in a fine sieve and pat dry; transfer to a bowl. Add the chives, lime juice, sesame oil and the 1 tablespoon of olive oil and toss.

2. Roll out the caviar ⅛ inch thick between 2 sheets of plastic wrap. Transfer the caviar to a cutting board and cut into ⅛-inch dice. Add the caviar to the bowl. Fold in the fish and season with salt and pepper. Spoon the tartare onto plates (using a 3-inch ring mold as a guide, if desired). Drizzle with olive oil, garnish with the tomatoes and herb sprigs and serve. —*Jacques Pépin*

Everything Twists

ACTIVE: 20 MIN; TOTAL: 1 HR 20 MIN

MAKES ABOUT 32 TWISTS ● ● ●

These seed-coated puff pastry twists were inspired by the "everything" bagel.

1½ tablespoons dehydrated chopped onion

1½ tablespoons sesame seeds

1 tablespoon poppy seeds

2 teaspoons caraway seeds

1½ teaspoons coarse sea salt

1 teaspoon garlic powder

One 14-ounce package all-butter puff pastry, thawed if frozen but still cold

1 egg beaten with 1½ teaspoons of water

1. In a bowl, mix the dehydrated onion; the sesame, poppy and caraway seeds; the salt and the garlic powder.

2. Line 3 large baking sheets with parchment. On a floured surface, roll out the puff pastry into an 11-by-14-inch rectangle; cut in half lengthwise. Brush with the egg wash and sprinkle evenly with the seed mixture. Cut the pastry crosswise into ¾-inch-wide strips. Twist the strips and transfer them to the baking sheets, leaving 2 inches in between each one. Freeze until firm, 30 minutes.

3. Preheat the oven to 375°. Bake the twists for 22 minutes, until golden. Switch the pans top to bottom and back to front halfway through baking. Let stand until cool enough to handle, about 10 minutes. Transfer to a platter and serve. —*Melissa Rubel*

MAKE AHEAD The unbaked twists can be stored between layers of parchment and frozen for up to 1 month.

Prosciutto-Fontina Pinwheels

ACTIVE: 25 MIN; TOTAL: 2 HR

MAKES ABOUT 6½ DOZEN

PINWHEELS ●

One 14-ounce package all-butter puff pastry, thawed if frozen but still cold

3 ounces thinly sliced prosciutto

¾ cup shredded Fontina cheese

Freshly ground pepper

1 egg beaten with 1½ teaspoons of water

1. On a floured surface, roll out the puff pastry to a 10½-by-15-inch rectangle; cut in half lengthwise. Top with the prosciutto and Fontina, leaving a ½-inch border along the far edge of each piece. Season with pepper. Starting at the near edge, roll each rectangle into a log; brush the border with the egg wash and pinch to seal. Transfer to a large baking sheet; freeze until firm, 30 minutes.

2. Line 2 large baking sheets with parchment. Working with one log at a time, trim the ends. Cut the log crosswise ¼ inch thick. Arrange the pinwheels 2 inches apart on the baking sheets. Freeze until firm. Preheat the oven to 375°. Bake for 20 minutes, until golden. Cut the remaining log, then freeze and bake; serve. —*Melissa Rubel*

MAKE AHEAD The frozen sliced pinwheels can be transferred to a resealable plastic bag and frozen for up to 1 month.

Fig-and-Stilton Squares

ACTIVE: 20 MIN; TOTAL: 3 HR 15 MIN

MAKES 4 DOZEN SQUARES ● ●

After baking flaky squares of puff pastry, F&W's Melissa Rubel tops them with sweet fig preserves and pungent blue cheese.

One 14-ounce package all-butter puff pastry, thawed if frozen but still cold

½ cup fig preserves

¾ cup crumbled Stilton cheese (4 ounces)

1. On a lightly floured work surface, roll out the puff pastry to a 10½-by-15-inch rectangle. Transfer the pastry to a large rimmed baking sheet and cut into 1¾-inch squares; you should have about 48 squares. Freeze until firm, about 30 minutes.

2. Preheat the oven to 375°. Line a large rimmed baking sheet with parchment paper. Arrange 12 squares on the sheet and cover with more parchment paper. Top the squares with another baking sheet, bottom side down. If you have another pair of baking sheets, repeat with 12 more squares. Bake the squares for about 35 minutes, until the pastry is golden. Transfer the squares to a rack to cool. Repeat to bake the remaining squares.

3. Return as many cooled squares as will fit to a baking sheet. Top each square with ½ teaspoon of the fig preserves. Sprinkle with the Stilton and bake for about 5 minutes, until the Stilton is melted. Serve warm or at room temperature. —*Melissa Rubel*

MAKE AHEAD The unbaked frozen pastry squares can be frozen in an airtight container for up to 1 month.

AUGUST CHOPPED
SALAD (P. 44)

salads

66 *Clint Eastwood came in and wanted a romaine salad. We don't have one on the menu. I ran next door to get the lettuce.* 99

—SEAN O'BRIEN, EXECUTIVE CHEF AND PARTNER,
MYTH, SAN FRANCISCO

CRUNCHY VEGETABLE SALAD WITH PEAS AND RADISHES

BLT SALAD WITH BLUE CHEESE

Crunchy Vegetable Salad with Sautéed Peas and Radishes

TOTAL: 50 MIN

4 SERVINGS ● ● ●

"I grew up in the French countryside," chef Laurent Gras says, "so vegetable-heavy dishes make me feel like I'm back home."

- 1 **cup cherry tomatoes (5 ounces)**
- 1 **pound fava beans, shelled (1 cup)**
- 8 **ounces fresh peas, shelled (½ cup)**
- ¼ **cup extra-virgin olive oil**
- 2 **tablespoons fresh lemon juice**

Kosher salt

- 4 **baby artichokes (about 1 pound)**
- 4 **medium radishes, quartered**
- 1 **bunch of watercress (6 ounces), tough stems discarded**
- 1 **teaspoon finely grated lemon zest**

1. Bring a medium saucepan of water to a boil. Fill a bowl with ice water. Cut a slit into the base of each cherry tomato and blanch them in the boiling water until their skins start to split, about 15 seconds. Using a slotted spoon, transfer the cherry tomatoes to the ice water to cool, then drain and peel them.

2. In the same water, cook the fava beans until just tender, about 2 minutes. Use a slotted spoon to transfer the fava beans to a plate and let cool slightly, then peel. Blanch the peas until just tender, about 2 minutes. Drain well.

3. In a medium bowl, whisk 3 tablespoons of the olive oil with the lemon juice and season with salt. With a paring knife, trim the artichoke bottoms and stems and snap off the tough outer leaves until you reach the light green inner leaves. Using a serrated knife, cut off the top third of the artichokes. Cut the artichokes in half

lengthwise. Using a teaspoon, remove the chokes, if there are any. Thinly slice the artichokes lengthwise, add the slices to the dressing and toss to coat. Add the peeled cherry tomatoes and the blanched fava beans to the bowl and toss again.

4. In a medium skillet, heat 1½ teaspoons of the olive oil. Add the quartered radishes and cook over moderate heat, stirring occasionally, until tender, about 2 minutes. Add the blanched peas and cook, stirring, for 1 minute longer. Season the radishes and peas with salt.

5. In a medium bowl, toss the watercress with the remaining 1½ teaspoons of olive oil and the grated lemon zest and divide the dressed watercress between 4 salad plates. Top each portion of watercress with some of the artichoke salad followed by the sautéed radishes and peas; serve the vegetable salads right away.

—*Laurent Gras*

BLT Salad with Blue Cheese

TOTAL: 35 MIN
4 SERVINGS

In his breadless version of the BLT sandwich, Miami chef Michael Schwartz replaces mayo with a wedge of blue cheese. Schwartz cures his own bacon, but the salad is delicious with any good artisanal bacon. His one piece of advice: Use thickly cut strips. "They can never be too thick," he says.

- 8 thick slices of bacon (4 ounces)
- 2 tablespoons minced shallot
- 1½ tablespoons sherry vinegar
- 3 tablespoons extra-virgin olive oil
- Salt and freshly ground pepper
- 1 large head of frisée, torn into bite-size pieces (8 cups)
- 2 pounds assorted tomatoes, large ones sliced or cut into wedges
- 6 ounces blue cheese, such as Stilton, cut into 4 equal wedges

1. In a skillet, cook the bacon over moderate heat until crisp, 3 minutes per side. Drain on paper towels. Cut the slices in half crosswise.

2. In a small bowl, combine the shallot, vinegar and olive oil and season with salt and pepper. In a large bowl, toss the frisée with the vinaigrette; mound on plates. Arrange the bacon, tomatoes and blue cheese around the frisée and serve. —*Michael Schwartz*

Mixed Green Salad with Fig-Yogurt Dressing

TOTAL: 35 MIN
4 SERVINGS ● ●

- ¼ cup plus 2 tablespoons dried figs, stemmed and halved
- 2 cups boiling water
- ½ cup plain low-fat yogurt
- 1 tablespoon fresh lemon juice
- 1 tablespoon balsamic vinegar
- Salt and freshly ground pepper
- 8 ounces mixed greens (8 cups)
- 1 cup shaved Parmigiano-Reggiano cheese (3 ounces)

1. In a small heatproof bowl, soak the figs in the boiling water until softened, about 15 minutes, then drain.

2. Transfer two-thirds of the soaked figs to a blender. Add the yogurt, lemon juice and vinegar and puree until smooth. Add the remaining figs to the blender and pulse once or twice, until the figs are coarsely chopped. Season the dressing with salt and pepper. In a large bowl, toss the greens with the dressing, top with the cheese shavings and serve right away.
—*Jessica Gilmartin and Patama Roj*

Spring Lettuce Salad with Roasted Asparagus

TOTAL: 25 MIN
6 SERVINGS ● ●

- 1 pound medium asparagus
- ⅓ cup plus 1 tablespoon extra-virgin olive oil
- ½ teaspoon finely grated lemon zest
- Kosher salt and freshly ground black pepper
- 1½ tablespoons fresh lemon juice
- 1 tablespoon Dijon mustard
- 10 ounces mixed spring lettuces
- One 1½-ounce piece of Parmigiano-Reggiano cheese, shaved into curls with a vegetable peeler

1. Preheat the oven to 450°. On a large rimmed baking sheet, toss the asparagus with 1 tablespoon of the olive oil and the grated lemon zest and season with salt and black pepper. Roast the asparagus for about 8 minutes, until the stalks are just tender and the tips begin to turn brown.

2. In a small bowl, whisk the lemon juice with the mustard and the remaining ⅓ cup of olive oil. Season with salt and pepper.

3. In a large bowl, toss the lettuces with all but 2 tablespoons of the dressing. Arrange the salad on plates and top with the roasted asparagus and cheese curls. Drizzle the remaining dressing over the asparagus and serve. —*Amber Huffman*

Seared Romaine Spears with Caesar Dressing

TOTAL: 30 MIN
10 SERVINGS ● ●

In this healthy incarnation of a Caesar salad, romaine develops an appealing smoky flavor on the grill, while low-fat mayonnaise stands in for egg yolks in the garlicky dressing.

- ¼ cup low-fat mayonnaise
- ¼ cup red wine vinegar
- 4 garlic cloves
- 1 tablespoon fresh lemon juice
- 2 teaspoons Dijon mustard
- ½ teaspoon Worcestershire sauce
- ¼ teaspoon Tabasco
- ½ cup plus 2 tablespoons vegetable oil
- Salt and freshly ground pepper
- 10 hearts of romaine, halved lengthwise
- 10 slices crusty peasant bread
- 3 ounces Parmigiano-Reggiano cheese, shaved

1. Light a grill. In a blender or mini food processor, blend the mayonnaise with the red wine vinegar, garlic cloves, lemon juice, Dijon mustard, Worcestershire sauce and Tabasco. With the machine on, gradually add ½ cup of the vegetable oil until the Caesar dressing is creamy. Season with salt and pepper, cover and refrigerate.

2. Lightly brush the hearts of romaine with 1 tablespoon of the vegetable oil and season them with salt and pepper. Grill the romaine hearts over moderately high heat, turning once or twice with tongs, until the lettuce is lightly charred but still crisp, about 3 minutes.

3. Lightly brush the bread with the remaining 1 tablespoon of oil. Grill, turning once, until toasted, about 2 minutes.

4. Spread half of the Caesar dressing on a large platter. Arrange the grilled hearts of romaine on top and brush with the remaining dressing. Garnish with the cheese shavings and serve the grilled bread alongside.
—*Kerry Simon*

Arugula Salad with Olives, Feta and Dill

ACTIVE: 20 MIN; TOTAL 1 HR 20 MIN

10 SERVINGS ● ●

To give arugula salad a slightly Greek twist, Cleveland chef Michael Symon tosses the greens with fresh dill, briny Greek feta cheese and kalamata olives. Symon dresses the salad with Greek extra-virgin olive oil, which he says has a pure flavor and is generally more affordable than olive oil from Italy.

- 1 red onion, very thinly sliced
- 1 garlic clove, minced
- 1 cup pitted kalamata olives, coarsely chopped
- ½ cup plus 2 tablespoons extra-virgin olive oil
- ¼ cup plus 2 tablespoons red wine vinegar
- Salt and freshly ground pepper
- 3 tablespoons chopped fresh dill
- 1 cup crumbled Greek feta cheese (5 ounces)
- 14 ounces baby arugula

In a large bowl, toss the onion, garlic and olives with the oil and vinegar and season with salt and pepper. Let stand at room temperature for 1 hour. Stir in the dill and feta, then add the arugula and toss gently. Serve right away. —*Michael Symon*

summer salad ideas

Raw Beet Salad with Mint and Quick-Pickled Onions Cover thinly sliced onions with white wine vinegar, season with salt and let stand for 10 minutes. Toss frisée and mint with olive oil; season with salt and pepper. Slice peeled Chioggia beets on a mandoline and arrange around the frisée on plates. Top with the onions.

Spicy Chayote Slaw with Lime and Cilantro Peel, halve and pit a chayote (a mild-flavored vegetable in the gourd family) and cut it into 2-inch matchsticks. In a bowl, cover thinly sliced red onion with fresh lime juice and let stand for 10 minutes. Whisk in olive oil. Add the chayote matchsticks and a minced seeded jalapeño, season with salt and pepper and toss. Just before serving, add finely chopped cilantro and toss.

Arugula-and-Endive Salad with Honeyed Pine Nuts

TOTAL: 25 MIN

4 SERVINGS ● ●

This salad replaces blue cheese's classic partner, honey, with a crunchy, brittle-like garnish made from honey and pine nuts. Pine nuts have a subtle flavor that goes especially well with milder honeys, but other nuts, like pecans and walnuts, work nicely here, too.

- ½ cup pine nuts (2½ ounces)
- 2 tablespoons plus 2 teaspoons honey, preferably clover
- 1½ tablespoons cider vinegar
- 2 teaspoons whole-grain mustard
- ½ teaspoon Dijon mustard
- ¼ cup extra-virgin olive oil
- Kosher salt and freshly ground black pepper
- 4 ounces baby arugula (4 cups)
- 2 Belgian endives—halved, cored and thinly sliced lengthwise
- 4 ounces blue cheese, crumbled (1 cup)

1. Line a baking sheet with parchment paper and lightly coat the parchment with cooking spray. In a nonstick skillet, combine the pine nuts with 2 tablespoons of the honey. Cook over moderately high heat, stirring, until the nuts are golden and coated with honey, 4 minutes. Pour the nuts and honey onto the baking sheet. Using a spatula, spread the nuts in an even layer; let cool.

2. In a small bowl, whisk the remaining 2 teaspoons of honey with the vinegar and the mustards. Gradually whisk in the oil; season with salt and pepper. In a large bowl, toss the arugula with the endives and blue cheese. Break the honeyed pine nuts into small pieces and add them to the salad. Add the dressing, toss to coat and serve at once. —*Susan Spungen*

Arugula Salad with Prosciutto and Oyster Mushrooms

TOTAL: 30 MIN

10 SERVINGS

When he was growing up in the Marche region of Italy, chef Fabio Trabocchi loved foraging for mushrooms in the woods around his house. In this elegant salad, he tosses lightly sautéed oyster mushrooms with arugula and tops them with thin slices of prosciutto and Pecorino Toscano.

- ¼ cup plus 2 tablespoons extra-virgin olive oil
- 1 pound oyster mushrooms, thickly sliced
- Salt and freshly ground pepper
- ¼ cup aged balsamic vinegar
- 1 teaspoon finely grated lemon zest
- 4 inner celery ribs, cut into 2-by-¼-inch matchsticks, plus ¼ cup celery leaves for garnish
- 10 ounces baby arugula (10 cups)
- 6 ounces Pecorino Toscano, shaved with a vegetable peeler (1½ cups)
- 6 ounces thinly sliced prosciutto di Parma

1. In a large nonstick skillet, heat 2 tablespoons of the olive oil. Add the mushrooms and season with salt and pepper. Cook over moderately high heat, stirring occasionally, until tender and lightly browned, about 6 minutes. Transfer the mushrooms to a bowl and let cool.

2. In a large bowl, whisk the vinegar with the lemon zest and the remaining ¼ cup of olive oil. Season with salt and pepper. Add the celery matchsticks, arugula and mushrooms and gently toss. Transfer the salad to a large platter or bowl, top with the cheese, prosciutto and celery leaves and serve right away. —*Fabio Trabocchi*

Warm Spinach Salad with Cannellini Beans and Shrimp

TOTAL: 25 MIN
4 SERVINGS

The combination of sweet shrimp and meaty little cannellini beans here transforms a simple warm spinach salad.

- 8 ounces baby spinach (7 cups)
- 3 slices of bacon, cut crosswise into ½-inch strips
- 1 pound shelled and deveined large shrimp

Kosher salt and freshly ground pepper

One 15-ounce can cannellini beans, drained and rinsed

- ¼ cup plus 1 tablespoon extra-virgin olive oil
- 1 small shallot, minced
- 1 tablespoon Dijon mustard
- ¼ cup red wine vinegar

1. Spread the spinach on a large platter. In a large skillet, cook the bacon over moderate heat until crisp, 4 minutes. Drain off all but 2 tablespoons of the fat. Season the shrimp with salt and pepper and cook with the bacon over moderately high heat until just white throughout, about 4 minutes. Add the beans, season with salt and pepper and toss until heated through, 1 minute. Scrape the shrimp and beans onto the bed of spinach.

2. In the same skillet, heat 1 tablespoon of the oil. Add the shallot and cook over moderately low heat until softened, 1 minute. Whisk in the mustard and vinegar, then whisk in the remaining ¼ cup of oil. Season the dressing with salt and pepper, pour over the salad and serve. —*Melissa Rubel*

Warm Fennel–and–Bitter Greens Salad

TOTAL: 20 MIN
6 SERVINGS ● ●

Danielle Custer (an F&W Best New Chef 1998) wilts basil and watercress in a hot skillet for a minute or two before tossing them with spinach and arugula. Here, F&W's Grace Parisi makes a quicker, crunchier version of Custer's dish with bitter greens, radishes, fennel and shaved Parmigiano-Reggiano cheese.

- 2 tablespoons red wine vinegar
- 1 teaspoon honey
- ¼ cup extra-virgin olive oil

Salt and freshly ground pepper

One 1-pound fennel bulb, cored and very thinly sliced

- 4 small radishes, very thinly sliced
- 1 bunch of watercress, thick stems discarded
- 5 ounces baby arugula (5 cups)
- 1 small head of radicchio, leaves torn
- ½ cup flat-leaf parsley leaves
- 2 ounces Parmigiano-Reggiano shavings (1 cup)

1. In a large bowl, whisk the red wine vinegar with the honey. Add the olive oil and whisk until emulsified. Season with salt and pepper. Add the remaining ingredients and toss well.

2. Heat a large, deep skillet until very hot. Add the dressed salad and toss over high heat just until barely wilted in spots, about 30 seconds. Transfer to plates and serve immediately. —*Grace Parisi*

Ensalada Verde with Idiazábal Cheese

TOTAL: 45 MIN
12 SERVINGS ● ● ●

The crowning touch in this salad is Idiazábal cheese, a semifirm Spanish sheep's-milk cheese that has a rich, buttery flavor and a slight smokiness (it was traditionally aged in stone chimneys).

- 3 tablespoons sherry vinegar
- 2 tablespoons very finely chopped shallot
- 1½ teaspoons very finely chopped thyme
- 1½ teaspoons whole-grain mustard
- 1½ teaspoons honey
- ¼ cup plus 2 tablespoons extra-virgin olive oil

Kosher salt and freshly ground pepper

- ¼ pound thin green beans, trimmed
- 3 romaine hearts, cut crosswise into ¼-inch-wide strips
- 1 bunch of watercress, thick stems discarded and leaves coarsely chopped
- 1 small head of frisée, coarsely chopped
- 2 ounces baby arugula (2 cups)
- 1 Granny Smith apple—halved, cored and thinly sliced
- 1 Bosc pear—halved, cored and thinly sliced
- 1 Hass avocado, cut into ½-inch dice
- ¼ pound Idiazábal or Manchego cheese, coarsely shredded

1. In a small bowl, mix the sherry vinegar with the shallot and thyme and let stand for 10 minutes. Whisk in the mustard, honey and olive oil and season the dressing with salt and pepper.

2. In a medium saucepan of boiling salted water, cook the green beans until they are crisp-tender, about 3 minutes. Drain and rinse the green beans under cold running water until they are cool; pat dry. Cut the green beans into ½-inch lengths.

3. In a large bowl, toss the green beans with the romaine hearts, watercress, frisée, arugula, apple, pear, avocado and Idiazábal cheese. Toss the salad with the dressing, season with salt and pepper and serve at once. —*Jose Garces*

salads

Kale-and-Avocado Salad

TOTAL: 25 MIN
1 SERVING ● ● ●

- 1 teaspoon sesame seeds
- 1 packed cup chopped kale leaves
- ⅛ teaspoon salt
- 1 Hass avocado, quartered
- 1 tablespoon fresh lime juice
- ½ packed cup arugula leaves
- 1 small tomato, coarsely chopped
- 1 radish, diced
- 2 large pitted green olives, diced
- 1 tablespoon chopped cilantro

1. In a skillet, toast the sesame seeds over moderate heat. Transfer to a plate.
2. In a bowl, knead the kale with the salt until it begins to wilt. Add the avocado and lime juice and mash until chunky. Add the arugula, tomato, radish, olives, cilantro and sesame seeds, toss gently and serve.
—Adina Niemerow

August Chopped Salad

TOTAL: 45 MIN
6 SERVINGS ● ●

At August, his flagship New Orleans restaurant, chef John Besh makes a chopped salad with 21 different vegetables and herbs, but this fantastic version uses just nine.

- 2 tablespoons Champagne vinegar
- ⅓ cup extra-virgin olive oil
- Salt and freshly ground pepper
- ½ pound prepared beet salad or cooked beets
- 18 baby carrots, halved lengthwise
- 8 ounces fingerling potatoes, sliced ½ inch thick
- 8 ounces marinated artichoke hearts, drained and chopped
- One 1-pound fennel bulb, thinly sliced on a mandoline
- 4 radishes, thinly sliced
- ½ seedless cucumber—peeled, quartered lengthwise and thinly sliced crosswise
- 3 ounces pea shoots
- 2 tablespoons chopped dill

1. In a large bowl, whisk the vinegar and olive oil and season with salt and pepper. Transfer 2 tablespoons of the dressing to a small bowl and toss with the beets.
2. Bring a saucepan of salted water to a boil. Fill a bowl with ice water. Cook the carrots for 5 minutes; using a slotted spoon, transfer to the ice water. Add the potatoes to the boiling water and cook for 8 minutes. Drain and add to the carrots; pat dry.
3. Add the carrots and potatoes to the dressing in the large bowl. Add the artichokes, fennel, radishes, cucumber, pea shoots and dill. Season with salt and pepper and toss to coat. Transfer the salad to plates, scatter the beets on top and serve right away.
—John Besh

Beet, Fennel and Jicama Salad with Macadamia Nut Dressing

TOTAL: 25 MIN
1 SERVING ● ●

DRESSING
- ¼ cup macadamia nuts
- 1 tablespoon water
- ¼ teaspoon lime zest
- 1 tablespoon fresh lime juice
- ¼ teaspoon ground cumin
- Pinch of salt
- Pinch of cayenne pepper

SALAD
- ½ cup diced peeled jicama
- ½ cup diced fennel
- ½ cup diced peeled raw beets
- ¼ cup chopped Belgian endive
- 4 cherry tomatoes, chopped
- Salt and freshly ground pepper

1. MAKE THE DRESSING: In a food processor, finely grind the macadamias. Add the remaining dressing ingredients and pulse until creamy; add more water, ½ teaspoon at a time, to thin out as desired.
2. MAKE THE SALAD: Transfer the dressing to a bowl. Add the jicama, fennel, beets, endive and tomatoes and season with salt and pepper. Toss well and serve.
—Adina Niemerow

Warm Chanterelle–and–Berry Salad with Cheddar

TOTAL: 40 MIN
4 SERVINGS ●

- 6 tablespoons plus 1 teaspoon extra-virgin olive oil
- ½ small sweet onion, sliced into ¼-inch-thick rings
- Salt and freshly ground pepper
- 1 pound chanterelle or hedgehog mushrooms, stems trimmed and large mushrooms halved
- 1 tablespoon plus 1 teaspoon red wine vinegar
- 1 teaspoon Dijon mustard
- 3 ounces baby arugula (3 cups)
- 1 cup blackberries
- 1 cup raspberries
- Four 2-ounce pieces of sharp cheddar cheese

1. In a large skillet, heat 1 tablespoon of oil until shimmering. Add the onion, season with salt and pepper and cook over high heat until richly browned, 2 minutes per side. Transfer the onion to a large bowl.
2. Add 3 tablespoons of the olive oil to the skillet, and when it is hot, add the chanterelles and season with salt and pepper. Cook over moderate heat until the liquid in the skillet has evaporated, about 7 minutes. Continue to cook over moderate heat, stirring occasionally, until the chanterelles are browned, about 5 minutes longer. Season with salt and pepper.
3. In a small bowl, combine the vinegar with the mustard and the remaining 2 tablespoons plus 1 teaspoon of olive oil; season the vinaigrette with salt and pepper. Add the arugula, blackberries and raspberries to the large bowl with the onion. Add the chanterelles and the vinaigrette and toss well. Put a piece of cheddar on each plate, divide the salad among the plates and serve. *—Eric Warnstedt*
MAKE AHEAD The onion and mushrooms can be kept at room temperature for up to 2 hours. Reheat gently before serving.

WARM CHANTERELLE—AND—
BERRY SALAD WITH CHEDDAR

Mexican Chopped Salad with Beets and Walnut Dressing

TOTAL: 30 MIN
4 SERVINGS ○

- 8 ounces walnut halves (2 cups)
- ½ cup extra-virgin olive oil
- ¼ cup fresh lime juice
- Salt and freshly ground pepper
- ¾ pound peeled roasted beets, cut into ⅓-inch cubes (see Note)
- 1 Fuji apple, cut into ⅓-inch cubes
- 1 Hass avocado, cubed
- 1 fennel bulb, cored and thinly sliced
- 4 ounces Manchego cheese, thinly shaved (1 cup)
- 5 ounces mesclun greens
- 2 cups tortilla chips, lightly crushed

1. Preheat the oven to 350°. Spread the walnuts on a baking sheet and toast for 10 to 12 minutes, until golden and fragrant. Let cool completely.

2. Transfer 1½ cups of the walnuts to a food processor. Add the oil and lime juice and pulse until the walnuts are coarsely chopped. Transfer to a bowl and season with salt and pepper. Add the beets, apple, avocado, fennel and Manchego and toss. Add the mesclun and tortilla chips, season with salt and pepper and toss again. Transfer the salad to plates, garnish with the remaining walnuts and serve right away. —*Dionicio Jimenez*

NOTE Vacuum-sealed roasted beets are available in specialty shops.

Turkish Tomato Salad with Fresh Herbs

TOTAL: 30 MIN
8 SERVINGS ○ ○ ○

Toasted pistachios add flavor and crunch to this jalapeño-spiked tomato salad from Turkish food expert Engin Akin.

- 1½ cups unsalted pistachios
- ½ cup pomegranate molasses
- ¼ cup extra-virgin olive oil
- Salt

- 2 pounds tomatoes, finely chopped, or quartered cherry tomatoes
- 4 bunches of scallions, finely chopped
- 2 cups chopped flat-leaf parsley leaves
- 1 cup chopped mint leaves
- 1 cucumber—peeled, seeded and cut into ½-inch chunks
- 2 jalapeños, seeded and minced

1. Preheat the oven to 350°. Spread the pistachios on a rimmed baking sheet and toast in the oven for about 8 minutes, or until lightly browned; let cool.

2. In a small bowl, whisk the pomegranate molasses with the olive oil until blended. Season the dressing with salt.

3. In a large bowl, toss the tomatoes with the scallions, parsley, mint, cucumber and jalapeños. Add the pomegranate dressing and toss well. Season with salt. Spoon the tomato salad onto a platter, sprinkle the pistachios over the top and serve.
—*Engin Akin*

Three-Pea Salad

TOTAL: 30 MIN
6 SERVINGS ○ ○ ○

This salad combines sugar snap peas, snow peas and green peas in a sherry vinaigrette blended with a touch of sour cream. It can be made into a main course by adding shaved Manchego cheese and serrano ham.

- 1 tablespoon minced shallot
- 1 tablespoon sherry vinegar
- 1 tablespoon sour cream or crème fraîche
- ¼ cup extra-virgin olive oil
- Salt and freshly ground pepper
- 8 ounces sugar snap peas
- 8 ounces snow peas, halved crosswise
- One 10-ounce box frozen baby peas

1. Bring a large saucepan of salted water to a boil. Fill a large bowl with ice water. In another large bowl, whisk the shallot, vinegar and sour cream together. Whisk in the olive oil until emulsified. Season with salt and pepper.

2. Add the sugar snap peas to the boiling water and blanch for 20 seconds. Add the snow peas and cook for 20 seconds. Add the frozen baby peas and cook for 20 seconds longer, until the sugar snaps and snow peas are crisp-tender and the baby peas are heated through. Drain and immediately transfer the colander to the ice water to stop the cooking. Drain again and pat the peas dry. Add the peas to the dressing, season with salt and pepper and toss to coat. Serve right away. —*Grace Parisi*

MAKE AHEAD The salad can be refrigerated overnight.

Beet Salad with Candied Marcona Almonds

ACTIVE: 45 MIN; TOTAL: 2 HR
8 SERVINGS ● ● ●

- 2½ pounds medium red or golden beets, scrubbed and trimmed
- ½ cup plus 2 tablespoons extra-virgin olive oil
- 1 tablespoon unsalted butter
- 2 tablespoons sugar
- 1 tablespoon light corn syrup
- Salt and cayenne pepper
- 1 cup marcona almonds (see Note)
- ½ cup fresh tangerine juice
- 2 tablespoons sherry vinegar
- 1 tablespoon Dijon mustard
- 1 tablespoon minced shallots
- 1 small head of frisée (4 ounces), torn into bite-size pieces
- Young pecorino cheese

1. Preheat the oven to 350°. In a large baking dish, toss the beets with 2 tablespoons of the olive oil. Cover with foil and bake for 1½ hours, or until tender. When cool enough to handle, peel the beets and cut them into ½-inch wedges.

2. Meanwhile, line a large rimmed baking sheet with parchment paper and lightly butter the paper. In a medium saucepan,

BEET SALAD WITH CANDIED MARCONA ALMONDS

CRUNCHY ASIAN PEA SALAD WITH HONEYED BACON

combine the 1 tablespoon of butter with the sugar, corn syrup and a pinch each of salt and cayenne and bring to a boil, stirring, to dissolve the sugar. Add the almonds and stir until evenly coated with the syrup. Scrape the almonds onto the parchment-lined baking sheet in an even layer. Bake with the beets for about 12 minutes, until golden and bubbling. Let the nuts cool for about 25 minutes, then break into small clusters.

3. In a small saucepan, simmer the tangerine juice over moderate heat until it is reduced to 2 tablespoons, about 15 minutes. Let cool, then transfer to a large bowl. Whisk in the sherry vinegar, Dijon mustard and shallots. Gradually whisk in the remaining ½ cup of olive oil and season the dressing with salt. Add the beets and frisée and toss the salad.

4. Transfer the salad to a platter or bowl. Garnish with the almonds, shave the pecorino on top and serve. —*Steve Corry*

NOTE Richer and sweeter than California almonds, Spanish marcona almonds are available from latienda.com.

MAKE AHEAD The peeled, roasted beets can be refrigerated overnight. Bring to room temperature before serving. The candied almonds can be kept in an airtight container at room temperature for up to 2 days.

Crunchy Asian Pea Salad with Honeyed Bacon

TOTAL: 30 MIN
4 SERVINGS ●

 6 thick slices of maple-cured
    bacon (about 6 ounces)
 2 tablespoons honey
 1 tablespoon soy sauce
 ½ teaspoon Chinese
    five-spice powder
 3 tablespoons pure olive oil
 2 tablespoons fresh lime juice
 ½ teaspoon finely grated lime zest

 1 tablespoon Asian fish sauce
 1 tablespoon chile oil
Salt and freshly ground pepper
 ½ pound snow peas, julienned
 6 ounces snow pea shoots
    (8 cups)
 2 tablespoons torn basil leaves
 2 tablespoons torn mint leaves

1. Preheat the broiler and position a rack 8 inches from the heat. Arrange the bacon slices on a baking sheet in a single layer. In a small bowl, stir together the honey, soy sauce and five-spice powder and brush liberally over the bacon. Broil for 10 minutes, turning once, until the bacon is browned and crisp. Transfer to a work surface and cut into ½-inch pieces. Let the bacon cool.

2. In a large bowl, whisk the olive oil with the lime juice, lime zest, fish sauce and chile oil and season with salt and pepper. Add the snow peas, pea shoots, basil, mint and bacon and toss. Serve right away. —*Ratha Chau*

●HEALTHY ●MAKE AHEAD ●VEGETARIAN ●STAFF FAVORITE

GREEN BEAN–AND–
TOMATO SALAD WITH
TARRAGON DRESSING

Green Bean–and–Tomato Salad with Tarragon Dressing

TOTAL: 30 MIN
12 SERVINGS ● ●

This supersimple bean-and-tomato salad tossed with a tarragon-flavored dressing is perfect for summertime picnics like the ones chef Paul Virant's mother would prepare when he was a child. "She would make tomato salad, potato salad and fried chicken the night before, so we'd have everything ready the next day," he says.

- 2 pounds green and yellow string beans
- ¼ cup extra-virgin olive oil
- 2 medium shallots, very finely chopped
- 2 tablespoons chopped tarragon
- Salt and freshly ground pepper
- 1 pint cherry tomatoes, halved

1. In a large pot of boiling salted water, cook the beans until just tender, about 4 minutes. Drain the beans and spread them on a large baking sheet to cool. Pat dry.
2. In a small bowl, whisk the olive oil with the shallots and tarragon and season with salt and pepper. Place the beans and tomatoes in a large bowl, add the dressing and toss well. Transfer to a platter and serve. —*Paul Virant*

MAKE AHEAD The cooked green beans and dressing can be refrigerated separately overnight. Bring to room temperature before tossing.

Yellow-Wax-Bean-and-Radish Salad with Cannellinis

ACTIVE: 25 MIN; TOTAL: 1 HR 40 MIN
PLUS OVERNIGHT SOAKING
10 SERVINGS ● ●

For a crunchy, summery salad, San Francisco chef Chris Cosentino tosses yellow wax beans, radish slivers, red onion slices, cannellini beans and fresh basil in a lemony vinaigrette. To save time, substitute canned cannellinis for the dried ones called for here.

- 2 cups dried cannellini beans (12 ounces), soaked overnight and drained
- 1 small yellow onion, peeled and halved
- 1 small carrot
- 1 small celery rib
- 1 pound yellow wax beans
- ½ cup extra-virgin olive oil
- ¼ cup red wine vinegar
- 1 tablespoon fresh lemon juice
- Salt and freshly ground black pepper
- 8 large radishes, sliced ¼ inch thick
- 1 small red onion, very thinly sliced
- ⅓ cup small basil leaves or chopped basil

1. In a large saucepan, cover the drained cannellini beans with 2 inches of water. Add the yellow onion, carrot and celery and bring to a boil. Simmer over low heat, stirring occasionally, until the cannellinis are tender, about 1 hour and 15 minutes. Drain the cannellinis; discard the onion, carrot and celery; let cool.
2. Meanwhile, bring a large saucepan of salted water to a boil. Fill a large bowl with ice water. Add the wax beans to the saucepan and cook until just tender, 3 minutes. Drain the beans and chill them quickly in the ice water. Drain and pat dry.
3. In a small bowl, combine the olive oil with the vinegar and lemon juice and season with salt and black pepper.
4. In a large bowl, toss the cannellini beans with the wax beans, radishes, red onion and basil. Add the vinaigrette and toss to coat. Season with salt and black pepper and serve right away. —*Chris Cosentino*

MAKE AHEAD The cooked wax beans and dressing can be refrigerated separately overnight. Bring to room temperature before combining with the remaining salad ingredients.

Tomato, Radicchio and Grilled-Peach Salad with Basil Oil

TOTAL: 30 MIN
6 SERVINGS ● ●

Gabriel Rucker (an F&W Best New Chef 2007) of Le Pigeon in Portland, Oregon, swears by the heirloom tomatoes from Viridian Farms (viridianfarms.com). Here, Rucker arranges the tomatoes under a salad of sweet grilled peaches tossed with radicchio and feta cheese.

- 1½ lightly packed cups basil leaves
- ¼ cup plus 1½ tablespoons extra-virgin olive oil
- Salt and freshly ground pepper
- 4 small peaches, peeled and cut into 2-inch wedges
- 1 tablespoon fresh lemon juice
- 1 small head of radicchio, cored and thinly sliced
- ¼ cup thinly sliced red onion
- ½ cup crumbled feta cheese
- 2 large tomatoes, thickly sliced

1. Bring a small saucepan of salted water to a boil. Add the basil leaves and blanch until just wilted. Drain the basil, run briefly under cold water, then squeeze dry; transfer to a blender. Add ¼ cup of the olive oil and puree until smooth; season the basil oil with salt and pepper.
2. Preheat a grill pan. Toss the peach wedges with ½ tablespoon of the olive oil and season with salt and pepper. Grill the peaches over high heat, turning once, until the wedges are lightly browned all over, about 3 minutes; let cool. Transfer the peaches to a bowl. Add the lemon juice and the remaining 1 tablespoon of olive oil and toss to coat. Add the radicchio, red onion and feta, season with salt and pepper and toss.
3. Arrange the tomato slices on a platter and mound the grilled peach and radicchio salad on top. Drizzle the salad with the basil oil and serve immediately. —*Gabriel Rucker*

Celery, Pear and Hazelnut Salad

 **TOTAL: 20 MIN**
6 SERVINGS ● ● ●

Seattle chef Jerry Traunfeld makes this refreshing salad with a trio of crunchy ingredients: celery, Asian pear and toasted hazelnuts. "Celery is underappreciated as a salad ingredient," he says. "And Asian pears also have that great crunch." Traunfeld prefers the sweet, oval-shaped DuChilly hazelnut over the rounder, more common variety. A good source for DuChilly nuts is Holmquist Hazelnut Orchards (holmquisthazelnuts.com).

½ cup hazelnuts
2 tablespoons cider vinegar
2 teaspoons whole-grain mustard
1 teaspoon kosher salt
¼ cup hazelnut oil
6 celery ribs, thinly sliced
on the bias
1 medium Asian pear, cut into
1½-by-⅜-inch matchsticks
¼ cup chopped dill

1. Preheat the oven to 350°. Spread the hazelnuts in a pie plate and toast for about 8 minutes, until lightly golden and fragrant. Let cool, then transfer to a clean kitchen towel and rub them together to remove the skins. Coarsely chop the hazelnuts.
2. In a large bowl, whisk the cider vinegar with the mustard and salt. Gradually whisk in the hazelnut oil. Add the celery, Asian pear, dill and hazelnuts and toss to coat. Serve immediately. —*Jerry Traunfeld*

Warm Brussels Sprout Salad with Caramelized Goat Cheese

 **TOTAL: 45 MIN**
4 SERVINGS

This salad from San Francisco chef Loretta Keller is a flavorful mix of brussels sprouts, smoked ham and pine nuts tossed in an apple dressing and topped with goat cheese. (Keller uses Cypress Grove Chèvre's Bermuda Triangle; cypressgrovechevre.com).

1 Granny Smith apple—peeled,
quartered and cored
2 tablespoons extra-virgin
olive oil
Kosher salt
1 tablespoon water
1 tablespoon cider vinegar
½ teaspoon Dijon mustard
½ teaspoon very finely
chopped shallot
½ cup plus 1 tablespoon
canola oil
Freshly ground black pepper
2 tablespoons pine nuts
One 6-ounce piece of smoked ham,
cut into ⅓-inch dice
1 pound brussels sprouts,
leaves separated and
cores discarded
1 Fuji apple, cut into
⅓-inch dice
2 tablespoons chopped
flat-leaf parsley
One 4-ounce piece of chilled
Bûcheron (semi-aged goat
cheese), quartered
1½ teaspoon snipped chives

1. Preheat the oven to 425°. In a small baking dish, toss the peeled Granny Smith apple quarters with 1 tablespoon of the olive oil and season with kosher salt. Roast the apple quarters for about 15 minutes, until they are very tender and browned in spots.
2. Scrape the apple and its juices into a blender. Add the water, cider vinegar, Dijon mustard, shallot and the remaining 1 tablespoon of olive oil to the blender. With the machine on, slowly pour in ½ cup of the canola oil and puree until smooth. Season the apple dressing with salt and pepper and refrigerate.
3. In a very large skillet, toast the pine nuts over moderate heat, shaking the skillet, until the nuts are golden and fragrant, about 4 minutes. Transfer the pine nuts to a small plate to cool.

4. In the same skillet, heat the remaining 1 tablespoon of canola oil. Add the ham and cook over moderately high heat until browned in spots, about 2 minutes. Add the brussels sprout leaves and Fuji apple and season with salt and pepper. Cook, stirring, until the leaves wilt slightly, about 3 minutes. Add the pine nuts, parsley and 6 tablespoons of the apple dressing and cook until warmed through, about 1 minute. (Reserve the remaining dressing for another use.) Season with salt and pepper and transfer to plates.
5. Heat a medium nonstick skillet over high heat. Set the goat cheese in the skillet and cook undisturbed until the cheese begins to bubble and a golden crust forms, about 1 minute per side. Carefully set the caramelized cheese on top of the warm salads, sprinkle with the chives and serve.
—*Loretta Keller*

MAKE AHEAD The apple dressing can be refrigerated for up to 3 days. Bring to room temperature and whisk to recombine before tossing.

Butter Bean, Tuna and Celery Salad

 **TOTAL: 20 MIN**
4 SERVINGS ●

Big, creamy butter beans make this tuna and celery salad terrifically hearty. The salad would also be delicious spooned over slices of grilled country bread.

2 tablespoons fresh lemon juice
2 teaspoons Dijon mustard
¼ cup plus 1 tablespoon
extra-virgin olive oil
¼ cup snipped chives
Kosher salt and freshly ground pepper
Four 3½-ounce cans Italian tuna
in olive oil, drained
3 celery stalks, with leaves,
thinly sliced on the bias
Two 15-ounce cans butter beans,
drained and rinsed
1½ tablespoons drained capers

1. In a small bowl, whisk the lemon juice with the mustard, then slowly whisk in the olive oil. Stir in the chives and season the lemon-mustard vinaigrette with salt and pepper.

2. In a large bowl, gently toss the drained tuna with the sliced celery, butter beans and capers. Add the lemon-mustard vinaigrette and toss to coat. Season the salad with salt and pepper and serve at once. —*Melissa Rubel*

SERVE WITH Crusty bread.

Celery Salad with Walnuts, Dates and Pecorino

 TOTAL: 20 MIN
12 SERVINGS ● ● ○ ○

1¼ cups walnuts
1 small shallot, minced
2 tablespoons sherry vinegar
2 tablespoons walnut oil
2 tablespoons extra-virgin olive oil
Kosher salt and freshly ground black pepper
2 bunches of celery (2 pounds), thinly sliced on the bias
¾ cup dried pitted Medjool dates, quartered lengthwise
3 ounces dry pecorino cheese, shaved with a vegetable peeler

1. Preheat the oven to 350°. Spread the walnuts in a pie plate and toast for about 8 minutes, until they are lightly golden and fragrant. Let cool completely, then coarsely chop.

2. In a small bowl, combine the shallot with the sherry vinegar. Whisk in the walnut oil and the olive oil and season the dressing with salt and pepper.

3. In a large bowl, toss the walnuts, celery, dates and pecorino. Add the dressing and toss. Serve at once. —*Melissa Rubel*

MAKE AHEAD The salad and dressing can be refrigerated separately for up to 1 day. Store the walnuts in an airtight container and add to the salad just before serving.

BUTTER BEAN, TUNA AND CELERY SALAD

CELERY SALAD WITH WALNUTS, DATES AND PECORINO

BLOOD ORANGE–AND–RED ONION SALAD

WATERMELON SALAD WITH FETA

Blood Orange–and–Red Onion Salad

 TOTAL: 35 MIN
4 SERVINGS ● ●

¼ small red onion, very thinly sliced

¼ cup rice wine vinegar

Maldon salt and freshly ground pepper

4 blood oranges

2 tablespoons extra-virgin olive oil

2 tablespoons torn basil leaves

1. In a bowl, toss the red onion with the vinegar and season with Maldon salt and white pepper. Let stand at room temperature until softened, 15 minutes. Drain.

2. Meanwhile, using a sharp knife, peel the oranges, removing all of the bitter white pith. Thinly slice the oranges crosswise, removing any pits. Arrange the oranges on a platter and scatter the red onion on top. Drizzle with the olive oil and season with Maldon salt and pepper. Garnish with the basil and serve. *—Mike Price*

Watermelon Salad with Feta

 TOTAL: 20 MIN
4 SERVINGS ● ● ●

This watermelon salad, tossed with Mediterranean ingredients like olives and feta, is sweet, salty and a little spicy.

¼ cup extra-virgin olive oil

1½ tablespoons fresh lemon juice

½ teaspoon harissa
or other hot sauce

Salt and freshly ground pepper

1½ pounds seedless watermelon,
rind removed and fruit sliced
¼ inch thick

½ small red onion, thinly sliced

¼ cup coarsely chopped
flat-leaf parsley

¼ cup pitted oil-cured
black olives, preferably
Moroccan, coarsely chopped

½ cup crumbled feta cheese

In a small bowl, whisk the olive oil with the lemon juice and harissa and season with salt and pepper. Arrange the watermelon slices on a platter and sprinkle with the onion, parsley, olives and feta. Drizzle the dressing on top and serve.
—Melissa Clark

Watermelon–and–Goat Cheese Salad

 TOTAL: 15 MIN
6 SERVINGS ●

1 pound seedless watermelon
chunks, cut into small slabs

6 ounces fresh goat cheese,
cut into 12 rounds

¼ teaspoon grated orange zest

1 teaspoon nigella seeds

2 tablespoons fresh orange juice

1 tablespoon fresh lemon juice

3 tablespoons extra-virgin olive oil

Salt and freshly ground pepper

1. Arrange the watermelon on 6 plates and top with the cheese. Sprinkle all over with the orange zest and nigella seeds.

2. In a small bowl, whisk the orange juice and lemon juice with the olive oil and season with salt and pepper. Drizzle the dressing over the watermelon and goat cheese and serve right away. —*Defne Koryürek*

Watermelon-and-Papaya Salad with Tequila Vinaigrette

 TOTAL: 25 MIN

4 SERVINGS ● ●

¼ cup fresh lime juice

2 tablespoons tequila

¼ cup plus 2 tablespoons
  extra-virgin olive oil

Salt and freshly ground
  black pepper

1 small papaya (¾ pound)—
  peeled, seeded and cut into
  1-by-½-inch batons (2 cups)

¾ pound seedless, rindless
  watermelon, cut into
  1-by-½-inch batons (2 cups)

½ pound jicama, peeled and cut into
  1-by-½-inch batons (2 cups)

5 ounces mesclun greens

1 Hass avocado, cut into
  ½-inch cubes

In a large bowl, whisk the lime juice with the tequila. Whisk in the olive oil and season the vinaigrette with salt and pepper. Add the papaya, watermelon, jicama and greens and toss well. Add the avocado and toss gently. Season with salt and pepper and serve right away. —*Dionicio Jimenez*

Roasted Carrot–and–Avocado Salad with Citrus Dressing

TOTAL: 50 MIN

6 SERVINGS ● ● ●

British star chef Jamie Oliver's favorite method for preparing carrots (as well as beets) is to parboil them, then toss them with a dressing and roast them to intensify their sweetness.

1 pound medium carrots

2 teaspoons cumin seeds

1 *chile de árbol*

Kosher salt and freshly ground
  black pepper

2 garlic cloves

1 teaspoon thyme leaves

⅓ cup plus 2 tablespoons
  extra-virgin olive oil

3 tablespoons red wine vinegar

1 orange, halved

1 lemon, halved

Four ½-inch-thick slices of
  ciabatta bread

3 Hass avocados, peeled and
  cut into 6 wedges each

8 ounces assorted greens,
  such as watercress,
  baby spinach or mesclun

2 ounces baby arugula (2 cups)

2 tablespoons unsalted roasted
  sunflower seeds

1 tablespoon roasted sesame seeds

1 tablespoon poppy seeds

3 tablespoons low-fat sour cream
  mixed with 1 tablespoon of water

1. Preheat the oven to 375°. In a skillet of boiling salted water, simmer the carrots, covered, over moderately low heat until crisp-tender, 10 minutes. Drain and transfer the carrots to a large roasting pan.

2. In a mortar, crush the cumin with the *chile de árbol,* ½ teaspoon of salt and ¼ teaspoon of pepper. Add the garlic and thyme and pound into a paste. Stir in 2 tablespoons each of the oil and vinegar.

3. Pour the cumin dressing over the carrots and toss to coat. Add the orange and lemon halves to the roasting pan, cut side down. Roast for about 25 minutes, until the carrots are tender.

4. Meanwhile, toast the ciabatta until the edges are golden brown. Tear the bread into bite-size pieces. In a salad bowl, gently toss the avocados with the watercress, arugula and ciabatta. In a small bowl, combine the sunflower, sesame and poppy seeds.

5. Using tongs, squeeze the hot orange and lemon halves into a measuring cup until you have about ⅓ cup of juice. Whisk in the remaining 1 tablespoon of red wine vinegar and ⅓ cup of olive oil and season with salt and pepper. Add the warm carrots to the salad bowl along with the citrus dressing and toss to coat. Transfer the salad to plates and drizzle with the sour cream. Sprinkle the salad with the seed mixture and serve. —*Jamie Oliver*

Green Papaya Salad with Curry-Lime Dressing

ACTIVE: 20 MIN; TOTAL: 50 MIN

4 SERVINGS ● ●

2 tablespoons Asian fish sauce

2 tablespoons fresh lime juice

1 tablespoon unseasoned
  rice vinegar

1 tablespoon mirin

½ teaspoon Thai red curry paste

½ teaspoon mild curry powder

3 tablespoons vegetable oil

One 2½-pound green papaya—peeled,
  seeded and finely julienned,
  preferably on a mandoline
  (6 cups)

¼ cup finely chopped cilantro

4 small scallions, thinly sliced

3 ounces *inari* (fried tofu skin),
  thinly sliced (see Note)

2 tablespoons finely shredded
  pickled ginger

Salt

In a large bowl, whisk the fish sauce with the lime juice, rice vinegar, mirin, curry paste, curry powder and vegetable oil. Add the green papaya, cilantro, scallions, *inari* and pickled ginger and toss well. Season the salad lightly with salt and refrigerate until chilled, about 30 minutes.
—*Nobuo Fukuda*

NOTE *Inari* is available at Asian markets. Look for it in the refrigerated section.

MAKE AHEAD The salad can be refrigerated overnight.

WHITE BEAN SOUP WITH
BACON AND HERBS (P. 65)

soups

" In our house, we always started with good homemade stock and then added whatever was around: beans, leftover sausage, shredded chicken. "

—TOM VALENTI, COOKBOOK AUTHOR AND CHEF AND OWNER, OUEST, NEW YORK CITY

SPRING VEGETABLE SOUP WITH TARRAGON

CREAMY BROCCOLI SOUP WITH CHEDDAR CRISPS

Spring Vegetable Soup with Tarragon

ACTIVE: 25 MIN; TOTAL: 1 HR

4 SERVINGS ● ●

In the summer, Napa winemaker Stéphane Vivier purees this lovely vegetable soup and serves it chilled. He always uses the freshest herbs he can find.

- 7 cups water
- 10 small red potatoes, quartered
- 2 medium carrots, sliced ¼ inch thick
- 2 celery ribs, sliced ¼ inch thick
- 1 medium onion, coarsely chopped
- 1 large leek, sliced ¼ inch thick
- ½ tablespoon kosher salt
- 1 pound green beans, cut into 1-inch lengths, or frozen peas
- 2 tablespoons chopped parsley
- 1 tablespoon chopped tarragon

Freshly ground pepper

1. In a large pot, combine the water with the potatoes, carrots, celery, onion and leek. Bring to a boil. Add the salt and simmer over moderately low heat for 30 minutes. **2.** Add the green beans and simmer until tender, 3 minutes. Stir in the parsley and tarragon. Season with pepper and serve. —*Stéphane Vivier*

Creamy Broccoli Soup with Cheddar Crisps

 TOTAL: 30 MIN

4 SERVINGS ● ●

For an ingenious twist on the classic combination of broccoli and melted cheese, Boston chef Barbara Lynch serves a broccoli soup with cheese crisps. She likes using Mimolette, an orange-hued semihard French cheese with a milder, nuttier flavor than cheddar, but cheddar is also delicious. The soup is equally good with cauliflower or celery root in place of the broccoli.

- 2 tablespoons extra-virgin olive oil
- ½ large white onion, chopped
- 3 small celery ribs, thinly sliced
- 1 garlic clove, minced
- 1½ pounds broccoli, cut into florets
- 3½ cups water

Salt and freshly ground pepper

Cheddar Crisps (recipe follows), for serving

1. In a large saucepan, heat the olive oil. Add the onion, celery and garlic and cook over moderately low heat, stirring occasionally, until softened, about 7 minutes. **2.** Add the broccoli and water and bring to a boil. Simmer over moderate heat until the broccoli is tender, 10 minutes. **3.** Transfer the contents of the saucepan to a blender and puree until smooth. Season with salt and pepper and serve with the Cheddar Crisps. —*Barbara Lynch*

MAKE AHEAD The broccoli soup can be refrigerated overnight.

CHEDDAR CRISPS

ACTIVE: 10 MIN; TOTAL: 35 MIN
MAKES 8 CRISPS ●

4 ounces sharp cheddar
cheese, coarsely shredded
(1 cup)

Preheat the oven to 350°. Line a baking sheet with parchment paper. Sprinkle the cheese on the sheet in eight 2-inch rounds. Bake for 18 minutes, until darkened slightly. Blot the crisps with paper towels and let cool (they'll harden as they cool). —BL

Corn Vichyssoise

TOTAL: 35 MIN
6 SERVINGS ● ●

Chef Joseph Humphrey of Murray Circle restaurant at Cavallo Point, an eco-lodge in Sausalito, California, simmers this soup with the corn cobs to deepen the flavor.

4 cups water
4 cups low-sodium
chicken broth
6 ears of corn, kernels cut
off the cobs and cobs
broken in half
1 medium onion, thinly sliced
4 garlic cloves, thinly sliced
2 celery ribs, thinly sliced
¼ cup dry vermouth
Salt and freshly ground
white pepper
3 tablespoons heavy cream
2 white mushrooms, thinly sliced
2 tablespoons chopped cilantro
Extra-virgin olive oil, for drizzling

In a saucepan, bring the water and broth to a boil with the corn kernels, cobs, onion, garlic, celery and vermouth. Simmer for 20 minutes. Discard the cobs. Puree the soup in a blender. Strain into a large, clean saucepan, season with salt and pepper and whisk in the cream. Serve the soup hot or chilled; garnish with the mushrooms, cilantro and olive oil.
—Joseph Humphrey

Raw Sweet Corn and Cashew Chowder

TOTAL: 15 MIN
4 SERVINGS ● ● ●

3¼ cups fresh yellow corn kernels
(from 4 large ears)
2 cups water
½ cup raw cashews
6 tablespoons extra-virgin olive oil
1 small garlic clove
2 teaspoons kosher salt
1½ teaspoons chopped cilantro
Freshly ground pepper

In a blender, combine 2¼ cups of the corn with the water, cashews, olive oil, garlic and salt and puree until smooth. Pour the soup into bowls. Garnish with the remaining 1 cup of corn kernels, the cilantro and a sprinkle of pepper, then serve.
—Ani Phyo

MAKE AHEAD The corn chowder can be refrigerated overnight.

Creamy Asparagus Soup

TOTAL: 30 MIN
6 SERVINGS ●

3 cups chicken stock or
low-sodium broth
1 pound pencil-thin asparagus,
tips reserved and stalks cut
into 1-inch lengths
½ small onion, thinly sliced
1 pound fresh ricotta (2 cups)
Salt and freshly ground white pepper
¼ cup salted roasted pistachios
2 scallions, cut into ½-inch lengths
1 teaspoon white wine vinegar
¼ cup extra-virgin olive oil

1. In a large saucepan, bring the stock to a boil. Add the asparagus tips and cook just until bright green, about 2 minutes. Using a slotted spoon, transfer the tips to a plate. Add the onion to the saucepan, cover and cook over moderate heat until softened, about 5 minutes. Add the asparagus stalks and cook until just tender, about 3 minutes.

2. Using a slotted spoon, transfer the onion and asparagus stalks to a blender. Add the ricotta and puree until smooth and creamy, adding a bit of the broth to loosen the puree. Return the puree to the saucepan; stir well and season with salt and white pepper. Add the reserved asparagus tips and simmer the soup until just heated through.

3. Meanwhile, in a mini chopper, pulse the pistachios, scallions, vinegar and oil to form a coarse paste. Season with salt and white pepper. Ladle the soup into shallow bowls and swirl in a bit of the scallion-pistachio pesto. —Grace Parisi

Gingery Sweet Potato Soup

ACTIVE: 25 MIN; TOTAL: 1 HR
1 SERVING ● ● ●

This recipe yields extra ginger broth; it makes a terrific cooking liquid for grains like quinoa.

1 quart water
1 small onion, coarsely chopped
2 garlic cloves, coarsely chopped
1 tablespoon coarsely chopped
peeled fresh ginger
1 stalk of fresh lemongrass,
thinly sliced crosswise
One ½-pound sweet potato, peeled
and cut into 2-inch cubes
½ teaspoon *sambal oelek*
or other Asian hot sauce
Salt
½ tablespoon chopped cilantro
Lime wedge, for serving

1. In a saucepan, bring the water to a boil with the onion, garlic, ginger, lemongrass and sweet potato. Cover and simmer for 25 minutes, until the potato is tender.

2. Transfer the sweet potato to a blender. Strain the broth. Add 1 cup to the blender, reserving the rest for another use; puree.

3. Return the soup to the saucepan. Stir in the *sambal oelek*, season with salt and simmer until heated. Transfer to a bowl, top with the cilantro and lime wedge and serve. —Adina Niemerow

Cauliflower Soup with Crispy Chorizo Bread Crumbs

TOTAL: 1 HR
12 SERVINGS ●●

- 4 tablespoons unsalted butter
- 1 medium onion, cut into ¼-inch dice
- 3 garlic cloves, crushed
- 3 thyme sprigs
- 1 bay leaf
- 2 medium heads of cauliflower, cut into 2-inch florets
- 6½ cups chicken stock or low-sodium broth
- ½ cup heavy cream
- Kosher salt and freshly ground pepper
- 3 ounces dry chorizo, finely chopped
- ¾ cup *panko* (Japanese bread crumbs)

1. In a large soup pot, melt the butter. Add the diced onion, crushed garlic cloves, thyme sprigs and bay leaf and cook over moderate heat, stirring occasionally, until the onion is softened, about 5 minutes. Add the cauliflower florets and chicken stock and bring to a simmer. Cover and cook over moderately low heat until the cauliflower is very tender when pierced with a fork, about 20 minutes. Discard the thyme sprigs and bay leaf.

2. In a blender or food processor, carefully puree the soup in batches until smooth. Pour the soup into a clean pot and set it over low heat. Stir in the heavy cream and season the soup with salt and pepper.

3. Meanwhile, in a medium skillet, cook the chopped chorizo over moderate heat until it is almost crisp, about 3 minutes. Add the *panko* and cook, stirring frequently, until the crumbs are crisp, about 5 minutes. Transfer the chorizo bread crumbs to a small bowl.

4. Ladle the soup into shallow bowls. Sprinkle with the chorizo bread crumbs and serve right away, before the bread crumbs get soggy. —*Melissa Rubel*

Yellow Squash Soup with Scallion Salad

TOTAL: 1 HR 15 MIN
6 SERVINGS ●●

- 1 tablespoon unsalted butter
- 1 pound small yellow squash, cut into 1-inch pieces
- 2 fresh bay leaves
- 1½ cups low-sodium chicken broth
- 1½ cups water
- 6 scallions, trimmed
- 1 tablespoon plus 1 teaspoon extra-virgin olive oil
- 1 cup buttermilk
- Salt and freshly ground white pepper
- ¾ cup finely grated Manchego cheese (2 ounces)
- 1 cup grape tomatoes, quartered
- 1 tablespoon minced tarragon
- 1 tablespoon minced parsley
- ¼ cup finely diced peeled cucumber
- 1 teaspoon lemon juice

1. In a saucepan, melt the butter. Add the yellow squash and bay leaves and cook over moderate heat for 8 minutes. Add the broth and water and bring to a boil. Simmer just until the squash is tender, 5 minutes.

2. Meanwhile, preheat a grill pan. Rub the scallions with 1 teaspoon of the oil and grill over high heat until lightly charred, 5 minutes. Cut into ½-inch pieces.

3. Transfer the squash and ½ cup of the broth to a blender; discard the bay leaves. Puree the soup; blend in the buttermilk and remaining broth. Season with salt and pepper. Keep warm or refrigerate until cold.

4. Heat a nonstick skillet over moderate heat. Spoon twelve 2-inch-wide mounds of the cheese into the skillet; cook over moderate heat until browned on the bottom. Off the heat, flip the crisps. Return to the heat and cook until browned. Cool on a rack.

5. Toss the tomatoes, tarragon, parsley, cucumber, lemon juice and the remaining 1 tablespoon of oil with the scallions. Season with salt and pepper. Serve the soup with the salad and crisps. —*Champe Speidel*

Silky Leek and Red Wine Soup

TOTAL: 45 MIN
4 SERVINGS ●

- Four 1-inch-thick slices of peasant bread (4 ounces), crusts removed
- 3½ tablespoons extra-virgin olive oil, plus more for brushing
- 1 garlic clove
- Pinch of saffron threads
- 3 medium leeks, thinly sliced crosswise (3 cups)
- ½ cup plus 1 tablespoon dry red wine
- 3 cups chicken stock
- ½ cup heavy cream
- Salt and freshly ground pepper
- ¼ cup freshly grated Parmigiano-Reggiano cheese

1. Preheat the oven to 350°. Arrange the bread slices on a baking sheet and brush with olive oil. Bake until crisp, about 10 minutes. Rub with the garlic and tear the bread into 1-inch pieces.

2. In a saucepan, heat 3 tablespoons of the oil. Add the saffron and all but ½ cup of the leeks. Cook over moderate heat until tender, 4 minutes. Add ½ cup of the red wine; reduce over high heat to 2 tablespoons. Add the stock; simmer for 3 minutes. Stir in the toasts and simmer 3 minutes.

3. Working in batches, puree the soup in a blender. Return the soup to the saucepan. Stir in the cream and the remaining 1 tablespoon of red wine, season with salt and pepper and keep warm.

4. In a nonstick skillet, heat the remaining ½ tablespoon of oil. Add the reserved leeks and cook over moderate heat until softened, 3 minutes. Using a heatproof spatula, form the leeks into four 2-inch rounds. Sprinkle 1 tablespoon of the cheese over each round. Cook over moderate heat until melted, about 3 minutes. Transfer the rounds to a plate and let cool until crisp.

5. Ladle the soup into bowls, top with the leek crisps and serve. —*Marcia Kiesel*

Sweet Potato, Chipotle and Apple Soup

ACTIVE: 35 MIN; TOTAL: 1 HR 20 MIN

6 SERVINGS ● ●

- 2 tablespoons vegetable oil, plus 1 cup for frying
- ½ white onion, finely chopped
- 2 garlic cloves, smashed
- 1 teaspoon finely grated fresh ginger
- 2 Gala apples—peeled, seeded and coarsely chopped
- 1 celery rib, thinly sliced crosswise
- 1¾ pounds sweet potatoes, peeled and thinly sliced
- 1 quart chicken stock
- 3 cups water
- 1 small canned chipotle in adobo sauce, seeded and minced

Salt and freshly ground white pepper

- ½ teaspoon cinnamon
- ½ teaspoon sugar
- 3 yellow corn tortillas, cut into ½-inch strips

1. In a soup pot, heat 2 tablespoons of the oil until shimmering. Add the onion, garlic and ginger and cook over low heat, stirring, until softened, 7 minutes. Add the apples and celery and cook for 5 minutes. Add the sweet potatoes and cook for 5 minutes. Add the chicken stock and water and bring to a boil. Cover partially and simmer over low heat until the fruit and vegetables are very tender, 45 minutes. Stir in the chipotle.

2. Working in batches, puree the soup in a blender until smooth. Season with salt and white pepper and return to the pot.

3. In a small bowl, mix the cinnamon and sugar with ½ teaspoon of salt. Heat the remaining 1 cup of oil in a medium skillet. Add the tortilla strips and fry over high heat, stirring, until crisp and golden, about 2 minutes. Drain on paper towels and sprinkle with the cinnamon-sugar mixture. Serve the soup in shallow bowls and garnish with the fried tortilla strips. —*Sue Torres*

SILKY LEEK AND RED WINE SOUP

SWEET POTATO, CHIPOTLE AND APPLE SOUP

ROASTED EGGPLANT–AND–LENTIL SOUP

FRESH SHELL BEAN SOUP

Smoky Tomato Soup with Gruyère Toasts

TOTAL: 40 MIN

4 SERVINGS ●

- 1 tablespoon unsalted butter
- 1 tablespoon extra-virgin olive oil
- 1 onion, cut into ¼-inch dice
- 2 garlic cloves, crushed
- 2 teaspoons sweet smoked paprika, preferably pimentón de la Vera
- 3½ pounds tomatoes, quartered
- ½ cup water
- 1 thyme sprig
- 1 bay leaf

Kosher salt and freshly ground pepper

- ¼ cup plus 2 tablespoons heavy cream

Eight ¼-inch-thick baguette slices, cut on the bias

- 2 ounces Gruyère cheese, coarsely grated (¾ cup)

1. In a soup pot, melt the butter in the oil. Add the onion and garlic and cook over moderately high heat until tender, 5 minutes. Add the paprika and cook until fragrant, 30 seconds. Add the tomatoes, water, thyme and bay leaf, season with salt and pepper and bring to a boil. Cover and simmer over moderate heat until the tomatoes break down, about 15 minutes. Discard the thyme sprig and bay leaf.

2. Preheat the broiler. In a blender, puree the soup in batches. Strain the soup back into the pot, pressing on the solids. Stir in the cream and season with salt and pepper.

3. Meanwhile, place the baguette slices on a baking sheet. Broil 6 inches from the heat until lightly toasted on both sides, about 2 minutes total. Top the toasts with the Gruyère and broil for about 30 seconds, until the cheese is bubbly. Ladle the soup into bowls and serve with the Gruyère toasts. —*Melissa Rubel*

Roasted Eggplant– and–Lentil Soup

ACTIVE: 15 MIN; TOTAL: 50 MIN

4 SERVINGS ● ●

One 1¼-pound eggplant, quartered lengthwise

- 2 tablespoons extra-virgin olive oil

Salt and freshly ground pepper

- 1 cup French green lentils (5½ ounces)
- 14 large sage leaves
- 2 cups chicken stock or low-sodium broth
- 1 cup 1 percent milk
- 1 tablespoon fresh lemon juice

1. Preheat the oven to 400°. Place the eggplant quarters on a rimmed baking sheet, skin side down. Drizzle with 1 tablespoon of the olive oil and season with salt and pepper. Bake until the eggplant is very tender, about 30 minutes.

2. Meanwhile, in a medium saucepan, cover the lentils with 2 inches of water. Add ½ teaspoon of salt and 2 sage leaves and bring to a boil. Simmer over low heat until the lentils are tender, about 20 minutes. Drain the lentils in a colander and discard the sage leaves.

3. With a spoon, scrape the eggplant flesh into a blender; discard the skin. Add 1 cup of the stock and puree until smooth; transfer to a clean saucepan. Add the lentils and the remaining 1 cup of stock to the blender and puree until smooth. Add the lentil puree to the eggplant puree in the saucepan.

4. Stir the milk and lemon juice into the soup and bring to a simmer. Season with salt and pepper; keep the soup hot over low heat, stirring occasionally.

5. In a small skillet, heat the remaining 1 tablespoon of olive oil. Add the remaining 12 sage leaves and cook over moderate heat until crisp, about 30 seconds per side. Ladle the soup into bowls, garnish with the fried sage leaves and serve.

—*Clark Frasier and Mark Gaier*

MAKE AHEAD The soup can be refrigerated overnight. Reheat gently.

Fresh Shell Bean Soup

ACTIVE: 1 HR; TOTAL: 1 HR 45 MIN
10 SERVINGS ● ●

As a young man in Boston's North End, a historically Italian neighborhood, Peter Pastan would watch customers at the Italian market ask for prosciutto skin. He had no idea what they did with it. Today Pastan cures his own meats at his two Washington, D.C., restaurants, Obelisk and 2Amys, then uses prosciutto skin to flavor and thicken soups like this tomatoey fresh shell bean soup. While the skin is optional here, it's easy to obtain—sometimes for free—from delis and meat counters.

3   tablespoons extra-virgin olive oil, plus more for drizzling
One 3-ounce slice of pancetta, finely diced (½ cup)
5   garlic cloves, smashed
3   medium carrots, diced
3   celery ribs, cut into ¼-inch dice, plus 10 celery leaves for garnish
1   large onion, cut into ½-inch dice
1   fennel bulb, diced
¼   cup chopped flat-leaf parsley
1   rosemary sprig
1   basil sprig
4   large plum tomatoes—peeled, seeded and cut into ½-inch dice
3   pounds fresh cranberry beans, shelled (3 cups; see Note)
2   medium Yukon Gold potatoes, peeled and cut into ½-inch cubes
One 3-by-3-inch piece of prosciutto skin (optional)
6   cups chicken stock
Salt and freshly ground pepper

1. In a large enameled cast-iron casserole, heat the 3 tablespoons of oil. Add the pancetta and cook over low heat, stirring occasionally, until golden, 4 minutes. Add the garlic, carrots, celery, onion, fennel, parsley, rosemary and basil and cook over moderate heat, stirring occasionally, until the vegetables are softened, 10 minutes.

2. Add the tomatoes, beans, potatoes and prosciutto skin to the casserole and cook, stirring, until the vegetables are just heated through, about 3 minutes. Add the chicken stock and bring to a simmer. Cook over moderately low heat until the beans are tender, about 40 minutes. Discard the prosciutto skin and the herb sprigs.

3. Partially mash the beans with a potato masher, or transfer 2 cups of the soup to a food processor or food mill and puree; return the puree to the casserole. Season the soup with salt and pepper. Ladle the soup into bowls and drizzle with olive oil. Garnish with the celery leaves and serve.

—*Peter Pastan*

SERVE WITH Crusty bread.

NOTE Any fresh shell bean can be used. Cooking time will vary according to the variety of bean.

Spicy Chickpea Soup

TOTAL: 30 MIN
6 SERVINGS ● ●

Cookbook author Pam Anderson uses chickpeas as the base for this creamy (though cream-free) Indian-flavored soup. To save time, Anderson purees the ingredients first, then simmers them. "Pureed legumes give you richness without having to enrich the soup," she says.

Two 19-ounce cans chickpeas, drained
One 13.5-ounce can light coconut milk
One 14.4-ounce can whole tomatoes, drained and chopped (½ cup)
¼   cup naturally sweetened apple juice
¼   cup cilantro leaves
½   teaspoon garam masala
½   teaspoon ground ginger
1   cup chicken stock or low-sodium broth
Salt and freshly ground black pepper
¼   cup plain low-fat yogurt
2   scallions, green parts only, thinly sliced

1. In a blender, combine the drained chickpeas with the coconut milk, chopped tomatoes, apple juice, cilantro leaves, garam masala and ground ginger and puree the mixture until smooth.

2. Transfer the puree to a medium saucepan. Stir in the chicken stock and bring to a simmer over moderately high heat, stirring occasionally. Season the liquid with salt and black pepper. Ladle the soup into bowls, top with the yogurt and scallion greens and serve right away.

—*Pam Anderson*

SERVE WITH Crispy Seeded Pita Chips (p. 34).

MAKE AHEAD The Spicy Chickpea Soup can be cooled and refrigerated overnight. Reheat gently.

● HEALTHY   ● MAKE AHEAD   ● VEGETARIAN   ● STAFF FAVORITE

CLASSIC CHICKEN NOODLE SOUP

perfecting chicken soup

From one deeply flavorful broth, F&W's Grace Parisi creates four exceptional soups by transforming a classic chicken soup with Korean, Ukrainian and West African ingredients.

Classic Chicken Noodle Soup

ACTIVE: 45 MIN; TOTAL: 3 HR

6 SERVINGS ● ●

One 3-pound chicken, neck reserved

3½ quarts water

4 carrots—2 coarsely chopped, 2 sliced ¼ inch thick

4 celery ribs—2 coarsely chopped, 2 sliced ¼ inch thick

1 unpeeled onion, quartered

1 large unpeeled garlic clove, smashed

1 teaspoon whole black peppercorns

1 large fresh bay leaf

6 parsley sprigs

2 thyme sprigs

Kosher salt

½ pound thin egg noodles

¼ cup finely chopped flat-leaf parsley

1. In a stockpot, combine the chicken and neck, water, chopped carrots and celery, onion, garlic, peppercorns and herbs; bring to a boil. Cover partially and simmer over low heat for 30 minutes. Transfer the chicken to a plate. Discard the skin. Pull the meat off the bones, cut into ½-inch pieces and refrigerate.

2. Return the bones to the pot. Simmer for about 1 hour. Strain the broth into a bowl and rinse out the pot. Return the broth to the pot and boil until reduced to 8 cups, 30 minutes. Season with salt.

3. Add the sliced carrots and celery to the broth, cover and simmer until just tender, 12 minutes. In a saucepan of boiling salted water, cook the noodles; drain and cool under running water. Add the noodles, chicken and parsley to the pot and bring to a simmer. Ladle the soup into bowls and serve hot.

Three Great Variations

1 Korean Chicken Soup Make the soup through Step 2. Cook ½ pound sliced shiitake mushroom caps in 2 tablespoons vegetable oil until browned and add to the soup along with ½ pound cooked udon noodles, ¼ cup julienned ginger, 12 ounces cubed firm tofu, 1 cup thinly sliced kimchi, 2 tablespoons fish sauce and 1 teaspoon sesame oil. Simmer for 5 minutes. Add the chicken and serve.

2 Ukrainian Chicken Soup Make the soup through Step 2. Cook 1 pound coarsely chopped green cabbage, 1 chopped onion and 1 cup thinly sliced pickles in butter until softened. Add ¼ cup tomato paste and 1 tablespoon sweet paprika; cook for 1 minute. Add the broth and simmer for 20 minutes. Add the chicken, ½ cup pickle juice and ¼ cup chopped dill. Serve with sour cream.

3 West African Chicken Soup Make the soup through Step 2. Cook 1 sliced onion, 2 chopped tomatoes, 2 tablespoons minced fresh ginger, 2 tablespoons curry powder and 1 tablespoon tomato paste in vegetable oil for 7 minutes. Add the broth, 1 cup unsweetened coconut milk and 1 sliced green banana. Simmer for 30 minutes. Add the chicken and serve with rice and cilantro.

Tofu, Eggplant and Shiitake Noodle Soup

TOTAL: 1 HR

4 SERVINGS ● ○

- 3 cups vegetable broth
- 2 cups water
- 2 whole lemongrass stalks, thinly sliced

Six ¼-inch-thick slices of fresh ginger, smashed lightly, plus 1½ teaspoons very finely chopped fresh ginger
- ¼ cup low-sodium soy sauce

Freshly ground white pepper
- 4 ounces rice vermicelli
- ¼ cup vegetable oil
- 1 pound small eggplant, peeled and cut into 1-inch cubes
- ¼ pound shiitake mushrooms, stems removed and caps quartered

Salt
- 2 garlic cloves, very finely chopped
- 1 pound firm tofu, cut into 1-inch cubes
- ½ pound napa cabbage, shredded (8 cups)
- ½ cup bean sprouts
- ¼ cup cilantro leaves
- 2 tablespoons mint leaves, torn into pieces

Lime wedges and hot sauce, for serving

1. In a medium soup pot, combine the vegetable broth, water, lemongrass, sliced ginger and soy sauce and season generously with white pepper. Bring to a simmer, cover and cook over low heat until flavorful, about 20 minutes. Strain the broth into a heatproof bowl, pressing on the solids. Discard the solids.

2. Meanwhile, bring a medium saucepan of water to a boil. Cook the rice vermicelli until al dente, about 5 minutes. Drain and cool under running water.

3. Wipe out the soup pot and heat the vegetable oil. Add the eggplant and shiitake mushrooms, season with salt and white pepper and cook the vegetables over high heat, stirring occasionally, until softened and browned, about 8 minutes. Stir in the chopped ginger and garlic and cook until fragrant, about 1 minute. Add the tofu and cook, stirring gently once or twice, until lightly browned, about 4 minutes. Add the vegetable broth along with the cabbage and noodles and simmer just until the cabbage is wilted, about 2 minutes longer. Stir in the bean sprouts, cilantro and mint and season the soup with salt and white pepper. Serve the soup in deep bowls, passing lime wedges and hot sauce at the table. —*Ratha Chau*

Chestnut Soup with Grappa Cream

ACTIVE: 35 MIN; TOTAL: 1 HR 15 MIN

10 SERVINGS ●

Growing up in Italy's Marche region, New York City chef Fabio Trabocchi roasted chestnuts in the fireplace to eat as a snack while playing cards with his family. At culinary school, he transformed those chestnuts into this luscious soup. Incredibly creamy, it's best served in small cups as an hors d'oeuvre.

- 2 tablespoons unsalted butter
- 2 ounces thinly sliced pancetta
- 2 medium shallots, sliced (½ cup)
- ½ cup diced peeled celery root
- ½ pound white mushrooms, sliced

One 14-ounce jar vacuum-packed roasted chestnuts, coarsely chopped
- 4 cups chicken stock or low-sodium broth
- ¼ cup Cognac
- 1 fresh bay leaf
- 1 sage sprig
- 1 thyme sprig, plus 1 tablespoon thyme leaves for garnish
- ¾ cup half-and-half

Salt and freshly ground white pepper
- 1 cup heavy cream
- 2 tablespoons grappa

1. In a large saucepan, melt 1 tablespoon of the butter. Add the pancetta and cook over moderate heat until lightly browned, about 5 minutes. Add the shallots and celery root and cook until the celery root is just tender, about 10 minutes. Transfer the vegetables to a bowl, leaving the pancetta and fat in the saucepan.

2. Add the remaining 1 tablespoon of butter to the saucepan along with the mushrooms and all but 2 tablespoons of the chestnuts. Cook over moderately high heat, stirring occasionally, until the mushrooms have released their liquid and are slightly softened, 6 minutes. Add 2 tablespoons of the chicken stock and the celery root mixture and cook for 1 minute. Add the Cognac and cook until evaporated, 2 minutes.

3. Add the bay leaf and sage and thyme sprigs to the saucepan along with the remaining chicken stock. Bring to a boil and simmer for 30 minutes, stirring occasionally. Discard the pancetta, bay leaf and sage and thyme sprigs.

4. Working in batches, puree the soup in a blender until creamy and smooth. Return the soup to the saucepan. Stir in the half-and-half, season with salt and white pepper and keep warm.

5. In a large bowl, using a handheld electric mixer, whip the cream until soft peaks form. Beat in the grappa and season with salt and white pepper.

6. Ladle the soup into small bowls. Dollop the grappa cream on top, garnish with the thyme leaves and the reserved 2 tablespoons of chestnuts and serve.
—*Fabio Trabocchi*

MAKE AHEAD The soup can be refrigerated for up to 3 days. Reheat gently before serving, adding a few tablespoons of water to thin it as needed.

Pepper Pot Soup

ACTIVE: 1 HR; TOTAL: 3 HR 35 MIN

8 TO 10 SERVINGS ● ●

Whenever she's in Jamaica, F&W's Marcia Kiesel makes sure to eat at least one bowl of pepper pot soup, a spicy West Indian stew that's loaded with meat, seafood and vegetables. At home, she loves serving the soup in the winter because it combines warming Scotch bonnet chiles and vitamin-rich spinach.

- **4** smoked ham hocks (about 3 pounds)
- **2** large onions—1 halved, 1 cut into ½-inch dice
- **2** Scotch bonnet chiles—1 whole, 1 seeded and minced
- **18** cups water
- **2½** pounds spinach, stemmed
- **3** tablespoons vegetable oil
- **6** large scallions, coarsely chopped
- **4** large garlic cloves, very finely chopped
- **2** large thyme sprigs
- **1** large green bell pepper, cut into ½-inch dice
- **1** tablespoon very finely chopped fresh ginger
- **1** teaspoon ground allspice
- **2½** pounds medium shrimp, shelled and deveined

Salt and freshly ground black pepper

1. In a large stockpot, cover the ham hocks, the halved onion and the whole Scotch bonnet chile with the water and bring to a boil. Cover partially and simmer over moderately low heat until the ham hocks are tender, about 1½ hours. Strain the stock (you should have about 12 cups). Remove the meat from the hocks, cut into bite-size pieces and refrigerate. Discard the onion and Scotch bonnet chile.

2. Meanwhile, heat a large saucepan. Rinse the spinach, add a few handfuls to the saucepan and cook, stirring, until

wilted. Repeat until all of the spinach has been wilted; transfer to a food processor and coarsely puree.

3. In the large pot, heat the vegetable oil. Add the diced onion, minced Scotch bonnet chile, scallions, garlic, thyme, bell pepper, ginger and allspice. Cover and cook over moderately low heat until the vegetables are softened, about 10 minutes. Add the stock and bring to a boil over high heat. Cover partially and simmer over low heat for 40 minutes. Add the spinach and simmer over low heat for another 15 minutes. Discard the thyme sprigs. Add the ham and shrimp and simmer until the shrimp are white throughout and just cooked, about 3 minutes. Season with salt and pepper and serve right away.
—*Marcia Kiesel*

White Bean Soup with Bacon and Herbs

ACTIVE: 30 MIN; TOTAL: 2 HR PLUS OVERNIGHT SOAKING

12 SERVINGS ● ● ●

Chef Jose Garces loads a light chicken broth with chunky Great Northern beans and tops it with a sprinkling of bacon. It's a variation on the *caldo gallego* (a Spanish white bean soup) that Garces serves at his Philadelphia tapas bar, Amada.

- **1¼** pounds thick-sliced bacon, cut crosswise into ¼-inch-wide strips
- **2** tablespoons extra-virgin olive oil
- **1** medium Spanish onion, finely chopped
- **1** large carrot, finely diced
- **2** celery ribs, finely diced
- **4** garlic cloves, very finely chopped
- **1** fresh bay leaf
- **2** teaspoons chopped fresh thyme leaves
- **2** teaspoons chopped fresh rosemary
- **1** pound Great Northern beans, soaked overnight and drained
- **10** cups chicken stock or low-sodium broth

Salt and freshly ground black pepper

1. Line a plate with paper towels. In a large soup pot, cook the bacon strips over moderate heat, stirring constantly, until they are browned and crisp, about 7 minutes. Use a slotted spoon to transfer the cooked bacon to the paper towel–lined plate to drain. Carefully pour the hot bacon fat into a heatproof glass measuring cup and set it aside.

2. Heat the olive oil in the large soup pot. Add the chopped onion and diced carrot and celery and cook over moderate heat, stirring occasionally, until the vegetables are softened, about 8 minutes. Stir in the chopped garlic, the bay leaf and 1 teaspoon each of the chopped thyme leaves and rosemary and cook, stirring frequently, until the aromatics are fragrant, about 2 minutes longer. Add the soaked and drained Great Northern beans, the chicken stock and 3 tablespoons of the reserved bacon fat and bring the soup to a boil. Simmer the soup over moderately low heat, stirring occasionally, until the beans are completely tender but not mushy, about 1½ hours longer.

3. Discard the bay leaf and stir the remaining chopped thyme leaves and rosemary into the soup. Season with salt and black pepper and ladle into shallow soup bowls. Garnish the white bean soup with the bacon and serve immediately.
—*Jose Garces*

MAKE AHEAD The cooled white bean soup and crispy bacon strips can be refrigerated separately in airtight containers for up to 3 days. Recrisp the bacon strips in a small skillet over moderately high heat and rewarm the soup over moderate heat, stirring frequently, before ladling into bowls to serve.

● **HEALTHY** ● **MAKE AHEAD** ● **VEGETARIAN** ● **STAFF FAVORITE**

Creamy Clam and White Bean Chowder

ACTIVE: 1 HR; TOTAL: 1 HR 50 MIN
PLUS 2 HR SOAKING

8 SERVINGS ●

1¼ cups dried cellini or Great Northern beans, rinsed and picked over, then soaked for 2 hours

Kosher salt

1¼ pounds butternut squash, peeled and cut into ½-inch dice (2 cups)

1 tablespoon extra-virgin olive oil

Freshly ground pepper

3 dozen littleneck clams, scrubbed

6 thick slices of bacon (4 ounces), cut crosswise into ¼-inch strips

2 tablespoons unsalted butter

1 medium onion, cut into ½-inch dice

3 large celery ribs, cut into ½-inch dice

¼ teaspoon crushed red pepper

4 large garlic cloves, minced

1⅓ cups dry white wine

1 cup heavy cream

Garlic Bread (recipe follows), for serving

1. In a saucepan, cover the beans with 2 inches of water and bring to a boil. Simmer over moderately low heat, stirring occasionally, until tender, about 1½ hours; add water as needed to keep the beans covered by 2 inches. Season the beans with salt and let stand for 5 minutes. Drain the beans, reserving 1½ cups of the cooking liquid.

2. Meanwhile, preheat the oven to 375°. On a rimmed baking sheet, toss the squash with the oil; season with salt and pepper. Bake for 20 minutes, until browned.

3. Set a colander over a bowl. In a skillet, cook the clams and 2 tablespoons of water over moderately high heat, covered, shaking the skillet a few times, until the clams open, 5 minutes. Transfer the opened clams to the colander; discard any that do not open. Remove the clams from their shells. Strain and reserve 1 cup of the clam broth.

4. In a saucepan, brown the bacon over moderately low heat, about 4 minutes. Stir in the butter. Add the onion, celery and crushed red pepper, cover and cook, stirring occasionally, until softened, 8 minutes. Add the garlic, cover and cook until fragrant, 4 minutes. Add the wine and boil until reduced by two-thirds, 6 minutes. Pour in the reserved clam broth, the reserved bean cooking liquid and the cream; simmer for 10 minutes. Stir in the beans, squash and clams; simmer just until heated through. Serve the chowder in bowls with the Garlic Bread alongside. —*Laurence Jossel*

GARLIC BREAD

 TOTAL: 10 MIN
8 SERVINGS ○

Eight ¾-inch slices of ciabatta

4 tablespoons unsalted butter

2 large garlic cloves, minced

Kosher salt and freshly ground pepper

¼ cup chopped parsley

1. Preheat the oven to 375°. Arrange the bread slices on a large baking sheet and bake for 6 minutes, until toasted.

2. Meanwhile, in a small skillet, melt the butter. Add the garlic and season with salt and pepper. Cook over moderately low heat until the garlic is golden, about 2 minutes. Stir in the parsley. Spoon the garlic butter over the toasts and serve right away. —*LJ*

Mussel and Chorizo Soup

TOTAL: 1 HR 15 MIN

8 SERVINGS ●

At Steve Corry's Five Fifty-Five in Portland, Maine, mussels from nearby Bangs Island are almost always on the menu. "People freak out if they're not there," says Corry, who often steams the mollusks in white wine and lemon juice scented with pickled cherry peppers and garlic. For this Mediterranean-inspired soup, however, he serves the mussels in a brothy liquid with plenty of chorizo.

½ cup dry white wine

1 tablespoon finely minced shallots

3 pounds mussels, scrubbed and debearded

2 tablespoons extra-virgin olive oil

5 ounces dry chorizo, finely diced (about ¾ cup)

2 medium carrots, finely diced

2 medium leeks, white and tender greens parts only, finely diced

1 small onion, finely diced

2 garlic cloves, minced

1 large plum tomato, finely diced

¼ teaspoon saffron threads, crumbled

3 cups low-sodium fish stock, clam juice or chicken broth

½ cup heavy cream

Salt and freshly ground white pepper

1 teaspoon chopped thyme

1. In a large, heavy pot, bring the wine with the shallots to a boil. Add the mussels, cover and cook over high heat until they open, about 5 minutes. Strain the cooking liquid into a large bowl and reserve. Remove the mussels from their shells, reserving some unshelled for garnish, if desired.

2. In the large pot, heat the olive oil. Add the chorizo, carrots, leeks and onion; cook over moderate heat, stirring occasionally, until the vegetables are softened, about 8 minutes. Spoon off all but 3 tablespoons of the fat. Add the garlic, diced tomato and saffron and cook over moderate heat until fragrant, about 4 minutes. Add the fish stock and reserved mussel cooking liquid and bring to a boil. Simmer the soup over low heat for 30 minutes.

3. Add the cream to the soup and simmer over moderately high heat for 3 minutes. Season with salt and pepper. Add the mussels and the thyme and simmer just until the mussels are heated through, about 1 minute. Ladle the soup into bowls, garnish with the mussel shells and serve hot. —*Steve Corry*

MUSSEL AND CHORIZO SOUP

Matzo Ball Soup with Dill-Horseradish Pistou

ACTIVE: 1 HR; TOTAL: 3 HR 15 MIN

10 SERVINGS ●

Instead of sprinkling his soup with the customary bits of chopped fresh dill, New York City chef Adam Perry Lang makes a vibrant horseradish and dill *pistou* (typically a condiment made with fresh basil, garlic and olive oil). A swirl of the *pistou* brightens up the soup enormously.

MATZO BALLS

8 large eggs, beaten

⅓ cup olive oil

1 cup seltzer or club soda

2 teaspoons kosher salt

1 teaspoon ground white pepper

½ teaspoon ground ginger

2 cups matzo meal (10 ounces)

PISTOU AND SOUP

½ cup extra-virgin olive oil

1 cup coarsely chopped dill

2 tablespoons finely grated fresh horseradish

1 garlic clove

making great chicken stock

To make full-flavored chicken stock, Thomas John, the executive chef of the Au Bon Pain chain, slow-simmers chicken bones for 2 hours with vegetables and herbs like onions, carrots, celery and parsley, as well as a knob of fresh ginger. For the most flexibility, he advises against salting the broth. "What if you decide to make a soup with something salty like chorizo?" he asks. "You can always salt later."

1 teaspoon salt

½ teaspoon ground white pepper

1 medium turnip, peeled and finely diced

1 celery rib, finely diced

1 large carrot, finely diced

5 quarts chicken stock, preferably homemade

8 cups diced chicken (¾-inch dice), from two 3½-pound chickens

1. MAKE THE MATZO BALLS: In a bowl, whisk the eggs with the olive oil, seltzer, salt, white pepper and ginger. Add the matzo meal and stir until moistened. Refrigerate until firm, at least 2 hours.

2. Line 2 baking sheets with wax paper. Scoop the matzo meal mixture into fifty 1-inch balls. Using lightly moistened hands, roll the matzo balls until smooth. Transfer to the baking sheets and refrigerate the matzo balls briefly.

3. MEANWHILE, MAKE THE PISTOU: In a blender or food processor, pulse the olive oil with the dill, fresh horseradish, garlic, salt and white pepper until the dill is finely chopped and a sauce has formed.

4. Bring a medium saucepan of water to a boil. Add the turnip, celery and carrot and cook until the vegetables are crisp-tender, about 5 minutes. Drain and refresh under cold water.

5. In a large pot of boiling salted water, simmer the matzo balls over very low heat, covered, until they are plump and cooked through, 25 to 30 minutes.

6. Meanwhile, in another large pot, heat the chicken stock with the drained and cooled vegetables. Using a slotted spoon, transfer the matzo balls to the soup; simmer for 5 minutes. Add the chicken and cook until heated through. Serve the matzo ball soup in bowls with a dollop of the dill-horseradish *pistou.* —Adam Perry Lang

MAKE AHEAD The recipe can be prepared through Step 3; refrigerate overnight.

Cambodian Chicken-and-Rice Soup with Shrimp

 TOTAL: 40 MIN

4 SERVINGS ● ●

Using prepared stock and preroasted chicken significantly cuts back on the prep time for this spicy, soothing and restorative chicken-and-rice soup.

One 3-pound rotisserie chicken

1 tablespoon vegetable oil

2 tablespoons very finely chopped fresh ginger

2 garlic cloves, very finely chopped

4 cups chicken stock or low-sodium broth

1 cup water

3 tablespoons Asian fish sauce

1 teaspoon honey

1 cup cooked jasmine rice

8 shelled and deveined medium shrimp, halved lengthwise (about ¼ pound)

2 tablespoons fresh lime juice

¼ cup chopped cilantro

2 tablespoons chopped basil

1 Thai chile, thinly sliced

Lime wedges, for serving

1. Using a cleaver or large, heavy kitchen knife, divide the rotisserie chicken into legs, thighs, breasts and wings. Cut each breast crosswise through the bones into 3 pieces. Remove the thigh bones and cut each thigh in half.

2. In a large saucepan, heat the vegetable oil. Add the chopped ginger and garlic and cook over moderate heat, stirring occasionally, until softened, about 3 minutes. Add the stock, water, fish sauce, honey and rice and bring to a boil. Add the chicken pieces and simmer for 5 minutes. Stir in the shrimp and cook just until opaque, about 1 minute. Stir in the lime juice, cilantro, basil and chile and serve right away, passing lime wedges at the table. —Ratha Chau

MATZO BALL SOUP WITH DILL-HORSERADISH PISTOU

CAMBODIAN CHICKEN-AND-RICE SOUP WITH SHRIMP

Chilled Russian Borscht

TOTAL: 45 MIN PLUS 4 HR CHILLING

6 TO 8 SERVINGS ● ● ●

This luscious chilled beet soup—served with a dollop of rich, tart sour cream and plenty of salady garnishes (boiled cubed potatoes, chopped hard-boiled eggs, crunchy diced radishes and fragrant, coarsely chopped dill and parsley)—seems the very essence of Russian cooking: sustaining food that still carries hints of its peasant roots.

- 2 **pounds medium beets (about 6 beets), peeled and quartered**
- 11 **cups water**
- ¼ **cup plus 1 tablespoon granulated sugar**
- ¼ **cup fresh lemon juice**
- 2 **tablespoons cider vinegar**

Salt and freshly ground black pepper

- 1 **medium Yukon Gold potato, peeled and cut into ½-inch cubes**
- 1 **pound Kirby cucumbers— peeled, seeded and cut into ½-inch cubes**
- 1 **cup finely diced radishes**
- 4 **scallions, thinly sliced**
- 3 **large hard-cooked eggs, peeled and coarsely chopped**
- ¼ **cup coarsely chopped dill**
- ¼ **cup coarsely chopped flat-leaf parsley**

Sour cream or crème fraîche, for serving

1. In a large pot, cover the peeled and quartered beets with the 11 cups of water and bring to a boil. Simmer over moderately low heat until the beets are tender when pierced with a fork, about 30 minutes. Using a slotted spoon, transfer the cooked beets to a plate.

2. Coarsely shred the beets in a food processor. Return them to the pot and add the granulated sugar, lemon juice and cider vinegar; season with salt and black pepper. Let the soup cool; cover and refrigerate until well chilled, for at least 4 hours or, preferably, overnight.

3. Meanwhile, bring a small saucepan of salted water to a boil. Add the potato cubes and cook until tender, about 7 minutes. Drain and cool under cold water. Pat dry and transfer to a medium bowl. Add the cucumbers, radishes, scallions, eggs, dill and parsley.

4. Ladle the chilled borscht into bowls. Garnish with the vegetable and chopped egg mixture, top with a generous dollop of sour cream and serve.

—*Anya von Bremzen*

MAKE AHEAD The borscht can be refrigerated for up to 3 days. Prepare the garnishes just before serving the soup.

● HEALTHY ● MAKE AHEAD ● VEGETARIAN ● STAFF FAVORITE

CHILLED SPRING PEA SOUP

CHILLED CUCUMBER SOUP WITH SALT-ROASTED SHRIMP

Chilled Spring Pea Soup

 TOTAL: 45 MIN
6 SERVINGS ● ●

Chef Daniel Boulud's delicious and clean-tasting soup—a mix of sweet peas, favas, pea shoots, snap peas and snow peas—is on the menu each spring at his Café Boulud in New York City. This version omits the labor-intensive fresh favas as well as the snow peas and pea shoots, instead using sugar snaps and frozen baby peas.

  8 slices of bacon
  1 tablespoon extra-virgin olive oil
  2 celery ribs, thinly sliced
  1 onion, thinly sliced
  1 leek, white and tender green parts only, thinly sliced
  5 cups chicken stock or low-sodium broth
Two 4-inch rosemary sprigs
Salt and freshly ground white pepper
  ½ pound sugar snap peas, thinly sliced
Two 10-ounce boxes frozen baby peas
  ¼ cup flat-leaf parsley leaves
  1 cup heavy cream
  1 garlic clove, minced

1. In a medium soup pot, cook the bacon over moderate heat until browned and crisp, about 6 minutes. Transfer the bacon to a plate. Pour off the fat in the pot.

2. In the same pot, heat the olive oil. Add the celery, onion and leek and cook over moderately low heat, stirring occasionally, until softened but not browned, about 7 minutes. Add the stock, 4 slices of the cooked bacon, 1 rosemary sprig and a pinch each of salt and white pepper. Simmer until the vegetables are very tender, about 15 minutes. Discard the bacon and rosemary. Using a slotted spoon, transfer the vegetables to a blender. Reserve the broth.

3. Meanwhile, bring a medium saucepan of salted water to a boil. Add the sugar snaps and cook for 3 minutes. Add the frozen baby peas and the parsley and cook just until heated through, about 1 minute; drain.

Add the sugar snaps, baby peas and parsley to the blender and puree until smooth, adding a few tablespoons of the broth to loosen the mixture. Transfer the soup and the remaining broth to a large bowl set in a larger bowl of ice water to cool.

4. In a small saucepan, bring the heavy cream, garlic and remaining rosemary sprig to a boil. Simmer over low heat until slightly reduced, about 5 minutes. Strain the garlic cream into a bowl and let cool.

5. Ladle the chilled pea soup into bowls and drizzle with the garlic cream. Crumble the remaining 4 slices of bacon into each bowl and serve. —*Daniel Boulud*

Chilled Cucumber Soup with Salt-Roasted Shrimp

TOTAL: 30 MIN PLUS OVERNIGHT CHILLING

4 SERVINGS ●

Made with lime, garlic and ginger, this cucumber soup from Jim Burke (an F&W Best New Chef 2008) is so light, refreshing and restorative that Burke's kitchen staff jokes that it's like a mini spa treatment. Salt-roasted shrimp, avocado and a hit of spicy chile oil add substance.

- 2 large English cucumbers (2 pounds total), halved lengthwise
- 3 cilantro sprigs, plus 2 teaspoons finely chopped cilantro
- 2 garlic cloves, crushed

One 1-inch piece of fresh ginger, coarsely chopped

- 3 tablespoons plus 1 teaspoon fresh lime juice

Kosher salt and freshly ground pepper

- ¼ pound large shrimp
- 1 Hass avocado, cut into thin slices
- 1 teaspoon hot chile oil

1. Using a juicer, juice the cucumbers into a large bowl (you should have about 3 cups of juice). Stir in the cilantro sprigs, garlic, ginger, 3 tablespoons of the lime juice, 2 teaspoons of salt and ¼ teaspoon of pepper. Cover and refrigerate overnight.

2. Spread ⅓ cup of salt in a skillet. Heat the skillet until the salt is hot. Add the shrimp and cook over moderately high heat, turning once, until pink, about 4 minutes. Remove the shrimp and let stand until cool enough to handle, about 5 minutes. Peel the shrimp and remove the intestinal vein. Cut the shrimp into ½-inch pieces and transfer to a bowl. Add the chopped cilantro, avocado and the remaining 1 teaspoon of lime juice.

3. Strain the cucumber juice through a fine strainer into a large measuring cup. Spoon the shrimp and avocado into shallow bowls and drizzle with the chile oil. Pour the cucumber soup around the shrimp and serve. —*Jim Burke*

Chilled Edamame Soup with Ginger Crème Fraîche

ACTIVE: 15 MIN; TOTAL: 45 MIN PLUS 3 HR CHILLING

6 SERVINGS ● ●

- 1 tablespoon unsalted butter
- 1 medium onion, finely chopped
- 4 cups chicken stock
- 2 cups frozen shelled edamame (10 ounces)

Salt

- ¼ cup crème fraîche
- 2 teaspoons finely grated fresh ginger

1. In a medium saucepan, melt the butter. Add the onion and cook over moderate heat until softened, about 7 minutes. Add 3 cups of the stock and simmer over low heat for 20 minutes. Add the edamame and cook until tender, about 10 minutes. Let cool slightly, then puree the soup in a blender until very smooth. Transfer the soup to a bowl and refrigerate until chilled, at least 3 hours.

2. Whisk the remaining 1 cup of chicken stock into the soup and season with salt. In a small bowl, combine the crème fraîche with the grated ginger. Ladle the soup into bowls, drizzle with the ginger crème fraîche and serve. —*Nobuo Fukuda*

Grilled-Vegetable Gazpacho

TOTAL: 45 MIN PLUS 2 HR CHILLING

10 SERVINGS ● ●

- 4 large garlic cloves, unpeeled
- 2 large red bell peppers, cored and quartered
- 2 large yellow bell peppers, cored and quartered
- 2 medium zucchini, sliced lengthwise ½ inch thick
- 1 large white onion, cut into ½-inch slabs
- 2 ears of corn, husked
- 2 tablespoons vegetable oil

Kosher salt and freshly ground pepper

- 1½ teaspoons ground cumin
- ½ teaspoon crushed red pepper
- 2 cups tomato juice
- ½ cup fresh orange juice
- 3 tablespoons fresh lemon juice
- 2 tablespoons red wine vinegar
- ¼ cup chopped cilantro
- 1 English cucumber, thinly sliced

1. Light a grill. Thread the garlic cloves onto a skewer. Lightly brush the garlic, bell peppers, zucchini, onion and corn with the vegetable oil and season with salt and pepper. Grill the vegetables over moderately high heat, turning frequently, until lightly charred and crisp-tender, about 10 minutes. Transfer the peppers to a bowl, cover with plastic and let steam for 10 minutes.

2. Meanwhile, remove the garlic cloves from the skewers, peel them and transfer to a large bowl. Using a large serrated knife, cut the charred corn kernels into the bowl. Peel the peppers and add them to the bowl along with the zucchini, onion, cumin, crushed red pepper, tomato juice, orange juice, lemon juice and vinegar.

3. Working in batches, puree the vegetable mixture in a blender or food processor. Pour the gazpacho into a clean bowl and season with salt and pepper. Cover and refrigerate until chilled, about 2 hours.

4. Stir in the cilantro, garnish with cucumber and serve. —*Kerry Simon*

CREAMY PASTA WITH
TOMATO CONFIT AND FRESH
GOAT CHEESE (P. 75)

pasta

"My grandma cooked her pasta sauces for what seemed like days. At home, my sauces take about 10 minutes."

—MICHAEL SCHLOW, CHEF AND RESTAURATEUR

FARFALLE WITH ZUCCHINI AND PARSLEY-ALMOND PESTO

FETTUCCINE WITH TOMATOES AND CRISPY CAPERS

Farfalle with Zucchini and Parsley-Almond Pesto

 TOTAL: 30 MIN
4 SERVINGS ● ● ●

Roasted almonds, Parmigiano-Reggiano cheese and parsley are combined here for a nutty, fresh-tasting pesto. This pasta dish is terrific served warm, but it can also be refrigerated and served as a salad.

- 1 pound farfalle
- 1 garlic clove
- ⅓ cup unsalted roasted almonds
- 1½ cups flat-leaf parsley leaves
- ½ cup plus 1 tablespoon extra-virgin olive oil
- ¼ cup freshly grated Parmigiano-Reggiano cheese

Kosher salt and freshly ground pepper
- 1 pound zucchini (2 medium), halved lengthwise and sliced crosswise ⅛ inch thick

Pinch of crushed red pepper

1. Bring a large pot of salted water to a boil. Add the farfalle and cook until it is al dente. Drain the farfalle.
2. Meanwhile, in a food processor, pulse the garlic clove until it is finely chopped. Add the almonds and pulse until they are coarsely chopped. Add the parsley and ½ cup of the olive oil and process until the parsley is finely chopped. Add the Parmigiano-Reggiano cheese and pulse just until the pesto is combined. Season with salt and pepper and scrape the pesto into a large, shallow serving bowl.
3. In a large skillet, heat the remaining 1 tablespoon of oil until shimmering. Add the zucchini and cook over moderately high heat until tender and browned in spots, 5 minutes. Add the red pepper and season with salt and pepper. Transfer the zucchini to the bowl with the pesto. Add the farfalle, toss and serve. —*Melissa Rubel*
WINE Fresh, lively Soave.

Fettuccine with Tomatoes and Crispy Capers

 TOTAL: 30 MIN
6 SERVINGS ●

Fried capers add a delectable, salty crunch to pasta tossed with fresh tomatoes and creamy prosciutto.

- ½ cup extra-virgin olive oil
- ¼ cup small capers, drained and patted dry
- ¼ cup cornstarch
- 4 oil-packed anchovies, chopped
- 2 large garlic cloves, thinly sliced
- 2 ounces thinly sliced prosciutto, cut into 1-inch-wide ribbons
- 2 tomatoes, coarsely chopped
- ½ teaspoon crushed red pepper
- 1 tablespoon thinly sliced basil
- 1 pound fettuccine

Freshly grated Parmigiano-Reggiano cheese, for serving

1. In a large skillet, heat the olive oil. In a small bowl, toss the capers with the cornstarch and transfer to a sieve; shake off the excess cornstarch. Add the coated capers to the oil and fry over high heat, tilting and gently shaking the pan, until the capers are crispy and golden, about 3 minutes. Drain the capers, reserving 2 tablespoons of the oil in the skillet. Spread the capers on a paper towel–lined plate.

2. Add the anchovies and garlic to the skillet and cook over high heat, stirring, until the garlic is golden and the anchovies dissolve, about 3 minutes. Add the prosciutto, separating the ribbons, and cook until lightly browned, about 1 minute. Add the tomatoes and crushed red pepper and cook just until the tomatoes begin to break down, about 3 minutes. Stir in the basil.

3. Meanwhile, in a large pot of boiling salted water, cook the pasta until al dente. Drain, reserving ½ cup of the cooking water. Return the pasta to the pot along with the reserved cooking water and pour the sauce on top. Toss over high heat just until the sauce is thickened, about 2 minutes. Serve the pasta in bowls, garnished with the crispy capers. Pass the grated cheese at the table. —*Grace Parisi*
WINE Dry, light Champagne.

Spaghetti with Spinach, Tomatoes and Goat Cheese

TOTAL: 30 MIN
4 SERVINGS

¾ pound spaghetti
¼ cup extra-virgin olive oil
2 garlic cloves, thinly sliced
Pinch of crushed red pepper
1 cup grape tomatoes
(6 ounces), halved
Kosher salt and freshly ground pepper
8 cups baby spinach (7 ounces)
¼ cup freshly grated pecorino cheese, plus more for serving
4 ounces fresh goat cheese, crumbled (1 cup)

1. In a large pot of boiling salted water, cook the spaghetti until it is al dente. Drain the spaghetti well, reserving ½ cup of the pasta cooking water.

2. Meanwhile, in a large skillet, heat the olive oil. Add the garlic and crushed red pepper and cook over moderate heat until the garlic is tender, about 3 minutes. Add the tomatoes, season with salt and pepper and cook over moderately high heat until the tomatoes begin to release their juices, about 2 minutes. Add the spinach and cook until wilted, about 2 minutes.

3. Add the spaghetti, the reserved ½ cup of pasta cooking water and the ¼ cup of pecorino to the skillet and toss over low heat until the pasta is coated with the sauce. Season with salt and pepper. Add the goat cheese and toss gently. Transfer the spaghetti to shallow bowls and serve, passing additional grated pecorino cheese at the table. —*Melissa Rubel*
WINE Lively, tart Sauvignon Blanc.

Creamy Pasta with Tomato Confit and Fresh Goat Cheese

TOTAL: 1 HR
4 SERVINGS

Terrance Brennan (an F&W Best New Chef 1995) cooks this pasta risotto-style by stirring in rich chicken stock a ladleful at a time. As the pasta releases its starch, the dish becomes delicately milky. Instead of finishing the dish with a knob of butter, he folds in fresh goat cheese, which turns creamy in the gentle heat. Brennan uses a little, tube-shaped pasta called ditalini, but any small cut works.

1 cup extra-virgin olive oil, for poaching
3 plum tomatoes—peeled, quartered and seeded
2 thyme sprigs
1 bay leaf
2 garlic cloves, minced
2 tablespoons unsalted butter
1 small onion, coarsely chopped

Kosher salt
½ pound ditalini or other small-cut pasta (1½ cups)
3½ cups chicken stock or low-sodium broth
½ cup soft fresh goat cheese (4 ounces)
½ cup tightly packed freshly grated Parmigiano-Reggiano cheese (2½ ounces), plus more for serving
Freshly ground pepper
2 tablespoons snipped chives
2 tablespoons finely shredded basil leaves

1. In a medium saucepan, combine the olive oil with the tomatoes, thyme, bay leaf and half of the garlic and bring to a simmer. Cook over low heat until the tomatoes are very tender, about 15 minutes. Discard the thyme and bay leaf. Using a slotted spoon, transfer the tomatoes to a work surface and coarsely chop them; reserve the olive oil for another use.

2. In a large saucepan, melt the butter. Add the onion and a pinch of salt; cook over moderate heat, stirring, until softened, 5 minutes. Add the pasta and cook, stirring, until golden in spots, about 2 minutes. Add the remaining garlic; cook for 1 minute.

3. Add ½ cup of the chicken stock to the pasta and cook over moderately high heat, stirring constantly, until nearly absorbed. Continue adding the chicken stock ½ cup at a time, stirring and cooking until it is nearly absorbed between additions. The pasta is done when it is al dente and suspended in a lightly thickened sauce, about 17 minutes total.

4. Stir the tomatoes into the pasta. Off the heat, add the goat cheese and Parmigiano-Reggiano and stir until melted. Season with salt and pepper, stir in the chives and basil and serve right away, passing additional Parmigiano-Reggiano at the table.
—*Terrance Brennan*
WINE Bright, tart Barbera.

Pasta Salad with Tomatoes, Arugula, Pine Nuts and Herb Dressing

TOTAL: 20 MIN
4 SERVINGS

For lighter winter meals, F&W's Melissa Rubel transforms a basic pasta salad with peppery arugula and a lively mayo-based dressing made with garlic, lemon juice and fresh herbs. She uses sweet grape tomatoes, which are delicious year-round.

- ¼ cup plus 3 tablespoons pine nuts
- 1 pound fusilli
- ½ cup cilantro leaves
- ½ cup basil leaves
- 2 teaspoons coarsely chopped oregano leaves
- 1 garlic clove
- ¼ cup mayonnaise
- ¼ cup extra-virgin olive oil
- 1½ tablespoons fresh lemon juice

Kosher salt and freshly ground black pepper

- 2½ cups baby arugula
- 1¼ cups grape tomatoes, halved
- ½ small red onion, cut into ¼-inch dice

1. Preheat the oven to 350°. In a pie plate, toast 3 tablespoons of the pine nuts until lightly golden and fragrant, about 5 minutes. Set aside to cool.

2. In a large pot of boiling salted water, cook the fusilli until it is al dente. Drain the pasta and rinse it under cold water, then drain again; transfer to a large bowl.

3. Meanwhile, in a food processor, combine the cilantro with the basil, oregano and garlic and pulse until coarsely chopped. Add the mayonnaise, olive oil, lemon juice and the remaining ¼ cup of pine nuts and process until smooth. Season the herb dressing with salt and pepper.

4. Toss the fusilli with the pine nuts, arugula, tomatoes, onion and dressing. Season the pasta salad with salt and pepper and serve. —*Melissa Rubel*

WINE Fresh, lively Soave.

Farfalle with Tomatoes and Green Vegetables

TOTAL: 25 MIN
6 SERVINGS ● ●

"I make this dish often in the early summer, when green vegetables like zucchini and spinach are just coming into the farmers' market," says Laurent Gras (an F&W Best New Chef 2002). "You can eat a lot of it and still feel good about yourself. It doesn't make you tired like heavier pasta dishes can."

- 1 pound ripe green tomatoes, such as Green Zebra
- ¼ cup extra-virgin olive oil
- 1 medium zucchini, halved lengthwise and thinly sliced crosswise

Kosher salt

- 1 pound farfalle
- 12 asparagus spears, cut into ½-inch lengths
- 2 cups baby spinach (1½ ounces)
- 1 tablespoon chopped fresh tarragon
- 2 ounces *ricotta salata* cheese, coarsely grated (⅔ cup)

1. Bring a saucepan of water to a boil. Fill a bowl with ice water. Using a paring knife, core the tomatoes and make a shallow X in the bottom of each one. Blanch the tomatoes in the boiling water until their skins just begin to split, about 30 seconds. Using a slotted spoon, transfer the tomatoes to the ice water to cool, then drain and peel. Halve the tomatoes and discard the seeds. Cut the tomato flesh into ½-inch dice.

2. Bring a pot or large saucepan of salted water to a boil. In a large skillet, heat the olive oil. Add the sliced zucchini and cook over moderate heat, stirring occasionally, until almost tender, about 3 minutes. Add the diced tomatoes and cook until they begin to break down, stirring occasionally, about 2 minutes. Season with salt.

3. Cook the farfalle in the boiling water until al dente, adding the asparagus to the pot 1 minute before the pasta is done. Drain the pasta and asparagus well, reserving ½ cup of the cooking water.

4. Return the pasta and asparagus to the pot. Add the zucchini-tomato mixture along with the baby spinach, chopped tarragon and the reserved pasta water and season with salt. Spoon the farfalle into bowls, sprinkle with the *ricotta salata* and serve right away. —*Laurent Gras*

WINE Zippy, fresh Pinot Bianco.

Farfalle with Yogurt and Zucchini

TOTAL: 25 MIN
4 TO 6 SERVINGS ● ●

The shredded zucchini cooks along with the farfalle in this tangy pasta.

- 1 pound farfalle
- 1½ pounds medium zucchini, coarsely shredded
- 4 tablespoons unsalted butter
- 1 cup plain whole-milk Greek yogurt
- 1 cup freshly grated Parmigiano-Reggiano cheese, plus more for serving

Freshly grated nutmeg

Kosher salt and freshly ground black pepper

1. Bring a large pot of salted water to a boil. Cook the farfalle until al dente; about 1 minute before the farfalle is done, add the shredded zucchini to the pot. Drain the farfalle and zucchini, reserving ¼ cup of the cooking water.

2. In a large, deep skillet, melt the butter. Off the heat, stir in the Greek yogurt and the cup of grated Parmigiano-Reggiano cheese; season with nutmeg, salt and pepper. Add the farfalle, zucchini and the reserved cooking water and cook over low heat, tossing, until the sauce coats the farfalle. Transfer the pasta to warmed bowls and serve with additional cheese. —*George Germon and Johanne Killeen*

WINE Fresh, minerally Vermentino.

Pasta with Cauliflower, Peppers and Walnut Pesto

TOTAL: 40 MIN
6 SERVINGS ● ●

This vegetable-loaded pasta is equally delicious warm or cold. Seattle chef Jerry Traunfeld created it with the Eastern Mediterranean staples of cauliflower and bell peppers, which taste great together, especially when they're tossed in a garlicky walnut pesto.

1½ lightly packed cups cilantro leaves

½ lightly packed cup
   flat-leaf parsley leaves

¾ cup walnuts

2 garlic cloves

½ cup extra-virgin olive oil

Kosher salt

¾ pound strozzapreti or orecchiette

1 small head of cauliflower
   (1½ pounds), cut into 1-inch
   florets (about 4 cups)

1 small red bell pepper, cut into
   2-by-¼-inch strips

1 small yellow bell pepper,
   cut into 2-by-¼-inch strips

Freshly ground pepper

1. In a food processor, pulse the cilantro, parsley, walnuts and garlic until finely chopped. Add 6 tablespoons of the oil and process until smooth. Season with salt.

2. In a large pot of boiling salted water, cook the pasta until al dente. Drain the pasta and reserve ¼ cup of the pasta water.

3. Meanwhile, in a large skillet, heat the remaining 2 tablespoons of oil. Add the cauliflower and season with salt. Cook over moderately high heat until browned in spots, 5 minutes. Add the bell peppers and cook until tender and brown in spots, 5 minutes. Scrape the vegetables into a bowl.

4. Add the pasta, pesto and the reserved pasta water to the vegetables; toss until the pasta is coated. Season with salt and pepper. Spoon into warm bowls and serve.
—*Jerry Traunfeld*

WINE Ripe, luxurious Chardonnay.

FARFALLE WITH TOMATOES AND GREEN VEGETABLES

PASTA WITH CAULIFLOWER, PEPPERS AND WALNUT PESTO

10-minute tomato sauce

A tablespoon of butter makes this speedy sauce especially luxurious. Michael Schlow (*an F&W Best New Chef 1996*) *recommends leaving the butter out if you plan to freeze the sauce, and adding it during reheating.*

MAKES ABOUT 3½ CUPS

In a food processor, pulse one 28-ounce can whole Italian tomatoes with their juices until finely chopped. In a large saucepan, heat ⅓ cup olive oil over moderately high heat. Add 10 basil leaves and cook until they begin to wilt, 10 seconds. Add a pinch of crushed red pepper, salt and black pepper. Add the tomatoes, bring to a boil and cook, stirring, until slightly thickened, about 6 minutes. Remove from the heat and stir in 1 tablespoon unsalted butter. Season with salt and pepper.

Angel Hair Pasta with Red Pepper Pesto and Basil

 ACTIVE: 20 MIN; TOTAL: 40 MIN
4 SERVINGS ● ○ ○

Lachlan Mackinnon-Patterson (an F&W Best New Chef 2005) of Frasca Food and Wine in Boulder, Colorado, creates a simple summery sauce by blending roasted red peppers with traditional pesto ingredients, like basil and pine nuts, to toss with cool angel hair pasta. The pesto freezes beautifully and is also delicious spread on grilled cheese sandwiches or swirled into soups.

- 3 medium red bell peppers
- 1 tablespoon pine nuts
- 1 small garlic clove, smashed
- ¼ cup basil leaves, plus 2 tablespoons chopped basil
- ¼ cup extra-virgin olive oil
- Kosher salt and freshly ground black pepper
- ½ pound angel hair pasta
- ½ cup shaved pecorino cheese

1. Roast the red peppers over a gas flame or under the broiler, turning occasionally, until charred all over. Transfer the peppers to a bowl, cover with plastic wrap and let cool. Peel, core and chop the peppers.
2. In a small skillet, toast the pine nuts over moderate heat until golden, about 4 minutes. Let cool.
3. Transfer the peppers and pine nuts to a blender. Add the garlic and whole basil leaves and blend until coarsely chopped. Add the olive oil and puree to a chunky pesto. Season with salt and pepper.
4. Bring a large saucepan of salted water to a boil. Add the pasta and cook until al dente. Drain and cool slightly under running water. Transfer to a serving bowl and add the red pepper pesto; toss well. Season the pasta with salt and black pepper. Top with the chopped basil and shaved pecorino and serve at room temperature. —*Lachlan Mackinnon-Patterson*
WINE Minerally, complex Sauvignon Blanc.

Gemelli with Creamy Red Pepper Sauce and Fresh Mozzarella

 TOTAL: 25 MIN
4 SERVINGS ● ○ ○

- ¾ pound gemelli
- 2 whole roasted red peppers from the deli counter (6 ounces)
- ¼ cup plus 2 tablespoons extra-virgin olive oil
- 2 oil-packed sun-dried tomato halves, drained
- 1 tablespoon tomato paste
- 1 garlic clove
- 9 large basil leaves
- Kosher salt and freshly ground pepper
- ½ pound salted fresh mozzarella cheese, cut into ½-inch dice

1. In a large pot of boiling salted water, cook the gemelli until al dente.
2. Meanwhile, in a blender, puree the roasted red peppers with the olive oil, sun-dried tomatoes, tomato paste, garlic and 3 basil leaves until smooth. Season the sauce with salt and pepper.
3. Scrape the sauce into a large bowl and toss with the pasta until well coated. Tear the remaining 6 basil leaves into the pasta and add the mozzarella. Toss the mozzarella, basil and pasta and serve warm or at room temperature. —*Melissa Rubel*
WINE Intense, fruity Zinfandel.

Triple-Tomato Penne

 TOTAL: 20 MIN
4 SERVINGS ● ● ○

Tomatoes in three forms—fresh, sun-dried and paste—come together in this thick, creamy, deeply tomatoey sauce.

- 1 pound penne
- 2 medium tomatoes, diced
- 4 oil-packed sun-dried tomatoes
- 2 tablespoons tomato paste
- 4 large basil leaves
- 1 garlic clove
- ⅓ cup extra-virgin olive oil
- Kosher salt and freshly ground pepper

TRIPLE-TOMATO PENNE

CRESPELLE WITH RICOTTA AND MARINARA

1. In a large pot of boiling salted water, cook the penne until al dente.

2. In a blender, puree the diced and sun-dried tomatoes with the tomato paste, basil, garlic and olive oil. Pour the sauce into a large bowl and season with salt and pepper.

3. Drain the pasta, add it to the sauce and toss to coat. Serve hot. —*Melissa Rubel*
WINE Dry, fruity sparkling wine.

Crespelle with Ricotta and Marinara

ACTIVE: 45 MIN; TOTAL: 2 HR 10 MIN
4 SERVINGS ● ●

In this recipe, adapted from *Wine Bar Food* (Clarkson Potter), chef Tony Mantuano fills *crespelle* (Italian crêpes) with lush ricotta and bakes them in a rich marinara sauce.

CRESPELLE

¾ cup all-purpose flour
½ teaspoon salt
2 large eggs
¾ cup milk
1 tablespoon melted unsalted butter

Olive oil

FILLING

1½ cups ricotta cheese
1 tablespoon chopped parsley
⅔ cup freshly grated Parmigiano-Reggiano cheese

Salt and freshly ground pepper

1½ cups marinara sauce

1. MAKE THE CRESPELLE: In a medium bowl, whisk the flour with the salt. In a small bowl, whisk the eggs with the milk. Whisk the egg mixture into the flour mixture. Whisk in the melted butter until just blended. Cover the batter and refrigerate for 1 hour.

2. Heat a 10-inch nonstick skillet over moderately high heat. With a paper towel, rub the skillet with olive oil. Pour in ¼ cup of the batter and tilt the skillet to distribute. Cook the *crespella* until golden brown on the bottom, 2 minutes. Flip and cook until browned in spots, 1 minute longer. Invert the *crespella* onto a baking sheet. Repeat with the remaining batter, rubbing the pan with oil as needed. You should have 8 *crespelle*.

3. MAKE THE FILLING: Preheat the oven to 375°. In a bowl, blend the ricotta with the parsley and ⅓ cup of the Parmigiano-Reggiano. Season with salt and pepper.

4. Lay the 8 *crespelle* on a surface. Spread 2 rounded tablespoons of filling over half of each *crespella*. Fold the *crespelle* in half, then fold them in half again into quarters.

5. Spread half of the marinara sauce in the bottom of a 9-by-13-inch baking dish. Arrange the filled *crespelle* in a single layer, overlapping them slightly. Top with the remaining sauce and sprinkle with the remaining ⅓ cup of cheese. Bake for 25 minutes, until golden brown and bubbling. —*Tony Mantuano*

WINE Cherry-inflected, earthy Sangiovese.

● HEALTHY ● MAKE AHEAD ● VEGETARIAN ● STAFF FAVORITE

PARMIGIANO-CRUSTED RIGATONI
WITH CAULIFLOWER AND PROSCIUTTO

Parmigiano-Crusted Rigatoni with Cauliflower and Prosciutto

TOTAL: 30 MIN
4 SERVINGS ●

3½ tablespoons extra-virgin olive oil
1 large garlic clove, thinly sliced
1 cup heavy cream
Kosher salt and freshly ground black pepper
¾ pound rigatoni
One 1¾-pound head of cauliflower, cut into 1-inch florets
1 cup *panko* (Japanese bread crumbs)
½ cup freshly grated Parmigiano-Reggiano cheese
3 ounces sliced prosciutto, cut into ¼-inch-wide ribbons

1. Preheat the broiler. Bring a large pot of salted water to a boil. In a medium skillet, heat 1 tablespoon of the olive oil. Add the sliced garlic and cook over moderate heat until lightly golden, about 3 minutes. Add the cream and simmer until thickened slightly, about 2 minutes. Season the garlic cream with salt and pepper.

2. Cook the rigatoni until al dente; about 6 minutes before the rigatoni is done, add the cauliflower florets to the pot. Drain the pasta and cauliflower, reserving 2 tablespoons of the cooking water.

3. Meanwhile, in a medium bowl, toss the *panko* with the Parmigiano cheese and the remaining 2½ tablespoons of olive oil; season with salt and pepper.

4. Return the rigatoni and cauliflower to the pot. Add the garlic cream, the prosciutto and the 2 tablespoons of reserved pasta water and toss until the pasta is coated. Scrape the pasta into a large, shallow baking dish and sprinkle the *panko* mixture evenly over the top. Broil for about 2 minutes, rotating constantly, until the topping is evenly browned. Serve hot.
—*Melissa Rubel*

WINE Cherry-inflected, earthy Sangiovese.

Pappardelle with Porcini and Pistachios

TOTAL: 45 MIN
6 SERVINGS

Manhattan chef Shea Gallante (an F&W Best New Chef 2005) loves pappardelle with porcini mushrooms: "It's great in its simplicity," he says. Roasted pistachios add a sweet nuttiness to the dish.

6 tablespoons unsalted butter
1 large red onion, cut into ¾-inch dice
1 pound fresh porcini or cremini mushrooms, thinly sliced
Salt and freshly ground pepper
1 shallot, minced
1 garlic clove, thinly sliced
2 cups chicken stock or low-sodium broth
2 tablespoons chopped flat-leaf parsley
½ cup unsalted roasted pistachios
½ teaspoon fresh lemon juice
1 small chile, such as red Thai chile, seeded and minced
1 pound pappardelle, preferably fresh
2 tablespoons extra-virgin olive oil
Freshly grated Parmigiano-Reggiano cheese, for serving

1. In a large, deep skillet, melt 4 tablespoons of the butter. Add the onion and cook over low heat, stirring occasionally, until softened but not browned, about 10 minutes. Using a slotted spoon, transfer the onion to a bowl; leave as much of the butter in the pan as possible.

2. Add the mushrooms to the skillet, season with salt and pepper and cook over high heat, stirring occasionally, until the liquid is evaporated and the mushrooms are golden, about 8 minutes. Stir in the shallot and garlic and cook for 1 minute. Return the onion to the skillet. Add the chicken stock and parsley and simmer over moderately high heat until the liquid is reduced to ¼ cup, about 8 minutes. Add the remaining 2 tablespoons of butter along with the pistachios, lemon juice and chile and stir until the butter is melted. Season with salt and pepper.

3. Meanwhile, cook the pappardelle in a large pot of boiling salted water until al dente. Drain the pasta, reserving ½ cup of the cooking water.

4. Add the pasta to the skillet along with the reserved cooking water and the oil. Cook over moderately high heat, tossing, until the pasta is coated with a thick sauce, about 2 minutes. Transfer the pasta to bowls and serve with the cheese. —*Shea Gallante*

MAKE AHEAD The recipe can be prepared through Step 2 and refrigerated overnight; let the mushroom sauce return to room temperature before proceeding.

WINE Bright, tart Barbera.

Pasta with Sausage, Basil and Mustard

TOTAL: 20 MIN
4 SERVINGS ●

In matching spicy sausage with a creamy mustard sauce and fragrant basil, British cookbook author Nigel Slater creates a hearty pasta dish that feels very English.

1 pound penne or medium shells
1 tablespoon extra-virgin olive oil
1½ pounds hot Italian sausages—casings removed, meat crumbled
¾ cup dry white wine
¾ cup heavy cream
3 tablespoons grainy mustard
Pinch of crushed red pepper
1 cup thinly sliced basil

1. Cook the pasta in a large pot of boiling salted water until al dente; drain.

2. Heat the oil in a large, deep skillet. Add the sausage meat and brown over moderately high heat. Add the wine and simmer until reduced by half. Add the cream, mustard and red pepper and simmer for 2 minutes. Stir in the pasta and basil and serve.
—*Nigel Slater*

WINE Zippy, fresh Pinot Bianco.

Pasta with Rosemary and Onion-Orange Marmalade

TOTAL: 40 MIN
4 FIRST-COURSE SERVINGS

- 3 tablespoons extra-virgin olive oil
- 3 ounces thinly sliced pancetta, finely chopped
- 1 medium onion, thinly sliced
- 2 teaspoons chopped rosemary
- 2 tablespoons orange marmalade

Salt and freshly ground pepper

- ½ pound dried pasta, such as garganelli, fusilli or rotini
- ¼ cup freshly grated Parmigiano-Reggiano cheese

1. In a saucepan, heat the oil. Add the pancetta and cook over moderate heat until browned and most of the fat has been rendered, 4 minutes. Add the onion and rosemary, cover and cook over moderately low heat, stirring occasionally, until the onion is tender and golden, 10 minutes. Stir in the marmalade; season with salt and pepper.

2. Bring a large saucepan of salted water to a boil. Add the pasta and cook until al dente. Drain the pasta, reserving ⅓ cup of the cooking water.

3. Return the pasta to the saucepan. Add the onion-orange mixture and the reserved cooking water; toss well. Season with salt and pepper and transfer to plates. Sprinkle with the cheese and serve right away.
—*Anna Imparato*

MAKE AHEAD The marmalade mixture can be made up to 4 hours ahead.
WINE Cherry-inflected, earthy Sangiovese.

Pasta with Artichokes and Rouget

TOTAL: 1 HR
8 SERVINGS ●

- 2 lemons, halved
- 4 large artichokes (about 1 pound each)
- ½ cup extra-virgin olive oil
- 2 garlic cloves, thinly sliced
- 20 cherry tomatoes, halved

Salt and freshly ground pepper
- 1 pound fettuccine
- 1 tablespoon chopped parsley
- 16 rouget (red mullet) fillets (about 2 ounces each)

1. Squeeze the lemons into a large bowl of water. Working with one artichoke at a time, snap off the outer leaves and trim off all but ½ inch of the stem. Using a sharp knife, cut off the leaves at the top of the heart. Peel the base and stem. Using a small spoon or a melon baller, scoop out the furry choke. Add the artichoke to the water and repeat with the remaining artichokes. Thinly slice the artichoke hearts and return them to the water.

2. In a large, deep skillet, heat ¼ cup plus 2 tablespoons of the oil until shimmering. Drain the artichokes and pat dry. Add the artichokes to the skillet and cook over high heat, stirring occasionally, until lightly browned in spots and barely tender, about 7 minutes. Add the garlic and cook, stirring, until lightly browned, about 2 minutes. Add the tomatoes and a generous pinch of salt and pepper and cook over low heat, smashing the tomatoes, until the artichokes are tender, about 5 minutes.

3. Meanwhile, in a large pot of boiling salted water, cook the pasta until al dente. Drain the pasta, reserving ¾ cup of the cooking water.

4. Add the pasta and the cooking water to the skillet and simmer, tossing, until the liquid is nearly absorbed, about 2 minutes. Stir in the parsley.

5. In a large nonstick skillet, heat the remaining 2 tablespoons of olive oil until shimmering. Season the fish with salt and pepper and add it to the skillet, skin side down. Cook over high heat, turning once, until crisp and cooked through, about 5 minutes. Transfer the pasta to a large platter and arrange the fish on top, skin side up. Serve right away.
—*Maurizio Quaranta*

WINE Zippy, fresh Pinot Bianco.

Linguine with Littleneck Clams and Genoa Salami

TOTAL: 25 MIN
4 SERVINGS ●

- ¾ pound linguine
- 3 tablespoons extra-virgin olive oil
- 2 garlic cloves, thinly sliced
- ¼ teaspoon crushed red pepper
- 30 littleneck clams, scrubbed
- ½ cup dry white wine
- ½ cup bottled clam broth
- 3 ounces sliced Genoa salami, cut into ½-inch strips
- ½ cup coarsely chopped flat-leaf parsley leaves

1. Bring a large pot of salted water to a boil. Add the linguine and cook until it is al dente. Drain the linguine.

2. Meanwhile, in a large, deep skillet, heat the olive oil. Add the garlic and cook over moderate heat until lightly golden, about 3 minutes. Add the crushed red pepper, clams and wine and bring to a boil. Add the clam broth, cover and cook over moderate heat until the clams open, about 5 minutes. Discard any that do not open.

3. Add the linguine, salami and parsley to the clam sauce and toss over low heat until combined. Transfer the linguine to shallow bowls and serve immediately.
—*Melissa Rubel*

SERVE WITH Crusty bread.
WINE Light, fresh Pinot Grigio.

Mexican-Style Chicken with Penne

TOTAL: 30 MIN
4 SERVINGS ●

- ¾ pound penne rigate
- 5 tablespoons extra-virgin olive oil
- 1 pound skinless, boneless chicken thighs, cut into 1-inch dice

Kosher salt and freshly ground pepper
- 1 onion, cut into ¼-inch dice
- 1 large garlic clove, minced

One 28-ounce can diced tomatoes, drained

PASTA WITH ROSEMARY AND ONION-ORANGE MARMALADE

MEXICAN-STYLE CHICKEN WITH PENNE

1 large chipotle in adobo sauce, seeded and minced, plus 2 teaspoons adobo sauce

½ cup frozen corn

¼ pound *queso blanco* or mozzarella cheese, coarsely grated (1⅓ cups)

¼ cup chopped cilantro leaves

1. In a large pot of salted boiling water, cook the penne until al dente.

2. Meanwhile, in a large, deep skillet, heat 3 tablespoons of the oil. Season the chicken with salt and pepper, add it to the skillet and cook over moderately high heat until lightly browned, about 4 minutes. Add the onion and garlic and cook over moderate heat until the onion is softened and the chicken is cooked through, about 4 minutes. Add the tomatoes, chipotle and adobo sauce and cook until heated through, about 2 minutes. Add the corn, season with salt and pepper and cook until the corn is heated through, 1 minute.

3. Add the penne and the remaining 2 table-spoons of oil to the sauce and toss to coat. Add 1 cup of the *queso blanco* and toss. Transfer the pasta to bowls, sprinkle with the remaining *queso blanco* and the cilantro and serve. —*Melissa Rubel*
WINE Intense, fruity Zinfandel.

Orzo Risotto with Sausage and Artichokes

 TOTAL: 45 MIN
4 SERVINGS

2 tablespoons extra-virgin olive oil

1 pound sweet Italian sausage, casings removed

1 large white onion, thinly sliced

1 large garlic clove, minced

1½ cups orzo (10 ounces)

2 cups chicken stock

Salt and freshly ground pepper

1 cup marinated artichokes, drained and quartered

1 cup frozen baby peas

3 tablespoons snipped chives

6 tablespoons grated Parmesan, plus more for serving

1. In a deep 10-inch skillet, heat the oil. Add the sausage and cook over high heat, pressing to flatten, until cooked through, 10 minutes. Transfer to a plate, leaving the fat in the pan. Break the sausage into bite-size pieces. Add the onion and garlic to the skillet. Cover and cook over moderate heat, stirring occasionally, until softened, 4 minutes. Add the orzo and cook, stirring, for 3 minutes. Add the stock and 2 cups of water and cook, stirring constantly, until the orzo is al dente, about 15 minutes. Season with salt and pepper.

2. Add the sausage, artichokes, peas, chives and cheese to the orzo. Cook until the peas are heated through and the cheese is melted. Serve with cheese. —*Grace Parisi*
WINE Intense, fruity Zinfandel.

●HEALTHY ●MAKE AHEAD ●VEGETARIAN ●STAFF FAVORITE

pasta

Baked Penne with Sausage and Creamy Ricotta

ACTIVE: 1 HR; TOTAL: 2 HR 15 MIN

8 SERVINGS ● ●

This hearty pasta dish is studded with chunks of Italian sausage and mixed with a quick garlic-infused tomato sauce. It's then topped with dollops of fresh ricotta and a sprinkling of both mozzarella and Parmigiano-Reggiano, which form a cheesy layer as the pasta bakes.

- 3 tablespoons extra-virgin olive oil
- 2 garlic cloves, smashed
- 1 pound hot or sweet Italian fennel sausage, casings removed
- One 28-ounce can tomato puree
- 1½ cups water
- 1½ teaspoons sugar
- 1 bay leaf
- ¼ teaspoon ground fennel
- Salt and freshly ground pepper
- 1 pound penne
- 3 cups Creamy Ricotta (p. 11)
- ½ pound fresh mozzarella, cut into ½-inch cubes
- ¼ cup freshly grated Parmigiano-Reggiano cheese

1. Preheat the oven to 400°. In a large saucepan, heat 1 tablespoon of the olive oil. Add the garlic and cook over moderate heat, stirring, until lightly browned, about 1 minute. Add the sausage and cook, breaking up the meat, until browned, about 8 minutes. Add the tomato puree, water, sugar, bay leaf and fennel. Season with salt and pepper and bring to a boil. Simmer over low heat until thickened, about 30 minutes. Remove the garlic, mash it to a paste and stir it back into the sauce; discard the bay leaf.

2. Meanwhile, bring a large pot of salted water to a boil. Add the penne and cook until al dente. Drain the pasta and return it to the pot. Stir in the remaining 2 tablespoons of olive oil. Using a slotted spoon, add the cooked sausage to the pasta, then add 1 cup of the tomato sauce and toss to coat the penne.

3. Spoon the pasta into a 9-by-13-inch baking dish. Pour the remaining tomato sauce over the pasta and dollop the Creamy Ricotta on top. Gently fold some of the ricotta into the pasta; you should have pockets of ricotta. Scatter the mozzarella on top and sprinkle with the Parmigiano-Reggiano. Bake the pasta for about 45 minutes, or until bubbling and golden on top. Let rest for 20 minutes before serving. —*Maria Helm Sinskey*

MAKE AHEAD The baked penne can be refrigerated overnight.

WINE Fruity, luscious Shiraz.

Smoky Pork Pappardelle

ACTIVE: 45 MIN; TOTAL: 3 HR 45 MIN

6 SERVINGS

For the luscious meat sauce here, Gerard Craft (an F&W Best New Chef 2008) braises pork with apples and honey, which adds some unexpected sweetness. Another surprise: He finishes the pasta with a sprinkling of smoked salt.

- One 2-pound piece of boneless pork shoulder
- Smoked sea salt
- 2 tablespoons canola oil
- 1 Granny Smith apple, cut into 1-inch dice
- 1 medium onion, cut into 1-inch dice
- 1 carrot, cut into 1-inch dice
- 1 celery rib, cut into 1-inch dice
- 2 garlic cloves, crushed
- 3 thyme sprigs
- ½ cup tomato paste
- 1 cup dry white wine
- 2 cups chicken stock or low-sodium broth
- ⅓ cup Champagne vinegar
- 3 tablespoons honey
- 3 tablespoons mascarpone cheese
- Freshly ground pepper
- 1 pound pappardelle
- 1 tablespoon chopped flat-leaf parsley
- Extra-virgin olive oil, for drizzling

1. Preheat the oven to 300°. Season the pork with 1½ tablespoons of smoked salt. In a medium enameled cast-iron casserole, heat the canola oil until shimmering. Add the pork and cook over moderately high heat, turning, until it is browned on all sides, about 15 minutes. Transfer the pork to a plate.

2. Add the diced apple, onion, carrot and celery, the crushed garlic and the thyme sprigs to the casserole and cook over moderate heat until beginning to brown, about 6 minutes. Add the tomato paste and cook, stirring, until it deepens in color, about 2 minutes. Add the white wine and bring to a boil. Add the chicken stock, Champagne vinegar and honey and bring to a simmer. Return the browned pork to the pot, cover and transfer the casserole to the oven. Braise the pork for about 3 hours, turning once halfway through, until the meat is very tender.

3. Transfer the braised pork to a plate. Strain the sauce into a large bowl, gently pressing on the solids with the back of a wooden spoon. Discard the solids and pour the sauce back into the pot. Using 2 forks, shred the pork, discarding any large pieces of fat. Transfer the shredded pork to the sauce and stir in the mascarpone cheese. Season the sauce with smoked salt and pepper. Cover and keep warm.

4. Meanwhile, bring a large pot of salted water to a boil. Add the pappardelle and cook until al dente. Drain the pasta and transfer it to the casserole with the pork sauce. Add the parsley and toss the pasta with the sauce and the parsley over moderate heat until well coated, about 1 minute. Transfer the pasta to warm shallow bowls. Drizzle with olive oil, sprinkle with smoked salt and serve immediately. —*Gerard Craft*

MAKE AHEAD The pork sauce can be refrigerated for up to 3 days. Rewarm before proceeding.

WINE Juicy, fresh Dolcetto.

Spaghetti with Rich Meat Ragù

TOTAL: 40 MIN
4 SERVINGS ●

To create the flavor of a long-simmered meat ragù in a fraction of the usual time, F&W's Melissa Rubel makes this delightful sauce with tomato paste and preseasoned Italian sausage, then finishes with whole milk for richness.

- ¾ pound spaghetti
- 2 tablespoons extra-virgin olive oil
- ½ pound ground beef chuck
- 3 sweet Italian sausages (10 ounces), casings removed
- 1 medium onion, cut into ¼-inch dice
- 2 garlic cloves, very finely chopped
- ¼ cup tomato paste
- 1½ cups chicken stock or low-sodium broth
- One 3-inch rosemary sprig
- Kosher salt and freshly ground black pepper
- ⅓ cup whole milk
- Freshly grated Parmigiano-Reggiano cheese, for serving

1. Bring a large pot of salted water to a boil. Add the spaghetti and cook until al dente. Drain the spaghetti.

weekday meat sauce

Brown 1 pound Italian sausage (casings removed) in olive oil. Add 2 sliced garlic cloves; cook 1 to 2 minutes longer. Add one 35-ounce can whole tomatoes, crushed, and ½ cup water; simmer until thick. Season with salt and pepper.

2. Meanwhile, in a large, deep skillet, heat the olive oil until shimmering. Add the ground beef and sausage and cook over moderately high heat, breaking up the meat with a spoon, until browned, about 6 minutes. Add the onion and garlic and cook over moderate heat until softened, about 4 minutes. Add the tomato paste and cook, stirring, until the meat is coated, about 3 minutes. Add the chicken stock and rosemary and season with salt and pepper. Simmer the sauce over moderate heat, stirring occasionally, until thickened, about 4 minutes. Add the milk and simmer, stirring, for 2 more minutes. Discard the rosemary sprig and season the meat sauce with salt and pepper.

3. Add the spaghetti to the sauce and toss over low heat until combined. Transfer to bowls and pass the grated Parmigiano-Reggiano cheese at the table.
—*Melissa Rubel*

WINE Cherry-inflected, earthy Sangiovese.

Baked Orecchiette with Pork Sugo

ACTIVE: 1 HR; TOTAL: 4 HR
8 SERVINGS ● ●

In Italian cuisine, *sugo* is a gravy or sauce. The *sugo* in this baked pasta derives its satisfying flavors from pork shoulder, red wine and tomatoes.

- 3¼ pounds boneless pork shoulder, cut into 1-inch pieces
- Kosher salt and freshly ground pepper
- 3 tablespoons extra-virgin olive oil
- 4 medium carrots, cut into ¼-inch dice
- 4 medium celery ribs, cut into ¼-inch dice
- 1 large sweet onion, cut into ¼-inch dice
- 4 garlic cloves, minced
- One 14-ounce can diced tomatoes
- 1½ cups dry red wine
- 4 thyme sprigs
- 5 cups chicken stock
- 2 tablespoons chopped flat-leaf parsley
- 1 tablespoon chopped oregano
- ½ teaspoon crushed red pepper
- 1½ pounds orecchiette
- 2 cups freshly grated Parmigiano-Reggiano cheese (7 ounces)

1. Season the pork shoulder with salt and pepper. In a large enameled cast-iron casserole, heat the olive oil until shimmering. Add the pork in a single layer and cook over moderately high heat until the pieces are golden brown all over, about 12 minutes. Add the diced carrots, celery and onion and the minced garlic and cook, stirring, until the vegetables are softened and browned in spots, about 8 minutes. Add the diced tomatoes and their juices and bring to a simmer, stirring occasionally. Add the wine and thyme sprigs and cook over high heat, stirring occasionally, until the wine is reduced by half, about 5 minutes. Pour in the stock and bring to a boil. Cover and simmer over low heat until the pork is very tender, about 2 hours.

2. Using a slotted spoon, transfer the pork and vegetables to a food processor; discard the thyme sprigs. Pulse just until the pork is shredded. Scrape the shredded pork and vegetables back into the casserole. Stir in the chopped parsley, oregano and crushed red pepper and season with salt and pepper.

3. Preheat the oven to 375°. Bring a large pot of salted water to a boil. Add the orecchiette and cook until it is still firm to the bite, about 5 minutes; drain well. Add the orecchiette to the casserole and toss with the pork sauce. Scrape the pasta into a very large baking dish and sprinkle all over with the Parmigiano-Reggiano. Bake the casserole in the upper third of the oven for about 35 minutes, until golden brown on top and bubbling. Let the baked pasta stand for 10 minutes before serving.
—*Ethan Stowell*

WINE Complex, aromatic Nebbiolo.

Celery Root and Mushroom Lasagna

ACTIVE: 1 HR 30 MIN; TOTAL: 3 HR

10 SERVINGS ● ●

- 1 cup dried porcini mushrooms
- 2 cups boiling water
- 4 tablespoons unsalted butter
- ¼ cup extra-virgin olive oil
- ¾ pound white mushrooms, thinly sliced (4 cups)

Salt and freshly ground white pepper

- ¼ pound thickly sliced prosciutto di Parma, cut into ¼-inch dice
- 2 medium shallots, finely chopped
- 1 fresh bay leaf
- 2 rosemary sprigs
- 2 sage sprigs
- 2 thyme sprigs
- 1 pound celery root, peeled and finely diced (1½ cups)
- 3 medium leeks, white and tender green parts only, finely chopped (3 cups)
- ½ cup dry Marsala
- 4 cups chicken stock
- 2½ cups heavy cream
- 1¾ cups freshly grated Parmigiano-Reggiano cheese
- 2 large eggs
- 1½ pounds lasagna noodles
- 1½ pounds fresh mozzarella, sliced
- 1 cup basil leaves

1. In a heatproof bowl, soak the porcini in the boiling water until softened, about 15 minutes. Drain and coarsely chop.

2. In a large saucepan, melt 2 tablespoons of the butter in 2 tablespoons of the olive oil. Add the white mushrooms and the porcini, season with salt and white pepper and cook over moderately high heat, stirring occasionally, until browned, about 10 minutes. Transfer the mushrooms to a bowl.

3. Add the remaining 2 tablespoons each of butter and olive oil to the saucepan. Add the prosciutto and shallots and cook over moderately low heat, stirring occasionally, until softened, 6 minutes. Using kitchen string, tie the bay leaf, rosemary, sage and thyme into a bundle. Add the bundle and the celery root to the saucepan; cook, stirring, until the celery root is crisp-tender, 6 minutes. Add the leeks and cook until the celery root is tender, 5 minutes.

4. Return the mushrooms to the saucepan and stir over moderate heat until hot, 2 minutes. Add the Marsala and cook until evaporated, 5 minutes. Pour in 2 cups of the chicken stock and simmer over moderate heat for 10 minutes. Add ½ cup of the cream; simmer for 3 minutes longer, until the mixture has reduced to 5 cups. Season the ragù with salt and white pepper.

5. In another large saucepan, combine the remaining 2 cups each of cream and stock and bring to a boil. Simmer over moderate heat until reduced to 3 cups, about 10 minutes. Off the heat, whisk in 1½ cups of the Parmigiano-Reggiano cheese. Whisk in the eggs. Puree the sauce in a blender until smooth. Season with salt and white pepper. Set ½ cup of the sauce aside.

6. Bring a very large pot of salted water to a boil and fill a large bowl with ice water. Cook the lasagna noodles until just barely al dente; drain and transfer to the ice water to cool. Drain the noodles and pat dry.

7. Preheat the oven to 350°. Butter a 9-by-13-inch baking dish. Line the bottom with a single layer of noodles, overlapping them slightly. Spread one-fifth of the vegetable ragù on top, followed by one-fifth each of the sauce, mozzarella and basil. Repeat to make four more layers, ending with a layer of noodles (you won't use all the noodles). Top with the reserved ½ cup of sauce and sprinkle with the remaining ¼ cup of Parmigiano-Reggiano cheese.

8. Bake the lasagna until bubbling and golden, about 1 hour. Let rest for 20 minutes before serving. —*Fabio Trabocchi*

MAKE AHEAD The assembled lasagna can be refrigerated overnight. Bring to room temperature before baking.

WINE Juicy, fresh Dolcetto.

Marja's Mac and Cheese

ACTIVE: 30 MIN; TOTAL: 1 HR 30 MIN

8 TO 10 SERVINGS ● ● ●

- ¾ pound elbow macaroni

Extra-virgin olive oil, for drizzling

- 1½ cups heavy cream
- 1 cup half-and-half
- 1 cup whole milk
- 2 large eggs
- ½ teaspoon freshly grated nutmeg
- ½ tablespoon kosher salt
- ¼ teaspoon freshly ground white pepper
- 1½ cups shredded extra-sharp cheddar cheese (4 ounces)
- 1½ cups shredded sharp cheddar cheese (4 ounces)
- 1½ cups shredded Monterey Jack cheese (4 ounces)
- 4 ounces cold cream cheese, cut into ½-inch cubes

1. Preheat the oven to 350°. In a large pot of boiling salted water, cook the macaroni for 3 minutes (it will still be very chewy). Drain the pasta and return it to the pot. Drizzle lightly with olive oil and toss well.

2. Butter a 10-by-15-inch baking dish. In a large bowl, whisk the heavy cream with the half-and-half, milk, eggs, nutmeg, salt and pepper. Stir in the shredded cheeses and the pasta. Spread the mac and cheese in the baking dish and scatter the cream cheese on top.

3. Bake the macaroni and cheese for 5 minutes. Using the back of a large spoon, spread the melted cream cheese cubes evenly over the surface. Bake for 40 minutes, until bubbling.

4. Remove the baking dish from the oven and preheat the broiler. Broil about 3 inches from the heat source until richly browned, about 2 minutes. Let the mac and cheese stand for at least 10 minutes and up to 20 minutes before serving.

—*Marja and Jean-Georges Vongerichten*

WINE Ripe, luxurious Chardonnay.

SHRIMP AND NOODLE SALAD WITH GINGER DRESSING

RED CURRY PEANUT NOODLES

Shrimp and Noodle Salad with Ginger Dressing

TOTAL: 30 MIN
4 TO 6 SERVINGS ● ●

Instead of spending time shredding cabbage and carrots, F&W's Grace Parisi uses prepackaged coleslaw mix. She tosses it with udon noodles and cooked shrimp, then adds a spicy, gingery dressing prepared with other easy-to-find supermarket ingredients, like bottled teriyaki sauce and chile-garlic sauce.

- 7 **ounces dried udon noodles or fettuccine (fettuccine broken in half)**
- 12 **ounces shredded coleslaw mix**
- 2 **scallions, white and green parts, thinly sliced**
- 1 **cup cilantro leaves**
- ¾ **pound cooked medium shrimp, halved lengthwise**
- ¼ **cup teriyaki sauce**
- 2 **tablespoons finely grated fresh ginger**
- ½ **teaspoon Chinese chile-garlic sauce**
- ¼ **cup plus 2 tablespoons vegetable oil**

Salt

Lime wedges, for serving

1. Bring a medium saucepan of salted water to a boil. Add the noodles and cook until al dente. Drain and rinse under cold running water. Pat the noodles dry and transfer them to a large bowl. Add the coleslaw mix, sliced scallions, cilantro leaves and halved shrimp.

2. In a blender, combine the teriyaki sauce with the grated ginger and chile-garlic sauce and puree until smooth. With the machine on, slowly add the vegetable oil in a thin stream and puree until the dressing is emulsified. Season lightly with salt. Add the dressing to the bowl with the udon noodles and toss well. Serve the noodle salad with lime wedges on the side.

—*Grace Parisi*

MAKE AHEAD The dressed salad can be refrigerated overnight. Add the shrimp just before serving.
WINE Dry, earthy sparkling wine.

Red Curry Peanut Noodles

 **TOTAL: 25 MIN**
4 SERVINGS ● ●

Red curry paste gives a fiery hit to the peanut sauce in these sesame noodles, a Chinese take-out classic.

- ¾ pound whole-wheat spaghetti
- ½ cup smooth peanut butter
- 1½ tablespoons fresh lime juice
- 1 tablespoon red curry paste
- ⅓ cup chicken stock or low-sodium broth
- ¼ cup plus 2 tablespoons packed cilantro leaves
- Kosher salt
- 1 cup mung bean sprouts (2½ ounces)
- 2 scallions, white and green parts quartered and thinly sliced lengthwise
- 1 carrot, coarsely grated
- ⅓ cup salted, roasted peanuts, coarsely chopped
- Lime wedges, for serving

1. Bring a large pot of salted water to a boil. Add the spaghetti and cook until it is al dente. Drain the pasta and rinse under cold water until cool. Drain very well.

2. Meanwhile, in a food processor, combine the peanut butter with the lime juice, red curry paste, chicken stock and ¼ cup of the cilantro leaves and puree. Season the peanut sauce with salt.

3. In a large bowl, toss the spaghetti with the peanut sauce, bean sprouts, sliced scallions and grated carrot until well coated. Season with salt. Transfer the peanut noodles to bowls and sprinkle with the remaining cilantro leaves and the chopped peanuts. Serve with lime wedges.
—*Melissa Rubel*
WINE Fresh, fruity rosé.

Leek Mac and Cheese

ACTIVE: 30 MIN; TOTAL: 1 HR 30 MIN
6 SERVINGS ● ● ●

Cooks usually reserve dark, tough leek greens for stock. Here, F&W's Grace Parisi sautés them until they're soft and supple, then folds them into a luscious macaroni and cheese made with nutty Manchego.

- 4 tablespoons unsalted butter
- Leek greens from 1½ pounds of leeks, thinly sliced
- Salt and freshly ground pepper
- 3 tablespoons all-purpose flour
- 3 cups half-and-half or whole milk
- 10 ounces Manchego cheese, shredded (2½ cups)
- 1 pound elbow macaroni

1. Preheat the oven to 350°. Melt 2 tablespoons of the butter in a large skillet. Add the leeks and cook over high heat, stirring just until slightly wilted, 5 minutes; season with salt and pepper. Cook over low heat until very tender, about 20 minutes.

2. Meanwhile, in a large saucepan, melt the remaining 2 tablespoons of butter. Add the flour and cook over moderately high heat, whisking, for 2 minutes. Add the half-and-half and bring to a boil, whisking until thickened, about 5 minutes. Remove from the heat. Add 2 cups of the cheese, season with salt and pepper and whisk the cheese sauce until melted.

3. In a large saucepan of boiling salted water, cook the macaroni until nearly al dente. Drain well. Add the macaroni and the cheese sauce to the leek greens and stir until combined.

4. Transfer the macaroni to an 8-by-11-inch baking dish and sprinkle with the remaining ½ cup of cheese. Bake for about 40 minutes, until bubbling. Turn the broiler on and broil the mac and cheese until golden brown on top, about 3 minutes. Let stand for 15 minutes before serving.
—*Grace Parisi*
WINE Intense, fruity Zinfandel.

Chinese Noodles with Cockles and Pork

ACTIVE: 25 MIN; TOTAL: 2 HR
4 SERVINGS ●

- 1 pound ground pork
- 1 tablespoon fermented black beans
- ¼ cup soy sauce
- 1½ teaspoons *sambal oelek*
- ⅔ cup chicken stock
- 1 teaspoon finely grated fresh ginger
- Pinch of sugar
- 3 medium garlic cloves, very finely chopped
- ½ pound butternut squash, peeled and diced
- ½ pound fresh Chinese egg noodles
- 2 medium shallots, very finely chopped
- 2 tablespoons vegetable oil
- 2 dozen cockles
- 2 cups chopped bok choy greens

1. In a large bowl, combine the ground pork with the fermented black beans, 2 tablespoons of the soy sauce and 1 teaspoon of the *sambal oelek*. Let marinate at room temperature for 30 minutes.

2. In a saucepan, simmer the chicken stock with the ginger, sugar, one-third of the garlic and the remaining 2 tablespoons of soy sauce and ½ teaspoon of *sambal* over low heat until reduced to ½ cup, 15 minutes.

3. Boil the squash in a large saucepan of salted water until just tender, 5 minutes; transfer to a plate. Boil the noodles in the water until al dente; drain and rinse.

4. In a wok, stir-fry the shallots and the remaining garlic in the oil, 2 minutes. Add the pork mixture and stir-fry until the meat is just white throughout. Add the cockles; pour in the ginger sauce and simmer until the cockles open, 2 minutes. Stir in the noodles, squash and bok choy and serve.
—*Suzanne Tracht*
WINE Fresh, fruity rosé.

STICKY GRILLED DRUMSTICKS
WITH PLUM SAUCE (P. 99)

poultry

*" My father was in the poultry business;
thankfully, everyone likes chicken. "*

—**KOREN GRIEVESON,** CHEF DE CUISINE, AVEC, CHICAGO

SPICY ROAST CHICKEN

QUICK-ROASTED CHICKEN WITH MUSTARD AND GARLIC

Spicy Roast Chicken

ACTIVE: 45 MIN; TOTAL: 2 HR

4 SERVINGS ●

CHICKEN

- ¼ cup Dijon mustard
- ½ tablespoon water
- ½ tablespoon ancho chile powder
- 5 garlic cloves, very finely chopped
- 3 tablespoons finely chopped sage leaves
- 3 tablespoons extra-virgin olive oil

Kosher salt and freshly ground black pepper

One 4-pound pastured chicken

- 2 tablespoons pickled jalapeño peppers, sliced, plus ¼ cup of the brine strained into a spray bottle
- 2 tablespoons chopped parsley
- 1 tablespoon fresh lemon juice
- 2 tablespoons unsalted butter

TOPPING

- 2 garlic cloves, smashed
- 2 tablespoons extra-virgin olive oil
- 1 cup fresh bread crumbs

Finely grated zest of 1 lemon

- 1 tablespoon chopped parsley
- ¼ teaspoon cayenne pepper

Salt

1. PREPARE THE CHICKEN: Preheat the oven to 350°. In a blender, puree the Dijon mustard, water, ancho chile powder, half of the chopped garlic, 1 tablespoon of the chopped sage, ½ teaspoon of the olive oil and ½ teaspoon each of salt and black pepper. Place the chicken breast side up in an ovenproof skillet and coat the skin with the mustard mixture.

2. Bake the chicken for 1 hour and 20 minutes, or until cooked through. Spray the chicken all over with the jalapeño brine; bake for 5 minutes longer. Let the chicken rest in the pan for 10 minutes.

3. In a skillet, cook the jalapeños, parsley, lemon juice, the remaining garlic and the remaining sage in the butter and remaining oil over moderate heat until fragrant.

4. MAKE THE TOPPING: In a skillet, brown the garlic in the oil over moderate heat; discard the garlic. Add the bread crumbs, zest, parsley and cayenne and stir until the crumbs are crisp. Season with salt.

5. Top the chicken with the jalapeño butter, sprinkle with the crumbs and serve.

—*Adam Perry Lang*

WINE Ripe, luxurious Chardonnay.

Quick-Roasted Chicken with Mustard and Garlic

ACTIVE: 20 MIN; TOTAL: 1 HR

4 SERVINGS ●

One 4-pound chicken

- 4 large garlic cloves, minced
- 2 tablespoons Dijon mustard
- 2 tablespoons dry white wine

2 tablespoons extra-virgin olive oil

1 tablespoon soy sauce

1 teaspoon Tabasco

1 teaspoon herbes de Provence

½ teaspoon salt

1. Preheat the oven to 450°. Using poultry shears, cut along each side of the chicken backbone and remove it. Turn the chicken breast side up and press on the breast bone to flatten the chicken. Using a sharp knife, cut partway through both sides of the joint between the thighs and the drumsticks. Cut partway through the joint between the wings and the breast.

2. In a bowl, mix all of the remaining ingredients. Turn the chicken breast down and spread it with half of the mustard mixture. Set the chicken in a large skillet skin side up; spread with the remaining mixture.

3. Set the skillet over high heat and cook the chicken until it starts to brown, 5 minutes. Transfer the skillet to the oven and roast the chicken for 30 minutes, until the skin is browned and the chicken is cooked through. Let the chicken rest for 5 minutes. Transfer to a cutting board, cut into 8 pieces and serve. —*Jacques Pépin*

SERVE WITH Mashed potatoes.

MAKE AHEAD The chicken can be prepared through Step 2 and refrigerated overnight.

WINE Fruity, low-oak Chardonnay.

Roast Chicken with Bread Salad

TOTAL: 1 HR 15 MIN PLUS 2 HR MARINATING

4 SERVINGS ●

One 3½-pound chicken

Kosher salt and freshly ground pepper

7 tablespoons extra-virgin olive oil

5 tablespoons fresh lemon juice

2 teaspoons finely grated lemon zest

One 1-pound loaf of sourdough bread, cut into 1-inch cubes

3 medium tomatoes, cut into ½-inch dice

1. In a large glass baking dish, season the chicken all over with salt and pepper. Rub with 2 tablespoons each of the olive oil and lemon juice as well as the lemon zest. Cover and refrigerate for at least 2 hours or up to 6 hours.

2. Preheat the oven to 450°. Spread the bread cubes in a medium roasting pan, then set a rack in the pan. Place the chicken on the rack, breast side up, and roast for about 20 minutes, until beginning to brown. Turn the chicken and roast breast side down for about 20 minutes, until beginning to brown. Reduce the oven temperature to 375°. Turn the chicken breast side up and roast for about 20 minutes longer, until an instant-read thermometer inserted in the thickest part of the thigh registers 165°. Transfer the bird to a cutting board and let rest for 10 minutes.

3. In a large bowl, toss the toasted bread cubes with the tomatoes and the remaining 5 tablespoons of olive oil and 3 tablespoons of lemon juice; season with salt and pepper. Carve the chicken and pour any juices over the bread salad.
—*Frank Ruta*

WINE Lively, fruity Merlot.

Smoky Bacon-Roasted Chicken

TOTAL: 1 HR 15 MIN PLUS OVERNIGHT MARINATING

4 SERVINGS

4 ounces sliced bacon, chopped

1 teaspoon sweet paprika

5 small garlic cloves—3 smashed, 2 minced

Salt and freshly ground pepper

One 4-pound chicken, quartered and wings removed

2 tablespoons extra-virgin olive oil

1 small onion, coarsely chopped

1 large carrot, cut into ½-inch pieces

2 small celery ribs, cut into ½-inch pieces

2 rosemary sprigs

2 cups low-sodium chicken broth

½ cup dry red wine

1. In a mini processor, puree the bacon, paprika, smashed garlic and a pinch each of salt and pepper to a paste. Loosen the skin on the chicken breasts and legs and spread the paste under the skin, pressing to even it out. Refrigerate the chicken for 4 hours or, preferably, overnight.

2. Preheat the oven to 350°. Heat the oil in a large ovenproof nonstick skillet. Season the chicken lightly with salt and pepper. Add to the skillet, skin side down, and cook over moderately high heat until golden, about 5 minutes. Turn and cook until lightly browned all over, about 2 minutes longer. Transfer the chicken to a plate.

3. Add the onion, carrot, celery, minced garlic and rosemary to the skillet and cook over moderate heat, stirring occasionally, until barely softened, about 6 minutes. Return the chicken to the pan, skin side up, and roast in the oven for about 25 minutes, until an instant-read thermometer inserted in the thickest part of the leg and breast registers 170°. Remove the skillet from the oven and preheat the broiler.

4. Meanwhile, in a medium saucepan, boil the chicken broth until reduced to ½ cup, about 15 minutes.

5. Transfer the chicken to a large platter, cover loosely with foil and keep warm. Spoon off the fat in the skillet. Add the red wine to the skillet and boil over high heat until the wine is almost completely evaporated, about 5 minutes. Pour in the reduced chicken broth and cook until slightly reduced, 2 to 3 minutes. Return the chicken to the skillet, skin side up. Broil 4 inches from the heat for about 1 minute, just until the skin is very crisp. Discard the rosemary sprigs. Transfer the chicken, sauce and vegetables to plates and serve.
—*Shea Gallante*

WINE Juicy, spicy Grenache.

● HEALTHY ● MAKE AHEAD ● VEGETARIAN ● STAFF FAVORITE

Chicken Breasts with Apricot-Onion Pan Sauce

TOTAL: 35 MIN
4 SERVINGS

After sautéing chicken breasts, F&W's Melissa Rubel adds onion and white wine to sweep up the delicious browned bits in the skillet, then sweetens the sauce slightly with dried apricots and apricot preserves.

3½ ounces dried apricots

Four 9-ounce boneless chicken
   breasts, with skin

Salt and freshly ground pepper

 1 tablespoon olive oil
 1 large onion, diced
 1 garlic clove, thinly sliced
 2 thyme sprigs
 1 bay leaf
 ½ cup dry white wine
1½ cups chicken stock
 2 tablespoons apricot preserves
 1 tablespoon unsalted butter

1. Preheat the oven to 350°. In a bowl, cover the apricots with hot water and let stand until soft, about 15 minutes; drain.
2. Meanwhile, dry the chicken with paper towels and season with salt and pepper. In a stainless steel skillet, heat the oil. Add the chicken, skin side down, and cook over moderately high heat until golden brown, 5 minutes. Flip and cook about 3 minutes longer. Transfer the chicken to a baking sheet and roast for about 14 minutes.
3. Add the onion, garlic, thyme and bay leaf to the skillet. Season with salt and cook over moderate heat until the onion is tender. Add the wine and reduce by half, scraping up the browned bits in the skillet. Add the chicken stock, apricots and apricot preserves and bring to a boil. Cook over high heat until the sauce thickens. Off the heat, swirl in the butter until melted. Discard the thyme sprigs and bay leaf. Season the sauce with salt and pepper. Transfer the chicken to plates, spoon the sauce on top and serve. —*Melissa Rubel*
WINE Lush, fragrant Viognier.

Curry-and-Yogurt-Braised Chicken Thighs

TOTAL: 50 MIN
4 SERVINGS ●

The creaminess of this quick-braised chicken curry comes from tangy Greek-style low-fat yogurt, which is cleverly blended with fresh tomatoes, corn kernels, serrano chile, ginger and curry powder for immense flavor.

 ¼ cup grapeseed or canola oil
1½ pounds skinless, boneless
    chicken thighs

Kosher salt and freshly ground
    black pepper

All-purpose flour, for dusting

 1 tablespoon very finely
    chopped fresh ginger
 1 medium garlic clove, very
    finely chopped
 1 serrano chile, thinly sliced
 1 red bell pepper—cored, seeded
    and cut into thin strips
 1 tablespoon Madras curry powder
 1 pound tomatoes, cored and
    coarsely chopped
 ½ cup fresh corn kernels
    (from 1 ear)
 ¼ cup Greek-style plain
    low-fat yogurt
 ½ cup water

Cilantro leaves, for garnish

1. In a large, deep skillet, heat the oil. Season the chicken thighs with salt and pepper and lightly dust with flour, tapping off the excess. Add the chicken to the skillet and cook over high heat, turning once, until lightly browned, 6 minutes. Transfer the chicken to a plate.
2. Add the ginger, garlic, chile and red bell pepper to the skillet and cook over high heat, stirring occasionally, until the vegetables are slightly softened, about 2 minutes. Stir in the curry powder and cook for 1 minute longer. Add the chopped tomatoes, corn kernels, Greek yogurt and water; stir until smooth. Season with salt and pepper.

3. Return the chicken and any accumulated juices to the skillet and bring to a boil. Cover and simmer over very low heat until the chicken is tender and the juices are slightly thickened, about 15 minutes. Sprinkle with cilantro and serve.
—*Grace Parisi*
SERVE WITH Steamed rice.
WINE Rustic, peppery Malbec.

Tangy Roasted Chicken Thighs with Artichoke Panzanella

ACTIVE: 45 MIN; TOTAL: 3 HR 30 MIN
4 SERVINGS

Panzanella, an Italian salad, is typically made with tomatoes, onions and chunks of bread. In her smart version, Chicago chef Koren Grieveson (an F&W Best New Chef 2008) combines grilled bread and sweet broiled tomatoes with marinated baby artichokes before dressing the warm salad with a lemony vinaigrette. It's fabulous served alongside the roasted chicken.

 4 large garlic cloves

One ¼-inch piece of fresh ginger,
    peeled and coarsely chopped

 2 teaspoons sweet paprika
 ½ teaspoon cayenne pepper
 ⅓ cup plus 1 tablespoon
    fresh lemon juice
 8 bone-in chicken thighs, with skin
    (2¾ pounds)
 2 tablespoons chopped
    cilantro leaves
 1 scallion, thinly sliced
 ½ cup extra-virgin olive oil
 ¼ cup chopped flat-leaf parsley

One ¾-pound loaf white country-style
    bread, sliced 1 inch thick

Kosher salt and freshly ground
    black pepper

12 ounces cherry tomatoes
 8 baby artichokes in oil, drained
    and halved lengthwise
 1 tablespoon grated lemon zest
 1 tablespoon canola oil
 ¼ cup chicken stock

1. In a mini food processor, pulse the garlic and ginger until chopped. Add the paprika, cayenne and ⅓ cup of the lemon juice and process until smooth; transfer to a bowl. Add the chicken, cilantro, scallion and 2 table-spoons each of the olive oil and parsley. Toss, cover and refrigerate for 3 hours.

2. Meanwhile, heat a grill pan. Brush the bread with 3 tablespoons of the olive oil and season with salt and pepper. Grill the bread over moderately high heat, turning once, until toasted, about 3 minutes. Let cool slightly, then tear into bite-size pieces.

3. Preheat the broiler. In a large, deep skil-let, toss the tomatoes with 1 tablespoon of the olive oil and season with salt and pep-per. Broil the tomatoes for 7 minutes, until they begin to burst. Using a spoon, lightly mash the tomatoes to release some of their juices. Let cool slightly, then add the bread, artichokes and lemon zest to the skillet.

4. Preheat the oven to 375°. Remove the chicken thighs from the marinade and pat dry. In a very large skillet, heat the canola oil. Season the chicken thighs with salt and pepper and add them to the skillet, skin side down. Cook over moderately high heat until browned, about 4 minutes. Turn the chicken, pour the chicken stock into the skillet and bring to a boil. Transfer the skillet to the oven. Roast the chicken for 15 minutes, until cooked through. Spoon ¼ cup of the pan drippings from the skil-let over the bread mixture.

5. In a small bowl, whisk the remaining 2 tablespoons of olive oil, 2 tablespoons of parsley and the remaining 1 tablespoon of lemon juice. Gently warm the bread mixture over moderate heat, tossing, until it is heated through, about 2 minutes. Remove from the heat. Pour the dressing over the bread salad and toss well. Season with salt and pepper.

6. Transfer the chicken to plates, spoon the bread salad alongside and serve.
—Koren Grieveson

WINE Peppery, refreshing Grüner Veltliner.

CHICKEN BREASTS WITH APRICOT-ONION PAN SAUCE

CURRY-AND-YOGURT-BRAISED CHICKEN THIGHS

HERB-AND-LEMON-
ROASTED CHICKEN

perfecting roast chicken

F&W's **Grace Parisi** *creates four flavorful sauces by scattering ingredients like lemons, tomatoes, chiles and dates in the roasting pan.*

Herb-and-Lemon-Roasted Chicken

ACTIVE: 30 MIN; TOTAL: 1 HR 45 MIN

4 SERVINGS

- 2 tablespoons unsalted butter, softened
- 5 garlic cloves, 1 minced
- ½ teaspoon minced rosemary plus 2 rosemary sprigs
- ½ teaspoon minced thyme plus 2 thyme sprigs
- ½ teaspoon finely grated lemon zest

Salt and freshly ground pepper

One 4-pound chicken, at room temperature

- 1 large onion, cut into 8 wedges
- 1 lemon, cut crosswise into 8 rounds
- ½ cup chicken stock or low-sodium broth

1. Preheat the oven to 425° and position a rack in the lower third of the oven. In a bowl, mix the butter with the minced garlic, minced herbs and the lemon zest and season with salt and pepper.

2. Pat the chicken dry. Rub half of the herb butter under the skin and the rest over the chicken; season with salt and pepper.

3. Set the chicken breast side up on a rack in a roasting pan. Scatter the onion, lemon, garlic cloves and herb sprigs and add ½ cup of water. Roast for 30 minutes, until the breast is firm and just beginning to brown in spots. Using tongs, turn the chicken breast-down and roast for 20 minutes longer, until the skin is lightly browned.

4. Using tongs, turn the chicken breast side up. Add another ½ cup of water. Roast for about 20 minutes longer, until an instant-read thermometer inserted in the inner thigh registers 175° to 180°.

5. Tilt the chicken to drain the cavity juices into the pan; transfer the bird to a cutting board. Remove the rack from the pan and spoon off the fat. Set the pan over high heat. Add the stock and cook, scraping up any browned bits. Press the lemon to release the juices. Carve the chicken and pass the chunky jus at the table.

WINE Light, crisp white Burgundy.

Three Great Variations

1 Moroccan Roasted Chicken
To the butter, add 1 teaspoon each of ground cumin, coriander and sweet paprika, plus ¼ teaspoon each of cayenne pepper and ground cinnamon. To the roasting pan, add 12 pitted dates, 12 dried apricots, 4 garlic cloves and 1 quartered onion.
WINE Fruity, soft Chenin Blanc.

2 Ginger-Roasted Chicken
To the butter, add 1 minced garlic clove and 1 tablespoon grated ginger. To the roasting pan, add 12 thin ginger slices, 4 garlic cloves, 2 seeded and thinly sliced serrano chiles, 1 quartered onion and 1 quartered lime. Stir in 1 tablespoon Asian fish sauce before serving.
WINE Vivid, lightly sweet Riesling.

3 Curry-Roasted Chicken
To the butter, add 1 minced garlic clove and 1 teaspoon Madras curry powder. To the roasting pan, add 4 garlic cloves; 2 cups seeded, diced tomatoes; 2 seeded, thinly sliced serrano chiles; and 1 quartered onion. Stir in 2 tablespoons Greek-style yogurt just before serving.
WINE Fresh, fruity rosé.

poultry

Mushroom-and-Goat-Cheese-Stuffed Chicken Thighs

TOTAL: 1 HR

4 SERVINGS

1 slice of bacon, finely chopped
Stems from 1 pound of white
    button or cremini mushrooms,
    finely chopped (4 ounces)
1 shallot, minced
Salt and freshly ground
    black pepper
1 teaspoon chopped thyme
2 ounces fresh goat cheese (¼ cup)
Eight 3- to 4-ounce boneless chicken
    thighs, with skin
1 tablespoon extra-virgin olive oil
1 teaspoon all-purpose flour
½ cup low-sodium
    chicken broth

1. Preheat the oven to 350°. In a medium skillet, cook the bacon over high heat, stirring, until crisp, about 6 minutes. Add the mushroom stems and shallot, season with salt and pepper and cook, stirring, until the stems are tender and lightly browned, about 8 minutes. Add the thyme and goat cheese and let cool slightly.

2. Arrange the chicken thighs on a work surface, skin side down. Using a meat pounder, lightly pound the thighs until they are a scant ½ inch thick. Spread the mushroom mixture evenly over the thighs and roll them up; the skin should almost wrap around the meat. Tie each bundle with kitchen string in 2 places.

3. In a large ovenproof skillet, heat the olive oil. Season the chicken with salt and pepper and add the bundles to the skillet. Cook over moderately high heat, turning, until lightly browned all over, about 5 minutes. Turn the chicken skin side up. Transfer to the oven and roast for about 12 minutes, until the chicken is cooked through. Light the broiler and broil 6 inches from the heat for about 1 minute, until the skin is browned and crispy. Transfer the chicken to a plate and cover loosely with foil.

4. Pour the chicken fat and pan drippings into a small bowl and skim off the fat, reserving 1 teaspoon in the skillet. Whisk in the flour and cook over moderate heat until foamy. Whisk in the broth and cook, scraping up any bits stuck to the pan with a wooden spoon, until slightly thickened, about 3 minutes. Pour the reserved pan drippings and any accumulated juices from the chicken into the sauce and season with salt and pepper. Remove the strings from the chicken thighs, drizzle with the gravy and serve. —*Grace Parisi*
WINE Fruity, light-bodied Beaujolais.

Pretzel-Crusted Chicken

ACTIVE: 15 MIN; TOTAL: 40 MIN
6 SERVINGS ● ● ●

This dish, from chef Ilene Rosen at the City Bakery in Manhattan, matches chicken with a classic NYC street-vendor combo: pretzels and mustard.

½ **pound hard pretzels, crushed**
½ **cup canola oil**
½ **cup whole-grain mustard**
2 **tablespoons Dijon mustard**
¼ **cup water**
3 **tablespoons red wine vinegar**
Salt and freshly ground pepper
6 **large skinless, boneless**
    chicken breast halves

1. Preheat the oven to 400°. In a food processor, pulse the pretzels until coarsely ground; you should have coarse chunks and fine crumbs. Transfer to a large, shallow bowl.

2. Wipe out the processor. Add the oil, mustards, water and vinegar and blend. Season with salt and pepper. Pour half the dressing into a bowl. Add the chicken and turn to coat, then dredge the chicken in the pretzels; transfer the chicken to a rack set over a rimmed baking sheet.

3. Bake in the upper third of the oven until cooked through, 20 to 25 minutes. Slice and serve warm or at room temperature with the remaining dressing. —*Ilene Rosen*
WINE Juicy, fresh Dolcetto.

Chicken Thighs with Garlicky Crumbs and Snap Peas

TOTAL: 1 HR

4 SERVINGS ●

5 oil-packed anchovy fillets,
    drained and chopped
2 cups fresh bread crumbs
12 garlic cloves, smashed
½ cup finely chopped
    flat-leaf parsley
½ cup plus 3 tablespoons
    extra-virgin olive oil
2½ pounds skinless, boneless
    chicken thighs
Salt
1 pound sugar snap peas
3 medium shallots, thinly sliced

1. In a food processor, combine 4 of the anchovy fillets with the bread crumbs, garlic, parsley and ½ cup of the olive oil; process until evenly blended.

2. Season the chicken thighs with salt. In a large bowl, toss the chicken with the bread crumb mixture. Cover and refrigerate for 15 minutes.

3. Light a grill or preheat a grill pan. Blanch the snap peas in boiling, salted water until bright green, 1 minute. Drain and pat dry.

4. Grill the chicken thighs over moderate heat until they are lightly charred, crisp and cooked through, about 10 minutes per side. Transfer the thighs to a platter.

5. In a large skillet, heat the remaining 3 tablespoons of olive oil. Add the shallots and the remaining anchovy fillet and cook over moderate heat, stirring occasionally, until the shallots are softened, about 5 minutes. Add the snap peas and cook, tossing a few times, until heated through, about 2 minutes. Season the snap peas with salt and transfer to a serving bowl. Serve the chicken with the snap peas.
—*Mario Batali*

MAKE AHEAD The chicken recipe can be prepared through Step 2 and refrigerated for up to 6 hours.
WINE Fresh, lively Soave.

Herb-Grilled Chicken with Goat Cheese Ravioli

TOTAL: 1 HR PLUS 4 HR MARINATING
6 SERVINGS

Six 8-ounce boneless chicken breast
    halves, with skin
1 tablespoon minced rosemary
1 tablespoon minced thyme
4 large garlic cloves, minced
¼ cup extra-virgin olive oil
Salt and freshly ground pepper
4 tablespoons unsalted butter
2 shallots, thinly sliced
2 tablespoons sliced basil leaves
2 tablespoons finely chopped
    baby spinach leaves
8 ounces soft goat cheese
1 package wonton wrappers
2 pounds fresh fava beans,
    shelled (2 cups)
½ cup pitted Taggiasca or
    kalamata olives

1. In a shallow baking dish, rub the chicken with the rosemary, thyme, half of the garlic and 2 tablespoons of the oil and season lightly with salt and pepper. Refrigerate for at least 4 hours or overnight. Return to room temperature before grilling.

2. In a skillet, melt 2 tablespoons of the butter. Add the shallots and remaining garlic and cook over moderate heat until softened, 2 minutes. Stir in the basil and spinach and let wilt. Remove from the heat. Stir in the goat cheese, season with salt and pepper and let cool. Transfer to a pastry bag fitted with a plain ½-inch tip.

3. Lay 4 wontons wrappers on a work surface; keep the rest covered with a damp towel. Lightly brush the edges of the wrappers with water. Spoon or pipe a scant teaspoon of the goat cheese mixture onto the center of each wrapper. Fold to form triangles. Press out any air bubbles, then press the edges to seal. Transfer to a baking sheet lined with plastic wrap and repeat to make about 48 ravioli; layer them between sheets of plastic wrap.

4. Fill a large bowl with ice water. Blanch the favas in boiling salted water for 1 minute. Drain and cool in the ice water, then drain again. Peel the fava beans.

5. Light a grill. Scrape as much of the marinade off the chicken as possible. Grill the chicken over moderately high heat, turning occasionally, until cooked through, about 15 minutes. Let rest for 10 minutes.

6. Meanwhile, cook the ravioli in boiling salted water until al dente, 5 minutes; drain gently. In a skillet, melt the remaining 2 tablespoons of butter in the remaining 2 tablespoons of oil. Add the ravioli, favas and olives; cook over moderate heat until just heated through, 1 minute. Serve with the chicken. —*Johnathan Sundstrom*
WINE Fresh, fruity rosé.

Sticky Grilled Drumsticks with Plum Sauce

 TOTAL: 40 MIN
4 SERVINGS

12 chicken drumsticks, with skin
2 tablespoons canola oil
Salt and freshly ground pepper
2 tablespoons unsalted butter
¼ cup finely chopped red onion
2 red or purple plums, pitted and
    cut into ½-inch pieces
¼ cup hot or sweet red pepper jelly
1 tablespoon Dijon mustard
¼ cup water

1. Light a grill. Rub the chicken with the oil and season with salt and pepper. Grill over moderate heat, turning occasionally, until cooked through, about 30 minutes.

2. Meanwhile, in a saucepan, melt the butter. Add the onion and cook over moderately low heat, stirring, until softened, 5 minutes. Add the plums and cook over moderately high heat, stirring, until softened and nearly broken down, 5 minutes. Add the pepper jelly and mustard and bring to a boil, stirring until the jelly is melted. Carefully transfer to a food processor. Add the water and puree. Season with salt and pepper.

3. Liberally brush the plum sauce over the chicken and grill, turning occasionally, until lightly caramelized, 5 minutes. Serve with any remaining sauce. —*Grace Parisi*
WINE Intense, fruity Zinfandel.

Green Jalapeño Hot Wings

TOTAL: 45 MIN
4 TO 6 SERVINGS ●

5 pounds chicken wings,
    split at the joints and tips
    reserved for stock (see Note)
Salt and freshly ground pepper
½ cup green jalapeño hot sauce
2 tablespoons coarsely chopped
    pickled jalapeños
1 stick unsalted butter
2 large garlic cloves, minced
½ cup plain nonfat yogurt
¼ cup mayonnaise
1 tablespoon apple cider vinegar
2 ounces blue cheese, crumbled
    (½ cup)
Celery sticks, for serving

1. Preheat the oven to 500° and position racks in the middle and upper thirds. Spread the wings on 2 baking sheets and season with salt and pepper. Roast for 40 minutes, turning once, until golden and crisp.

2. Meanwhile, in a mini food processor, puree the hot sauce and pickled jalapeños. In a saucepan, cook the butter with the garlic over moderate heat just until fragrant, about 2 minutes. Add the puree to the saucepan and bring to a simmer. Transfer to a large bowl. Rinse out the processor.

3. Add the yogurt, mayonnaise, vinegar and blue cheese to the processor and pulse until fairly smooth. Season with salt and pepper and transfer to a small bowl.

4. Transfer the wings to the bowl with the hot sauce and toss to coat. Pour the wings and sauce onto a platter and serve, passing the dip and celery. —*Grace Parisi*
NOTE Precut chicken wings are available at supermarkets.
WINE Dry, fruity sparkling wine.

●HEALTHY ●MAKE AHEAD ●VEGETARIAN ●STAFF FAVORITE

ROASTED CHICKEN LEGS WITH POTATOES AND KALE

BUTTERMILK CHICKEN WITH CRISPY CORNFLAKES

Roasted Chicken Legs with Potatoes and Kale

ACTIVE: 10 MIN; TOTAL: 1 HR

8 SERVINGS

In this one-pan dish, chicken legs roast on a bed of potatoes and kale; the meaty juices keep the vegetables moist. Cutting the joint slightly between the drumstick and thigh helps the chicken legs cook through faster.

- 1½ pounds tender young kale, stems and inner ribs removed
- 1½ pounds medium Yukon Gold potatoes, scrubbed and sliced ¼ inch thick
- 1 medium onion, very thinly sliced
- ¼ cup extra-virgin olive oil
- Salt and freshly ground black pepper
- Eight 10-ounce whole chicken legs, with skin
- 1 teaspoon paprika
- Lemon wedges, for serving

1. Preheat the oven to 450°. In a very large roasting pan, toss the kale, potato slices and sliced onion with the olive oil. Season with salt and black pepper and spread the vegetables in an even layer.

2. Set the chicken legs on a cutting board, skin side down. Using a sharp knife, slice halfway through the joint between the drumsticks and thighs. Season the chicken with salt and pepper, sprinkle with the paprika and set on the vegetables.

3. Cover the roasting pan with foil. Roast the chicken in the upper third of the oven for 20 minutes. Remove the foil and roast for 30 minutes longer, until the chicken is golden and cooked through and the potatoes and kale are tender. Transfer the chicken to plates and spoon the vegetables alongside. Serve with lemon wedges.
—*Grace Parisi*

WINE Ripe, luxurious Chardonnay.

Buttermilk Chicken with Crispy Cornflakes

TOTAL: 45 MIN PLUS OVERNIGHT MARINATING

4 SERVINGS ●

- 1 quart buttermilk
- 3 garlic cloves, smashed with the side of a knife

Kosher salt

- 4 whole chicken legs, with skin, separated into drumsticks and thighs

Tabasco

- 1½ cups cornflakes, coarsely crushed
- ¼ cup chopped flat-leaf parsley

Freshly ground black pepper

- 3 tablespoons unsalted butter, melted

1. In a large bowl, combine the buttermilk, smashed garlic cloves and 2 tablespoons of kosher salt. With a sharp knife, make shallow 1-inch-long slashes in all of the chicken pieces. Rub the chicken generously with Tabasco, then add the chicken to the buttermilk, turning to coat the pieces. Cover the bowl with plastic wrap and let the chicken marinate in the refrigerator overnight.

2. Light a grill. Remove the chicken pieces from the marinade and grill them over moderate heat, turning often, until the skin is browned and charred in spots and the chicken pieces are cooked through, about 30 minutes.

3. In a wide, shallow dish, toss the crushed cornflakes with the chopped parsley and season with salt and black pepper. Brush the grilled chicken pieces with the melted butter. Using tongs, roll the buttered chicken pieces in the seasoned cornflake mixture. Transfer the cornflake-crusted chicken to a medium platter and serve, passing Tabasco at the table.
—*Kristin Donnelly*

WINE Ripe, juicy Pinot Noir.

Red Curry Chicken Kebabs with Minty Yogurt Sauce

TOTAL: 30 MIN PLUS 2 HR MARINATING

8 TO 10 SERVINGS ●

For spicy chicken kebabs as addictive as buffalo wings, chef Kerry Simon creates a fantastically simple marinade using nothing more than jarred red curry paste, vegetable oil and salt.

- 2½ tablespoons Thai red curry paste
- ½ cup vegetable oil

Kosher salt

- 2½ pounds skinless, boneless chicken breast halves, cut into 1-inch cubes
- ¾ cup plain low-fat yogurt
- ¼ cup low-fat mayonnaise
- 1 tablespoon honey
- 1 tablespoon fresh lime juice
- 1 tablespoon finely chopped mint

1. In a large bowl, mix the Thai red curry paste with the vegetable oil and 2 teaspoons of salt. Add the chicken breast cubes and toss to coat with the marinade. Let the chicken stand at room temperature for up to 2 hours, or cover and refrigerate overnight.

2. Light a grill. In a medium bowl, whisk the low-fat yogurt with the mayonnaise, honey, lime juice and chopped mint and season with salt.

3. Thread the marinated chicken cubes onto 10 skewers, leaving ¼ inch between the cubes. Grill the chicken over moderately high heat, turning the skewers frequently, until the chicken cubes are lightly charred and cooked through, about 8 minutes. Serve the kebabs right away, passing the minty yogurt sauce at the table.
—*Kerry Simon*

MAKE AHEAD The yogurt sauce can be covered and refrigerated overnight. The chicken can be refrigerated in the red curry marinade overnight.

WINE Vivid, lightly sweet Riesling.

Chicken with Piquillos

ACTIVE: 35 MIN; TOTAL: 2 HR 15 MIN

4 SERVINGS ● ●

Pilar Sanchez, an elderly home cook who lives in Asturias, Spain, taught chef Mario Batali and writer Mark Bittman how to make *pollo casero,* a luscious chicken in a rich white wine and piquillo pepper sauce. When they asked where she buys her poultry, Sanchez told them to go to her yard and listen for the "singing in the field" from the chickens she raises.

One 3½-pound chicken, cut into 8 pieces

- 2 garlic cloves, sliced

Kosher salt

- 2 tablespoons extra-virgin olive oil
- 1 large onion, coarsely chopped

One 9-ounce jar piquillo peppers, drained

- 1 cup dry white wine

1. Rub the chicken with the garlic and 1 tablespoon of kosher salt. Cover and refrigerate for 1 hour.

2. Heat the olive oil in a large, deep skillet. Scrape the garlic off of the chicken pieces. Add the chicken to the skillet in a single layer and cook over moderately high heat, turning occasionally, until browned all over, about 12 minutes. Transfer the chicken to a platter.

3. Add the onion to the skillet and cook over low heat, stirring occasionally, until very tender, about 10 minutes. Add the piquillo peppers and white wine and bring to a simmer, scraping up any browned bits.

4. Return the chicken and any accumulated juices to the skillet. Cover partially and cook over low heat until the chicken is tender and cooked through and the sauce is thickened, about 30 minutes. Transfer the chicken to a platter, spoon the sauce on top and serve. —*Mario Batali*

MAKE AHEAD The chicken can be refrigerated overnight; rewarm before serving.

WINE Fresh, fruity rosé.

● HEALTHY ● MAKE AHEAD ● VEGETARIAN ● STAFF FAVORITE

poultry

Olive-Brined Chicken with Grilled Onions and Paprika Oil

TOTAL: 1 HR PLUS OVERNIGHT MARINATING

12 SERVINGS

A brine made with green olives, lemons and a slew of bay leaves does most of the work of flavoring this dish. "I like to use fresh bay leaves whenever possible," says Paul Virant (an F&W Best New Chef 2007). "They have a more fragrant, floral pungency." To add an extra layer of smokiness, Virant brushes the chicken with a quick pimentón-infused oil.

- 2 quarts water
- ½ cup kosher salt
- ¼ cup sugar
- ¼ cup herbes de Provence

Finely grated zest and juice of 2 lemons

- 1 cup pitted Spanish green olives, smashed
- 10 bay leaves
- 12 whole chicken legs, with skin, separated into drumsticks and thighs
- ½ cup vegetable oil
- 1 tablespoon hot pimentón de la Vera (smoked Spanish paprika)
- 2 tablespoons chopped thyme
- 3 large Vidalia or other sweet onions, sliced crosswise ½ inch thick

Salt and freshly ground pepper

- ½ cup pimiento-stuffed Spanish olives, sliced crosswise ¼ inch thick
- ½ cup flat-leaf parsley leaves

1. In a large saucepan, combine the water, kosher salt, sugar, herbes de Provence, lemon zest and juice, smashed olives and bay leaves and simmer to dissolve the salt. Pour the brine into a very large, nonreactive bowl or stockpot and let cool to room temperature, stirring occasionally. Submerge the chicken in the brine and cover, or put the chicken and brine in a heavy-duty plastic bag. Refrigerate overnight.

2. In a small saucepan, whisk together the vegetable oil, pimentón de la Vera and 1 tablespoon of the chopped thyme. Place over moderate heat until hot.

3. Light a grill. Brush the onion slices with some of the paprika oil. Season with salt and pepper and sprinkle with the remaining 1 tablespoon of thyme. Grill the onions over moderately high heat, turning once, until lightly charred and crisp-tender, about 4 minutes per side. Transfer the onions to a large platter. Toss to separate the rings and drizzle with 2 tablespoons of the paprika oil. Add the sliced olives and parsley and toss again.

4. Remove the chicken pieces from the brine and pat dry. Season with salt and pepper. Grill the chicken over moderate heat, turning often, until the skin is nicely charred and the meat is cooked through, about 25 minutes. Toward the end of cooking, brush the chicken all over with the paprika oil. Transfer the chicken to the platter with the onions and serve.
—Paul Virant

MAKE AHEAD The smoked-paprika oil can be refrigerated for up to 1 week.

WINE Fresh, fruity rosé.

Moroccan Chicken with Apricot-and-Olive Relish

ACTIVE: 30 MIN; TOTAL: 3 HR 15 MIN

4 SERVINGS

This grilled chicken dish transforms the sweet-savory elements of a Moroccan tagine—apricots, olives, couscous—into a light, summery meal. The marinade and relish are both flavored with eucalyptus honey, which has a deep, herbal quality that's delicious with the smoky chicken. Plus, the honey caramelizes on the grill, which makes the chicken extra-crispy.

- ¼ cup eucalyptus honey
- ¼ cup plus 1 tablespoon canola oil
- 3 tablespoons fresh lemon juice
- 2 teaspoons grated fresh ginger
- 1 garlic clove, minced

- 1 teaspoon ground cumin
- ½ teaspoon ground coriander
- ½ teaspoon cinnamon
- ½ teaspoon sweet pimentón de la Vera (smoked Spanish paprika)
- ⅛ teaspoon cayenne pepper
- 1 teaspoon kosher salt
- ¼ teaspoon freshly ground pepper
- 8 bone-in chicken thighs, with skin (2¾ pounds)

Boiling water

- 1 cup dried apricots
- 2 medium shallots, thinly sliced
- 20 green olives, such as Cerignola or Picholine, pitted (½ cup)
- 2 tablespoons chopped cilantro

1. In a bowl, whisk the honey with ¼ cup of the canola oil and the lemon juice, grated ginger, garlic, cumin, coriander, cinnamon, pimentón, cayenne, salt and black pepper. Arrange the chicken in a glass baking dish. Pour the marinade on top and turn to coat. Refrigerate for 2 hours, turning once.

2. Preheat the oven to 400°. Drain the chicken and transfer to a rimmed baking sheet; reserve the marinade. Cover with foil and bake for about 35 minutes, until cooked through. Remove the foil and discard any juices from the baking sheet.

3. Meanwhile, in a small bowl, pour boiling water over the apricots to cover and let stand until plump, 8 minutes; drain.

4. In a skillet, heat the remaining 1 tablespoon of oil. Add the shallots and cook over moderate heat until softened, 6 minutes. Add the apricots, olives and the reserved marinade and bring to a simmer. Cook over moderately high heat until the marinade glazes the apricots and olives, 2 minutes. Stir the cilantro into the relish.

5. Light a grill or preheat a grill pan. Grill the chicken over moderately high heat, turning once, until the skin is charred in spots and crisp, 6 minutes. Transfer to plates, top with the relish and serve. —Susan Spungen

SERVE WITH Couscous.

WINE Fruity, luscious Shiraz.

Chicken Stir-Fry with Asparagus and Cashews

TOTAL: 40 MIN
4 SERVINGS ●

½ cup raw cashews
1½ pounds skinless, boneless chicken breasts, cut into 1½-inch pieces
2 tablespoons Asian fish sauce
2 tablespoons vegetable oil
½ cup chicken stock or low-sodium broth
1 pound asparagus, sliced on the diagonal 1 inch thick
1 tablespoon oyster sauce
1 tablespoon fresh lime juice
⅛ teaspoon cayenne pepper
½ cup chopped basil
¼ cup chopped chives
Freshly ground black pepper

1. Preheat the oven to 350°. Spread the cashews in a pie plate and toast in the oven for about 8 minutes, until they are nicely browned and fragrant. Let cool.
2. In a medium bowl, toss the chicken with 1 tablespoon of the fish sauce. In a wok or large skillet, heat the oil until shimmering. Add the chicken in an even layer and cook over high heat, turning once, until browned and just cooked throughout, about 4 minutes. Using a slotted spoon, transfer the chicken to a clean bowl.

asian sauces for stir-fries

Black Bean Fermented soy beans give this salty, garlicky sauce its distinctive flavor.

Hoisin Sweet and spicy, hoisin is great with poultry and shellfish.

Oyster This savory-sweet sauce, made with cooked oysters, is surprisingly versatile.

3. Pour the chicken stock into the wok and bring to a simmer, scraping up any browned bits. Add the asparagus slices, cover and cook over moderate heat until they are crisp-tender, about 3 minutes. Using a slotted spoon, transfer the asparagus to the bowl along with the chicken.
4. Add the remaining 1 tablespoon of fish sauce to the wok along with the oyster sauce, lime juice and cayenne pepper. Simmer until the sauce is reduced to ⅓ cup, about 2 minutes. Return the chicken pieces and sliced asparagus to the wok and toss to heat through. Remove the wok from the heat and stir in the cashews, basil and chives. Season the stir-fry with black pepper and serve right away.
—*Stéphane Vivier*
SERVE WITH Steamed rice.
WINE Intense, spicy Shiraz.

Smoky-Hot Ginger Chicken Stir-Fry

ACTIVE: 25 MIN; TOTAL: 1 HR 25 MIN
4 SERVINGS ● ●

1¼ pounds skinless, boneless chicken thighs, cut into ½-inch pieces
2 tablespoons cornstarch
2 tablespoons Shaoxing wine
2 tablespoons peanut oil
10 dried red chiles
¼ cup finely chopped fresh ginger
1 tablespoon light brown sugar
2 tablespoons soy sauce
1 tablespoon rice vinegar
2 tablespoons snipped chives

1. In a medium bowl, toss the chicken, cornstarch and wine; let stand for 1 hour.
2. In a wok, heat the oil. Add the chiles and stir-fry them over moderate heat until they begin to darken, about 1 minute. Using a slotted spoon, transfer them to a plate.
3. When the oil in the wok is shimmering, add half the chicken; stir-fry over high heat until lightly browned and cooked through, 3 minutes. Transfer to the plate with the chiles. Repeat with the second batch.

4. Return all the stir-fried chicken and chiles to the wok. Add the chopped ginger and cook, stirring constantly, until the ginger is fragrant, about 1 minute. Add the brown sugar and stir-fry until the chicken pieces are lightly caramelized, about 1 minute longer. Add the soy sauce, rice vinegar and snipped chives to the wok and stir-fry until the sauce is just thickened, about 30 seconds. Serve the stir-fried chicken immediately.
—*Kylie Kwong*
SERVE WITH Steamed rice.
WINE Vivid, lightly sweet Riesling.

Asian Chicken Salad with Wasabi Dressing

TOTAL: 40 MIN
4 SERVINGS ●

Packed with Asian pear, cucumber and bean sprouts, this delectable poached-chicken salad offers a double hit of wasabi. First, wasabi powder is whisked into the dressing—a blend of mayonnaise, rice vinegar and sesame oil—then the salad is garnished with crunchy wasabi peas.

4 skinless, boneless chicken breast halves (1¾ pounds)
½ cup mayonnaise
¼ cup rice vinegar
2½ tablespoons wasabi powder
1½ teaspoons Asian sesame oil
1½ tablespoons water
Kosher salt and freshly ground black pepper
2 heads of Boston lettuce, torn into bite-size pieces
1 large Asian pear—halved, cored and thinly sliced
½ seedless cucumber, halved lengthwise and thinly sliced on the bias
2 scallions, white and green parts thinly sliced
1 cup mung bean sprouts
½ cup roasted wasabi peas, coarsely chopped

1. In a large saucepan, cover the chicken breasts with water and bring to a gentle simmer. Cook over moderately low heat until the chicken is white throughout, about 12 minutes. Transfer the poached chicken breasts to a plate and let stand until cooled slightly, about 10 minutes.

2. Meanwhile, in a small bowl, whisk the mayonnaise with the rice vinegar, wasabi powder, Asian sesame oil and 1½ tablespoons of water. Season the wasabi dressing with salt and black pepper.

3. In a large serving bowl, toss the lettuce with the Asian pear slices, cucumber, scallions, bean sprouts and ⅔ cup of the wasabi dressing. Slice the chicken breasts crosswise ¼ inch thick and lay the slices on top of the salad. Spoon the remaining wasabi dressing over the chicken breasts, sprinkle with the chopped wasabi peas and serve the chicken salad immediately. —*Melissa Rubel*

WINE Tart, citrusy Riesling.

Chicken Salad with Blue Cheese and Grapes

TOTAL: 30 MIN
4 TO 6 SERVINGS ●

F&W's Grace Parisi considered many classic salads, like Waldorf and Cobb, before deciding on this take on chicken salad, which mixes store-bought roasted chicken with blue cheese, grapes, celery and sunflower seeds. She sometimes likes eating the salad wrapped in Bibb lettuce leaves.

¼ cup plus 2 tablespoons
    mayonnaise
1½ tablespoons white wine vinegar
3 ounces crumbled mild
    blue cheese, such as Maytag
    (¾ cup)
2½ cups diced roasted chicken
    (from 1 rotisserie chicken)
1½ cups halved red and green grapes
2 celery ribs, finely diced
3 tablespoons chopped
    flat-leaf parsley

Salt and freshly ground pepper
¼ cup salted roasted
    sunflower seeds

In a large bowl, whisk the mayonnaise with the vinegar. Fold in the blue cheese, breaking it up with a fork. Add the chicken, red and green grapes, celery and parsley and fold gently. Season with salt and pepper. Fold in the sunflower seeds and serve. —*Grace Parisi*

MAKE AHEAD The chicken salad can be refrigerated overnight.

WINE Lively, fruity Merlot.

Circassian Chicken Salad

ACTIVE: 45 MIN; TOTAL: 2 HR
6 SERVINGS ● ●

This traditional Turkish chicken salad in a light, creamy walnut-and-garlic sauce supposedly got its name because its color resembles the pale complexions of the Circassian beauties in the sultan's harem during the Ottoman Empire. This version is served with a refreshing salad of baby arugula and roasted beets in a vinegary dressing.

One 4-pound chicken, left whole
1 onion, quartered
1 carrot, halved
6 black peppercorns
1 pound medium beets,
    peeled and cut into
    ½-inch wedges
¼ cup plus 2 tablespoons
    extra-virgin olive oil
Salt and freshly ground
    black pepper
4 teaspoons red wine vinegar
One 1-ounce slice of baguette,
    toasted
⅔ cup walnuts
1 small garlic clove
1 teaspoon Aleppo pepper or
    ancho chile powder
4 ounces baby arugula
Toasted pita bread triangles,
    for serving

1. Preheat the oven to 400°. Put the whole chicken, quartered onion, carrot halves and peppercorns in a large soup pot and add enough water to cover the chicken. Bring to a boil, skimming off any scum with a spoon. Simmer until the chicken is cooked, about 45 minutes.

2. Carefully remove the chicken from the pot and pull the meat from the bones; discard the skin. Return the bones to the pot and simmer for 30 minutes longer.

3. Meanwhile, put the beet wedges in a medium baking dish. Add 2 tablespoons of the olive oil and ¼ cup of water and season with salt and pepper. Cover with foil and roast for about 1 hour, until the beets are very tender. Let cool. Stir the vinegar and 2 tablespoons of the olive oil into the pan juices.

4. Shred the chicken and transfer it to a bowl. Strain the chicken broth from the soup pot. Pour 1 cup into a bowl and save the rest for another use. Add the bread to the broth and let stand until softened. In a blender or food processor, pulse the walnuts with the garlic until finely chopped. Add the soaked bread and puree until creamy and smooth. If necessary, add a few extra tablespoons of broth until the sauce is the consistency of thin sour cream. Season with salt and pepper. Stir the sauce into the chicken and season with salt and pepper.

5. In a small skillet, heat the remaining 2 tablespoons of olive oil with the Aleppo pepper over moderate heat until fragrant, about 1 minute. Drizzle the spicy oil over the chicken salad.

6. Arrange the arugula on a platter and top with the beets and their dressing. Spoon the chicken salad alongside and serve with the pita. —*Defne Koryürek*

MAKE AHEAD The chicken salad and roasted beets can be refrigerated separately overnight. Bring to room temperature before serving.

WINE Fruity, light-bodied Beaujolais.

GRILLED-CHICKEN BANH MI AND VIETNAMESE CHICKEN SALAD

QUICK CHICKEN-AND-CHEESE TAMALES

Grilled-Chicken Banh Mi

TOTAL: 1 HR 30 MIN PLUS 3 HR MARINATING AND PICKLING

4 SERVINGS ● ●

A popular Vietnamese sandwich, *banh mi* combines sweet, sour, crunchy and soft in one delicious—and portable—package.

MARINADE

- 1 cup Asian fish sauce
- 1 cup fresh lime juice
- ½ cup sugar
- 8 garlic cloves, minced
- 4 red Thai chiles, thinly sliced
- 1 tablespoon kosher salt
- 8 skinless, boneless chicken breast halves (3½ pounds)

PICKLED VEGETABLES

- ½ cup water
- ¼ cup rice vinegar
- ¼ cup sugar
- ½ teaspoon kosher salt

Pinch of crushed red pepper

- 3 large carrots, julienned on a mandoline
- ¼ pound daikon radish, julienned on a mandoline

BANH MI

Four 8-inch baguettes, split and grilled

- ¼ cup mayonnaise
- 1 cucumber, thinly sliced lengthwise
- 10 large cilantro sprigs
- 1 jalapeño, thinly sliced

1. MAKE THE MARINADE: In a bowl, whisk the fish sauce with the lime juice, sugar, garlic, Thai chiles and salt. Put the chicken in a resealable plastic bag with all but ¼ cup of the marinade. Reserve the remaining marinade for the Vietnamese Chicken Salad (recipe follows). Seal the bag and refrigerate the chicken for 3 hours.

2. PICKLE THE VEGETABLES: In a small saucepan, bring the water, vinegar, sugar, salt and crushed red pepper to a boil. Transfer the brine to a large bowl and let cool to room temperature. Add the carrots and daikon and cover to keep them submerged. Refrigerate the vegetables for at least 30 minutes and up to 3 days.

3. MAKE THE BANH MI: Light a grill. Remove the chicken from the marinade and pat dry. Grill the chicken over moderate heat, turning once, until just cooked through, about 14 minutes. Transfer to a work surface and let rest for 5 minutes.

4. Drain 1 cup of the pickled vegetables. Slice 6 of the chicken breasts. Reserve the remaining pickled vegetables and 2 breasts for the Vietnamese Chicken Salad.

5. Spread the cut sides of the baguettes with mayonnaise. Arrange the cucumber slices on the bottom halves. Top with the chicken and the pickled carrots and daikon. Garnish with the cilantro sprigs and jalapeño. Close the sandwiches and serve.

—*Nick Fauchald*

WINE Bright, tart Barbera.

VIETNAMESE CHICKEN SALAD

TOTAL: 15 MIN
4 SERVINGS ●

The extra chicken, pickled vegetables and marinade from the Grilled-Chicken Banh Mi recipe on the previous page can be transformed into a salad in just 15 minutes.

- ¼ cup reserved chicken marinade
- 1 tablespoon vegetable oil
- 5 cups shredded green cabbage
- 2 reserved grilled chicken-breast halves, sliced ⅓ inch thick
- 1 medium shallot, thinly sliced
- 1 cup reserved pickled carrots and daikon, drained
- ¼ cup finely chopped mint
- ¼ cup finely chopped cilantro, plus 6 large cilantro sprigs for garnish

Salt and freshly ground pepper

In a bowl, whisk the marinade with the oil. Add the cabbage, chicken, shallot, pickled carrots and daikon and chopped mint and cilantro and toss. Season with salt and pepper and garnish with cilantro sprigs. —NF

Quick Chicken-and-Cheese Tamales

TOTAL: 45 MIN
6 SERVINGS ●

Rotisserie chicken and cheese are mixed into a quick tamale dough that's wrapped in plastic and steamed.

- 2 cups masa harina
- 1 teaspoon baking powder
- 1¼ teaspoons kosher salt
- 1¼ cups cool water
- ½ cup solid vegetable shortening (3 ounces), softened
- ½ cup chicken stock or low-sodium broth
- 2½ cups shredded chicken (from 1 rotisserie chicken)
- ¼ pound sharp cheddar cheese, shredded (1 packed cup)
- ½ cup chopped cilantro
- 2 scallions, finely chopped

Hot sauce, for serving

1. In a food processor, pulse the masa harina with the baking powder and salt. Add the water and pulse to moisten the masa harina. Add the vegetable shortening in clumps and drizzle with the chicken stock. Process until smooth and evenly blended, scraping the side of the bowl occasionally. Transfer the dough to a large bowl and stir in the shredded chicken, shredded cheese, chopped cilantro and scallions.

2. Tear twelve 12-inch-square sheets of plastic wrap. Working with 6 at a time, spoon a scant ½ cup of the tamale mixture onto the center of each sheet. With lightly moistened hands, press the tamales into 4-by-2-inch rectangles about ½ inch thick. Fold up the squares of plastic around the tamales, twist the ends securely and then fold them under to make packets. Repeat to form the remaining tamales.

3. Arrange the tamales seam side down in the bottom of a large bamboo (or other) steamer. Steam over 2 inches of boiling water for 25 minutes. Let the tamales cool slightly, then carefully transfer them to a large platter: Cut the ends of the plastic-wrapped packets and slide the tamales out onto the platter. Serve the tamales with hot sauce. —*Grace Parisi*

WINE Lively, fruity Merlot.

Chipotle Chicken Burritos

ACTIVE: 1 HR; TOTAL: 1 HR 30 MIN
4 SERVINGS

- 2 pounds skinless, boneless chicken thighs
- 1 medium onion, quartered, plus 1 small onion cut into ½-inch dice
- 3 garlic cloves, crushed
- 2 bay leaves
- 1 tablespoon vegetable oil
- ½ teaspoon dark brown sugar
- 1 large chipotle in adobo, stemmed, plus 1 tablespoon adobo sauce
- 1 cup canned diced tomatoes, with juices

Kosher salt and freshly ground pepper
- ½ cup sour cream
- 3 tablespoons canned chopped green chiles, drained
- 1½ teaspoons water

Four 12-inch flour tortillas, warmed
- 6 ounces Monterey Jack cheese, shredded (1½ cups)

One 15-ounce can black beans—drained, rinsed and patted dry
- 2 cups shredded iceberg lettuce
- ½ cup prepared pico de gallo salsa
- 1 small Hass avocado—halved, peeled and cut lengthwise into 12 slices

1. In a large saucepan, combine the chicken thighs, quartered onion, garlic and bay leaves. Add enough water to cover the chicken and bring to a simmer. Cover and cook over moderately low heat until the chicken is fork-tender, 1 hour. Remove the chicken and shred it into bite-size pieces. Transfer the chicken to a medium bowl.

2. Meanwhile, in a skillet, heat the oil. Add the diced onion and brown sugar and cook over moderately high heat until the onion is golden brown, 10 minutes. Add the chipotle, adobo sauce and tomatoes and simmer over moderately low heat until thickened, 10 minutes. Transfer the mixture to a food processor and blend until smooth. Pour over the shredded chicken and season with salt and pepper.

3. In a blender, combine the sour cream with the green chiles and water and puree until smooth. Season with salt and pepper.

4. Sprinkle the tortillas with the cheese. Spoon the chicken mixture down the center of the tortillas. Top the chicken with the black beans, lettuce, salsa, avocado and green-chile sour cream. Bring the sides of the tortillas toward the center of the filling. Fold the bottom of the tortilla up over the filling and continue to roll until the burrito closes. Serve immediately.
—*Joanna Garnett Raeppold*

WINE Lively, fruity Merlot.

poultry

Braised Chicken and Greens with Gnocchi

ACTIVE: 1 HR; TOTAL: 2 HR

4 SERVINGS

- 1 tablespoon extra-virgin olive oil
- 2 ounces thinly sliced soppressata

Four 6-ounce bone-in chicken thighs, with skin

Salt and freshly ground black pepper

- 1 large yellow onion, finely chopped
- 1 large carrot, finely chopped
- 1 garlic clove, thinly sliced
- ½ cup dry white wine
- 2 cups chicken stock or low-sodium broth
- 1 thyme sprig
- 1 pound sturdy greens, such as kale or turnip greens, stemmed and leaves coarsely chopped
- 2 tablespoons unsalted butter
- 1 pound fresh or frozen gnocchi

Freshly grated young pecorino cheese, for serving

1. Preheat the oven to 325°. In a large, deep ovenproof skillet, heat the olive oil. Add the soppressata slices in a single layer and cook over high heat, turning once, until they are crispy, about 3 minutes. Transfer the soppressata to a paper towel–lined plate and let cool.

2. Season the chicken thighs with salt and pepper and add them to the skillet. Cook over moderately high heat, turning once, until browned, about 8 minutes. Transfer the chicken to a plate.

3. Add the onion, carrot and garlic to the skillet and cook over moderately low heat, stirring, until softened, about 8 minutes. Add the wine and cook until nearly evaporated, scraping up any browned bits stuck to the pan, about 5 minutes. Add the stock and bring to a boil. Nestle the chicken and thyme into the broth and cover tightly. Transfer to the oven and cook for about 1 hour, until the chicken is very tender.

4. Transfer the chicken thighs to a plate and pull the meat from the bones. Discard the skin and spoon off as much fat as possible from the broth in the skillet.

5. Add the greens to the skillet, cover and cook over moderate heat until they are wilted, about 5 minutes. Return the chicken to the skillet and stir in the butter. Cover and keep warm.

6. Bring a large pot of salted water to a boil. Add the gnocchi and cook according to the package directions. Using a slotted spoon, transfer the gnocchi to the chicken and greens ragout and gently stir to combine. Spoon the ragout into wide bowls. Crumble the crisp soppressata on top and serve, passing the pecorino at the table.
—Payton Curry

MAKE AHEAD The braised chicken can be prepared through Step 3. Let cool completely, cover and refrigerate overnight. Shred the chicken while it is cold, and bring the broth to a simmer over moderate heat before adding the greens.

WINE Intense, fruity Zinfandel.

Mexican Chicken Pozole Verde

ACTIVE: 45 MIN; TOTAL: 1 HR 15 MIN

6 TO 8 SERVINGS ●

There are many variations on pozole, a traditional hominy-based Mexican stew associated with the Pacific coast state of Guerrero. Food and travel writer Anya von Bremzen's version, a green pozole, derives much of its flavor from tangy ingredients like tomatillos, cilantro and green chiles.

- 7 cups chicken stock
- 2 cups water
- 4 bone-in chicken breast halves, with skin
- 1 pound tomatillos, husked and halved
- 1 small onion, quartered
- 2 poblano chiles—cored, seeded and quartered
- 2 jalapeños, seeded and quartered
- 4 large garlic cloves, smashed
- ½ cup chopped cilantro
- 1 tablespoon oregano leaves

Salt and freshly ground pepper

- 1 tablespoon vegetable oil

Three 15-ounce cans hominy, drained

Finely shredded iceberg lettuce, sliced radishes, chopped onion, diced avocado, sour cream, tortilla chips and lime wedges, for serving

1. In a large enameled cast-iron casserole, bring the chicken stock and water to a boil. Add the chicken breasts skin side down, cover and simmer over very low heat until they're tender and cooked through, about 25 minutes. Transfer the chicken breasts to a plate and shred the meat; discard the bones and skin. Skim any fat from the cooking liquid and reserve.

2. In a blender, combine the halved tomatillos with the quartered onion, poblanos and jalapeños, smashed garlic, chopped cilantro and oregano. Pulse until coarsely chopped, scraping down the side. With the machine on, add 1 cup of the cooking liquid and puree until smooth. Season the tomatillo puree with salt and pepper.

3. In a large, deep skillet, heat the vegetable oil until shimmering. Add the tomatillo puree and cook over moderate heat, stirring occasionally, until the sauce turns a deep green, about 12 minutes.

4. Pour the green sauce into the cooking liquid in the casserole. Add the hominy and bring to a simmer over moderate heat. Add the chicken, season with salt and pepper and cook just until heated through. Serve the pozole in deep bowls, passing the lettuce, radishes, onion, avocado, sour cream, tortilla chips and lime wedges at the table.
—Anya von Bremzen

MAKE AHEAD The pozole verde can be prepared through Step 3 and refrigerated, covered, overnight.

WINE Full-bodied, rich Pinot Gris.

Sautéed Chicken with Olives and Roasted Lemons

TOTAL: 35 MIN
4 SERVINGS ●

This piquant dish from chef Lidia Bastianich's Missouri restaurant, Lidia's Kansas City, is a flavorful way to prepare skinless chicken breasts.

- 2 lemons, sliced ¼ inch thick
- ¼ cup extra-virgin olive oil, plus more for drizzling
- Salt and freshly ground black pepper
- Four 6-ounce skinless, boneless chicken breast halves
- All-purpose flour, for dusting
- ½ cup pitted green Sicilian or Spanish olives, sliced
- 2 tablespoons drained capers
- 1 cup chicken stock or low-sodium broth
- 3 tablespoons unsalted butter, cut into small dice
- 2 tablespoons chopped parsley

1. Preheat the oven to 375°. Line a baking sheet with lightly oiled parchment paper. Arrange the lemon slices on the paper in a single layer. Lightly drizzle the slices with oil and season with salt and pepper. Roast for about 20 minutes, until the slices begin to brown around the edges.

2. In a medium, deep skillet, heat the ¼ cup of olive oil. Season the chicken breasts with salt and pepper and dust them with flour, shaking off the excess. Cook the chicken over high heat, turning once, until the breasts are golden, about 6 minutes.

3. Add the olives, capers and stock to the skillet and bring to a boil. Cook over high heat until the stock is reduced to ⅓ cup, about 5 minutes. Add the roasted lemons, butter and parsley, season with salt and pepper and simmer just until the chicken is cooked through, about 1 minute. Transfer to plates and serve. —*Lidia Bastianich*

SERVE WITH Sautéed baby spinach.

WINE Earthy, medium-bodied Tempranillo.

MEXICAN CHICKEN POZOLE VERDE

SAUTÉED CHICKEN WITH OLIVES AND ROASTED LEMONS

Braised Chicken with Olives and Sweet Peppers

ACTIVE: 1 HR 15 MIN;

TOTAL: 3 HR 30 MIN

8 SERVINGS ●

Plump, meaty green olives punch up the flavor in this homey chicken dish, which is loaded with soft, sweet roasted red and yellow bell peppers and onions.

- 4 red bell peppers
- 4 yellow bell peppers
- ¼ cup plus 2 tablespoons extra-virgin olive oil
- 8 bone-in chicken drumsticks, with skin
- 8 bone-in chicken thighs, with skin

Kosher salt and freshly ground pepper

- 2 carrots, cut into ½-inch dice
- 2 celery ribs, cut into ½-inch dice
- 3 garlic cloves, halved
- 2 teaspoons thyme leaves
- 2 large sweet onions, halved and thinly sliced
- 2 cups dry white wine
- 2 cups chicken stock or low-sodium broth
- ½ pound large green Italian olives, such as Castelvetrano or Cerignola
- 2 tablespoons chopped flat-leaf parsley

Crusty bread, for serving

pastured chicken

Chickens raised on grass have such superior taste that NYC chef Adam Perry Lang wants to get into chicken farming. You can find farms that produce pastured chickens at LocalHarvest.org, which lists sources by zip code.

---

1. Preheat the oven to 400°. On a large rimmed baking sheet, rub the bell peppers with 1 tablespoon of the olive oil. Roast the peppers for about 45 minutes, turning them halfway through, until the skins are blistered. When cool enough to handle, peel the bell peppers and slice them into ½-inch-wide strips. Lower the oven temperature to 350°.

2. Meanwhile, season the chicken pieces with salt and pepper. In a very large skillet, heat 3 tablespoons of the olive oil until shimmering. Working in 2 batches, cook the chicken over moderately high heat until it is golden all over, about 10 minutes per batch. Transfer the browned chicken pieces to a large roasting pan.

3. Add the carrots, celery, garlic, thyme and half of the onions to the skillet and cook over moderate heat until the onion is translucent, about 5 minutes. Using a slotted spoon, transfer the vegetables to the roasting pan with the chicken. Discard the fat from the skillet.

4. Set the skillet over high heat. Add the white wine and bring to a boil, scraping up the browned bits from the bottom of the pan. Pour the wine over the chicken. Add the chicken stock to the roasting pan, cover with foil and transfer to the oven. Braise the chicken for about 1½ hours, until it's falling off the bone.

5. Transfer the chicken to a serving dish and cover with foil. Set the roasting pan over high heat and boil the juices for 15 minutes. Season the sauce with salt and pepper.

6. Meanwhile, in a large skillet, heat the remaining 2 tablespoons of olive oil. Add the remaining sliced onion and cook over moderate heat until tender, 8 minutes. Stir the onion, peppers and olives into the sauce and simmer until heated through, about 1 minute. Pour the sauce and vegetables over the chicken, sprinkle with parsley and serve with crusty bread. —*Ethan Stowell*

WINE Ripe, juicy Pinot Noir.

Spicy Chicken Cacciatore

ACTIVE: 25 MIN; TOTAL: 1 HR

4 SERVINGS ●●

Although this Italian standard has suffered at the hands of lesser chefs, Boston chef Barbara Lynch redeems it. She ably deconstructs what is often a heavy sauce into its vivid components: bright red strips of bell pepper, sweet slices of onion, hot pickled peppers and fresh chopped tomatoes.

- 2 tablespoons extra-virgin olive oil
- 8 boneless chicken thighs, with skin

Salt and freshly ground pepper

- 1 medium onion, thinly sliced
- 1 red bell pepper, thinly sliced
- 2 pickled hot peppers, thinly sliced
- 3 garlic cloves, thinly sliced
- ½ cup dry red wine
- 1½ cups chicken stock
- 1 pound ripe plum tomatoes, coarsely chopped
- 2 tablespoons chopped flat-leaf parsley

1. In a deep skillet, heat the olive oil. Season the chicken thighs with salt and pepper and add the chicken to the skillet, skin side down. Cook over moderately high heat, turning once until lightly browned and crisp, about 8 minutes. Transfer to a plate.

2. Add the onion, bell pepper, pickled peppers and garlic and cook over low heat, stirring occasionally, until softened, about 10 minutes. Pour in the wine and simmer, stirring occasionally, until nearly evaporated, about 5 minutes.

3. Add the chicken stock and tomatoes to the skillet and season lightly with salt and pepper. Return the chicken to the pan, nestling it skin side up in the vegetables, and bring to a simmer. Cover partially and cook over moderate heat for 30 minutes, until the chicken is tender and the sauce is reduced by half. Sprinkle with the parsley and serve. —*Barbara Lynch*

SERVE WITH Farro Risotto (p. 254).

WINE Cherry-inflected, earthy Sangiovese.

Chicken Goulash with Biscuit Dumplings

TOTAL: 45 MIN
4 SERVINGS ●

The chicken stock and sour cream serve a dual purpose here: They moisten the biscuits and enrich the thick, velvety sauce.

- 2 pounds skinless, boneless chicken thighs, cut into 2-inch pieces
- Kosher salt and freshly ground black pepper
- 1½ cups all-purpose flour, plus more for dusting
- 5 tablespoons cold unsalted butter, cubed
- 2 tablespoons extra-virgin olive oil
- 2 teaspoons baking powder
- 2½ cups chicken stock or low-sodium broth
- 1 cup sour cream
- 1 large white onion, very finely chopped
- 1 red bell pepper, finely diced
- 2 medium garlic cloves, very finely chopped
- 2 tablespoons hot Hungarian paprika
- ¾ teaspoon caraway seeds
- 1 teaspoon thyme leaves

1. Preheat the oven to 425°. Season the chicken with salt and pepper and dust lightly with flour. In a large, deep ovenproof skillet, melt 1 tablespoon of the butter in the olive oil. Add the chicken and cook over high heat, turning once, until browned, about 7 minutes. Using a slotted spoon, transfer the chicken to a plate.

2. Meanwhile, in a food processor, pulse the 1½ cups of flour, the baking powder, ½ teaspoon of salt and ¼ teaspoon of pepper. Pulse in the remaining 4 tablespoons of butter until the mixture resembles coarse meal. Whisk ½ cup of the stock with ½ cup of the sour cream and drizzle over the dry ingredients; pulse until a dough forms.

3. Add the onion, bell pepper and garlic to the skillet and cook over high heat, stirring occasionally, until softened, about 3 minutes. Return the chicken to the skillet. Stir in the paprika and caraway and cook for 30 seconds. Add the remaining 2 cups of chicken stock and ½ cup of sour cream and stir until smooth. Add the thyme leaves and bring to a boil.

4. Scoop twelve 3-tablespoon-size mounds of biscuit dough over the chicken. Transfer the skillet to the oven and bake for 20 minutes, until the sauce is bubbling and the biscuits are cooked. Turn on the broiler and broil for 2 minutes, until the biscuits are golden. Serve in bowls, spooning the biscuits on top. —*Grace Parisi*
WINE Ripe, luxurious Chardonnay.

Caramelized Black Pepper Chicken

TOTAL: 35 MIN
4 SERVINGS ●●

At the Slanted Door in San Francisco, chef Charles Phan prepares spectacular Vietnamese specialties like this intensely sweet and savory peppered chicken.

- ½ cup dark brown sugar
- 3 tablespoons Asian fish sauce
- ¼ cup water
- 3 tablespoons rice vinegar
- 1 teaspoon very finely chopped garlic
- 1 teaspoon finely grated fresh ginger
- 1 teaspoon coarsely ground black pepper
- 2 fresh Thai chiles, halved
- 1 tablespoon canola oil
- 1 shallot, thinly sliced
- 1 pound skinless, boneless chicken thighs, cut into 1-inch pieces
- 4 cilantro sprigs

1. In a small bowl, combine the brown sugar, fish sauce, water, rice vinegar, garlic, ginger, black pepper and chiles.

2. Heat the oil in a large, deep skillet. Add the shallot and cook over moderate heat until softened, about 4 minutes. Add the fish sauce mixture and chicken and simmer over high heat until the chicken is cooked, about 10 minutes. Garnish with cilantro sprigs and serve. —*Charles Phan*
SERVE WITH Jasmine rice.
WINE Vivid, lightly sweet Riesling.

Green Chicken Masala

TOTAL: 45 MIN
4 TO 6 SERVINGS ●●

- 2 cups cilantro leaves
- 1 cup mint leaves
- 1 jalapeño, coarsely chopped
- 4 garlic cloves, crushed
- ¼ cup fresh lemon juice
- ½ cup water
- 2 tablespoons canola oil
- 1 onion, finely chopped
- 8 skinless, boneless chicken thighs (1¾ pounds), cut into 1-inch pieces
- 1½ teaspoons turmeric
- ½ teaspoon cinnamon
- ½ teaspoon ground cardamom
- ⅛ teaspoon ground cloves
- 1 cup unsweetened coconut milk
- Kosher salt
- Basmati rice, for serving

1. In a blender, combine the cilantro, mint, jalapeño, garlic, lemon juice and water and puree until smooth.

2. In a large, deep skillet, heat the oil. Add the onion and cook over moderately high heat, stirring frequently, until softened, about 5 minutes. Add the chicken and turmeric and cook, stirring occasionally, until golden in spots, about 7 minutes. Add the cinnamon, cardamom and cloves and cook for 1 minute. Add the cilantro puree and coconut milk, season with salt and bring to a boil. Simmer over low heat until the sauce is slightly reduced and the chicken is tender, about 15 minutes. Serve with basmati rice. —*Vikram Sunderam*
WINE Spicy American Gewürztraminer.

poultry

Chicken Tikka

TOTAL: 30 MIN PLUS 2 HR MARINATING
4 TO 6 SERVINGS

- 1 tablespoon mustard seeds
- 1 teaspoon Chinese five-spice powder
- 1 teaspoon freshly ground black pepper
- 1 teaspoon turmeric
- 1 teaspoon cayenne pepper
- 1 bay leaf
- 2 tablespoons very finely chopped fresh ginger
- 4 garlic cloves, very finely chopped
- 1 cup plain whole-milk yogurt

Kosher salt

- 2 pounds skinless, boneless chicken thighs, cut into 2-inch pieces
- 2 tablespoons unsalted butter, melted

Cilantro and Yogurt Sauce (p. 199), for serving

1. In a spice grinder, pulse the mustard seeds with the five-spice powder, black pepper, turmeric, cayenne pepper and bay leaf until fine. Transfer the spice powder to a medium bowl. Add the chopped ginger, garlic and yogurt and season with salt. Add the chicken pieces and turn to coat. Refrigerate for 2 hours.

2. Light a grill. Remove the chicken from the marinade and brush the pieces with the melted butter. Season with salt. Oil the grate and grill the chicken over high heat, turning occasionally, until the chicken is lightly charred and cooked through, about 8 minutes. Serve right away, with the Cilantro and Yogurt Sauce.
—*Vikram Sunderam*

SERVE WITH Warm naan.

MAKE AHEAD The chicken can be covered and refrigerated in the yogurt marinade for up to 8 hours.

WINE Complex, elegant Pinot Noir.

Chicken in Vinegar Sauce

 TOTAL: 40 MIN
4 SERVINGS ●

Master French chef Paul Bocuse's recipe reflects his interest in lightening up the classics. For his *poulet au vinaigre de vin,* he's swapped fresh tomatoes for tomato paste, used lower-acid rice vinegar in place of red wine vinegar and significantly reduced the amount of butter.

- 4 tablespoons unsalted butter
- 1 tablespoon extra-virgin olive oil
- 4 garlic cloves, unpeeled

One 3¾-pound chicken, cut into 10 pieces

Kosher salt and freshly ground pepper

- ½ cup rice vinegar
- 2 medium tomatoes, seeded and cut into ½-inch dice
- 2 tablespoons chopped flat-leaf parsley

1. In a large, deep skillet, melt 2 tablespoons of the butter in the olive oil. Add the whole garlic cloves. Season the chicken with salt and pepper and add it to the skillet. Cook over moderately high heat until lightly browned all over, about 8 minutes. Add the rice vinegar and diced tomatoes and bring to a simmer. Cover and simmer over moderately low heat until the chicken is cooked through, about 15 minutes. Transfer the chicken pieces to a large serving platter and keep warm.

2. Boil the sauce over moderately high heat until slightly thickened, about 4 minutes. Remove from the heat.

3. Peel the garlic cloves and mash them into the sauce. Whisk in the remaining 2 tablespoons of butter and stir in the chopped parsley; season the sauce with salt and pepper. Pour the sauce over the chicken and serve right away.
—*Paul Bocuse*

SERVE WITH Crusty bread.

WINE Dry, rich Champagne.

Chicken Hot Pot with Mushrooms and Tofu

ACTIVE: 20 MIN; TOTAL: 1 HR
8 SERVINGS

Cooks in Asia serve hot pots communally, setting a big pot of bubbling broth on the table alongside a platter of raw ingredients (like vegetables and thinly sliced chicken) for dipping. It's a fun way for guests to feel like they have a hand in making their own meal. In his version, Seattle chef Ethan Stowell (an F&W Best New Chef 2008) gives each person an individual bowl of sliced mushrooms, tofu and scallions, then adds piping hot chicken broth loaded with chunks of tender cooked chicken.

- 12 cups chicken stock or low-sodium broth
- 1 pound honshimeji or cremini mushrooms—stems removed and reserved, caps thinly sliced

One 2-inch piece of ginger, thinly sliced

- 2 large garlic cloves, crushed

Kosher salt

- 6 skinless, boneless chicken thighs (about 1¾ pounds), trimmed and sliced into ¼-inch strips

One 14-ounce package firm tofu, drained and cut into ½-inch dice

- 4 scallions, thinly sliced

Asian sesame oil, for drizzling

1. In a large soup pot, bring the stock, mushroom stems, ginger and garlic to a simmer. Cook over low heat for 30 minutes. Strain the stock into a large bowl and return it to the pot. Season the broth with salt.

2. Bring the enriched broth to a boil; add the chicken. Cook until the chicken is white throughout, about 4 minutes. Divide the mushroom caps, tofu and scallions among eight soup bowls and serve, passing the broth and sesame oil. —*Ethan Stowell*

MAKE AHEAD The enriched chicken broth can be refrigerated for up to 3 days.

WINE Fruity, low-oak Chardonnay.

CHICKEN HOT POT WITH
MUSHROOMS AND TOFU

poultry

Chicken with White Wine and Crème Fraîche

ACTIVE: 1 HR; TOTAL: 1 HR 30 MIN

4 SERVINGS

- 2 tablespoons olive oil
- One 3½-pound chicken, cut into 8 pieces
- Kosher salt and freshly ground black pepper
- 1 cup chicken stock
- 1 cup water
- ½ cup dry white wine
- 1 carrot, halved lengthwise
- 1 celery rib, halved lengthwise
- 1 leek, white and tender green parts only, quartered lengthwise
- 1 medium onion, halved
- 2 garlic cloves, halved
- 2 bay leaves
- 1 clove
- ½ teaspoon whole peppercorns
- ½ cup crème fraîche
- 2 tablespoons unsalted butter

1. In a large skillet, heat 1 tablespoon of the oil. Season the chicken with salt and pepper and cook in a single layer over moderately high heat, skin side down, until the skin is golden and beginning to crisp, about 5 minutes. Transfer to a plate.

2. Add the chicken stock, water and white wine to the skillet and cook over moderate heat, scraping up any browned bits from the bottom. Add the carrot, celery, leek, onion, garlic, bay leaves, clove and peppercorns and bring to a simmer. Return the chicken pieces to the skillet, skin side up. Cover, reduce the heat to low and simmer until the chicken is cooked through, 20 minutes. Transfer the chicken to a plate and cover loosely with foil.

3. Strain the cooking liquid into a small saucepan. Bring to a boil, then simmer over moderately high heat until reduced to ⅔ cup, 20 minutes. Remove from the heat. Whisk in the crème fraîche and butter and season with salt and pepper. Keep warm.

4. In a medium skillet, heat the remaining 1 tablespoon of oil. Add the chicken skin side down; cook over moderately high heat until the skin is crisp, 2 minutes. Transfer to plates, ladle the sauce on top and serve.
—*Pierre Jancou*

MAKE AHEAD The chicken can be prepared through Step 2 and refrigerated overnight in the poaching liquid.

WINE Light, crisp white Burgundy.

Skillet Chicken-and-Mushroom Potpie

 TOTAL: 45 MIN

6 SERVINGS ●

This one-skillet dish—prepared with store-bought rotisserie chicken and slices of buttered white bread in place of the usual labor-intensive puff pastry crust—proves that making potpie doesn't have to take a long time.

- 4 tablespoons unsalted butter, softened
- 1 onion, finely chopped
- ½ pound shiitake mushrooms, stemmed, caps thinly sliced
- 2 carrots, thinly sliced
- Salt and freshly ground pepper
- 3 tablespoons all-purpose flour
- 1 teaspoon sweet paprika
- 1 cup chicken stock or low-sodium broth
- 2 tablespoons Madeira
- 2 cups whole milk
- 3 cups shredded chicken (from 1 rotisserie chicken)
- ½ cup frozen baby peas
- Eight 1-inch-thick slices of bakery white country bread (about 1 pound), crusts removed

1. Preheat the oven to 425°. In a large ovenproof nonstick skillet, melt 2 tablespoons of the butter. Add the onion, mushrooms and carrots and season lightly with salt and pepper. Cover and cook over high heat, stirring once, until the vegetables are just softened, about 1 minute. Uncover and cook, stirring frequently, until lightly browned, about 5 minutes. Stir in the flour and paprika and cook, stirring, for 1 minute. Add the stock and Madeira and cook, stirring, until blended. Add the milk and bring to a gentle boil. Stir in the chicken and peas and season with salt and pepper. Remove from the heat.

2. Arrange the bread over the chicken mixture, trimming it to fit snugly in a single layer. Brush the bread with the remaining 2 tablespoons of butter. Bake for about 20 minutes, until the filling is bubbling and the bread is golden. Serve right away.
—*Grace Parisi*

WINE Fresh, fruity rosé.

Chicken-and-Sausage Gumbo

TOTAL: 1 HR 5 MIN

6 SERVINGS ●

- One 1½-pound whole bone-in chicken breast, with skin
- Kosher salt and freshly ground black pepper
- 1 tablespoon vegetable oil
- 1 pound andouille sausage links
- 2 celery ribs, cut into ⅓-inch dice
- 1 red bell pepper, diced
- 1 medium onion, diced
- 4 garlic cloves, minced
- ¼ cup all-purpose flour
- 2 tablespoons tomato paste
- 4 cups low-sodium chicken broth
- One 15-ounce can diced tomatoes
- 3 scallions, thinly sliced
- 2 cups cooked white long-grain rice
- Tabasco, for serving

1. Season the chicken with salt and pepper. In a heavy pot, heat the oil until shimmering. Add the chicken skin side down and cook over moderately high heat until browned on the bottom, 5 minutes; turn over and cook until browned on the second side, 4 minutes. Transfer to a plate and discard the skin.

2. In the same pan, brown the sausages over moderately high heat, 5 minutes. Transfer to the plate with the chicken.

CHICKEN WITH WHITE WINE AND CRÈME FRAÎCHE

SKILLET CHICKEN-AND-MUSHROOM POTPIE

3. Pour off all but 1 tablespoon of the fat from the pot. Add the celery, bell pepper and onion and cook over moderate heat until the vegetables are lightly browned, about 10 minutes. Add the garlic and cook for 1 minute. Stir in the flour and the tomato paste and cook, stirring, until the flour smells nutty, 5 minutes. Add the broth and tomatoes; bring to a simmer. Add the chicken and sausages and simmer over low heat until the chicken is cooked through, about 15 minutes.

4. Transfer the chicken and sausages to a cutting board. Shred the chicken into small pieces. Slice the sausages into ½-inch-thick rounds. Return both to the pot and stir in the scallions and rice. Simmer until heated through, about 1 minute. Season the gumbo with salt and pepper and serve, passing Tabasco at the table.
—*Amber Huffman*

WINE Ripe, luxurious Chardonnay.

White Bean and Chicken Soup

ACTIVE: 35 MIN; TOTAL: 1 HR 35 MIN
8 SERVINGS ●

- 3 pounds skinless, boneless chicken thighs, cut into 1-inch dice
- Kosher salt and freshly ground pepper
- 2 tablespoons vegetable oil
- 2 medium onions, diced
- 3 garlic cloves, minced
- 1 jalapeño, minced
- 2 tablespoons all-purpose flour
- 2 tablespoons chile powder blend
- 2 teaspoons ground cumin
- 1 teaspoon dried oregano, crushed
- ½ teaspoon cayenne pepper
- 8 cups chicken stock or low-sodium broth
- Three 15-ounce cans navy beans, drained
- Tortilla chips, sour cream, shredded Monterey Jack cheese, cilantro and diced avocado, for serving

1. Season the chicken with salt and pepper. In a large enameled cast-iron casserole, heat the oil until shimmering. Add half of the chicken at a time and cook over moderately high heat until lightly browned all over, about 8 minutes per batch. Using a slotted spoon, transfer the chicken to a plate.

2. Add the onions to the casserole and cook over moderate heat, stirring, until tender, 5 minutes. Add the garlic and jalapeño and cook until fragrant. Add the flour, chile powder, cumin, oregano and cayenne and cook, stirring constantly, until fragrant. Add the stock, navy beans and chicken and bring to a simmer. Cover and cook over low heat until the chicken is very tender, 30 minutes.

3. Uncover and simmer the soup over moderate heat until slightly thickened, about 30 minutes longer. Season with salt and pepper and serve with the chips, sour cream, cheese, cilantro and avocado. —*Melissa Rubel*

WINE Minerally, complex Sauvignon Blanc.

● HEALTHY ● MAKE AHEAD ● VEGETARIAN ● STAFF FAVORITE

poultry

Green Chile–Chicken and Pink Bean Stew

TOTAL: 30 MIN
4 SERVINGS ● ●

Canned green chiles contribute flavor and heat to this thick chicken stew, which is made doubly satisfying by the addition of pink beans. Similar to pinto and kidney beans, pink beans give this recipe a nice Latin feel.

- 2 tablespoons vegetable oil
- 1½ pounds skinless, boneless chicken thighs, cut into 1-inch dice
- Kosher salt and freshly ground black pepper
- 1 white onion, cut into ½-inch dice
- 2 garlic cloves, very finely chopped
- 1¼ teaspoons ground cumin
- One 19-ounce can pink beans, drained and rinsed
- Two 4-ounce cans green chiles, drained
- 1¾ cups chicken stock or low-sodium broth
- 2 tablespoons chopped cilantro
- Lime wedges, for serving

1. In a medium soup pot, heat the vegetable oil until shimmering. Season the diced chicken thighs with salt and pepper and cook over moderately high heat until browned on both sides, about 5 minutes. Add the onion and garlic and cook over moderate heat until softened, about 4 minutes. Stir in the cumin and cook until fragrant, about 1 minute.
2. Add the pink beans, green chiles and stock to the chicken and bring to a simmer. Cook over moderately low heat, stirring occasionally, until the stew has thickened, about 10 minutes. Stir in the cilantro and season with salt and pepper. Ladle the stew into bowls and serve with lime wedges. —*Melissa Rubel*

WINE Rustic, peppery Malbec.

Red Chile–Chicken Enchiladas

ACTIVE: 45 MIN; TOTAL: 1 HR 30 MIN
8 SERVINGS ●
SAUCE

- 3 each of *guajillo* and ancho chiles, stemmed and seeded
- 3 cups hot water
- 1 medium onion, quartered
- 3 large garlic cloves
- 1 tablespoon ground cumin
- 1½ teaspoons ground coriander
- ½ teaspoon dried oregano, preferably Mexican
- 2 tablespoons extra-virgin olive oil
- 2½ cups canned tomato sauce (20 ounces)
- 1 cup water
- Salt and freshly ground pepper
ENCHILADAS

- 2 tablespoons extra-virgin olive oil
- 1 large onion, thinly sliced (3 cups)
- ½ cup low-sodium chicken broth
- 4 cups shredded cooked chicken
- 1 teaspoon ground cumin
- ¼ cup chopped cilantro
- ¾ pound Monterey Jack cheese, shredded (3 cups)
- Salt and freshly ground pepper
- Vegetable oil, for frying
- 16 corn tortillas
- Chopped red onion, cilantro, hot sauce and sour cream, for serving

1. MAKE THE SAUCE: In a microwave-safe bowl, cover the chiles with the hot water. Microwave at high power for 2 minutes, until softened. Transfer the chiles to a blender along with 1 cup of their soaking liquid and the onion, garlic, cumin, coriander and oregano; puree until smooth.
2. In a saucepan, heat the oil over moderately low heat. Add the tomato sauce and the water. Strain the chile sauce through a fine sieve into the saucepan, scraping to remove the skins. Cook, stirring occasionally, until slightly reduced, 15 minutes. Season with salt and pepper. Spoon ¾ cup of the sauce into 2 shallow baking dishes.

3. MEANWHILE, MAKE THE ENCHILADAS: Preheat the oven to 350°. In a large skillet, heat the oil. Add the onion and cook over moderate heat until lightly browned, 10 minutes. Add the broth and cook until the onions are soft and the broth has evaporated, 10 minutes. Transfer to a bowl and let cool. Stir in the chicken, cumin, cilantro and half of the cheese. Season with salt and pepper.
4. Wipe out the skillet and heat ¼ inch of vegetable oil in it. Fry the tortillas one at a time over low heat just until pliable, about 10 seconds each. Transfer to a paper towel–lined baking sheet and pat dry. Spoon ¼ cup of the chicken filling onto each tortilla and roll up into a tight cylinder, lining the filled cylinders up in the baking dishes, seam side down. Spoon the remaining enchilada sauce on top, spreading it to cover the enchiladas. Sprinkle the remaining shredded Monterey Jack cheese over the top.
5. Cover the enchiladas with foil and bake for 45 minutes, until the chicken filling is heated through and the cheese is bubbling; remove the foil halfway through cooking. Let the enchiladas cool for 10 minutes before transferring to plates. Serve with chopped red onion, cilantro, hot sauce and sour cream. —*Grace Parisi*

WINE Lively, fruity Merlot.

Jerk Cornish Game Hens

ACTIVE: 1 HR; TOTAL: 2 HR PLUS OVERNIGHT MARINATING
4 SERVINGS

- 4 Scotch bonnet or habanero chiles, stemmed and halved
- 5 scallions, cut into 2-inch lengths
- 2 teaspoons chopped thyme
- 1 teaspoon garlic powder
- ¼ cup light brown sugar
- 1 tablespoon soy sauce
- 1 tablespoon dark rum
- 2 tablespoons water
- Salt and freshly ground black pepper
- Four 2-pound Cornish game hens

1. In a blender, puree the chiles with the scallions, thyme, garlic powder, brown sugar, soy, rum and water. Season with 1 tablespoon of salt and ½ teaspoon of pepper.

2. Using kitchen scissors, cut out the backbone of each hen. Press down on the breasts to flatten the hens. Set them in a baking dish and coat them all over with the jerk paste. Cover and refrigerate overnight.

3. Preheat the oven to 300°. Set the hens on 2 large rimmed baking sheets and bake for 45 minutes, until firm but not browned or cooked through.

4. Meanwhile, light a grill. Grill the hens over moderately high heat, turning occasionally, until cooked through and lightly charred in spots, about 20 minutes. Transfer to a platter and let rest for 10 minutes before serving. —*Bradford Thompson*
WINE Dry, fruity sparkling wine.

Roast Squabs with Bacon and Grapes

ACTIVE: 35 MIN; TOTAL: 1 HR
8 SERVINGS

- 1 stick unsalted butter, softened
- 2 tablespoons juniper berries, crushed

Salt and freshly ground pepper
Vegetable oil, for frying

- 8 squabs
- 8 slices of bacon, halved
- 3 cups red or green seedless grapes

1. Preheat the oven to 450°. In a small bowl, blend the butter with the juniper berries and season with salt and pepper.

2. In a skillet, heat ¼ inch of oil until shimmering. Season the squabs with salt and pepper. Add 4 of the squabs, breast side down, and cook over moderately high heat, turning a few times, until richly browned all over, 12 minutes. Repeat with the remaining squabs, adding more oil as needed.

3. Arrange the squabs breast side up on a large rimmed baking sheet. Rub the cavities with the juniper butter. Arrange 2 bacon halves on each squab breast. Scatter the

grapes around the squab and roast in the upper third of the oven for about 15 minutes, until an instant-read thermometer inserted in the thickest part of the legs registers 125° for medium-rare. Transfer to a carving board and let rest for about 5 minutes.

4. Cut each squab in half through the breast bone. Transfer to plates. Spoon the grapes and roasting juices on top and serve.
—*Florence Daniel Marzotto*
WINE Bright, tart Barbera.

Apricot-Glazed Turkey with Fresh Herb Gravy

ACTIVE: 30 MIN; TOTAL: 4 HR
12 SERVINGS ● ●
TURKEY

One 16-pound fresh turkey
- 1 tablespoon canola oil

Salt and freshly ground pepper
- 1 lemon, halved
- 6 garlic cloves, crushed
- 6 large thyme springs
- 4 large rosemary sprigs
- 4 large sage sprigs
- 1 fresh bay leaf

GLAZE
- ¾ cup apricot jam
- 1½ tablespoons fresh lemon juice
- 2 teaspoons grated lemon zest
- 1½ tablespoons minced sage

Salt and freshly ground pepper
GRAVY
- 3 cups turkey stock, chicken stock or low-sodium broth
- 4 tablespoons unsalted butter
- ¼ cup all-purpose flour
- 2 tablespoons chopped parsley
- 1 tablespoon minced sage
- 1 teaspoon chopped thyme

Salt and freshly ground pepper

1. MAKE THE TURKEY: Preheat the oven to 350°. Remove the turkey from the refrigerator at least 30 minutes before roasting. Pat the turkey dry and set it on a V-shaped rack in a large roasting pan. Rub the turkey all over with the canola oil and season it

inside and out with salt and pepper. Stuff the cavity with the lemon halves, crushed garlic, thyme, rosemary, sage and bay leaf. Roast the turkey for about 2½ hours, until the skin is golden all over and an instant-read thermometer inserted between the leg and thigh registers 165°.

2. MEANWHILE, MAKE THE GLAZE: In a bowl, mix together the jam, lemon juice, lemon zest and sage; season with salt and pepper. Microwave until thinned slightly, about 20 seconds.

3. Brush the turkey with half of the glaze and roast for about 15 minutes, until the skin is mahogany-colored. Brush the turkey with the remaining glaze and roast for about 15 minutes longer, until the skin is deep mahogany and an instant-read thermometer inserted between the leg and thigh registers 175°. Tilt the turkey to drain all the juices from the cavity into the roasting pan. Transfer the turkey to a carving board and let rest for 45 minutes.

4. MAKE THE GRAVY: Skim the fat from the drippings in the roasting pan (alternatively, carefully pour the juices into a heat-proof gravy separator and pour the skimmed juices back into the pan). Set the roasting pan over high heat and bring the liquid to a boil. Pour in the turkey stock and cook for 2 minutes, using a wooden spoon to scrape up the browned bits from the bottom of the pan.

5. In a medium saucepan, melt the butter. Add the flour and cook over moderate heat until smooth, about 2 minutes. Strain 3½ cups of the liquid in the roasting pan into the saucepan and whisk to blend. Bring the gravy to a simmer and cook over moderately low heat, whisking occasionally, until slightly thickened, about 5 minutes. Stir in the parsley, sage and thyme and season with salt and pepper. Pour the gravy into a small pitcher. Carve the turkey and serve with the gravy.
—*Melissa Rubel*
WINE Light, crisp white Burgundy.

CITRUS-MARINATED TURKEY

Citrus-Marinated Turkey

ACTIVE: 1 HR 30 MIN; TOTAL: 5 HR
PLUS 2 DAYS BRINING AND
MARINATING

12 SERVINGS ●

Chef Jose Garces (of Amada, Tinto and Distrito restaurants in Philadelphia, and Mercat a la Planxa in Chicago) uses turkey instead of pork in his riff on *cochinita pibil*. In the traditional Yucatán dish, slow-roasted pork marinates in citrus and annatto paste (a condiment made from achiote seeds that adds an orange hue to foods). Here, Garces brines and marinates turkey to make the meat especially succulent.

BRINE

- 1 gallon water
- 2 cups apple cider
- 2 cups kosher salt
- 2 cups sugar
- One 15-pound fresh turkey, giblets and neck reserved, liver discarded

MARINADE

- 10 roasted garlic cloves (see Note)
- 10 raw garlic cloves
- 1¾ cups plus 3 tablespoons vegetable oil
- ¾ cup fresh orange juice
- ¼ cup cider vinegar
- ¼ cup kosher salt
- 3 tablespoons fresh lime juice
- 3 tablespoons dried oregano
- 3 chipotles in adobo
- 2 tablespoons annatto paste (see Note)
- 1 tablespoon ground cumin
- 1 teaspoon ground allspice

TURKEY

- 9 cups chicken or turkey stock or low-sodium chicken broth
- 3 tablespoons canola oil
- 3 shallots, coarsely chopped
- 2 carrots, coarsely chopped
- 2 celery ribs, coarsely chopped
- 1 onion, coarsely chopped
- 10 roasted garlic cloves (see Note)
- 8 black peppercorns
- 2 tablespoons unsalted butter
- 2 tablespoons all-purpose flour
- Salt and freshly ground pepper

1. BRINE THE TURKEY: In a very large bowl, stir the water, apple cider, kosher salt and sugar until the salt and sugar are dissolved. Line a large stockpot with a large, sturdy doubled plastic bag. Put the turkey in the bag, neck first. Pour in the brine and seal the bag, pressing out as much air as possible. Brine the turkey in the refrigerator for 24 hours.

2. MARINATE THE TURKEY: Remove the turkey from the brine and discard the brine. Pat the turkey dry and transfer to a large rimmed baking sheet. In a blender, combine the roasted garlic with the 10 raw garlic cloves, the vegetable oil, orange juice, cider vinegar, kosher salt, lime juice, oregano, chipotles, annatto paste, cumin and allspice. Puree until smooth. Slather the turkey inside and out with the marinade, cover and refrigerate the coated turkey for 24 hours.

3. COOK THE TURKEY: Preheat the oven to 325°. Lift the turkey out of the marinade and set on a rack in a roasting pan. Brush the breast with some of the marinade. Pour 1½ cups of the stock into the bottom of the pan and cover the turkey very loosely with foil. Roast the turkey for 2 hours. Remove the foil and add another 1½ cups of the stock to the pan. Continue roasting for about 2½ hours longer, until an instant-read thermometer inserted in the thickest part of the thigh registers 175°.

4. Meanwhile, in a large saucepan, heat the canola oil. Add the turkey giblets and neck and cook over moderate heat, stirring occasionally, until browned. Transfer the giblets and neck to a plate. Add the chopped shallots, carrots, celery and onion to the pan and cook, stirring occasionally, until the vegetables are softened, about 5 minutes. Return the turkey parts to the saucepan. Stir in the roasted garlic and black peppercorns, add the remaining 6 cups of stock and bring to a boil over moderate heat. Simmer over low heat until the stock is reduced to 4 cups, about 1½ hours. Strain the enriched stock into a heatproof bowl and discard the solids.

5. Transfer the roast turkey to a cutting board and remove the roasting rack from the pan. Pour the pan juices into a bowl and skim off the fat, reserving 2 tablespoons of the skimmed fat (alternatively, you can use a gravy separator). Transfer the reserved fat to a medium saucepan. Add the butter and flour to the pan and cook over high heat, whisking constantly, until the mixture is golden brown, about 2 minutes. Add the enriched stock and bring to a boil. Simmer over moderate heat until the gravy is reduced to 3 cups, about 10 minutes.

6. Place the roasting pan over 1 burner on high heat. Add the strained, defatted pan drippings (there should be about 1 cup) and use a wooden spoon to scrape up any bits stuck to the bottom of the pan. Strain the pan drippings into the gravy and season with salt and pepper; keep warm.

7. Carve the turkey and transfer the slices to a large serving platter. Serve the carved turkey right away, with the warm gravy.
—*Jose Garces*

NOTE To roast the garlic for this recipe, place 20 unpeeled cloves in a small baking dish and drizzle them with 2 tablespoons of canola oil. Cover the baking dish with foil and roast the garlic at 375° for about 40 minutes, until the cloves are tender and caramelized. Let the garlic cool, then squeeze the cloves from their skins. Jose Garces likes using El Yucateco brand achiote annatto paste. It's available at elyucateco.com.

WINE Earthy, medium-bodied Tempranillo.

● HEALTHY ●MAKE AHEAD ●VEGETARIAN ●STAFF FAVORITE

poultry

Grilled Butterflied Turkey with Caraway-Ancho Gravy

ACTIVE: 30 MIN; TOTAL: 3 HR

12 SERVINGS ●

- 2 cups smoking chips, preferably applewood
- 1 tablespoon pure ancho chile powder
- 1½ teaspoons caraway seeds
- 1½ teaspoons dried onion flakes

Kosher salt and freshly ground pepper

- 1 stick unsalted butter, softened

One 15-pound fresh turkey, butterflied (see Note)

- 3 tablespoons all-purpose flour
- 2 cups turkey stock

1. Preheat the grill to low heat. Using heavy-duty aluminum foil, make two 1-cup packets of smoke chips. Poke holes in one side of each packet to create vents.

2. In a spice grinder, combine the ancho powder, caraway seeds and dried onion with 1½ teaspoons of kosher salt and ½ teaspoon of ground pepper and pulse until finely ground. Transfer to a small bowl and stir in the butter. Reserve 3 tablespoons of the seasoned butter for the gravy.

3. Starting from the neck end of the turkey, carefully slip your hands between the skin and flesh. Slip your hands as far down the legs as possible. Rub half of the remaining butter under the skin and place the bird skin side up in 3 stacked sturdy disposable roasting pans. Rub some of the remaining butter over the skin.

4. Place one of the chip packets directly on the heat source and replace the grate. Set the roasting pans on the grate. Cover and grill the turkey for 1 hour, basting occasionally with the remaining butter.

5. Place the second chip packet on the grill. Using 2 pairs of tongs, carefully transfer the turkey to the grill, skin side up. Turn off one of the burners and grill over low heat, turning twice, until an instant-read thermometer inserted in the thigh registers 175°, about 1½ hours longer.

6. Pour the pan juices into a heatproof measuring cup; skim off the fat (there should be 1 cup of juices). In a saucepan, melt the reserved 3 tablespoons of seasoned butter. Whisk in the flour, then whisk over moderate heat for 2 minutes. Whisk in the stock and pan juices and bring to a boil; simmer over moderate heat until thickened.

7. Carve the turkey and serve with the caraway-ancho gravy. —*Grace Parisi*

NOTE Ask your butcher to remove the backbone and crack the breastbone so the turkey will lie flat on the grill.

MAKE AHEAD The seasoned butter can be frozen for up to 1 week.

WINE Intense, fruity Zinfandel.

Roast Duck with Citrus Pan Sauce

ACTIVE: 20 MIN; TOTAL: 3 HR

4 SERVINGS

One 5½-pound Pekin or Long Island duck, neck reserved

Salt and freshly ground black pepper

- 1 navel orange—one half cut into wedges, one half juiced
- 1 lemon—one half cut into wedges, one half juiced
- 2 cups water
- 2 tablespoons coriander seeds
- ½ teaspoon soy sauce
- ½ tablespoon unsalted butter, softened
- 1 tablespoon all-purpose flour

1. Preheat the oven to 325°. Prick the duck all over with a sharp knife. Season the cavity with salt and pepper and stuff it with the orange and lemon wedges.

2. In a medium roasting pan, combine the water, coriander seeds and duck neck. Place the duck on a rack, season with salt and pepper, set it in the roasting pan and cover with foil. Bring the water to a boil over high heat. Transfer the duck to the oven and roast for 1 hour, until most of the fat has been rendered.

3. Transfer the duck to a work surface. Increase the oven temperature to 350°. Strain the pan juices into a medium bowl and skim off the fat. Return the duck to the roasting pan and prick it all over a second time. Roast uncovered for 1 hour.

4. Increase the oven temperature to 400°. Tip any juices from the cavity into the roasting pan and transfer the duck to a large rimmed baking sheet. Roast the duck for 45 minutes longer, until the meat is very tender and the skin is crisp.

5. Meanwhile, set the roasting pan over moderately high heat. Add the orange and lemon juices and boil for 1 minute. Add the reserved pan juices and the soy sauce and boil for 1 minute longer. Pour the liquid into a small saucepan and bring to a simmer over moderate heat.

6. In a medium bowl, make a paste with the butter and flour. Whisk in ¼ cup of the hot liquid until smooth, then scrape the mixture back into the saucepan. Simmer over low heat, whisking, until the sauce has thickened, about 2 minutes. Season with salt and pepper.

7. Transfer the duck to a board and let rest for 10 minutes. Carve the duck and serve with the citrus sauce. —*Marcia Kiesel*

WINE Firm, complex Cabernet Sauvignon.

Cumin-Scented Duck Breasts with Peach Succotash

TOTAL: 1 HR

4 SERVINGS ●

- 1 tablespoon cumin seeds

Four 8-ounce White Pekin duck breasts

Salt and freshly ground pepper

- 2 ears of corn (unshucked)
- 1 large red bell pepper
- 4 tablespoons unsalted butter
- 2 large peaches—halved, pitted and cut into ½-inch dice
- 2 tablespoons water
- 2 tablespoons canola oil

Cilantro sprigs, for garnish

1. In a skillet, toast the cumin seeds over high heat just until fragrant, about 1 minute. Transfer to a spice grinder and let cool completely. Coarsely grind the seeds.

2. Using a sharp paring knife, score the skin of the duck breasts in a shallow crosshatch pattern, spacing the cuts about ½ inch apart. Rub the duck breasts all over with the cumin and season with salt and pepper. Let the spice-rubbed duck stand at room temperature for 30 minutes.

3. Meanwhile, preheat the broiler. Arrange the corn and bell pepper on a rimmed baking sheet and broil 8 inches from the heat, turning, until charred, 8 minutes. Transfer the bell pepper to a bowl, cover with plastic wrap and let steam for 10 minutes.

4. Shuck the corn. Using a serrated knife, cut the kernels from the cobs. Peel, core and finely chop the bell pepper.

5. In a large saucepan, melt the butter. Add the corn, bell pepper, peaches and water and season with salt and pepper. Cook over high heat, stirring, until the peaches are just softened, about 5 minutes.

6. In a large skillet, heat the canola oil. Add the duck breasts skin side down and cook over low heat until the skin is deeply browned, about 15 minutes; spoon off the fat as it accumulates in the pan. Turn the duck breasts over and cook for 8 minutes longer for medium. Transfer to a cutting board and let rest for 5 minutes.

7. Thinly slice the duck breasts crosswise and arrange the slices on plates. Spoon the peach succotash alongside, garnish with the cilantro sprigs and serve.

—*Stuart Brioza*

WINE Complex, aromatic Chenin Blanc.

Honey-Glazed Duck with Savoy Cabbage

TOTAL: 50 MIN

6 SERVINGS

- ¼ cup grapeseed oil
- 1 tablespoon very finely chopped fresh ginger
- 2 garlic cloves, minced
- One 2-pound Savoy cabbage, cored and cut into 1-inch pieces
- 2 tablespoons chicken stock or low-sodium broth
- Salt and freshly ground pepper
- ¼ cup snipped chives
- 1 cup fresh orange juice
- ¼ cup honey
- 1 thyme sprig
- ½ teaspoon coriander seeds
- One 2-inch cinnamon stick
- Six 7-ounce White Pekin duck breasts

1. Preheat the oven to 400°. In a large, deep skillet, heat the oil. Add the ginger and garlic and cook over low heat just until fragrant, about 1 minute. Add the cabbage and cook over low heat, tossing, until wilted, about 5 minutes. Add the stock and season with salt and pepper. Cover and cook the cabbage until tender, about 10 minutes. Stir in the chives.

2. Meanwhile, in a small saucepan, combine the orange juice, honey, thyme, coriander seeds and cinnamon stick and bring to a boil. Simmer over moderate heat, stirring occasionally, until reduced to a glaze, about 10 minutes; strain.

3. Heat a large ovenproof skillet. Using a sharp knife, score the duck skin in a crosshatch pattern and season with salt and pepper. Add the duck to the skillet, skin side down, and cook over low heat until the skin is golden, about 20 minutes. Spoon off the fat as it accumulates in the pan. Turn the duck over and brush the skin with the glaze. Transfer the skillet to the oven and roast the duck for about 6 minutes, until an instant-read thermometer inserted in the thickest part of a breast registers 135°. Let the duck rest for 5 minutes, then transfer to plates. Rewarm the cabbage and serve it alongside the duck.

—*David Bouley*

MAKE AHEAD The glaze can be made up to 4 hours ahead.

WINE Ripe, juicy Pinot Noir.

Duck with Miso-Almond Butter

TOTAL: 50 MIN PLUS OVERNIGHT MARINATING

4 SERVINGS ● ●

- 1 garlic clove, minced
- 3 tablespoons white miso paste
- 3 tablespoons extra-virgin olive oil
- 2 Moulard duck breasts (1½ pounds total), fat trimmed and skin scored in a crosshatch pattern
- 1 cup plus 2 tablespoons marcona almonds (see Note on p. 47)
- ¼ cup plus 1 tablespoon water
- 1 tablespoon honey
- ¼ teaspoon *sambal oelek*
- Kosher salt

1. In a bowl, mix the garlic and 1 tablespoon each of the miso and the oil. Set the duck in a glass baking dish and rub all over with the miso mixture; refrigerate overnight.

2. In a blender, process 1 cup of the almonds, the water, honey, *sambal oelek,* 2 tablespoons of the oil and the remaining 2 tablespoons of miso until smooth. Press the miso butter through a strainer into a small bowl.

3. Preheat the oven to 450°. Rinse the marinade off the duck; pat dry. Lightly season the skin with salt. Heat a large ovenproof skillet. Add the duck skin side down and cook over high heat until some fat is rendered, about 1 minute. Reduce the heat to moderate and cook until the skin is golden, about 7 minutes. Transfer the skillet to the oven and roast for about 10 minutes, until the duck is slightly firm to the touch and the meat is medium. Transfer to a cutting board and let rest for 10 minutes.

4. Coarsely chop the remaining 2 tablespoons of almonds. Spoon the miso-almond butter onto plates. Thinly slice the duck breasts crosswise and arrange the slices on the almond butter. Garnish with the chopped almonds and serve.

—*Stephanie Izard*

SERVE WITH Blanched baby bok choy.

WINE Rich Alsace Gewürztraminer.

HONEY-TAMARIND
BABY BACK RIBS (P. 129)

pork & veal

66 *Whatever you cook on the bone always stays nice.* 99

—JEAN-GEORGES VONGERICHTEN,
INTERNATIONAL CHEF AND RESTAURATEUR

CITRUS-MARINATED PORK RIB ROAST

HARISSA-CRUSTED PORK CROWN ROAST

Garlic-and-Spice-Rubbed Pork Loin Roast

ACTIVE: 20 MIN; TOTAL: 2 HR 15 MIN

10 SERVINGS

- 6 large garlic cloves, coarsely chopped
- 2 tablespoons coarsely chopped rosemary
- 1 tablespoon whole fennel seeds
- 1 teaspoon ground fennel
- 2 teaspoons crushed red pepper
- 2 teaspoons freshly ground black pepper
- ¼ cup extra-virgin olive oil

One 10-rib pork loin roast (5½ pounds)—chine bone removed, fat trimmed to ¼ inch, rib bones frenched (see Note)

Salt

1. Preheat the oven to 400°. In a mini processor, combine the garlic with the rosemary, fennel seeds, ground fennel, crushed red pepper, black pepper and oil and process to a paste. Set the pork on a large rimmed baking sheet and cut shallow score marks all over the fat. Spread 1 tablespoon of the garlic paste on the underside of the roast; spread the remaining paste all over the scored fat and meaty parts of the roast. Season all over with salt.

2. Roast the pork, fat side up, for 1 hour. Reduce the oven temperature to 325° and continue roasting for about 35 minutes, or until an instant-read thermometer inserted into the thickest part of the meat registers 150°. Transfer the roast to a carving board and let rest for 15 minutes. Carve the roast into chops and serve. —*Ryan Hardy*

NOTE Have your butcher french (remove the meat from) the rib bones for you.

WINE Juicy, spicy Grenache.

Citrus-Marinated Pork Rib Roast

ACTIVE: 45 MIN; TOTAL: 2 HR 30 MIN

PLUS OVERNIGHT MARINATING

10 SERVINGS ●

Two 5-bone pork rib roasts (about 4 pounds each)

- 6 garlic cloves
- 6 whole cloves
- 3 lemons, zest removed in strips and lemons juiced
- 3 oranges, zest removed in strips and oranges juiced
- 20 fresh bay leaves
- 8 rosemary sprigs
- 2 tablespoons fennel seeds, chopped
- 1 tablespoon juniper berries, coarsely chopped
- ½ cup extra-virgin olive oil

Salt and freshly ground pepper

Roasted small apples and pears (see Note), for garnish

1. Using a paring knife, make three 1-inch-deep slits on the fatty side of each pork rib roast closest to the bones. Stud the garlic cloves with the whole cloves and stuff them into the slits.

2. In a baking dish, combine the lemon and orange zests and juices with the bay leaves, rosemary sprigs, fennel seeds, juniper berries and ¼ cup of the olive oil. Add the pork and turn to coat. Cover and refrigerate overnight, turning occasionally. Bring the pork rib roasts to room temperature before roasting.

3. Preheat the oven to 350°. Scrape off the marinade and generously season the pork with salt and pepper. In a very large skillet, heat the remaining ¼ cup of olive oil. Add the pork and brown over moderate heat, turning occasionally, about 15 minutes.

4. Transfer the pork rib roasts to a large roasting pan. Roast for about 1 hour and 20 minutes, rotating the pan once or twice, until an instant-read thermometer inserted into the thickest part of the meat registers 140°. Transfer the pork to a cutting board and let rest for 20 minutes. Cut the pork between the rib bones into 10 chops. Transfer to plates, garnish with the apples and pears and serve. —*Fabio Trabocchi*

NOTE Score the apples to prevent the skin from splitting. Roast the fruit at 350° for about 1 hour, until tender.

WINE Complex, aromatic Nebbiolo.

Harissa-Crusted Pork Crown Roast

ACTIVE: 1 HR; TOTAL: 3 HR 45 MIN
12 SERVINGS ●

One 8½-pound crown roast pork, tied, bones frenched

7 dried New Mexico or pasilla chiles (1½ ounces), stemmed and seeded

2 dried ancho chiles (½ ounce), stemmed and seeded

5 large garlic cloves, 4 cloves thinly sliced

¾ cup extra-virgin olive oil

Kosher salt

1½ teaspoons ground coriander

½ teaspoon caraway seeds

One 1¼-pound loaf seeded rye bread, cut into 1-inch cubes

8 scallions, sliced crosswise into thirds and thinly sliced lengthwise

16 dried Turkish apricots (5½ ounces), quartered

3 tablespoons golden raisins

1½ cups low-sodium chicken broth

Freshly ground pepper

1. Remove the pork from the refrigerator 1 hour ahead. Preheat the oven to 350°. In a bowl, cover the chiles with hot water. Let stand until softened, 15 minutes.

2. Transfer the chiles and ½ cup of their soaking liquid to a blender. Add the whole garlic clove, 6 tablespoons of the olive oil, 2½ teaspoons of salt and the coriander and caraway. Blend until smooth. Transfer the *harissa* to a small bowl.

3. Spread the rye bread on a large rimmed baking sheet and toast in the oven for 12 minutes, until the edges begin to brown. Transfer to a bowl. In a large skillet, heat the remaining 6 tablespoons of oil. Add the scallions and the sliced garlic and cook over moderately high heat until the garlic is lightly golden, about 4 minutes. Add the mixture to the bread and toss; add the apricots, raisins and broth, season with salt and pepper and toss again. Transfer to an 8½-by-11-inch baking dish and cover with foil.

4. Increase the oven temperature to 425°. Line a baking sheet with foil. Place the pork on the baking sheet and season generously inside and out with salt and pepper. Roast the pork for 30 minutes, or until the outside begins to brown. Spread 1 cup of the *harissa* all over the roast. Reduce the oven temperature to 350° and cook for 1 hour and 15 minutes longer, or until an instant-read thermometer inserted in the thickest part of the roast reaches 145°. Remove

from the oven and let the roast rest on the baking sheet for 15 minutes.

5. Meanwhile, bake the dressing in the oven for 15 minutes, until warmed through.

6. Preheat the broiler. Transfer the roast to a cutting board. Drizzle any pork juices from the baking sheet over the dressing. Broil until crisp on top, about 2 minutes.

7. Slice the pork between the ribs and serve with the dressing. Drizzle with any juices left on the cutting board. Pass the remaining *harissa* at the table.
—*Melissa Rubel*

WINE Intense, fruity Zinfandel.

Bacon-Crusted Pork Loin Roasts

ACTIVE: 20 MIN; TOTAL: 1 HR 45 MIN
PLUS OVERNIGHT MARINATING
10 TO 12 SERVINGS ●

12 ounces sliced bacon, chopped

3 tablespoons yellow mustard seeds

2 tablespoons caraway seeds

2 tablespoons vegetable oil

2 teaspoons ground ginger

Two 4-rib bone-in pork loin roasts (3½ pounds each)—chine bones removed

Salt and freshly ground black pepper

1. In a food processor, combine the bacon, mustard seeds, caraway seeds, vegetable oil and ground ginger and process to a paste. Set the pork loin roasts on a large rimmed baking sheet. Spread the bacon paste over the meaty side of the roasts and refrigerate overnight.

2. Preheat the oven to 400°. Bring the roasts to room temperature and season all over with salt and pepper. Set the pork in a roasting pan, fat side up. Roast in the upper third of the oven for about 1 hour and 15 minutes, until an instant-read thermometer inserted in the thickest part of the roasts registers 150°. Transfer to a carving board and let rest for 10 minutes. Carve and serve. —*Marcia Kiesel*

WINE Intense, fruity Zinfandel.

Pork Rib Roast with Balsamic Onion Marmalade

ACTIVE: 45 MIN; TOTAL: 2 HR 45 MIN
PLUS 24 HR MARINATING

4 SERVINGS

- 1 tablespoon crushed red pepper
- 1½ teaspoons black peppercorns
- 1½ teaspoons juniper berries
- 1½ teaspoons allspice berries
- 3 bay leaves
- 8 cups water
- 1 tablespoon ground cumin
- 1 tablespoon soy sauce
- 1 small onion, halved, plus 4 medium onions, halved and thinly sliced
- 2 garlic cloves, crushed
- 2 thyme sprigs

One 3¼-pound bone-in center-cut pork roast (about 4 ribs), cut through the chine bone

- 1 tablespoon vegetable oil

Pinch of ground cloves

Kosher salt and freshly ground black pepper

- ¼ cup dark brown sugar
- ⅔ cup balsamic vinegar
- 1½ teaspoons orange zest

1. In a mortar, combine the crushed red pepper with the peppercorns, juniper berries, allspice berries and bay leaves; crush the seasonings together with a pestle. Transfer the spices to a large pot and add the water, cumin, soy sauce, halved small onion, crushed garlic and thyme sprigs. Submerge the pork roast in the brine, meat side down. Cover and refrigerate for 24 hours, turning the roast over once.

2. Meanwhile, in a medium skillet, heat the vegetable oil. Add the sliced onions and cook over moderate heat until softened, about 20 minutes. Season with the ground cloves and salt and black pepper. Add the brown sugar and cook over moderately low heat, stirring, until the skillet is dry, about 10 minutes. Add the balsamic vinegar and orange zest and cook over moderately low heat, stirring occasionally, until the marmalade is very thick, 30 minutes. Transfer the marmalade to a bowl, cover and refrigerate.

3. Remove the pork roast from the marinade 1 hour before cooking and let stand at room temperature. Pat the pork roast dry with paper towels and wipe off any spices sticking to it. Season the pork with salt and place it on a rack in a roasting pan.

4. Preheat the oven to 450°. Cook the pork roast for 15 minutes, then reduce the oven temperature to 375° and cook it for about 1 hour and 10 minutes longer, until an instant-read thermometer inserted in the thickest part of the pork roast registers 140°. Transfer the roast to a carving board and let rest for 15 minutes. Carve the roast between the bones into chops. Transfer the chops to plates and serve right away, with the onion marmalade.

—*Thomas Odermatt*

WINE Dry, rich Champagne.

Juniper-Brined Double-Cut Pork Chops

ACTIVE: 30 MIN; TOTAL: 1 HR 15 MIN
PLUS 2 HR 30 MIN BRINING

8 SERVINGS ● ●

- 1 gallon cold water
- ½ cup kosher salt
- ¼ cup sugar
- 2 bay leaves
- 2 tablespoons cracked black peppercorns
- 8 juniper berries, lightly crushed with the side of a knife

Zest from ½ orange, removed in strips with a vegetable peeler

- 2 rosemary sprigs
- 4 bone-in double-cut pork rib chops (about 1½ pounds each)
- 2 tablespoons extra-virgin olive oil

1. In a large stockpot, bring 4 cups of the cold water to a boil. Remove the pot from the heat and stir in the kosher salt, sugar, bay leaves, black peppercorns, juniper berries, orange zest and one of the rosemary sprigs until the salt and sugar dissolve. Add the remaining 12 cups of cold water and let the brine cool to room temperature. Add the pork chops and let stand at room temperature for 2½ hours. Drain the pork chops. Pick off the spices and pat the chops dry.

2. Preheat the oven to 350°. Heat a large ovenproof skillet until very hot. Add the olive oil, and when it shimmers, add the brined pork chops. Cook the chops over high heat, turning them occasionally, until they are crusty and brown on both sides, about 10 minutes.

3. Stand the pork chops upright in the skillet and add the remaining rosemary sprig. Transfer the skillet to the oven and roast the chops for about 35 minutes, until an instant-read thermometer inserted near the bone registers 140°. Transfer the chops to a cutting board and let them rest for about 10 minutes; reserve the drippings in the skillet.

4. Using a boning knife, cut the pork chops between the bones, then run the blade along the bones to separate the meat. Transfer to plates, spoon the pan drippings over the meat and serve right away.

—*Jessica and Joshua Applestone*

SERVE WITH Roasted potatoes.

WINE Deep, velvety Merlot.

Spice-Roasted Ribs with Apricot Glaze

ACTIVE: 30 MIN; TOTAL: 3 HR

6 SERVINGS

F&W Senior Test Kitchen Associate Grace Parisi uses sweet pimentón de la Vera (Spanish smoked paprika) to sneak a just-barbecued flavor into these sticky baby back ribs, which are among the more affordable cuts of pork.

1 teaspoon caraway seeds

2 tablespoons sweet pimentón de la Vera (smoked Spanish paprika)

1 tablespoon ground cumin

1 teaspoon garlic powder

2 tablespoons kosher salt

2 teaspoons freshly ground pepper

½ cup apricot preserves

1 tablespoon Dijon mustard

3 racks baby back ribs (7 pounds)

1. Preheat the oven to 300°. In a spice grinder, pulse the caraway seeds to a coarse powder. Add the pimentón, cumin, garlic powder, salt and pepper and pulse to blend. Transfer 2 tablespoons of the spice mixture to a small saucepan and stir in the apricot preserves and mustard.

2. Using a kitchen towel, grasp and pull off the papery membrane from the underside of each rack of ribs. Place the ribs side by side in a large roasting pan and rub both sides with the remaining spice mixture. Cover tightly with foil and roast for 1½ hours, or until the meat is almost tender.

3. Pour the pan juices into the saucepan with the apricot preserves. Cover the ribs again and roast for about 30 minutes longer, until very tender. Pour any remaining pan juices into the saucepan.

4. Preheat the broiler. Bring the pan juices and apricot preserves to a boil and simmer over moderate heat until slightly thickened, about 10 minutes.

5. Arrange the ribs concave side up; brush them with half of the glaze, allowing it to pool in the center of the rack. Broil 10 inches from the heat until browned, 10 minutes. Turn the racks, brush with the remaining glaze and broil until caramelized, about 10 minutes. Transfer the rack to a cutting board and cut into ribs. —*Grace Parisi*

MAKE AHEAD The ribs can be prepared through Step 3 and refrigerated overnight. Rewarm in a 325° oven before glazing.

WINE Intense, fruity Zinfandel.

JUNIPER-BRINED DOUBLE-CUT PORK CHOPS

SPICE-ROASTED RIBS WITH APRICOT GLAZE

pork & veal

Cider-Brined Double-Cut Pork Chops

TOTAL: 50 MIN PLUS OVERNIGHT BRINING

4 SERVINGS

- 5 cups apple cider
- ¼ cup light brown sugar
- Kosher salt
- 4 bone-in double-cut pork chops (about 1 pound each)
- ¾ cup yellow mustard
- ¼ cup whole-grain mustard
- ¼ cup dark brown sugar
- ⅓ cup apple cider vinegar
- ¼ cup water
- 2 teaspoons Worcestershire sauce
- 1 garlic clove, minced
- 2 tablespoons unsalted butter
- Tabasco
- Freshly ground pepper

1. In a medium bowl, whisk the apple cider with the light brown sugar and ¼ cup of kosher salt until the salt and sugar are dissolved. Pour the brine into a large plastic bag. Add the pork chops, seal and refrigerate overnight.

2. Light a grill. In a small saucepan, combine the yellow and whole-grain mustards with the dark brown sugar, cider vinegar, water, Worcestershire sauce and garlic. Simmer over moderate heat, stirring occasionally, until thickened, about 10 minutes. Stir in the butter and season with Tabasco and salt and pepper. Keep warm.

3. Remove the chops from the brine and pat dry with paper towels. Season the chops with salt and pepper. Grill over high heat until the pork is nicely browned, about 5 minutes per side. Reduce the heat to moderate or, if using a charcoal grill, move the coals to one side and transfer the pork chops so they're opposite the coals. Continue cooking the chops until an instant-read thermometer inserted in the thickest part of the chops registers 145° for medium-well, 10 to 15 minutes. Let rest 5 minutes, then serve with the sauce. —*Nick Fauchald*

MAKE AHEAD The mustard sauce can be refrigerated for up to 2 days. Reheat the sauce gently before serving.

WINE Tart, citrusy Riesling.

Vietnamese Glazed Skinny Pork Chops

TOTAL: 30 MIN PLUS OVERNIGHT MARINATING

4 SERVINGS ●

"I love the way the Vietnamese grill pork chops," says F&W's Marcia Kiesel, who co-authored *The Simple Art of Vietnamese Cooking* with chef Binh Duong. "They pound the chops thin for maximum exposure to the heat and then marinate them in a sweet-and-salty sauce that caramelizes as quickly as the pork chops cook on the grill."

- 2 tablespoons vegetable oil
- ¼ cup honey
- ¼ cup Asian fish sauce
- 4 garlic cloves, minced
- 2 medium shallots, very finely chopped
- 2 teaspoons freshly ground pepper
- 8 thin center-cut pork loin chops on the bone (about 6 ounces each)
- Salt
- ¼ cup chopped salted peanuts
- Jasmine Rice with Carrot Relish (p. 259), for serving

1. In a large bowl, combine the vegetable oil with the honey, fish sauce, garlic, shallots and pepper. Add the pork chops, turn to coat thoroughly with the marinade and refrigerate overnight.

2. Light a grill. Lightly season the pork chops with salt. Brush the grill with oil and cook the pork chops over very high heat until nicely charred and just cooked through, about 3 minutes per side. Scatter the peanuts on top and serve right away, with Jasmine Rice with Carrot Relish. —*Marcia Kiesel*

WINE Full-bodied, minerally Riesling.

Asian Glazed Baby Back Ribs

ACTIVE: 30 MIN; TOTAL: 1 HR 30 MIN

4 SERVINGS ● ●

- ¼ cup ground coriander
- ½ teaspoon Chinese five-spice powder
- Kosher salt
- 2 racks baby back ribs (about 4 pounds)
- ¼ cup cider vinegar
- 3 tablespoons Asian fish sauce
- ½ cup mango chutney
- ¼ cup Worcestershire sauce
- ¼ cup plus 2 tablespoons fresh lemon juice
- 1 tablespoon honey
- 1 teaspoon crushed red pepper
- ½ packed cup cilantro leaves
- ½ cup mayonnaise
- 2 tablespoons fresh lime juice
- 1 tablespoon water

1. Preheat the oven to 350°. In a small bowl, combine the coriander and five-spice powder with 1 tablespoon of kosher salt. Rub the spice mix on both sides of the ribs and transfer them to a large rimmed baking sheet. Add the cider vinegar and 2 tablespoons of the fish sauce to the baking sheet and cover with foil. Roast the ribs for about 1 hour, until just tender.

2. Meanwhile, in a blender, combine the mango chutney, Worcestershire sauce, lemon juice, honey, crushed red pepper and the remaining 1 tablespoon of fish sauce and puree until smooth. Transfer the chutney glaze to a bowl.

3. Rinse out the blender. Add the cilantro leaves, mayonnaise, lime juice and water and puree the cilantro sauce until smooth. Season the cilantro sauce with salt and transfer to a serving bowl.

4. Remove the ribs from the oven. Preheat the broiler and position a rack 8 inches from the heat source. Pour off any liquid on the baking sheet. Brush half of the chutney glaze on the ribs and broil for about 4 minutes, until they are sizzling and browned. Turn the racks and brush with the remaining glaze. Broil for 4 minutes longer, until browned. Transfer the racks to a cutting board and cut in between the bones. Serve the ribs, passing the cilantro sauce on the side. —*Ratha Chau*

MAKE AHEAD The ribs and cilantro sauce can be refrigerated overnight. Reheat the ribs before serving.

WINE Rustic, peppery Malbec.

Sticky Marmalade-Glazed Baby Back Ribs

 **TOTAL: 30 MIN**
4 SERVINGS ●

Using baby back ribs that are precut shortens the cooking time significantly. These ribs are tossed in a marinade with ground fennel and a touch of crushed red pepper, then coated in a marvelously sweet and sticky orange-marmalade glaze.

- 2 **racks baby back ribs (4¾ pounds), cut into individual ribs**
- 1 **tablespoon vegetable oil**
- 1½ **teaspoons ground fennel**
- ¾ **teaspoon crushed red pepper**
- **Kosher salt and freshly ground black pepper**
- 1 **cup orange marmalade**
- 1 **teaspoon minced rosemary**

1. Preheat the oven to 450°. In a large roasting pan, toss the ribs with the oil, fennel and crushed red pepper and season with salt and black pepper. Spread the ribs in an even layer and roast for about 20 minutes, until cooked through.

2. Meanwhile, in a small saucepan, warm the marmalade over moderate heat until it becomes pourable, about 1 minute.

3. Turn the broiler on. In a very large bowl, toss the ribs with the marmalade until well coated. Return the ribs to the roasting pan, meat side up, and scrape any marmalade left in the bowl over the ribs. Broil the ribs 6 inches from the heat for about 3 minutes,

basting twice with the juices, until golden all over and charred in spots. Sprinkle the ribs with the minced rosemary and transfer to plates. Spoon any juices from the roasting pan over the ribs and serve. —*Melissa Rubel*

WINE Intense, fruity Zinfandel.

Honey-Tamarind Baby Back Ribs

ACTIVE: 20 MIN; TOTAL: 3 HR
4 SERVINGS ●

Naturally tart tamarind keeps the honey-based barbecue sauce here from becoming too sweet for the luscious, slow-cooked ribs. Opt for dark, runny tamarind concentrate instead of tamarind pulp, which needs to be soaked and strained before using; it's available at Asian markets.

- 2 **racks baby back ribs (5¼ pounds)**
- **Kosher salt and freshly ground black pepper**
- ½ **cup clover honey or other mild honey**
- ¼ **cup ketchup**
- 2 **tablespoons soy sauce**
- 2 **teaspoons grated fresh ginger**
- 1½ **teaspoons tamarind concentrate**
- 2 **garlic cloves, coarsely chopped**
- ½ **teaspoon Asian chile paste, such as** *sambal oelek*

1. Preheat the oven to 275°. Line a rimmed baking sheet with foil. Put the ribs on the baking sheet and season on both sides with salt and black pepper. Bake the ribs, meaty side up, for 2½ hours, or until tender.

2. Meanwhile, in a food processor, blend the honey, ketchup, soy sauce, ginger, tamarind, garlic and chile paste until smooth.

3. Increase the oven temperature to 450°. Drain the fat from the baking sheet. Brush the ribs with the barbecue sauce. Roast the ribs, bony side up, for 10 minutes, until richly browned. Turn the ribs over, brush with more sauce and roast for 5 minutes, until browned.

Brush the ribs with the remaining barbecue sauce and roast for 5 minutes longer, until deeply browned and glossy. Transfer to a board and let stand 5 minutes. Cut the racks into ribs and serve. —*Susan Spungen*

VARIATION Grill the ribs over moderately low heat, turning and brushing frequently with the sauce, until cooked through.

SERVE WITH Asian coleslaw.

WINE Juicy, spicy Grenache.

Cream-and-Lemon-Braised Pork Shoulder

ACTIVE: 30 MIN; TOTAL: 4 HR 30 MIN
8 SERVINGS ●

- **One 7-pound bone-in pork picnic shoulder, with skin**
- 1 **head of garlic, halved crosswise**
- 2 **sage sprigs**
- 2 **cups heavy cream**
- 5 **cups water**
- 1 **lemon**
- **Salt and freshly ground pepper**
- 2 **tablespoons vegetable oil**

1. Preheat the oven to 300°. In an enameled cast-iron casserole, add the pork, garlic, sage, cream and water. Using a vegetable peeler, remove the zest from the lemon in strips. Add the zest to the casserole. Halve the lemon and squeeze in the juice. Season with salt and pepper; bring to a boil. Cover the casserole and braise the pork in the oven for 3 hours, until the meat is very tender.

2. Transfer the pork to a plate and pat dry. Strain the liquid into a heatproof bowl and skim off the fat. Return the liquid to the casserole and boil until reduced to 2 cups, 45 minutes. Season with salt and pepper.

3. Meanwhile, in a large, deep skillet, heat the oil. Carefully add the pork, skin side down, and cook over moderately high heat, turning, until the skin is crisp, 15 minutes; use 2 pairs of tongs to steady the pork. Transfer the pork to a cutting board, skin side up, and slice it ¼ inch thick. Serve with the gravy. —*Chris Mattera*

WINE Cherry-inflected, earthy Sangiovese.

PORK BRAISED IN
CHAMPAGNE VINEGAR

Pork Braised in Champagne Vinegar

ACTIVE: 45 MIN; TOTAL: 4 HR

4 SERVINGS ●●

One 3½-pound bone-in pork picnic
    shoulder, with skin
3 garlic cloves, thinly sliced
Salt and freshly ground pepper
¼ cup extra-virgin olive oil
2 cups thinly sliced shallots
1 teaspoon ground cumin
1 teaspoon ground coriander
1 teaspoon powdered mustard
¾ cup Champagne vinegar
2 cups dry sparkling wine
2 cups chicken stock
2 large sage sprigs
1 pound red grapes, stemmed
2 tablespoons unsalted butter
2 tablespoons chopped parsley
2 tablespoons snipped chives

1. Preheat the oven to 300°. Score the pork skin in a crosshatch pattern. Make deep slits all over the pork and insert a garlic slice into each. Season with salt and pepper.
2. In a large enameled cast-iron casserole, heat the oil. Add the pork and cook over moderate heat, turning, until browned, about 12 minutes. Transfer to a plate.
3. Add the shallots to the pot and cook over low heat, stirring, until lightly browned, 5 minutes. Stir in the cumin, coriander and mustard. Add the vinegar and scrape up any browned bits from the bottom of the pot. Add the wine, stock and sage and bring to a boil. Return the pork and accumulated juices to the pot. Cover and braise in the oven for 3 hours, or until the pork is very tender.
4. Transfer the pork to a platter and cover with foil. Set the pot over high heat and boil the liquid until slightly reduced and thickened, 10 minutes. Add the grapes and boil until they begin to soften, 8 minutes. Remove from the heat and whisk in the butter, parsley and chives. Slice the pork and serve with the sauce. —*David Page*
WINE Dry, rich Champagne.

Slow-Cooked Pork Shoulder with Cherry Tomatoes

ACTIVE: 45 MIN; TOTAL: 4 HR 30 MIN
PLUS OVERNIGHT CURING

10 SERVINGS ●

1 tablespoon plus 1 teaspoon
    coriander seeds
2 teaspoons fennel seeds
2 teaspoons black peppercorns
½ star anise pod
4 garlic cloves, crushed, plus
    1 teaspoon minced garlic
1 tablespoon kosher salt
¼ cup extra-virgin
    olive oil
One 5-pound boneless
    pork shoulder roast
2 cups dry red wine
2 pints cherry tomatoes or small
    late-season tomatoes, halved
1 teaspoon finely chopped
    lemon zest
1 tablespoon plus 1 teaspoon
    chopped flat-leaf parsley

1. In a spice grinder, grind the coriander, fennel, peppercorns and star anise to a fine powder. Transfer the spices to a bowl and stir in the crushed garlic, salt and 2 tablespoons of the olive oil. Rub the spice mixture all over the pork shoulder roast, wrap it in plastic and refrigerate overnight. Unwrap the pork and let it return to room temperature before proceeding.
2. Preheat the oven to 300°. Set the pork shoulder on a rack in a medium roasting pan. Pour the wine into the pan and roast the meat for about 4 hours, until an instant-read thermometer inserted in the center registers 180°. Transfer the pork to a carving board, cover loosely with foil and let rest for about 15 minutes.
3. Meanwhile, toss the tomatoes with the remaining 2 tablespoons of oil and spread them on a rimmed baking sheet. Roast for about 1 hour, or until softened.
4. In a small bowl, stir the minced garlic with the lemon zest and parsley. Thinly slice the pork, sprinkle with the parsley mixture and serve alongside the roasted cherry tomatoes. —*Peter Hoffman*
SERVE WITH Fresh Shell Bean Stew (p. 269).
WINE Round, deep-flavored Syrah.

Carolina-Style Pulled Pork

ACTIVE: 30 MIN; TOTAL: 9 HR PLUS
OVERNIGHT MARINATING

8 TO 10 SERVINGS ●

¼ cup dark brown sugar
2 tablespoons sweet paprika
2 tablespoons chile powder
1 tablespoon dry mustard
Kosher salt and freshly ground pepper
One 7½-pound bone-in pork
    shoulder, skin removed and thick
    layer of fat scored
¾ cup cider vinegar
¼ cup yellow mustard
2 tablespoons honey
Toasted buns, for serving

1. In a bowl, mix the brown sugar with the paprika, chile powder, dry mustard and 2 tablespoons each of salt and pepper; rub the spice mixture all over the pork. Refrigerate the pork, covered, overnight.
2. Light a grill. Set a drip pan in the center of the grill bottom, and surround with a single layer of lit coals. Place the pork fat side up on the grill over the drip pan. Cover and cook for about 8 hours, or until an instant-read thermometer inserted in the thickest part registers 175°. Replenish with a layer of lit coals every hour as needed to maintain a steady temperature of 200° to 250° inside the grill. Transfer the pork to a rimmed baking sheet and cover loosely with foil; let rest for 30 minutes.
3. In a bowl, whisk the vinegar, mustard, honey and 2 teaspoons of pepper. Pull the pork from the bone in large shreds. Add the pork to the mustard sauce and toss. Season with salt and serve with the buns. —*Nick Fauchald*
WINE Fruity, luscious Shiraz.

Pork Cheek and Black-Eyed Pea Chili

ACTIVE: 45 MIN; TOTAL: 3 HR 15 MIN

10 SERVINGS ●●

1 tablespoon ground coriander

1 tablespoon sweet smoked paprika

1 teaspoon ground cumin

5 pounds cleaned and trimmed pork cheeks (see Note)

Salt and freshly ground pepper

¼ cup extra-virgin olive oil

1 pound slab bacon, cut into ½-inch dice

1 onion, finely chopped

3 garlic cloves, minced

2 jalapeños, seeded and very finely chopped

2 red bell peppers, finely diced

One 12-ounce bottle amber ale or porter

2 cups chicken stock or low-sodium broth

2 cups canned whole Italian tomatoes, crushed

2 canned chipotles in adobo, seeded and minced

1 pound dried black-eyed peas, picked over and rinsed

1 small cinnamon stick

Shredded smoked cheddar cheese, cilantro leaves and crème fraîche, for serving

1. In a large bowl, combine the coriander, paprika and cumin and toss with the pork cheeks. Season with salt and pepper.

2. In a large enameled cast-iron casserole, heat 2 tablespoons of the oil. Add half of the pork and cook over moderately high heat, turning once, until browned, about 8 minutes. Transfer the pork to a plate. Add the remaining 2 tablespoons of oil and brown the remaining pork over moderate heat. Transfer the pork to the plate.

3. Add the bacon to the casserole and cook over moderate heat, stirring occasionally, until browned and slightly crisp, about 7 minutes. Add the onion, garlic, jalapeños and bell peppers and cook, stirring occasionally, until softened, 5 minutes.

4. Return the pork to the casserole along with any juices. Add the ale, stock, tomatoes, chipotles, black-eyed peas and cinnamon stick and bring to a boil. Cover and cook over very low heat until the meat and beans are tender, about 2½ hours. Season with salt and pepper. Spoon off the fat from the surface and discard the cinnamon stick. Serve the chili in bowls. Pass the smoked cheddar, cilantro and crème fraîche at the table. —*Michael Symon*

SERVE WITH Toasted Cornmeal Corn Bread (p. 297).

NOTE You can substitute 5 pounds of pork shoulder for the pork cheeks. Cut the shoulder into 2-inch chunks and proceed with the recipe. Add 30 minutes to the cooking time in Step 4.

MAKE AHEAD The pork cheek chili can be refrigerated for up to 5 days.

WINE Rustic, peppery Malbec.

Simple Pork Posole

ACTIVE: 20 MIN; TOTAL: 2 HR 30 MIN

8 SERVINGS ●

Mexican *posole* is a thick, hearty soup made with hominy (dried corn kernels with the hull and germ removed). The flavorful condiments—jalapeño, onion, cilantro and lime wedges—are essential to the dish.

roasting a suckling pig

TECHNIQUE · TECHNIQUE

What could be more dramatic and festive than roasting your own suckling pig? Special-order a pig from your butcher or go to mcreynoldsfarms.com.

1. On a nonflammable surface, such as brick, cement or gravel, build a 6-by-2-foot hardwood log or charcoal fire.

2. Rig a 20-pound suckling pig onto a spit fitted with a spit fork to grip the rear haunches. Using a heavy-duty trussing needle and twine, tie the pig to the spit behind the head and close to the tail. Stuff the belly with 10 crushed garlic cloves, 5 rosemary sprigs and 5 thyme sprigs. Using a small trussing needle and twine, sew the belly shut. Brush the pig with olive oil.

3. Mount the spit on its tripods so that it stands 1 foot off the ground, just to the side of a long edge of the fire. Lay 2 aluminum roasting pans or 2 sheets of heavy-duty foil under the pig to catch the drippings. Turn on the spit.

4. Set an oven thermometer on an upturned cinder block close to the pig. The ambient temperature should stay between 225° and 250°. Add a layer of fresh coal every 30 minutes, as needed; although you will likely use a total of 20 pounds of coal, it's a good idea to keep up to 60 pounds of coal on hand.

5. Roast the pig for about 2 hours, or until a meat thermometer inserted in the thickest part of the shoulder and rear haunch registers 145°.

6. Remove the spit from the heat and let the pig rest for 30 minutes. Transfer the pig to a large work surface lined with heavy-duty foil. Untie the pig from the spit. Discard the twine, peel off the skin, carve the meat, sprinkle with fleur de sel or sea salt and serve.

4 pounds pork butt, cut into
1½-inch cubes
1 head of garlic, halved crosswise
1 onion, quartered
10 cups water
Two 28-ounce cans hominy,
drained and rinsed
2 tablespoons dried oregano
½ teaspoon cayenne pepper
Kosher salt and freshly ground pepper
Chopped cilantro, chopped red onion,
chopped jalapeño and lime
wedges, for serving

1. In a large soup pot, bring the pork, garlic, onion and water to a simmer. Cover and cook over low heat until the pork is very tender, about 2 hours.
2. Transfer the pork to a large bowl. Strain the broth into the bowl; discard the garlic and onion. Return the pork and broth to the pot and skim any fat. Stir in the hominy, oregano and cayenne and season with salt and black pepper. Bring to a simmer. Ladle the *posole* into bowls. Pass with the cilantro, red onion, jalapeño and lime wedges at the table. —*Ethan Stowell*
WINE Intense, fruity Zinfandel.

Yucatán Pork Stew with Ancho Chiles and Lime Juice

ACTIVE: 40 MIN; TOTAL: 3 HR 40 MIN
8 SERVINGS ● ●
¼ cup vegetable oil
4½ pounds trimmed boneless pork
shoulder, cut into 2-inch pieces
Salt and freshly ground pepper
2 large white onions, cut into
½-inch pieces
8 garlic cloves, smashed
1 pound carrots, cut into
2-inch lengths
3 ancho chiles, seeded and cut into
very thin strips with scissors
3 bay leaves
Pinch of ground cloves
¼ cup fresh lime juice
6 cups chicken stock

6 plum tomatoes, quartered
lengthwise
2 tablespoons chopped cilantro
Steamed white rice and sliced
jalapeños, for serving

1. In an enameled cast-iron casserole, heat the oil until shimmering. Season the pork with salt and pepper and add half of it to the casserole. Cook over moderate heat, turning, until browned all over, 10 minutes. Transfer to a plate. Brown the remaining pork.
2. Return the pork to the casserole along with any accumulated juices. Stir in the onions, garlic, carrots, chiles, bay leaves, cloves, lime juice and stock. Season with salt and pepper; bring to a boil. Add the tomatoes, nestling them into the liquid. Cover and cook over low heat until the pork is very tender and the carrots are cooked through, about 3 hours. Discard the bay leaves and stir in the cilantro. Serve with rice and sliced jalapeños. —*Tia Harrison*
WINE Rustic, peppery Malbec.

Smoked Ham with Apple-Riesling Sauce

ACTIVE: 25 MIN; TOTAL: 5 HR
20 TO 25 SERVINGS ●
One 18-pound bone-in smoked ham,
skin removed and fat scored in
a crosshatch pattern
2 cups water
1 bottle Riesling, preferably off-dry
6 red apples such as Empire—
halved, cored and skin peeled
in stripes
2 tablespoons unsalted butter
6 scallions, coarsely chopped
1 teaspoon hot paprika
2 tablespoons Calvados
Salt

1. Preheat the oven to 325°. Set the ham fat side up in a large roasting pan. Add the water to the pan and bake for 2 hours.
2. Pour the wine over the ham. Roast for 30 minutes. Increase the oven to 350°. Baste the ham and arrange the apples around it.

Roast for 35 minutes; baste the ham once. Remove the apples, then peel and chop.
3. Bake the ham for 1 hour and 15 minutes, basting frequently, until an instant-read thermometer registers 170°. Transfer to a carving board; let rest for 15 minutes.
4. Strain the pan juices into a bowl and skim off the fat. In a deep skillet, melt the butter. Add the scallions and paprika; cook over moderately high heat until the scallions are wilted. Add the Calvados. Carefully ignite the Calvados. Add the apples and pan juices and cook until the apples are just heated. Season the sauce with salt. Carve the ham and serve with the sauce. —*Marcia Kiesel*
WINE Vivid, lightly sweet Riesling.

Fried Pork Rolls with Ham

TOTAL: 50 MIN
4 SERVINGS ●
Eight ½-inch-thick boneless pork loin
chops (3 ounces each)
Freshly ground pepper
8 thin slices of serrano ham
All-purpose flour, for dusting
2 large eggs
1 tablespoon milk
1¼ cups dry bread crumbs
Pure olive oil, for frying
Mayonnaise, for serving

1. Working with one chop at a time, place in a plastic bag and pound into a ¼-inch-thick cutlet. Arrange the cutlets on a surface and season with pepper. Cover each cutlet with a slice of ham; starting with the short end, roll into a cylinder. Dust with the flour.
2. In a bowl, beat the eggs with the milk. Put the bread crumbs in another bowl. Dip the pork rolls in the egg, then in the bread crumbs, pressing them. Transfer to a plate.
3. In a skillet, heat ¼ inch of oil until shimmering. Add the rolls and fry over moderate heat until an instant-read thermometer inserted in the center registers 155°, 5 minutes. Transfer the rolls to paper towels. Serve hot, with mayonnaise. —*Mario Batali*
WINE Earthy, medium-bodied Tempranillo.

Roasted Pork Tenderloin with Raisin-Ginger Pan Sauce

TOTAL: 1 HR
4 SERVINGS ●

One 1¼-pound pork tenderloin
2 teaspoons vegetable oil
Salt and freshly ground pepper
½ cup naturally sweetened
apple juice
½ cup low-sodium chicken broth
1 tablespoon low-sodium soy sauce
3 tablespoons golden raisins
½ teaspoon ground ginger
¼ teaspoon cornstarch dissolved in
1 teaspoon of water

1. Preheat the oven to 350°. Coat the pork with the oil; season with salt and pepper. In a large nonstick ovenproof skillet, cook the pork over moderately high heat until browned all over, 3 minutes per side. Transfer the skillet to the oven and roast for about 18 minutes, turning twice, until an instant-read thermometer inserted in the thickest part of the meat registers 140°.
2. Transfer the pork to a carving board and let rest for 10 minutes. Add the apple juice, broth, soy sauce, raisins and ginger to the skillet and bring to a boil. Cook until the liquid has reduced by half, 4 minutes. Stir in the cornstarch slurry and cook, stirring, until thick enough to coat a spoon, about 30 seconds; remove from the heat.
3. Carve the pork and arrange in shallow bowls. Stir any carving juices into the pan sauce. Spoon the sauce over the pork and serve. —*Pam Anderson*
WINE Dry, fruity sparkling wine.

Stir-Fried Five-Spice Pork with Lettuce Cups

TOTAL: 35 MIN
4 SERVINGS

1 tablespoon peanut oil
1½ pounds boneless pork shoulder,
outer fat trimmed and
pork cut into ½-inch dice
1 small onion, cut into ⅓-inch dice
1 carrot, halved lengthwise
and thinly sliced crosswise
1 celery rib, thinly sliced on the bias
¾ teaspoon Chinese five-spice
powder
⅓ cup canned whole water chestnuts,
drained and coarsely chopped
3 tablespoons chicken stock
or low-sodium broth
2½ tablespoons hoisin sauce
8 basil leaves, torn into pieces
2 scallions, thinly sliced
½ teaspoon Asian sesame oil
Kosher salt and freshly ground pepper
Iceberg lettuce leaves, for serving

1. In a skillet, heat the oil until shimmering. Add the pork and stir-fry over high heat until browned and just cooked through, 5 minutes. Transfer the pork to a plate.
2. Add the onion, carrot and celery to the skillet and cook over moderate heat until tender, 4 minutes, Add the five-spice powder and cook until fragrant, 30 seconds. Stir in the water chestnuts, stock and hoisin, scraping up the brown bits from the bottom of the pan. Return the pork to the skillet and stir-fry until heated through and coated with sauce, 1 minute. Remove from the heat and stir in the basil, scallions and sesame oil; season with salt and pepper. Spoon into bowls and serve with lettuce leaves for wrapping. —*Melissa Rubel*
WINE Ripe, juicy Pinot Noir.

Spicy Pork Po'boys

TOTAL: 30 MIN
4 SERVINGS

1½ pounds ground pork
1½ teaspoons paprika
1¼ teaspoons dried thyme
¾ teaspoon cayenne pepper
¾ teaspoon garlic powder
Kosher salt and freshly ground
black pepper
½ cup mayonnaise
1½ tablespoons Dijon mustard
2 kosher dill pickles, minced
½ small shallot, minced
Four 8-inch soft baguettes, split
2 cups shredded iceberg lettuce
2 tomatoes, thinly sliced
Hot sauce, for serving

1. Preheat a grill pan. In a large bowl, using your hands, mix the ground pork with the paprika, thyme, cayenne pepper, garlic powder, 1½ teaspoons of kosher salt and ¼ teaspoon of black pepper. Form the pork into twelve ½-inch-thick patties. Grill the pork patties over moderate heat, turning once, until they are cooked through, about 8 minutes total.
2. Meanwhile, mix the mayonnaise with the mustard, pickles and shallot and season with salt and pepper. Spread the mayonnaise on both sides of the baguettes.
3. Place 3 pork patties on the bottom of each baguette and top with the lettuce, tomato and a few splashes of hot sauce. Close the sandwiches and serve.
—*Melissa Rubel*
WINE Round, deep-flavored Syrah.

Pork with Arugula, Prosciutto and Tomatoes

TOTAL: 30 MIN
4 SERVINGS ● ●

2 tablespoons olive oil
5 ounces thinly sliced prosciutto,
finely chopped
2 large garlic cloves, minced
1½ pounds pork tenderloin, cut into
1-inch-thick medallions
Salt and freshly ground pepper
2 tablespoons balsamic vinegar
1 pound arugula, stems discarded
and leaves chopped
1 pound plum tomatoes, chopped

1. In a large skillet, heat the oil. Add the prosciutto and garlic and cook over moderate heat, stirring, until the garlic is golden, about 4 minutes. Transfer to a plate.
2. Season the pork with salt and pepper, add to the skillet and cook over moderately high heat until well browned on the outside and

ROASTED PORK TENDERLOIN WITH RAISIN-GINGER PAN SAUCE

STIR-FRIED FIVE-SPICE PORK WITH LETTUCE CUPS

medium within, 3 to 4 minutes per side. Transfer to a plate and keep warm.

3. Add the balsamic to the skillet and cook until nearly evaporated, scraping up any browned bits. Add the arugula and toss until wilted, 2 minutes. Add the tomatoes, prosciutto and garlic. Cook over high heat for 2 minutes, stirring; season with salt and pepper. Transfer the arugula to a platter, top with the pork and serve. —*Nancy Verde Barr*
WINE Dry, light Champagne.

Lemongrass Pork with Pickled Carrots

TOTAL: 50 MIN

4 SERVINGS

½ cup distilled white vinegar
½ cup granulated sugar
½ teaspoon salt
 3 carrots, cut into matchsticks
½ packed cup brown sugar
¼ cup Asian fish sauce

 3 tablespoons canola oil
1½ pounds boneless pork shoulder, sliced ¼ inch thick
 4 fresh Thai bird or serrano chiles
 2 garlic cloves, minced
 3 large shallots, very thinly sliced
 3 stalks of fresh lemongrass, tender inner bulb only, minced
 1 tablespoon grated fresh ginger
¼ cup chicken stock
Rice vermicelli, bean sprouts, sliced cucumber, mint and chopped roasted peanuts, for serving

1. In a bowl, mix the vinegar with the granulated sugar and the salt until they dissolve. Add the carrots and let stand until just softened, about 30 minutes.

2. Meanwhile, in a saucepan, combine the brown sugar with the fish sauce. Cook over moderate heat, stirring occasionally, until the sugar is dissolved and the sauce is thick, about 4 minutes. Pour into a bowl.

3. In a large skillet, heat the oil until almost smoking. Add half the pork and cook over high heat until browned in spots, about 2 minutes per side. Using a slotted spoon, transfer the pork to a platter. Repeat with the remaining pork.

4. Add the chiles, garlic, shallots, lemongrass and ginger to the skillet and cook over moderate heat until fragrant, 1 minute. Add the stock and cook, scraping up any browned bits from the bottom of the pan, 1 minute. Add the sauce and cook over moderate heat, stirring, until thickened, 3 minutes.

5. Cut the pork into 2-inch strips. Return the pork and any accumulated juices to the skillet and cook until the meat is coated with sauce, about 30 seconds. Transfer to plates. Drain the carrots, sprinkle over the pork and serve at once, with the rice noodles, bean sprouts, sliced cucumber, mint and chopped peanuts. —*Charles Phan*
WINE Vivid, lightly sweet Riesling.

Coconut-Rice Crêpes Filled with Pork

TOTAL: 1 HR
4 SERVINGS

- 1 cup rice flour
- ¼ cup unsweetened coconut milk
- 1 large egg
- 1 teaspoon ground turmeric
- 2 scallions, very finely chopped

Salt and freshly ground black pepper

- ½ cup Asian fish sauce
- ¼ cup sugar
- 2 tablespoons distilled white vinegar
- 2 tablespoons fresh lime juice
- 2 Thai chiles, thinly sliced
- 1 red onion, very finely chopped
- 2 garlic cloves, very finely chopped
- 2 tablespoons minced fresh ginger
- ¼ cup shredded carrots
- 2 tablespoons vegetable oil, plus more for frying
- 1 pound ground pork

- 1 head of red leaf lettuce; chopped roasted peanuts; mung bean sprouts; and mint, cilantro and basil leaves, for serving

1. In a medium bowl, whisk the rice flour with the coconut milk, egg, turmeric, half of the scallions and ½ teaspoon each of salt and black pepper. Whisk in enough tepid water (about 1 cup) for the batter to resemble thin pancake batter.

2. In a small bowl, whisk the fish sauce, sugar, vinegar, lime juice, Thai chiles and 2 tablespoons of water. Add one-third of the chopped red onion, and half each of the garlic and ginger. Stir in the carrots.

3. In a large skillet, heat the 2 tablespoons of vegetable oil. Add the remaining onion, garlic and ginger and cook over moderately high heat until softened, about 5 minutes. Add the pork, season lightly with salt and pepper and cook over high heat, stirring occasionally, until browned and cooked through, about 8 minutes. Stir in the remaining scallions. Transfer the pork to a bowl and keep warm.

4. Preheat the oven to 250°. Brush a small nonstick skillet or crêpe pan very lightly with oil and heat until very hot. Pour in about 3 tablespoons of the crêpe batter and swirl the pan to coat evenly with the batter. Cook over moderately high heat until the edge is just turning brown and the crêpe is nearly set, about 1 minute. Drizzle a few drops of oil around the edge and flip the crêpe to cook the other side, about 20 seconds. Turn the crêpe out onto a baking sheet and keep warm in the oven; repeat with the remaining batter to make 7 more crêpes.

5. Transfer the crêpes to a platter along with the lettuce leaves, sprouts and herbs. Serve alongside the pork, with the chopped peanuts and carrot-chile sauce in separate bowls. Wrap the crêpes and fillings in the lettuce leaves to eat. —*Ratha Chau*

VINE Peppery, refreshing Grüner Veltliner.

Asian Pork, Mushroom and Noodle Stir-Fry

 TOTAL: 45 MIN
4 SERVINGS ●

This stir-fry calls for succulent pork tenderloin, meaty shiitake mushrooms, sweet bok choy and chewy noodles—either Japanese curly noodles (available in the international aisle of supermarkets) or instant ramen (minus the flavor packet).

- 8 ounces Japanese curly noodles or instant ramen
- ¾ cup chicken stock or low-sodium broth
- 3 tablespoons soy sauce
- 1 tablespoon Shaoxing or dry sherry (see Note)
- 2 teaspoons Asian sesame oil
- ½ teaspoon crushed red pepper
- 1½ teaspoons cornstarch
- 1 tablespoon water
- 3 tablespoons vegetable oil
- 3 large garlic cloves, very thinly sliced
- 2 large eggs, beaten
- 1 pound pork tenderloin, cut into ½-inch dice

Kosher salt and freshly ground black pepper

- 10 ounces shiitake mushrooms, stems removed and caps thinly sliced
- 2 heads of baby bok choy, cut crosswise into ¼-inch-thick slices

1. Cook the noodles according to the package directions, then drain and rinse under cold water. In a measuring cup, mix the stock with the soy sauce, Shaoxing, sesame oil and crushed red pepper. In a small bowl, mix the cornstarch with the water.

2. In a very large skillet, heat 2 tablespoons of the vegetable oil. Add the sliced garlic and cook over moderate heat until golden, about 3 minutes. Using a slotted spoon,

transfer the garlic slices to a plate. Add the beaten eggs to the skillet and cook, stirring frequently, until they are set, about 1 minute. Transfer the eggs to the plate with the garlic. Season the diced pork with salt and black pepper. Add the pork to the skillet and stir-fry over moderately high heat until the pork is browned and just cooked through, about 3 minutes. Using a slotted spoon, transfer the cooked pork to the plate with the garlic and egg.

3. In the same skillet, heat the remaining 1 tablespoon of vegetable oil. Add the sliced shiitake mushrooms, season with salt and black pepper and cook over moderate heat, stirring frequently, until the mushrooms are tender, about 4 minutes. Add the baby bok choy slices and cook until they are softened, about 3 minutes. Add the drained noodles and soy sauce and cornstarch mixtures and cook over moderate heat, tossing, until the sauce thickens and coats the noodles, about 2 minutes. Add the garlic slices, cooked eggs and pork and any accumulated juices from the plate to the skillet and cook, tossing, until the pork is heated through and all the ingredients are well combined, about 1 minute longer. Transfer the stir-fry to bowls and serve right away.
—*Melissa Rubel*

NOTE Shaoxing is an aged Chinese rice wine often used in cooking. Look for bottles in Asian markets (where it will likely be seasoned with salt to ensure that it can be used only for cooking), or substitute dry sherry.

WINE Complex, elegant Pinot Noir.

Mixed Grill with Rib Eyes, Sausages and Bacon Chops

TOTAL: 45 MIN
10 SERVINGS

For a cowboy picnic at California's Prather Ranch, San Francisco chef Chris Cosentino served copious amounts of meat; this included Italian sausages, Prather's rib

eyes and "caveman" bacon chops. Ask your butcher to cut these unusually large pork chops from near the shoulder, leaving the belly meat attached.

Three 1-pound bone-in rib eye steaks (1½ inches thick)
Five 1-pound bone-in pork chops, cut from the shoulder end, belly left on (1 inch thick)
3 pounds Italian sausage
Olive oil, for brushing
Halen Môn sea salt or other coarse sea salt (see Note)
Freshly ground black pepper
Salsa Picante (p. 377), for serving
Salsa Verde (p. 376), for serving

1. Light a grill. Brush the rib eyes, pork chops and Italian sausages with olive oil and season with coarse sea salt and black pepper. When the coals are hot, rake them to one side of the grill. Grill the seasoned, oil-brushed meat directly over the coals for 3 minutes, rotating the rib eyes and chops halfway through to create a crosshatch pattern, if desired. Turn the meat and grill for 3 minutes longer on the second side.

2. Move the pork chops to the side of the grill opposite the coals. Cover and grill the meat for about 10 minutes longer, turning once, until an instant-read thermometer inserted in the thickest part of the chops registers 150° for medium-well, and in the rib eyes, 130° for medium-rare. Transfer the sausages, steaks and chops to a carving board and let them rest for 5 minutes. Carve the steaks and chops into thick slices off the bone and serve right away, with the Italian sausages and the Salsa Picante and Salsa Verde alongside.
—*Chris Cosentino*

NOTE Halen Môn sea salt is a crunchy, flaky white sea salt harvested in Wales. It is available in gourmet stores and online from chefshop.com.

WINE Intense, fruity Zinfandel.

Pan-Seared Sausages with Apples

TOTAL: 30 MIN
4 SERVINGS

At Farm Bloomington market-restaurant in Bloomington, Indiana, chef Daniel Orr sells Midwestern sausages, including bratwurst from Fiedler Family Farms in Rome, Indiana (fiedlerfamilyfarms.com). Non-Hoosier sweet Italian sausages will work in this recipe, too. Be sure to use cooking apples that will hold their shape, like Granny Smiths, Winesaps or Rome Beauties.

1 tablespoon extra-virgin olive oil
4 sweet Italian sausages (about 1 pound), pricked with a fork
½ cup water
2 Granny Smith apples, peeled and thinly sliced
½ teaspoon fennel seeds
1 tablespoon cider vinegar
Salt and freshly ground black pepper
Cheesy Grits with Scallions (p. 253), for serving

1. In a large skillet, heat the olive oil. Add the pricked Italian sausages to the skillet and cook over moderate heat, turning occasionally, until the sausages are browned but not cooked through, about 5 minutes.

2. Pour the ½ cup of water into the skillet. Cover and cook until the water is nearly evaporated and the sausages are firm, about 7 minutes longer. Add the sliced apples and fennel seeds and cook, stirring occasionally, until the apples are tender and browned, about 8 minutes. Stir in the cider vinegar and season with salt and black pepper. Serve the sausages and apples in bowls atop the Cheesy Grits with Scallions. —*Daniel Orr*

WINE Complex, aromatic Chenin Blanc.

Meat Loaf with Red Wine Glaze

ACTIVE: 40 MIN; TOTAL: 2 HR

6 SERVINGS ●

- 2 slices of white sandwich bread, torn into pieces
- ½ cup milk
- 1 large egg
- 1 large egg yolk
- 2 tablespoons chopped parsley
- 1½ teaspoons finely chopped sage leaves
- 1 teaspoon finely chopped thyme leaves
- 1 tablespoon kosher salt

Pinch of freshly ground black pepper

Pinch of freshly grated nutmeg

Pinch of cayenne pepper

- ¾ cup freshly grated Parmigiano-Reggiano cheese
- ¼ cup plain dry bread crumbs
- 2 tablespoons unsalted butter
- 1 medium white onion, finely diced
- 4 garlic cloves, minced
- 1 pound ground lamb
- ½ pound ground pork
- ½ pound ground veal

Vegetable oil, for brushing

- 1¼ cups dry red wine
- ¼ cup sugar
- 1 tomato, finely chopped
- 1 teaspoon unsulfured molasses

Pinch of ground allspice

1. Preheat the oven to 350°. In a bowl, combine the bread with the milk and mash to a paste. Add the whole egg, egg yolk, parsley, sage, thyme, salt, pepper, nutmeg and cayenne and stir until smooth. Add the cheese and bread crumbs and mix well.

2. In a medium skillet, melt the butter. Add the onion and cook over moderate heat until softened, about 7 minutes. Add the garlic and cook just until fragrant, 1 minute longer. Let cool, then transfer to the bowl. Add the lamb, pork and veal and knead until evenly combined.

3. Brush a medium oval baking dish with oil. Transfer the meat loaf mixture to the dish and pat it into a 4-by-12-inch oval loaf. Bake for about 50 minutes, or until firm but not quite cooked through.

4. Meanwhile, in a medium saucepan, combine the red wine with the sugar, chopped tomato, molasses and allspice and bring to a boil over moderate heat, stirring to dissolve the sugar. Boil until the glaze is thick and syrupy, about 15 minutes.

5. Brush half of the glaze over the meat loaf. Continue baking for about 20 minutes longer, until an instant-read thermometer inserted in the center registers 150°; brush once more with the remaining glaze during baking. Let rest for 15 minutes, then thickly slice and serve. —*Shea Gallante*

WINE Rich, ripe Cabernet Sauvignon.

Fontina-Stuffed Veal Meatballs

ACTIVE: 1 HR 15 MIN; TOTAL: 2 HR

6 SERVINGS

- 5 tablespoons extra-virgin olive oil
- 1 medium onion, cut into ¼-inch dice
- 3 garlic cloves—2 minced, 1 thinly sliced
- 1 teaspoon thyme leaves
- ¼ teaspoon minced rosemary

Kosher salt and freshly ground black pepper

- 2 slices of white sandwich bread, crusts removed and bread torn into 1-inch pieces
- ⅓ cup whole milk
- 1½ pounds ground veal
- 1 egg, lightly beaten
- ¼ cup freshly grated Parmigiano-Reggiano cheese
- 3 ounces Italian Fontina cheese, cut into ½-inch cubes
- 2 tablespoons tomato paste

One 28-ounce can diced tomatoes, with juices

1. In a medium skillet, heat 2 tablespoons of the olive oil. Add the diced onion and minced garlic and cook over moderate heat until softened, about 8 minutes. Stir in the thyme leaves and minced rosemary and season with salt and pepper. Transfer to a large bowl and let stand until cool, about 10 minutes.

2. In a small bowl, soak the bread pieces in the milk until absorbed, about 5 minutes. Squeeze the milk from the bread and transfer the bread to the bowl with the onion. Add the veal, egg, Parmigiano-Reggiano and 2½ teaspoons of kosher salt and ½ teaspoon of black pepper. Mix with clean hands until well combined.

3. Scoop 1½-tablespoon-size balls from the veal mixture. Stuff a cube of Fontina into the center of each meatball and roll to enclose the cheese. Transfer the meatballs to a rimmed baking sheet and refrigerate for 30 minutes.

4. In a large nonstick skillet, heat 2 tablespoons of the olive oil. Cook the meatballs in batches over moderately high heat until browned all over, about 6 minutes. Return the meatballs to the baking sheet.

5. In the same skillet, heat the remaining 1 tablespoon of olive oil. Add the sliced garlic clove and cook over moderately high heat until it is lightly golden, about 3 minutes. Add the tomato paste and cook, stirring constantly, for 1 minute. Add the diced tomatoes and bring to a simmer. Add the meatballs and any accumulated pan juices to the tomato sauce. Cover and cook over moderately low heat, turning the meatballs once, until they are cooked through, about 10 minutes.

6. Using a slotted spoon, transfer the meatballs to bowls or plates. Simmer the sauce over moderate heat until thickened slightly, about 2 minutes. Season with salt and pepper and pour over the meatballs. —*Melissa Rubel*

SERVE WITH Crusty bread.

WINE Bright, tart Barbera.

FONTINA-STUFFED
VEAL MEATBALLS

Veal Chops with Cognac Sauce

TOTAL: 1 HR

6 SERVINGS

"Cognac, cream and truffle butter—how can you possibly go wrong?" asks F&W's Grace Parisi. Here, she combines these three rich ingredients in a decadent sauce for juicy pan-roasted veal chops.

- ¼ cup vegetable oil
- 6 sage sprigs

Salt

Six 12-ounce veal rib chops (about 1¼ inches thick)

Freshly ground pepper

All-purpose flour, for dusting

- 2 tablespoons unsalted butter
- 2 tablespoons extra-virgin olive oil
- 2 large shallots, minced
- ½ cup Cognac
- ½ cup heavy cream
- 1½ cups chicken stock or low-sodium broth
- 2 tablespoons white truffle butter (see Note)

1. Preheat the oven to 375°. In a small skillet, heat the vegetable oil. Add the sage sprigs and fry over high heat until deep green and translucent, about 1 minute. Transfer to a paper towel–lined plate to cool. Season with salt.

2. Season the veal chops with salt and pepper and dust lightly with flour, patting off the excess. In a large skillet, melt 1 tablespoon of butter in the olive oil. Add half of the veal chops and cook over high heat, turning once, until golden brown, about 7 minutes. Transfer to a large baking pan and repeat with the remaining chops, lowering the heat to moderate.

3. Roast the veal chops for 15 minutes, or until an instant-read thermometer inserted near the bone registers 140°.

4. Meanwhile, pour off the fat in the skillet. Add the remaining 1 tablespoon of butter and the shallots and cook over moderate heat until softened, about 3 minutes. Remove from the heat. Add the Cognac, return to the heat and boil over moderately high heat, scraping up any bits stuck to the bottom, until the pan is nearly dry, 2 minutes. Add the cream and stock and bring to a boil. Season with salt and pepper and boil over moderately high heat until reduced to ¾ cup, about 15 minutes.

5. Strain the sauce into a saucepan, season with salt and pepper and whisk in the truffle butter over low heat until incorporated.

6. Transfer the veal to plates and spoon the sauce on top. Garnish the chops with the fried sage sprigs and serve right away. —*Grace Parisi*

SERVE WITH Spaetzle.

NOTE D'Artagnan (dartagnan.com) makes white truffle butter.

WINE Rich, complex white Burgundy.

Smoky Tomato-Braised Veal Shoulder with Potatoes

ACTIVE: 45 MIN; TOTAL: 3 HR 15 MIN

8 SERVINGS ● ●

Humanely raised veal is becoming more widely available at top butcher shops, among them Avedano's in San Francisco. Tia Harrison, the head butcher at Avedano's, recommends choosing veal shoulder or rump roast, which are more economical than other cuts of veal but still delicious. Harrison likes to braise them; here, canned fire-roasted tomatoes give the dish a smoky flavor.

- 2 tablespoons vegetable oil

One 6-pound boneless veal shoulder, cut into 8 equal chunks

Kosher salt and freshly ground pepper

- 2 cups dry red wine

One 28-ounce can whole fire-roasted tomatoes, crushed

- 1 cup chicken stock

One 6-ounce can tomato paste

- 5 garlic cloves, smashed
- 3 bay leaves

Three 3-inch rosemary sprigs

- 2 star anise pods
- 3 celery ribs, cut into ½-inch dice
- 2 carrots, cut into ½-inch dice
- 1 onion, cut into ½-inch dice
- 2 pounds fingerling potatoes, sliced crosswise ¼ inch thick
- 2 teaspoons finely grated lemon zest

1. In a large enameled cast-iron casserole, heat the vegetable oil until shimmering. Season the veal with salt and pepper. Add 4 pieces of the veal to the casserole and cook over moderately high heat until browned all over, about 10 minutes. Transfer the browned veal to a large plate and repeat with the remaining 4 pieces.

2. Add the red wine to the casserole and bring to a boil, scraping up the browned bits from the bottom. Return the veal and any accumulated juices to the casserole. Add the fire-roasted tomatoes, chicken stock, tomato paste, garlic, bay leaves, rosemary, star anise, celery, carrots and onion and bring to a simmer. Cover and cook over moderately low heat until the veal is tender, about 2 hours.

3. Add the potatoes to the casserole, cover and cook until tender, about 30 minutes. Season the stew with salt and pepper.

4. Discard the bay leaves, rosemary sprigs and star anise. Transfer the veal to large, shallow bowls. Spoon the potatoes and sauce over the veal, sprinkle with lemon zest and serve. —*Tia Harrison*

MAKE AHEAD The braised veal can be refrigerated for up to 3 days. Reheat gently before serving.

WINE Complex, elegant Pinot Noir.

Veal Scallopine with Charred Cherry Tomato Salad

TOTAL: 25 MIN

4 SERVINGS ●

Charred tomatoes add their warm, tangy juices to an arugula salad served with quick-grilled veal scallopine in this fast version of a steak salad.

2 tablespoons extra-virgin olive oil

2 tablespoons sherry vinegar

1 small shallot, minced

1 teaspoon Dijon mustard

Kosher salt and freshly ground pepper

1 pint cherry tomatoes

Four 4-ounce veal cutlets

4 cups baby arugula (4 ounces)

½ cup shaved Parmigiano-Reggiano cheese (1½ ounces)

1. Light a grill. In a large bowl, whisk the olive oil with the sherry vinegar, minced shallot and Dijon mustard. Season the vinaigrette with salt and pepper.

2. Heat a medium cast-iron skillet on the grill. Add the tomatoes and cook over high heat, shaking the pan a few times, until the tomatoes are charred and the skins begin to split, about 4 minutes. Add the tomatoes to the vinaigrette and lightly smash the tomatoes to release some of their juices.

3. Season the veal with salt and pepper. Lightly oil the grill grate. Grill the veal, turning once, until just cooked through, about 2 minutes. Transfer to plates.

4. Add the arugula and the cheese shavings to the tomatoes and toss well. Place the salad alongside the veal and serve. —*Nick Fauchald*

WINE Fruity, light-bodied Beaujolais.

Roasted Veal Chops with Grapes

 **TOTAL: 25 MIN**
4 SERVINGS ●

In this recipe from cookbook author Melissa Clark, juicy red grapes roast alongside tender veal chops, cooking down to an intensely fruity condiment.

1 pound seedless red grapes

3 tablespoons sherry vinegar

2½ tablespoons unsalted butter, softened

½ teaspoon sugar

Salt and freshly ground pepper

Four 1-inch-thick veal rib chops (about 8 ounces each)

1. Preheat the oven to 500°. On a sturdy rimmed baking sheet, toss the grapes with the vinegar, 1½ tablespoons of the butter and the sugar; season with salt and pepper. Roast for about 10 minutes, shaking the baking sheet halfway through, until the grapes are hot and the pan is sizzling.

2. Rub the veal chops with the remaining 1 tablespoon of butter and season with salt and pepper. Push the grapes to one side of the baking sheet. Add the veal chops and roast for about 5 minutes, or until sizzling underneath. Turn the chops and roast for 5 minutes longer for medium-rare meat. Transfer the veal chops to a platter, scrape the grapes and juices on top and serve. —*Melissa Clark*

WINE Complex, elegant Pinot Noir.

Osso Buco with Citrus Gremolata

ACTIVE: 1 HR; TOTAL: 4 HR
8 SERVINGS ●

8 meaty veal shanks, cut 1½ inches thick (7 pounds)

Kosher salt and freshly ground black pepper

6 tablespoons extra-virgin olive oil

6 carrots, cut into ¼-inch dice

6 celery ribs, cut into ¼-inch dice

2 onions, cut into ¼-inch dice

6 garlic cloves—4 whole, 2 minced

3 bay leaves

4 cups chicken stock or low-sodium broth

2 cups dry white wine

One 15-ounce can diced Italian tomatoes

6 thyme sprigs

Two 2½-inch strips of orange zest, very finely chopped

Two 2½-inch strips of lemon zest, very finely chopped

2 tablespoons very finely chopped flat-leaf parsley

1. Preheat the oven to 375°. Season the veal shanks with salt and black pepper. In a very large, deep skillet, heat 3 tablespoons of the olive oil until shimmering. Working in batches, cook the veal shanks over moderately high heat until they are browned on both sides, about 8 minutes total per batch. Transfer the osso buco to a large roasting pan.

2. Add the remaining 3 tablespoons of olive oil to the skillet. Add the diced carrots, celery, onions, 4 whole garlic cloves and the bay leaves and cook over moderate heat until they are softened, about 12 minutes. Add the chicken stock, white wine, diced tomatoes and thyme sprigs and bring to a boil. Pour the vegetables and liquid over the veal, cover the roasting pan with foil and transfer to the oven. Braise the shanks for about 2½ hours, until very tender.

3. Meanwhile, in a small bowl, mix the chopped orange zest, lemon zest and parsley with the 2 minced garlic cloves. Lightly season the gremolata with salt and black pepper.

4. Transfer the veal shanks to a baking sheet and cover them with aluminum foil. Carefully strain the cooking liquid into a large bowl. Reserve the vegetables; discard the bay leaves and thyme sprigs. Pour the cooking liquid back into the roasting pan and boil over high heat until it is reduced by half, about 25 minutes. Season the sauce with salt and black pepper. Stir in the reserved vegetables and simmer over moderately low heat for 2 minutes. Transfer the osso buco to shallow bowls. Spoon the sauce and vegetables on top and sprinkle lightly with the citrus gremolata. Serve with the remaining gremolata at the table. —*Ethan Stowell*

SERVE WITH Polenta.

MAKE AHEAD The osso buco can be refrigerated for up to 2 days. Reheat gently before serving.

WINE Bright, tart Barbera.

GRILLED BEEF TENDERLOIN WITH
ANCHO-JALAPEÑO BUTTER (P. 145)

beef, lamb & game

BEEF TENDERLOIN STEAK WITH CELERY ROOT GRATIN

MEXICAN SPICE-RUBBED RIB EYE WITH LIME BUTTER

Beef Tenderloin Steaks with Celery Root Gratin

ACTIVE: 20 MIN; TOTAL: 1 HR 45 MIN

4 SERVINGS ●

William Abitbol, owner and chef of the Paris wine bar Alfred, serves tenderloin steak in a rich pan sauce along with a creamy gratin of nutty celery root rather than the usual potato.

One 2-pound celery root—peeled, quartered and sliced crosswise ⅛ inch thick

Salt and freshly ground pepper

Pinch of freshly grated nutmeg

1 cup heavy cream

5 tablespoons unsalted butter, 1 tablespoon cut into small pieces

1 tablespoon extra-virgin olive oil

Four 6-ounce trimmed beef tenderloin steaks, about 2 inches thick

½ cup veal demiglace

4 rosemary sprigs, for garnish

1. Preheat the oven to 375°. Spread one-fourth of the celery root slices in a shallow 1-quart gratin dish. Season with salt, pepper and nutmeg. Repeat with the remaining celery root slices to create 4 layers; season between each layer. Pour the cream over the celery root and dot with the 1 tablespoon of butter pieces. Cover with foil and bake for 30 minutes. Remove the foil and bake for about 30 minutes longer, until browned on top and the celery root is tender when pierced with a knife. Let stand for 15 minutes. Leave the oven on.

2. In a large ovenproof skillet, melt 1 tablespoon of the butter in the olive oil. Season the steaks with salt and pepper and cook over moderately high heat until a brown crust forms on the bottom, about 3 minutes. Turn the steaks, transfer the skillet to the oven and cook for about 12 minutes for medium-rare. Transfer the steaks to dinner plates.

3. Add the veal demiglace to the skillet and bring to a boil. Remove the skillet from the heat and whisk in the remaining 3 tablespoons of butter, 1 tablespoon at a time. Season the sauce with salt and pepper. Spoon the sauce over and around the steaks. Garnish each steak with a sprig of rosemary and serve hot, with the celery root gratin. —*William Abitbol*

WINE Firm, complex Cabernet Sauvignon.

Mexican Spice-Rubbed Rib Eyes with Lime Butter

TOTAL: 30 MIN

4 SERVINGS

4 tablespoons unsalted butter, softened

1 small garlic clove, minced

¼ teaspoon finely grated lime zest

1 tablespoon fresh lime juice

Kosher salt

1½ teaspoons sweet paprika

1½ teaspoons ground cumin

1½ teaspoons chipotle powder

Four 12-ounce boneless rib eye
    steaks, 1 inch thick

Vegetable oil, for the grill

1. Light a grill or preheat a large grill pan. In a small bowl, combine the softened butter, garlic, lime zest, lime juice and a pinch of salt. In another bowl, combine the paprika, cumin and chipotle powder with 1½ teaspoons of kosher salt. Rub the mixture all over the steaks.

2. Oil the grate and grill the steaks over moderately high heat, turning once, until slightly charred and medium-rare, about 12 minutes. Transfer the steaks to plates and top with the lime butter. Let the steaks stand for 3 to 4 minutes before serving.
—*Bernie Kantak*

WINE Rustic, peppery Malbec.

Grilled Beef Tenderloin with Ancho-Jalapeño Butter

ACTIVE: 25 MIN; TOTAL: 1 HR

8 SERVINGS

This dish of sliced tenderloin and grilled bread smeared with chile butter recalls the traditional meal of beef, butter and bread served at "beefsteaks," the nearly forgotten New York and New Jersey banquets where utensils are shunned.

  2 sticks unsalted butter, softened

  2 medium shallots, minced

  2 jalapeños, minced

  3 teaspoons ancho chile powder

Kosher salt

  2 tablespoons dark brown sugar

  1 tablespoon sweet
      smoked paprika

  1 teaspoon freshly ground
      black pepper

One 2½-pound beef tenderloin, tied

  8 thick slices of crusty bread

1. Set up a grill for indirect grilling, with the coals on one side, and heat to 450°. In a bowl, mix the butter, shallots, jalapeños and chile powder; season with salt. Transfer to

a sheet of plastic wrap and roll into a 1½-inch-thick log; refrigerate for 15 minutes.

2. In a bowl, mix the brown sugar, paprika, pepper and 1 tablespoon of salt. Rub the beef with the spice mixture. Oil the grate and grill the beef directly over the coals, turning, until charred, 12 minutes.

3. Move the beef away from the coals. Cover and grill for 25 minutes, or until an instant-read thermometer inserted in the thickest part of the tenderloin registers 130° for medium-rare. Transfer to a carving board; let rest for 10 minutes.

4. Grill the bread directly over the coals until toasted. Spread the bread with half of the ancho-jalapeño butter. Slice the remaining butter and transfer to a plate.

5. Slice the beef and serve with the toasts and ancho-jalapeño butter.
—*Nick Fauchald*

SERVE WITH Charred cherry tomatoes.

MAKE AHEAD The ancho-jalapeño butter can be refrigerated for up to 1 week.

WINE Deep, velvety Merlot.

Curry-Glazed Beef Tenderloins

ACTIVE: 20 MIN; TOTAL: 1 HR PLUS OVERNIGHT MARINATING

16 TO 18 SERVINGS ●

Inspired by a recipe from cookbook author Eileen Yin-Fei Lo, F&W's Marcia Kiesel transforms beef tenderloin into a deliciously sweet and savory roast with a glaze of honey, curry powder and soy sauce.

1¼ cups mushroom soy sauce
      or tamari

⅓ cup honey

¼ cup curry powder

Two 4-pound trimmed beef
      tenderloin roasts,
      each halved crosswise

¼ cup vegetable oil

1. In a bowl, whisk the mushroom soy sauce with the honey and curry powder. Score the top and bottom of the beef tenderloins in a crosshatch pattern about ½ inch deep. Transfer the meat to 2 large resealable

plastic bags and pour in the marinade. Turn the tenderloins to coat with the marinade, seal the bags and refrigerate overnight.

2. Preheat the oven to 500°. Transfer the tenderloins and the marinade to a large rimmed baking sheet. Rub the tops of the tenderloins with the vegetable oil. Roast the tenderloins in the upper third of the oven, basting every 8 to 10 minutes, for about 30 minutes, until an instant-read thermometer inserted in the thickest part of the roasts registers 125° for medium-rare. Transfer the tenderloins to a carving board and let rest for 10 minutes. Slice the tenderloins and serve warm or at room temperature.
—*Marcia Kiesel*

WINE Rich, ripe Cabernet Sauvignon.

Grilled Strip Steak with Warm Shallot Vinaigrette

TOTAL: 25 MIN

4 SERVINGS

¾ cup sliced shallots (2 large)

½ cup extra-virgin olive oil

2½ tablespoons sherry vinegar

  2 teaspoons Dijon mustard

¼ cup flat-leaf parsley leaves

Salt and freshly ground pepper

Two 1-pound boneless New York strip
      steaks, 1 inch thick

1. In a small saucepan, cook the shallots in the olive oil over low heat, stirring frequently, until softened but not browned, about 10 minutes. Transfer the shallots and oil to a blender and let cool briefly. Add the vinegar and mustard and puree until smooth. Add the parsley and pulse until finely chopped. Season the vinaigrette with salt and pepper.

2. Meanwhile, light a grill or preheat a grill pan. Season the steaks with salt and pepper and grill over moderately high heat, turning once, until medium-rare, 10 to 12 minutes. Let the steaks rest for 5 minutes. Transfer to plates, top with the vinaigrette and serve.
—*Grace Parisi*

WINE Rustic, peppery Malbec.

beef, lamb & game

Carne Asada with Black Beans

TOTAL: 1 HR PLUS OVERNIGHT MARINATING

6 SERVINGS

At Frontera Grill in Chicago, Rick Bayless serves a classic Mexican combination of grilled marinated steak, fried plantains, slow-cooked black beans and guacamole. The minimalist version here features spice-marinated rib eye steaks, canned black beans and avocado slices.

- 2 tablespoons vegetable oil
- 4 garlic cloves, minced
- 1/3 cup ancho chile powder
- 2 tablespoons cider vinegar
- 1½ teaspoons dried oregano
- Salt
- Six 12-ounce boneless rib eye steaks, about 1 inch thick
- 1 dry chorizo (3 ounces), thinly sliced
- 1 large white onion, finely chopped
- Two 15-ounce cans black beans
- Avocado slices and lime wedges, for serving

1. In a small saucepan, heat 1 tablespoon of the vegetable oil. Add the garlic and cook over moderate heat until fragrant, about 1 minute. Add the chile powder, vinegar, 1 teaspoon of the oregano and ¾ cup of water and cook over very low heat, whisking occasionally, until the marinade is slightly thickened, about 3 minutes. Season with salt. Transfer the marinade to a large baking dish and let cool completely. Add the steaks and turn to coat. Cover and refrigerate overnight.

2. Light a grill. In a large saucepan, heat the remaining 1 tablespoon of vegetable oil. Add the chorizo slices and cook over moderate heat until crisp, about 4 minutes. Using a slotted spoon, transfer the chorizo to a bowl; reserve it for another use. Add the chopped white onion to the saucepan along with the remaining ½ teaspoon of oregano and cook until the onion is softened, about 6 minutes. Add the beans with their liquid and simmer until slightly thickened, about 10 minutes. Season the beans lightly with salt.

3. Grill the rib eye steaks over moderately high heat, turning once, about 12 minutes for medium-rare meat. Serve the steaks with the black beans, avocado slices and lime wedges. —*Rick Bayless*

MAKE AHEAD The ancho-chile marinade can be refrigerated for up to 1 week. The cooked black beans can be refrigerated for up to 2 days.

WINE Intense, spicy Syrah.

Steak, Chicken and Vegetable Tacos

ACTIVE: 1 HR 45 MIN; TOTAL: 2 HR 30 MIN PLUS OVERNIGHT MARINATING

MAKES 36 TACOS

New York City chef Sue Torres takes tacos seriously: At her restaurant Sueños, a "tortilla lady" hand-presses the tortillas in the main dining room. But Torres still wants her guests to have fun eating them. "I like offering lots of options, so everyone can play with different flavor combinations," she says. The skirt steak—marinated in Coca-Cola and tamarind—is one of her best options. She discovered the recipe while traveling through Oaxaca. "Mexicans love Coke. They'd offer it to me at breakfast," she says.

STEAK

- 2 ounces pressed tamarind from a block, cut into ¾-inch pieces
- ¾ cup hot water
- 4 unpeeled garlic cloves
- 3 scallions, chopped
- 1½ teaspoons thyme leaves
- 1 tablespoon pure ancho chile powder
- 2 tablespoons extra-virgin olive oil
- ¾ cup Coca-Cola
- Salt and freshly ground pepper
- 1½ pounds skirt steak, cut into 4-inch lengths

VEGETABLES AND CHICKEN

- ½ cup extra-virgin olive oil
- 2 garlic cloves, minced
- 1 serrano chile, thinly sliced
- 2 medium zucchini, thinly sliced lengthwise
- 2 chayote—peeled, halved lengthwise, pitted and thinly sliced crosswise
- 2 large carrots, thinly sliced on a sharp angle
- 1 fennel bulb—trimmed, cored and thinly sliced
- Salt and freshly ground pepper
- 4 skinless, boneless chicken breast halves, butterflied
- 36 corn tortillas, warmed
- Salsa Verde (p. 376), Pico de Gallo (p. 377), cilantro sprigs and sour cream, for serving

1. PREPARE THE STEAK: In a microwave-safe bowl, combine the tamarind and water and microwave on high power for 2 minutes. Cover and let stand until the tamarind is softened, about 30 minutes.

2. Meanwhile, preheat a skillet. Add the garlic and cook over moderate heat, turning occasionally, until the cloves are blackened in spots, about 8 minutes. Peel the garlic.

3. Mash the tamarind to a pulp. Strain the tamarind puree through a fine sieve into a blender. Discard the seeds and fibers. Add the peeled garlic and the scallions, thyme, chile powder and olive oil to the blender and puree until smooth. With the machine on, add the Coca-Cola in a thin stream until blended. Season generously with salt and pepper. Transfer the mixture to a shallow baking dish. Add the steak and turn to coat. Cover and refrigerate overnight.

4. PREPARE THE VEGETABLES AND CHICKEN: Preheat a grill pan. In a large bowl, combine the olive oil, garlic and serrano chile. Add the sliced vegetables and a generous pinch each of salt and pepper and toss to coat. Grill the vegetables over high heat, turning occasionally, until tender and lightly charred, about 8 minutes. Transfer the vegetables to a cutting board and coarsely chop them.

5. Brush the chicken with some of the remaining oil from the vegetable bowl and season with salt and pepper. Grill the chicken over high heat, turning once, until cooked through and lightly charred, about 8 minutes. Let rest for 10 minutes, then cut into thin strips.

6. Scrape most of the marinade off the steaks. Grill the steaks over high heat, turning, until charred in spots, 10 minutes for medium-rare. Transfer the steaks to a cutting board and let rest for 10 minutes, then thinly slice across the grain.

7. Mound the steak, chicken and vegetables in 3 bowls and serve the fillings with the tortillas, Salsa Verde, Pico de Gallo, cilantro and sour cream. —*Sue Torres*
WINE Juicy, fresh Dolcetto.

Grilled Skirt Steak with Fregola-Orange Salad

TOTAL: 45 MIN
6 SERVINGS

This Mediterranean-inspired skirt-steak dish is a wonderful pairing of just-seared slices of beef with cool and crisp fennel, chewy *fregola* (the Sardinian dot-shaped pasta) and juicy oranges, finished with a drizzle of briny black olive tapenade.

- ¼ cup *fregola*
- 1 pound skirt steak, cut crosswise into 6-inch pieces
- 1 tablespoon pure chile powder, such as ancho
- Salt and freshly ground pepper
- ½ small red onion, sliced into ¼-inch slabs
- 2 tablespoons fresh lemon juice
- ¼ cup extra-virgin olive oil
- 1 fennel bulb—halved, cored and thinly sliced crosswise
- 2 medium navel oranges—peeled, quartered lengthwise and thinly sliced crosswise
- 5 ounces baby arugula
- 4 large radishes, thinly sliced
- ¼ cup black olive tapenade

1. Light a grill or preheat the broiler. In a saucepan of boiling salted water, cook the *fregola* until al dente, about 20 minutes. Drain and cool under running water; shake off the excess water.

2. Meanwhile, rub the steak with the chile powder and season with salt and pepper. Grill the steak and the onion slabs over high heat for about 8 minutes, turning occasionally, for medium-rare meat and tender onions. Let the steak rest for about 10 minutes. Let the onions cool slightly, then coarsely chop them.

3. In a large bowl, whisk the lemon juice into the olive oil and season with salt and pepper. Add the fennel, oranges, arugula, radishes, *fregola* and grilled onion and toss the salad well. Thinly slice the skirt steak across the grain and arrange on plates. Spoon the tapenade over the meat, mound the salad alongside and serve.
—*Michael Schwartz*
WINE Rich, ripe Cabernet Sauvignon.

Grilled Skirt Steak with Chimichurri Sauce

TOTAL: 25 MIN
8 SERVINGS ●

New York Times columnist Mark Bittman uses a tangy, salsa-esque Argentinean sauce to complement rich skirt steak.

- 2 cups chopped parsley
- ⅔ cup extra-virgin olive oil
- 6 tablespoons fresh lemon juice
- 2 tablespoons minced garlic
- 2 teaspoons crushed red pepper
- Salt and freshly ground pepper
- 4 pounds skirt steak

1. Light a grill. In a bowl, mix the parsley, olive oil, lemon juice, garlic and crushed red pepper; season with salt and pepper.

2. Season the steak with salt and pepper and grill over high heat until the meat is charred outside and rare within, about 2 minutes per side. Transfer to a carving board and let rest for 5 minutes. Thinly slice the steak across the grain. Serve right away, passing the chimichurri sauce at the table.
—*Mark Bittman*
WINE Round, deep-flavored Syrah.

Skirt Steak with Creamed Corn and Poblanos

TOTAL: 45 MIN
4 SERVINGS

- 2 poblano chiles
- ¼ cup extra-virgin olive oil
- 1 medium onion, thinly sliced
- 1½ cups fresh or thawed frozen corn kernels
- 1 cup sour cream
- Salt and freshly ground pepper
- 1½ pounds skirt steak, cut into 6-inch pieces

1. Roast the poblanos directly over a gas flame or under a broiler, turning, until charred all over. Transfer to a bowl, cover with plastic wrap and let stand for 10 minutes. Peel, core and seed the chiles, then cut them into thin strips.

2. In a medium saucepan, heat 2 tablespoons of the olive oil until shimmering. Add the onion and cook over moderate heat, stirring, until softened, about 5 minutes. Add the corn and poblano strips and cook until the corn is tender, about 2 minutes. Stir in the sour cream and season with salt and pepper. Keep the creamed corn warm over very low heat.

3. Light a grill or preheat a grill pan. Rub the steak with the remaining 2 tablespoons of oil; season with salt and pepper. Grill over high heat, turning once, until lightly charred, about 6 minutes. Let the steak rest for 5 minutes, then thinly slice across the grain. Serve with the corn and poblanos.
—*Dionicio Jimenez*
WINE Rustic, peppery Malbec.

SKIRT STEAK WITH SALSA VERDE AND RICOTTA SALATA

PAN-SEARED SKIRT STEAKS WITH ANCHOVIES AND LIME

Skirt Steak with Salsa Verde and Ricotta Salata

TOTAL: 45 MIN PLUS OVERNIGHT MARINATING

12 SERVINGS ●

Cut from the underside of a cow, below the rib cage, skirt steak is a quick-cooking cut well suited for a hot grill. Here, Paul Virant (an F&W Best New Chef 2007) tenderizes the meat in a wine-and-vinegar-based marinade flavored with both hot and sweet smoked paprika, then smears the grilled steak with a tangy, anchovy-loaded salsa verde.

MARINADE

½ cup vegetable oil

¼ cup dry red wine

¼ cup red wine vinegar

1 small red onion, minced

3 garlic cloves, minced

1 tablespoon tomato paste

½ tablespoon ground cumin

1 teaspoon freshly ground
   black pepper

½ teaspoon sweet pimentón de la
   Vera (smoked Spanish paprika)

½ teaspoon hot pimentón
   de la Vera

Finely grated zest and juice
   of 1 lemon

5½ pounds skirt steak

SALSA VERDE

1½ cups extra-virgin olive oil

10 anchovy fillets, minced

4 medium shallots, very
   finely chopped

¼ cup chopped flat-leaf
   parsley

2 tablespoons drained
   capers, chopped

2 tablespoons very finely
   chopped chives

1 tablespoon minced tarragon

Salt and freshly ground
   black pepper

1 cup shredded *ricotta salata*
   (1 ounce)

1. MARINATE THE STEAK: In a food processor, combine all of the marinade ingredients and process to blend. In a large, shallow dish, pour the marinade over the steak and turn to coat. Cover and refrigerate overnight. Bring to room temperature before grilling.

2. MAKE THE SALSA VERDE: In a bowl, combine the olive oil with the anchovies, shallots, parsley, capers, chives and tarragon. Season with salt and pepper and whisk until blended.

3. Light a grill. Pat the steak dry, season with salt and grill over high heat until medium-rare, 3 minutes per side. Transfer the meat to a carving board; let rest for 5 minutes.

4. Thinly slice the skirt steak across the grain and arrange the slices on a platter. Drizzle with some of the salsa verde and sprinkle with the *ricotta salata.* Serve immediately, passing the remaining salsa verde at the table. —*Paul Virant*

MAKE AHEAD The salsa verde can be refrigerated overnight. Bring to room temperature before serving.

WINE Rustic, peppery Malbec.

Pan-Seared Skirt Steaks with Anchovies and Lime

TOTAL: 30 MIN
4 SERVINGS

Chef Jacques Pépin's mother-in-law, who was from Puerto Rico, seasoned her steaks liberally with lime juice before and after cooking, then served them with a sauce that included anchovies and garlic. This is Pépin's quicker version of her recipe.

Four 6-ounce skirt steaks
1 tablespoon fresh lime juice, plus lime wedges for serving
Kosher salt and freshly ground pepper
1 tablespoon extra-virgin olive oil
One 2-ounce can anchovy fillets packed in oil, drained and minced
2 scallions, minced
1 large garlic clove, minced
¼ cup water

1. Rub the steaks with the lime juice and salt and pepper. Let stand for 10 minutes.
2. In a skillet, heat the olive oil. Add the steaks and cook over moderately high heat, turning once, until medium-rare, 4 minutes; transfer to plates and keep warm.
3. Add the anchovies, scallions and garlic to the skillet and cook over moderate heat, stirring, 30 seconds. Add the water and simmer until the sauce has thickened, scraping up the browned bits from the bottom, 30 seconds. Pour the sauce over the steaks and serve with lime wedges. —*Jacques Pépin*

WINE Fresh, fruity rosé.

Skirt Steak with Salsa Verde

TOTAL: 30 MIN
4 SERVINGS

One 3-inch piece of baguette, cubed
1 cup flat-leaf parsley leaves
½ cup basil leaves
3 tablespoons capers, drained
2 garlic cloves, smashed
2 anchovy fillets, chopped
2 tablespoons white wine vinegar
⅔ cup extra-virgin olive oil
1½ pounds skirt steak
Salt and freshly ground black pepper

1. Light a grill. In a food processor, pulse the baguette, parsley, basil, capers, garlic, anchovies and vinegar until coarsely chopped. With the machine on, gradually add the olive oil.
2. Season the steak with salt and pepper. Grill over high heat until medium-rare, 8 minutes; transfer to a carving board and let rest for 5 minutes. Slice across the grain and serve with the salsa verde.
—*Nick Fauchald*

MAKE AHEAD The salsa verde can be refrigerated overnight. Bring to room temperature before serving.

WINE Rustic, peppery Malbec.

Hanger Steaks with Bourbon and Green Peppercorn Sauce

ACTIVE: 25 MIN; TOTAL: 1 HR
10 SERVINGS

Tanya Cauthen, owner of Belmont Butchery in Richmond, Virginia, likes to teach customers how to work with many different cuts of meat. Here, she makes a hearty pan sauce with bourbon, demiglace and green peppercorns that's tasty with any kind of steak.

2 tablespoons extra-virgin olive oil
Three 1½-pound hanger steaks
Salt and freshly ground black pepper
2 tablespoons plus 1 teaspoon unsalted butter
1 large shallot, finely chopped
¼ cup bourbon
1 cup beef or veal demiglace (see Note)
1 tablespoon drained brined green peppercorns, coarsely chopped

1. Preheat the oven to 300°. In a skillet, heat the olive oil. Season the steaks with salt and black pepper and add to the skillet. Cook over high heat, turning, until browned all over, 20 minutes. Transfer the steaks to a baking sheet and roast for 10 minutes, until an instant-read thermometer inserted in the thickest part of a steak registers 135°. Transfer to a cutting board and let rest for 10 minutes.

2. Meanwhile, pour off the fat from the skillet. Add 2 tablespoons of the butter and let melt. Add the shallot and cook over moderate heat until softened. Carefully add the bourbon and scrape up any browned bits. Add the demiglace and bring to a boil. Simmer for about 5 minutes. Stir in the green peppercorns. Off the heat, swirl in the remaining 1 teaspoon of butter. Slice the steaks across the grain and serve with the sauce. —*Tanya Cauthen*

NOTE Demiglace is available at specialty food shops or from dartagnan.com.

WINE Firm, complex Cabernet Sauvignon.

beef, lamb & game

Korean Grilled Beef

TOTAL: 20 MIN PLUS 4 HR MARINATING
4 SERVINGS ●

- 1 cup apple juice
- ½ cup soy sauce
- 2 tablespoons Asian sesame oil
- ⅓ cup sugar
- 6 large garlic cloves, minced
- 5 scallions, thinly sliced
- 2 tablespoons toasted sesame seeds
- 1½ teaspoons freshly ground pepper
- Five ½-inch-thick boneless rib eye steaks (2 pounds), pounded ⅛ inch thick and cut into 4 pieces each
- Lettuce and steamed rice, for serving

1. In a large nonreactive bowl, whisk the apple juice with the soy sauce, sesame oil, sugar, garlic, scallions, sesame seeds and pepper. Add the steaks and toss to coat. Cover and refrigerate for at least 4 hours or up to 24 hours.

2. Light a grill. Remove the meat from the marinade and grill over high heat, turning once, until lightly charred outside and slightly pink in the center, about 30 seconds per side. Transfer to a platter and serve with lettuce and rice. —*Julia Yoon*

WINE Intense, fruity Zinfandel.

Braised Short Ribs

ACTIVE: 1 HR; TOTAL: 3 HR 15 MIN
PLUS OVERNIGHT MARINATING
6 SERVINGS ●

Tom Colicchio (an F&W Best New Chef 1991) is a master with meat; his tender, succulent braised short ribs are much in demand at his three Craft restaurants.

- 2 tablespoons canola oil
- 6 flanken-style short ribs, with bones, cut 2 inches thick (about 4 pounds; see Note)
- Kosher salt and freshly ground pepper
- 1 large onion, finely chopped
- 2 carrots, sliced
- 3 celery ribs, sliced
- 3 garlic cloves, thickly sliced
- One 750-milliliter bottle dry red wine, such as Cabernet Sauvignon
- 4 thyme sprigs
- 3 cups chicken stock

1. In a large skillet, heat the oil. Season the ribs with salt and pepper. Add them to the skillet and cook over moderate heat, turning once, until browned and crusty, about 18 minutes. Transfer the ribs to a shallow baking dish in a single layer.

2. Add the onion, carrots, celery and garlic to the skillet and cook over low heat, stirring occasionally, until very soft and lightly browned, about 20 minutes. Add the wine and thyme sprigs and bring to a boil over high heat. Pour the hot marinade over the ribs and let cool. Cover and refrigerate overnight, turning the ribs once.

3. Preheat the oven to 350°. Transfer the ribs and marinade to a large enameled cast-iron casserole. Add the chicken stock and bring to a boil. Cover and cook in the lower third of the oven for about 1½ hours, until the meat is tender but not falling apart. Uncover and braise for 45 minutes longer, turning the ribs once or twice, until the sauce is reduced by about half and the meat is very tender.

4. Transfer the meat to a clean shallow baking dish, discarding the bones as they fall off. Strain the sauce into a heatproof measuring cup and skim off as much fat as possible. Pour the sauce over the meat; there should be about 2 cups.

5. Preheat the broiler. Broil the meat, turning once or twice, until glazed and sizzling, about 10 minutes. Transfer the meat to plates, spoon the sauce on top and serve. —*Tom Colicchio*

NOTE Flanken-style short ribs (short ribs cut across the bones instead of parallel to them) can be ordered at butcher shops.

MAKE AHEAD The short ribs can be prepared through Step 4 and refrigerated for up to 2 days.

WINE Earthy, medium-bodied Tempranillo.

Flank Steak with Tamarind Glaze and Orange Gremolata

TOTAL: 50 MIN
4 SERVINGS

- 1½ cups water
- ½ cup coarsely chopped fresh ginger
- ¼ cup honey
- ¼ cup ketchup
- ¼ cup tamarind concentrate (see Note)
- 2 chipotle chiles in adobo, stemmed and finely chopped
- 3 garlic cloves—2 smashed, 1 minced
- 1 tablespoon apple cider vinegar
- Kosher salt
- ¼ cup finely chopped parsley leaves
- 2 teaspoons grated orange zest
- Freshly ground pepper
- One 1¾-pound flank steak

1. Light a grill. In a medium saucepan, combine the water, ginger, honey, ketchup, tamarind concentrate, chipotle chiles, smashed garlic and cider vinegar; bring to a boil, stirring. Simmer over low heat until thickened, about 20 minutes. Strain the tamarind glaze and season with salt.

2. Meanwhile, in a bowl, mix the minced garlic with the parsley and orange zest. Season the gremolata with salt and pepper.

3. Season the flank steak with salt and pepper and grill over high heat until the meat is well browned and an instant-read thermometer inserted into the thickest part registers 125° for medium-rare, 5 minutes per side. During the last 2 minutes of cooking, liberally brush the steak with the tamarind glaze.

4. Transfer the steak to a cutting board and let rest for 5 minutes. Thinly slice the steak across the grain on the diagonal and garnish with the orange gremolata. Serve, passing any remaining glaze at the table. —*Nick Fauchald*

NOTE Tamarind concentrate is available from Asian markets and kalustyans.com.

WINE Juicy, spicy Grenache.

FLANK STEAK WITH TAMARIND
GLAZE AND ORANGE GREMOLATA

Braised Beef Short Ribs with Spices

ACTIVE: 30 MIN; TOTAL: 3 HR

4 SERVINGS

- 1 tablespoon dried porcini mushrooms
- 1½ teaspoons black peppercorns
- 1 teaspoon kosher salt
- 1½ teaspoons ground coriander
- 1½ teaspoons powdered ginger
- 1½ teaspoons smoked sweet paprika
- ½ teaspoon ground cloves
- 5 pounds flanken-style short ribs, 1 inch thick, boned and trimmed of excess fat (see Note on p. 153)
- 2 tablespoons extra-virgin olive oil
- 1 medium onion, thinly sliced
- 1 large carrot, thinly sliced
- 2 inner celery ribs, thinly sliced
- 2 garlic cloves, thickly sliced
- 2 cups dry red wine
- 2 cups beef stock or low-sodium broth
- ¼ cup sugar

1. Preheat the oven to 300°. In a spice grinder, pulse the porcini, peppercorns and salt to a fine powder. Add the coriander, ginger, paprika and cloves and pulse to combine. Rub the spices all over the short ribs.
2. Heat the oil in a large skillet. Add the short ribs and cook over moderate heat, turning, until lightly browned all over, about 12 minutes; don't let the spices burn.

grass-fed beef

Cows that graze on pasture rather than being fed grains produce leaner, more flavorful meat. Grass-fed beef is rich in omega-3 fatty acids and usually free of hormones and antibiotics. For information and sources, go to *eatwild.com*.

3. Scatter the onion, carrot, celery and garlic in a medium roasting pan. Set the short ribs on top, cover tightly with foil and roast for about 2½ hours, until tender.
4. Meanwhile, pour off the fat in the skillet and return it to high heat. Add the wine, stock and sugar and bring to a boil, scraping up any bits from the bottom of the pan. Simmer over moderately high heat until reduced to 1 cup, about 15 minutes. Transfer the glaze to a heatproof cup.
5. Preheat the broiler. Transfer the short ribs to a plate and pour the pan juices and vegetables into a bowl. Skim off all of the fat. Transfer the pan juices and vegetables to a blender. Add ½ cup of the glaze and puree the pan sauce until very smooth.
6. Return the short ribs to the roasting pan and brush with ¼ cup of the glaze. Broil 8 inches from the heat for about 3 minutes, until caramelized and sizzling. Turn the ribs and repeat the process with the remaining ¼ cup of glaze. Serve the ribs with the pan sauce. —*Shea Gallante*
MAKE AHEAD The short ribs can be prepared through Step 3 and refrigerated overnight. Broil just before serving.
WINE Juicy, spicy Grenache.

Slow-Braised Short Ribs with Spinach

ACTIVE: 1 HR 30 MIN;

TOTAL: 6 HR 30 MIN

10 SERVINGS ●

Cholent is a traditional Jewish stew of meat, beans, potatoes and barley. In his kosher-for-Passover version, chef Adam Perry Lang first roasts short ribs, then braises them with porcini mushrooms until the meat is fall-apart tender. He finishes the *cholent* by stirring matzo farfel (crushed matzo) into the pan juices until it plumps up. Baby spinach and crunchy sea salt complete the dish.

- 2 tablespoons garlic salt
- 1 tablespoon sweet paprika

Kosher salt and freshly ground pepper
- ½ cup canola oil

- Two 3-bone sections of short ribs (about 9 pounds total), trimmed of excess fat
- 1 ounce dried porcini mushrooms (3 cups)
- 3 cups boiling water
- ⅓ cup extra-virgin olive oil
- 1 very large white onion, diced
- 2 carrots, finely diced
- 4 celery ribs, finely diced
- 8 garlic cloves, crushed
- 1 pound white button mushrooms, stemmed and quartered
- 1 cup dry white wine
- 3 cups beef stock or low-sodium broth
- 8 ounces matzo farfel (4 cups), finely crushed (see Note)
- 4 cups baby spinach (4 ounces)
- 2 tablespoons chopped flat-leaf parsley

Coarse sea salt

1. Preheat the oven to 275°. Set a large rack in a very large roasting pan. In a small bowl, combine the garlic salt with the sweet paprika, 1 tablespoon of kosher salt and 2 tablespoons of black pepper. Stir in ¼ cup of the canola oil. Rub the spice paste on both sides of the short ribs and transfer to the rack in the roasting pan, meaty side up. Roast for 4 hours, until the meat is tender and pulls away from the bones. Transfer the short ribs to a platter and pour off the fat in the roasting pan. Increase the oven temperature to 325°.
2. Meanwhile, in a medium heatproof bowl, soak the porcini in the boiling water until they are softened, about 20 minutes. Drain the porcini and reserve 2 cups of the soaking liquid. Rinse and coarsely chop the porcini mushrooms.
3. Place the roasting pan over a burner and add the olive oil. Add the onion, carrots, celery, garlic, white mushrooms and chopped porcini mushrooms and cook over moderately high heat, stirring, until the vegetables are softened and beginning

to brown, about 10 minutes. Add the wine and cook, scraping up any browned bits stuck to the bottom of the pan, until the wine has evaporated, about 5 minutes. Add the beef stock, the reserved 2 cups of porcini mushroom soaking liquid and 3 cups of water and bring to a boil. Season with salt and pepper.

4. Return the short ribs to the roasting pan, meaty side up. Cover the pan very tightly with foil and braise in the oven for 1 hour and 15 minutes, until the meat is tender. Remove the foil and spoon off as much fat as possible from the pan juices. Transfer the short ribs to a platter.

5. Meanwhile, in a large skillet, heat the remaining ¼ cup of canola oil. Add the matzo farfel and cook over moderately high heat, stirring, until lightly toasted, about 5 minutes. Stir the toasted farfel into the pan juices in the roasting pan.

6. Return the short ribs to the pan, nestling them into the liquid, and roast uncovered for 15 minutes, until the matzo farfel is moistened and plump.

7. Transfer the short ribs to a cutting board. Remove the bones and slice the meat across the grain. Stir the spinach into the farfel, season with salt and pepper and let wilt. Spoon the farfel onto a platter and top with the meat. Sprinkle the parsley and coarse sea salt on top and serve.
—*Adam Perry Lang*

NOTE Matzo farfel is available in the kosher section of supermarkets during Passover. To make this dish without observing the holiday's dietary restrictions, substitute pearled barley. Stir 1½ cups of pearled barley into the sautéed vegetables in Step 3 and toast for 2 to 3 minutes before adding the wine, then proceed with the recipe (eliminating Step 5 altogether).

MAKE AHEAD The recipe can be prepared through Step 4 and refrigerated for up to 2 days. Slice the meat cold and rewarm, covered, in a 325° oven.

WINE Juicy, spicy Grenache.

Slow-Roasted and Grilled Spiced Short Ribs

ACTIVE: 30 MIN; TOTAL: 4 HR 15 MIN PLUS OVERNIGHT MARINATING

4 SERVINGS

- 2 tablespoons ground ginger
- 2 tablespoons chile powder
- 1 tablespoon pimentón de la Vera (smoked sweet paprika)
- 1 tablespoon minced garlic
- Kosher salt and freshly ground pepper
- ¼ cup vegetable oil
- 6½ pounds meaty flanken-style short ribs (see Note)
- 24 cipollini onions, peeled
- 2 tablespoons extra-virgin olive oil, plus more for drizzling
- Hazelnut Romesco Sauce (recipe follows)
- Lemon wedges, for serving

1. In a bowl, combine the ginger with the chile powder, pimentón, garlic, 1 tablespoon each of kosher salt and pepper and the vegetable oil. Rub the mixture all over the short ribs. Transfer to 2 resealable plastic bags and refrigerate overnight.

2. Preheat the oven to 325°. Arrange the ribs on a large rack set over a large rimmed baking sheet. Bake for about 1 hour and 30 minutes, or until most of the fat has been rendered. Remove the ribs from the rack and set them directly on the baking sheet. Cover with foil and bake for about 2 hours longer, or until tender. Let cool slightly, then discard the bones and trim any gristle, keeping each piece of meat intact.

3. Increase the oven temperature to 425°. On another large rimmed baking sheet, toss the cipollini onions with the 2 tablespoons of olive oil. Season the onions with salt and pepper and roast for about 15 minutes, or until golden brown and tender.

4. Light a grill or preheat the broiler. Drizzle the ribs with olive oil; grill over high heat for 2 minutes per side, or until nicely charred. Serve with the roasted onions, Romesco and lemon wedges. —*Michael Schwartz*

NOTE Flanken-style short ribs (short ribs cut across the bones instead of parallel to them) can be ordered at butcher shops.

MAKE AHEAD The short ribs can be prepared through Step 2 and refrigerated overnight. Let the meat return to room temperature before proceeding.

WINE Intense, fruity Zinfandel.

HAZELNUT ROMESCO SAUCE

TOTAL: 30 MIN
MAKES ABOUT 1½ CUPS ● ●

- 1 small red bell pepper
- 1 tablespoon unsalted butter
- ¼ cup plus 1 tablespoon extra-virgin olive oil
- ½ cup cubed sourdough bread (½ inch)
- 2 tablespoons sherry vinegar
- 1 tablespoon tomato paste
- 1 large garlic clove, very finely chopped
- ½ cup skinned roasted hazelnuts, chopped
- Salt and freshly ground black pepper

1. Roast the red bell pepper directly over a gas flame or under a preheated broiler, turning, until charred all over. Transfer to a plate and let cool. Discard the charred skin and the stem and seeds. Coarsely chop the bell pepper.

2. In a medium skillet, melt the butter in 1 tablespoon of the olive oil. Add the bread cubes and cook over moderate heat, tossing, until crisp, about 3 minutes. Let cool.

3. In a food processor, combine the roasted red pepper with the toasted bread cubes, sherry vinegar, tomato paste, chopped garlic and roasted hazelnuts and puree. With the machine on, slowly pour in the remaining ¼ cup of olive oil. Season the *romesco* sauce with salt and pepper.
—*MS*

MAKE AHEAD The *romesco* sauce can be refrigerated for up to 3 days. Let return to room temperature before serving.

Short Rib Stew

ACTIVE: 45 MIN; TOTAL: 3 HR 30 MIN
8 SERVINGS ●

When Ethan Stowell (an F&W Best New Chef 2008) was growing up, his father was the family cook; beef stew was one of his specialties. Unlike his dad, who favored rump roast, Stowell uses short ribs, a marbled cut that turns fabulously succulent when slow-simmered.

3½ pounds boneless beef short
ribs, cut into 1½-inch pieces
¼ cup all-purpose flour
3 tablespoons extra-virgin
olive oil
2 cups dry red wine
3 cups veal or chicken stock
6 carrots, cut into ½-inch dice
1½ pounds Yukon Gold potatoes,
peeled and cut into ½-inch dice
3 medium parsnips, peeled and
cut into ½-inch dice
1 large onion, cut into 1-inch dice
½ pound cremini mushrooms,
quartered
1 tablespoon thyme leaves,
chopped
8 sage leaves, coarsely chopped
Kosher salt and freshly ground pepper

1. In a large bowl, toss the short ribs with the flour. In a large enameled cast-iron casserole, heat the oil. Working in batches, cook the short ribs over moderately high heat until browned all over, about 6 minutes per batch. Discard the oil.

2. Return the meat and any juices to the casserole. Add the wine and boil until reduced by half, 8 minutes. Add the stock and bring to a simmer. Cover and cook over low heat until the meat is tender, 2 hours.

3. Skim any fat from the stew. Stir in the carrots, potatoes, parsnips, onion, mushrooms, thyme and sage. Cover and simmer over low heat until the vegetables are tender, about 35 minutes. Season with salt and pepper and serve. —*Ethan Stowell*

WINE Fruity, luscious Shiraz.

Horseradish Brisket

ACTIVE: 50 MIN; TOTAL: 4 HR 30 MIN
8 SERVINGS ●

Prepared horseradish punches up the rich flavors of this dish: It's both rubbed on the meat and whisked into the gravy. Like most braised meats, the brisket here tastes even better on the second or even third day.

One 5½-pound first-cut brisket
Kosher salt and freshly ground
black pepper
3½ tablespoons vegetable oil
2 medium onions, halved and
thinly sliced
4 garlic cloves, minced
4 carrots, cut crosswise
1 inch thick
2 medium parsnips, halved
lengthwise and cut
crosswise 1 inch thick
2 celery ribs, cut into
1-inch pieces
½ cup prepared white horseradish,
drained
2 cups dry red wine
2 bay leaves, preferably fresh
3 cups beef stock or
low-sodium broth
4 medium Yukon Gold potatoes,
peeled and cut into
1½-inch pieces

1. Preheat the oven to 325°. Season the brisket generously with salt and pepper. In a very large enameled cast-iron casserole, heat 3 tablespoons of the vegetable oil. Cook the brisket on both sides over moderately high heat until browned all over, about 12 minutes. Using tongs, carefully transfer the brisket to a rimmed baking sheet, fat side up.

2. Pour off all but 3 tablespoons of the fat from the casserole. Add the onions and half of the garlic and cook over moderate heat until softened, about 3 minutes. Add the carrots, parsnips and celery and cook over moderate heat until browned in spots, about 6 minutes.

3. Meanwhile, in a small bowl, mix ¼ cup of the prepared horseradish with the remaining garlic and ½ tablespoon of vegetable oil. Spread the garlic-horseradish paste on the fat side of the brisket.

4. Pour the red wine into the casserole, bring to a boil and cook over high heat, scraping up the brown bits from the bottom of the pot, about 1 minute. Push the vegetables to the side of the casserole and add the bay leaves. Set the brisket horseradish side up in the center of the casserole. Pour the beef stock around the brisket and bring to a simmer over moderate heat. Cover the casserole, transfer to the oven and cook for 1 hour.

5. Scatter the potatoes around the brisket, cover and cook for about 2 hours longer, until the meat is very tender. Increase the oven temperature to 350°. Remove the lid and roast for about 30 minutes, until the brisket is browned on top and the gravy has thickened.

6. Carefully transfer the brisket to a carving board and let rest for 30 minutes. Discard the bay leaves. Using a slotted spoon, transfer the vegetables to a serving platter and cover with foil to keep warm.

7. Pour the cooking liquid into a fat separator and let stand until the fat rises to the surface. Pour the cooking liquid into a gravy boat; discard the fat. Whisk the remaining ¼ cup of horseradish into the gravy and season with salt and pepper.

8. Thinly slice the brisket across the grain and transfer to the platter with the vegetables. Spoon some of the gravy over the brisket and vegetables and serve, passing the remaining gravy at the table.
—*Gail Simmons*

MAKE AHEAD The recipe can be prepared through Step 5 and refrigerated overnight. To reheat, skim the fat from the surface of the cooking liquid. Slice the cold brisket, return it to the casserole and reheat gently. Transfer to a platter and serve.

WINE Fruity, luscious Shiraz.

Red Wine–Braised Beef

ACTIVE: 1 HR; TOTAL: 3 HR 30 MIN
PLUS OVERNIGHT MARINATING
10 SERVINGS ●

Peter Pastan, chef and owner of Obelisk restaurant in Washington, D.C., loves the beef flatiron (or top blade) steak from the shoulder because it stays tender and flavorful even after long braising.

MARINADE

- 1 **cup crushed red grapes with seeds**
- 5 **garlic cloves, smashed**
- 5 **parsley sprigs**
- 3 **bay leaves**
- 1 **rosemary sprig**
- 3 **tablespoons extra-virgin olive oil**
- 2 **teaspoons kosher salt**
- 1 **small dried red chile, crushed**
- 1 **whole 5-pound beef flatiron roast, with membrane and fat layer (see Note)**

BRAISE

- ¼ **cup extra-virgin olive oil**
- 1 **large onion, thinly sliced**
- 5 **garlic cloves, smashed**
- 4 **small carrots, sliced ½ inch thick**
- 3 **celery ribs, sliced 1 inch thick**

Three 3-inch strips of orange zest, removed with a vegetable peeler

- 2 **cups fruity red wine, such as Syrah**
- 2 **cups beef or chicken stock or low-sodium broth**

Salt and freshly ground black pepper

1. MARINATE THE ROAST: In a large, shallow glass or ceramic dish, combine the crushed grapes, smashed garlic cloves, parsley sprigs, bay leaves, rosemary sprig, olive oil, salt and dried red chile. Add the flatiron roast and turn to coat the meat with the marinade. Cover with plastic wrap and refrigerate overnight, turning the beef a few times.

2. MAKE THE BRAISE: Preheat the oven to 325°. Remove the flatiron roast from the grape-and-herb marinade and pat the meat dry with paper towels. Strain the marinade through a food mill and reserve. Set a medium flameproof roasting pan over moderately high heat. Add 2 tablespoons of olive oil and heat until shimmering. Add the beef and cook over moderately high heat, turning once, until it is browned on all sides, about 10 minutes total; transfer the meat to a large plate.

3. Add the remaining 2 tablespoons of olive oil to the roasting pan along with the sliced onion, smashed garlic, sliced carrots, sliced celery and orange zest strips. Cook over low heat, stirring occasionally, until the vegetables are softened, about 10 minutes. Add the red wine, bring to a boil and cook over moderately high heat until the wine is reduced by one-third, about 5 minutes. Add the beef or chicken stock and bring to a boil. Stir in the reserved marinade. Add the beef and cover the pan with foil. Transfer the roasting pan to the oven and braise the meat for about 2½ hours, turning once halfway through, until the beef is very tender.

4. Transfer the beef to a carving board and thickly slice across the grain. Arrange the slices on a large serving platter. Skim any fat from the braising liquid; spoon the liquid over the meat along with some of the vegetables and serve right away.
—*Peter Pastan*

NOTE The beef flatiron is usually precut and sold as individual steaks. The whole flatiron roast called for in this recipe will need to be ordered from the butcher in advance.

MAKE AHEAD The beef can be cooked, cooled and refrigerated in its braising liquid up to 3 days ahead. Skim off the fat and reheat gently before proceeding with the recipe.

WINE Intense, spicy Shiraz.

Horseradish-Crusted Roast Beef

ACTIVE: 10 MIN; TOTAL: 2 HR 30 MIN
8 TO 10 SERVINGS ●

To showcase the grass-fed beef they sell at Fleisher's, their upstate New York butcher shop, Joshua and Jessica Applestone make a simple roast beef using any number of cuts, including rib loin (prime rib), top round or a tied sirloin tip. The roast—deliciously crusted with horseradish and black peppercorns—is perfect hot out of the oven, but it's also amazing cold on a sandwich: Thinly slice it and serve it on white bread with horseradish mayonnaise and juicy tomatoes.

One 6-pound sirloin tip roast, preferably grass-fed, tied

- ½ **cup prepared horseradish**
- 2 **tablespoons kosher salt**
- 2 **tablespoons Dijon mustard**
- 2 **tablespoons finely chopped parsley**
- 1 **tablespoon coarsely ground black pepper**
- 1 **tablespoon sugar**
- 1 **tablespoon sherry vinegar**

1. Preheat the oven to 375°. Set a rack in a large, deep roasting pan and place the beef roast on the rack.

2. In a small bowl, blend the horseradish with the salt, Dijon mustard, chopped parsley, ground pepper, sugar and sherry vinegar to form a paste. Slather the paste all over the top and sides of the meat. Roast in the lower third of the oven for about 2 hours, until an instant-read thermometer inserted in the center of the roast registers 125°. Transfer the roast to a cutting board and let rest for at least 20 minutes.

3. Discard the string; thinly slice the beef across the grain. Transfer to a platter and serve. —*Jessica and Joshua Applestone*

MAKE AHEAD The unsliced roast can be refrigerated for up to 3 days. The sliced beef can be refrigerated overnight.

WINE Intense, fruity Zinfandel.

CLASSIC POT ROAST

perfecting pot roast

*F&W's **Grace Parisi** refines—and redefines—this quintessential wintry roast by experimenting with four flavorful braising liquids.*

Classic Pot Roast

ACTIVE: 1 HR; TOTAL: 4 HR

8 SERVINGS ●

One 4-pound chuck eye roast or other chuck roast, tied

Kosher salt and freshly ground pepper

All-purpose flour, for dusting

- ¼ cup extra-virgin olive oil
- 1 large onion, coarsely chopped
- 3 garlic cloves
- 4 cups beef stock or low-sodium broth
- 6 thyme sprigs, 6 parsley sprigs and 2 bay leaves, tied
- ½ pound white button mushrooms, quartered
- 1 pound large carrots, sliced diagonally ½ inch thick
- 1½ pounds Yukon Gold potatoes, peeled and cut into 2-inch chunks
- 1½ teaspoons cornstarch mixed with 2 tablespoons water

1. Preheat the oven to 300°. Season the roast with salt and pepper and dust with flour. In a medium enameled cast-iron pot, heat 2 tablespoons of the oil. Add the roast; cook over moderate heat, turning, until browned all over, 20 minutes. Transfer to a plate.

2. Add the onion and garlic to the pot and cook, stirring, until softened, 5 minutes. Add the stock and herb bundle and bring to a boil. Return the meat to the pot, cover and transfer to the oven. Braise for 2½ hours, or until tender, turning once halfway through.

3. Meanwhile, in a medium skillet, heat the remaining 2 tablespoons of olive oil. Add the mushrooms, season with salt and pepper and cook over high heat until golden, about 8 minutes.

4. Transfer the roast to a plate. Strain the cooking liquid into a bowl and discard the solids. Skim the fat off the cooking liquid and return the liquid and meat to the pot. Add the mushrooms, carrots and potatoes. Cover and braise in the oven for 30 minutes, until the vegetables are tender.

5. Transfer the roast to a work surface. Using a slotted spoon, transfer the vegetables to a deep serving platter; cover. Boil the liquid until reduced to 3½ cups. Stir the cornstarch slurry and whisk it into the simmering liquid until thickened.

6. Remove the strings from the roast and cut into thick slices; arrange on the platter and pour the sauce on top.

SERVE WITH Buttered egg noodles and prepared horseradish.

WINE Rich, ripe Cabernet Sauvignon.

Three Great Variations

1 Japanese-Inspired Pot Roast
Add 6 slices ginger with the onion and garlic. Replace 1 cup of the stock with ½ cup each of mirin and soy sauce. Omit the herb bundle and add ½ star anise pod. Replace the button mushrooms with shiitake caps and the potatoes with peeled daikon. Cook for 45 minutes.
WINE Rustic, peppery Malbec.

2 Beer-Braised Pot Roast
Before adding the onion, cook 12 ounces diced bacon; transfer half to a plate. Replace 1 cup of the stock with 12 ounces amber ale. Omit the mushrooms and carrots; replace the potatoes with parsnips cut ¾ inch thick and cook for 45 minutes. Garnish with reserved bacon.
WINE Intense, fruity Zinfandel.

3 Spicy Ancho Chile Pot Roast
Soak 4 large stemmed and seeded ancho chiles in ½ cup boiling water for 20 minutes. In a food processor or blender, puree the chiles with their soaking liquid and add the chile puree with the beef stock. Omit the mushrooms and carrots.
WINE Intense, spicy Shiraz.

beef, lamb & game

Roast Leg of Lamb with Red Wine Sauce

ACTIVE: 30 MIN; TOTAL: 2 HR 15 MIN
6 SERVINGS

¼ cup extra-virgin olive oil
¼ cup Dijon mustard
3 garlic cloves, finely chopped
1 tablespoon chopped sage
1 tablespoon chopped parsley
2 teaspoons chopped rosemary
One 7-pound bone-in leg of lamb
Salt and freshly ground pepper
1 medium onion, coarsely chopped
1 celery rib, coarsely chopped
1 carrot, thinly sliced
½ cup dry red wine
2 tablespoons tomato paste
1 cup veal demiglace
   (see Note on p. 149)
1 cup water

1. Preheat the oven to 375°. In a bowl, mix 2 tablespoons of the oil with the mustard, garlic and herbs. Coat the lamb with the mixture; season with salt and pepper.

2. In a large roasting pan, toss the onion, celery and carrot with the remaining oil. Place the lamb fat side up on the vegetables. Roast for 1 hour and 40 minutes, until an instant-read thermometer inserted in the thickest part registers 130°. Transfer the lamb to a carving board and let rest for 15 minutes.

3. Set the roasting pan over 2 burners. Pour in the red wine and bring to a boil over moderately high heat. Boil until reduced to ¼ cup, using a wooden spoon to scrape up the browned bits from the bottom of the pan. Stir in the tomato paste and simmer for 1 minute longer. Add the veal demiglace and water and simmer, stirring occasionally, until the sauce is reduced to 2 cups, about 5 minutes. Strain the sauce into a small saucepan, pressing on the solids. Season with salt and pepper and keep hot.

4. Carve the lamb and serve the slices with the red wine sauce. —*Stu Stein*

WINE Round, deep-flavored Syrah.

Merlot-Braised Lamb Shoulder with Lemon Gremolata

ACTIVE: 45 MIN; TOTAL: 3 HR 15 MIN
6 SERVINGS ●

One 3-pound boneless lamb
   shoulder roast, tied
3 garlic cloves, thinly sliced,
   plus 1 very finely chopped
   garlic clove
Salt and freshly ground
   black pepper
¼ cup extra-virgin olive oil
1 cup pearl onions, peeled
2 cups Merlot or other
   dry red wine
1 cup beef stock
One 15-ounce can diced
   tomatoes, drained
One 3-inch rosemary sprig
   plus 1 teaspoon chopped
   rosemary leaves
Two 1-inch-wide strips of lemon
   zest, removed with a
   vegetable peeler, plus
   1 teaspoon very finely
   chopped lemon zest
3 medium carrots, cut into
   2-inch pieces
1 fennel bulb, cut into 8 wedges
   attached at the core
1 tablespoon very finely
   chopped flat-leaf parsley
Pinch of crushed red pepper

1. Preheat the oven to 325°. Using a sharp knife, make deep slits all over the lamb roast and fill each slit with a garlic slice. Season the lamb with salt and pepper.

2. In a large enameled cast-iron casserole, heat the olive oil. Add the lamb and cook over moderate heat, turning, until the roast is browned and crusty, about 12 minutes. Transfer the lamb to a plate and pour off the fat in the casserole.

3. Add the pearl onions to the casserole and cook over low heat until lightly browned, about 5 minutes. Add the wine and scrape up any browned bits from the bottom of the casserole. Add the stock, tomatoes, rosemary sprig and lemon zest strips and bring to a boil. Return the lamb and any accumulated juices to the casserole and cover.

4. Transfer the covered casserole to the oven and braise the lamb for 1½ hours, until the meat is nearly tender. Add the carrots and fennel wedges, cover and braise for about 45 minutes longer, until the vegetables and lamb are tender.

5. Transfer the lamb and vegetables to a platter and cover with foil. Discard the rosemary sprigs and lemon zest. Boil the braising liquid over high heat until it is reduced by half, about 15 minutes.

6. Meanwhile, in a small bowl, toss the parsley with the crushed red pepper, chopped rosemary, chopped lemon zest and chopped garlic.

7. Discard the strings from the lamb and slice the meat. Transfer to a platter and garnish with the parsley-lemon gremolata. Serve with the sauce and vegetables. —*David Page and Barbara Shinn*

MAKE AHEAD The lamb can be refrigerated, sliced or unsliced, with the vegetables in the braising sauce for up to 2 days. Reheat gently in a 325° oven or on the stovetop before serving.

WINE Deep, velvety Merlot.

Skillet-Roasted Lamb Loins with Herbs

TOTAL: 1 HR
8 SERVINGS

Cathal Armstrong (an F&W Best New Chef 2006) recalls that his family always celebrated the end of Lent with lamb, and that preparing the meal became an all-day event that left the adults "snoring on the couch." Armstrong's preparation for lamb nowadays isn't exhausting at all: He rubs the loins with herbs, garlic and shallots, then ties them up, sears them and finishes them in the oven. The result is tender, delicately flavored meat.

3 tablespoons extra-virgin
    olive oil

2 garlic cloves, very
    finely chopped

1 large shallot, very
    finely chopped

1 teaspoon very finely
    chopped rosemary

1 teaspoon very finely
    chopped sage

1 teaspoon very finely
    chopped marjoram

1 teaspoon very finely
    chopped thyme

2 boneless lamb loins—with
    tenderloins attached, thin
    layer of fat and rib apron
    left on (about 3 pounds),
    at room temperature

Salt and freshly ground
    black pepper

1. In a small bowl, combine 2 tablespoons of the oil with the garlic, shallot and herbs. Lay the loins on a work surface, fat side down, and season with salt and pepper. Spread the herb paste all over the lamb. Roll each loin over the tenderloin and rib apron to make a neat roulade. With butcher's twine, tie the meat at 1-inch intervals. Season the lamb with salt and pepper.

2. Preheat the oven to 350°. In a 12-inch skillet (preferably cast-iron), heat the remaining 1 tablespoon of olive oil until shimmering. Add the lamb loins and cook over moderate heat, turning, until browned all over, about 20 minutes total.

3. Transfer the skillet to the oven and roast the loins for 10 minutes, until an instant-read thermometer inserted in the thickest part registers 125°. Transfer the loins to a carving board to rest for 10 minutes.

4. Cut off the strings. Carve the loins into 1-inch-thick slices and serve.

—*Cathal Armstrong*

SERVE WITH Slow-Roasted Tomatoes (p. 236) and boiled baby new potatoes.

WINE Ripe, juicy Pinot Noir.

Oven-Roasted Lamb Chops with Mint Chimichurri

TOTAL: 50 MIN

4 SERVINGS

For this playful twist on British roast lamb with mint jelly, Australian chef Luke Mangan serves lamb chops with a piquant condiment of fresh mint and jalapeño.

2 cups mint leaves

1 small jalapeño, seeded
    and coarsely chopped

1 small shallot, coarsely
    chopped

1 garlic clove, coarsely
    chopped

2 tablespoons red wine
    vinegar

Pinch of sugar

½ cup plus 3 tablespoons
    extra-virgin olive oil

Salt

2 six-rib racks of lamb
    (about 1½ pounds each)

Freshly ground pepper

6 ounces snow peas

1 red Thai chile, seeded
    and very finely chopped

1 tablespoon chopped cilantro

¼ cup roasted almonds, chopped

1. In a blender, puree the mint leaves, chopped jalapeño, shallot and garlic, vinegar, sugar and ½ cup of the olive oil. Season the mint chimichurri with salt.

2. Preheat the oven to 450°. In a large ovenproof skillet, heat 2 tablespoons of the olive oil until shimmering. Season the lamb racks with salt and pepper; add to the skillet, fat side down, and brown over high heat, turning once. Transfer the skillet to the oven and roast the lamb for 12 minutes, until medium-rare. Transfer the lamb racks to a carving board; let rest for about 10 minutes.

3. Meanwhile, bring a medium saucepan of salted water to a boil. Add the snow peas and blanch them until crisp-tender, about 1 minute. Drain and pat dry.

4. In a small bowl, mix the chile, cilantro, blanched snow peas, chopped almonds and the remaining 1 tablespoon of olive oil; season the snow pea salad with salt.

5. Carve the racks into chops and set 3 on each plate. Dollop the lamb chops with some of the mint chimichurri and serve the snow pea salad alongside.

—*Luke Mangan*

WINE Firm, complex Cabernet Sauvignon.

Grilled Herbed Baby Lamb Chops

 TOTAL: 25 MIN

4 SERVINGS

In Spain, *chuletillas de cordero* (teeny lamb chops) are about the size of lollipops. On an installment of his TV series *Spain . . . On the Road Again,* Mario Batali rubbed these juicy chops with a mixture of rosemary, lavender, sugar and red wine vinegar, which imparted a wonderful herbal tang while the meat grilled.

Twelve 4-ounce baby lamb
    rib chops

2 tablespoons extra-virgin
    olive oil

2 tablespoons red wine vinegar

1 tablespoon sugar

2 teaspoons very finely
    chopped fresh rosemary

2 teaspoons chopped
    dried lavender buds

Coarse salt and freshly ground
    black pepper

Light a grill. Rub the lamb all over with the olive oil and drizzle with the red wine vinegar. In a small bowl, combine the sugar, rosemary and lavender and season with salt and black pepper. Rub the herb mixture all over the lamb chops and grill the herb-rubbed chops over high heat, turning occasionally, about 8 minutes for medium-rare meat. Transfer to a platter, season with salt and black pepper and serve.

—*Mario Batali*

WINE Earthy, medium-bodied Tempranillo.

beef, lamb & game

Herb-and-Spice Lamb Chops with Minted Asparagus

TOTAL: 50 MIN PLUS OVERNIGHT MARINATING

6 SERVINGS

MARINADE

- 1 cup extra-virgin olive oil
- 4 garlic cloves, thickly sliced
- ¼ cup rosemary leaves
- 3 tablespoons flat-leaf parsley leaves
- 2 tablespoons marjoram or oregano leaves
- 2 tablespoons kosher salt
- 1 tablespoon freshly ground black pepper
- 1 tablespoon ground fennel
- 1½ teaspoons ground cumin
- 1½ teaspoons ground cardamom
- 1 teaspoon balsamic vinegar
- 12 lamb loin chops, 1½ inches thick

ASPARAGUS

- ¼ cup extra-virgin olive oil
- 2 large garlic cloves, minced
- 1 shallot, minced
- 1 teaspoon finely grated lemon zest
- ¼ cup mint leaves

Salt and freshly ground pepper

- 1½ pounds pencil-thin asparagus

1. MARINATE THE LAMB: In a saucepan, combine ¼ cup of the oil with the garlic and cook over moderate heat, stirring frequently, until golden, 4 minutes. Transfer the garlic oil to a blender. Add the rosemary, parsley, marjoram, salt, pepper, fennel, cumin, cardamom, vinegar and the remaining ¾ cup of oil and puree until smooth.

2. Arrange the lamb chops in a shallow baking dish. Pour the marinade on top, turn to coat and refrigerate overnight. Return to room temperature before grilling.

3. PREPARE THE ASPARAGUS: In a small saucepan, heat the olive oil. Add the garlic and shallot and simmer over moderate heat until fragrant and softened, about 3 minutes. Transfer to a blender, add the lemon zest and let cool. Add the mint and

a generous pinch each of salt and pepper and puree to a chunky paste.

4. In a large skillet of boiling salted water, cook the asparagus until crisp-tender, about 4 minutes. Drain the asparagus and run under cold water to cool; pat dry. Transfer the asparagus to a platter and drizzle with the mint dressing.

5. Light a grill. Remove the lamb chops from the marinade and grill over high heat, turning occasionally, until browned, about 10 minutes for medium-rare meat. Serve the lamb chops with the asparagus. —*Jason Wilson*

WINE Juicy, spicy Grenache.

Pot-Roasted Lamb Shanks with Cannellini Beans

ACTIVE: 30 MIN; TOTAL: 2 HR 30 MIN PLUS OVERNIGHT SOAKING

4 SERVINGS ●

- 1½ cups dried cannellini beans, soaked overnight and drained
- 1 bay leaf
- 4 meaty lamb shanks

Salt and freshly ground pepper

- 4 large unpeeled garlic cloves
- 3 cups chicken stock
- 1 teaspoon sherry vinegar
- 1 teaspoon chopped fresh thyme

1. In a large saucepan, cover the beans and the bay leaf with 2 inches of water and bring to a boil. Simmer over low heat until the beans are tender, about 2 hours. Drain the beans and discard the bay leaf.

2. Meanwhile, preheat the oven to 300°. Heat an enameled cast-iron casserole that's large enough to hold the lamb shanks in a single layer. Season the shanks with salt and pepper and cook over moderate heat, turning a few times, until lightly browned all over, about 15 minutes. Nestle the garlic cloves among the shanks. Cover and cook in the oven for about 1 hour and 45 minutes, turning three times, until the shanks are very tender.

3. Reduce the oven temperature to 200°. Transfer the shanks to a small roasting pan and the garlic cloves to a small bowl. Cover the shanks with foil and keep warm in the oven. Strain the juices from the casserole into a bowl and skim off the fat. Return the juices to the casserole, add the chicken stock and set the casserole over a burner. Boil over high heat until the juices have reduced to 2 cups, about 12 minutes.

4. Peel the garlic cloves and add the sherry vinegar. With a fork, mash to a paste. Add the garlic paste to the juices in the casserole and stir in the beans and thyme. Simmer over low heat for 5 minutes. Season with salt and pepper.

5. Place the lamb shanks on plates and serve with the beans. —*Marcia Kiesel*

SERVE WITH Chard with Orange and Bacon (p. 223).

MAKE AHEAD The beans can be prepared through Step 1 and refrigerated overnight in their liquid. The lamb can be prepared through Step 2 and refrigerated overnight.

WINE Deep, velvety Merlot.

Merguez-Spiced Lamb Shanks with Chickpeas

ACTIVE: 45 MIN; TOTAL: 2 HR 15 MIN

8 SERVINGS ●

The braising liquid for this supremely tender lamb dish includes many of the ingredients that make up merguez, a North African spice blend typically used to flavor sausages of the same name. Lamb shanks are great for serving at dinner parties, as they look so dramatic, but lamb stew meat—cut from the shoulder or the leg—is equally delicious.

- 1 tablespoon cumin seeds
- 1 tablespoon fennel seeds
- 1 tablespoon coriander seeds
- ¼ cup sweet paprika
- 1 tablespoon freshly ground black pepper
- 2 teaspoons sugar
- 1 teaspoon ground allspice

POT-ROASTED LAMB SHANKS WITH CANNELLINI BEANS

MERGUEZ-SPICED LAMB SHANKS WITH CHICKPEAS

1½ teaspoons cayenne pepper

8 lamb shanks
(about 1 pound each)

Salt

1 cup all-purpose flour

2 tablespoons unsalted butter

¼ cup extra-virgin olive oil

1 medium sweet onion,
coarsely chopped

2 tablespoons tomato paste

2 quarts chicken stock

One 14-ounce can crushed
tomatoes

Two 15-ounce cans chickpeas,
drained

Harissa, for serving (see Note)

1. In a small skillet, toast the cumin, fennel and coriander seeds over moderately low heat until just fragrant, about 1 minute; let cool completely. Grind the toasted seeds to a powder in a spice grinder; transfer to an airtight container. Stir in the paprika, black pepper, sugar, allspice and cayenne and cover the merguez spice blend until ready to use.

2. Preheat the oven to 325°. Season the lamb with salt and dredge in the flour, shaking off the excess. In a large enameled cast- iron casserole, melt the butter in the olive oil. Add 4 of the lamb shanks; cook over moderately high heat, turning frequently, until well browned all over, about 8 minutes. Transfer the lamb shanks to a plate and repeat with the remaining 4 shanks. Discard all but 1 tablespoon of the fat from the casserole.

3. Reduce the heat to moderate. Add the onion to the casserole and cook, stirring, until lightly browned, 5 minutes. Stir in 4 tablespoons of the spice blend along with the tomato paste and cook until aromatic, 2 minutes. Add 1 cup of the chicken stock and scrape up the browned bits from the bottom of the pot. Stir in the tomatoes.

4. Return the lamb to the casserole and pour in any accumulated juices. Add the chickpeas. Pour in just enough of the chicken stock to cover the meat and bring to a simmer. Cover the casserole and transfer to the oven. Braise the shanks for 1½ hours, or until the meat is tender and pulling away from the bones.

5. Transfer the braised lamb shanks to a large, deep platter. Using a large spoon, skim the fat from the surface of the sauce. Spoon the sauce over the shanks and serve, passing *harissa* at the table.
—*Tanya Cauthen*

SERVE WITH Couscous.

NOTE *Harissa* is a North African chile paste. It is available at specialty shops or from kalustyans.com.

MAKE AHEAD The braised shanks can be refrigerated in the sauce for up to 3 days. Reheat gently before serving.

WINE Juicy, spicy Grenache.

Lamb Chops with Harissa-Yogurt Sauce

TOTAL: 25 MIN
4 SERVINGS

These delectable lamb chops from F&W's Nick Fauchald require just minutes to grill—not much more time than it takes to make the sauce, a hot-and-cool combination of spicy *harissa* and Greek yogurt. At casual get-togethers, Fauchald and his guests grab the chops directly off the grill, then dip them in the sauce—no plates or platters are required.

- 1 cup plain Greek-style yogurt
- 1½ tablespoons *harissa* (see Note on p. 161)
- 1½ tablespoons fresh lemon juice
- Salt and freshly ground pepper
- 8 lamb rib chops, about 1 inch thick, trimmed of excess fat
- Finely grated lemon zest, for serving

1. Light a grill. In a small bowl, combine the yogurt with the *harissa* and lemon juice and season with salt and pepper.
2. Season the lamb chops with salt and pepper and grill over high heat, turning once, about 4 minutes for medium-rare. Sprinkle the lamb chops with lemon zest and serve with the yogurt sauce.
—*Nick Fauchald*

WINE Earthy, medium-bodied Tempranillo.

rib chops vs. loin chops

Rib and loin lamb chops are both tender cuts that are great for dry-cooking methods like grilling. Rib chops are small rounds of meat attached to bones; loin chops are shaped like T-bone steaks and have some strip and some tenderloin.

Lamb Chops with Spicy Thai Peanut Sauce

TOTAL: 25 MIN
4 SERVINGS ●

A nutty paste does double duty as a rub and a sauce for these grilled lamb chops from meat master Bruce Aidells.

- 2 large garlic cloves
- ⅓ cup cilantro leaves
- ⅓ cup unsalted natural peanut butter
- 2 tablespoons peanut oil
- 2 tablespoons ketchup
- 1 tablespoon Thai green curry paste
- 1 tablespoon fresh lime juice
- 1 tablespoon Asian fish sauce
- 1 tablespoon soy sauce
- 1 teaspoon sugar
- 8 lamb loin chops, about 1 inch thick

1. In a food processor, pulse the garlic cloves and cilantro leaves until finely chopped. Add the peanut butter, peanut oil, ketchup, Thai green curry paste, fresh lime juice, Asian fish sauce, soy sauce and sugar and pulse until a paste forms. Spread ¼ cup of the peanut paste all over the lamb chops.
2. In a small saucepan, whisk the remaining peanut paste with ⅓ cup of water until smooth. Warm the peanut sauce over low heat until pourable.
3. Light a grill. Grill the paste-coated lamb chops over moderately high heat for 4 minutes per side, or until an instant-read thermometer inserted in the thickest part of a chop registers 125° to 130° for medium-rare. Transfer the chops to a serving platter. Spoon some of the warm peanut sauce over the chops and serve right away, passing the extra peanut sauce at the table.
—*Bruce Aidells*

MAKE AHEAD The spicy peanut paste can be prepared up to 1 day ahead. Bring to room temperature before coating the lamb.

WINE Fruity, luscious Shiraz.

Lamb Rogan Josh

ACTIVE: 35 MIN; TOTAL: 1 HR 45 MIN
4 TO 6 SERVINGS ● ●

The name of this succulent Indian stew translates roughly as "red lamb."

- ¼ cup canola oil
- 2 pounds boneless lamb shoulder, cut into 1-inch pieces
- Kosher salt
- 2 onions, thinly sliced (3 cups)
- 2 tablespoons very finely chopped fresh ginger
- 2 garlic cloves, very finely chopped
- 1 tablespoon plus 1 teaspoon Madras curry powder
- 1 teaspoon turmeric
- ½ teaspoon cayenne pepper
- 2 bay leaves
- One 14-ounce can tomato puree
- 1 cup plain whole-milk yogurt
- 2 cups water
- 1 teaspoon garam masala
- Cilantro leaves, for garnish
- Basmati rice and warm naan, for serving

1. In a large enameled cast-iron casserole, heat the oil. Season the lamb pieces with salt and cook over high heat, stirring occasionally, until the lamb is browned all over, about 12 minutes; using a slotted spoon, transfer the lamb to a plate.
2. Add the sliced onions to the casserole and cook over moderate heat, stirring frequently, until they are lightly browned, about 4 minutes. Add the chopped ginger, garlic, curry, turmeric, cayenne and bay leaves and cook for 2 minutes. Stir in the tomato puree, yogurt and water. Bring the sauce to a boil and season with salt.
3. Return the lamb and any juices to the casserole. Cover partially and simmer over low heat until the lamb is very tender, about 1 hour. Stir in the garam masala; cook for 5 minutes. Discard the bay leaves. Garnish with cilantro. Serve with rice and naan. —*Vikram Sunderam*

WINE Round, deep-flavored Syrah.

Grilled Coconut-Curry Lamb Chops with Red Pepper Sauce

TOTAL: 40 MIN PLUS OVERNIGHT MARINATING

4 SERVINGS

- ¾ cup plus 1 tablespoon chicken stock or low-sodium broth
- ¼ cup plus ½ tablespoon unseasoned rice vinegar
- ½ cup unsweetened coconut milk
- ¼ cup mirin
- ¼ cup Asian fish sauce
- 2 tablespoons mild curry powder
- 2 tablespoons creamy peanut butter
- 1 teaspoon Chinese mustard
- 8 lamb rib chops
- 1 red bell pepper
- 1 tablespoon vegetable oil

Salt

- ½ seedless cucumber, peeled and thinly sliced

1. In a medium bowl, whisk ¾ cup of the chicken stock and ¼ cup of the rice vinegar with the coconut milk, mirin, fish sauce, curry powder, peanut butter and Chinese mustard. Transfer to a large resealable plastic bag. Add the lamb chops and turn to coat them completely. Seal the bag and refrigerate overnight.

2. Roast the red bell pepper over a gas flame or under a broiler, turning, until the pepper skin is blackened all over. Transfer the charred pepper to a small bowl, cover with plastic wrap and let cool. Peel the pepper and discard the core and seeds. Transfer the pepper to a blender. Add the remaining 1 tablespoon of stock and ½ tablespoon of rice vinegar and puree until smooth. With the machine on, add the oil and puree until creamy and smooth. Season the red pepper sauce with salt.

3. In a small bowl, toss the cucumber with a pinch of salt and let stand until softened slightly, about 5 minutes.

4. Light a grill or preheat a grill pan. Drain the lamb chops and grill over high heat, turning once, until charred outside and medium-rare within, about 7 minutes. Transfer the chops to plates and serve with the red pepper sauce and cucumber. —*Nobuo Fukuda*

MAKE AHEAD The red pepper sauce can be refrigerated overnight.

WINE Intense, spicy Shiraz.

Moroccan Spiced Lamb with Date Barbecue Sauce

ACTIVE: 1 HR; TOTAL: 2 HR PLUS 6 HR MARINATING

8 SERVINGS ●

- 1 tablespoon plus 1½ teaspoons ground coriander
- 2¾ teaspoons ground cumin
- 2¾ teaspoons sweet paprika
- 2¾ teaspoons ground ginger
- 1½ teaspoons cinnamon

Freshly ground black pepper

Salt

- ½ cup extra-virgin olive oil

One 5-pound butterflied leg of lamb, trimmed of excess fat

- 8 medium garlic cloves— 4 thinly sliced, 4 minced
- 1 medium onion, finely chopped
- ¼ cup tomato paste
- 3 cups low-sodium beef broth
- 2 tablespoons honey
- ¼ teaspoon saffron, crumbled into 1 tablespoon of water
- ½ teaspoon cayenne pepper
- 8 large pitted Medjool dates, minced (3 ounces)
- ¼ cup fresh lemon juice
- 20 large pitted green olives, finely chopped
- ¼ cup finely chopped mint
- ¼ cup finely chopped cilantro

1. In a bowl, combine the coriander, cumin, paprika, ginger, cinnamon and 1 teaspoon of black pepper. Set aside 3 tablespoons of the spice mixture for the barbecue sauce. Stir 1 teaspoon of salt and ¼ cup of olive oil into the remaining spice mixture.

2. Using a small, sharp knife, make ½-inch-deep slits all over the lamb. Press the garlic slices into the slits. Coat the lamb with the spiced oil, making sure to rub it in the slits. Cover with plastic wrap and refrigerate for at least 6 hours.

3. In a medium saucepan, heat the remaining ¼ cup of olive oil. Add the chopped onion and minced garlic and cook over moderately low heat, stirring occasionally, until softened, about 10 minutes. Add the reserved 3 tablespoons of spice mixture and cook, stirring occasionally, until fragrant, about 4 minutes.

4. Add the tomato paste and cook, stirring, for about 1 minute. Add the beef broth, honey, saffron water and cayenne pepper and simmer over high heat until slightly thickened, about 8 minutes. Add the dates and simmer over low heat, stirring occasionally, until they break down and the sauce is thick and glossy, about 15 minutes. Remove from the heat. Stir in the lemon juice and season with salt and black pepper. Reserve ½ cup of the date barbecue sauce for glazing the lamb.

5. Light a grill. Lightly season the lamb with salt and black pepper and grill over moderate heat, turning once, until the lamb is nicely charred all over and an instant-read thermometer inserted in the thickest part of the leg registers 130°, about 15 minutes per side. During the last 3 minutes of grilling, brush the reserved date barbecue sauce all over the lamb. Transfer the grilled lamb to a carving board and let rest for 10 minutes.

6. In a small bowl, toss the olives with the mint and cilantro. Slice the lamb across the grain and serve with the date barbecue sauce and olive relish. —*Kristin Donnelly*

MAKE AHEAD The date barbecue sauce can be refrigerated for up to 3 days.

WINE Rich, ripe Cabernet Sauvignon.

MOROCCAN LAMB-AND-
VEGETABLE COUSCOUS

Moroccan Lamb-and-Vegetable Couscous

ACTIVE: 1 HR; TOTAL: 3 HR 40 MIN

8 SERVINGS

Loaded with tender lamb and poached vegetables, this classic couscous is spiced with generous amounts of cumin.

- 4½ tablespoons unsalted butter
- 1 tablespoon extra-virgin olive oil
- 1 large Spanish onion, thinly sliced

Large pinch of saffron threads

- 4 meaty lamb shanks (about 1 pound each)

Salt and freshly ground black pepper

- 1 tablespoon sweet paprika, plus more for dusting
- 2 teaspoons ground cumin

Large pinch of cayenne pepper

- 3 large plum tomatoes—peeled, seeded and quartered
- 10 parsley sprigs and 1 large thyme sprig, tied with kitchen string
- 3 medium boiling potatoes, cut into 1½-inch chunks
- 3 large celery ribs, cut into 2-inch lengths
- 2 large carrots, cut into 2-inch lengths
- 2 red bell peppers, cut into 2-inch pieces
- 3 medium zucchini, cut into 2-inch pieces
- 2 cups frozen lima beans
- 2 cups couscous
- ¼ cup slivered mint leaves

Harissa, for serving

1. In a very large, enameled cast-iron casserole, melt 3 tablespoons of the butter in the olive oil. Add the onion and cook over moderate heat, stirring occasionally, until just softened, about 5 minutes. In a small bowl, crumble the saffron into 2 tablespoons of hot water and let stand for at least 10 minutes.

2. Season the lamb shanks with salt and black pepper and dust with paprika. Add the lamb shanks to the casserole and cook over moderate heat, turning occasionally, until the shanks are well browned, about 7 minutes. Stir in the 1 tablespoon of paprika, the cumin and cayenne and cook, stirring, until fragrant, about 1 minute. Add the tomatoes and 3 quarts of water and bring to a boil over moderately high heat. Skim off any fat and add the saffron and its soaking liquid, the parsley bundle and a large pinch of salt. Reduce the heat to low, cover partially and simmer until the lamb is tender, about 2 hours.

3. Transfer the lamb shanks to a large plate and cover with foil. Add the potatoes, celery and carrots to the casserole, cover and simmer over moderate heat until almost tender, 10 minutes. Add the red peppers and zucchini and simmer uncovered until all the vegetables are tender, 10 minutes longer. Remove from the heat and discard the parsley bundle; set aside 1 cup of the cooking liquid. Stir in the frozen lima beans.

4. Remove the meat from the lamb shanks and cut it into ¾-inch pieces. Return the meat to the stew.

5. In a large saucepan, melt the remaining 1½ tablespoons of butter. Add the couscous and cook over moderate heat, stirring, until lightly toasted, about 3 minutes. Stir in 2 cups of water, the reserved 1 cup of cooking liquid and a large pinch of salt and bring to a boil. Cover, remove from the heat and let stand until the liquid has been absorbed, about 10 minutes. Fluff with a fork.

6. Season the stew with salt and black pepper. Mound the couscous on a platter. Ladle one-third of the lamb and vegetables around the couscous and moisten with a little of the cooking liquid. Sprinkle the lamb stew and couscous with the mint and serve the remaining stew on the side, passing the *harissa* at the table.

—*Anya von Bremzen*

MAKE AHEAD The lamb stew can be made through Step 4 and refrigerated for up to 3 days; reheat gently.

WINE Lively, fruity Merlot.

Lamb Tagine with Green Olives and Lemon

ACTIVE: 35 MIN; TOTAL: 2 HR 45 MIN

PLUS 4 HR MARINATING

8 SERVINGS ●●

- ¼ cup extra-virgin olive oil
- 5 garlic cloves, minced

Two 2½-inch strips of lemon zest

- 2 teaspoons ground ginger
- 2 teaspoons sweet paprika
- 2 teaspoons ground coriander
- 1 teaspoon ground cumin
- 1 teaspoon freshly ground black pepper
- ¼ teaspoon cayenne pepper
- ¼ teaspoon ground cloves

Pinch of saffron threads, crumbled

One 3-inch cinnamon stick

Kosher salt

- 3½ pounds boneless lamb shoulder, cut into 1-inch pieces
- 4 cups water
- 6 large carrots, thinly sliced
- 1 onion, cut into ¼-inch dice
- 2 cups pitted green Picholine olives, rinsed
- 1 cup flat-leaf parsley, chopped
- 1 cup cilantro leaves, chopped
- 3 tablespoons fresh lemon juice

1. In a large bowl, mix the olive oil, garlic, lemon zest, ginger, paprika, coriander, cumin, black pepper, cayenne, cloves, saffron, cinnamon stick and 1 tablespoon of kosher salt. Add the lamb and toss to coat. Refrigerate for 4 to 6 hours.

2. Scrape the lamb and spices into a tagine or a medium enameled cast-iron casserole; discard the lemon zest. Add the water, carrots and onion and bring to a simmer. Cover and cook over low heat until the lamb is very tender, about 2 hours.

3. Spoon off any fat from the broth. Stir in the olives, season with salt and cook for 2 minutes. Remove from the heat and stir in the parsley, cilantro and lemon juice. Ladle into bowls and serve. —*Ethan Stowell*

WINE Round, deep-flavored Syrah.

beef, lamb & game

Sweet Onions Stuffed with Spiced Lamb

ACTIVE: 30 MIN; TOTAL: 1 HR 45 MIN

6 SERVINGS ●●

- 1½ cups chicken stock or low-sodium broth
- ½ cup dried apricots, chopped
- 1 teaspoon finely grated lemon zest
- 6 medium sweet onions (10 ounces each), unpeeled
- 4 tablespoons unsalted butter
- ½ pound ground lamb
- ½ teaspoon cinnamon
- Salt and freshly ground pepper
- 3 tablespoons finely chopped mint
- 3 tablespoons finely chopped flat-leaf parsley
- 2 tablespoons coarse dry bread crumbs
- ¼ cup water

1. Preheat the oven to 400°. In a small saucepan, combine the chicken stock, chopped dried apricots and grated lemon zest and bring to a boil. Simmer over moderate heat until the apricots are plump and the liquid is reduced to a few tablespoons, about 10 minutes.

2. Meanwhile, cut the top third off of each onion; reserve the tops. Using a melon baller or small spoon, remove the center of each onion, leaving a 2-layer shell. Coarsely chop the centers. Trim off the root ends and stand the onions upright in a medium baking dish; leave room for the onion tops.

3. In a large skillet, melt 3 tablespoons of the butter. Add the chopped onions and cook over moderate heat, stirring occasionally, until very soft, about 12 minutes. Add the lamb and cinnamon, season with salt and pepper and cook over moderately high heat, stirring occasionally, until the lamb is cooked through and any liquid has evaporated, about 8 minutes. Remove from the heat. Stir in the apricots and 2 tablespoons each of the mint and parsley. Let cool slightly.

4. Spoon the lamb filling into the onion shells, packing it in tightly and mounding it over the onions. Sprinkle the bread crumbs on top and dot with the remaining 1 tablespoon of butter. Set the onion tops beside the stuffed onions and add the water to the dish. Cover with foil and bake for 40 minutes. Uncover and bake for about 20 minutes longer, until the onions are tender and the tops are golden. Let the onions rest for 10 minutes, then sprinkle with the remaining 1 tablespoon each of mint and parsley. Partially cover with the onion tops, transfer to plates and serve.

—*Michael Schwartz*

MAKE AHEAD The lamb-stuffed onions can be baked up to 8 hours ahead. Reheat before serving.

WINE Juicy, fresh Dolcetto.

Lamb Sausage with Lentils and Sautéed Pears

ACTIVE: 30 MIN; TOTAL: 1 HR 20 MIN

6 SERVINGS

- 2 cups brown lentils (14 ounces)
- 4 cups boiling water
- ¾ cup extra-virgin olive oil
- 2 carrots, diced
- 1 onion, diced
- 1 celery rib, diced
- Salt and freshly ground black pepper
- 3 tablespoons cider vinegar
- 1 cup roasted red peppers (8 ounces), preferably piquillo, cut into thin strips
- 1¼ pounds merguez sausage
- 2 ripe Bartlett pears, cored and cut into eighths

1. In a large heatproof bowl, cover the lentils with the boiling water and let stand for 30 minutes. Drain.

2. In a large saucepan, heat 2 tablespoons of the olive oil. Add the diced carrots, onion and celery and cook over moderate heat, stirring occasionally, until softened, about

8 minutes. Add the soaked and drained lentils and 1½ cups of water and season with salt and black pepper. Cover and cook over low heat until the lentils are just tender and the liquid is absorbed, about 20 minutes. Stir in ½ cup of the olive oil, the cider vinegar and the roasted red peppers and season with salt and black pepper. Transfer the lentil mixture to a serving platter.

3. In a large skillet, heat the remaining 2 tablespoons of olive oil. Add the merguez sausage and cook over moderate heat, turning occasionally, until browned and cooked through, about 8 minutes. Arrange the sausages around the lentils and pour over any accumulated juices.

4. Return the skillet to high heat. Add the pears and cook, turning once, until lightly browned, about 2 minutes. Transfer to the platter and serve right away.

—*Defne Koryürek*

MAKE AHEAD The cooked lentils can be refrigerated overnight. Reheat them gently before serving.

WINE Juicy, spicy Grenache.

Grilled Beef-and-Lamb Köfte

ACTIVE: 30 MIN; TOTAL: 1 HR 30 MIN

6 SERVINGS

Turkey's small, oval *köfte* are like a cross between a meatball and a hamburger. These juicy *köfte* from Dükkan, Defne Koryürek's Istanbul butcher shop, are simply flavored with onion and parsley.

- 3 ounces stale baguette (about ⅓ of a standard baguette), torn into small pieces
- ½ cup hot water
- ¼ cup finely chopped onion
- ¼ cup very finely chopped flat-leaf parsley
- 1 large egg
- 1½ teaspoons kosher salt
- ½ teaspoon freshly ground black pepper
- 1 pound ground beef chuck

½ pound ground lamb
Olive oil, for brushing
Warm pita bread or mashed potatoes,
    for serving

1. In a large bowl, soak the bread in the hot water until absorbed, about 5 minutes. Add the onion, parsley, egg, salt and pepper and knead until combined. Knead in the beef and lamb until combined.

2. Line a large baking sheet with plastic wrap. Using moistened hands, roll the meat mixture into 18 oval patties. Cover and refrigerate the patties for at least 1 hour.

3. Preheat a grill pan. Brush the *köfte* with olive oil and grill over moderately high heat, turning occasionally, until browned and cooked through, about 7 minutes. Serve the *köfte* immediately, with warm pita bread or mashed potatoes.

—*Defne Koryürek*

MAKE AHEAD The uncooked *köfte* can be refrigerated overnight.

WINE Fruity, luscious Shiraz.

Grilled Mini Meat Loaves

TOTAL: 35 MIN
4 SERVINGS ●

Marcia Kiesel, F&W's Test Kitchen supervisor, learned this recipe from her sister, Susie, who created it one day when she was craving meat loaf but didn't want to turn on the oven. The mini meat loaves—made with just seven ingredients, including cubes of fresh mozzarella that become warm and gooey—cook directly on the grill for less than 10 minutes.

Two ⅓-inch-thick slices of firm
    white bread, cut into ½-inch
    pieces
  4 scallions, thinly sliced
½ cup chopped basil
  3 tablespoons extra-virgin olive oil,
    plus more for rubbing
  1 pound ground beef chuck
  2 tablespoons freshly grated
    Parmigiano-Reggiano cheese
Kosher salt and freshly ground pepper

Four 1½-inch cubes of fresh
    mozzarella
  4 medium tomatoes,
    halved crosswise

1. In a food processor, pulse the bread, scallions, basil and 1 tablespoon of the olive oil until the bread is coarsely chopped.

2. Transfer the mixture to a large bowl. Add the ground chuck, grated cheese, 1 teaspoon of salt, ½ teaspoon of pepper and the remaining 2 tablespoons of oil and blend well. Shape the meat into 4 thick 5-inch-long ovals. Make an indentation in the center of each meat loaf and tuck in a piece of mozzarella, then cover the cheese with the meat mixture to enclose it. Reshape the meat into ovals with slightly tapered ends.

3. Light a grill. Rub the meat loaves with olive oil and grill over high heat, turning, until well browned all over and firm to the touch, about 8 minutes total; the loaves should still be slightly pink in the center.

4. Rub the cut sides of the tomatoes with olive oil and season with salt and pepper. Grill the tomatoes cut side down until lightly charred, about 1 minute. Turn and grill until the tomato juices begin bubbling, about 1 minute longer. Serve the meat loaves right away, with the tomatoes.

—*Marcia Kiesel*

MAKE AHEAD The uncooked meat loaves can be refrigerated overnight. Bring to room temperature before grilling.

WINE Intense, fruity Zinfandel.

Neapolitan Meat Loaf with Pine Nuts and Raisins

ACTIVE: 20 MIN; TOTAL: 1 HR
4 SERVINGS ●

This meat loaf is comfort food at its most luxe. Ground beef chuck and pork mixed with golden raisins, pine nuts and Provolone cheese become juicy and delectable as the meat bakes, while a combination of pine nuts and Provolone gives the loaf a golden crust.

¼ cup pine nuts
¼ cup golden raisins
½ cup hot water
  4 slices of white sandwich bread,
    crusts removed and bread torn
    into pieces
¼ cup milk
  1 large egg, lightly beaten
½ pound ground beef chuck
½ pound ground pork
  1 teaspoon kosher salt
½ teaspoon freshly ground pepper
  2 tablespoons extra-virgin olive oil,
    plus more for drizzling
½ cup plus 2 tablespoons freshly
    grated aged provolone cheese

1. Preheat the oven to 425°. Spread the pine nuts in a pie plate and toast in the oven until golden, about 2 minutes. Let cool.

2. In a small bowl, soak the raisins in the hot water until plump, 10 minutes. Drain.

3. In a large bowl, soak the bread in the milk until soft, 10 minutes. Using a fork, mash the bread thoroughly, then beat in the egg until fluffy. Add the ground meats to the bowl along with the raisins, salt, pepper, 2 tablespoons of the pine nuts, the 2 tablespoons of oil and ½ cup of the cheese. Blend until just incorporated.

4. Oil a large rimmed baking sheet. Transfer the meat mixture to the prepared baking sheet and form it into a 4-by-8-inch loaf. Drizzle the meat loaf with olive oil. Sprinkle with the remaining 2 tablespoons each of the pine nuts and the provolone cheese, pressing to help them adhere.

5. Bake the meat loaf in the upper third of the oven for about 25 minutes, until browned on top and an instant-read thermometer inserted in the thickest part registers 165°. Remove from the oven and let stand for about 10 minutes. Cut into thick slices and serve. —*Anna Imparato*

MAKE AHEAD The uncooked meat loaf can be refrigerated overnight. Bring to room temperature before baking.

WINE Complex, aromatic Nebbiolo.

Crosshatch Hot Dogs on Grilled Croissants

TOTAL: 30 MIN
4 SERVINGS ●

These sweet-savory glazed hot dogs were inspired by a dish that F&W's Marcia Kiesel discovered at a Manhattan Chinatown restaurant. They're cut in a crosshatch pattern, which makes the franks cook even faster, and served in a grilled butter-and-mustard-brushed croissant.

- 1 tablespoon plus 1 teaspoon honey
- 1 tablespoon plus 1 teaspoon sherry vinegar
- 6 cups finely shredded green cabbage (from ½ small head)
- 3 fresh red chiles such as Fresno, seeded and thinly sliced

Salt

- 2 tablespoons unsalted butter, softened
- 2 tablespoons Dijon mustard
- 4 croissants, split but still attached on one side
- 4 large hot dogs
- 2 tablespoons ketchup
- 1 tablespoon soy sauce
- ½ teaspoon vegetable oil
- 1 large garlic clove, very finely chopped

1. In a large bowl, stir the honey with the sherry vinegar until the honey is dissolved. Add the shredded cabbage and red chiles, season with salt and toss. Let stand until the cabbage is slightly softened, tossing a few times, about 15 minutes.

2. Meanwhile, in a small bowl, blend the butter and mustard. Gently spread the cut sides of the croissants with the mixture.

3. Light a grill. Thread each hot dog lengthwise onto a thick metal or wooden skewer. With a small, sharp knife, make cuts at an angle in 3 rows down each hot dog, about ½ inch apart, cutting partway into the hot dog. The cuts should look like rounded half circles. Lightly run the knife down the center of the cuts to halve the half circles.

4. On a large plate, mix the ketchup with the soy sauce, oil and garlic. Turn to coat each hot dog with the mixture.

5. Grill the croissants over high heat, cut side down, until toasted, about 30 seconds. Turn and grill the other side for about 10 seconds. Grill the hot dogs over high heat until they are nicely charred all over and the cuts open up, about 2 minutes total; the hot dogs should resemble pine cones. Mound the cabbage salad on one half of each croissant, set the hot dogs on top and serve. —*Marcia Kiesel*

MAKE AHEAD The cabbage salad can be refrigerated overnight. The cut hot dogs can marinate overnight in the refrigerator.

WINE Bright, tart Barbera.

Hot Dogs with Grilled Coleslaw

TOTAL: 25 MIN
10 SERVINGS ●

One 3-pound head of green cabbage, cut through the core into 8 wedges

Vegetable oil, for brushing

Salt and freshly ground pepper

- 4½ tablespoons mayonnaise
- 4½ tablespoons cider vinegar
- 3 pickled jalapeños, seeded and very finely chopped, plus 2 teaspoons pickling liquid from the jar
- 10 hot dog buns, split
- 10 hot dogs

1. Light a grill. Brush the cabbage wedges with vegetable oil and season with salt and pepper. Grill the cabbage over high heat until charred, about 3 minutes per side. Transfer to a work surface. When the cabbage is cool enough to handle, finely slice it crosswise with a sharp knife.

2. In a large bowl, whisk the mayonnaise with the cider vinegar, jalapeños and pickling liquid. Add the shredded cabbage and toss well. Season the grilled coleslaw with salt and pepper and toss again.

3. Grill the hot dog buns over high heat until crisp, about 30 seconds. Grill the hot dogs over high heat, turning several times, until lightly charred and heated through, about 4 minutes. Place the hot dogs in the toasted buns, top with the grilled coleslaw and serve. —*Kristin Donnelly*

SERVE WITH Crisp beer.

Beef-and-Lamb Cheddar Burgers with Caper Remoulade

TOTAL: 30 MIN
4 SERVINGS

- 4 cornichons, coarsely chopped
- 3 tablespoons parsley leaves, coarsely chopped
- 2 teaspoons drained capers
- 1 garlic clove
- ½ cup mayonnaise
- 1 tablespoon whole-grain mustard
- ¾ pound ground beef, preferably 80 percent lean
- ½ pound ground lamb

Kosher salt and freshly ground black pepper

- 4 English muffins, split
- 4 thin slices of aged cheddar, preferably farmhouse

Tomato slices and thinly sliced English cucumber, for garnish (optional)

1. Light a grill. In a mini food processor, pulse the cornichons with the parsley leaves, capers and garlic clove until finely chopped. Add the mayonnaise and mustard and pulse until the caper remoulade ingredients are blended.

2. In a large bowl, use your hands to gently mix the ground beef with the ground lamb just until well combined, and season generously with kosher salt and black pepper. Form the meat mixture into four 1-inch-thick patties and make a slight indentation in the center of each one with your thumb. Season the burgers with a little more kosher salt and black pepper.

HOT DOGS WITH GRILLED COLESLAW

BEEF-AND-LAMB CHEDDAR BURGER WITH CAPER REMOULADE

3. Place the English muffin halves cut side down on the grill and cook until toasted, about 1 minute. Flip the muffins and grill for 30 seconds longer. Transfer the toasted muffin halves to a work surface, cut side up, and spread the bottom halves with the caper remoulade.

4. Grill the beef-and-lamb burgers over high heat until they are nicely charred on the bottom, about 4 minutes. Flip the burgers, top them with the cheddar cheese and grill until the meat is cooked to medium and the cheese melts, about 4 minutes longer. Transfer the burgers to the toasted English muffins and let rest for 5 minutes. Top the burgers with the tomatoes and cucumbers, close the burgers and serve.
—*Nick Fauchald*

MAKE AHEAD The caper remoulade can be refrigerated in an airtight container for up to 3 days.

WINE Rustic, peppery Malbec.

Juicy Texas Burgers

ACTIVE: 25 MIN; TOTAL: 50 MIN

4 SERVINGS

Chef, cookbook author and TV personality Bobby Flay created this recipe for his wife, Stephanie March, whom he describes as "a Texan who loves brisket and coleslaw."

COLESLAW

- ¾ cup mayonnaise
- ½ small onion, finely shredded
- 3 tablespoons cider vinegar
- 2 tablespoons sugar
- 2 teaspoons celery seeds
- 8 cups shredded green cabbage
- 1 large carrot, finely shredded

Salt and freshly ground pepper

BURGERS

- 2 pounds ground beef chuck

Vegetable oil, for rubbing

Salt and freshly ground pepper

- ¾ cup barbecue sauce
- 4 hamburger buns, split

Sliced pickles

1. MAKE THE COLESLAW: In a large bowl, whisk the mayonnaise with the shredded onion, cider vinegar, sugar and celery seeds. Add the shredded cabbage and carrot, season with salt and pepper and toss well. Let stand until the cabbage is slightly softened, about 25 minutes.

2. MAKE THE BURGERS: Light a grill. Form the beef into 4 patties, rub with oil and season with salt and pepper. Sear over high heat, turning once, for 5 minutes for medium-rare. Brush with ½ cup of the barbecue sauce and grill until glazed, about 1 minute per side.

3. Grill the buns and brush them with the remaining barbecue sauce. Top with the burgers, pickles and coleslaw and serve.
—*Bobby Flay*

WINE Intense, fruity Zinfandel.

● HEALTHY ● MAKE AHEAD ○ VEGETARIAN ● STAFF FAVORITE

SEARED BISON STRIP LOIN AND BURRATA SALSA (P. 379)

GOAT CHILI WITH EYE OF THE GOAT BEANS

Seared Bison Strip Loin with Juniper and Fennel

ACTIVE: 15 MIN; TOTAL: 2 HR

10 SERVINGS ●

San Francisco chef Chris Cosentino spices his bison strip loin with juniper, since juniper berries often grow where bison graze; the bison can also be replaced with a beef strip loin. For putting a good crust on a juicy steak, Cosentino says, "A hot stone is awesome!" Sometimes known as cooking *a la plancha*, the method requires heating a smooth stone or cast-iron griddle over hot coals, creating a surface ideal for searing, no oil required. Pizza stones work well here.

- 2 **tablespoons black peppercorns**
- 2 **tablespoons fennel seeds**
- 1 **tablespoon juniper berries**

One 5-pound bison or beef strip loin

Salt

Burrata Salsa (p. 379), for serving

1. In a spice grinder, grind the black peppercorns, fennel seeds and juniper berries to a coarse powder. Season the strip loin with salt and rub with the spice mixture. Let the meat stand at room temperature for 1 hour.

2. Light a grill. Place a large pizza stone on the grate and heat until it is very hot, about 10 minutes. (To test the temperature, place a lemon slice or a few drops of water on the stone; the lemon should caramelize on contact and the water should bounce off the surface.) Set the strip loin on the hot stone and cook for about 30 minutes, turning once or twice, until the outside is richly browned and an instant-read thermometer inserted in the thickest part of the meat registers 125° for medium-rare.

3. Transfer the steak to a work surface and let rest for 10 minutes. Carve into thick slices and serve with the Burrata Salsa. —*Chris Cosentino*

SERVE WITH Grilled spring onions or scallions and red onion slices.

WINE Complex, aromatic Nebbiolo.

Goat Chili with Eye of the Goat Beans

ACTIVE: 1 HR; TOTAL: 3 HR 30 MIN
PLUS OVERNIGHT MARINATING AND
4 HR SOAKING

8 SERVINGS ● ●

- 3 dried árbol chiles, stemmed and seeded
- 1 dried guajillo chile, stemmed and seeded
- 1 ancho chile, stemmed and seeded
- 1½ cups boiling water
- 1 teaspoon cumin seeds
- 1 teaspoon dried oregano
- 1 garlic clove, chopped
- 1 teaspoon hot pimentón de la Vera (smoked Spanish paprika)
- Kosher salt
- 2 pounds trimmed boneless goat or pork shoulder, cut into 1-inch cubes
- 2 cups dried Eye of the Goat or red kidney beans, rinsed and picked over, then soaked for 4 hours and drained (see Note)
- 1 thick slice of bacon (1 ounce), cut crosswise into ¼-inch strips
- 3 tablespoons extra-virgin olive oil
- 1 large onion, cut into ½-inch dice
- 1 cup dark Mexican beer, such as Negra Modelo
- 2 cups chicken stock or low-sodium broth
- Freshly ground pepper
- Sour cream, cilantro sprigs and lime wedges, for serving

1. In a heatproof bowl, soak the árbol, guajillo and ancho chiles in the boiling water until softened, about 20 minutes. Drain the chiles, reserving ⅓ cup of the soaking liquid. Coarsely chop the chiles.

2. In a small skillet, toast the cumin seeds over moderate heat until fragrant, about 20 seconds. Transfer the seeds to a blender. Add the chiles and their reserved soaking liquid along with the oregano, garlic, paprika and 1 tablespoon of salt. Puree until smooth. Scrape the chile puree into a large nonreactive bowl or baking dish. Add the goat and toss to coat thoroughly. Cover and refrigerate overnight.

3. In a large saucepan, cover the soaked and drained beans with 2 inches of water and bring to a boil. Simmer over low heat, stirring occasionally, until tender, 1 hour; add more water as needed to keep them covered by 2 inches. When the beans are just tender but still al dente, season them with salt and let stand in their cooking liquid for 5 minutes.

4. Preheat the oven to 375°. In a large enameled cast-iron casserole, cook the bacon over moderate heat until the fat has rendered, about 3 minutes. Using a slotted spoon, transfer the bacon to a large plate. Add the olive oil to the casserole. Working in batches, cook the chile-goat mixture over moderately high heat, turning a few times, until richly browned all over, about 4 minutes. Transfer the browned goat to the plate with the bacon.

5. Add the onion to the casserole and cook over moderately low heat, stirring occasionally, until softened, about 10 minutes. Add the goat and bacon and any accumulated juices and stir well. Add the beer and boil over high heat until reduced by half, 8 minutes. Add the stock and bring to a simmer.

6. Cover the casserole, transfer it to the oven and bake for about 30 minutes, until the goat is tender when pierced with a fork. Add the beans and bake, uncovered, for about 10 minutes, until they are warmed through. Remove the casserole from the oven and let rest for 10 minutes. Season with salt and pepper. Transfer the chili to bowls and serve with the sour cream, cilantro sprigs and lime wedges. —*Laurence Jossel*

NOTE Named for their resemblance to goats' eyes, Eye of the Goat beans are available from ranchogordo.com.

MAKE AHEAD The chili can be refrigerated for up to 3 days. Reheat gently.

WINE Cherry-inflected, earthy Sangiovese.

Cambozola Cheeseburgers with Herbed Fries

TOTAL: 45 MIN
4 SERVINGS

- 1½ quarts vegetable oil
- 4 medium baking potatoes, scrubbed but not peeled and cut into ¾-inch-thick sticks
- 2 tablespoons chopped mixed herbs, such as parsley, thyme and rosemary
- Salt
- 1¼ pounds ground Kobe-style beef or sirloin
- 4 brioche buns, split and toasted
- Eight ⅛-inch-thick slices of Cambozola or other triple-cream cheese (see Note)
- Arugula leaves, torn

1. Line a large rimmed baking sheet with paper towels. In a large saucepan, heat the vegetable oil to 300°. Add the potatoes and fry until softened but not browned, about 10 minutes. Spread the fries on the baking sheet to drain.

2. Heat the frying oil to 350°. Line a large bowl with paper towels. Return the fries to the oil and cook until they are golden brown, about 6 minutes. Transfer the fries to the bowl, sprinkle with the chopped mixed herbs and salt and toss gently to coat the fries. Transfer the herbed fries to dinner plates.

3. Meanwhile, preheat a grill pan. Use your hands to gently form the beef into 4 patties and season them generously with salt. Grill the patties over moderately high heat, turning once, about 3 minutes per side for medium-rare meat. Transfer the burgers to the toasted brioche buns, top each burger with 2 slices of the Cambozola cheese and some arugula leaves and serve right away, with the herbed fries.
—*Joshua Henderson*

NOTE Cambozola is a creamy hybrid of Camembert and Gorgonzola.

WINE Fruity, light-bodied Beaujolais.

PAN-ROASTED SALMON WITH
TOMATO VINAIGRETTE (P. 176)

fish

" When fish tastes like the sea, there's no need to hide the flavor in heavy sauces. "

—CATHAL ARMSTRONG, CHEF AND RESTAURATEUR, ALEXANDRIA, VIRGINIA

SALMON WITH OYSTER MUSHROOMS AND PEPPERS

GRILLED TUNA WITH SMOKED-ALMOND ROMESCO SAUCE

Grilled Tuna with Tomato-Cilantro Salsa

 **TOTAL: 35 MIN**
6 SERVINGS ●

- 2 pounds tomatoes, cut into ½-inch dice
- 6 scallions, thinly sliced
- 2 lightly packed cups cilantro leaves
- 1 lightly packed cup mint leaves
- 1 serrano chile, seeded and minced
- 2 tablespoons freshly squeezed lemon juice
- 2 tablespoons freshly squeezed lime juice
- 3 tablespoons extra-virgin olive oil

Kosher salt and freshly ground black pepper

Six 6-ounce tuna steaks, cut ¾ inch thick

Lime wedges, for garnish

1. Light a grill. On a large cutting board, pile the tomatoes with the scallions, cilantro, mint and serrano chile. Using a large knife, finely chop all the ingredients together until they become a salsa. Transfer the salsa to a bowl and stir in the lemon juice, lime juice and 2 tablespoons of the olive oil. Season with salt and pepper.

2. Brush the tuna steaks with the remaining 1 tablespoon of olive oil and season with salt and black pepper. Grill the tuna steaks over moderately high heat until they are cooked to desired doneness, 1 minute per side for medium-rare or 2 minutes per side for medium. Transfer the tuna steaks to plates, spoon the salsa all around and serve with lime wedges.

—*Jamie Oliver*

MAKE AHEAD The salsa can be refrigerated overnight. Bring to room temperature before serving.

WINE Fresh, fruity rosé.

Salmon with Oyster Mushrooms and Peppers

 **TOTAL: 45 MIN**
6 SERVINGS

- 3 tablespoons unsalted butter
- 1 large white onion, very thinly sliced
- 2 red or yellow bell peppers, sliced ½ inch thick
- ½ pound oyster mushrooms, thickly sliced
- 2 garlic cloves, very finely chopped
- ¼ cup dry white wine
- ¼ cup finely chopped flat-leaf parsley

Salt and freshly ground black pepper

- 1 tablespoon extra-virgin olive oil

Six 8-ounce salmon fillets, with skin

Lemon wedges, for serving

1. Preheat the oven to 450°. In a large skillet, melt the butter. Add the onion and cook over moderate heat, stirring frequently, until softened, about 6 minutes. Add the bell peppers and cook until just softened, about 5 minutes. Add the mushrooms, garlic and wine and cook, stirring occasionally, until the mushrooms are tender and just beginning to brown, about 8 minutes. Stir in the parsley, season with salt and pepper and keep warm.

2. Heat a very large ovenproof skillet until hot. Add the olive oil and swirl the skillet to coat. Season the salmon fillets with salt and pepper and add them to the skillet, skin side down. Cook the salmon over high heat until the skin is crisp, 3 minutes. Turn the fillets, transfer to the oven and roast for 10 minutes, until just cooked through.

3. Spoon the mushrooms and peppers onto plates, top with the salmon, skin side up, and serve with lemon wedges.

—Maria Hines

WINE Fresh, fruity rosé.

Pan-Seared Tuna Steaks with Capers and Oregano

TOTAL: 35 MIN
4 SERVINGS ●

- ¼ cup capers, drained
- 2 tablespoons chopped fresh oregano
- 1 small shallot, minced
- 1½ tablespoons extra-virgin olive oil, plus more for drizzling
- Salt and freshly ground black pepper
- Four 6-ounce tuna steaks, cut ¾ inch thick
- 4 anchovy fillets, chopped
- 1 cup dry red wine
- 2 tablespoons cold unsalted butter, cut into 2 pieces
- 4 packed cups baby arugula

1. In a small bowl, combine the capers with the oregano, shallot and ½ tablespoon of the olive oil. Season with salt and pepper.

2. In a skillet, heat the remaining 1 tablespoon of oil until shimmering. Season the steaks with salt and pepper; add to the skillet and cook over high heat, turning once, until browned and medium-rare, about 4 minutes. Transfer the steaks to a platter.

3. Add the anchovies to the skillet and cook over moderate heat, mashing with a fork until dissolved, about 1 minute. Add the wine and boil until reduced by half, about 4 minutes. Remove the skillet from the heat and swirl in the butter, 1 piece at a time, until blended and smooth. Season the red wine sauce with salt and pepper.

4. In a medium bowl, drizzle the arugula with olive oil and season with salt. Mound the arugula alongside the tuna. Pour the red wine sauce around the tuna steaks, top them with the caper mixture and serve.

—Jane Sigal

WINE Bright, tart Barbera.

Grilled Tuna with Smoked-Almond Romesco Sauce

TOTAL: 30 MIN
4 SERVINGS ●

Smoked almonds and a touch of pimentón de la Vera (powdered, smoked Spanish red peppers) add fabulous smoky flavors to the Catalan sauce *romesco*, a mixture of tomatoes, bell peppers, garlic and almonds.

- ¼ cup plus 2 tablespoons smoked almonds (2½ ounces)
- One 3-inch piece of baguette, cubed
- 1 garlic clove
- 1 cup canned diced tomatoes
- 2 roasted red bell peppers from a jar, drained
- 2 tablespoons sherry vinegar
- ¼ teaspoon pimentón de la Vera
- ½ cup extra-virgin olive oil
- Kosher salt and freshly ground pepper
- Four 1-inch-thick tuna steaks

1. Light a grill. In a food processor, coarsely chop the almonds, bread cubes and garlic. Add the tomatoes, roasted red peppers, sherry vinegar and pimentón; puree until

smooth. With the machine on, gradually add the oil. Season with salt and pepper.

2. Season the tuna with salt and pepper. Grill over moderate heat, turning once, for 6 minutes for medium-rare, or 8 minutes for medium. Transfer the tuna to plates. Spoon some of the *romesco* sauce over the fish and pass the rest at the table.

—Nick Fauchald

MAKE AHEAD The *romesco* sauce can be refrigerated for up to 1 week. Bring to room temperature before serving.

WINE Complex, elegant Pinot Noir.

Grilled Salmon with Dill Pickle Butter

TOTAL: 20 MIN
4 SERVINGS

Salmon is an excellent low-maintenance ingredient for the grill because it doesn't need careful testing for doneness—the fish is wonderful cooked anywhere from rare to medium. Here, fillets are topped with a tangy pickle-studded butter as soon as they come off the grill.

- 4 tablespoons unsalted butter, softened
- ¼ cup finely diced dill pickles
- 1 teaspoon minced tarragon
- ½ teaspoon Dijon mustard
- Salt and freshly ground pepper
- Four 6-ounce salmon fillets, with skin
- Extra-virgin olive oil, for rubbing

1. Light a grill. In a small bowl, blend the butter with the diced pickles, tarragon and mustard and season with salt and pepper.

2. Rub the salmon with oil and season with salt and pepper. Grill over moderately high heat, skin side down, until the skin is lightly charred and crisp, about 3 minutes. Using a metal spatula, turn the fillets and grill until barely done in the center, about 4 minutes longer. Transfer the salmon to plates. Top with the dill pickle butter and serve.

—Marcia Kiesel

SERVE WITH Corn and cherry tomatoes.

WINE Fruity, light-bodied Beaujolais.

Pan-Roasted Salmon with Tomato Vinaigrette

TOTAL: 30 MIN
4 SERVINGS ● ●

1 pint grape tomatoes, halved

Salt

1 medium shallot, thinly sliced

1 tablespoon drained capers

2 tablespoons red wine vinegar

3 tablespoons extra-virgin olive oil

Four 7-ounce center-cut salmon fillets, with skin

Freshly ground pepper

½ teaspoon ground cumin

2 tablespoons canola oil

1 tablespoon minced parsley

1 tablespoon chopped basil

1. Preheat the oven to 425°. In a bowl, toss the tomatoes with ½ teaspoon of salt and the shallot, capers and vinegar.

2. In a medium ovenproof skillet, heat 1 tablespoon of the olive oil. Season the salmon with salt and pepper and add to the skillet, skin side up. Cook over moderately high heat until browned on the bottom, about 3 minutes. Carefully flip the fish. Transfer the skillet to the oven and roast the fish until cooked through, about 7 minutes; transfer to plates and pour off any fat in the skillet.

3. Place the skillet over moderate heat and add the tomato mixture along with the cumin, canola oil and the remaining 2 tablespoons of olive oil. Cook, scraping up any bits stuck to the skillet, until the tomatoes just soften, about 2 minutes. Pour over the salmon, sprinkle with the parsley and basil and serve. —*Ted Allen*

WINE Dry, fruity sparkling wine.

Pan-Fried Salmon with Citrus Vinaigrette

TOTAL: 45 MIN
8 SERVINGS ●

2 pounds asparagus, stalks peeled

¼ cup extra-virgin olive oil, plus more for drizzling

¼ cup fresh orange juice

¼ cup fresh lemon juice

2 tablespoons fresh lime juice

1 medium shallot, minced

2 tablespoons snipped chives

Salt and freshly ground pepper

3 tablespoons vegetable oil

Eight 6-ounce skinless salmon fillets

1. In a large skillet of boiling salted water, cook the asparagus until bright green and crisp-tender, about 3 minutes. Drain and rinse with cold water. Pat the asparagus dry and transfer to a serving platter. Drizzle with olive oil and toss gently to coat.

2. In a saucepan, combine the orange, lemon and lime juices and simmer over moderate heat until reduced by half, about 10 minutes. Pour into a heatproof bowl and let cool to room temperature. Whisk in the shallot, chives and the ¼ cup of olive oil. Season with salt and pepper.

3. In each of 2 large skillets, heat 1½ tablespoons of vegetable oil until shimmering. Season the salmon fillets with salt and pepper and add 4 to each skillet. Cook over moderately high heat until browned and just cooked, about 3 minutes per side.

4. Transfer the salmon to plates and spoon some of the citrus vinaigrette on top. Serve with the asparagus, passing the extra vinaigrette at the table. —*Cathal Armstrong*

WINE Fruity, low-oak Chardonnay.

Indian Coconut Fish Curry

TOTAL: 45 MIN
6 SERVINGS

⅓ cup unsweetened shredded coconut

¼ cup chopped onion

2 large garlic cloves, chopped

2 medium serrano chiles, chopped

1½ tablespoons minced fresh ginger

⅓ cup plus ¾ cup unsweetened coconut milk

3 tablespoons vegetable oil

½ teaspoon yellow mustard seeds

8 curry leaves, preferably fresh (see Note)

2 teaspoons ground fennel

1 tablespoon ground coriander

¼ teaspoon ground cardamom

¼ teaspoon turmeric

¼ teaspoon cayenne pepper

¼ teaspoon ground fenugreek

1 tablespoon tamarind concentrate dissolved in 1 tablespoon of water

⅔ cup water

½ cup chopped canned tomatoes, drained

Pinch of sugar

15 cherry tomatoes, halved

2¼ pounds skinless salmon fillet, cut into 1¼-inch chunks

Salt

Chopped cilantro leaves, for garnish

1. In a mini food processor, combine the coconut, onion, garlic, serrano and ginger with the ⅓ cup coconut milk and process to a paste.

2. In a large, deep skillet, heat the vegetable oil. Add the yellow mustard seeds and curry leaves and cook over moderately high heat until the seeds pop, about 1 minute. Add the coconut paste and cook over moderate heat, stirring, until fragrant, about 4 minutes. Add the ground fennel, coriander, cardamom, turmeric, cayenne and fenugreek and cook, stirring, until fragrant, about 2 minutes. Add the remaining ¾ cup of coconut milk and the tamarind paste, water, tomatoes and sugar. Bring to a simmer, scraping up any bits from the skillet. Simmer over low heat for 10 minutes.

3. Add the cherry tomatoes to the sauce and simmer over moderate heat until just starting to soften, about 1 minute. Season the salmon with salt, add it to the skillet and simmer over moderate heat, stirring gently a few times, until just cooked through, about 3 minutes. Sprinkle with cilantro leaves and serve. —*Anya von Bremzen*

NOTE Fresh curry leaves, which resemble small bay leaves and have a savory flavor, are available from kalustyans.com.

WINE Spicy American Gewürztraminer.

INDIAN COCONUT FISH CURRY

fish

Sesame-and-Curry-Crusted Salmon with Tomato Salad

TOTAL: 30 MIN
4 SERVINGS

Rather than pan-roasting individual pieces of salmon, F&W's Grace Parisi prefers to cook a large fillet to keep the fish moist. She mixes chile flakes into her curry rub to add a spicy kick.

1 tablespoon sesame seeds
1 teaspoon curry powder
¼ teaspoon crushed red pepper
One 1¼-pound center-cut skinless
    salmon fillet
Salt and freshly ground pepper
1 tablespoon plus 1 teaspoon
    Dijon mustard
2 tablespoons extra-virgin
    olive oil
1 tablespoon fresh lemon juice
1 pint grape tomatoes, halved
1 serrano chile, seeded and minced
½ cup coarsely chopped cilantro

1. Preheat the oven to 425°. In a spice grinder, combine the sesame seeds, curry powder and crushed red pepper and pulse until coarsely ground. Season the salmon with salt and pepper, brush one side of the fillet with 1 tablespoon of the mustard and coat with the sesame seed mixture.
2. In a large ovenproof nonstick skillet, heat 1 tablespoon of the olive oil. Add the salmon, coated side down, and cook over moderately high heat until lightly browned, about 3 minutes. Carefully flip the salmon. Transfer the skillet to the oven and roast for about 10 minutes, until the salmon is just cooked through. Transfer the salmon to a cutting board.
3. In a large bowl, whisk the lemon juice with the remaining 1 teaspoon of mustard and 1 tablespoon of olive oil. Season the dressing with salt and pepper. Add the tomatoes, serrano chile and cilantro and toss. Cut the salmon into 4 pieces and serve right away with the tomato salad.
—*Grace Parisi*

CUMIN-FENNEL RUB VARIATION In a spice grinder, grind 1 tablespoon of fennel seeds with 1 teaspoon of cumin seeds and 1 teaspoon of finely grated lemon zest. After brushing the fish with the mustard, rub the spice mixture on the fish.

FENNEL-PARSLEY SALAD VARIATION Omit the serrano chile and replace the tomatoes with 1 shaved fennel bulb and the cilantro with 1 cup of flat-leaf parsley leaves.

FISH VARIATION Mahimahi or tuna.

WINE Ripe, juicy Pinot Noir.

Salmon in Tomato-Olive Sauce

TOTAL: 40 MIN
4 SERVINGS ●

5 tablespoons extra-virgin olive oil
1 medium onion, finely chopped
4 garlic cloves, finely chopped
2 pounds plum tomatoes,
    coarsely chopped
1 tablespoon chopped fresh oregano
2 bay leaves
½ cup pitted kalamata olives, sliced
⅓ cup drained capers
⅓ cup sliced pickled jalapeños
Four 7-ounce center-cut salmon fillets,
    with skin
Salt and freshly ground pepper

1. Preheat the oven to 375°. In a large saucepan, heat ¼ cup of the olive oil until shimmering. Add the onion and garlic and cook over moderately high heat, stirring occasionally, until softened, about 5 minutes. Add the tomatoes, oregano and bay leaves and cook, stirring occasionally, until the tomatoes are just beginning to break down, about 5 minutes. Stir in the olives, capers and jalapeños and simmer for 2 minutes longer. Discard the bay leaves.
2. In a large ovenproof skillet, heat the remaining 1 tablespoon of oil until shimmering. Season the salmon with salt and pepper and add to the skillet, skin side down. Cook over high heat until the skin begins to brown, 4 minutes. Transfer the skillet to the oven and roast the fish for

about 10 minutes, until slightly rare on the inside. Transfer to plates, spoon the sauce all around and serve. —*Dionicio Jimenez*

SERVE WITH Yellow rice.

WINE Ripe, juicy Pinot Noir.

Creamy Indian Spiced Halibut Curry

TOTAL: 40 MIN
4 TO 6 SERVINGS ● ●

2 tablespoons canola oil
1 onion, minced
2 tablespoons finely chopped
    fresh ginger
4 garlic cloves, minced
1 teaspoon cayenne pepper
1 teaspoon turmeric
1 teaspoon ground coriander
1 cup plain whole-milk yogurt
1 cup heavy cream
1 tablespoon garam masala
Pinch of saffron threads, crumbled
Kosher salt
2 pounds skinless halibut fillets,
    cut into 4-inch pieces
Basmati rice and warm naan,
    for serving

1. In large, deep skillet, heat the oil. Add the onion, ginger and garlic and cook over moderate heat, stirring frequently, until lightly browned, about 6 minutes. Add the cayenne, turmeric and coriander and cook for 1 minute, stirring. Whisk in the yogurt, then add the cream, garam masala and saffron and bring to a boil. Reduce the heat and simmer the sauce until slightly thickened, about 10 minutes. Season with salt.
2. Add the halibut to the sauce and turn to coat. Cook over moderate heat, turning once, until the fish is cooked through, about 10 minutes. Serve the curry with basmati rice and warm naan.
—*Vikram Sunderam*

MAKE AHEAD The recipe can be prepared through Step 1 and refrigerated overnight. Bring to a simmer before proceeding.

WINE Lush, fragrant Viognier.

Halibut with Grilled Ratatouille

TOTAL: 50 MIN

4 SERVINGS ●

Vegetable oil, for brushing

3 medium tomatoes, halved crosswise and seeded

1 medium onion, sliced ½ inch thick

1 medium zucchini, halved lengthwise

1 medium yellow squash, halved lengthwise

1 red bell pepper

Salt and freshly ground black pepper

2 tablespoons red wine vinegar

2 tablespoons drained capers

2 anchovy fillets, minced

¼ cup extra-virgin olive oil

3 tablespoons thinly sliced basil leaves

Four 6- to 7-ounce skinless halibut fillets

1. Light a grill. Brush all of the vegetables with vegetable oil and lightly season with salt and pepper. Grill the tomatoes, onion, zucchini and yellow squash over moderate heat, turning once, until charred and just tender, about 3 minutes per side. Grill the bell pepper on four sides until charred all over, about 3 minutes per side. Peel the tomatoes and bell pepper. Cut all of the vegetables into ½-inch dice.

2. In a large bowl, whisk the vinegar with the capers and anchovies. Gradually whisk in the olive oil. Add the diced vegetables and the basil and toss gently. Season the ratatouille with salt and pepper.

3. Brush the halibut with vegetable oil and season with salt and pepper. Grill the fillets over high heat, turning once, until they are lightly charred and just cooked through, about 3 minutes per side. Transfer the halibut fillets to plates and serve with the grilled ratatouille. —*Nick Fauchald*

WINE Zesty, fresh Albariño.

Halibut with Parsley-Lemon Sauce

TOTAL: 40 MIN

4 SERVINGS

Any other meaty but delicately flavored fish, such as wild striped bass or red snapper, would also work with this bright, lemony parsley sauce.

¼ cup extra-virgin olive oil

2 large shallots, thinly sliced

1 cup water

½ cup heavy cream

4 loosely packed cups flat-leaf parsley

2 teaspoons fresh lemon juice

Kosher salt and freshly ground black pepper

Four ½-inch-thick halibut steaks (1½ pounds)

1. In a medium saucepan, heat 2 tablespoons of the olive oil. Add the thinly sliced shallots and cook over moderate heat, stirring occasionally, until softened, about 5 minutes. Add the water and simmer until reduced by half, about 6 minutes. Add the heavy cream and simmer until reduced by one-third, about 6 more minutes. Let cool for about 10 minutes.

2. Stir the parsley leaves into the saucepan. Transfer the sauce to a blender and coarsely puree. Return the sauce to the saucepan. Stir in the fresh lemon juice, season the sauce with salt and black pepper and keep warm.

3. In each of 2 large nonstick skillets, heat 1 tablespoon of the remaining olive oil until shimmering. Season the halibut steaks with salt and black pepper and cook them over high heat, turning once, until they are browned and just cooked, about 2 minutes per side. Transfer the seared halibut steaks to plates. Serve with the parsley sauce. —*Marcia Kiesel*

SERVE WITH Roasted potatoes.

WINE Minerally, complex Sauvignon Blanc.

Halibut with Pork-and-Peanut Ragù and Cilantro Sauce

TOTAL: 45 MIN

4 SERVINGS

2 lightly packed cups cilantro leaves

⅓ cup extra-virgin olive oil

2 tablespoons white balsamic vinegar

2 teaspoons Dijon mustard

¾ teaspoon honey

Kosher salt and freshly ground black pepper

¼ cup salted roasted peanuts

3 tablespoons peanut oil

1 medium shallot, minced

1 medium garlic clove, minced

½ pound ground pork

1½ tablespoons sugar

1 tablespoon white miso paste

1 teaspoon tamarind concentrate

1½ teaspoons fresh lime juice

Four 6-ounce skinless halibut fillets

1. In a blender, puree the cilantro, olive oil, vinegar, mustard and honey. Season the sauce with salt and pepper. In a mini processor, finely grind the peanuts.

2. Heat 1 tablespoon of the peanut oil in a saucepan. Add the shallot and garlic and cook over moderate heat, stirring, until softened, 3 minutes. Add the pork and cook over moderately high heat, breaking up the meat, until browned, 4 minutes.

3. Add the sugar, miso, tamarind, ground peanuts and ½ cup of water to the pork. Simmer over moderately low heat until thickened, 2 minutes. Season with salt and pepper; stir in the lime juice and keep warm.

4. In a nonstick skillet, heat the remaining 2 tablespoons of peanut oil. Season the fish with salt and pepper; cook over moderately high heat until browned and just cooked through, 4 minutes per side. Spoon the pork ragù onto plates and top with the fish. Drizzle with the cilantro sauce and serve. —*Stephanie Izard*

WINE Rich Alsace Gewürztraminer.

Swordfish Sicilian-Style

TOTAL: 20 MIN
4 TO 6 SERVINGS ● ●

An herb-infused dressing brightens just-grilled swordfish steaks in this recipe from cookbook genius Marcella Hazan.

2 tablespoons fresh lemon juice
2 teaspoons salt
2 teaspoons chopped fresh oregano
¼ cup extra-virgin olive oil
Freshly ground pepper
2 pounds swordfish steaks,
cut ½ inch thick

1. Light a grill. In a small bowl, mix the lemon juice with the salt until the salt dissolves. Stir in the oregano. Whisk in the olive oil and season generously with pepper.

sustainable seafood

A growing number of chefs are eco-activists who buy only sustainable seafood. To do the same, check out Monterey Bay Aquarium's Seafood Watch (mbayaq.org) and Environmental Defense's Oceans program (environmentaldefense.org). Below, four sustainable choices:

Atlantic Mackerel This fish matures quickly, which helps keep the population plentiful.

Farmed Striped Bass Farmed striped bass are raised in ponds and tanks that limit pollution.

Wild Alaskan Salmon All Alaskan salmon varieties are sourced from eco-sound fisheries.

Wild Pacific Halibut This meaty northern Pacific fish is protected by a quota system.

2. Grill the swordfish steaks over high heat, turning once, until cooked through, 6 to 7 minutes. Transfer the swordfish to a platter. Prick each steak in several places with a fork. Using a spoon, beat the dressing, then drizzle it over the fish. Serve at once.
—*Marcella Hazan*

WINE Rich, complex white Burgundy.

Roasted Sea Bass with Potatoes, Olives and Tomatoes

ACTIVE: 25 MIN; TOTAL: 1 HR
8 SERVINGS ●

Piedmontese chef Maurizio Quaranta roasts sea bass with potatoes, olives and tomatoes until the fish is crisp and succulent. His special touch is spooning toasted warm pine nuts over the fish before serving.

2 pounds Yukon Gold potatoes,
peeled and sliced ½ inch thick
1 pound tomatoes, cut into
large chunks
¾ cup pitted green olives
¼ cup torn basil leaves
½ cup plus 3 tablespoons
extra-virgin olive oil
Salt and freshly ground pepper
Two 3-pound sea bass, cleaned
½ cup pine nuts

1. Preheat the oven to 425°. In a very large roasting pan, toss the potatoes, tomatoes, olives and basil with ½ cup of the olive oil. Season with salt and pepper.
2. Make 3 shallow slashes in both sides of each fish. Rub each fish with 1 tablespoon of the olive oil and season with salt and pepper. Set the fish in the roasting pan, tucking them into the vegetables. Roast for about 40 minutes, until the vegetables are tender and the fish are cooked through.
3. Meanwhile, in a small skillet, toast the pine nuts in the remaining 1 tablespoon of oil over moderate heat, stirring, until golden, about 3 minutes. Spoon the nuts over the fish and vegetables and serve right away. —*Maurizio Quaranta*

WINE Minerally, complex Sauvignon Blanc.

Oven-Steamed Sea Bass with Wild Mushrooms

TOTAL: 35 MIN
4 SERVINGS

6 tablespoons unsalted
butter, softened
2 garlic cloves, very
finely chopped
½ pound shiitake mushrooms,
stems discarded and caps
thinly sliced
½ pound oyster mushrooms,
thickly sliced
Salt and freshly ground
black pepper
Four 6-ounce sea bass fillets,
with skin, pin bones removed
2 tablespoons soy sauce
2 tablespoons sake

1. Preheat the oven to 500°. In a small bowl, combine the softened butter and chopped garlic. In a large skillet, melt half of the garlic butter. Add the sliced shiitake and oyster mushrooms and cook over high heat, stirring occasionally, until the mushrooms are tender and just beginning to brown, about 8 minutes. Season the mushrooms lightly with salt and black pepper.
2. Tear 4 sheets of heavy-duty aluminum foil, about 14 inches square. Spoon a quarter of the warm mushrooms onto the center of each of the foil squares and top with the sea bass fillets, skin side down. Spread the remaining garlic butter over the fillets and drizzle with the soy sauce and sake. Fold the foil over the fish and seal the edges of the packets. Set them seam side up on a sturdy baking sheet. Bake for 15 minutes, until the fish is tender. Transfer the fish to plates, spoon the mushrooms and juices on top and serve.
—*Nobuo Fukuda*

SERVE WITH Rice and vegetables.
MAKE AHEAD The garlic butter can be refrigerated for up to 2 days.
WINE Complex, elegant Pinot Noir.

SWORDFISH SICILIAN-STYLE

ROASTED SEA BASS WITH POTATOES, OLIVES AND TOMATOES

Sea Bass Fillets with Parsley Sauce

 TOTAL: 40 MIN

4 SERVINGS ●

Bob Chambers, a private chef and former F&W staffer, created this delectable dish of sea bass fried in butter and served with an easy lemony sauce.

1¾ cups fresh bread crumbs

1 cup finely chopped flat-leaf
parsley leaves

Salt and freshly ground pepper

4 tablespoons unsalted butter

1 shallot, minced

1½ cups chicken stock or
low-sodium broth

3 tablespoons fresh lemon juice

3 tablespoons crème fraîche

¼ cup extra-virgin olive oil

All-purpose flour, for dredging

2 large eggs, beaten

Four 6-ounce sea bass fillets

1. In a large bowl, mix 1½ cups of the fresh bread crumbs with ½ cup of the chopped parsley, 1½ teaspoons of salt and ½ teaspoon of pepper.

2. In a small saucepan, melt 2 tablespoons of the butter. Add the shallot and cook over moderate heat until translucent, about 1 minute. Add the chicken stock and lemon juice and boil over high heat until reduced to 1 cup, about 15 minutes.

3. Whisk the crème fraîche into the sauce along with the remaining ½ cup of chopped parsley and ¼ cup of bread crumbs. Scrape the sauce into a blender and puree. Strain the sauce back into the saucepan and rewarm gently.

4. In a skillet, melt the remaining 2 tablespoons of butter in the oil over moderate heat. Put the flour and eggs in 2 shallow bowls. Season the sea bass fillets with salt and pepper, then dredge them in flour, dip in the beaten eggs and coat with the bread

crumb mixture. When the butter starts to brown slightly, add the fillets to the skillet and cook until browned on the bottom, 3 minutes. Flip the fillets and cook until the fish is just white throughout, 2 to 3 minutes longer. Transfer the fish to plates, spoon the parsley sauce alongside and serve.

—*Bob Chambers*

LEMON-HAZELNUT BROWN BUTTER SAUCE VARIATION Preheat the oven to 350°. On a baking sheet, toast ½ cup of hazelnuts for 8 minutes, until fragrant. Using a clean kitchen towel, rub the skins off the nuts. Coarsely chop the hazelnuts. In a skillet, cook 4 tablespoons of unsalted butter over moderate heat until browned, about 4 minutes. Add the chopped nuts and 2 tablespoons of fresh lemon juice. Season with salt and pepper and pour over the fish.

FISH VARIATION Striped bass or red snapper.

WINE Lively, tart Sauvignon Blanc.

● HEALTHY ● MAKE AHEAD ● VEGETARIAN ● STAFF FAVORITE

Steamed Sea Bass with Crispy Caper Bread Crumbs

TOTAL: 30 MIN
4 SERVINGS •

- 2 thick slices of bakery white peasant bread (about 4 ounces), crusts removed and bread torn into 2-inch pieces
- ¼ cup extra-virgin olive oil
- 1 large anchovy fillet, chopped
- 1 garlic clove, sliced
- Scant ½ teaspoon crushed red pepper
- 1 tablespoon drained capers
- 2 tablespoons coarsely chopped flat-leaf parsley
- ½ teaspoon finely grated lemon zest
- Salt and freshly ground pepper
- 4 teaspoons unsalted butter, softened, plus more for the pie plate
- Four 7-ounce sea bass fillets, cut 1 inch thick
- 8 thin lemon slices
- 1 tablespoon dry white wine

1. In a food processor, pulse the bread until coarse crumbs form. In a medium skillet, heat the oil until shimmering. Add the anchovy, garlic and crushed red pepper and cook over high heat, stirring, until the anchovy dissolves and the garlic is just beginning to brown, about 30 seconds.

Stir in the bread crumbs and capers and cook over moderately low heat, stirring constantly, until the bread is golden and crisp, about 8 minutes. Off the heat, stir in the parsley and lemon zest and season the bread crumbs with salt and pepper.

2. Meanwhile, lightly butter a 9-inch glass pie plate. Arrange the fish fillets skin side down in the plate. Season with salt and pepper and dot with the 4 teaspoons of butter. Place 2 lemon slices on each fillet and drizzle with the wine.

3. Make a steamer by arranging 3 small balls of aluminum foil in a very large, deep skillet. Add 1 inch of water to the skillet and bring to a boil. Carefully set the pie plate on the foil balls, cover the skillet with a tight-fitting lid or aluminum foil and steam for about 8 minutes, until the fish flakes with a fork. (Alternatively, steam the fish in a bowl in a bamboo steamer.)

4. Transfer the sea bass to shallow bowls and spoon the broth on top. Push the lemon slices off to the side and top the fillets with the toasted bread crumbs. Serve right away. —*Grace Parisi*

WINE Lively, tart Sauvignon Blanc.

Fish Fry with Ramp Aioli

TOTAL: 1 HR
6 SERVINGS

- 4 large ramps or scallions, cut into 2-inch lengths
- ½ cup mayonnaise
- 2 tablespoons soy sauce
- 1 tablespoon fresh lemon juice
- 1½ teaspoons apricot jam
- 1 teaspoon grated fresh ginger
- 1 small garlic clove
- 1 teaspoon dry English mustard mixed with 1 tablespoon of water
- ½ cup extra-virgin olive oil
- Kosher salt
- 1 quart vegetable oil, for frying
- 4 skinless sea bass fillets (about 1¾ pounds), cut crosswise into 1-inch-wide strips

- 2 cups buttermilk
- 1 cup all-purpose flour
- ½ teaspoon Old Bay seasoning
- ½ teaspoon ground coriander
- Lemon wedges, for serving

1. Blanch the ramps in boiling water just until bright green, 30 seconds. Drain, cool under water and pat dry.

2. In a blender, puree the ramps, mayonnaise, soy sauce, lemon juice, apricot jam, ginger, garlic and mustard paste until smooth. With the machine on, drizzle in the olive oil until emulsified. Season the aioli with salt, transfer to a bowl and refrigerate.

3. In a large saucepan, heat the vegetable oil to 375°. Set a rack on a baking sheet and cover the rack with paper towels.

4. In a bowl, coat the fish with the buttermilk. In a resealable plastic bag, combine the flour, Old Bay, coriander and 1 teaspoon of salt. Drain the fish and transfer to the bag. Seal the bag and shake until the fish is coated. Remove the fish, shaking off excess flour.

5. Working in batches, fry the fish over high heat, turning once, until golden and cooked through, 3 minutes. Transfer to the rack and sprinkle with salt. Serve hot, with the aioli and lemon wedges. —*Shea Gallante*

WINE Vivid, lightly sweet Riesling.

Striped Bass with Caramelized Brussels Sprouts

TOTAL: 45 MIN
4 SERVINGS

- ½ cup mayonnaise
- ¼ cup extra-virgin olive oil
- 1 garlic clove, minced
- ½ teaspoon finely grated lemon zest
- 1 teaspoon fresh lemon juice
- Salt and freshly ground pepper
- One 3-ounce piece of pancetta, sliced ¼ inch thick and cut into ½-inch pieces
- 1 pound brussels sprouts, halved lengthwise
- 2 large thyme sprigs, plus 4 small sprigs for garnish

bamboo steamer

Ian Schnoebelen of Iris in New Orleans is fond of his two-level bamboo steamer for cooking fish: "I put aromatics like ginger or star anise on the bottom level and fish like halibut on top," he says (*from $10; cooking.com*).

2 tablespoons vegetable oil
Four 6- to 7-ounce wild striped bass or
    grouper fillets, with skin
Sweet paprika, for garnish

1. Preheat the oven to 425°. In a bowl, whisk the mayonnaise with 2 tablespoons of the olive oil and the garlic, lemon zest and lemon juice; season with salt and pepper.
2. In a large ovenproof skillet, heat the remaining 2 tablespoons of olive oil. Add the pancetta and cook over moderate heat until golden, 4 minutes. Add the brussels sprouts, cut side down, and the large thyme sprigs. Cook over moderately high heat without stirring until the brussels sprouts start to brown, 4 minutes. Transfer the skillet to the bottom third of the oven and roast for 10 minutes, until the brussels sprouts are tender and browned all over; discard the thyme sprigs.
3. Meanwhile, in another ovenproof skillet, heat the vegetable oil until shimmering. Make 3 slashes in the skin of each fillet, season with salt and pepper and add to the skillet, skin side down. Cook over moderately high heat until the skin is browned, 4 minutes. Turn the fillets and transfer the skillet to the upper third of the oven. Roast for 4 minutes, until just white throughout.
4. Transfer the bass to plates, sprinkle with paprika and garnish with the small thyme springs. Serve with the brussels sprouts and garlic mayonnaise. —*Michael Schwartz*
WINE Ripe, juicy Pinot Noir.

Ginger-and-Lemon-Steamed Striped Bass with Fennel Salad

TOTAL: 30 MIN
4 SERVINGS ●

Two 2-pound whole striped bass,
    cleaned and heads removed
One 2-inch piece of fresh ginger,
    peeled and thinly sliced
1 lemon, thinly sliced
1 fennel bulb—halved,
    cored and very thinly sliced,
    plus ¼ cup fennel fronds

Kosher salt
¼ cup extra-virgin olive oil
3 tablespoons fresh lemon juice
2 tablespoons snipped chives

1. Stuff the cavities of the striped bass with the ginger, lemon and fennel fronds. Season inside and outside with salt.
2. Position a wire rack in a large, deep skillet filled with ⅛ inch of water. Bring the water to a simmer. Set the fish on the rack, cover and steam over moderately low heat until cooked through, 18 minutes.
3. Meanwhile, in a bowl, toss the sliced fennel with 2 tablespoons each of the oil and the lemon juice; season with salt. Let stand for 15 minutes.
4. Transfer the fish to a platter. Drizzle with the remaining 2 tablespoons of oil and 1 tablespoon of lemon juice; sprinkle with the chives. Serve with the fennel salad.
—*Laurent Gras*
WINE Dry, light Champagne.

Steamed Red Snapper Packets

ACTIVE: 1 HR; TOTAL: 3 HR
6 SERVINGS ●
FISH TEA
1 tablespoon canola oil
1 onion, thinly sliced
3 garlic cloves, thinly sliced
1 fennel bulb, thinly sliced
1 carrot, thinly sliced
5 pounds red snapper bones,
    coarsely chopped and rinsed
3 ripe tomatoes, coarsely chopped
4 oil-packed anchovies
1 orange, zest removed with a
    vegetable peeler, orange halved
¼ Scotch bonnet chile
3 sprigs each of parsley, basil
    and mint, tied in a bundle
2 quarts cold water
Salt and freshly ground pepper
FISH
2 tablespoons canola oil,
    plus more for brushing

4 garlic cloves, thinly sliced
4 carrots, thinly sliced diagonally
1 bunch of scallions,
    cut into 3-inch lengths
18 okra, halved lengthwise
½ Scotch bonnet or habanero chile,
    seeded and minced
2 tomatoes, cut into eighths
Pinch of ground allspice
Salt and freshly ground pepper
Six 7-ounce red snapper fillets
    (about 1½ inches thick),
    skin lightly scored

1. MAKE THE FISH TEA: In a large pot, heat the oil. Add the onion, garlic, fennel and carrot; cook over moderate heat until softened, 15 minutes. Add the bones; cook until just beginning to turn opaque, 10 minutes. Add the tomatoes, anchovies and zest. Squeeze the orange juice into the pot; add the halves to the pot along with the chile, herb bundle and water and bring to a boil. Simmer over moderately low heat until very flavorful, 1 hour. Strain the broth; season with salt and pepper.
2. MAKE THE FISH: Preheat the oven to 500°. In a large skillet, heat the 2 tablespoons of canola oil. Add the garlic and carrots and cook over moderately high heat, stirring, until they are barely tender, 3 minutes. Add the scallions, okra and chile; cook for 2 minutes, stirring occasionally. Add the tomatoes and cook, stirring, for 1 minute. Stir in the allspice and season with salt and pepper. Let cool slightly.
3. Place six 12-inch squares of aluminum foil on a surface, shiny side down; brush with oil. Season the fillets with salt and pepper; place one in the center of each piece of foil. Spoon the vegetables over the fillets. Fold up the sides of the foil; seal each packet.
4. Arrange the packets on a baking sheet and bake for 18 minutes, until the fish is tender and the vegetables cooked. Transfer the packets to plates. Pour the fish tea into cups and serve. —*Bradford Thompson*
WINE Fresh, minerally Vermentino.

GRAPPA-CURED
STRIPED BASS

Grappa-Cured Striped Bass

TOTAL: 30 MIN PLUS 24 HR CURING
8 FIRST-COURSE SERVINGS ● ●

Grappa, an Italian spirit, is made from grape pomace (the skins, seeds and stems left over from winemaking). Its slight earthiness and high alcohol make it perfect for curing fish.

- 1 tablespoon fennel seeds
- 1 small red onion, very thinly sliced

Fennel fronds from 1 fennel bulb

- ¼ cup kosher salt
- 2 tablespoons sugar

One 2-pound striped bass fillet, with skin

- 1 cup grappa

Toasted baguette slices, extra-virgin olive oil and coarse sea salt, for serving

1. In a small skillet, toast the fennel seeds over moderate heat until fragrant, about 1 minute. Let cool.

2. On a rimmed baking sheet, spread the onion slices in the same shape as the fish fillet. Top the onions with most of the fennel fronds, reserving a few for garnish. In a small bowl, mix the salt with the sugar and fennel seeds and sprinkle over the fennel fronds. Set the fish on the curing mixture, skin side up, and pour the grappa over the fillet. Cover with plastic wrap. Set a baking sheet on top of the fish and weigh it down with heavy cans. Refrigerate for 24 to 36 hours.

3. Drain the fish. Scrape off the curing mixture; transfer the fish to a cutting board, skin side down. Using a thin-bladed knife and starting at the tail end, thinly slice the fish on the diagonal. Avoid the darker flesh near the skin. Serve the slices on toasts drizzled with olive oil, sprinkled lightly with coarse sea salt and garnished with the reserved fennel fronds. —*David Page*

MAKE AHEAD The cured fish fillet can be refrigerated for up to 2 days once the curing mixture is scraped off.

WINE Dry, fruity sparkling wine.

Spiced Catfish with Avocado

TOTAL: 45 MIN
12 SERVINGS ●

FISH

- 1 tablespoon coriander seeds
- 1 tablespoon cumin seeds
- 1 tablespoon dried thyme
- 1 tablespoon dried oregano
- 2 teaspoons chipotle chile powder
- 2 teaspoons ancho chile powder
- 2 teaspoons salt
- 1 teaspoon sugar
- 1 teaspoon ground mace
- 1 teaspoon cinnamon
- ½ teaspoon freshly grated nutmeg
- 4 medium yellow onions, chopped
- 4 garlic cloves
- 2 tablespoons poppy seeds
- ¼ cup extra-virgin olive oil
- 4 pounds catfish fillets, cut into 1-inch pieces
- 2 cups water

AVOCADO SALAD

- 2 medium red onions, finely diced
- ⅔ cup fresh lime juice

Kosher salt

- 4 ripe Hass avocados, diced

Basmati rice, for serving

1. PREPARE THE FISH: In a skillet, toast the coriander and cumin seeds over moderate heat until fragrant, 1 minute; transfer to a spice grinder and let cool, then finely grind them. In a bowl, mix the coriander, cumin, thyme, oregano, chile powders, salt, sugar, mace, cinnamon and nutmeg.

2. In a food processor, puree the onions, garlic and poppy seeds. In a casserole, heat 3 tablespoons of the oil. Add the onion puree and cook over moderately high heat, stirring, until the moisture has evaporated and the puree begins to brown, 5 minutes. Add the remaining 1 tablespoon of oil and the spice mixture and cook until fragrant.

3. Arrange the catfish in the casserole in a single layer. Pour in the water, cover and cook over low heat, stirring occasionally, for 5 minutes. Transfer the fish to a bowl. Boil the sauce, uncovered, until it has thickened, 5 minutes longer. Return the fish to the casserole and keep warm.

4. MEANWHILE, PREPARE THE AVOCADO SALAD: In a large bowl, toss the onion with the lime juice and season with salt. Add the diced avocados and toss.

5. Scoop the rice into bowls. Spoon the fish and sauce over the rice and mound the avocado salad alongside. —*Mini Kahlon*

WINE Vivid, lightly sweet Riesling.

Red Snapper with Zucchini and Black Olive Tapenade

TOTAL: 30 MIN
6 SERVINGS ●

- 2 tablespoons sherry vinegar
- ½ cup extra-virgin olive oil
- 1½ tablespoons small capers
- 6 sun-dried tomato halves in oil, finely chopped
- ¼ cup thinly sliced basil leaves

Salt and freshly ground pepper

- 1 pound small zucchini, sliced on the diagonal ½ inch thick

Six 7-ounce center-cut red snapper fillets

- ¼ cup black olive tapenade
- 1 teaspoon Cognac

1. In a bowl, whisk the vinegar with 5 tablespoons of the oil. Stir in the capers, tomatoes and basil; season with salt and pepper.

2. In a nonstick skillet, heat the remaining oil. Add the zucchini and cook over high heat until golden and just tender, 4 minutes. Season with salt and pepper. Using a slotted spoon, add the zucchini to the dressing.

3. Heat the skillet until the oil is shimmering. Season the fish with salt and pepper and add it to the skillet, skin side down. Cook over high heat, turning once, until golden outside and white throughout, 10 minutes. Transfer to plates and spoon the zucchini alongside. In a bowl, mix the black olive tapenade with the Cognac and spoon over the fish. Serve right away. —*Terrance Brennan*

WINE Fresh, fruity rosé.

Fish Tacos with Creamy Lime Guacamole and Cabbage Slaw

TOTAL: 45 MIN
10 SERVINGS ● ●

Fish tacos are beloved by California surfers, but the fish is often beer-battered and fried. Chef Kerry Simon's healthier version includes grilled red snapper and guacamole made with low-fat sour cream.

- 2 Hass avocados—halved, pitted and peeled
- ¼ cup low-fat sour cream or Greek yogurt
- 1 small jalapeño, seeded and thinly sliced
- 2 tablespoons very finely chopped red onion
- 2 tablespoons chopped cilantro
- 5 tablespoons fresh lime juice
- Kosher salt and freshly ground black pepper
- 1 small head of napa cabbage, shredded (4 cups)
- 2 tablespoons vegetable oil, plus more for brushing
- 2 pounds thick red snapper fillets, with skin, cut crosswise into ten 2-inch-wide strips
- Ten 7-inch flour tortillas, warmed
- 2 medium tomatoes, thinly sliced
- Hot sauce, for serving
- Lime wedges, for serving

1. Light a grill. In a medium bowl, mash the avocados, sour cream, jalapeño, red onion, cilantro and 3 tablespoons of the lime juice. Season with salt and pepper and press a piece of plastic wrap directly onto the surface of the guacamole.

2. In a large bowl, toss the cabbage with the 2 tablespoons of vegetable oil and the remaining 2 tablespoons of lime juice. Season the slaw with salt and pepper.

3. Brush the fish with oil and season with salt and pepper. Grill over moderately high heat until lightly charred and cooked through, about 10 minutes. Transfer the fish to a platter and pull off the skin.

4. To assemble each taco, spread a dollop of guacamole on a tortilla. Top with a piece of fish, a few tomato slices and a large spoonful of the cabbage slaw. Serve with the hot sauce and lime wedges.
—*Kerry Simon*

MAKE AHEAD The guacamole can be made up to 4 hours ahead and refrigerated.
WINE Ripe, luxurious Chardonnay.

Seared Cod with Spicy Mussel Aioli

TOTAL: 30 MIN
4 SERVINGS ● ●

From Eric Ripert of Manhattan's Le Bernardin comes this simple, sophisticated dish that relies on store-bought mayonnaise to enrich the sublime garlicky mussel sauce.

- ⅓ cup dry white wine
- 2 dozen mussels
- ½ cup mayonnaise
- 2 garlic cloves, minced
- 2 tablespoons chopped parsley
- 2 teaspoons fresh lemon juice
- Cayenne pepper
- Salt and freshly ground black pepper
- 1 tablespoon vegetable oil
- Four 6-ounce skinless cod fillets
- 1 roasted red bell pepper, cut into thin strips, for garnish

1. Bring the wine to a boil in a medium saucepan. Add the mussels, cover and cook over high heat until they open, shaking the pan a few times, about 3 minutes. Discard any that do not open. Transfer the mussels and their liquid to a large bowl. Shell the mussels. Rinse out the pan. Pour the mussel liquid back into the pan, stopping before you reach the grit at the bottom.

2. In a bowl, mix the mayonnaise with the garlic, parsley and lemon juice. Season the aioli with cayenne, salt and black pepper.

3. Heat the oil in a large skillet. Season the cod with salt and pepper and cook over moderate heat until lightly browned, about 4 minutes per side.

4. Bring the mussel liquid to a boil; remove from the heat. Whisk in the aioli, then stir in the mussels. Transfer the cod to bowls and spoon the mussel aioli around it. Garnish with the pepper strips and serve.
—*Eric Ripert*

WINE Rich, complex white Burgundy.

Seared Cod with Provençal Vegetables

TOTAL: 1 HR
4 SERVINGS ●

- 1 lemon, halved
- 8 baby artichokes (about 1 pound)
- 3 tablespoons extra-virgin olive oil
- ½ medium onion, thinly sliced
- ½ each of green, red and yellow bell peppers, thinly sliced lengthwise
- 2 garlic cloves, thinly sliced
- 1 teaspoon thyme leaves
- Kosher salt and freshly ground pepper
- 2 tablespoons dry white wine
- Four 6-ounce skinless cod fillets

1. Bring a saucepan of salted water to a boil. Squeeze the lemon halves into a bowl of water, then add the halves. Working with 1 artichoke at a time, snap off all of the dark green leaves. Using a sharp knife, slice off the top half of the leaves, peel and trim the stem and add to the lemon water. Add the artichokes to the boiling water and cook until just tender, 20 minutes. Drain and let cool.

2. Meanwhile, in a medium skillet, heat 1 tablespoon of the oil. Add the onion, bell peppers, garlic and thyme and season with salt and pepper. Cook over moderate heat, stirring, until the vegetables begin to soften, 5 minutes. Add the wine, cover and cook over low heat, stirring, until the vegetables are tender, 25 minutes. Transfer to a bowl.

3. Wipe out the skillet and heat 1 tablespoon of the oil. Add the artichokes and cook over moderately high heat until lightly browned and the outer leaves begin to crisp, about 7 minutes. Season with salt and pepper, add the bell peppers and keep warm.

FISH TACOS WITH LIME GUACAMOLE AND CABBAGE SLAW   PAN-SEARED COD WITH PRESERVED-LEMON AIOLI

4. In a large nonstick skillet, heat the remaining 1 tablespoon of olive oil. Season the cod fillets with salt and pepper and cook over moderately high heat, turning once, until the fillets are lightly browned and slightly firm, about 4 minutes per side. Transfer the seared cod to plates, garnish with the peppers and artichokes and serve immediately.
—*Arnaud Bradol*

MAKE AHEAD The cooked peppers and artichokes can be refrigerated overnight. Rewarm before serving.

WINE Juicy, spicy Grenache.

Pan-Seared Cod with Preserved-Lemon Aioli

 **TOTAL: 20 MIN**
4 SERVINGS

To give skinless cod fillets a golden crust, F&W's Melissa Rubel dusts them with finely milled Wondra flour before cooking them. She then serves the fish alongside a creamy preserved-lemon aioli that can double as a terrific dipping sauce for roasted potatoes.

- 1 cup mayonnaise
- 1 **preserved lemon, peel only, finely chopped (see Note)**
- 1 garlic clove, chopped
- 1 tablespoon water

Pinch of cayenne pepper

- 5 **tablespoons extra-virgin olive oil**

Kosher salt and freshly ground black pepper

Four 6-ounce skinless cod fillets

- ¼ cup Wondra flour

1. In a blender, puree the mayonnaise with the preserved lemon peel, chopped garlic, water, cayenne and 3 tablespoons of the olive oil. Season the preserved-lemon aioli with salt and black pepper and scrape it into a small bowl.

2. In a large nonstick skillet, heat the remaining 2 tablespoons of olive oil. Season the cod fillets with salt and black pepper and dust them with the Wondra flour. Cook the cod fillets over moderately high heat, turning once, until they are golden on the outside and white throughout, about 10 minutes total. Transfer the seared cod fillets to 4 plates and serve right away with the preserved-lemon aioli.
—*Melissa Rubel*

NOTE Preserved lemons are a traditional Moroccan ingredient made by macerating whole lemons in lemon juice and salt until very soft. The lemon pulp is often discarded and the peel is used. They are available at specialty food shops and from kalustyans.com.

MAKE AHEAD The preserved-lemon aioli can be kept in an airtight container in the refrigerator for up to 4 days.

WINE Zesty, fresh Albariño.

●HEALTHY ●MAKE AHEAD ○VEGETARIAN ●STAFF FAVORITE

CRUNCHY FISH STICKS
WITH TARTAR SAUCE

Crunchy Fish Sticks with Tartar Sauce

TOTAL: 30 MIN
6 SERVINGS ●

In this clever recipe, cod strips are dredged in flour and potato flakes and fried to create crunchy fish sticks, then served with a sun-dried-tomato tartar sauce.

½   cup mayonnaise
4   oil-packed sun-dried tomatoes, finely chopped
3   sweet gherkins, finely chopped
2   tablespoons finely chopped red onion
2   tablespoons finely chopped dill
1   teaspoon fresh lemon juice, plus lemon wedges for serving
Salt
Cayenne pepper
2   large eggs
2   tablespoons water
¾   cup all-purpose flour
1   cup instant potato flakes
1¾ pounds cod fillets, cut into 4-by-¾-inch strips
Vegetable oil, for frying

1. In a small bowl, combine the mayonnaise with the sun-dried tomatoes, gherkins, red onion, dill and lemon juice. Season the tartar sauce with salt and cayenne.
2. In a shallow bowl, whisk the eggs with the water. In another shallow bowl, mix ½ cup of the flour with salt and cayenne. In a third shallow bowl, combine the potato flakes with the remaining ¼ cup of flour and season with salt and cayenne. Line a baking sheet with wax paper and another one with paper towels.
3. Working in batches, dredge the cod in the flour, tapping off the excess. Dip the cod in the egg, allow any excess to drip back into the bowl, then coat the cod in the potato flakes, pressing to help them adhere. Transfer to the wax paper–lined baking sheet.
4. In a large, deep skillet, heat 1½ inches of oil to 325°. Working in 2 batches, fry the cod in the hot oil, turning once, until deep golden and crispy, about 3 minutes. Using a slotted spoon, transfer the fish to the paper towel–lined baking sheet and sprinkle lightly with salt. Repeat with the remaining fish. Serve immediately with the tartar sauce and lemon wedges. —*Grace Parisi*
MAKE AHEAD The tartar sauce can be refrigerated for 1 week.
WINE Creamy, supple Pinot Blanc.

Lemongrass-Marinated Pompano with Dipping Sauce

ACTIVE: 30 MIN; TOTAL: 1 HR 30 MIN
4 SERVINGS ● ●

When *Top Chef* Season 3 winner Hung Huynh cooks small pompano, he trims the head, tail and fins, then cuts the fish into rectangular quarters: "I love to think I invented that presentation," he says. But the recipe is just as good with pompano fillets: The crispy-skinned fish is delicious with the hot-sweet-tangy dipping sauce.

DIPPING SAUCE
Juice of 2 limes
2   tablespoons Asian fish sauce
2   Thai chiles, minced
2   tablespoons sugar
MARINADE AND FISH
2   garlic cloves, chopped
2   scallions, whites chopped, greens sliced for garnish
1   large stalk of lemongrass, bottom two-thirds chopped
1   tablespoon chopped cilantro stems, plus sprigs for garnish
2   teaspoons sugar
1   tablespoon fresh lime juice
1   tablespoon kosher salt
½   teaspoon freshly ground pepper
Four 6-ounce pompano fillets, with skin
2   tablespoons vegetable oil
Lime wedges, for serving

1. MAKE THE DIPPING SAUCE: In a bowl, stir the lime juice with the fish sauce, chiles and sugar until the sugar is dissolved.
2. MARINATE THE FISH: In a mini processor, puree the garlic, scallion whites, lemongrass, cilantro stems, sugar, lime juice, salt and pepper to a paste. Rub the paste all over the pompano. Put the fish on a plate, cover and refrigerate for 1 hour.
3. Scrape the marinade from the fish. In a large nonstick skillet, heat the oil. Add the fish skin side down and cook over moderately high heat until the skin is crisp, about 3 minutes. Turn the fillets, lower the heat to moderate and cook until just opaque throughout, about 2 minutes longer; transfer to plates, skin side up, and garnish with scallion greens and cilantro sprigs. Serve with lime wedges and the dipping sauce. —*Hung Huynh*
WINE Tart, citrusy Riesling.

Black Cod with Miso

TOTAL: 30 MIN PLUS OVERNIGHT MARINATING
6 SERVINGS ● ●

3   tablespoons mirin
3   tablespoons sake
½   cup white miso paste
⅓   cup sugar
Six 6- to 7-ounce skinless black cod fillets, cut 1½ inches thick
Vegetable oil, for grilling
Pickled ginger, for serving

1. In a small saucepan, bring the mirin and sake to a boil. Whisk in the miso until dissolved. Add the sugar and cook over moderate heat, whisking, just until dissolved. Transfer the marinade to a large baking dish and let cool. Add the fish and turn to coat. Cover and refrigerate overnight.
2. Preheat the oven to 400°. Heat a grill pan and oil it. Scrape the marinade off the fish. Add the fish to the grill pan and cook over high heat until browned, 2 minutes. Flip the fish onto a heavy rimmed baking sheet and roast in the oven for 10 minutes, until flaky. Transfer to plates and serve with pickled ginger. —*Nobu Matsuhisa*
MAKE AHEAD The marinade can be refrigerated for up to 1 week.
WINE Rich Alsace Gewürztraminer.

Grilled Spanish Mackerel with Cauliflower "Tabbouleh"

ACTIVE: 45 MIN; TOTAL: 1 HR 45 MIN

6 SERVINGS ●

When Seattle chef (and F&W Best New Chef 2006) Jason Wilson worked in Singapore, he picked up a trick: using freshly grated cauliflower in a version of tabbouleh, a Middle Eastern salad usually made with bulgur wheat. At Crush, Wilson mixes salted, grated cauliflower with preserved lemon, garlic and plenty of chopped parsley, then serves it with yellowtail, prepared sashimi-style, or with grilled *kampachi*, a slightly fatty fish from Hawaii; Spanish mackerel is equally tasty.

- 1 tablespoon chopped fresh marjoram or oregano
- 1 teaspoon ground fennel
- 1 teaspoon finely grated orange zest
- ¾ cup plus 2 tablespoons extra-virgin olive oil
- ½ cup snipped chives
- ¼ cup plus 2 tablespoons chopped flat-leaf parsley
- 2 shallots, minced

Salt and freshly ground pepper

Six 7-ounce Spanish mackerel fillets, with skin

- 1 small head of cauliflower (1½ pounds), cut into florets
- 1 garlic clove, minced
- 1 tablespoon ground cumin
- 1 teaspoon mild or hot smoked paprika
- 1½ teaspoons minced preserved lemon, rind only (see Note)
- 1 tablespoon chopped mint
- 1 small tomato, seeded and diced
- 2 tablespoons sherry vinegar

1. In a medium bowl, mix the marjoram, ground fennel and orange zest with ½ cup of the olive oil, ¼ cup of the chives, 2 tablespoons of the parsley and half of the minced shallots. Season the marinade with salt and pepper and transfer it to a shallow baking dish. Add the mackerel, turn to coat and refrigerate for 1 hour.

2. Meanwhile, fit a food processor with a coarse shredding disk. With the machine on, drop the cauliflower florets through the feed tube without pressing and process until finely grated. Transfer the cauliflower to a medium bowl and toss with 1 tablespoon of salt. Let stand at room temperature for 30 minutes.

3. Drain the cauliflower and squeeze out any liquid; return the cauliflower to the bowl.

4. In a small skillet, heat the remaining 6 tablespoons of olive oil. Add the minced garlic, cumin and paprika and the remaining minced shallot and cook until the mixture is fragrant, about 2 minutes. Let cool slightly, then pour the mixture over the cauliflower. Add the preserved lemon rind, mint, tomato, sherry vinegar and the remaining ¼ cup each of parsley and chives to the cauliflower. Season the tabbouleh with salt and pepper and toss.

5. Light a grill. Grill the fish fillets over moderately high heat, turning once or twice, until they are nicely charred in spots, about 7 minutes. Serve the fish with the cauliflower tabbouleh. —*Jason Wilson*

NOTE Preserved lemons are a common Moroccan ingredient made from lemons that have been preserved in lemon juice and salt. Look for them at specialty food stores or kalustyans.com.

WINE Fresh, lively Soave.

Roasted Branzino with Caper Butter

 TOTAL: 40 MIN

8 SERVINGS

"It's almost impossible to end up with dry, overcooked fish when cooking it whole," says Steve Corry (an F&W Best New Chef 2007). "The bones protect against extreme heat, plus they add flavor and moisture." Here, Corry pan-roasts whole branzino (Mediterranean sea bass) stuffed with lemon slices and rosemary sprigs.

- 1 stick unsalted butter, softened
- 1 tablespoon finely chopped capers
- 1 tablespoon fresh lemon juice
- 1 tablespoon chopped parsley

Salt

Four 1- to 1¼-pound whole branzino or striped bass, scaled and gutted

- 1 lemon, sliced into 8 rounds
- 4 large rosemary sprigs
- 3 tablespoons extra-virgin olive oil

1. Preheat the oven to 425°. In a medium bowl, mix the butter with the capers, lemon juice and parsley and season with salt. Keep at room temperature.

2. Season the branzino cavities with salt and stuff 2 lemon rounds and 1 rosemary sprig in each. Season the fish with salt.

3. In a large nonstick ovenproof skillet, heat 2 tablespoons of the olive oil until shimmering. Add 2 of the branzino and cook over high heat until the skin is browned and crisp, about 3 minutes per side. Transfer the fish to a large rimmed baking sheet. Repeat with the remaining 1 tablespoon of olive oil and 2 stuffed branzino. Roast the fish in the oven for about 10 minutes, until just cooked through.

4. Serve the branzino whole or filleted, passing the caper butter at the table. —*Steve Corry*

WINE Fresh, minerally Vermentino.

Skate with Mushrooms and Hazelnuts

 TOTAL: 45 MIN

4 SERVINGS

This luscious dish from renowned French chef Daniel Boulud is deceptively simple: skate stuffed with duxelles, a mixture of mushrooms and shallots.

- ½ cup hazelnuts
- 3 medium shallots, very finely chopped
- 2 garlic cloves, halved
- 6 tablespoons unsalted butter, softened

½ pound shiitake mushrooms, stems discarded and caps cut into 1-inch pieces

2 thyme sprigs

Salt and freshly ground pepper

Four 6-ounce skate wings

2 tablespoons vegetable oil

½ lemon—peeled, sectioned and diced

2 teaspoons fresh lemon juice

1. Preheat the oven to 350°. Spread the hazelnuts in a pie plate and toast for 10 minutes. Let cool, then transfer to a kitchen towel and rub them together to remove the skins. Transfer the hazelnuts to a work surface; coarsely chop.

2. In a medium skillet, cook the shallots and garlic in 2 tablespoons of the butter over moderately low heat until softened, 4 minutes. Add the mushrooms and thyme; season with salt and pepper. Cook, stirring occasionally, until the mushrooms are tender, 5 minutes. Discard the garlic and thyme. Reserve ⅓ of the mixture. In a food processor, puree the remaining mushroom mixture. Season with salt and pepper.

3. Cut each skate wing in half crosswise and season with salt and pepper. Spread 4 of the skate pieces with ½ tablespoon of the softened butter and top each with one-quarter of the mushroom puree. Cover with the remaining skate wing, pressing the packets together.

4. In a large skillet, heat the oil until shimmering. Add the skate packets and cook over high heat until browned and crisp on the bottom, 4 minutes. Flip the packets, lower the heat to moderate and add the remaining 2 tablespoons of butter, the reserved mushroom mixture, the hazelnuts, diced lemon and lemon juice. Cook until the skate is just white throughout, 4 minutes. Transfer the skate to plates, top with the mushrooms, nuts and lemon and serve. —*Daniel Boulud*

SERVE WITH Creamy Spinach (p. 223).

WINE Rich, complex white Burgundy.

ROASTED BRANZINO WITH CAPER BUTTER

SKATE WITH MUSHROOMS AND HAZELNUTS

Barramundi with Tomato-Basil Salsa

TOTAL: 30 MIN
4 SERVINGS ●

Barramundi, a flaky white fish native to the waters around Australia, is delicious here, but any sea bass will work with this basil-inflected salsa.

- 4 medium tomatoes—peeled, seeded and cut into ½-inch dice
- ½ small red onion, minced
- 2 tablespoons finely chopped basil
- 3 tablespoons extra-virgin olive oil
- Four 6-ounce barramundi or sea bass fillets, with skin
- Salt
- 2 limes, halved crosswise
- 1 tablespoon unseasoned rice vinegar

1. In a medium bowl, toss the tomatoes with the onion, basil and 1 tablespoon of the olive oil.
2. In a skillet, heat the remaining 2 tablespoons of oil until shimmering. Season the fish with salt and add to the skillet, skin side down. Cook over high heat until the skin is crisp, 3 minutes. Flip and cook over moderate heat until just white throughout, 2 minutes longer. Transfer to plates.
3. Place the limes in the skillet, cut side down. Cook over moderately high heat until browned; transfer them to the plates.
4. Stir the vinegar into the salsa and season with salt. Spoon the salsa alongside the barramundi and serve. —*Luke Mangan*
WINE Fruity, low-oak Chardonnay.

Sautéed Trout with Citrus-Olive Relish

TOTAL: 25 MIN
4 SERVINGS ●

- 2 navel oranges
- 1 small lemon
- 1 teaspoon finely grated orange zest
- ½ teaspoon finely grated lemon zest
- ¼ cup pitted green olives, thinly sliced
- 2 tablespoons chopped parsley
- 1 teaspoon minced garlic
- ¼ cup extra-virgin olive oil
- 2 tablespoons red wine vinegar
- Salt and freshly ground black pepper
- 1 tablespoon vegetable oil
- Four 6-ounce skinless trout fillets
- All-purpose flour, for dusting

1. Using a sharp knife, peel the bitter white pith from the oranges and lemon; be sure to remove all of the pith. Working over a bowl, cut in between the membranes to release the sections. Add the grated orange and lemon zests, olives, parsley, garlic, olive oil and vinegar. Season the relish with salt and pepper and toss gently.

2. In a large nonstick skillet, heat the vegetable oil. Season the trout fillets with salt and pepper and dust with flour. Add the trout to the skillet and cook over moderately high heat until browned on the bottom, about 2 minutes. Turn the fillets, reduce the heat to moderate and cook until just white throughout, about 3 minutes. Transfer the fillets to plates or a platter, spoon the relish on top and serve.
—*Clark Frasier and Mark Gaier*
SERVE WITH Quinoa salad.
WINE Full-bodied, minerally Riesling.

Cornmeal-Fried Trout with Grapefruit and Fried Sage

TOTAL: 35 MIN
4 SERVINGS

Coating skinless trout fillets with cornmeal before frying them creates a crunchy crust with a pleasant sweetness.

- 1 large red grapefruit
- All-purpose flour, for dusting
- 1 large egg lightly beaten with 1 tablespoon of water
- Yellow cornmeal, for dredging
- Four 6-ounce skinless trout fillets
- Salt and freshly ground black pepper
- 3 tablespoons unsalted butter, chilled
- 8 large sage leaves
- Vegetable oil, for frying
- ¼ cup water

1. Using a sharp knife, remove the peel and bitter white pith from the grapefruit. Working over a medium bowl, carefully cut in between the membranes to release the sections into the bowl. Squeeze the remaining juice into a separate bowl.
2. Put the flour, beaten egg and cornmeal in 3 wide, shallow bowls. Season the trout fillets with salt and pepper and lightly dust them with flour, tapping off the excess. Dip the fillets in the egg, then dredge them in the cornmeal.

smoking fish in a flash

Chefs like Michael Anthony *of New York City's Gramercy Tavern are toying with a new technique: smoking fish to order.*

Line a 9-by-13-inch roasting pan with foil; spread with ½ cup dry applewood chips. Cover loosely with foil and char over moderately low heat until heavy smoke gives way to light wisps, about 7 minutes. Place four 4-ounce, skin-on trout fillets skin side down on an oiled rack set 2 inches above the chips. Season the fish with salt and cover with foil; smoke over low heat until just cooked, 5 minutes. Remove the skins, transfer the fish fillets to plates and serve.

3. In a large skillet, melt 1 tablespoon of the butter. Add the sage leaves and cook over moderate heat, turning once, until crisp, about 2 minutes per side. Transfer the sage leaves to paper towels to drain. Add ¼ inch of oil to the skillet and heat until shimmering. Carefully add the trout fillets and fry them over moderately high heat until they are golden brown and just cooked through, about 3 minutes per side. Divide the fillets among 4 plates.

4. Discard the frying oil and wipe out the skillet with paper towels. Add the grapefruit juice and water to the skillet and bring to a boil; cook for 1 minute. Reduce the heat to moderate, add the grapefruit sections and simmer the sauce for 1 minute. Remove the skillet from the heat and swirl in the remaining 2 tablespoons of butter, 1 tablespoon at a time. Season with salt and pepper and spoon the sauce and grapefruit sections over the trout fillets. Garnish each trout fillet with 2 fried sage leaves and serve immediately.
—*Marcia Kiesel*

PUMPKIN SEED CRUST VARIATION In a food processor, pulse ½ cup of raw, unsalted pumpkin seeds until coarsely ground. After dusting the fish fillets with flour and dipping them in the beaten egg, dredge them in the pumpkin seeds instead of the cornmeal and fry as directed.

FISH VARIATION Catfish or tilapia.
WINE Fruity, low-oak Chardonnay.

Pan-Fried Smoked-Trout Cakes with Lemony Salad

TOTAL: 35 MIN
4 SERVINGS ●

These crispy pan-fried cakes highlight the intense flavors of smoked trout; the lemony salad served alongside adds a lovely light twang.

¼ cup mayonnaise
1 large egg, lightly beaten
2 tablespoons very finely chopped scallion greens

1 tablespoon capers in brine, drained and coarsely chopped
2 teaspoons Dijon mustard
3 tablespoons fresh lemon juice, plus lemon wedges for serving
Freshly ground pepper
½ pound boneless smoked trout fillet, skin removed and trout flaked (about 2 cups)
1 cup *panko* (Japanese bread crumbs)
3½ tablespoons extra-virgin olive oil
Salt
4 cups mâche or watercress

1. In a large bowl, mix the mayonnaise with the lightly beaten egg, finely chopped scallion greens, chopped capers, Dijon mustard, 2 tablespoons of the lemon juice and ½ teaspoon of pepper. Add the flaked smoked trout and toss to combine. Fold in ½ cup of the *panko*.

2. Spread the remaining ½ cup of *panko* bread crumbs on a plate. Form the trout mixture into eight 1-inch-thick cakes, add them to the plate and turn to coat with the *panko*.

3. In a large skillet, heat 2 tablespoons of the olive oil until shimmering. Add the cakes to the skillet and cook over moderate heat, turning once, until browned and heated through, about 6 minutes. Transfer the trout cakes to plates.

4. In a medium bowl, whisk the remaining 1½ tablespoons of olive oil with the remaining 1 tablespoon of lemon juice and season the dressing with salt and pepper. Add the mâche and toss to coat. Transfer the salad to the plates with the trout cakes and serve right away, with lemon wedges.
—*Nick Fauchald*

MAKE AHEAD The uncooked trout cakes can be prepared through Step 2 and refrigerated overnight.
WINE Light, fresh Pinot Grigio.

Grilled Trout with Grilled Romaine Salad

TOTAL: 25 MIN
12 SERVINGS ●

Paul Virant (an F&W Best New Chef 2007) created this dish on the fly while he was visiting his brother Tom in Washington, D.C., one Memorial Day. "I wanted to do the entire dish on the grill so I wouldn't have to go inside," he says. The lemony vinaigrette is delicious on the crispy trout and the smoky charred lettuce; Virant liberally dresses both, before and after grilling.

4 garlic cloves, minced
2 teaspoons finely grated lemon zest
¼ cup plus 2 tablespoons fresh lemon juice
1 cup extra-virgin olive oil
Salt and freshly ground pepper
3 heads of romaine lettuce (1½ pounds each)—tough outer leaves discarded, heads halved lengthwise through the cores
Twelve 6-ounce trout fillets, with skin

1. Light a grill. In a bowl, whisk the garlic with the lemon zest, lemon juice and oil and season with salt and pepper. Drizzle the cut side of each romaine lettuce half with 1 tablespoon of the dressing and season with salt and pepper. Grill over high heat until lightly charred, about 1 minute per side. Cut each piece of romaine in half lengthwise and transfer to a platter.

2. Brush the trout fillets on both sides with some of the remaining dressing and season with salt and pepper. Grill the trout fillets over high heat, skin side down, until the skin is lightly charred and crisp, about 3 minutes. Turn the trout fillets over and cook for 1 minute longer. Place a trout fillet over each romaine quarter, drizzle with the remaining dressing and serve right away. —*Paul Virant*
WINE Vivid, lightly sweet Riesling.

POP-OPEN CLAMS
WITH HORSERADISH-
TABASCO SAUCE (P. 209)

shellfish

" I often grab a handful of mussels at the end of the dinner shift and cook them at home for a late-night snack. "

—ETHAN STOWELL, CHEF AND RESTAURATEUR, SEATTLE

GRILLED SOUR CREAM—MARINATED SHRIMP

SHRIMP-AND-AVOCADO SALAD WITH MANGO DRESSING

Grilled Sour Cream–Marinated Shrimp

TOTAL: 30 MIN PLUS 3 HR MARINATING
4 FIRST-COURSE SERVINGS

Instead of marinating shrimp in yogurt that's been drained for hours, as is traditional in India, chef Suvir Saran uses sour cream—it's faster and, he thinks, tastier.

- 1 cup sour cream
- 6 garlic cloves, minced
- 1 teaspoon cumin seeds
- 1 teaspoon garam masala
- 1 teaspoon cracked white and black peppercorns
- 1 teaspoon ground cumin
- 1 teaspoon ground ginger
- ½ teaspoon turmeric
- 16 jumbo shrimp, shelled and deveined

Salt

- 3 tablespoons unsalted butter, melted
- ½ teaspoon *chat masala*, for sprinkling (see Note)

Lime wedges, for serving

1. In a large, shallow dish, whisk the sour cream with the garlic, cumin seeds, garam masala, peppercorns, ground cumin, ginger and turmeric. Add the shrimp and coat thoroughly with the marinade. Cover and refrigerate for 3 hours.

2. Light a grill. Remove the shrimp from the marinade and thread onto skewers; season with salt. Oil the grates and grill over high heat until almost cooked through, 2 minutes per side. Brush the shrimp with the butter and grill until glazed and just cooked through. Sprinkle the shrimp with the *chat masala* and serve with lime wedges. —*Suvir Saran*

NOTE *Chat masala* is a spicy, tangy Indian spice blend. It is available at Indian markets and kalustyans.com.

WINE Rich Alsace Gewürztraminer.

Shrimp-and-Avocado Salad with Mango Dressing

TOTAL: 1 HR

4 SERVINGS ● ●

Bradford Thompson (an F&W Best New Chef 2004) simmers shrimp in a fragrant broth made with lager, chile and fresh ginger, then serves them with avocado and a light mango dressing.

SHRIMP

- 1 lemon, halved
- 6 cups water
- 1 small onion, sliced
- 2 tablespoons kosher salt
- 1 Scotch bonnet or habanero chile, halved
- 1 tablespoon finely grated fresh ginger

One 12-ounce bottle of lager, such as Red Stripe

- 2 pounds large shrimp, shelled and deveined

DRESSING

1 mango, peeled and finely diced (1½ cups)
¼ cup rice vinegar
2 tablespoons fresh lime juice
1 teaspoon Dijon mustard
½ cup canola oil
1 tablespoon chopped cilantro
½ teaspoon finely grated lime zest
¼ teaspoon minced Scotch bonnet or habanero chile
¼ cup thinly sliced red onion
Salt and freshly ground black pepper
2 Hass avocados, sliced
Lime wedges, for serving

1. PREPARE THE SHRIMP: Squeeze the lemon halves into a large saucepan, then add them to the pan. Add the water, onion, salt, Scotch bonnet, ginger and beer and bring to a boil. Cover and simmer for 15 minutes. Add the shrimp and cook for 3 minutes, just until pink. Drain the shrimp and spread on a platter. Refrigerate until chilled. Halve the shrimp horizontally.

2. MEANWHILE, MAKE THE DRESSING: In a blender, combine ⅓ cup of the diced mango with the vinegar, lime juice and mustard and puree until smooth. With the machine on, add the oil in a thin stream and blend until very smooth. Add the cilantro, lime zest and minced Scotch bonnet and pulse just to combine.

3. Transfer the dressing to a large bowl. Add the shrimp, red onion and the remaining mango and season with salt and pepper. Toss to coat. Arrange the avocado slices around a large platter. Mound the shrimp salad in the center and garnish with lime wedges. Serve right away.
—*Bradford Thompson*

MAKE AHEAD The cooked shrimp and mango dressing can be refrigerated separately overnight. Toss the shrimp with the mango dressing before serving.
WINE Lively, tart Sauvignon Blanc.

Grilled Shrimp with Mangoes and Chile

 TOTAL: 40 MIN
4 SERVINGS

3 tablespoons extra-virgin olive oil, plus more for drizzling
2 tablespoons white wine vinegar
1 small shallot, minced
1 garlic clove, minced (optional)
1 red Thai chile, minced
1 tablespoon finely grated fresh ginger
1 tablespoon chopped cilantro
1 mango, peeled and cut into ¼-inch dice
Salt
2 pounds large shrimp, shelled and deveined
Freshly ground pepper
1 cup baby arugula

1. Light a grill or preheat a grill pan. In a medium bowl, stir the 3 tablespoons of olive oil with the vinegar, shallot, garlic, chile, ginger and cilantro. Fold in the mango and season with salt.

2. Drizzle the shrimp with oil, toss to coat and season with salt and pepper. Grill the shrimp over high heat, turning once, until lightly charred and just cooked through, about 4 minutes.

3. Transfer the shrimp to plates and top with the mango salsa. Mound the arugula leaves alongside and drizzle with olive oil. Season with salt and pepper and serve right away. —*Luke Mangan*
WINE Full-bodied, rich Pinot Gris.

Shrimp-and-Poblano Salad with Tortillas

 TOTAL: 45 MIN
4 SERVINGS

Because shrimp can dry out on the grill, F&W's Marcia Kiesel wraps them in cured meat so they stay succulent. Here she uses salami, which adds an instantly rich and garlicky flavor to the shellfish. You can also wrap the shrimp in bacon or prosciutto.

3 large ears of corn, shucked
2 large poblano chiles
1 large red bell pepper
3 tablespoons vegetable oil, plus more for brushing
2 tablespoons fresh lime juice
2 tablespoons chopped cilantro
1 garlic clove, minced
Salt and freshly ground pepper
2 dozen medium shrimp (about 10 ounces), shelled and deveined
12 thin slices of salami (3 ounces), halved
Four 8-inch flour tortillas

1. Light a grill. In a large saucepan of boiling water, cook the corn until just tender, about 4 minutes. Drain and let cool, then cut the kernels from the cobs into a large bowl.

2. Grill the poblanos and red pepper over high heat, turning, until charred all over and tender, about 5 minutes for the poblanos and 8 minutes for the red pepper. Transfer to a rimmed baking sheet to cool. Remove the charred skins, seeds and stems and cut the poblanos and red pepper into 2-by-½-inch strips. Add them to the corn.

3. In a small bowl, mix the 3 tablespoons of oil with the lime juice, cilantro and garlic. Pour the dressing over the corn and season with salt and pepper; toss well.

4. Brush the shrimp with oil and season lightly with salt and pepper. Wrap each shrimp in a half slice of salami and skewer 6 shrimp onto each of 4 metal skewers. Grill over high heat, turning once, until the salami is crisp and the shrimp are just cooked through, about 1½ minutes per side. Transfer the shrimp to a plate. Generously brush the flour tortillas with oil and grill over high heat until blistered and charred, about 1 minute per side.

5. Remove the shrimp from the skewers. Add them to the corn salad and toss well. Transfer the salad to plates and serve with the grilled tortillas. —*Marcia Kiesel*
WINE Creamy, supple Pinot Blanc.

Chipotle Shrimp Tostadas

TOTAL: 40 MIN
4 SERVINGS ● ●

To create this Southwestern-inspired dish, F&W's Melissa Rubel tosses shrimp with chipotle chile powder (made from dried, smoked jalapeños), grills them, then layers them on top of crunchy fried corn tortillas and crisp, citrusy slaw.

- 1 teaspoon vegetable oil, plus more for frying
- 4 corn tortillas

Kosher salt

- 24 large shelled and deveined shrimp (about 1 pound)
- 1 teaspoon chipotle chile powder
- 4 cups shredded cabbage or coleslaw mix
- 1 medium tomato, seeded and cut into ¼-inch dice
- 2 scallions, thinly sliced
- ¼ cup sour cream
- 1½ teaspoons fresh lime juice
- 1 Hass avocado, thinly sliced
- 2 medium radishes, thinly sliced
- ¼ cup cilantro leaves

Lime wedges, for serving

1. In a medium, deep skillet, heat ¼ inch of vegetable oil until hot. Fry one tortilla at a time over moderately high heat until lightly golden on both sides, about 2 minutes. Drain the tortillas on paper towels and sprinkle with salt.

making shrimp broth

Save shrimp shells to make a fragrant, versatile broth. Bring shells and water to a boil; lower the heat, cover and simmer for 30 minutes. Strain and use in place of water in grits, polenta or rice, or as a base for soups and sauces.

2. Preheat a grill pan. In a medium bowl, toss the shrimp with the 1 teaspoon of vegetable oil and the chipotle chile powder. Season the shrimp with salt. Grill the shrimp over moderately high heat, turning once, until they are browned in spots and cooked through, about 4 minutes.

3. In a medium bowl, toss the cabbage with the tomato, scallions, sour cream and lime juice and season with salt. Set the tortillas on plates and top with the cabbage slaw, chipotle shrimp, avocado, radishes and cilantro. Serve with lime wedges.
—*Melissa Rubel*
WINE Fresh, fruity rosé.

Jumbo Shrimp with Mushrooms and Garlic

TOTAL: 30 MIN
4 SERVINGS

- 4 garlic cloves, thinly sliced
- ¼ cup plus 2 tablespoons pure olive oil
- ½ pound shiitake mushrooms, stems discarded and caps thickly sliced
- 2 pounds jumbo shrimp, butterflied in their shells (see Note)

Salt and freshly ground pepper

- ¼ cup water
- 1 cup coarsely chopped cilantro leaves
- 2 tablespoons unsalted butter

Yellow rice and lime wedges, for serving

1. In a large skillet, cook the sliced garlic in the olive oil over moderate heat, stirring occasionally, until lightly browned and fragrant, about 1 minute. Using a slotted spoon, transfer the browned garlic slices to a plate. Add the shiitake mushrooms to the skillet and cook over high heat, stirring occasionally, until the mushrooms are browned, about 7 minutes.

2. Season the shrimp with salt and pepper and add them to the skillet. Cook over high

heat, stirring occasionally, until the shrimp are nearly cooked through, 7 to 8 minutes. Add the water and cook just until evaporated. Add the cilantro leaves and butter to the skillet and stir to coat. Transfer the shrimp and mushrooms to a platter and garnish with the sliced garlic. Serve the shrimp with yellow rice and lime wedges.
—*Dionicio Jimenez*
NOTE If you can't get pre-butterflied shrimp, use a pair of kitchen scissors to cut down the back of each shrimp, leaving the shells intact.
WINE Lively, tart Sauvignon Blanc.

Garlic Shrimp with Polenta

TOTAL: 45 MIN
4 SERVINGS ● ●

This Venetian classic known as *schie con polenta* features briny shrimp laced with garlic and spooned with their pan juices over creamy white polenta. The dish is traditionally made with tiny gray shrimp from the Venetian lagoon; any size shrimp will work, though, as long as they are very fresh.

- 6½ cups water

Salt

- 1¾ cups white polenta (10 ounces)
- 2 tablespoons unsalted butter

Freshly ground pepper

- ½ cup extra-virgin olive oil
- 2 pounds shrimp, shelled and deveined
- 2 large garlic cloves, very finely chopped

1. In a large saucepan, combine the water with a large pinch of salt and bring to a boil. Add the polenta in a thin stream, whisking constantly.

2. Reduce the heat to low and simmer, stirring constantly with a wooden spoon, until the polenta is thick and the grains are tender, about 20 minutes. Stir in the butter, season the polenta with salt and pepper and keep warm.

3. In a very large skillet, heat the olive oil until shimmering. Season the shrimp with salt and pepper. Add them to the skillet and cook over high heat until they are lightly browned on one side, about 2 minutes. Add the garlic, turn the shrimp over and cook until they are cooked through, about 1 minute longer.

4. Transfer the polenta to shallow bowls. Top with the shrimp and some of the garlic oil from the skillet. Serve right away.
—*Florence Daniel Marzotto*

WINE Lush, fragrant Viognier.

Ginger-Garlic Shrimp with Tangy Tomato Sauce

TOTAL: 1 HR PLUS 2 HR MARINATING
10 SERVINGS ●

The marinade for these shrimp—a piquant mix of lemon juice, garlic, ginger, basil and parsley—would be equally good with pork or chicken. The dipping sauce is almost chutney-like, with chunks of whole tomatoes; lemongrass and lime juice add tang.

SHRIMP

- ½ cup vegetable oil
- ¼ cup finely chopped parsley
- 2 tablespoons minced garlic
- 2 tablespoons finely chopped basil
- 1 tablespoon minced fresh ginger
- 2 tablespoons fresh lemon juice
- 2 teaspoons kosher salt
- 1 teaspoon crushed red pepper
- 2½ pounds large shrimp, shelled and deveined

DIPPING SAUCE

- 1 tablespoon vegetable oil
- 1 tablespoon minced fresh ginger
- 1 large garlic clove, minced
- 3 stalks of fresh lemongrass, tender inner bulb only, very finely chopped
- 1½ pounds tomatoes—peeled, seeded and coarsely chopped
- 1 tablespoon fresh lime juice
- 2 tablespoons chopped cilantro
Kosher salt

1. MARINATE THE SHRIMP: In a large bowl, mix the vegetable oil with the parsley, garlic, basil, ginger, lemon juice, salt and crushed red pepper. Add the shrimp and toss to coat. Cover and refrigerate for at least 2 hours and up to 4 hours.

2. MEANWHILE, MAKE THE SAUCE: In a medium saucepan, heat the vegetable oil. Stir in the ginger, garlic and lemongrass and cook over moderate heat until fragrant, about 2 minutes. Add the tomatoes and cook over moderate heat, stirring occasionally, until the sauce is slightly thickened, about 10 minutes. Let cool to room temperature, then stir in the lime juice and cilantro. Season with salt. Transfer the sauce to ramekins.

3. Light a grill. Loosely thread the shrimp onto 10 skewers. Grill over moderately high heat, turning once, until lightly charred and cooked through, about 5 minutes. Transfer the grilled shrimp to plates and serve with the tomato sauce.
—*Kerry Simon*

WINE Zesty, fresh Albariño.

Mango Shrimp

TOTAL: 30 MIN PLUS 2 HR MARINATING
4 TO 6 SERVINGS

- ¼ cup raw cashews
- 1 tablespoon very finely chopped fresh ginger
- 4 garlic cloves
- 1 jalapeño, halved and seeded
- 1 tablespoon mustard seeds
- 1 teaspoon garam masala
- 1 teaspoon ground turmeric
- ½ cup mango nectar
- 2 tablespoons fresh lemon juice
- 1 cup plain whole-milk yogurt
Kosher salt
- 1½ pounds shelled and deveined large shrimp
- 2 tablespoons unsalted butter, melted
Cilantro and Yogurt Sauce (recipe follows), for serving

1. In a blender, combine the cashews, chopped ginger, garlic cloves, halved jalapeño, mustard seeds, garam masala and turmeric and pulse until all the ingredients are finely chopped. Add the mango nectar and lemon juice and puree until smooth, scraping down the side of the bowl. Add the yogurt and 1 tablespoon of salt and pulse to blend. Pour the mixture into a large bowl. Add the shrimp and toss to coat. Cover and refrigerate for 2 hours, stirring once or twice.

2. Light a grill. Thread the shrimp on pairs of skewers, being sure to leave on some of the marinade. Brush the shrimp with the melted butter and sprinkle with salt. Oil the grate and grill the shrimp over high heat, turning occasionally, until they are lightly charred and cooked through, about 8 minutes. Serve the grilled shrimp with the Cilantro and Yogurt Sauce.
—*Vikram Sunderam*

SERVE WITH Warm naan or pita.
WINE Fresh, minerally Vermentino.

CILANTRO AND YOGURT SAUCE

TOTAL: 15 MIN
MAKES 1½ CUPS ●

This bright, cooling, yogurty sauce comes together instantly in a blender.

- 2 cups cilantro leaves
- 1 cup mint leaves
- 1 jalapeño, seeded and coarsely chopped
- 4 garlic cloves, crushed
- 1 teaspoon ground cumin
- 1 tablespoon fresh lemon juice
- 1 cup plain whole-milk yogurt
Kosher salt

In a blender, combine the cilantro and mint leaves, the chopped jalapeño, crushed garlic, cumin and lemon juice and puree to a paste. Add the yogurt and puree until smooth. Season the sauce with salt and transfer to a small serving dish. —*VS*

MAKE AHEAD The sauce can be refrigerated for up to 2 days.

shellfish

Barbecued Shrimp with Cheese Grits

ACTIVE: 40 MIN; TOTAL: 1 HR 20 MIN

6 SERVINGS

- 2 tablespoons unsalted butter
- 1 small onion, cut into ¼-inch dice
- 2 garlic cloves, minced
- 1¼ cups ketchup
- ¼ cup bourbon
- 3 tablespoons cider vinegar
- 2 tablespoons molasses
- 2 tablespoons honey
- 2 teaspoons Tabasco
- 1 teaspoon chopped thyme
- ½ teaspoon cayenne pepper

Kosher salt and freshly ground black pepper
- 1½ pounds shelled and deveined large shrimp
- 1 tablespoon vegetable oil

Cheese Grits (recipe follows), for serving

1. In a medium saucepan, melt the butter. Add the onion and cook over moderate heat until softened, about 5 minutes. Add the garlic and cook until fragrant, about 1 minute. Stir in the ketchup, bourbon, cider vinegar, molasses, honey, Tabasco, thyme and cayenne. Simmer over low heat until thickened, about 40 minutes.

2. Transfer the barbecue sauce to a blender and puree until smooth. Season with salt and pepper. Pour ⅓ cup of the sauce into a small bowl and reserve the rest.

3. Preheat a grill pan. Season the shrimp with salt and pepper and brush on both sides with the ⅓ cup of barbecue sauce. Grease the grill pan with the oil. Grill the shrimp over moderate heat, turning once, until cooked through, about 4 minutes. Transfer to plates and serve with Cheese Grits and the remaining barbecue sauce. *—Amber Huffman*

MAKE AHEAD The barbecue sauce can be refrigerated for up to a week.

WINE Ripe, juicy Pinot Noir.

CHEESE GRITS

 TOTAL: 25 MIN
6 SERVINGS

- 4 cups low-sodium chicken broth
- 1 garlic clove, very finely chopped
- 1 cup old-fashioned grits
- 4 ounces extra-sharp cheddar cheese, shredded (1½ cups)
- 4 tablespoons unsalted butter
- 2 tablespoons heavy cream

Kosher salt and freshly ground black pepper

In a medium saucepan, bring the broth to a boil. Add the garlic and slowly stir in the grits. Reduce the heat to moderately low and cook, stirring frequently, until the grits are tender, 20 minutes. Remove the saucepan from the heat and stir in the cheese, butter and cream. Season with salt and pepper and serve immediately. *—AH*

Creole Shrimp with Garlic and Lemon

 TOTAL: 30 MIN
4 FIRST-COURSE SERVINGS ●

- 1 pound large shrimp, shelled and deveined
- 1½ tablespoons very finely chopped garlic
- 1 tablespoon Creole seasoning
- 1 red bell pepper, finely chopped
- 2 tablespoons vegetable oil

Juice of 2 lemons
- ¼ cup chopped parsley

1. In a bowl, toss the shrimp with the garlic, Creole seasoning and bell pepper.

2. In a skillet, sauté the shrimp in the vegetable oil over moderately high heat, turning the shrimp once, until they are just white throughout, about 3 minutes per side. Add the lemon juice and parsley to the skillet and toss well. Transfer the shrimp to a serving dish. *—Tory McPhail*

WINE Light, fresh Pinot Grigio.

Stir-Fried Shrimp with Bacon, Mint and Chiles

 TOTAL: 25 MIN
4 SERVINGS ● ●

Chef Jerry Traunfeld of Poppy in Seattle adds a handful of mint to brighten this hot, sweet and smoky stir-fry.

- 2 teaspoons vegetable oil
- ¼ pound thickly sliced bacon, cut crosswise ¼ inch thick
- 3 garlic cloves, minced
- 8 Thai chiles or 4 serrano chiles
- 1½ pounds shelled and deveined large shrimp

Salt and freshly ground pepper
- ¼ cup vermouth or dry white wine
- 6 tablespoons chopped mint

In a large skillet, heat the oil. Add the bacon and cook over moderate heat, stirring occasionally, until most of the fat has been rendered. Spoon off all but 1 tablespoon of the fat from the skillet. Add the garlic and chiles and stir-fry until fragrant, about 1 minute. Add the shrimp, season with salt and pepper and stir-fry over moderately high heat until pink and curled, about 3 minutes. Add the vermouth and cook until nearly evaporated, about 1 minute. Stir in the mint. Transfer to plates and serve. *—Jerry Traunfeld*

WINE Fruity, low-oak Chardonnay.

Crispy Shrimp with Noodle and Bean Sprout Salad

TOTAL: 1 HR

4 SERVINGS ●

- ½ cup unsalted roasted peanuts
- ¼ cup sake
- 2 tablespoons soy sauce
- 2 tablespoons mirin
- ½ cup fresh lime juice
- ¼ cup Asian fish sauce
- ¼ cup Thai sweet chile sauce
- ¼ cup water
- 1 garlic clove, smashed
- 1 small Thai chile, coarsely chopped

BARBECUED SHRIMP WITH CHEESE GRITS

CREOLE SHRIMP WITH GARLIC AND LEMON

½ **pound bean sprouts**

½ **pound rice vermicelli**

One 12-ounce seedless English
   cucumber—peeled, seeded and
   cut into 2-inch matchsticks

½ **cup torn mint leaves**

3 **scallions, thinly sliced**

1 **pound large shrimp, shelled
   and deveined**

½ **cup all-purpose flour**

2 **large eggs, beaten**

1 **cup *panko* (Japanese bread
   crumbs)**

3 **cups vegetable oil, for frying**

Salt

1. In a medium saucepan, warm the peanuts over moderate heat, about 1 minute. Add the sake, soy sauce and mirin and cook over low heat, stirring, until the liquid is reduced and coats the peanuts, about 5 minutes. Spread the peanuts on a parchment paper–lined plate and let cool.

2. In a blender, add the lime juice, fish sauce, chile sauce, water, garlic and Thai chile and puree the dressing until smooth.

3. Bring a large pot of water to a boil and fill a bowl with ice water. Add the bean sprouts to the boiling water and blanch for 10 seconds. Using a slotted spoon, transfer the bean sprouts to the ice water to cool, then drain and pat dry. Fill the bowl with more ice water. Add the rice vermicelli to the pot and cook until tender, about 5 minutes. Drain the noodles and transfer them to the ice water to cool. Drain again, shaking off the excess water; pat dry with paper towels. Wipe out the bowl. Cut the noodles into 4-inch lengths and return them to the bowl. Add the bean sprouts, cucumber, mint and scallions.

4. Put the shrimp in a large resealable plastic bag. Add the flour, seal and shake to coat. Tap the excess flour off the shrimp. Put the eggs and *panko* in 2 separate bowls

and line a baking sheet with wax paper. Working in batches, dip the shrimp in the egg, then in the *panko*. Press the crumbs to help them adhere. Transfer the shrimp to the baking sheet.

5. In a large, deep skillet, heat the oil to 340°. Add half of the shrimp and fry over high heat, turning once, until they are golden, about 2 minutes. Drain the fried shrimp on paper towels and sprinkle them with salt. Repeat with the remaining breaded shrimp.

6. Coarsely chop the peanuts. Add the dressing to the rice noodles and toss to coat. Transfer the noodle salad to a platter and top with the shrimp and chopped peanuts. Serve right away.
—*Nobuo Fukuda*

MAKE AHEAD The peanuts can be stored in an airtight container for 2 days. The dressing can be refrigerated for 2 days.
WINE Peppery, refreshing Grüner Veltliner.

●**HEALTHY** ●**MAKE AHEAD** ●**VEGETARIAN** ●**STAFF FAVORITE**

ROASTED LOBSTER WITH
VERJUS AND TARRAGON

Roasted Lobsters with Verjus and Tarragon

TOTAL: 40 MIN
4 SERVINGS ●

Four 1½-pound live lobsters

2 teaspoons dried tarragon, crumbled

1 teaspoon smoked paprika

Salt and freshly ground pepper

¾ cup verjus (see Note)

¾ cup extra-virgin olive oil

2 jalapeños, seeded and minced

2 tablespoons finely chopped fresh tarragon

2 tablespoons finely chopped flat-leaf parsley

1 tablespoon minced shallot

Lemon wedges, for serving

1. Preheat the oven to 450°. Plunge the lobsters headfirst into a very large pot of boiling salted water and cook just until they stop moving, about 2 minutes. Transfer to a cutting board and let cool slightly.

2. Using a heavy knife, split the lobsters in half lengthwise. Wrap the claws in a clean towel and, using the back of the knife, crack the claws in several spots. Transfer the lobsters, cut side up, to 2 baking sheets.

3. In a small bowl, mix the dried tarragon with the paprika and a generous pinch each of salt and pepper. Sprinkle the mixture over the lobsters and drizzle with ½ cup of the verjus and ¼ cup of the olive oil. Roast for 12 minutes, until the lobster meat is opaque; transfer the lobsters to a large platter.

4. Meanwhile, in a bowl, stir the jalapeños, fresh tarragon, parsley and shallot with the remaining ¼ cup of verjus and ½ cup of oil. Season with salt and pepper. Spoon the dressing over the lobsters and serve with the lemon wedges. —*David Page*

NOTE Verjus, a tart, unfermented juice made primarily from unripe wine grapes, is available from Wölffer Estate ($6 for 375 ml; wolffer.com) and Terra Sonoma ($17 for 375 ml; terrasonoma.com).

WINE Fruity, low-oak Chardonnay.

Baja Fried-Shrimp Tacos

TOTAL: 50 MIN
4 SERVINGS ●

½ cup mayonnaise

1 chipotle in adobo, stemmed

½ cup plus 1 tablespoon buttermilk

Kosher salt and freshly ground pepper

1½ tablespoons unsalted butter

½ small green cabbage, shredded (about 3 cups)

2 large carrots, shredded

Vegetable oil, for frying

24 large shrimp (about 1¼ pounds), shelled and deveined

2 cups *panko* (Japanese bread crumbs)

12 corn tortillas, warmed

4 pickled jalapeños, thinly sliced

½ small red onion, thinly sliced

½ cup coarsely chopped cilantro leaves

2½ ounces *queso fresco* or mild feta, crumbled (½ cup)

Lime wedges, for serving

1. In a mini food processor, blend the mayonnaise with the chipotle and 1 tablespoon of the buttermilk. Season with salt and pepper and refrigerate.

2. Heat a large skillet until very hot. Add the butter, cabbage and carrots and cook over high heat until the cabbage is browned in spots, about 2 minutes. Season with salt and pepper and transfer to a bowl.

3. In a large saucepan, heat 2½ inches of vegetable oil to 350°. In a medium bowl, toss the shrimp with the remaining ½ cup of buttermilk. Put the *panko* in another bowl. Coat each shrimp with the *panko* and fry in batches until golden, about 2 minutes per batch. Drain on paper towels.

4. Spoon some of the cabbage into the center of each tortilla and top with 2 shrimp. Drizzle with the mayonnaise and sprinkle with some of the pickled jalapeños, red onion, cilantro and *queso fresco*. Serve with lime wedges. —*Michael Rypka*

WINE Fresh, fruity rosé.

Lobster and Fennel Salad

TOTAL: 1 HR
4 SERVINGS ●

Four 1½-pound live lobsters

2 cups cold water

3 tablespoons fresh lemon juice

1 large fennel bulb—halved, cored and sliced paper-thin on a mandoline

½ cup mayonnaise

2 teaspoons chopped tarragon

Salt and freshly ground pepper

3 packed cups arugula leaves (3 ounces)

1 shallot, very thinly sliced

¼ cup cilantro leaves

1. Cook the lobsters in a large pot of salted boiling water until they are bright red, about 7 minutes. Reserve 2 tablespoons of the cooking water, then drain the lobsters. Transfer to a large rimmed baking sheet and let them cool slightly.

2. Twist the lobster tails from the bodies. With scissors, cut down the length of each tail shell and remove the meat. Cut the tails in half lengthwise and discard the dark intestine. Crack the claws and remove the meat. Cover the lobster and refrigerate.

3. Meanwhile, in a large bowl, mix the cold water with 1 tablespoon of the lemon juice. Add the fennel and refrigerate for about 25 minutes, until the fennel is very crisp.

4. In a bowl, mix the mayonnaise with the tarragon, the reserved lobster cooking liquid and the remaining 2 tablespoons of lemon juice. Season with salt and pepper.

5. Drain the fennel and pat dry with paper towels; transfer to a large bowl. Add the arugula, shallot and cilantro leaves and toss well. Add all but ¼ cup of the dressing to the bowl and toss well.

6. Arrange the salad on plates and top each one with a claw and half a lobster tail. Drizzle the lobster with the remaining dressing and serve at once.
—*Cathal Armstrong*

WINE Fresh, lively Soave.

Lobster BLTs

TOTAL: 45 MIN
4 SERVINGS ●

Manhattan chef Shea Gallante's delectable BLT is filled with crunchy bacon, chunks of sweet lobster (replacing the usual lettuce) and herb-spiked mayonnaise. "When you add lobster to a sandwich, there's no way it won't be great," he says.

- ½ cup mayonnaise
- 2 tablespoons fresh lime juice
- 1 small shallot, very finely chopped
- 1 small garlic clove, mashed
- 2 tablespoons snipped chives
- 1 tablespoon finely chopped tarragon
- 1 teaspoon sweet paprika
- ½ teaspoon celery seeds
- 2 tablespoons extra-virgin olive oil
- Salt and freshly ground black pepper
- 2 cups coarsely chopped cooked lobster meat (about 1 pound), from two 1¼-pound lobsters
- 6 ounces sliced bacon
- 2 tablespoons unsalted butter, softened
- 4 brioche rolls, split
- 1 tomato, thickly sliced

cooking lobster tails

To keep lobster tails from curling during cooking, insert a bamboo or metal skewer lengthwise through the middle of each tail before boiling, steaming or grilling. Remove the skewers before serving.

1. In a medium bowl, whisk the mayonnaise with the lime juice, shallot, garlic, chives, tarragon, paprika, celery seeds and olive oil. Season with salt and pepper and fold in the cooked lobster meat. Refrigerate the lobster salad until chilled.

2. In a large skillet, cook the bacon over moderately high heat until crisp, 7 minutes. Transfer to paper towels to drain.

3. Preheat a grill pan. Spread the butter on the cut sides of the rolls. Grill the rolls cut side down over moderate heat until they are toasted, about 3 minutes. Transfer the rolls to plates. Mound the lobster salad on the grilled rolls. Top with the crisp bacon and tomato slices, close the sandwiches and serve right away.

—*Shea Gallante*

MAKE AHEAD The recipe can be prepared through Step 1 and refrigerated, covered, for up to 8 hours.

WINE Full-bodied, minerally Riesling.

Curry Crab Rundown

TOTAL: 45 MIN
6 SERVINGS ● ●

Rundown is a classic Caribbean recipe that involves cooking foods like crab, mackerel or lobster in coconut milk. The word *rundown* refers to the simmering down of the coconut milk.

- 2 tablespoons canola oil
- 1 medium onion, finely chopped
- 2 garlic cloves, very finely chopped
- 2 teaspoons finely grated fresh ginger
- 2 teaspoons curry powder
- 1 teaspoon ground turmeric
- ¾ teaspoon ground allspice
- 3 tomatoes—peeled, seeded and coarsely chopped
- ½ teaspoon very finely chopped Scotch bonnet or habanero chile
- 1 teaspoon chopped thyme
- Salt and freshly ground black pepper
- 2 cups unsweetened coconut milk (from two 14-ounce cans)
- 1 cup water
- 1 pound lump crabmeat
- ¾ cup chopped cilantro
- Grilled naan and hot sauce, for serving

1. In a deep, medium skillet, heat the canola oil. Add the onion and cook over moderate heat, stirring occasionally, until softened, about 5 minutes. Add the garlic and ginger and cook, stirring, until fragrant, about 2 minutes. Stir in the curry powder, turmeric and allspice and cook, stirring, until fragrant, about 2 minutes. Add the chopped tomatoes, Scotch bonnet chile pepper and thyme and season with salt and pepper. Cook, stirring occasionally, until the tomatoes are just beginning to soften, about 2 minutes. Pour in the coconut milk and water and bring to a boil. Simmer over low heat, stirring occasionally, until the sauce is reduced by one-third, about 15 minutes.

2. Stir the crab into the sauce and cook just until heated through, about 2 minutes. Stir in the cilantro and serve with grilled naan and hot sauce.

—*Bradford Thompson*

MAKE AHEAD The crab rundown can be refrigerated overnight.

WINE Full-bodied, rich Pinot Gris.

Chile-Lime Crab Salad with Tomato and Avocado

TOTAL: 30 MIN
4 FIRST-COURSE SERVINGS ●

The mix of fresh crab, avocado and juicy heirloom tomatoes here is a classic combination. But New Orleans chef Sue Zemanick (an F&W Best New Chef 2008) puts a new spin on the salad by tossing it with a vibrant, spicy dressing flavored with jalapeño, lime juice, garlic and honey.

5 tablespoons fresh lime juice

2½ tablespoons extra-virgin
olive oil

2½ tablespoons vegetable oil

1 tablespoon very finely
chopped jalapeño

1 tablespoon chopped
cilantro, plus additional
cilantro leaves for garnish

½ tablespoon honey

½ teaspoon very finely
chopped garlic

Salt and freshly ground
black pepper

½ pound lump crabmeat,
picked over

1½ Hass avocados, cut into
½-inch dice

⅓ cup very finely chopped
red onion

1 large ripe heirloom
tomato, cut into four
½-inch-thick slices

Tortilla chips, for serving

1. In a small bowl, combine the lime juice with the olive oil, vegetable oil, jalapeño, chopped cilantro, honey and garlic. Season the dressing with salt and pepper.

2. In another small bowl, toss the crab with 3 tablespoons of the dressing and season with salt and pepper. In a medium bowl, gently toss the avocado with the red onion and 2 tablespoons of the dressing; season with salt and pepper.

3. Place a tomato slice on each of 4 salad plates and season with salt. Top with the dressed avocado and the crab salad and garnish with the cilantro leaves. Drizzle the remaining dressing on top and serve the salad with tortilla chips.

—*Sue Zemanick*

VARIATION To turn these into a passed hors d'oeuvre, spoon chopped cherry tomatoes into glasses, then top with the crab, avocado and remaining dressing. Serve with small forks.

WINE Ripe, luxurious Chardonnay.

CURRY CRAB RUNDOWN

CHILE-LIME CRAB SALAD WITH TOMATO AND AVOCADO

Scallops with Roasted Cauliflower and Raisins

ACTIVE: 30 MIN; TOTAL: 1 HR

4 SERVINGS ●●

- 1 head of cauliflower (about 2 pounds), cut into florets
- ½ cup extra-virgin olive oil
- Salt and freshly ground pepper
- ½ cup pine nuts
- 1 cup golden raisins
- ¼ cup *saba* or aged balsamic vinegar (see Note)
- ¼ cup water
- 1 small shallot, very finely chopped
- 8 jumbo sea scallops (about 2 ounces each)
- ⅓ cup tarragon leaves

1. Preheat the oven to 425°. In a medium bowl, toss the cauliflower with 2 tablespoons of the olive oil and season with salt and pepper. Spread the cauliflower on a large rimmed baking sheet and roast for about 50 minutes, stirring once or twice, until tender and browned in spots. Spread the pine nuts on a pie plate and toast for about 3 minutes, until golden.

2. Meanwhile, in a small, microwave-safe bowl, combine the raisins, *saba* and water and microwave at high power for 3 minutes. Cover and let stand until the raisins are plump, about 30 minutes.

3. Strain the soaking liquid into a small saucepan and simmer until reduced to 2 tablespoons, about 3 minutes. Transfer to a bowl and let cool. Whisk in ¼ cup of the olive oil and the shallot and season the dressing with salt and pepper. Set the raisins aside.

4. In a large skillet, heat the remaining 2 tablespoons of oil until smoking. Season the scallops with salt and pepper and add them to the skillet in a single layer. Cook over high heat until deeply browned on the bottom, about 3 minutes. Turn and cook the scallops until lightly browned, about 2 minutes longer.

5. In a bowl, gently toss the cauliflower with the pine nuts, raisins, tarragon and dressing. Season with salt and pepper and transfer to plates. Top with the scallops and serve right away. —*Payton Curry*
NOTE *Saba* is the sweet reduction of grape must; thick and syrupy, it's similar to aged balsamic vinegar.

WINE Fresh, minerally Vermentino.

Seared Scallops with Bacon-Braised Chard

 TOTAL: 45 MIN
4 SERVINGS

"When you learn how to cook scallops with a crisp golden crust, they're just so good," says *Top Chef* Season 4 winner Stephanie Izard. To help brown the scallops, she adds butter to the pan halfway through cooking.

- 2 thick slices of bacon, cut crosswise into ¼-inch strips
- 1 small onion, cut into ¼-inch dice
- 2 garlic cloves, minced
- 1 medium tomato, seeded and diced
- 1¾ pounds rainbow chard, stems sliced crosswise ½ inch thick and leaves cut into 1-inch strips
- 2 teaspoons soy sauce
- Kosher salt and freshly ground pepper
- 12 large sea scallops (1½ pounds)
- 2 tablespoons extra-virgin olive oil
- 1 tablespoon unsalted butter

1. In a large, deep skillet, cook the bacon over moderate heat until crisp, 4 minutes. Spoon off all but 2 tablespoons of the fat. Add the onion to the skillet and cook, stirring, until slightly softened, 3 minutes. Add the garlic and stir until tender but not browned, 2 minutes. Add the tomato and cook until it begins to break down, 2 minutes. Add the chard stems and cook until crisp-tender, 4 minutes. Add the chard leaves and cook over moderately high heat, tossing, until wilted, 5 minutes; drain off any liquid. Add the soy sauce and cook until the leaves are tender, 2 minutes longer. Season with salt and pepper and keep warm.

2. Season the scallops with salt and pepper. In another large skillet, heat the oil until just smoking. Add the scallops and cook over high heat for 30 seconds. Reduce the heat to moderate and cook until golden on the bottom, about 3 minutes. Turn the scallops and add the butter. Cook, spooning the butter on the scallops, until just white throughout, about 3 minutes. Spoon the chard onto plates, top with the scallops and serve.
—*Stephanie Izard*

WINE Spicy American Gewürztraminer.

Grilled Scallops with Mexican Corn Salad

 TOTAL: 40 MIN
4 SERVINGS

- 1 garlic clove, minced
- 1 tablespoon minced red onion
- 2 tablespoons fresh lime juice
- 8 small ears of corn, husked
- Vegetable oil, for brushing
- ⅓ cup mayonnaise
- 1 teaspoon pure ancho chile powder
- 4 ounces *cotija* or *ricotta salata* cheese, crumbled (1¼ cups)
- Salt and freshly ground pepper
- Hot sauce
- 12 large sea scallops
- Lime wedges, for serving

1. Light a grill. In a large bowl, toss the garlic and onion with the lime juice and let stand for 10 minutes.

2. Brush the corn with oil and grill over moderate heat until charred and just tender, about 10 minutes. Transfer to a work surface and cut the kernels off the cobs.

3. Whisk the mayonnaise and chile into the garlic mixture. Add the cheese and corn. Season with salt, pepper and hot sauce.

4. Brush the scallops with oil and season with salt and pepper. Grill over high heat until nicely browned and barely cooked through, about 3 minutes per side. Top the corn salad with the scallops. Serve with lime wedges. —*Nick Fauchald*
WINE Ripe, luxurious Chardonnay.

GRILLED SCALLOPS WITH
MEXICAN CORN SALAD

Mussels with Speck, Lemon and Oregano

TOTAL: 30 MIN
4 FIRST-COURSE SERVINGS ●

Ethan Stowell (an F&W Best New Chef 2008) loves mussels all year round, but he's particularly fond of the summer ones from Washington's Puget Sound. "I often grab a couple handfuls of mussels at the end of the dinner shift and cook them at home for a late-night snack," he says.

- ¼ cup extra-virgin olive oil
- One 3-ounce piece of *speck* (smoked, cured ham), cut into ¼-inch dice
- 3 garlic cloves, thinly sliced
- 2 pounds mussels, scrubbed
- ¾ cup dry white wine
- 2 tablespoons fresh lemon juice
- 1 tablespoon finely chopped flat-leaf parsley
- 2 teaspoons finely chopped oregano
- Freshly ground pepper

In a large soup pot, heat the olive oil. Add the *speck* and garlic and cook over moderate heat until the garlic is tender, about 4 minutes. Add the mussels and wine and bring to a simmer. Cover and cook over moderately high heat until the mussels have opened, about 5 minutes. Remove the pot from the heat and stir in the lemon juice, parsley and oregano and season with pepper. Spoon the mussels and their broth into warm bowls and serve. —*Ethan Stowell*
SERVE WITH Warm, crusty bread.
WINE Minerally, complex Sauvignon Blanc.

Clams with Black Bean Sauce

TOTAL: 35 MIN
4 SERVINGS ●

These tender Cantonese-style clams with bok choy in an earthy and savory sauce have a number of common Chinese flavors: the pungent taste of fermented, salted black beans, the tangy jolt of fresh ginger, the dryness of Chinese rice wine and the saline tang of shellfish.

- ½ pound dried Chinese wheat noodles or tagliatelle
- 1½ tablespoons vegetable oil, plus more for tossing
- 1 cup chicken stock or low-sodium broth
- 2 tablespoons Shaoxing rice wine or dry sherry
- 1 tablespoon soy sauce
- 1 tablespoon Chinese oyster sauce
- 2 teaspoons cornstarch
- 1 teaspoon sugar
- 1 teaspoon Asian sesame oil
- 3 garlic cloves, minced
- 1 large scallion, minced
- 1 tablespoon very finely chopped fresh ginger
- 2 tablespoons fermented black beans, rinsed and coarsely chopped
- ½ teaspoon crushed red pepper
- ¼ cup minced red bell pepper
- 2 pounds littleneck clams or cockles, scrubbed
- 2 cups tightly packed, coarsely chopped bok choy leaves (from 1 medium head)

1. In a large saucepan of boiling salted water, cook the noodles until al dente, about 5 minutes. Drain, rinse under cold water and drain again. Toss the noodles with a little vegetable oil.
2. In a small bowl, whisk the chicken stock with the rice wine, soy sauce, oyster sauce, cornstarch, sugar and sesame oil.
3. In a wok, heat the 1½ tablespoons of vegetable oil until shimmering. Add the garlic, scallion, ginger, black beans and crushed red pepper and stir-fry over high heat until fragrant, about 1 minute. Add the red bell pepper and stir-fry for about 30 seconds. Add the clams and stir-fry over moderate heat until most of them have opened, about 3 minutes longer.
4. Add the coarsely chopped bok choy and stir-fry until wilted. Stir the sauce and add it to the wok. Cook over moderately high heat, stirring, until the sauce thickens and all the clams are opened, about 1 minute; discard any clams that don't open. Add the noodles and toss well. Transfer to bowls and serve right away.
—*Anya von Bremzen*
WINE Fruity, soft Chenin Blanc.

top seafood matches

2007 Txomin Etxaniz ($26) Getaria, a quaint Basque fishing village in northern Spain, is home to Txakoli, light-bodied, crisp and lively effervescent wines like this lime-scented one.

2007 Cape Mentelle Sauvignon Blanc Sémillon ($18) This peachy blend from Australia's Margaret River region is made with grapes grown near the Indian Ocean.

2007 Ajello Majus Grillo Catarratto ($12) Two indigenous grape varieties from Sicily's southwestern coast are combined to make this bright, nutmeg-spiced white.

Seared Scallops with Beet Salad and Horseradish Cream

ACTIVE: 20 MIN; TOTAL: 1 HR 40 MIN

4 FIRST-COURSE SERVINGS

Borscht is the inspiration for the vibrant beet accompaniment to these seared jumbo scallops from Shea Gallante of Cru in New York City. After roasting the vegetables, Gallante coarsely chops them, mixes them with a raspberry vinaigrette and then tops them with a terrific warm horseradish cream. "I used to hate beets, but now I like them, especially roasted and served with horseradish," he says.

- 1 **pound large unpeeled beets, cut into 1-inch wedges**
- **Salt and freshly ground pepper**
- ½ **cup water**
- ¼ **cup plus 2 tablespoons extra-virgin olive oil**
- 1 **tablespoon raspberry vinegar**
- 1 **small shallot, minced**
- 1 **tablespoon drained prepared horseradish**
- ½ **cup crème fraîche**
- 1 **teaspoon fresh lemon juice**
- 12 **jumbo scallops (about 1½ pounds)**

1. Preheat the oven to 375°. Put the beet wedges in a medium baking dish, season with salt and pepper and add the water. Cover the dish tightly with foil and bake for about 1½ hours, or until the beets are tender. Let cool slightly.

2. Peel the roasted beets and transfer to a food processor. Pulse several times, just until coarsely chopped. Transfer the chopped beets to a bowl and stir in ¼ cup of the olive oil, the raspberry vinegar and a pinch each of salt and pepper.

3. In a small skillet, combine the minced shallot with the horseradish, crème fraîche and lemon juice and season with salt and pepper. Cook over low heat, stirring occasionally, just until the crème fraîche is melted, 1 to 2 minutes. Keep the sauce warm over low heat.

4. Meanwhile, in a large skillet, heat the remaining 2 tablespoons of olive oil until nearly smoking. Using a paring knife, score a shallow crosshatch pattern into one side of each scallop. Season the scallops with salt and pepper and add them to the skillet, scored side down. Cook over high heat until the bottom is browned, about 3 minutes. Turn and cook until the scallops are lightly browned on the second side and just cooked through, 1 to 2 minutes; don't let the scallops become opaque.

5. Spoon the roasted beet salad onto plates and top with the seared scallops. Drizzle the warm horseradish cream all around and serve. —Shea Gallante

MAKE AHEAD The roasted beet salad can be refrigerated overnight. Bring the salad back to room temperature before making the sauce and cooking the scallops.

WINE Fresh, fruity rosé.

Pop-Open Clams with Horseradish-Tabasco Sauce

TOTAL: 15 MIN

4 FIRST-COURSE SERVINGS

"You can't get lazier than this," says F&W's Marcia Kiesel, who simply puts clams on a hot grill and waits a minute or two for them to open and start sizzling. Then she takes them off the heat and tops them with a spicy sauce spiked with horseradish and Tabasco.

- 4 **tablespoons unsalted butter, softened**
- 2 **tablespoons drained horseradish**
- 1 **tablespoon Tabasco**
- ¼ **teaspoon finely grated lemon zest**
- 1 **tablespoon fresh lemon juice**
- ¼ **teaspoon sweet pimentón de la Vera (Spanish smoked paprika)**
- **Salt**
- 2 **dozen littleneck clams, scrubbed**
- **Grilled slices of crusty white bread, for serving**

1. Light a grill. In a small bowl, blend the butter with the horseradish, Tabasco, lemon zest, lemon juice and pimentón de la Vera. Season with salt.

2. Arrange the clams over high heat and grill until they pop open, about 25 seconds. Using tongs, carefully turn the clams over so the meat side is down. Grill for about 20 seconds longer, until the clam juices start simmering. Transfer the clams to a serving bowl. Top each clam with about ½ teaspoon of the horseradish-Tabasco sauce and serve with the grilled bread. —Marcia Kiesel

WINE Dry, earthy sparkling wine.

Gwyneth's Clams

TOTAL: 20 MIN

4 SERVINGS ●

Confronted with a pile of clams and a bottle of Albariño, a crisp white wine from the Galicia region in Spain, actress Gwyneth Paltrow spontaneously created this tasty recipe. It couldn't be simpler: The wine becomes infused with garlic and bay leaves while it steams open the clams. A splash of olive oil completes the dish.

- 4 **dozen littleneck clams, scrubbed**
- 1 **head of garlic, halved horizontally**
- 3 **bay leaves, preferably fresh**
- 1½ **cups dry white wine, preferably Albariño**
- 2 **tablespoons extra-virgin olive oil**
- **Crusty bread, for serving**

Put the clams, garlic, bay leaves and wine in a large skillet. Bring the wine to a boil over moderately high heat. Cover with a tight-fitting lid and cook until the clams open, about 10 minutes; discard any clams that don't open. Using a slotted spoon, transfer the clams to 4 bowls. Stir the olive oil into the broth, and then pour over the clams. Serve hot, with crusty bread. —Gwyneth Paltrow

WINE Zesty, fresh Albariño.

SAUVIGNON BLANC–STEAMED
MUSSELS WITH GARLIC TOASTS

perfecting mussels

F&W's **Grace Parisi** *shares a classic recipe for mussels in white wine, then creates amazing alternatives with clam broth, sake and lager.*

Sauvignon Blanc–Steamed Mussels with Garlic Toasts

TOTAL: 20 MIN

4 SERVINGS

- 4 thick slices of white peasant bread
- ¼ cup extra-virgin olive oil, plus more for brushing
- 2 garlic cloves—1 left whole, 1 thinly sliced
- 1 medium shallot, minced

Salt and freshly ground pepper

- 4 pounds mussels, scrubbed
- 1½ cups Sauvignon Blanc or other dry white wine
- 4 tablespoons unsalted butter, at room temperature
- ¼ cup coarsely chopped flat-leaf parsley

1. Preheat the broiler. Brush the bread with olive oil and transfer to a baking sheet. Broil the bread a few inches from the heat, turning once, for 2 minutes, until golden and toasted. Lightly rub the whole garlic clove over the toasts.

2. In a large, deep pot, heat the ¼ cup of olive oil. Add the shallot and sliced garlic, season lightly with salt and pepper and cook over high heat, stirring, until the garlic is softened and lightly browned, about 3 minutes. Add the mussels and cook, stirring, for 1 minute. Add the wine, cover and steam the mussels until they open, about 5 minutes. Remove from the heat. Using a slotted spoon, transfer the mussels to 4 deep bowls, discarding any mussels that do not open.

3. Add the butter and parsley to the broth, swirling and shaking the pot until the butter melts. Slowly pour the broth over the mussels, stopping before you reach the grit at the bottom of the pot. Serve the mussels with the garlic toasts.

WINE Lively, tart Sauvignon Blanc.

Three Great Variations

1 Mussels with Crème Fraîche, Jalapeños and Cilantro

Cook 2 tablespoons thinly sliced pickled jalapeños with the garlic and shallot. Substitute bottled clam broth for the white wine, chopped cilantro for the parsley and ⅓ cup crème fraîche for the butter. Stir in 1 tablespoon freshly squeezed lime juice at the end.

WINE Fruity, soft Chenin Blanc.

2 Sake-Steamed Mussels with Ginger, Miso and Spinach

Cook 2 tablespoons very finely chopped fresh ginger with the garlic and shallot. Substitute dry sake for the white wine and 5 ounces baby spinach leaves for the chopped parsley. Add 2 tablespoons white miso (Japanese fermented soybean paste) along with the butter.

WINE Vivid, lightly sweet Riesling.

3 Lager-Steamed Mussels with Mustard, Kielbasa and Dill

Quarter and thinly slice ½ pound kielbasa sausage. Cook the kielbasa with the garlic and shallot. Substitute lager or another light-bodied beer for the white wine and dill for the chopped parsley. Add 2 tablespoons whole-grain mustard along with the butter.

WINE Dry, earthy sparkling wine.

THAI SEAFOOD NOODLE SALAD

LIGURIAN SEAFOOD SOUP

Thai Seafood Noodle Salad

TOTAL: 1 HR

6 SERVINGS ● ●

  6 ounces rice vermicelli
  2 red Thai chiles, thinly sliced
  2 garlic cloves, thinly sliced
  ¼ cup sugar
  ½ cup fresh lime juice
  ⅓ cup Asian fish sauce
  2 tablespoons boiling water
  ½ pound medium shrimp, shelled
     and deveined
  ½ pound bay scallops
  ½ pound small squid, bodies cut into
     ½-inch rings and tentacles halved
  3 plum tomatoes, seeded and diced
  1 cup bean sprouts
  1 cup mint leaves
  ½ small red onion, thinly sliced
  ½ cup salted roasted peanuts
  6 lettuce leaves, for serving
Cilantro leaves, for garnish

1. In a medium bowl, cover the vermicelli with cold water and soak for 30 minutes.

2. Meanwhile, in a mortar, pound the chiles and garlic to a paste with 1 tablespoon of the sugar. Add the lime juice, fish sauce, boiling water and the remaining 3 tablespoons of sugar and pound until the sugar is dissolved. Let stand for 30 minutes.

3. Bring a large saucepan of water to a boil. Fill a bowl with ice water. Add the shrimp to the boiling water and cook until white throughout and curled, 2 to 3 minutes. Using a slotted spoon, transfer the shrimp to the ice water. Add the scallops to the boiling water and cook until white and firm, 2 to 3 minutes. Transfer the scallops to the ice water. Add the squid to the boiling water and cook just until firm, about 45 seconds. Transfer the squid to the ice water. Drain all of the seafood and pat dry.

4. Bring a fresh saucepan of water to a boil and refill the bowl with ice water. Drain the vermicelli, add to the boiling water and cook just until al dente, about 1 minute. Drain and transfer to the ice water. Drain again and pat dry. Cut the vermicelli into 3-inch lengths.

5. In a large bowl, toss the seafood with the vermicelli, tomatoes, bean sprouts, mint, red onion, peanuts and chile dressing. Line a platter with the lettuce leaves and top with the seafood salad. Garnish with cilantro and serve.

—Anya von Bremzen

WINE Zesty, fresh Albariño.

Ligurian Seafood Soup

ACTIVE: 1 HR; TOTAL: 1 HR 30 MIN

10 SERVINGS ●

  ¼ cup extra-virgin olive oil,
     plus more for serving
  1 large sweet onion,
     thinly sliced
  2 garlic cloves, thinly sliced

¼ cup finely chopped
flat-leaf parsley

½ teaspoon crushed red pepper

One 28-ounce can whole
peeled Italian tomatoes,
drained and chopped

2 strips of orange zest (optional)

Salt and freshly ground
black pepper

Four 8-ounce skinless halibut or
other meaty white fish fillets

2 cups pitted green and black
olives, such as Picholine and
kalamata (about ¾ pound)

2 pounds large shrimp,
shelled and deveined

1 pound cleaned squid,
bodies cut into ½-inch rings

20 littleneck clams, scrubbed

1 pound mussels, scrubbed
and debearded

2 cups bottled clam juice

1 cup dry white wine

Grilled bread, for serving (optional)

1. Preheat the oven to 450°. In a large enameled cast-iron casserole, heat the ¼ cup of olive oil. Add the onion and garlic, cover partially and cook over low heat, stirring occasionally, until softened, about 8 minutes. Add the parsley and crushed red pepper and cook over moderate heat, stirring, for 1 minute. Add the tomatoes and cook until almost all of the liquid has evaporated, about 5 minutes. Add the orange zest, season with salt and black pepper and remove from the heat.

2. Arrange the halibut fillets in the casserole and season with salt and pepper. Scatter the olives over the fish fillets and top with the shrimp and calamari. Season lightly with salt and pepper. Tuck in the clams and mussels, hinge sides down.

3. In a medium saucepan, bring the clam juice and white wine to a boil. Pour the hot liquid over the seafood. Cover and bake for about 30 minutes, or until the mussels and clams open, the shrimp are pink, the

calamari is opaque and the halibut is cooked through. Transfer any unopened clams and mussels to the saucepan and add 1 cup of the cooking liquid from the casserole. Cover and simmer until the shellfish open, about 3 minutes; discard any that don't open.

4. Spoon into bowls and serve right away, passing grilled bread and additional olive oil at the table. —*Richard Betts*

WINE Fresh, lively Soave.

Octopus Salad with Potatoes and Green Beans

ACTIVE: 30 MIN; TOTAL: 1 HR 30 MIN

8 FIRST-COURSE SERVINGS ● ● ●

Octopus becomes delicate and tender when slowly simmered. Tossed in a salad with potatoes and green beans, then dressed with garlic and parsley, it makes for a lovely and satisfying dish.

1 onion, halved

1 carrot, chopped

1 celery rib, chopped

1 bay leaf

1½ pounds octopus tentacles,
separated

½ pound green beans, cut into
1½-inch lengths

1½ pounds Yukon Gold potatoes

1 garlic clove, minced

1 tablespoon chopped parsley

¼ cup extra-virgin olive oil

Salt and freshly ground pepper

1. Fill a large saucepan with water, add the onion, carrot, celery and bay leaf and bring to a boil. Add the octopus and simmer over moderate heat for 1 hour, until the tentacles are tender. Let the octopus cool in the liquid, then drain. Using a paper towel, wipe the purple skin off the tentacles, leaving the suckers intact. Cut the tentacles into 1-inch pieces.

2. Meanwhile, in a saucepan of boiling salted water, cook the green beans until tender, 5 minutes. Using a slotted spoon, transfer the beans to a plate and pat dry.

Add the potatoes to the boiling water and cook until tender, 25 minutes. Let cool slightly, then peel and dice the potatoes.

3. In a large bowl, combine the octopus with the potatoes, green beans, garlic, parsley and olive oil and season with salt and pepper. Serve warm or at room temperature. —*Maurizio Quaranta*

WINE Light, crisp white Burgundy.

Warm Seafood Salad with Pistachios and Capers

TOTAL: 30 MIN

4 FIRST-COURSE SERVINGS ● ●

2 anchovy fillets, coarsely chopped

1 tablespoon coarsely chopped
unsalted pistachios

1 tablespoon capers, drained

1 garlic clove, coarsely chopped

¼ cup extra-virgin olive oil

1 tablespoon fresh lemon juice

½ pound medium shrimp—
shelled, deveined and
halved lengthwise

½ pound cleaned squid, bodies cut
into ¼-inch-thick rings and
tentacles left whole

1. In a mortar, pound the anchovies with the pistachios, capers, garlic and 1 tablespoon of the olive oil until fairly smooth. Stir in the remaining 3 tablespoons of olive oil and the lemon juice.

2. Bring a medium saucepan of salted water to a boil. Add the shrimp and cook until just white throughout, 20 seconds. Using a slotted spoon, transfer the shrimp to a bowl. Add the squid to the saucepan and cook until just firm, 20 seconds. Drain the squid and transfer them to the bowl.

3. Add the dressing to the bowl with the seafood and toss to coat. Mound the salad on plates and serve. —*Jane Sigal*

SERVE WITH Crusty bread.

MAKE AHEAD The pistachio dressing can be made up to 4 hours ahead and kept at room temperature.

WINE Fresh, minerally Vermentino.

shellfish

Bouillabaisse

TOTAL: 2 HR

8 SERVINGS

This classic Provençal seafood stew is delicately flavored with fennel and pastis, a licorice-flavored aperitif. Make or buy a good fish stock and add different seafood at different times, so nothing is under- or overcooked. The *rouille*, a sauce made with cayenne, garlic, bread crumbs and olive oil, is the perfect finishing touch.

ROUILLE

One 3-inch piece of baguette, cut into ½-inch dice

3 tablespoons water

2 garlic cloves

½ teaspoon cayenne pepper

½ teaspoon kosher salt

3 tablespoons extra-virgin olive oil

BOUILLABAISSE

3 tablespoons extra-virgin olive oil, plus more for drizzling

2 leeks, white and light green parts only, thinly sliced

1 onion, cut into ¼-inch dice

1 fennel bulb—fronds reserved, bulb cored and cut into ¼-inch dice

4 garlic cloves, 3 coarsely chopped

2 tomatoes, cut into ½-inch dice

2 bay leaves

Pinch of saffron threads

2 tablespoons pastis or Pernod

5 cups store-bought fish stock

One 2-pound live lobster

Eight ½-inch-thick baguette slices, cut on the bias

3 Yukon Gold potatoes (1½ pounds), peeled and cut into ½-inch dice

¼ teaspoon cayenne pepper

Salt and freshly ground pepper

2 dozen littleneck clams, scrubbed

1 pound monkfish, cut into sixteen 1½-inch pieces

1 pound skinless red snapper fillets, cut into sixteen 1½-inch pieces

1 pound skinless halibut fillet, cut into sixteen 1½-inch pieces

1. MAKE THE ROUILLE: In a mini food processor, sprinkle the diced bread with the water and let stand until the water is absorbed, about 5 minutes. Add the garlic cloves, cayenne pepper and salt and process until the bread and garlic are coarsely chopped. With the machine on, drizzle in the olive oil and process until the *rouille* is smooth. Transfer the *rouille* to a bowl and refrigerate.

2. MAKE THE BOUILLABAISSE: In a very large, deep skillet, heat the 3 tablespoons of olive oil. Add the leeks, onion, diced fennel bulb and chopped garlic and cook over moderate heat until the vegetables are translucent, about 5 minutes. Add the tomatoes and cook until they begin to break down, about 5 minutes. Add the bay leaves, saffron and pastis and bring to a boil. Add the fish stock and bring to a simmer. Cook over low heat until the vegetables are very tender, about 20 minutes. Discard the bay leaves.

3. In a food processor, pulse the vegetables and broth to a coarse puree. Strain through a fine sieve set over the skillet.

4. Bring a large pot of water to a boil. Add the lobster and cook until it turns bright red, about 4 minutes. Drain and rinse the lobster under cold water until cool enough to handle. Remove the tail, claw and knuckle meat and cut into 1-inch pieces.

5. Preheat the broiler. Arrange the baguette slices on a baking sheet and broil them 6 inches from the heat for about 1 minute per side, until the slices are golden brown around the edges. Rub each slice with the remaining whole garlic clove and drizzle lightly with olive oil.

6. Add the potatoes and cayenne pepper to the broth and bring to a simmer. Cook over moderately high heat until the potatoes are just tender, about 10 minutes; season with salt and black pepper. Add the clams, cover and cook over moderate heat until they just begin to open, about 3 minutes. Add the monkfish, cover and simmer for 2 minutes. Add the lobster, snapper and halibut, cover and simmer until the clams are open and all the fish is cooked through, about 4 minutes.

7. Set a baguette toast in each of 8 shallow bowls. Ladle the fish and broth over the toasts and top each serving with 1 tablespoon of the *rouille*. Sprinkle with fennel fronds and serve. —*Ethan Stowell*

WINE Lush, fragrant Viognier.

Seafood Paella

ACTIVE: 45 MIN; TOTAL: 1 HR 30 MIN PLUS 3 HR MARINATING

12 SERVINGS ● ●

1 teaspoon paprika

¼ cup extra-virgin olive oil

Salt

8 bone-in chicken thighs, with skin

Four 6-ounce sole fillets, halved lengthwise

2 large pinches of saffron threads

4 cups vegetable stock, chicken stock or low-sodium broth

Freshly ground pepper

1 pound dry chorizo, sliced ¼ inch thick

8 small cleaned squid, bodies cut crosswise into ¼-inch rings and tentacles halved

2 yellow onions, finely chopped

4 garlic cloves, minced

2 cups arborio or other short-grain rice

1 cup frozen peas

1 pound littleneck clams, scrubbed

1 pound mussels, scrubbed and debearded

½ pound lump crabmeat, well-drained and picked over

2 tablespoons chopped flat-leaf parsley

1. In a bowl, mix the paprika, 1 tablespoon of the oil and ¼ teaspoon of salt. Add the chicken and turn to coat. Cover and refrigerate for at least 3 hours or overnight.

2. Arrange the sole in a single layer in a baking dish. In a bowl, combine 1 tablespoon of the olive oil with 1 pinch of the saffron. Drizzle the oil over the fish and let stand at room temperature for 30 minutes.

3. Meanwhile, in a saucepan, combine the vegetable stock with the remaining pinch of saffron and season with salt and pepper. Bring to a simmer, cover and keep warm.

4. In a 14-inch paella pan or cast-iron skillet, heat the remaining 2 tablespoons of olive oil. Add the chicken and cook over moderately high heat, turning, until browned all over, 15 minutes; transfer to a platter.

5. Add the chorizo to the pan and cook until lightly browned, about 3 minutes. Transfer the chorizo to the platter with the chicken. Pour off and reserve any excess fat in the pan; leave a thin layer of fat coating the bottom. Add the squid and cook until just white throughout, about 2 minutes. Transfer the squid to the platter with the chicken.

6. Return 2 tablespoons of the reserved fat to the pan. Add the onion and garlic, season with salt and pepper and cook, stirring occasionally, until translucent, about 5 minutes. Transfer to the platter.

7. Return another 2 tablespoons of the reserved fat to the pan. Stir in the rice and cook over moderately high heat for 2 minutes. Add the chicken, chorizo, squid and onion mixture to the pan along with any accumulated juices. Stir in the peas. Gently pour the warmed stock into the pan. Cover and cook for 10 minutes.

8. Using tongs, nestle the clams and the mussels into the rice. Cover and cook for 10 minutes. Arrange the sole fillets and the crabmeat on the rice. Cover and cook for 5 minutes longer, until the sole is cooked through and the rice is tender. Remove the pan from the heat and let the paella stand for 5 minutes. Discard any mussels or clams that have not opened. Sprinkle the paella with the parsley and serve.
—*David Joud*

WINE Juicy, spicy Grenache.

BOUILLABAISSE

SEAFOOD PAELLA

shellfish

Vineyard Sea Grill

TOTAL: 45 MIN
4 SERVINGS ●

One 2¼-pound live lobster

2 pounds razor or littleneck clams, scrubbed

¼ cup extra-virgin olive oil

2 tablespoons red wine vinegar

Salt

¼ cup coarsely chopped flat-leaf parsley

Lemon wedges, for serving

1. Light a grill. Bring a large pot of water to a boil and fill a large bowl with ice water. Plunge the lobster into the boiling water headfirst and cook for 2 minutes. Using tongs, transfer the lobster to the ice water to cool; drain and pat dry. Place the lobster on a work surface and, using kitchen shears, cut down the center of the underside from tail to head to break through the shell. Using a heavy knife and a kitchen mallet, cut the body in half. Remove both claws.

2. Set the lobster, cut side up, on a rimmed baking sheet and add the razor clams. Drizzle with 2 tablespoons of the olive oil and 1 tablespoon of the red wine vinegar. Grill the lobster claws, turning occasionally, for 5 minutes. Add the lobster halves, cut side up, and the razor clams to the grill. Cover and grill over high heat until the lobster meat is almost opaque and the razor clam shells are beginning to open, about 3 minutes. Turn the lobster halves and claws and continue grilling until the lobster meat is lightly charred and cooked through and the razor clam shells are open and the juices are bubbling, about 5 minutes longer. Discard any clams that don't open.

3. Transfer the grilled lobster and clams to a platter and drizzle with the remaining 2 tablespoons of olive oil and 1 tablespoon of red wine vinegar. Season with salt and garnish with the chopped parsley. Serve with lemon wedges.
—*Mario Batali*

WINE Rich, complex white Burgundy.

Mussel-and-Squid Pilaf with Sweet Spices and Dill

ACTIVE: 30 MIN; TOTAL: 2 HR 15 MIN
6 SERVINGS

Spices like cinnamon and allspice, plus some dried currants, give this dish a slightly sweet edge.

1½ cups arborio rice (¾ pound), rinsed

Kosher salt

2 garlic cloves, halved

2 pounds mussels, scrubbed

⅓ cup extra-virgin olive oil

1 medium onion, cut into ½-inch dice

Large pinch of saffron threads

1 tablespoon dried currants

One 1½-inch cinnamon stick

¼ teaspoon ground allspice

¾ pound cleaned squid, bodies sliced crosswise into ¼-inch rings and large tentacles halved

4 scallions, white and green parts, finely chopped

2 tablespoons chopped dill

1. In a large bowl, cover the rinsed arborio rice with 2 inches of hot water. Add 2 tablespoons of kosher salt and stir thoroughly to dissolve. Let the rice soak for 40 minutes, then drain.

2. Meanwhile, in a large saucepan, combine the halved garlic cloves with 1 cup of water. Bring the water to a boil and add the scrubbed mussels. Cover the saucepan and cook over high heat, shaking the pan vigorously a few times, until the mussels open, about 4 minutes. Discard any mussel shells that do not open. Use a slotted spoon to transfer the mussels to a medium bowl. Remove and discard the halved garlic cloves. Pour the mussel cooking liquid into a heatproof measuring cup and measure out 2 cups; add water if necessary. Remove the mussels from their shells and transfer them to a medium bowl. Discard the mussel shells.

3. In a large, deep skillet, heat the olive oil. Add the diced onion and cook over moderate heat, stirring occasionally, until the onion is softened, about 8 minutes. Crumble in the saffron threads and stir in the dried currants, the cinnamon stick and the allspice. Add the squid and cook, stirring, until the tentacles begin to curl, about 1 minute. Add the soaked and drained rice and cook over moderately high heat, stirring, until the rice starts to stick together, about 3 minutes. Stir in the mussels, the reserved 2 cups of mussel cooking liquid and ½ teaspoon of salt. Cover the skillet and cook the pilaf over moderate heat for about 12 minutes. Stir in the chopped scallions.

4. Cover the mussel-and-squid pilaf with a clean kitchen towel, then cover with the lid and cook over low heat for 10 minutes more without peeking. Remove the pilaf from the heat and keep it in a warm place, covered, for 45 minutes. Stir in the chopped dill, discard the cinnamon stick and serve the pilaf in shallow bowls.
—*Semsa Denizsel*

MAKE AHEAD The prepared mussel-and-squid pilaf can be kept in the covered skillet at room temperature for up to 2 hours before serving.

WINE Intense, spicy Shiraz.

Shrimp-and-Crab Gumbo

ACTIVE: 1 HR 15 MIN; TOTAL: 4 HR
15 SERVINGS ● ●

This gumbo from Donald Link, chef-owner of Herbsaint in New Orleans, owes its flavor to the roux, a mixture of flour and oil that is cooked until it takes on a nutty taste and the color of coffee.

STOCK

3 tablespoons vegetable oil

3 pounds medium shrimp, shelled and deveined, shells reserved

2 tablespoons tomato paste

1 gallon plus 2 cups clam juice or fish stock

1 medium onion,
  finely chopped
2 celery ribs, chopped
1 large carrot, chopped
8 bay leaves

ROUX

1½ cups all-purpose flour
1 cup vegetable oil

GUMBO

¼ cup vegetable oil
4 large garlic cloves, very
  finely chopped
1 large Spanish onion,
  finely chopped
2 celery ribs, finely chopped
2 cups canned crushed
  tomatoes
1 large green bell pepper,
  finely chopped
1 pound okra, cut into
  ½-inch rounds
1 tablespoon chile powder
1 tablespoon paprika
1½ tablespoons filé powder
1 tablespoon dried oregano
1 teaspoon dried thyme
1 teaspoon cayenne pepper
1 teaspoon freshly ground
  white pepper

Salt

1 pound lump crabmeat,
  picked over

Sliced scallions, for garnish

Tabasco, for serving

1. MAKE THE STOCK: In a large stockpot, heat the vegetable oil. Add the reserved shrimp shells and cook over high heat, stirring, until the shells are starting to brown, about 5 minutes. Add the tomato paste and cook, stirring, until it begins to stick to the bottom of the pot, about 2 minutes. Add the clam juice, onion, celery, carrot and bay leaves and bring to a boil. Simmer over moderately low heat, stirring occasionally, for about 25 minutes. Strain the shrimp stock into a large heatproof bowl, pressing on the solids.

2. MEANWHILE, MAKE THE ROUX: In a medium saucepan, whisk the flour with the vegetable oil to make a smooth paste. Cook the paste over moderate heat, stirring frequently, until the roux turns golden brown, about 30 minutes. Increase the heat to moderately high and cook, stirring, until the roux is dark brown, about 10 minutes longer. Scrape the roux into a medium bowl and reserve.

3. MAKE THE GUMBO: In the large stockpot, heat 2 tablespoons of the vegetable oil. Add the garlic, onion and celery; cook over moderate heat, stirring, until the vegetables are softened, about 8 minutes. Scrape in the roux and cook until bubbling. Stir in the strained shrimp stock and crushed tomatoes and bring to a boil over high heat. Reduce the heat to moderately low. Simmer, stirring occasionally, for 1½ hours, until no floury taste remains; skim any oil from the surface as necessary.

4. In a medium skillet, heat the remaining 2 tablespoons of vegetable oil. Add the green pepper, okra, chile powder, paprika, filé powder, oregano, thyme, cayenne and white pepper. Season with salt and cook over moderately low heat, stirring constantly, until the mixture is fragrant, about 5 minutes. Stir in a ladleful of the simmering gumbo and scrape up the browned bits from the bottom of the skillet. Scrape the contents of the skillet into the gumbo; cook over moderately low heat, stirring, until richly flavored, about 1 hour.

5. Add the shelled shrimp to the gumbo and cook just until they are white throughout, about 2 minutes. Stir in the crabmeat and season with salt. Garnish the gumbo with sliced scallions and serve, passing Tabasco sauce at the table.
—Donald Link

SERVE WITH Steamed rice.

MAKE AHEAD The gumbo can be prepared through Step 4 up to 2 days ahead. Reheat before adding the shrimp and crab.

WINE Fresh, fruity rosé.

Fusilli with Shrimp and Grated Pressed Caviar

TOTAL: 35 MIN
4 SERVINGS

¾ pound fusilli
1 large shallot, very finely
  chopped
¼ pound white mushrooms,
  sliced ½ inch thick (2 cups)
2 tablespoons extra-virgin
  olive oil
½ cup dry white wine
1 cup light cream

Salt and freshly ground pepper

¾ pound large shrimp—shelled,
  deveined and halved lengthwise
2 tablespoons very finely
  chopped chives
1 tablespoon pressed caviar
  (1 ounce; see Note), frozen

Freshly grated Parmigiano-Reggiano
  cheese, for garnish

1. In a large pot of boiling salted water, cook the fusilli until al dente. Drain the pasta and return it to the pot.

2. In a large skillet, cook the shallot and mushrooms in the olive oil over moderately high heat, stirring, until softened, 5 minutes. Add the wine and boil over high heat for 1 minute. Add the cream, season with salt and pepper and bring to a boil. Stir in the shrimp and chives and simmer over moderately high heat until the shrimp are just white throughout, about 1 minute.

3. Add the shrimp and sauce to the fusilli and toss. Season lightly with salt and pepper; transfer to bowls. Coarsely shred the caviar over the pasta on a frozen box grater (this will prevent the caviar from sticking). Garnish with the Parmigiano-Reggiano cheese and serve immediately.
—Jacques Pépin

NOTE Pressed caviar, the paste made from fish eggs that break during the packing of traditional caviar, is available from californiacaviar.com.

WINE Fruity, low-oak Chardonnay.

CRISP TOMATO, ZUCCHINI AND
EGGPLANT BREAD GRATIN (P. 229)

vegetables

GRILL-ROASTED VEGETABLES WITH PINE NUT PESTO

SWEET-AND-SOUR CARROTS

Grill-Roasted Vegetables with Pine Nut Pesto

ACTIVE: 40 MIN; TOTAL: 1 HR 30 MIN

12 SERVINGS ● ●

Quintessential fall vegetables—brussels sprouts, parsnips, butternut squash and carrots—are cooked on the grill until they're tender and lightly charred, then tossed in a cheesy pine nut pesto.

- 1 **pound carrots,**
  cut into 1-inch pieces
- 1 **pound parsnips,**
  cut into 1-inch pieces
- 1 **pound brussels sprouts,**
  halved lengthwise
- One **2½-pound butternut squash—**
  peeled, seeded and cut into
  ½-by-1½-inch pieces
- 2 **large shallots, cut into**
  ½-inch wedges
- 6 **thyme sprigs**
- ½ **cup extra-virgin olive oil**

Kosher salt and freshly ground
  black pepper
- ¼ **cup plus 2 tablespoons**
  pine nuts
- 1 **tablespoon unsalted butter**
- 1 **large garlic clove,**
  thinly sliced
- ¼ **cup freshly grated Parmigiano-**
  Reggiano cheese

1. In a large bowl, toss the carrot and parsnip pieces with the brussels sprouts, butternut squash, shallots, thyme sprigs and ¼ cup of the olive oil. Season generously with salt and pepper.

2. Preheat a gas grill to high heat (about 425°). Place 2 perforated grill pans directly on the grate to heat for about 10 minutes. Divide the vegetables between the grill pans and grill over high heat, stirring and turning them occasionally, until the vegetables are tender and lightly charred in spots, about 50 minutes. Alternatively, roast the vegetables in a large roasting pan in a 425° oven, stirring them occasionally, until tender.

3. Meanwhile, in a small skillet, heat 1 tablespoon of the olive oil. Add the pine nuts and cook over low heat, stirring constantly, until they are lightly browned, about 2 minutes. Add the butter and sliced garlic clove and cook, stirring, until the pine nuts are browned and the garlic is golden, about 2 minutes. Let cool, then transfer to a mini processor. Add the grated Parmigiano-Reggiano cheese and the remaining 3 tablespoons of olive oil and pulse to a chunky puree. Season the pine nut pesto with salt.

4. Transfer the grilled vegetables to a large serving bowl and toss with the pine nut pesto. Serve hot or warm. —*Grace Parisi*

MAKE AHEAD The pine nut pesto can be refrigerated overnight. Bring to room temperature before proceeding.

Sweet-and-Sour Carrots

ACTIVE: 15 MIN; TOTAL: 1 HR

10 SERVINGS ● ● ●

For this decidedly modern take on French glazed carrots, a fragrant (nonalcoholic) elderflower cordial stands in for sugar, and crushed pink peppercorns give the glaze an unexpected kick.

- 2 pounds small or baby carrots, peeled and tops trimmed
- 2 tablespoons extra-virgin olive oil

Salt

- ½ cup fresh orange juice
- ¼ cup fresh lemon juice
- ¼ cup elderflower cordial (see Note)
- 1 tablespoon pink peppercorns, coarsely ground in a mortar
- 2 tablespoons unsalted butter
- 2 tablespoons chopped fresh cilantro

1. Arrange the carrots in a single layer in a skillet just large enough to hold them. Add the olive oil, a pinch of salt and just enough water to cover. Simmer over moderate heat until the carrots are tender, about 45 minutes.

2. Add the orange and lemon juices, elderflower cordial and pink peppercorns to the skillet and simmer for 3 minutes over moderate heat.

3. Remove the skillet from the heat and swirl in the butter. Stir in the chopped cilantro, season with salt and transfer the carrots to a serving bowl.

—*Jean-Georges Vongerichten*

NOTE The Bottle Green Drinks Company brand of nonalcoholic elderflower cordial is available from specialty food markets and chefswarehouse.com.

MAKE AHEAD The Sweet-and-Sour Carrots can be prepared through Step 2 and refrigerated overnight. Reheat them gently before swirling in the butter.

Carrots with Fried-Shallot Gremolata

 TOTAL: 30 MIN

4 SERVINGS ● ● ●

- 1 pound baby carrots of varying colors, tops trimmed to ¼ inch

Salt

- 1 tablespoon extra-virgin olive oil
- 1 teaspoon finely grated lemon zest

Freshly ground black pepper

- 1½ cups vegetable oil, for frying
- 4 shallots, thinly sliced crosswise (1¼ cups)
- ¼ cup rice flour or cornstarch
- ½ cup finely chopped flat-leaf parsley

1. Place the carrots in a medium saucepan, cover them with water, add a pinch of salt and bring to a boil. Cook the carrots over high heat until they are tender, about 10 minutes.

2. Drain the cooked carrots and return them to the saucepan. Toss the carrots with the olive oil and half of the grated lemon zest. Season the carrots with salt and black pepper.

3. Meanwhile, in a small saucepan fitted with a frying thermometer, heat the vegetable oil to 300°. In a small bowl, toss the sliced shallots with the rice flour, separating the shallots into rings. Transfer the floured shallots to a strainer and tap off the excess flour. Add the flour-dusted shallots to the hot oil and fry just until golden and crisp, about 2 minutes. Using a slotted spoon, transfer the fried shallots to paper towels to drain.

4. In a small bowl, toss the fried shallots with the parsley and the remaining lemon zest. Transfer the carrots to plates and garnish with the gremolata. Serve right away.

—*Parke Ulrich*

MAKE AHEAD The carrots can be prepared through Step 1 and refrigerated overnight.

Honeyed Carrots with Currants and Saffron

 TOTAL: 45 MIN

10 SERVINGS ● ●

A casserole of vegetables, fruit and sometimes meat, the Jewish dish tzimmes is often flavored with honey and cinnamon and cooked very slowly. Here, sliced carrots are quickly simmered with orange juice, honey, ginger and a pinch of saffron, then simmered with dried currants.

- ¼ cup canola oil
- 3½ pounds carrots, sliced on the diagonal ⅓ inch thick
- 2 teaspoons finely julienned fresh ginger
- 1 teaspoon ground turmeric

Pinch of saffron threads, crumbled

- ½ cup fresh orange juice
- 3 tablespoons honey
- 1 cup chicken stock or low-sodium broth
- ¼ cup dried currants

Salt and freshly ground black pepper

In a large saucepan, heat the canola oil. Add the sliced carrots and cook over moderately high heat, stirring occasionally, until heated through, about 5 minutes. Add the julienned fresh ginger, turmeric and saffron and cook, stirring, until fragrant, about 3 minutes. Add the orange juice and honey and cook, stirring frequently, until the juice is reduced to a glaze that coats the carrots, about 8 minutes. Add the stock and currants, season with salt and black pepper and cook over moderate heat, stirring occasionally, until the carrots are tender and the liquid is thickened, about 10 minutes. Transfer to a bowl and serve hot or at room temperature.

—*Adam Perry Lang*

MAKE AHEAD The cooked carrots can be covered and refrigerated for up to 1 day. Bring to room temperature or warm gently before serving.

Vichy Carrot Puree

ACTIVE: 25 MIN; TOTAL: 1 HR

8 SERVINGS ● ● ○ ○

- 2 pounds carrots, coarsely chopped
- 3 cups sparkling water
- 4 tablespoons unsalted butter
- Kosher salt
- 1 tablespoon finely chopped cilantro or parsley
- Freshly ground pepper

1. In a large saucepan, cover the carrots with the sparkling water and bring to a boil over moderately high heat. Stir in 3 tablespoons of the butter and 2 teaspoons of salt. Reduce the heat to moderate and simmer the carrots until they are tender when pierced with a knife and the cooking liquid is reduced to ¼ cup, about 25 minutes.

weeknight vegetables

Some ideas for quick vegetable dishes from Maine chefs **Clark Frasier** *and* **Mark Gaier.**

Bok Choy Stir-fry halved baby bok choy with sliced scallions and diced ham until crisp-tender.

String Beans Toss blanched beans with toasted pine nuts, shaved pecorino and extra-virgin olive oil.

Kohlrabi Sauté diced kohlrabi with crushed chile flakes, then add chopped garlic and deglaze with red wine vinegar.

Shallots Toss whole medium shallots with honey and dried lavender. Roast until soft.

Winter Lettuce Toss hearty lettuce with grapefruit sections, red onion slices and sherry vinegar–walnut oil vinaigrette.

2. Transfer the carrots and their cooking liquid to a food processor and let cool for 10 minutes. Add the remaining 1 tablespoon of butter and process the carrots until smooth. Add the chopped cilantro and pulse until just incorporated. Season the carrot puree with salt and pepper and transfer to a medium bowl. Serve the Vichy Carrot Puree right away.
—*Florence Daniel Marzotto*

MAKE AHEAD The Vichy Carrot Puree can be refrigerated overnight. Reheat gently before serving.

Ginger-Roasted Parsnips

ACTIVE: 15 MIN; TOTAL: 1 HR

4 SERVINGS ● ● ○

"Parsnips are our favorite root vegetable," says Maine chef Clark Frasier. "We grow them through the winter in our garden at Arrows Restaurant, and they're the best parsnips you'll ever taste. The temperature change concentrates the sugar, which makes the parsnips even sweeter and more intensely flavored."

- 2 tablespoons extra-virgin olive oil
- 1¼ pounds small parsnips, peeled and quartered
- 1½ tablespoons very finely chopped fresh ginger
- Salt and freshly ground black pepper

Preheat the oven to 325°. Pour the olive oil into a 9-by-13-inch baking dish. Add the quartered parsnips and chopped ginger, season with salt and black pepper and toss to coat the parsnips with the seasonings. Cover the pan with foil and bake until the parsnips are tender, about 40 minutes. Serve right away.
—*Clark Frasier and Mark Gaier*

MAKE AHEAD The parsnips can be roasted up to 4 hours ahead and kept in the covered baking dish at room temperature. Just before serving, reheat them, covered, in a 350° oven.

Creamed Spinach and Parsnips

TOTAL: 40 MIN

12 SERVINGS ●

- 4 tablespoons unsalted butter
- 2 tablespoons vegetable oil
- 2 pounds small parsnips, cut into ¾-inch pieces
- 2 large shallots, thinly sliced
- 1 cup turkey stock or canned low-sodium broth
- 1 teaspoon chopped thyme
- Salt and freshly ground black pepper
- 1¼ pounds baby spinach (20 cups)
- 2 tablespoons all-purpose flour
- 2 cups half-and-half or whole milk
- ½ teaspoon freshly grated nutmeg

1. In a large, deep skillet, melt 2 tablespoons of the butter in the oil. Add the parsnips and cook over moderately high heat, stirring occasionally, until lightly browned, about 6 minutes. Add the shallots and cook, stirring, until softened, about 2 minutes. Add the stock and thyme and bring to a boil. Season with salt and pepper, cover and simmer over low heat until the parsnips are tender, about 8 minutes.

2. Meanwhile, fill a large, deep pot with 2 inches of water and bring to a boil. Add the spinach in large handfuls and blanch, stirring, just until wilted, about 10 seconds. Drain and cool under running water. Squeeze the spinach dry and coarsely chop it, then stir the spinach into the parsnips.

3. In a medium saucepan, melt the remaining 2 tablespoons of butter and cook over moderately high heat until lightly browned, about 4 minutes. Whisk in the flour and cook, whisking, for 1 minute. Whisk in the half-and-half and nutmeg, season with salt and pepper and bring the sauce to a boil, whisking until thickened, about 2 minutes. Stir the sauce into the spinach and parsnips and bring to a simmer. Transfer to a bowl and serve. —*Grace Parisi*

MAKE AHEAD The creamed vegetables can be refrigerated for up to 3 days and rewarmed over low heat. Stir in a little stock if the cream sauce is too thick.

Creamy Spinach

TOTAL: 20 MIN
4 SERVINGS ●

6 tightly packed cups fresh spinach (6 ounces)
½ cup heavy cream
1 teaspoon unsalted butter
Salt and freshly ground pepper

1. Bring a large saucepan of salted water to a boil. Add the spinach and blanch until bright green, 30 seconds. Transfer the spinach to a bowl of ice water to cool. Drain, squeezing out the excess water.
2. In a medium saucepan, bring the heavy cream to a simmer. Pour the cream into a food processor and add one-third of the spinach. Process to a smooth puree. Scrape the puree into the saucepan. Add the remaining spinach and bring to a simmer, stirring. Stir in the butter, season with salt and pepper and serve. —Daniel Boulud

Sweet-and-Sour Catalan Spinach

TOTAL: 45 MIN
12 SERVINGS ● ●

A syrup of honey and sherry vinegar drizzled on top of just-wilted spinach gives this sweet-and-sour dish its satisfying flavor. A relatively light dish, it's a great addition to a hearty holiday menu.

1 tablespoon canola oil
1 shallot, minced
½ cup sherry vinegar
1 thyme sprig
1 tablespoon honey
¼ cup pine nuts
2½ pounds baby spinach
3 tablespoons extra-virgin olive oil
Salt and freshly ground pepper
¼ cup currants

1. In a small saucepan, heat 2 teaspoons of the canola oil. Add the shallot and cook over low heat until softened, about 3 minutes. Add the vinegar and thyme sprig and bring to a boil. Simmer over low heat until the vinegar is reduced to 2 tablespoons, about 20 minutes. Discard the thyme sprig and stir the honey into the vinegar.
2. In a small skillet, toast the pine nuts in the remaining 1 teaspoon of canola oil over moderate heat, stirring constantly, until golden, about 5 minutes. Transfer the pine nuts to a plate and let cool.
3. Fill a soup pot with ½ inch of water and bring to a boil. Add the spinach in handfuls, stirring until wilted. When the spinach is wilted, transfer to a colander and squeeze out the excess water. Wipe out the pot.
4. Heat the olive oil in the pot and add the spinach. Season with salt and pepper and cook, stirring, until heated through, about 5 minutes. Transfer the spinach to a platter and garnish with the currants and toasted pine nuts. Drizzle the sherry vinegar syrup on top and serve right away. —Jose Garces

MAKE AHEAD The recipe can be prepared through Step 3 up to 1 day ahead. Refrigerate the spinach. The pine nuts can be stored in an airtight container for up to 3 days.

Sautéed Rainbow Chard with Garlic and Lemon

TOTAL: 1 HR
10 SERVINGS ● ●

½ cup extra-virgin olive oil
3 large garlic cloves, thinly sliced
4 pounds rainbow or ruby chard— thick stems discarded, inner ribs removed and cut into 2-inch lengths, leaves cut into 2-inch ribbons
Salt and freshly ground pepper
½ teaspoon finely grated lemon zest

1. In a large pot, heat ¼ cup plus 2 tablespoons of the olive oil. Stir in the garlic and cook over moderately high heat until lightly golden, about 1 minute. Add the chard leaves in large handfuls, allowing each batch to wilt slightly before adding more. Season the chard with salt and pepper and cook, stirring, until the leaves are softened and most of the liquid has evaporated, about 8 minutes. Transfer the chard to a bowl. Wipe out the pot.
2. Add the remaining 2 tablespoons of olive oil to the pot. Add the chard ribs and cook over moderately high heat, stirring occasionally, until crisp-tender, about 5 minutes. Stir in the chard leaves and season with salt and pepper. Transfer to a bowl, sprinkle with the lemon zest and serve right away. —Fabio Trabocchi

Chard with Orange and Bacon

TOTAL: 30 MIN
4 SERVINGS ●

These citrusy greens are delicious with swordfish or pork.

2 pounds Swiss chard, stems discarded and leaves coarsely chopped
3 tablespoons unsalted butter
4 thin slices of lean-cut bacon, sliced crosswise ½ inch thick
1 cup fresh orange juice
¼ teaspoon finely grated orange zest
Salt

1. In a large pot of boiling salted water, cook the chard until bright green and tender, about 2 minutes. Drain, squeezing out any excess water from the leaves.
2. In a skillet, melt 1 tablespoon of the butter. Add the bacon and cook over moderate heat until crisp, 5 minutes. Transfer all but 1 tablespoon of the bacon to a plate.
3. Pour the orange juice into the skillet and boil over high heat until reduced to ¼ cup, about 4 minutes. Stir in the remaining 2 tablespoons of butter. Add the orange zest and the chard, season with salt and stir to coat. Transfer to a bowl, top with the reserved bacon and serve. —Marcia Kiesel

vegetables

Kale and Squash with Pickled Peppers and Shaved Cheese

ACTIVE: 1 HR; TOTAL: 1 HR 45 MIN

10 SERVINGS ● ●

This satisfying salad is a mixture of unexpected ingredients: tender roasted squash, Tuscan kale sautéed with garlic, nutty Manchego cheese and quickly pickled chiles. New York City chef Peter Hoffman likes to use colorful gold and red chiles, specifically Trinidads and Grenada Seasonings, which he finds at Manhattan's Union Square Greenmarket.

1	Red Kuri squash (2 pounds)—peeled, halved and cut into ⅓-inch-thick slices
1½	cups extra-virgin olive oil
	Salt and freshly ground pepper
¾	pound mixed mild and spicy chile peppers, such as Anaheims and red Fresnos, seeded and thinly sliced (about 4 cups)
¼	cup white wine vinegar
2	pounds Tuscan kale, stems and inner ribs discarded, large leaves torn in half
3	garlic cloves, thinly sliced
½	pound Manchego cheese, preferably young, thickly shaved

1. Preheat the oven to 375°. On a rimmed baking sheet, toss the squash with ¼ cup of the olive oil and season with salt and pepper. Roast for about 30 minutes, or until softened and lightly browned.

2. Heat ¼ cup of the olive oil in a large skillet. Add the chiles and cook over low heat, stirring, until softened but not browned, about 12 minutes. Remove from the heat and stir in the white wine vinegar and ½ cup of olive oil. Season with salt and pepper and let cool.

3. Meanwhile, in a large pot of boiling salted water, cook the kale until wilted, about 5 minutes. Drain and shake out all of the excess water.

4. Heat the remaining ½ cup of olive oil in a large skillet. Add the garlic and cook over high heat until golden, about 1 minute. Using a slotted spoon, transfer the garlic to a plate. Add the kale to the skillet and cook, stirring occasionally, until just tender but still bright green, about 8 minutes. Stir in the reserved garlic and season the kale with salt and pepper.

5. Mound the kale on a platter. Garnish with the pickled chile peppers and drizzle with a little of the pickling liquid. Top with the roasted squash and Manchego shavings and serve. —*Peter Hoffman*

Kale with Roasted Onion Rings

 TOTAL: 45 MIN

8 SERVINGS ● ● ●

1	large sweet onion, cut into ⅓-inch-thick rings
½	cup extra-virgin olive oil, plus more for drizzling
	Salt and freshly ground pepper
2½	pounds kale, preferably Tuscan kale, thick stems discarded
2	large shallots, thinly sliced
3	large garlic cloves, minced

1. Preheat the oven to 425°. On a large rimmed baking sheet, toss the onion with 2 tablespoons of the oil and season with salt and pepper. Roast for about 35 minutes, until richly browned on the bottom.

2. Meanwhile, in a large pot of boiling salted water, blanch the kale until just tender, 4 minutes, and drain. When it's cool enough to handle, squeeze the excess water from the kale and coarsely chop the leaves.

3. In a large, deep skillet, heat the remaining 6 tablespoons of olive oil. Add the shallots and garlic and cook over moderately low heat until softened, about 7 minutes. Add the kale, toss well and cook over moderate heat until hot throughout and evenly coated with the shallots and garlic, about 2 minutes. Season with salt and pepper. Transfer the kale to a large bowl. Garnish with the roasted onion rings, drizzle with olive oil and serve. —*Steve Corry*

MAKE AHEAD The kale and roasted onion rings can be refrigerated separately overnight. Reheat the kale on the stove and the onion rings in a hot oven.

Crispy Onion Rings

 TOTAL: 30 MIN

10 SERVINGS ● ●

Thick onion rings are coated in an ultralight batter and quickly fried for this sensational vegetable tempura. Any vegetable that slices nicely, like delicata squash, fennel or zucchini, would be great here, as long as it takes to the batter—that is, the batter stays on.

3	cups all-purpose flour
⅓	cup cornstarch
1	teaspoon baking powder
2	teaspoons kosher salt, plus more for sprinkling
3 to 4	cups club soda, chilled
1	quart vegetable oil, for frying
2	large Spanish onions, cut crosswise into ½-inch rings

1. In a large bowl, whisk the flour with the cornstarch, baking powder and the 2 teaspoons of kosher salt. Whisk in 3 cups of the club soda until the batter is smooth. Add more club soda, about 1 tablespoon at a time, until the mixture is the consistency of thin pancake batter. Let stand for 10 minutes.

2. Meanwhile, in a large saucepan fitted with a frying thermometer, heat the vegetable oil to 380°. Dip 8 onion rings in the batter, letting the excess batter drip back into the bowl. Fry the onion rings in the hot oil over high heat, turning occasionally, until they are golden and crispy, about 3 minutes. Transfer the onion rings to a paper towel–lined baking sheet and sprinkle them lightly with salt. Repeat with the remaining onion rings and batter; serve the fried onion rings hot or warm. —*Peter Hoffman*

vegetables

Stewed Broccoli Rabe with Spicy Tomato Sauce

ACTIVE: 35 MIN; TOTAL: 1 HR 30 MIN

10 SERVINGS ●●○○

This sautéed broccoli rabe from Ryan Hardy, chef at the Little Nell hotel in Aspen, Colorado, is a pleasant departure from the standard version simply made with garlic and chiles, although Hardy's dish does include those ingredients. He mixes them with fennel and red onions into a satisfying tomato sauce that balances the bitter greens, and adds lovely color, too.

- 2 medium fennel bulbs, cored and coarsely chopped
- 2 medium carrots, coarsely chopped
- ⅔ cup extra-virgin olive oil
- 4 medium red onions, finely chopped
- 8 medium garlic cloves, very finely chopped
- 4 rosemary sprigs
- 2 teaspoons crushed red pepper

Two 35-ounce cans whole peeled Italian tomatoes, drained and chopped

- 4 pounds broccoli rabe, large stems discarded

Salt

1. In a food processor, finely chop the fennel and carrots. In a large saucepan, heat ⅓ cup of the olive oil. Add the onions, garlic, rosemary and the chopped fennel and carrots and cook over moderately low heat, stirring often, until the onions are very tender and starting to brown, about 25 minutes.

2. Add the crushed red pepper to the pan and cook over moderately low heat, stirring, for 1 minute. Add the chopped tomatoes and cook, stirring occasionally, until the sauce is thick, about 10 minutes; discard the rosemary sprigs.

3. Meanwhile, in a large pot of boiling salted water, cook the broccoli rabe until bright green, about 4 minutes. Drain and let cool, then coarsely chop.

4. In a large, deep skillet, heat the remaining ⅓ cup of olive oil. Add the broccoli rabe and cook over moderately high heat, stirring occasionally, until starting to brown, about 4 minutes. Add the tomato sauce and simmer over low heat until very thick, about 15 minutes. Season with salt. Transfer the broccoli rabe to a bowl and serve. —Ryan Hardy

Balsamic-Glazed Cipollini with Lemon and Bay Leaves

ACTIVE: 30 MIN; TOTAL: 2 HR

10 SERVINGS ●●

Called *cipollini agrodólce* in Italian for their sweet-and-sour vinegar glaze (*agro* means sour; *dolce,* sweet), these soft and tangy onions are a fantastic accompaniment to any rich roasted meat.

- ⅓ cup sugar
- 1 tablespoon water
- 4 tablespoons unsalted butter
- ½ cup plus 2 tablespoons balsamic vinegar
- 1½ pounds cipollini onions

Strips of zest from 1 lemon

- 4 fresh bay leaves
- 3 cups chicken stock

Salt and freshly ground pepper

1. In a large saucepan, dissolve the sugar in the water. Cook over moderate heat without stirring until a medium-amber caramel forms, about 5 minutes. Off the heat, carefully add the butter and ½ cup of the balsamic vinegar. Return the saucepan to the heat and cook until the caramel is completely melted.

2. Add the onions, lemon zest, bay leaves and chicken stock to the caramel in the saucepan and bring to a boil. Season lightly with salt and pepper and simmer over moderately low heat until the onions are very tender and glazed and the liquid is syrupy, about 1½ hours. Stir in the remaining 2 tablespoons of balsamic vinegar and season with salt and pepper. —Fabio Trabocchi

MAKE AHEAD The glazed onions can be refrigerated for up to 1 week. Reheat gently before serving.

Cauliflower Curry

ACTIVE: 25 MIN; TOTAL: 1 HR

6 SERVINGS ○

This curry gets its lively flavors from cumin, coriander and hot green chile.

- 1 large red onion, diced
- 2 teaspoons coriander seeds
- 1 teaspoon cumin seeds
- 1 cup water
- 2 tablespoons vegetable oil
- 1 small jalapeño, thinly sliced

One 2-pound head of cauliflower, cut into 1-inch florets

Kosher salt

- 1 medium tomato, seeded and diced
- 2 tablespoons minced cilantro

1. In a blender, puree half of the diced onion with the coriander and cumin seeds and ¼ cup of the water.

2. In a large skillet, heat the vegetable oil. Add the remaining diced onion and the jalapeño slices. Cook the vegetables over moderately high heat, stirring a few times, until the onion begins to brown, about 5 minutes. Scrape in the onion puree from the blender. Pour ¼ cup of the water into the blender, swirl it around, then pour it into the skillet. Cook over moderate heat, stirring occasionally, until the onion sauce begins to stick to the bottom of the skillet and turn brown, about 10 minutes.

3. Stir in the remaining ½ cup of water, scraping up the browned bits from the bottom of the skillet. Stir in the cauliflower and season with salt. Cover and cook over moderately low heat, stirring occasionally, until the cauliflower is tender, about 30 minutes. Stir in the diced tomato and the minced cilantro and cook until warmed through, about 1 minute. Serve. —Raghavan Iyer

CAULIFLOWER CURRY

CARAMELIZED BROCCOLI WITH GARLIC

Caramelized Broccoli with Garlic

TOTAL: 35 MIN
4 SERVINGS ● ● ●

- 3 tablespoons extra-virgin olive oil
- 2 heads of broccoli (1¼ pounds total), stems peeled and heads halved lengthwise
- ½ cup water
- 3 garlic cloves, thinly sliced
- Pinch of crushed red pepper
- Salt and freshly ground black pepper
- 2 tablespoons fresh lemon juice

1. In a large, deep skillet, heat 2 tablespoons of the olive oil. Add the broccoli cut side down, cover and cook over moderate heat until richly browned on the bottom, about 8 minutes. Add the water, cover and cook until the broccoli is just tender and the water has evaporated, about 7 minutes.

2. Add the remaining 1 tablespoon of olive oil to the skillet along with the garlic and the crushed red pepper. Cook until the garlic is golden brown, about 3 minutes. Season the broccoli with salt and pepper, drizzle with the lemon juice and serve.
—*David Gingrass*

Crunchy Broccoli Slaw

TOTAL: 30 MIN
4 SERVINGS ● ● ● ●

Most people throw away broccoli stems, preferring to eat the florets. But cut into long, thin strips with a fine julienne peeler, the sweet and crunchy stems are perfect in a fresh-tasting slaw with carrots, scallions and salty sunflower seeds.

- ¼ cup plus 2 tablespoons mayonnaise
- 2 tablespoons rice vinegar
- 2 tablespoons pure vegetable oil
- 1 teaspoon finely grated fresh ginger
- Salt and freshly ground black pepper
- Stems from 3 pounds of broccoli, peeled and julienned (3 cups)
- 2 carrots, finely julienned
- 2 scallions, white and green parts cut into 1-inch lengths and thinly sliced lengthwise
- 2 tablespoons coarsely chopped cilantro
- 2 tablespoons salted roasted sunflower seeds, for garnish

In a food processor, process the mayonnaise, rice vinegar, vegetable oil and grated ginger until smooth. Transfer the dressing to a large serving bowl and season with salt and pepper. Add the broccoli, carrots, scallions and cilantro and toss. Garnish with the sunflower seeds and serve.
—*Grace Parisi*

Piquillo Peppers with Balsamic and Parmesan

 TOTAL: 15 MIN
6 SERVINGS ●

In this simple, vibrant dish, piquillo peppers are served as a carpaccio with splashes of aged balsamic vinegar, fruity olive oil and a sprinkling of grated cheese.

One 7-ounce jar of piquillo peppers, drained and halved
¼ cup chopped flat-leaf parsley
½ cup extra-virgin olive oil
Salt and freshly ground pepper
1 tablespoon aged balsamic vinegar
One 2-ounce chunk of Parmigiano-Reggiano cheese

Arrange the peppers in concentric circles on a platter. In a blender, combine the parsley and oil and puree until smooth; season with salt and pepper. Drizzle the parsley oil and then the vinegar over the peppers. Shave the cheese on top, preferably with a Microplane grater. —*Anya von Bremzen*

Roasted Red Peppers with Tonnato Sauce

 TOTAL: 45 MIN
8 SERVINGS ● ● ●

Tonnato sauce—a smooth puree of olive oil–packed tuna, mayonnaise, capers and anchovies—is traditionally served in Piedmont with roasted veal. At his Brooklyn, New York, restaurant, Franny's, chef Andrew Feinberg tops the sauce with a layer of wood oven–roasted peppers and serves it with bread.

4 large red bell peppers
6 tablespoons extra-virgin olive oil
½ cup mayonnaise
Two 6-ounce cans Italian tuna packed in olive oil, drained
2 tablespoons fresh lemon juice
4 teaspoons small capers, drained
16 oil-packed anchovy fillets, drained
Salt and freshly ground pepper
2 tablespoons chopped flat-leaf parsley, for garnish
Crusty bread, for serving

1. Light a grill or preheat the broiler. Rub the peppers with 1 tablespoon of the olive oil and grill until charred all over and softened, turning occasionally, about 15 minutes. Transfer the peppers to a bowl, cover with plastic wrap and let cool. Peel, quarter and seed the peppers.

2. Meanwhile, in a food processor, combine 2 tablespoons of olive oil with the mayonnaise, tuna, lemon juice, 2 teaspoons of the capers and 8 of the anchovies. Puree until the *tonnato* sauce is smooth.

3. Spread the *tonnato* sauce on a large platter and arrange the roasted peppers on top. Garnish with the remaining 2 teaspoons of capers and 8 anchovies. Season lightly with salt and pepper and drizzle with the remaining 3 tablespoons of olive oil. Garnish with the parsley and serve with crusty bread. —*Andrew Feinberg*

Tangy Twice-Cooked Eggplant with Red Peppers

ACTIVE: 45 MIN; TOTAL: 2 HR
4 TO 6 SERVINGS ● ● ●

1½ pounds large Italian eggplants, peeled and cut crosswise into 1-inch-thick rounds
Kosher salt
⅔ cup vegetable oil
2 large red peppers, thinly sliced
1 large Spanish onion, thinly sliced
3 garlic cloves, thinly sliced
1 tablespoon sweet smoked paprika
¼ cup sherry vinegar
½ cup chopped parsley
2 tablespoons fresh lemon juice

1. Line a large rimmed baking sheet with paper towels. Arrange the eggplant slices in a single layer on the paper towels and sprinkle them with salt. Let stand for 1 hour. Pat the eggplant dry with paper towels.

2. In a large skillet, heat ⅓ cup of the vegetable oil until shimmering. Add half of the eggplant and cook over moderately high heat, turning once, until browned and tender, about 8 minutes. Using a slotted spoon, transfer the eggplant to fresh paper towels to drain. Repeat with the remaining ⅓ cup of vegetable oil and eggplant.

best summer produce

Eggplant Eggplants from the farmers' market are often much sweeter than supermarket varieties. Look for firm eggplants that are heavy for their size, with tight, smooth, shiny skin and bright-green stems.

Peppers There are loads of heirloom pepper varieties, ranging from mild and sweet to fiery hot, that never make it to supermarkets. The freshest are weighty, with sturdy, green stems; avoid any that rattle.

Corn is best eaten within a day or so of picking because its sugars begin turning starchy soon after it's picked. Look for ears with husks that are green, moist and tight.

Squash When choosing summer squash, like zucchini, look for ones that are firm, heavy and free of nicks. At farmers' markets, you can often find squash so fresh that they still have their flowers attached.

Tomatoes Deeply flavored heirloom tomatoes, which come in many shapes and colors, are often too delicate to ship, but they are available at farmers' markets. Tomatoes should be heavy and barely yield to touch.

3. Add the peppers, onion and garlic to the skillet and cook over moderate heat, stirring occasionally, until softened, about 10 minutes. Stir in the paprika and cook until fragrant, about 1 minute.

4. Return the eggplant to the skillet, stir gently to coat and cook for 5 minutes. Stir in the sherry vinegar and simmer for 1 minute. Remove from the heat. Stir in the parsley and lemon juice and season with salt. Let cool to room temperature, then refrigerate until lightly chilled, about 20 minutes, before serving. —*Michael Solomonov*

Japanese Spiced Eggplant

TOTAL: 25 MIN
4 SERVINGS ● ●

Allen Susser of Chef Allen's in Aventura, Florida, likes to sprinkle eggplant with *togarashi*, a tangerine-scented Japanese spice blend of chiles, sesame seeds and dried seaweed, then glaze it with soy sauce and mirin.

1½ pounds large Japanese eggplants, cut crosswise 1 inch thick
Togarashi, for sprinkling (see Note)
¼ cup canola oil
¼ cup Asian sesame oil
2 tablespoons mirin
2 tablespoons low-sodium soy sauce

Lightly sprinkle the eggplants on both sides with *togarashi*. In a very large skillet, heat 2 tablespoons each of the canola and sesame oils until shimmering. Add the eggplant and cook over moderately high heat until browned on the bottom, 4 minutes. Brush the eggplant with the remaining canola and sesame oil, turn and cook until deeply browned on the bottom and tender. Add the mirin and soy sauce to the skillet. Turn the eggplant and cook until glazed, 1 minute; transfer to a platter, sprinkle with more *togarashi* and serve. —*Allen Susser*

NOTE *Togarashi* spice blend is available at Asian markets.

Eggplant, Chickpea and Tomato Curry

TOTAL: 35 MIN
4 SERVINGS

Madras curry powder is a blend of many spices, including cardamom, chiles, coriander and cumin. Since it is hotter than regular curry powder, it adds a delicious kick to this Indian-style late-summer stew of eggplant, tomatoes and chickpeas in a sublime coconut-ginger broth. Prepare the recipe with vegetable stock for an excellent vegetarian main course.

2 tablespoons extra-virgin olive oil
2 red onions, each cut into 8 wedges
One ½-inch piece of fresh ginger, peeled and minced
2 garlic cloves, minced
1½ tablespoons Madras curry powder
1 eggplant (1½ pounds), cut into 1-inch dice
One 14-ounce can chickpeas, drained
1 cup chicken stock or low-sodium broth
¾ cup unsweetened coconut milk
12 cherry tomatoes, halved
Kosher salt and freshly ground pepper
½ cup cilantro leaves

1. In a very large, deep skillet, heat the olive oil. Add the onions and cook over moderate heat until they begin to soften, about 3 minutes. Add the ginger and garlic and cook until fragrant, about 1 minute. Add the curry powder and cook until fragrant, about 30 seconds. Add the eggplant, chickpeas, stock and coconut milk and bring to a simmer. Cover and cook over moderate heat until the eggplant begins to soften, about 8 minutes.

2. Stir the tomatoes into the curry, cover and simmer until the eggplant is tender, about 3 minutes longer. Season with salt and pepper. Stir in the cilantro and serve. —*Melissa Rubel*

Crisp Tomato, Zucchini and Eggplant Bread Gratin

ACTIVE: 30 MIN; TOTAL: 1 HR 30 MIN
6 SERVINGS ● ● ○ ○

½ medium eggplant, sliced crosswise ¼ inch thick
1 medium zucchini or yellow squash, sliced ¼ inch thick
Kosher salt
6 tablespoons extra-virgin olive oil
4 garlic cloves, minced or mashed
One 14-ounce loaf rustic white bread, crusts removed and bread sliced ½ inch thick
Freshly ground pepper
½ cup torn basil leaves
3 medium tomatoes, sliced ½ inch thick
1 teaspoon thyme leaves

1. Preheat the oven to 400°. In a colander, toss the eggplant and zucchini with 1 teaspoon of salt; let stand 20 minutes. Drain and gently squeeze out any excess liquid.

2. Meanwhile, in a bowl, stir the oil with the garlic. Coat a 9-by-13-inch baking dish with 1½ teaspoons of the garlic oil. Tear the bread into 2-inch pieces and line the bottom of the baking dish with bread, fitting the pieces tightly together. Drizzle the bread with 2 tablespoons of the garlic oil and season with salt and pepper. Sprinkle the bread with half of the basil.

3. In a bowl, toss the eggplant and zucchini with 2 tablespoons of the garlic oil and season with salt and pepper. Sprinkle the tomatoes with salt and pepper. Arrange the eggplant, zucchini and tomatoes over the bread, overlapping if necessary. Sprinkle with the thyme leaves, salt and pepper and drizzle with the remaining garlic oil.

4. Bake for 40 minutes, until the vegetables begin to brown and the bottom of the bread is golden brown. Let stand until slightly cooled, about 10 minutes. Sprinkle with the remaining basil, cut into pieces and serve hot or at room temperature. —*Jerry Traunfeld*

EGGPLANT PARMESAN WITH
CRISP BREAD CRUMB TOPPING

Eggplant Parmesan with Crisp Bread Crumb Topping

ACTIVE: 1 HR 30 MIN; TOTAL: 2 HR 30 MIN

8 SERVINGS ● ○ ○

This is the ultimate eggplant Parmesan: delicate slices of fried eggplant nestled in a bright, tangy tomato sauce, layered with gooey fresh mozzarella and topped with crisp bread crumbs.

- 3 tablespoons extra-virgin olive oil, plus about 2 cups for frying
- 1 onion, finely chopped
- 3 garlic cloves, very finely chopped

Two 28-ounce cans whole, peeled Italian tomatoes, drained

Kosher salt and freshly ground pepper

- 8 small eggplants (½ pound each), cut lengthwise ½ inch thick
- 3 tablespoons coarsely chopped basil
- 1 pound lightly salted fresh mozzarella, thinly sliced and torn into small pieces
- 1 cup freshly grated Parmigiano-Reggiano cheese
- 3 tablespoons dry bread crumbs

1. In a large skillet, heat the 3 tablespoons of olive oil. Add the onion and garlic and cook over moderate heat until tender, about 5 minutes. Using your hands, crush the whole tomatoes into the skillet. Bring to a simmer and cook over moderately low heat, stirring occasionally, until the sauce is very thick, about 25 minutes. Transfer the tomato sauce to a food processor and puree until smooth. Season with salt and pepper.

2. Meanwhile, in a very large skillet, heat ¼ inch of olive oil. Season the eggplant slices with salt and pepper. Working in several batches, cook the eggplant over moderately high heat, turning once, until the slices are golden on both sides, about 8 minutes per batch; add more olive oil to the skillet between batches. Drain the eggplant slices on paper towels.

3. Preheat the oven to 400°. Spread 1 cup of the tomato sauce in a 9-by-13-inch glass or ceramic baking dish. Arrange one-third of the fried eggplant slices in the baking dish; sprinkle all over with 1 tablespoon of the chopped basil. Top with one-third of the mozzarella pieces and sprinkle with ⅓ cup of the grated Parmigiano-Reggiano. Repeat this layering twice. Sprinkle the bread crumbs all over the top of the eggplant Parmesan. Bake in the upper third of the oven for about 45 minutes, until the top of the eggplant Parmesan is golden and the tomato sauce is bubbling. Let stand for 15 minutes before serving. —*Ethan Stowell*

SERVE WITH Green salad and crusty Italian or peasant bread.

NOTE This dish is extremely versatile. The eggplant can be sliced lengthwise or crosswise before it's fried. In addition, the eggplant Parmesan can be baked in a glass or ceramic baking dish that is round, oval, rectangular or square.

MAKE AHEAD The assembled eggplant Parmesan can be covered with plastic wrap and refrigerated for up to 1 day. Bring the eggplant Parmesan to room temperature before baking.

Artichokes Stuffed with Anchovies, Garlic and Mint

TOTAL: 2 HR

10 SERVINGS ● ●

For his take on a classic Roman dish, Peter Pastan, chef and owner of Obelisk in Washington, D.C., stuffs artichokes with anchovies, garlic and mint, then braises them so the flavors of the filling infuse the pan juices. To season the artichokes while keeping them from browning before cooking, Pastan rubs them with a salted lemon half, a technique he learned from a Turkish woman who worked for him at Obelisk.

- 6 oil-packed anchovy fillets, drained and very finely chopped
- 6 small garlic cloves, very finely chopped
- 1 cup finely chopped parsley
- 2 tablespoons finely chopped mint
- ½ cup plus 2 tablespoons extra-virgin olive oil

Salt and freshly ground black pepper

- 1 lemon, halved

Salt

- 20 baby artichokes
- 3 cups water

1. In a bowl, combine the anchovies, garlic, parsley, mint and 5 tablespoons of the oil. Season the stuffing with salt and pepper.

2. Dip the cut side of one of the lemon halves in salt. Working with one artichoke at a time, snap off the tough outer leaves. Using a small, sharp knife, cut off the top third of the artichoke and trim and peel the base. Using a ¼-inch melon baller, scoop out the hairy choke. Squeeze a little of the juice from the unsalted lemon half into the cavity. Rub the exterior of the artichoke all over with the salted lemon half. Repeat with the remaining artichokes. Using a small spoon, fill the artichokes with the anchovy stuffing.

3. In a large, deep skillet, heat the remaining 5 tablespoons of olive oil. Set the stuffed artichokes in the skillet, stem side up, and cook over moderately high heat until nicely browned, about 5 minutes.

4. Add the water to the skillet and bring to a boil. Reduce the heat to moderate, cover and cook for about 15 minutes, until the artichokes are tender when pierced with a knife. Transfer the artichokes to a serving platter.

5. Raise the heat to high and boil the cooking liquid until reduced to a syrupy glaze. Season with salt and pepper and pour the glaze over the artichokes. Serve at room temperature. —*Peter Pastan*

vegetables

Herb-and-Lemon-Poached Baby Artichokes

ACTIVE: 30 MIN; TOTAL: 1 HR 30 MIN

4 SERVINGS ● ● ○

William Abitbol, chef-owner of the Paris wine bar Alfred (his middle name), sources a special variety of small Provençal artichoke known as *artichaut poivrade* (also called just *poivrade*) for this simple dish, but standard baby artichokes are just as delicious here. The artichokes are infused with flavor from their aromatic poaching liquid, a mixture of lemon, thyme, rosemary, sage, bay leaves and olive oil.

- 1 cup water
- 4 lemons, halved
- 12 baby artichokes (about 1½ pounds)
- 1 cup olive oil, plus more for serving
- 1 cup dry white wine
- ¾ cup finely chopped red onion
- ¼ teaspoon coriander seeds
- ¼ teaspoon black peppercorns
- 2 thyme sprigs
- 2 rosemary sprigs
- 2 sage leaves
- 4 bay leaves, preferably fresh

Fine sea salt

1. In a large, deep skillet, combine the water with the juice of 2 of the lemons; add the 4 lemons to the water in the skillet. Working with one baby artichoke at a time, snap off all of the dark green outer leaves. Using a sharp knife, slice off the top half of the leaves and peel and trim the stem. Drop the baby artichokes into the lemon-infused water.

2. Add the 1 cup of olive oil and the white wine, onion, coriander seeds, peppercorns, thyme, rosemary, sage and bay leaves to the skillet. Bring to a simmer over moderately high heat, then reduce the heat to low. Cover and simmer until the artichokes are tender when pierced with a fork, about 20 minutes. Let the artichokes cool in the cooking liquid for 30 minutes.

3. Transfer the artichokes to a work surface; discard the cooking liquid. Cut the artichokes in half lengthwise and arrange them on a platter. Drizzle the artichokes with a little olive oil, sprinkle with salt and serve warm or at room temperature.
—*William Abitbol*

MAKE AHEAD The poached baby artichokes can be drained and refrigerated overnight. Let the artichokes return to room temperature before serving.

Grilled Baby Leeks with Romesco Sauce

 TOTAL: 40 MIN

4 SERVINGS ● ● ○

- 1 small ancho chile, seeded
- 3 tablespoons hazelnuts
- Two ½-inch-thick slices of baguette, toasted and torn into 1-inch pieces
- 3 tablespoons roasted almonds, preferably marcona, coarsely chopped (see Note on p. 47)
- 1 garlic clove, chopped
- 2 plum tomatoes—peeled, seeded and coarsely chopped
- 1 roasted red pepper from a jar, cut into 1-inch pieces
- ½ tablespoon sherry vinegar
- ¼ cup extra-virgin olive oil, plus more for brushing
- 1 tablespoon chopped flat-leaf parsley

Salt and freshly ground black pepper

- 16 baby leeks or thick scallions, trimmed

1. Light a grill. Preheat the oven to 350°. In a small heatproof bowl, cover the ancho with hot water and soak until softened, about 15 minutes. Drain.

2. Meanwhile, in a pie plate, toast the hazelnuts in the oven for about 10 minutes, or until fragrant and lightly browned. Let the hazelnuts cool, then transfer them to a kitchen towel and rub them together to remove the skins. Transfer the hazelnuts to a work surface and let cool completely, then coarsely chop.

3. In a food processor, combine the ancho with the hazelnuts, toasted baguette, almonds and garlic and process to a smooth paste. Add the tomatoes, roasted red pepper and vinegar and puree. With the machine on, slowly pour in the ¼ cup of olive oil and process until blended and smooth. Scrape the *romesco* sauce into a bowl, stir in the parsley and season with salt and black pepper.

4. Brush the leeks with oil and season with salt and pepper. Grill over high heat until charred all over, about 3 minutes. Serve the grilled leeks hot or warm, with the *romesco* sauce alongside.
—*Tony Mantuano*

MAKE AHEAD The *romesco* sauce can be refrigerated for up to 2 days. Bring to room temperature before serving.

Mushrooms and Leeks with Pecorino Fonduta

 TOTAL: 45 MIN

8 SERVINGS ○

"Mushrooms need something to wake them up," says chef Shea Gallante. He makes this dish at his Manhattan restaurant Cru with morels that are poached in butter, then topped with pecorino *fonduta*, Italy's take on fondue.

- 1 stick unsalted butter
- 2 pounds leeks, white and tender green parts only, thinly sliced
- 4 garlic cloves, thinly sliced
- 1 pound assorted mushrooms, such as oysters and stemmed shiitake, thickly sliced
- ¾ teaspoon finely chopped rosemary leaves

Salt and freshly ground pepper

- 1 cup heavy cream
- ½ cup freshly grated Parmigiano-Reggiano cheese

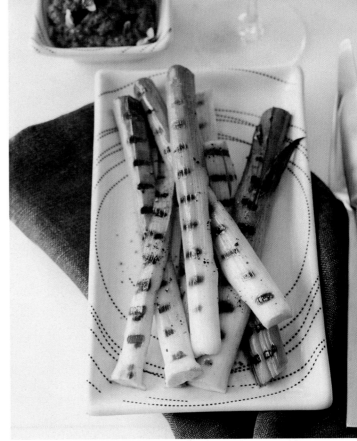

HERB-AND-LEMON-POACHED BABY ARTICHOKES · · · · · · · · GRILLED BABY LEEKS WITH ROMESCO SAUCE

¼ cup freshly grated young
   pecorino, such as Fiore Sardo
   or Toscano

2 teaspoons *vin cotto* (see Note)
   or balsamic vinegar

Grilled or toasted Italian bread,
   for serving

1. In a large, deep skillet, melt the butter. Add the leeks and garlic and cook over moderately low heat until softened, about 10 minutes. Add the mushrooms and cook, stirring occasionally, until tender and any exuded liquid has evaporated, about 20 minutes. Stir in the rosemary and season with salt and pepper; keep warm.

2. Meanwhile, in a small saucepan, bring the heavy cream to a boil. Cook over moderate heat until reduced to ⅔ cup, about 7 minutes. Remove the saucepan from the heat and stir in the Parmigiano-Reggiano and pecorino until melted. Strain the *fonduta* into a medium bowl.

3. Spoon the sautéed mushrooms and leeks onto a platter and drizzle with the *vin cotto.* Spoon the pecorino *fonduta* on top and serve immediately, with the grilled Italian bread. —*Shea Gallante*

NOTE *Vin cotto* ("cooked wine"), a sweet, tangy grape must condiment, is available at specialty food stores and igourmet.com.

Steamed Leeks with Mustard-Shallot Vinaigrette

⏱ **TOTAL: 35 MIN**
4 SERVINGS ● ● ○ ○

Leeks are among the sweetest members of the onion family, making them a perfect match for the tangy mustard vinaigrette here.

2 **large leeks, cut into**
   2-by-½-inch strips

1 **small shallot, very finely**
   chopped

1 **tablespoon Dijon mustard**

1 **tablespoon red wine vinegar**

1 **teaspoon balsamic vinegar**

¼ **cup extra-virgin olive oil**

Salt and freshly ground
   black pepper

1 **tablespoon chopped parsley**

1. In a saucepan fitted with a steamer basket, bring 1 inch of water to a boil. Add the leeks, cover and steam until just tender, about 5 minutes. Drain the leeks, pat dry and refrigerate until chilled, 10 minutes.

2. Meanwhile, in a small bowl, combine the shallot with the mustard and the red wine and balsamic vinegars. Whisk in the olive oil and season with salt and black pepper.

3. Mound the steamed leeks on plates. Drizzle them with the vinaigrette, sprinkle with the parsley and serve.
—*Stéphane Vivier*

MAKE AHEAD The steamed leeks and the mustard-shallot vinaigrette can be refrigerated separately overnight.

● HEALTHY ● MAKE AHEAD ● VEGETARIAN ● STAFF FAVORITE

ZUCCHINI RIBBONS WITH CRANBERRY BEANS AND PECANS

ZUCCHINI NOODLES WITH RAW TOMATO MARINARA

Zucchini Ribbons with Cranberry Beans and Pecans

TOTAL: 45 MIN
4 SERVINGS ● ●

Monica Pope (an F&W Best New Chef 1996) loves the organic pecans from Rio Grande Organics in Quemado Valley, Texas (riograndeorganics.com). At her Houston restaurant, T'afia, she uses the nuts to garnish a salad of quickly grilled zucchini ribbons and creamy-fleshed cranberry beans. Pecan oil enhances the pecans' sweet flavor, but the dish is equally delicious without it.

- 1 cup shelled cranberry beans (from 1 pound unshelled)
- 1 teaspoon Dijon mustard
- 2 tablespoons sherry vinegar
- 1 tablespoon pecan oil (see Note)
- 2 tablespoons grapeseed oil, plus more for brushing
- 1 teaspoon minced shallot
- 1 teaspoon finely chopped fresh tarragon
- 1 teaspoon finely grated lemon zest

Salt and freshly ground pepper
- 1¼ pounds small zucchini, sliced lengthwise ⅛ inch thick on a mandoline
- 8 mint leaves, torn
- ⅔ cup shaved Parmigiano-Reggiano cheese (2 ounces)
- ¼ cup pecan halves

1. In a medium saucepan of boiling water, cook the cranberry beans until tender, about 20 minutes; drain.

2. In a large bowl, whisk the mustard with the vinegar. Gradually whisk in the pecan oil and the 2 tablespoons of grapeseed oil. Whisk in the shallot, tarragon and lemon zest and season with salt and pepper. Add the warm beans to the dressing and toss.

3. Preheat a grill pan. Lightly brush the zucchini with oil; season with salt and pepper. Grill over high heat, turning once, until the

zucchini is crisp-tender, about 2 minutes. Add the zucchini to the beans, then the mint, and toss. Mound the zucchini on plates, top with the cheese and pecans and serve.
—*Monica Pope*

NOTE Pecan oil is available at specialty food stores and frenchfarm.com.

Squash and Zucchini "Linguine" with Goat Cheese

TOTAL: 45 MIN
6 SERVINGS ● ●

Cleveland chef Douglas Katz of Fire Food & Drink buys his goat cheese from a local urban producer, Lake Erie Creamery (lakeeriecreamery.com). To showcase the creamy cheese, Katz serves it over strands of zucchini and yellow squash that look like linguine.

- **2 tablespoons fresh lemon juice**
- **Salt and freshly ground black pepper**
- **¼ cup plus 2 tablespoons extra-virgin olive oil**
- **1 tablespoon chopped flat-leaf parsley**
- **1 tablespoon snipped chives**
- **3 pounds yellow squash and zucchini**
- **4 ounces shiitake mushrooms, stems discarded and caps thinly sliced**
- **1 small shallot, very finely chopped**
- **1 garlic clove, very finely chopped**
- **Pinch of crushed red pepper**
- **¼ cup pine nuts**
- **4 ounces fresh goat cheese, crumbled**

1. In a large bowl, whisk together the lemon juice, salt and pepper. Whisk in ¼ cup of the olive oil and add the chopped parsley and snipped chives.

2. Using the julienne setting on a mandoline or julienne peeler, remove the outer layer of the squash and zucchini in long, thin strips. Reserve the seedy core for another use.

3. Fill a bowl with ice water. In a large saucepan of boiling salted water, blanch the squash and zucchini until slightly wilted, 30 seconds. Drain and transfer to the ice water to cool. Drain and pat thoroughly dry. Add the squash and zucchini to the dressing and toss to coat.

4. In a medium skillet, heat the remaining 2 tablespoons of olive oil. Add the shiitake and cook over high heat until lightly browned, about 5 minutes. Add the shallot, garlic and crushed red pepper and season with salt. Cook until the garlic and shallot are fragrant. Add the shiitake to the squash and toss. Wipe out the skillet.

5. Add the pine nuts to the skillet and toast over moderately high heat, stirring, until golden, about 3 minutes. Transfer the nuts to a plate to cool. Scatter the goat cheese over the squash and zucchini, sprinkle with the pine nuts and serve right away.
—*Douglas Katz*

Zucchini Noodles with Raw Tomato Marinara

TOTAL: 25 MIN
4 SERVINGS ● ●

- **1¼ pounds tomatoes, diced**
- **2 dry-packed or oil-packed sun-dried tomato halves**
- **½ cup basil leaves**
- **¼ cup extra-virgin olive oil**
- **1 tablespoon fresh lemon juice**
- **1 soft Medjool date, pitted and minced**
- **1 small garlic clove**
- **1 teaspoon thyme leaves**
- **1 teaspoon coarsley chopped flat-leaf parsley**
- **Kosher salt and freshly ground pepper**
- **4 medium zucchini (1¾ pounds)**

1. In a blender, combine the fresh tomatoes with the sun-dried tomatoes, basil, olive oil, lemon juice, date, garlic, thyme and parsley and puree until smooth. Season the raw tomato marinara sauce with salt and pepper.

2. Using a mandoline, cut the zucchini lengthwise into ⅛-inch-thick slices, then cut the slices lengthwise into ⅛-inch-wide strips resembling spaghetti. Transfer the zucchini noodles to a bowl. Add the marinara sauce, toss to coat and serve immediately.
—*Ani Phyo*

MAKE AHEAD The marinara can be refrigerated for up to 2 days.

Grilled Endives with Marjoram

TOTAL: 20 MIN
6 SERVINGS ●

Endives pick up a wonderfully smoky flavor on the grill. Superchef Mario Batali tosses endives with a lemony dressing, cooks them until they're tender but still a little crisp, then tops them with shavings of Provatura (an Italian cheese that's similar to mozzarella but firmer). Young provolone is an easy to find substitute.

- **¼ cup extra-virgin olive oil**
- **Finely grated zest and juice of 1 lemon**
- **Salt and freshly ground black pepper**
- **6 Belgian endives, halved lengthwise**
- **2 tablespoons finely chopped marjoram**
- **One 4-ounce piece of young provolone, shaved**

1. Light a grill or preheat a grill pan. In a small bowl, whisk the olive oil with the lemon zest and lemon juice and season with salt and pepper. In a large bowl, toss the endive halves with all but 2 tablespoons of the dressing.

2. Grill the endive halves over moderate heat, turning once, until lightly charred and just cooked through, about 5 minutes. Transfer the endives to a platter, cut side up. Drizzle with the remaining 2 tablespoons of dressing and sprinkle with the marjoram. Scatter the provolone shavings on top of the endives and serve.
—*Mario Batali*

vegetables

Pancetta-Wrapped Asparagus with Citronette

TOTAL: 50 MIN

6 SERVINGS

In this riff on the traditional antipasto of prosciutto-wrapped asparagus, spears are wrapped in pancetta and grilled. (Unlike prosciutto, pancetta becomes nicely crispy when cooked.) Adding a bit of tanginess is the *citronette,* a marvelously bright-tasting mustardy-orange dressing.

- 2 pounds medium asparagus
- ½ pound very thinly sliced pancetta

  Finely grated zest and juice of 1 orange
- 2 teaspoons Dijon mustard
- ¼ cup extra-virgin olive oil

  Salt and freshly ground pepper
- 2 teaspoons chopped thyme

1. Tightly wrap each asparagus spear in a slice of pancetta and refrigerate until chilled, about 20 minutes.

2. Light a grill or preheat a grill pan. In a small bowl, stir the orange zest and juice with the mustard and olive oil; season with salt and pepper. Grill the asparagus over moderate heat, turning often, until they are just tender and the pancetta is crisp, about 5 minutes total. Transfer the asparagus to a platter and drizzle with the dressing. Sprinkle with the thyme and serve. —*Mario Batali*

MAKE AHEAD The uncooked pancetta-wrapped asparagus can be covered and refrigerated overnight.

Asparagus and Grilled Shiitake with Soy Vinaigrette

 TOTAL: 45 MIN

8 TO 10 SERVINGS ● ● ●

This early-summer dish is based on a recipe from chef Jean-Georges Vongerichten's New York restaurant Perry Street. The cooks there top the asparagus and mushrooms with a runny poached egg.

- 2 tablespoons extra-virgin olive oil, plus more for drizzling
- 2 tablespoons soy sauce
- 1 tablespoon fresh lemon juice
- 1 tablespoon rice vinegar
- 2 tablespoons chopped fresh tarragon

  Salt and freshly ground black pepper
- 1½ pounds shiitake mushrooms, stemmed
- 2 pounds thin asparagus

1. Light a grill. In a small bowl, mix the 2 tablespoons of olive oil with the soy sauce, lemon juice, vinegar and tarragon. Season the vinaigrette with salt and pepper.

2. Brush the shiitake mushroom caps with 2 tablespoons of the soy vinaigrette; season with salt and black pepper. Grill over moderate heat, turning once, until just tender, about 6 minutes. Transfer the shiitake to a bowl; cut any large shiitake into quarters. Add 4 tablespoons of the soy vinaigrette and toss to coat.

3. Bring a large skillet of salted water to a boil. Fill a large bowl with ice water. Add the asparagus to the skillet and cook until they are just crisp-tender, about 3 minutes. Drain the asparagus and transfer them to the ice water to cool. Drain and pat dry with paper towels.

4. Arrange the blanched and drained asparagus on a large serving platter. Drizzle the asparagus with olive oil and season with salt and black pepper. Spoon the grilled shiitake over the asparagus, drizzle any remaining soy vinaigrette on top of the vegetables and serve right away. —*Jean-Georges Vongerichten*

MAKE AHEAD The soy vinaigrette, grilled shiitake and blanched asparagus can each be refrigerated separately overnight. Reheat the shiitake in a 400° oven for about 4 minutes and bring the asparagus and vinaigrette to room temperature before assembling and serving.

Slow-Roasted Tomatoes

ACTIVE: 25 MIN; TOTAL: 2 HR

8 SERVINGS ● ● ●

This dish is outstanding because it can be made with less-than-perfect tomatoes.

- ¾ cup chopped basil
- ¼ cup extra-virgin olive oil
- ¼ cup pitted Niçoise olives, chopped
- 2 teaspoons chopped rosemary
- 8 large plum tomatoes, sliced crosswise ⅓ inch thick

  Salt and freshly ground pepper

1. Preheat the oven to 275°. In a mini food processor, process the basil, olive oil, olives and rosemary to a paste.

2. Arrange the tomato slices on a large rimmed baking sheet and season with salt and pepper. Spread about 1 teaspoon of the tapenade over each tomato slice. Bake for 1½ hours, until very tender. Serve hot or warm. —*Cathal Armstrong*

Skillet-Charred Cherry Tomatoes with Basil

 TOTAL: 15 MIN

10 SERVINGS ● ●

Chef Chris Cosentino remembers charring tomatoes when he was a line cook under Mark Miller at Red Sage in Washington, D.C. "Mark always said, 'It needs fleck,'" Cosentino says, referring to the blackened bits on the skins. "The fire brings out the sweetness in the tomatoes."

- 1 tablespoon extra-virgin olive oil
- 2½ pints cherry tomatoes
- 24 squash blossoms (optional)
- ¼ cup small basil leaves or chopped basil

  Salt and freshly ground pepper

1. Heat a 12-inch cast-iron skillet over high heat until smoking, 5 minutes. Add the olive oil, tomatoes and squash blossoms and cook until the tomatoes are lightly charred and about to burst, 3 minutes.

2. Off the heat, stir in the basil. Season with salt and pepper and serve right away. —*Chris Cosentino*

SKILLET-CHARRED CHERRY
TOMATOES WITH BASIL

SWEET CORN SUCCOTASH

Tomatoes with Sesame-Miso Sauce and Plum Vinaigrette

TOTAL: 45 MIN
6 SERVINGS ● ●

At Lantern, her restaurant in Chapel Hill, North Carolina, chef Andrea Reusing combines her focus on local foods with her predilection for Asian flavors. In the tangy vinaigrette here, *ume* plum vinegar adds a lovely salty edge that's delicious with tomatoes. A clever sauce made with toasted sesame seeds and miso lends the salad a nutty richness.

- ⅓ cup sesame seeds
- ¼ cup mayonnaise
- 2 tablespoons white miso
- 1½ teaspoons dry sake
- 3 tablespoons water
- 2 tablespoons *ume* (Japanese plum) vinegar (see Note)
- 2 tablespoons fresh lemon juice
- 2 teaspoons Asian sesame oil
- 1 tablespoon mirin
- ¼ cup canola oil
- Salt
- 2 pounds heirloom tomatoes, peeled and cut into wedges
- 4 scallions, thinly sliced crosswise
- 1 sheet of nori (dried seaweed), crumbled, for garnish

1. In a small skillet, toast the sesame seeds over moderate heat until golden, about 3 minutes; transfer the seeds to a spice grinder and let cool. Finely grind the seeds and transfer them to a bowl. Whisk in the mayonnaise, miso and dry sake, then whisk in the water.

2. In a large bowl, whisk the *ume* vinegar with the lemon juice, sesame oil and mirin. Gradually whisk in the canola oil and season with salt. Add the tomatoes and scallions and toss. Spoon the salad with its juices onto a large platter and drizzle with the sesame-miso sauce. Garnish the salad with the nori and serve. —*Andrea Reusing*

NOTE *Ume* vinegar is available in the Asian foods aisle of most grocery stores.

New Mexican Street Corn

ACTIVE: 20 MIN; TOTAL: 50 MIN
4 SERVINGS ●

Joseph Wrede (an F&W Best New Chef 2000) of Joseph's Table in Taos, New Mexico, makes a killer version of a popular Mexican snack: grilled corn brushed with flavored mayonnaise and rolled in grated cheese.

- 4 ears of corn
- Salt and freshly ground pepper
- ¼ cup mayonnaise
- 1 chipotle chile in adobo sauce
- 1½ teaspoons snipped chives
- 2 tablespoons extra-virgin olive oil
- 2 ounces grated *cotija* cheese
- Lime wedges, for serving

1. Preheat the oven to 425°. Peel back the corn husks, leaving them attached. Discard the silk. Season the corn with salt and pepper. Replace the husks, wrap each ear in foil, transfer to a baking sheet and roast for 30 minutes, until just tender.

2. In a mini food processor, blend the mayonnaise with the chipotle. Add the chives; pulse. Add the oil; process until smooth.

3. Light a grill. Peel back the husks, leaving them attached. Brush the corn with half of the mayonnaise. Using the husks as a handle, grill the corn until lightly charred. Brush it with the remaining mayonnaise and roll in the cheese; serve with the lime wedges. —*Joseph Wrede*

Sweet Corn Succotash

TOTAL: 45 MIN
4 SERVINGS ●

Birmingham, Alabama, chef Chris Hastings uses fresh field peas such as black-eyed peas in his succotash, but green peas are a nicely sweet, easy-to-find alternative.

- 2 cups fresh green peas
- 1 tablespoon canola oil
- 1 thick slice of bacon, finely diced
- 1 small onion, finely chopped
- ½ pound okra, sliced ½ inch thick
- 3 medium tomatoes—peeled, seeded and coarsely chopped
- 3 ears of corn, kernels cut off
- Salt and freshly ground pepper
- 2 tablespoons unsalted butter
- ¼ cup slivered basil leaves

1. In a large pot of boiling salted water, cook the peas until tender, 5 minutes. Drain, reserving ¾ cup of the cooking liquid.

2. In a deep skillet, heat the oil. Add the bacon and cook over moderately high heat until browned. Add the onion and cook until just softened. Add the okra and cook for 8 minutes. Add the tomatoes and corn and cook until the tomatoes break down. Add the peas with the cooking liquid and season with salt and pepper. Simmer for 2 minutes. Stir in the butter and basil and serve. —*Chris Hastings*

Sweet Pea Puree with Jalapeños

TOTAL: 25 MIN
8 TO 10 SERVINGS ● ●

Roasting jalapeños before incorporating them into this silken puree gives the dish a subtle smokiness. Use sweet fresh peas if you can find them; frozen peas are a fine substitute.

- 2 jalapeños
- 4 pounds fresh peas, shelled, or 4 cups (1¼ pounds) thawed frozen baby peas
- ¼ cup water
- 1 tablespoon unsalted butter
- Salt

1. Roast the jalapeños directly over a gas flame or under the broiler, turning, until charred all over. Transfer to a small bowl, cover with plastic wrap and let cool. Peel, seed and coarsely chop the jalapeños.

2. In a blender, puree the jalapeños with the peas and water. Transfer the puree to a medium saucepan.

3. Cook the puree over moderate heat, stirring occasionally, until piping hot, about 3 minutes. Stir in the butter, season with salt and serve.

—*Jean-Georges Vongerichten*

vegetables

Crisp Pickled Vegetables

TOTAL: 45 MIN PLUS 2 DAYS PICKLING

10 SERVINGS ● ● ○

With a rich meal, Manhattan chef Adam Perry Lang likes serving crisp, tangy vegetables to lighten things up. He marinates them for a couple of days in a mix of vinegar, sugar and, for a hint of spice, *guajillo* chiles. The vegetables can be served as a starter or alongside the main course.

- 3 cups cauliflower florets
- ½ pound baby carrots, halved lengthwise
- 1 fennel bulb, cored and cut into 2-by-½-inch matchsticks
- 1 red bell pepper, cut into 2-by-½-inch matchsticks
- 1 zucchini (½ pound), cut into 2-by-½-inch matchsticks
- ½ pound yellow wax beans or green beans, cut into 2-inch lengths
- 3 dried *guajillo* chiles, seeded and cut into thin strips

Boiling water

- 3 cups cider vinegar
- ½ cup white wine vinegar
- ¾ cup sugar
- 1 tablespoon kosher salt
- 1 teaspoon coriander seeds
- 1 teaspoon black peppercorns
- 1 tablespoon julienned fresh ginger
- 1 bay leaf
- 8 garlic cloves, smashed

Extra-virgin olive oil, for drizzling

- ¼ cup chopped flat-leaf parsley, for garnish
- ¼ cup snipped chives, for garnish

1. In a large, deep nonreactive bowl or heatproof glass jar, toss together the cauliflower florets, baby carrots, fennel, red bell pepper and zucchini matchsticks and yellow wax beans.

2. In a medium heatproof bowl, cover the *guajillo* chiles with boiling water and let stand until softened, about 10 minutes. Drain the chiles and transfer them to a large saucepan. Add the cider vinegar, white wine vinegar, sugar, salt, coriander seeds, black peppercorns, julienned ginger, bay leaf and smashed garlic cloves. Add 3 cups of water to the saucepan and bring to a boil over moderate heat, stirring to dissolve the sugar.

3. Pour the hot liquid and aromatics over the vegetables and cover the bowl with a plate to keep the vegetables submerged in the pickling liquid. Let cool to room temperature, then cover the bowl with plastic wrap and refrigerate the vegetables for 2 to 3 days.

4. Use a slotted spoon to transfer the pickled vegetables to a large serving platter. Drizzle the vegetables with olive oil, garnish them with the chopped parsley and snipped chives and serve.
—*Adam Perry Lang*

MAKE AHEAD The drained pickled vegetables can be refrigerated in a covered container for up to 3 days.

Fresh Vegetable Curry

ACTIVE: 20 MIN; TOTAL: 1 HR

4 TO 6 SERVINGS ● ○

- 2 tablespoons canola oil
- 1 small onion, thinly sliced
- 2 tablespoons finely julienned fresh ginger (from a 2-inch piece)
- 1 jalapeño, seeded and cut into thin strips
- 2 bay leaves
- 3 garlic cloves, very finely chopped
- 1 teaspoon turmeric
- 2 small tomatoes, coarsely chopped

One 14-ounce can unsweetened coconut milk

- ¼ cup water

Kosher salt

- 3 carrots, quartered lengthwise and cut into 1-inch pieces
- 1 pound butternut squash (neck only), peeled and cut into 1-by-½-inch pieces (1½ cups)
- ½ pound thin green beans, cut into 1-inch pieces

Basmati rice, for serving

1. In a large, deep skillet, heat the canola oil. Add the sliced onion, julienned ginger, jalapeño strips and bay leaves and cook over moderate heat, stirring occasionally, until the vegetables are softened, 5 minutes. Add the chopped garlic and the turmeric and cook, stirring, for 2 more minutes. Add the chopped tomatoes and mash lightly until just beginning to soften, 2 minutes. Add the coconut milk and water; season with salt. Bring to a boil.

2. Add the carrots, cover and simmer over low heat until crisp-tender, about 12 minutes. Add the squash and beans, cover and simmer until tender, 15 minutes. Discard the bay leaves. Serve with basmati rice.
—*Vikram Sunderam*

inexpensive peeler

"I use drugstore **razors** for peeling delicate vegetables like baby carrots because they waste less," explains Chicago chef Graham Elliot Bowles (an F&W Best New Chef 2004).

CRISP PICKLED VEGETABLES

FRESH VEGETABLE CURRY

Celery Root and Turnip Puree

ACTIVE: 25 MIN; TOTAL: 1 HR 10 MIN
8 SERVINGS ● ● ○

One 1-pound celery root,
    peeled and coarsely
    chopped (about 2 cups)
  1 pound medium turnips,
    peeled and coarsely
    chopped (about 3 cups)
  4 tablespoons unsalted butter
Kosher salt
  ¼ cup whole milk, warmed
Freshly ground pepper

1. In a large saucepan, add the celery root and turnips and just enough cold water to cover; bring to a boil. Stir in 3 tablespoons of the butter and 2 teaspoons of salt. Reduce the heat to moderate and simmer until the celery root and turnips are tender and the cooking liquid is reduced to ¼ cup, about 35 minutes.

2. Carefully transfer the cooked celery root and turnips with their cooking liquid to a food processor and let the vegetables cool for about 10 minutes. Add the remaining 1 tablespoon of butter and the warm milk and process until the mixture is completely smooth. Season the celery root–turnip puree with salt and pepper, transfer to a medium bowl and serve right away.
—*Florence Daniel Marzotto*

MAKE AHEAD The Celery Root and Turnip Puree can be refrigerated overnight. Gently reheat in the microwave or over low heat, stirring a few times, before serving.

Chestnut Puree

TOTAL: 20 MIN
8 SERVINGS ● ● ○

Two 14-ounce jars vacuum-
    packed roasted chestnuts
  2 cups water
1¾ cups milk, warmed

  4 tablespoons unsalted
    butter, melted
Salt and freshly ground
    black pepper

In a medium saucepan, cover the roasted chestnuts with the 2 cups of water and bring to a boil. Cover and simmer over moderate heat until the chestnuts are heated through, about 5 minutes. Drain the hot chestnuts and transfer them immediately to a food processor. Add the warm milk and melted butter and process until the mixture is completely smooth. Season the Chestnut Puree with salt and black pepper, transfer to a medium bowl and serve right away.
—*Florence Daniel Marzotto*

MAKE AHEAD The cooled Chestnut Puree can be refrigerated in an airtight container overnight. Gently reheat the puree in the microwave or over low heat, stirring a few times, before serving.

●HEALTHY ●MAKE AHEAD ○VEGETARIAN ●STAFF FAVORITE

241

vegetables

Crunchy Baked Fennel

ACTIVE: 35 MIN; TOTAL: 2 HR

12 SERVINGS ●●

Slices of sweet roasted fennel topped with herbed bread crumbs make for a fabulous freezer-to-oven side. (Of course, the dish can also be baked without freezing.)

- 10 medium fennel bulbs—halved, cored and sliced ½ inch thick
- 1 cup extra-virgin olive oil
- Kosher salt and freshly ground pepper
- 2 cups *panko* (Japanese bread crumbs)
- 1 cup finely grated Parmigiano-Reggiano cheese
- 2 tablespoons all-purpose flour
- 2 tablespoons unsalted butter
- 2 garlic cloves, very finely chopped
- 2 shallots, very finely chopped
- 2 teaspoons chopped thyme
- 2 tablespoons chopped flat-leaf parsley
- ¼ cup dry white wine

1. Preheat the oven to 375°. On 2 large rimmed baking sheets, drizzle the fennel with ½ cup of the olive oil; season with salt and pepper. Bake for 45 minutes, until softened. Let cool for 30 minutes.

2. In a skillet, toast the *panko* over moderate heat until golden, 3 minutes. Transfer to a bowl; stir in the cheese and flour.

3. In the same skillet, melt the butter. Add the garlic, shallots and thyme and cook over moderate heat until the garlic is softened, 5 minutes; add to the *panko*. Stir in the remaining ½ cup of oil and the parsley. Season with salt and pepper.

4. Preheat the oven to 400°. Spread half of the fennel in a 9-by-13-inch glass or ceramic baking dish. Pour the wine over the fennel, then sprinkle half of the *panko* on top. Repeat with the remaining fennel and *panko*. Cover and bake for 20 minutes,

then remove the foil and bake for 10 minutes longer, until the topping is browned and crisp. Serve hot. —*Rachel Soszynski*

MAKE AHEAD The unbaked gratin can be wrapped in foil and frozen for up to a week. Bake the foil-wrapped dish straight from the freezer for 25 minutes, then remove the foil and bake for 15 minutes longer.

Fennel Gratin with Crispy Bread Crumb Topping

ACTIVE: 30 MIN; TOTAL: 2 HR

10 SERVINGS ●●

This gratin combines tender braised fennel, crunchy bread crumbs and an over-the-top Parmigiano-Reggiano cream sauce. For added color, finely chop some of the fennel fronds as a garnish.

- Salt
- 5 fennel bulbs (5 pounds), quartered
- 2 tablespoons unsalted butter
- 2 garlic cloves, very finely chopped
- 1 quart heavy cream
- 1½ cups freshly grated Parmigiano-Reggiano cheese
- 2 large eggs, lightly beaten
- Freshly ground white pepper
- ½ cup fresh bread crumbs
- 2 tablespoons finely chopped flat-leaf parsley
- 1 tablespoon extra-virgin olive oil

1. Preheat the oven to 350°. Bring a large pot of salted water to a boil. Add the fennel and cook until crisp-tender, about 10 minutes. Drain and pat dry.

2. In a medium saucepan, melt the butter. Add the garlic and cook over moderate heat until softened, about 2 minutes. Add the cream and cook until reduced to 2 cups, about 20 minutes. Off the heat, whisk in 1 cup of the cheese. Gradually add the eggs and whisk until incorporated. Transfer the sauce to a blender and puree until smooth. Season with salt and white pepper.

3. In a small bowl, mix the bread crumbs with the chopped parsley and the remaining ½ cup of Parmigiano-Reggiano cheese. Season the bread crumb mixture lightly with salt and white pepper.

4. Arrange the fennel in a single layer in a 9-by-13-inch baking dish. Pour the cream sauce over the fennel, sprinkle with the bread crumb mixture and drizzle with the olive oil. Bake the gratin for about 45 minutes, until the fennel is tender, the sauce is bubbling and the crumbs are browned on top. Let the gratin stand for 15 minutes before serving. —*Fabio Trabocchi*

MAKE AHEAD The assembled gratin can be covered with plastic and refrigerated overnight. Bring to room temperature before baking.

Callaloo Stew

TOTAL: 30 MIN

6 SERVINGS ●●

Callaloo (sometimes called amaranth) is a spinach-like vegetable with large, heart-shaped leaves. Jamaicans cook it in water with oil and seasonings to make a silky stew eaten at breakfast with ackee (a Caribbean fruit) and saltfish, or as a side dish. Callaloo is available at many Caribbean markets in the U.S., but fresh spinach is a good substitute.

- 3 ounces salt pork, cut into 3 pieces
- 2 tablespoons unsalted butter
- 1 teaspoon annatto powder
- 1 large Spanish onion, thinly sliced
- ¼ cup water
- 2 pounds callaloo, thick stems trimmed, or spinach
- Salt and freshly ground black pepper

In a large soup pot, cook the pork over moderate heat, turning frequently, until it begins to brown and some of the fat is rendered, about 5 minutes. Add the butter and annatto and cook, stirring, until

the butter is melted. Stir in the sliced onion, cover and cook over low heat until softened, about 5 minutes. Add the water and bring to a boil. Add half of the callaloo, cover and cook until just barely wilted. Add the remaining callaloo, cover and cook until fully wilted, about 5 minutes longer. Discard the salt pork pieces, season the callaloo with salt and black pepper and serve right away.
—*Bradford Thompson*

MAKE AHEAD The callaloo can be refrigerated overnight.

Savoy Cabbage and Rutabaga Slaw

TOTAL: 35 MIN

4 SERVINGS ●

Blanched strips of rutabaga and chopped walnuts add crunch to this wintry slaw. Molasses gives the dressing a vibrant but not cloying sweetness.

One ½-pound rutabaga, peeled
  and cut into 2-by-¼-inch strips
¾ cup walnut halves
1½ tablespoons molasses,
  preferably sorghum
  (see Note)
1½ tablespoons fresh
  lemon juice
1½ tablespoons white vinegar
¼ cup plus 2 tablespoons
  extra-virgin olive oil
Salt and freshly ground pepper
One 1-pound Savoy cabbage,
  cored and finely shredded

1. Preheat the oven to 350°. Bring a saucepan of salted water to a boil and fill a bowl with ice water. Blanch the rutabaga in the boiling water until crisp-tender, about 3 minutes. Drain and transfer to the ice water to cool. Drain and pat dry.

2. Spread the walnuts on a baking sheet; toast for about 9 minutes, until fragrant and golden. Let cool; coarsely chop.

3. In a medium bowl, whisk the molasses with the lemon juice and vinegar. Gradually whisk in the olive oil. Season the dressing with salt and pepper. Add the cabbage, rutabaga and walnuts and toss well. Let the slaw stand at room temperature for 5 minutes before serving. —*Daniel Orr*

NOTE Sorghum molasses is a traditional Southern ingredient made by boiling down the juice of pressed sorghum (a grain related to millet). You can order it from fancysyrups.com.

Vegetable Stew with Crisp Ham and Garlic

TOTAL: 50 MIN

6 SERVINGS ●

This recipe is an adaptation of the enticing stew served at Nicolás Jimenez's Restaurante Túbal in Navarra, Spain. Jimenez updates the dish by reducing the cooking time, which keeps the vegetables' flavors bright. He also lightens the recipe by using less flour in the sauce.

½ lemon
3 large artichokes (¾ pound each)
Salt
2 cups baby spinach (2 ounces)
1 pound fingerling potatoes,
  scrubbed but not peeled
1 cardoon rib or celery rib,
  peeled and cut into 1-inch
  lengths
¾ pound green beans, halved
  lengthwise
6 tablespoons extra-virgin
  olive oil
3 garlic cloves, thinly sliced
4 ounces thinly sliced serrano
  ham, cut into 1-inch pieces
  (see Note)
1 tablespoon all-purpose flour

1. Fill a large bowl with water and squeeze the lemon half into it. Working with 1 artichoke at a time and using a sharp knife, cut off the top two-thirds of the leaves. Pull off the outer leaves until you reach the tender yellow leaves. Scrape out the choke with a melon baller or a spoon. Trim the base and peel the stem, then thickly slice the heart and add it to the lemon water. Repeat with the remaining artichokes.

2. In a large saucepan of boiling salted water, cook the spinach just until wilted, about 1 minute. Using a slotted spoon, transfer the spinach to a colander. Let cool slightly, then squeeze dry and chop finely. Transfer to a small bowl.

3. Meanwhile, add the potatoes to the boiling water and cook until tender, about 15 minutes. Using a slotted spoon, transfer the potatoes to a large bowl.

4. Add the cardoon or celery to the boiling water and cook until tender, about 8 minutes for cardoon, 3 minutes for celery. Using the slotted spoon, add the celery to the potatoes. Cook the beans in the boiling water until just tender, 2 minutes; using the slotted spoon, add the beans to the potatoes.

5. Drain the artichoke slices and add them to the boiling water. Cook until tender, about 8 minutes. Using the slotted spoon, add the artichokes to the potatoes; reserve 1¼ cups of the cooking water.

6. In a large skillet, heat 2 tablespoons of the oil. Add the garlic and cook over moderately high heat until softened and beginning to brown, about 1 minute. Add the ham and stir until the ham and garlic are lightly browned and crisp, about 2 minutes.

7. Add the blanched vegetables and half of the chopped spinach to the skillet and cook, stirring, until warm. Transfer to a shallow bowl and season with salt if necessary. Add the remaining ¼ cup of olive oil to the skillet, stir in the flour and cook until sizzling. Add the reserved 1¼ cups of cooking water and the remaining chopped spinach and cook, stirring, until the sauce is creamy, about 3 minutes. Drizzle the sauce over the vegetables and serve.
—*Nicolás Jimenez*

NOTE Serrano ham is a dry-cured, air-dried Spanish ham similar to prosciutto. Look for it at specialty stores or order it from tienda.com.

FARRO SALAD WITH
FRIED CAULIFLOWER AND
PROSCIUTTO (P. 255)

potatoes, grains & beans

*66 On a leisurely, rainy Sunday,
you might want to put a clay pot full
of beans in the fireplace. 99*

—STEVE SANDO, OWNER, RANCHO GORDO, NAPA

HERBED POTATO GRATIN WITH GARLIC AND MANCHEGO

PAN-ROASTED FINGERLING POTATOES WITH PANCETTA

Herbed Potato Gratin with Roasted Garlic and Manchego

ACTIVE: 30 MIN; TOTAL: 3 HR

12 SERVINGS ● ○

The combination of sharp, nutty Manchego and smoky San Simón cheeses gives this gratin a rich, complex flavor. Smoked gouda is a fine substitute for the San Simón.

- 3 heads of garlic, cloves separated but not peeled
- 1 tablespoon extra-virgin olive oil
- 1 quart half-and-half
- 1 tablespoon chopped thyme
- 1 teaspoon chopped rosemary

Salt and freshly ground
    black pepper

- 5 pounds Yukon Gold potatoes, peeled and very thinly sliced
- 9 ounces aged Manchego cheese, coarsely shredded (2 cups)
- 5 ounces San Simón or smoked Gouda cheese, shredded (1 cup)

1. Preheat the oven to 375°. In a 9-inch cake pan, drizzle the garlic cloves with the olive oil. Cover with foil and roast for 40 minutes, until tender. Let cool, then squeeze out the cloves.

2. Mash the garlic to a paste and transfer to a saucepan. Add the half-and-half, thyme and rosemary and bring to a boil. Simmer over very low heat until reduced to 3 cups, about 20 minutes; season with salt and pepper.

3. Arrange one-fourth of the potatoes in the bottom of a 9-by-13-inch baking dish. Top with one-fourth of the cheeses and drizzle lightly with the garlic cream. Repeat with the remaining potatoes, cheese and cream. Pour any remaining cream on top and press the top layer to submerge it.

4. Bake the gratin for about 1½ hours, until golden and bubbling. Let cool for 20 minutes, then cut into squares and serve.
—*Jose Garces*

Pan-Roasted Fingerling Potatoes with Pancetta

TOTAL: 50 MIN

10 SERVINGS

- 2 pounds fingerling potatoes, cut into ½-inch rounds
- ¼ cup extra-virgin olive oil
- ½ pound thickly sliced pancetta, cut into ⅓-inch dice

Salt and freshly ground pepper

- 1 onion, thinly sliced
- ¼ cup finely chopped dill

1. Boil the potatoes until just tender, about 8 minutes. Drain and pat dry.

2. In a cast-iron skillet, heat the oil. Add the pancetta and cook over moderate heat until lightly browned, 3 minutes. Using a slotted spoon, transfer the pancetta to a bowl.

3. Add the potatoes to the skillet, season with salt and pepper and cook, stirring occasionally, until lightly browned, 10 minutes. Add the onion and cook until softened and the potatoes are golden brown, 10 minutes. Stir in the pancetta and cook for 2 minutes longer. Transfer to a bowl; toss with the dill right before serving. —*Fabio Trabocchi*

Sweet Potato Gratin with Chile-Spiced Pecans

ACTIVE: 25 MIN; TOTAL: 2 HR

12 SERVINGS ● ●

5 pounds sweet potatoes

4 tablespoons unsalted butter

2 cups pecans (8 ounces)

2 tablespoons sugar

1 teaspoon chipotle chile powder

Kosher salt

¼ cup honey

½ teaspoon cinnamon

¼ teaspoon ground allspice

⅛ teaspoon ground cloves

½ cup heavy cream

Freshly ground pepper

2 cups mini marshmallows

1. Preheat the oven to 375°. Roast the sweet potatoes on a large baking sheet for about 1 hour and 10 minutes, until tender.

2. Meanwhile, in a skillet, melt the butter. Add the pecans, sugar and chipotle powder and cook over moderate heat, stirring, until the sugar starts to caramelize and the pecans are well coated, 8 minutes. Spread the pecans on a parchment-lined baking sheet, sprinkle with salt and let cool.

3. Cut the potatoes in half lengthwise and scoop the flesh into a food processor; discard the skins. Add the honey, cinnamon, allspice and cloves and puree. Add the cream and puree. Season with salt and pepper.

4. Scrape the potatoes into a 9-by-13-inch baking dish; scatter the marshmallows on top. Bake in the top third of the oven for 25 minutes, until the marshmallows are golden. Sprinkle with the chile-spiced pecans and serve. —*Jose Garces*

MAKE AHEAD The sweet potato puree can be refrigerated overnight. The nuts can be kept in an airtight container for 3 days.

Golden Potato and Porcini Gratin

ACTIVE: 30 MIN; TOTAL: 2 HR

10 SERVINGS ● ●

1 cup dried porcini mushrooms (1 ounce)

1 cup hot water

½ cup dry white wine

3 garlic cloves, halved

4 thyme sprigs

2½ cups heavy cream

1½ cups freshly grated Parmigiano-Reggiano cheese (5 ounces)

1 tablespoon kosher salt

⅛ teaspoon cayenne pepper

2 pounds Yukon Gold potatoes, peeled and sliced ⅛ inch thick on a mandoline

1. Preheat the oven to 350°. In a small bowl, cover the porcini with the hot water and let soak until softened, about 15 minutes. Using a slotted spoon, remove the porcini from the soaking liquid; discard the liquid. Rinse and coarsely chop the porcini.

2. In a large saucepan, combine the white wine, halved garlic cloves and thyme sprigs and boil over high heat until the wine has reduced by half, about 3 minutes. Add the heavy cream, 1 cup of the Parmigiano-Reggiano cheese, the salt and cayenne pepper and bring to boil. Remove from the heat; discard the thyme sprigs and garlic cloves.

3. Arrange half of the potato slices in an even layer in a shallow 10-by-15-inch baking dish. Spread the chopped porcini evenly over the potatoes. Top with the remaining potato slices. Pour the cream mixture on top and shake the dish to distribute the cream. Sprinkle the potatoes with the remaining ½ cup of grated cheese. Bake for 1 hour and 10 minutes, or until the potatoes are tender and the top is richly browned. Let the gratin rest for 15 minutes, then serve hot.

—*Richard Betts*

Potato Kugel with Fried Shallots

ACTIVE: 45 MIN; TOTAL: 2 HR

10 SERVINGS ● ●

1 cup vegetable oil

4 large shallots, thinly sliced

5 pounds Idaho potatoes, peeled and coarsely shredded

1 large yellow onion, coarsely grated

⅓ cup potato starch

1 tablespoon kosher salt

½ teaspoon freshly ground pepper

Pinch of freshly grated nutmeg

5 large eggs, beaten

2 large egg yolks, beaten

½ cup extra-virgin olive oil

1 cup boiling water

1. Preheat the oven to 450°. In a medium saucepan, heat the vegetable oil until shimmering. Add the shallots and cook over high heat, stirring occasionally, until golden and crisp, about 6 minutes. Using a slotted spoon, transfer the shallots to a plate. Reserve the shallot oil.

2. Working in batches, squeeze out as much liquid as possible from the potatoes, transferring them to a bowl as you go. Add the onion, potato starch, salt, pepper and nutmeg and stir well. Stir in the eggs, yolks, olive oil, boiling water and fried shallots.

3. Heat two 8-by-11½-inch flameproof or enameled cast-iron baking dishes over high heat until they are very hot. Add 2 tablespoons of the shallot oil to each baking dish and heat until smoking. Carefully spread the potato mixture in the dishes.

4. Transfer the kugels to the oven and bake for 20 minutes. Lower the temperature to 375° and bake for 40 minutes longer, until golden and crisp on the sides.

5. Preheat the broiler. Broil the potato kugels as close to the heat as possible for about 2 minutes, until they are browned and crisp on top. Let the kugels stand for 20 minutes before cutting into squares and serving. —*Adam Perry Lang*

potatoes, grains & beans

Mashed Potatoes with Crème Fraîche and Chives

ACTIVE: 40 MIN; TOTAL: 1 HR

12 SERVINGS ● ○ ○

These are the perfect mashed potatoes: creamy, fluffy and slightly tangy thanks to the addition of crème fraîche. The chopped chives add an appealing freshness, but purists can omit them.

- 6 pounds Yukon Gold potatoes, peeled and halved
- 2 cups whole milk
- 1½ sticks unsalted butter
- Kosher salt
- 1 cup crème fraîche
- ½ cup finely chopped chives
- Freshly ground pepper

1. In a large pot, cover the potatoes with cold water and bring to a boil. Cover and cook over moderate heat until the potatoes are tender, about 20 minutes; drain. Press the potatoes through a ricer into a large saucepan set over low heat.

2. Meanwhile, in a small saucepan, combine the milk with 10 tablespoons of the butter and 1 tablespoon of salt and cook over moderate heat until the butter is melted, about 3 minutes.

3. Pour the hot milk over the riced potatoes and cook over moderate heat, stirring occasionally, until blended, about 2 minutes. Stir in the crème fraîche, the remaining 2 tablespoons of butter and the chives and cook until the potatoes are heated through, about 5 minutes. Season with salt and pepper, transfer the mashed potatoes to a bowl and serve. —*Rachel Soszynski*

MAKE AHEAD The mashed potatoes can be kept covered at room temperature for up to 3 hours. Reheat before serving.

Meyer Lemon Gnocchi

TOTAL: 1 HR 15 MIN

8 SERVINGS

For supertender gnocchi, Maine chef Steve Corry (an F&W Best New Chef 2007) is careful not to overwork the dough. After draining the gnocchi, he sautés them until they're slightly crispy, then tosses them in a lemony sauce. Instead of sprinkling the gnocchi with Parmesan cheese, Corry likes to top them with shaved *bottarga*—dried and salted gray mullet roe—but they're also delicious without it.

- 1 pound baking potatoes, peeled and cut into 2-inch chunks
- 3 large egg yolks
- Finely grated zest of 2 lemons, preferably Meyer lemons
- 2 tablespoons plus 1 teaspoon extra-virgin olive oil
- 1½ teaspoons salt
- ¾ cup all-purpose flour
- ½ cup low-sodium chicken broth
- 1 stick plus 2 tablespoons unsalted butter, cut into pieces and chilled
- 1 tablespoon fresh lemon juice
- Salt
- Snipped chives, for garnish
- *Bottarga* (optional; see Note)

1. In a medium saucepan, cover the potatoes with water and bring to a boil. Simmer over moderately high heat until the potatoes are tender, about 8 minutes. Drain the potatoes, then return them to the pan; shake over moderately high heat until dry.

2. Working over a large rimmed baking sheet, rice the hot potatoes in an even layer. In a small bowl, whisk the egg yolks with the lemon zest, 1 teaspoon of olive oil and the salt and pour over the potatoes. Sprinkle the flour over the potatoes and stir gently just until a dough forms.

3. On a work surface, gently roll the dough into four ½-inch-thick ropes. Using a sharp knife, cut each rope into ½-inch pieces. Roll each piece against the tines of a fork to make ridges. Transfer the gnocchi to the baking sheet, cover with plastic and refrigerate.

4. In a small saucepan, bring the chicken broth to a simmer. Remove from the heat and whisk in the stick of butter a few pieces at a time until the sauce is creamy. Warm the sauce on low heat if necessary. Stir in the lemon juice and season with salt.

5. In a large pot of boiling salted water, cook the gnocchi until they rise to the surface, then cook them for 1 minute longer. Gently drain the gnocchi, toss with the remaining 2 tablespoons of olive oil and transfer to a baking sheet until cool.

6. In a large nonstick skillet, melt 1 tablespoon of the butter. Add half of the gnocchi and cook in a single layer over high heat until browned on the bottom, 2 minutes. Transfer to a large bowl and repeat with the remaining 1 tablespoon of butter and gnocchi.

7. Reheat the sauce; pour it over the gnocchi and fold gently with a rubber spatula until they are evenly coated. Transfer to a platter and garnish with the chives. Grate the *bottarga* on top and serve. —*Steve Corry*

NOTE *Bottarga* is available from specialty food shops and gourmetsardinia.com.

Tzatziki Potato Salad

TOTAL: 30 MIN

6 SERVINGS ● ● ○ ○

Tzatziki is a traditional Greek appetizer (or *meze*) made with yogurt and cucumbers. Here, tzatziki and mayonnaise form the base for an incredibly tasty potato salad tossed with dill, mint and serrano chile.

vegetable scrub gloves

Danish-designed Skruba textured nylon gloves—which remove dirt from potatoes, root vegetables and mushrooms with a quick brush of the hand—can be cleaned in the dishwasher (*$12; stonewallkitchen.com*).

2½ pounds Yukon Gold potatoes, peeled and cut into ¾-inch cubes

¾ cup Greek-style plain fat-free yogurt

¼ cup mayonnaise

3 Kirby cucumbers—peeled, seeded and cut into ½-inch cubes

1 serrano chile, seeded and thinly sliced

¼ cup coarsely chopped mint

1 tablespoon chopped dill

Salt and freshly ground pepper

1. Bring a large saucepan of salted water to a boil. Add the potatoes and cook over high heat until tender, about 9 minutes. Drain, gently shaking out the excess water. Spread the potatoes on a baking sheet in a single layer and freeze for about 10 minutes, just until no longer warm.

2. Meanwhile, in a large bowl, whisk the yogurt with the mayonnaise until smooth. Add the cucumbers, chile, mint and dill. Fold in the potatoes, season with salt and pepper and serve. —*Grace Parisi*

MAKE AHEAD The potato salad can be refrigerated for 2 days.

Warm Potato Salad with Pancetta and Brown Butter Dressing

TOTAL: 40 MIN
6 SERVINGS ●

Golden pancetta and brown butter enrich a tangy, mustardy dressing for creamy fingerling potatoes.

Salt

2 pounds fingerling potatoes, sliced ½ inch thick

4 tablespoons unsalted butter

3 ounces thickly sliced pancetta, cut into ¼-inch dice

1 shallot, minced

One 2-inch rosemary sprig

2 tablespoons sherry vinegar

1 tablespoon grainy mustard

Freshly ground pepper

2 tablespoons snipped chives

1. Bring a large saucepan of salted water to a boil. Add the potatoes and cook over high heat until tender, about 10 minutes. Drain, shaking off any excess water.

2. Meanwhile, in a large skillet, melt 1 tablespoon of the butter. Add the pancetta and cook over moderate heat, stirring frequently, until just beginning to brown, about 3 minutes. Add the remaining 3 tablespoons of butter and cook, stirring occasionally, until the pancetta is golden and the butter is just beginning to brown, about 2 minutes. Add the shallot and rosemary sprig and cook, stirring, for 2 minutes. Remove the skillet from the heat and discard the rosemary sprig.

3. Whisk the vinegar and mustard into the pancetta mixture; season with salt and pepper. Add the potatoes and chives and toss to coat. Serve the potato salad warm or at room temperature. —*Grace Parisi*

Cheddar-Stuffed Potatoes

ACTIVE: 40 MIN; TOTAL: 2 HR 45 MIN
6 SERVINGS ● ○

These overstuffed potatoes can be eaten as a main course (they're certainly big enough) or as a side dish with, say, juicy steak. For a side, use a smaller potato and adjust the filling accordingly.

6 medium baking potatoes (3¾ pounds), scrubbed

1 stick unsalted butter, at room temperature

1 tablespoon extra-virgin olive oil

½ pound cremini mushrooms, sliced ¼ inch thick

Kosher salt and freshly ground black pepper

6 ounces sharp white cheddar cheese, coarsely shredded (2 cups)

½ cup plus 2 tablespoons freshly grated Parmigiano-Reggiano cheese

½ cup sour cream

¼ cup snipped chives

1. Preheat the oven to 400°. Place the potatoes on a rimmed baking sheet and bake for 1½ hours, or until tender when pierced with a knife. Let stand until cool enough to handle.

2. Reduce the oven temperature to 350°. Meanwhile, in a medium skillet, melt 1 tablespoon of the butter in the olive oil. Add the sliced cremini mushrooms and cook over moderately high heat, stirring occasionally, until they are golden brown around the edges and tender, about 4 minutes. Season generously with salt and black pepper and transfer the mushrooms to a large bowl.

3. Cut off the top fourth of each potato. Scoop the flesh from the tops of the potatoes into the bowl with the sautéed mushrooms; discard the skins. Scoop the flesh from the potatoes into the bowl, leaving a ¼ inch of shell. Place the potato shells on the baking sheet.

4. While the potato flesh is still warm, add the remaining 7 tablespoons of butter, 1 cup of the cheddar cheese, ½ cup of the Parmigiano-Reggiano cheese, the sour cream and 3 tablespoons of the snipped chives to the bowl. Using a potato masher, whisk or pastry blender, mash the filling until the potatoes are almost smooth, the cheese is incorporated and the butter has melted. Season the potato filling with salt and black pepper.

5. Mound the potato, mushroom and cheese filling into the empty potato shells and top with the remaining 1 cup of shredded cheddar cheese and 2 tablespoons of grated Parmigiano-Reggiano cheese. Bake the stuffed potatoes for 30 minutes, until the filling is heated through and the cheese on top is lightly golden. Sprinkle the potatoes with the remaining 1 tablespoon of snipped chives and serve. —*Melissa Rubel*

MAKE AHEAD The stuffed potatoes can be covered and refrigerated overnight. Bring to room temperature before baking.

potatoes, grains & beans

Porcini-Potato Cake with Green Salad

TOTAL: 1 HR 30 MIN

6 SERVINGS ●

Dried porcini mushrooms—which cost about $50 a pound—and aged Gruyère cheese push an ordinary potato pancake into superluxe territory. "Sprinkle it with a bit of truffle salt, and it's off the charts," says F&W's Grace Parisi.

> 1 cup dried porcini mushrooms (1 ounce)
>
> 2 cups boiling water
>
> 3 tablespoons unsalted butter
>
> 2 medium shallots, minced
>
> Kosher salt and freshly ground black pepper
>
> 1½ cups coarsely shredded Gruyère cheese (6 ounces)
>
> 4 pounds Yukon Gold potatoes, peeled and coarsely shredded
>
> 1 medium onion, finely chopped
>
> ½ cup extra-virgin olive oil
>
> 2 tablespoons fresh lemon juice
>
> 1 tablespoon walnut oil
>
> 6 ounces mixed baby greens, such as mesclun and arugula
>
> 1 cup grape tomatoes, halved
>
> Truffle salt (optional)

1. In a small heatproof bowl, cover the dried porcini with the boiling water and let stand until the mushrooms are softened, about 25 minutes. Drain, rinse off any grit and finely chop the porcini mushrooms; discard the soaking liquid.

2. In a medium skillet, heat 1 tablespoon of the butter. Add the minced shallots and cook over moderate heat, stirring occasionally, until softened, about 4 minutes. Add the chopped porcini, season lightly with salt and black pepper and cook until fragrant, about 3 minutes. Let cool, then stir in the Gruyère cheese.

3. Meanwhile, in a large bowl, toss the potatoes and onion with 1 tablespoon of kosher salt and let stand for 15 minutes. Working with a handful at a time, squeeze as much of the liquid as possible from the potato-and-onion mixture into a large bowl. Transfer the squeezed potatoes and onion to a work surface. Let the liquid in the bowl stand for 5 minutes to allow the potato starch to settle to the bottom. Pour off the liquid, leaving only the starch in the bowl. Return the potatoes and onion to the bowl and toss with the starch. Season generously with black pepper.

4. Preheat the oven to 375°. In a 12-inch nonstick ovenproof skillet, melt the remaining 2 tablespoons of butter in 2 tablespoons of the olive oil. Remove from the heat. Add half of the potato-onion mixture, pressing it into an even layer with a spatula. Spoon the porcini-Gruyère mixture over the potatoes, leaving a 1-inch border all around the outside. Top with the remaining potato-onion mixture and press to seal the potato cake.

5. Cook the potato cake over moderately high heat, shaking the pan occasionally, until the bottom is golden brown, about 7 minutes. Carefully slide the potato cake onto a large, flat plate. Invert the skillet over the cake and, using oven mitts or towels, carefully invert the cake back into the skillet. Drizzle 2 tablespoons of olive oil around the edge and cook the potato cake for 5 minutes. Transfer the skillet to the oven and bake the potato cake for 30 minutes, until it is cooked through and golden on the bottom. Slide the potato cake onto a plate.

6. In a large bowl, whisk the remaining ¼ cup of olive oil with the lemon juice and walnut oil. Season with salt and pepper. Add the baby greens and tomatoes and toss. Cut the potato cake into wedges and sprinkle them with the truffle salt, if using. Serve with the salad.

—*Grace Parisi*

MAKE AHEAD The porcini-potato cake can be made up to 4 hours ahead; reheat in a 350° oven.

Roasted Potato Skewers

ACTIVE: 20 MIN; TOTAL: 1 HR

4 SERVINGS

For this aromatic side dish, F&W's Marcia Kiesel spears cubes of slab bacon with fragrant rosemary sprigs, then threads the bacon and red potatoes onto skewers.

> 6 ounces meaty slab bacon, cut into sixteen ½-inch cubes
>
> 4 rosemary sprigs, cut into sixteen 1-inch pieces
>
> 16 small red potatoes (1½ pounds)
>
> Extra-virgin olive oil, for drizzling
>
> Salt and freshly ground pepper

1. Preheat the oven to 350°. Spear the bacon cubes with the rosemary sprigs. Alternately thread the potatoes and the bacon onto four 10-inch metal skewers.

2. Lay the skewers on a large rimmed baking sheet. Drizzle them with olive oil and season with salt and pepper. Bake for about 40 minutes, until the bacon is crisp and the potatoes are tender.

—*Marcia Kiesel*

Warm Potato Salad with Arugula

ACTIVE: 15 MIN; TOTAL: 40 MIN

12 SERVINGS ● ●

> 3 pounds white potatoes, scrubbed
>
> ¼ cup plus 3 tablespoons extra-virgin olive oil
>
> Salt and freshly ground black pepper
>
> 2 tablespoons grainy mustard
>
> 1½ tablespoons sherry vinegar
>
> 1 small sweet onion, thinly sliced
>
> 5 ounces baby arugula

1. Preheat the oven to 425°. Cut the potatoes into ½-inch wedges. Scatter the potato wedges on 2 large rimmed baking sheets, drizzle with 3 tablespoons of the olive oil and toss until coated. Season with salt and pepper and roast for about 25 minutes, until browned and crisp.

2. In a small bowl, whisk the remaining ¼ cup of olive oil with the mustard and vinegar; season with salt and pepper. In a large bowl, toss the potatoes with the onion and arugula. Top with the dressing, toss again and serve. —*Paul Virant*

Crispy Potato Latkes

TOTAL: 1 HR

MAKES ABOUT 40 LATKES ● ● ●

Renée Simmons, mother of F&W's Gail Simmons (a *Top Chef* judge, pictured below right), uses the grating disk of a food processor to make tangles of long potato strands that fry up extra-crispy.

- 3½ **pounds baking potatoes, peeled and halved**
- 1 **large yellow onion, cut into 8 wedges**
- ½ **cup all-purpose flour**
- 2 **large eggs, lightly beaten**
- 2 **tablespoons chopped dill**
- 1½ **teaspoons salt**
- ¼ **teaspoon baking powder**

Canola oil, for frying

Pink Applesauce (p. 383) and sour cream, for serving

1. Set a large strainer over a bowl. In a food processor fitted with the shredding disk, shred the potatoes and onion in batches. Add each batch to the strainer; let stand for 5 minutes, then squeeze dry. Drain off all the liquid in the bowl and add the shredded potatoes and onion. Stir in the flour, eggs, dill, salt and baking powder. Scrape the mixture back into the strainer and set it over a bowl; let stand for 5 minutes.

2. In a very large skillet, heat ¼ inch of canola oil until shimmering. Spoon 2 tablespoons of the potato mixture into the canola oil for each latke, pressing slightly to flatten. Fry over moderate heat, turning once, until the latkes are golden and crisp on both sides, about 7 minutes. Drain the latkes on a paper towel–lined baking sheet. Serve the latkes hot, with Pink Applesauce and sour cream. —*Renée Simmons*

WARM POTATO SALAD WITH ARUGULA

CRISPY POTATO LATKES AND PINK APPLESAUCE (P. 383)

potatoes, grains & beans

Crispy Cornmeal Fritters

TOTAL: 1 HR

6 SERVINGS ●

These slightly sweet, crispy cornmeal fritters are served all over Jamaica, where they are called "festival," supposedly because eating them is like having a festival in your mouth.

- 2 cups all-purpose flour
- ½ cup fine cornmeal
- 2 packed tablespoons light brown sugar
- 2 teaspoons baking powder
- 1 teaspoon salt
- 4 tablespoons cold unsalted butter, cut into ½-inch cubes
- 1 cup evaporated milk
- 1 quart vegetable oil, for frying

1. In a large bowl, whisk together the flour, cornmeal, brown sugar, baking powder and salt. Using a pastry blender or 2 knives, cut in the chilled butter cubes until the mixture resembles coarse meal. Add the evaporated milk and stir until a dough forms. Turn the dough out onto a lightly floured work surface and knead just until smooth, about 1 minute. Cover the dough with plastic wrap and let stand at room temperature for 15 minutes.

2. On a lightly floured work surface, use your hands to roll the dough out into a long, thick rope. Cut the dough into 24 even pieces and roll each piece into a 9-inch rope. Bring both ends together and twist each rope tightly.

3. In a large saucepan fitted with a deep-frying thermometer, heat the vegetable oil to 350°. Fry the cornmeal twists in batches of about 8 at a time until golden all over, 2 to 3 minutes. Drain the fritters on paper towels and serve hot.

—*Bradford Thompson*

MAKE AHEAD The recipe can be prepared through Step 2 and kept at room temperature, covered, for up to 1 hour.

Oat Risotto with Peas and Pecorino

TOTAL: 35 MIN

6 SERVINGS ● ●

F&W's Grace Parisi simmers steel-cut oats risotto-style in chicken stock until they're tender, then stirs in nutty pecorino cheese and sweet baby peas.

- 2 tablespoons unsalted butter
- 1 leek, white and tender green parts only, halved lengthwise and thinly sliced crosswise
- 1 cup steel-cut oats, such as McCann's
- 5 cups chicken stock or low-sodium broth
- Salt and freshly ground white pepper
- 1 cup frozen baby peas (5 ounces), thawed
- 1 scallion, thinly sliced
- 1 cup pecorino shavings

In a large saucepan, melt the butter. Add the sliced leek and cook over moderate heat, stirring occasionally, until softened, about 5 minutes. Stir in the steel-cut oats and cook, stirring constantly, for about 1 minute. Pour 1 cup of the chicken stock into the saucepan and simmer over moderate heat, stirring frequently, until the stock is nearly absorbed. Continue cooking the oats, adding 1 cup of chicken stock at a time and cooking and stirring until the liquid is nearly absorbed between additions. The risotto is done when the oats are chewy-tender and suspended in a thick sauce, about 25 minutes total. Season the risotto with salt and white pepper. Stir in the thawed peas, sliced scallion and ¾ cup of the shaved pecorino cheese and cook until the peas are heated through, about 1 minute longer. Transfer the oat risotto to shallow serving bowls and sprinkle with the remaining shaved pecorino cheese. Serve the hot risotto right away.

—*Grace Parisi*

Vegetable Couscous Pilaf

TOTAL: 40 MIN

4 SERVINGS ●

This Moroccan-style vegetable pilaf gets its complex flavor from ground cumin, caraway seeds and roasted almonds.

- ¼ cup extra-virgin olive oil
- 1 medium carrot, thinly sliced
- 1 medium parsnip, thinly sliced
- 1 medium yellow squash, cut into ¾-inch pieces
- 1 medium zucchini, cut into ¾-inch pieces
- 1 medium onion, finely diced
- 1 garlic clove, minced
- Salt and freshly ground black pepper
- 1½ teaspoons ground cumin
- ½ teaspoon smoked paprika
- ¼ teaspoon caraway seeds
- 1½ cups couscous
- 2¼ cups chicken stock or low-sodium broth
- ½ cup diced dried apricots
- ½ cup salted roasted almonds, coarsely chopped
- ¼ cup chopped cilantro

In a large, deep skillet, heat the olive oil. Add the carrot and parsnip and cook over high heat, stirring frequently, until lightly browned and crisp-tender, about 5 minutes. Add the yellow squash, zucchini, onion and garlic and season with salt and pepper. Cook, stirring frequently, until the vegetables are lightly browned in spots, about 5 minutes. Stir in the cumin, paprika and caraway seeds and cook, stirring, until fragrant. Add the couscous and cook, stirring frequently, until lightly toasted, about 2 minutes. Stir in the stock and apricots and season with salt and pepper. Cover and let stand off the heat until the couscous is tender and the liquid is absorbed, about 5 minutes. Fluff with a fork, stir in the almonds and cilantro and serve.

—*Grace Parisi*

SERVE WITH Plain yogurt.

Cheesy Grits with Scallions

TOTAL: 40 MIN
4 SERVINGS ● ●

Slivers of scallion add zip to these comforting cheese grits.

3 cups water
2 cups milk
1 small onion, very
    finely chopped
2 garlic cloves, very
    finely chopped
2 tablespoons extra-virgin
    olive oil
½ teaspoon salt
1 cup grits (not instant)
½ cup shredded sharp cheddar
4 scallions, thinly sliced
½ teaspoon finely chopped
    thyme leaves

In a large saucepan, combine the water, milk, onion, garlic, olive oil and salt, and bring to a boil. Simmer over moderate heat until the onion and garlic are softened, about 3 minutes. Return to a boil and whisk in the grits. Cook over low heat, stirring frequently with a wooden spoon, until the grits are tender, about 25 minutes. Add the cheese, scallions and thyme and stir until the cheese has melted. Transfer to bowls and serve the grits right away.
—*Daniel Orr*

Eggplant Risotto with Tomatoes and Basil

TOTAL: 1 HR
4 SERVINGS

Loaded with eggplant, tomatoes and basil, this summery risotto evokes another Mediterranean classic, ratatouille.

¼ cup extra-virgin olive oil
One 1-pound eggplant, peeled
    and cut into ½-inch dice
3 garlic cloves, very
    finely chopped
Salt
4¼ cups chicken stock or
    low-sodium chicken broth
1 small onion, very finely chopped
1 pound tomatoes, coarsely
    chopped
1 cup arborio rice
1 tablespoon unsalted butter
½ cup crumbled *ricotta salata*
    (2 ounces)
2 tablespoons freshly grated
    Parmigiano-Reggiano cheese
½ cup julienned basil
Freshly ground pepper

1. In a large skillet, heat 3 tablespoons of the olive oil. Add the diced eggplant and cook over moderately high heat, stirring occasionally, until browned all over, about 10 minutes. Add the chopped garlic, season with salt and cook, stirring, until fragrant, about 1 minute longer. Remove the skillet from the heat.

2. In a medium saucepan, bring the chicken stock to a simmer. In a large saucepan, heat the remaining 1 tablespoon of olive oil. Add the chopped onion and cook over moderate heat, stirring occasionally, until softened, about 5 minutes. Add all but ¼ cup of the chopped tomatoes and cook, stirring, until softened, about 3 minutes. Add the rice and cook, stirring, until thoroughly coated, about 2 minutes.

3. Add 1 cup of the hot stock to the rice and cook, stirring, until the stock is nearly absorbed, about 3 minutes. Continue adding hot stock 1 cup at a time, stirring until it is absorbed between additions. The risotto is done when the rice is al dente and suspended in a creamy liquid, about 25 minutes total.

4. Remove the risotto from the heat. Stir in the butter, then stir in the *ricotta salata* and Parmigiano-Reggiano cheeses. Stir in the eggplant and basil along with the remaining ¼ cup of tomatoes. Season the risotto with salt and pepper and transfer to bowls. Serve right away. —*Jane Sigal*
MAKE AHEAD The eggplant can be cooked through Step 1 and kept at room temperature for up to 4 hours.

Grilled-Eggplant Risotto

ACTIVE: 40 MIN; TOTAL: 1 HR
6 SERVINGS ● ●

For this supersimple risotto, Missouri chef Jonathan Justus grills eggplant until smoky and charred, then blends the creamy flesh into the cooked rice. Just before serving, he sprinkles on sumac, a tart Middle Eastern spice made from the dried berry.

1 large eggplant (about 1½ pounds)
2½ tablespoons extra-virgin
    olive oil
1 tablespoon unsalted butter
¼ cup finely chopped onion
2 tablespoons minced shallot
1 tablespoon minced garlic
1½ cups arborio rice
¼ cup dry white wine
3 cups hot vegetable stock
    or broth
¼ cup heavy cream
Salt and freshly ground pepper
2 tablespoons minced
    flat-leaf parsley
2 scallions, thinly sliced
Ground sumac (see Note)

1. Light a grill. Rub the eggplant with ½ tablespoon of the oil and grill over moderate heat, turning occasionally, until charred and soft, 20 minutes; let cool slightly. Halve the eggplant lengthwise and scoop the pulp into a blender. Puree until creamy.

2. In a large saucepan, melt the butter in the remaining 2 tablespoons of oil. Add the onion, shallot, garlic and rice and cook over moderate heat, stirring, until fragrant, 5 minutes. Add the wine and cook until it is absorbed. Add the vegetable stock ½ cup at a time; stir constantly until it is absorbed before adding more. Cook until the rice is al dente, 20 minutes total.

3. Stir in the eggplant and cream; season with salt and pepper. Stir in the parsley and scallions. Spoon into bowls, sprinkle with sumac and serve. —*Jonathan Justus*
NOTE Sumac is available at specialty shops and from kalustyans.com.

Risotto with Baby Greens

ACTIVE: 1 HR; TOTAL: 2 HR

8 SERVINGS ● ●

STOCK

- 2 quarts plus 3 cups water
- 1 large onion, sliced
- 3 medium carrots, coarsely chopped
- 1 medium leek, white and light green parts only, coarsely chopped
- 1 large celery rib, coarsely chopped
- 4 garlic cloves
- 2 bay leaves
- 2 thyme sprigs
- 2 cloves

RISOTTO

- 5 tablespoons unsalted butter
- 1 large shallot, very finely chopped
- 5 ounces baby greens, such as pea shoots, spinach or arugula (6 packed cups)
- Salt and freshly ground pepper
- 1 tablespoon vegetable oil
- 2 cups arborio rice
- Freshly grated Parmigiano-Reggiano cheese, for serving

1. MAKE THE STOCK: In a large saucepan, combine the water with the sliced onion, the chopped carrots, leek, and celery, the garlic cloves, bay leaves, thyme sprigs and cloves and bring to a boil. Reduce the heat to moderate, cover and simmer for 50 minutes. Strain the stock through a fine-mesh sieve into a medium saucepan; cover and keep warm.

2. MAKE THE RISOTTO: In a medium skillet, melt 2 tablespoons of the butter. Add half of the chopped shallot and cook over moderate heat, stirring occasionally, until softened, about 3 minutes. Add the baby greens a handful at a time, stirring between batches until the leaves are wilted. Season the baby greens with salt and pepper and set aside.

3. In a large saucepan, melt 1 tablespoon of the butter in the vegetable oil. Add the remaining chopped shallot and cook over moderate heat until the shallot is softened, about 5 minutes. Add the arborio rice and cook over moderately high heat, stirring to coat the grains, about 2 minutes. Add 1 cup of the warm vegetable stock and cook, stirring constantly, until it is nearly absorbed. Continue adding the stock ½ cup at a time, stirring until it is nearly absorbed between additions. The risotto is done when the rice is al dente and suspended in a thick, creamy sauce, about 25 minutes total.

4. Stir the wilted greens and the remaining 2 tablespoons of butter into the risotto and season with salt and pepper. Serve at once, passing the cheese at the table.
—*Florence Daniel Marzotto*

MAKE AHEAD The vegetable stock and the wilted greens can be refrigerated separately overnight.

Farro Risotto

 TOTAL: 45 MIN

4 SERVINGS ● ●

Boston chef Barbara Lynch slowly stirs nutty grains of farro (a type of wheat) with onion and white wine, then adds cream, butter and Parmigiano-Reggiano cheese. The result isn't really a classic risotto, but more like a creamy pasta dish.

- 2 tablespoons extra-virgin olive oil
- 1 small white onion, finely chopped
- 10 ounces farro (1½ cups)
- ¼ cup dry white wine
- 3 cups water
- ½ cup heavy cream
- ¼ cup freshly grated Parmigiano-Reggiano cheese
- 2 teaspoons unsalted butter
- Salt and freshly ground black pepper

1. In a saucepan, heat the oil. Add the onion and cook over moderate heat until softened, 6 minutes. Add the farro and cook for 1 minute, stirring. Add the wine and cook, stirring until it is absorbed, 2 minutes.

2. Add the water 1 cup at a time and cook, stirring until absorbed between additions, until the farro is al dente and suspended in thick, creamy liquid, about 25 minutes.

3. Stir in the cream, cheese and butter; simmer until thick, 5 minutes. Season with salt and pepper and serve. —*Barbara Lynch*

Farro with Chanterelles, Green Beans and Mascarpone

 TOTAL: 40 MIN

6 SERVINGS ●

- 1 pound farro
- Salt
- ¾ pound green beans
- 2 tablespoons unsalted butter
- 1 garlic clove, minced
- ½ pound chanterelle mushrooms, thickly sliced
- Freshly ground pepper
- 1 cup mascarpone (8 ounces)
- ¼ cup snipped chives

1. In a medium saucepan, cover the farro with 2 inches of water, season with salt and bring to a boil. Cover and cook over moderately low heat until the grains are al dente; drain and return to the pot.

2. Meanwhile, in another medium saucepan of boiling salted water, cook the beans until crisp-tender, 5 minutes. Drain and pat dry. Cut the beans into 1-inch lengths.

3. In a skillet, melt the butter. Add the garlic and mushrooms and cook over moderately high heat, stirring occasionally, until the mushrooms are lightly browned, 8 minutes. Add the beans, season with salt and pepper and cook until heated through.

4. Stir the mascarpone and chives into the farro and season lightly with salt and pepper. Spoon into bowls, top with the mushrooms and beans and serve.
—*Johnathan Sundstrom*

Farro Salad with Fried Cauliflower and Prosciutto

TOTAL: 1 HR 30 MIN

8 SERVINGS ● ●

Cooks in Italy fry cauliflower to bring out its nuttiness. Here, Ethan Stowell (an F&W Best New Chef 2008) deep-fries cauliflower for a salad with salty prosciutto and chewy farro.

- 1 pound farro
- 2 carrots, halved crosswise
- 1 small onion, halved
- 1 celery rib, halved crosswise
- 2 garlic cloves, crushed
- 1 bay leaf

Canola oil, for frying

- 2 large heads of cauliflower (2½ pounds each), cut into 1-inch florets
- ½ pound prosciutto, sliced ¼ inch thick and cut into ¼-inch dice
- ½ cup extra-virgin olive oil
- 5 tablespoons fresh lemon juice
- ¼ cup chopped flat-leaf parsley
- 2 teaspoons chopped marjoram

Kosher salt and freshly ground pepper

1. In a large saucepan, combine the farro, carrots, onion, celery, garlic and bay leaf. Add enough cold water to cover the farro by 1 inch and bring to a simmer over high heat. Reduce the heat to moderate and cook until the farro is tender but chewy, 15 minutes; drain. Spread the farro on a rimmed baking sheet to cool. Discard the carrots, onion, celery, garlic and bay leaf.
2. Meanwhile, in a large saucepan, heat 1 inch of canola oil over moderately high heat until a deep-fry thermometer registers 350°. Fry the cauliflower in batches until golden, 5 minutes per batch; drain.
3. In a bowl, mix the farro, cauliflower, prosciutto, olive oil, lemon juice and herbs. Season with salt and pepper and serve.
—*Ethan Stowell*
SERVE WITH Green salad.

Kasha with Red Onions, Sage and Currants

TOTAL: 30 MIN

6 SERVINGS ● ●

Seattle chef Jerry Traunfeld enjoys using kasha, the toasted buckwheat groats that are a staple in Eastern Europe. To keep kasha from getting mushy, Traunfeld mixes it with egg whites before cooking it in a nonstick skillet. Here, he flavors the nutty grains with sweet currants and earthy sage to make an excellent vegetarian side dish.

- 1 cup coarse kasha
- 2 egg whites
- ¼ cup extra-virgin olive oil
- 2 medium red onions, cut into ¼-inch wedges
- 1 tablespoon thinly sliced sage
- 1 tablespoon kosher salt
- 2 cups hot water
- 1 tablespoon balsamic vinegar
- ¼ cup dried currants

1. In a nonstick skillet, mix the kasha with the egg whites. Set the skillet over moderate heat and cook, stirring constantly, until the kasha smells toasted and the grains are separate, about 5 minutes.
2. In a saucepan, heat the olive oil until shimmering. Add the onions and cook over high heat until tender and browned in spots, about 8 minutes. Add the sage and salt and cook for 30 seconds longer. Add the kasha, water and vinegar and bring to a simmer. Cover and cook over low heat until the water has been absorbed, about 12 minutes. Add the currants, fluff the kasha with a fork and serve.
—*Jerry Traunfeld*

Quinoa Salad with Roasted Peppers and Tomatoes

TOTAL: 1 HR

10 SERVINGS ●

Quinoa simmered in water and orange juice gives a citrus hit to this tabbouleh-like salad with tomato, cucumber and roasted bell pepper.

- ¼ cup plus 1 tablespoon extra-virgin olive oil
- 2 cups quinoa (11 ounces), rinsed and drained
- 2 cups fresh orange juice
- 2 cups water

Kosher salt

- 1 large red bell pepper
- 1 large yellow bell pepper
- ½ cup pine nuts
- 1 tablespoon white wine vinegar
- 1 medium cucumber—peeled, halved, seeded and finely diced
- 1 large beefsteak tomato, seeded and finely diced
- ¼ cup finely chopped basil
- ¼ cup finely chopped mint

Freshly ground black pepper

1. In a medium saucepan, heat the 1 tablespoon of olive oil. Add the quinoa and cook over moderately high heat, stirring, until lightly browned, about 4 minutes. Add the orange juice, water and a generous pinch of salt and bring to a boil. Cover and cook over low heat until the liquid is absorbed, about 15 minutes. Fluff the quinoa with a fork and spread on a baking sheet to cool.
2. Meanwhile, roast the red and yellow peppers directly over a gas flame or under the broiler, turning occasionally, until charred all over. Transfer the peppers to a bowl, cover and let steam for 10 minutes. Peel and seed them and cut into ¼-inch dice.
3. In a medium skillet, toast the pine nuts over moderate heat, stirring occasionally, until golden and fragrant, about 5 minutes. Transfer the pine nuts to a plate to cool.
4. In a large bowl, whisk the remaining ¼ cup of olive oil with the vinegar. Add the quinoa, peppers, pine nuts, cucumber, tomato, basil and mint and toss well, breaking up any lumps of quinoa. Season the salad with salt and pepper and serve.
—*Kerry Simon*

MAKE AHEAD The undressed, cooked quinoa and the diced roasted peppers can be refrigerated separately overnight.

QUINOA SALAD WITH PICKLED RADISHES AND FETA

BARLEY SALAD WITH PARSLEY AND WALNUTS

Lemony Quinoa Salad with Pine Nuts and Olives

 **TOTAL: 25 MIN**
1 SERVING ● ●

½ cup water

¼ cup quinoa, rinsed and drained

2 teaspoons pine nuts

2 tablespoons coarsely chopped cilantro

1 tablespoon fresh lemon juice

2 teaspoons chopped pitted green olives, such as Picholine

Salt

1. In a small saucepan, boil the water. Add the quinoa, cover and cook over low heat for about 12 minutes, until al dente. Transfer to a bowl.

2. In a skillet, toast the pine nuts over moderate heat until golden, 2 minutes. Add them to the quinoa along with the cilantro, lemon juice and olives. Season with salt and serve. —*Adina Niemerow*

Quinoa Salad with Pickled Radishes and Feta

ACTIVE: 30 MIN; TOTAL: 1 HR 15 MIN
6 SERVINGS ● ● ● ●

1 cup red wine vinegar

1½ tablespoons sugar

4 medium radishes, very thinly sliced

½ pound thin green beans

1 cup quinoa, rinsed and drained

1 large English cucumber— halved lengthwise, seeded and cut into ¼-inch dice

3½ tablespoons extra-virgin olive oil

Kosher salt and freshly ground black pepper

2 tablespoons chopped flat-leaf parsley

3 tablespoons fresh lemon juice

6 ounces Greek feta cheese, thinly sliced

1. In a small saucepan, bring the red wine vinegar to a simmer with the sugar. Remove from the heat and add the radish slices. Let stand until cool, about 1 hour.

2. Meanwhile, in a large saucepan of salted boiling water, blanch the green beans until they are crisp-tender, about 3 minutes. Drain and rinse the beans under cold water until cool. Pat the beans dry and cut them into 1½-inch lengths.

3. In a medium saucepan, bring 1¾ cups of water to a boil. Add the quinoa, cover and simmer over low heat until all of the water has been absorbed, about 12 minutes. Uncover and let stand until cool, about 10 minutes.

4. In a medium bowl, toss the cucumber with ½ tablespoon of the olive oil and season with salt and pepper. In a large bowl, toss the quinoa with the parsley, lemon juice and the remaining 3 tablespoons of olive oil; season with salt and pepper. Drain

the radishes and add them to the quinoa along with the beans, cucumber and feta. Toss well and serve. —*Giuseppe Tentori*
MAKE AHEAD The quinoa salad can be refrigerated for up to 3 hours.

Barley Salad with Parsley and Walnuts

TOTAL: 40 MIN
6 SERVINGS ● ●

Barley is versatile enough to be served warm or at room temperature, as in this terrific salad with walnuts, parsley and bits of salty *ricotta salata* cheese in a lemon-garlic vinaigrette. The salad can be served as a main course or as a side for grilled chicken or pork.

1¼ cups pearled barley (9 ounces)
1 cup walnut halves (4 ounces)
3 tablespoons fresh lemon juice
⅓ cup extra-virgin olive oil
1 garlic clove, minced
½ teaspoon finely grated lemon zest
Salt and freshly ground pepper
1 cup packed flat-leaf parsley leaves
4 ounces *ricotta salata,* crumbled (about 1 cup)

1. Preheat the oven to 350°. In a large saucepan of boiling salted water, cook the barley over high heat until tender, about 25 minutes. Drain the barley and rinse under cold water to cool thoroughly. Drain again, shaking out the excess water.
2. Meanwhile, spread the walnuts halves in a pie plate and toast for 10 to 12 minutes, until golden and fragrant. Transfer to a cutting board and let cool. Coarsely chop the nuts.
3. In a large bowl, whisk the lemon juice with the olive oil, garlic and lemon zest and season with salt and pepper. Add the barley, parsley and *ricotta salata* and toss gently. Add the toasted walnuts, toss again and serve. —*Grace Parisi*
MAKE AHEAD The salad can be refrigerated overnight.

Hung's Clay Pot Rice
ACTIVE: 30 MIN; TOTAL: 1 HR PLUS 1 HR SOAKING
4 SERVINGS ●

As a student at the Culinary Institute of America in Hyde Park, New York, *Top Chef* Season 3 winner Hung Huynh learned to cook with the Chinese trinity—GGS, or ginger, garlic and scallions. He uses all three here to flavor his earthy mushroom-and-bacon-studded clay pot rice.

1 cup short-grain rice (7 ounces)
3 ounces mixed mushrooms, such as oyster and stemmed shiitake, quartered if large (2 cups)
2 scallions, coarsely chopped
1 tablespoon plus 1 teaspoon low-sodium soy sauce
Salt and freshly ground pepper
2 thick slices of fatty bacon, cut into ½-inch dice (½ cup)
2 garlic cloves, minced
2 teaspoons minced fresh ginger
½ cup ginkgo nuts (optional; see Note)
1 cup water
1 tablespoon vegetable oil

1. In a bowl, cover the rice with water and let soak until the grains turn white, about 1 hour. Drain the rice.
2. In another bowl, toss the mushrooms and scallions with 1 tablespoon of the soy sauce and season with salt and pepper; let marinate for 10 minutes.
3. In a small enameled cast-iron casserole, clay pot or medium saucepan, cook the bacon over moderate heat until the fat is rendered and the bacon is crisp, about 5 minutes. Add the garlic and ginger and cook, stirring, until fragrant, about 1 minute. Add the soaked rice and stir to coat with the fat. Add the ginkgo nuts, marinated mushrooms and scallions, the water and the remaining 1 teaspoon of soy sauce. Bring to a boil over moderately high heat. Drizzle the oil around the edge of the pot so it runs down the inside.

4. Cover the pot and cook over low heat until the rice is tender and the liquid has been absorbed, 10 minutes. Raise the heat to high, cover and cook until the rice is sizzling and a crust forms on the bottom, about 5 minutes. Remove the pot from the heat and let stand, covered, for 5 minutes. Fluff the rice with a fork and serve. —*Hung Huynh*
NOTE Ginkgo nuts, which are slightly sweet and have a soft texture like soybeans, are available in Chinese markets.

Shiitake Sticky Rice
TOTAL: 45 MIN PLUS OVERNIGHT SOAKING
4 SERVINGS ●

1½ tablespoons vegetable oil
1 medium onion, cut into ¼-inch dice
½ pound shiitake mushrooms, stems discarded and caps cut into 1-inch pieces
2 Chinese sausages, cut into ¼-inch rounds
¼ cup dry white wine
1½ cups Asian short-grain sticky rice, soaked overnight and drained
1½ cups chicken stock
2 teaspoons low-sodium soy sauce
1 teaspoon kosher salt
2 tablespoons chopped parsley

1. In a medium saucepan, heat the oil. Add the onion and cook over moderate heat until softened, about 5 minutes. Add the shiitake and cook, stirring occasionally, until softened, about 4 minutes. Add the Chinese sausages and wine and bring to a boil over moderately high heat. Stir in the rice, chicken stock, soy sauce and salt and bring to a boil, stirring a few times.
2. Cover the rice and cook over low heat until the stock is absorbed and the rice is tender, about 12 minutes. Let the rice stand, covered, for 5 minutes, then stir in the parsley and serve. —*Marcia Kiesel*

Pistachio-Apricot Biryani

ACTIVE: 1 HR; TOTAL: 2 HR

6 SERVINGS

Many Indian restaurants call any spiced rice dish *biryani,* but New York City chef and cookbook author Suvir Saran insists that *biryani* must be layered. Here, he boils rice like pasta to make it fluffy, then layers it in a casserole dish with yogurt, pistachios and apricots. In traditional Indian kitchens, the *biryani* would then be cooked in a clay or tin pot over coal embers, but Saran swears by his Emile Henry casserole dish, which heats slowly and evenly.

- 2 cups dried apricots (10 ounces), cut into 1-inch pieces
- 2½ cups basmati rice
- 2 tablespoons vegetable oil, plus more for frying
- 1 large red onion, thinly sliced
- 1 teaspoon saffron threads
- ½ cup milk
- 2 teaspoons cumin seeds
- 3 garlic cloves, very finely chopped

One 2-inch piece of fresh ginger, peeled and finely julienned (¼ cup)

- 2 cups plain yogurt
- ½ teaspoon cayenne pepper
- 1 cup water
- 2½ cups unsalted shelled pistachios (8½ ounces), ½ cup chopped for garnish
- 1 tablespoon garam masala

Salt

- 4 tablespoons unsalted butter, melted
- 2 serrano chiles, seeded and very finely chopped
- ½ cup finely chopped mint
- ¼ cup finely chopped cilantro

1. In a large bowl, cover the dried apricots with warm water and let stand for about 1 hour, then drain. In a medium bowl, cover the rice with water and let soak for about 30 minutes, then drain.

2. Meanwhile, in a medium saucepan, heat 1 inch of vegetable oil to 325°. Add the onion slices and fry, stirring occasionally, until browned and crisp, about 7 minutes. Drain on paper towels.

3. In a large saucepan, toast the saffron over moderately high heat for 30 seconds. Transfer to a small bowl and let cool. Crumble the threads and add the milk.

4. In the same large saucepan, heat the 2 tablespoons of oil. Add the cumin seeds and cook over moderately high heat until fragrant. Add the garlic and 2 tablespoons of the ginger and cook over moderately high heat until the garlic is golden. Add the yogurt, cayenne pepper and the cup of water and simmer over low heat, stirring occasionally, for 5 minutes. Add the apricots, whole pistachios and garam masala and simmer for 5 minutes, stirring occasionally. Season with salt.

5. Preheat the oven to 325°. In another large saucepan of boiling salted water, cook the rice until al dente. Drain and return to the saucepan. Stir in half of the saffron milk, cover and set aside. Add the remaining saffron milk to the pistachio-yogurt mixture.

6. Spread half of the pistachio-yogurt mixture in a large, deep casserole or Dutch oven. Drizzle 1 tablespoon of the melted butter over the mixture and top with half of the chiles and fried onion and 1 tablespoon of the ginger. Spread half of the rice in the casserole and drizzle with 1 tablespoon of the melted butter. Spread with the remaining pistachio-yogurt mixture, drizzle with 1 tablespoon of the butter and scatter the remaining chiles, fried onion and 1 tablespoon of ginger on top. Cover with the remaining rice and drizzle on the remaining 1 tablespoon of melted butter. Cover the casserole tightly with foil, then cover with a lid.

7. Bake the *biryani* for about 15 minutes, until heated through. Uncover the *biryani,* garnish with the chopped pistachios, mint and cilantro and serve immediately.

—*Suvir Saran*

Crab-and-Andouille Jambalaya

 TOTAL: 40 MIN

4 SERVINGS

- ¼ cup extra-virgin olive oil
- 12 ounces andouille sausage or kielbasa, quartered lengthwise and cut into ¾-inch pieces
- 1 large onion, coarsely chopped
- 1 red bell pepper, finely chopped
- 1 celery rib, finely chopped
- 2 large garlic cloves, very finely chopped
- 1 teaspoon Old Bay seasoning
- 1¼ cups jasmine rice (9 ounces), rinsed
- 1½ cups chicken stock or low-sodium broth
- 1½ cups water
- 1 thyme sprig

Salt and freshly ground black pepper

- 8 ounces lump crabmeat
- 3 scallions, finely chopped

Hot sauce, for serving

1. In a medium enameled cast-iron casserole, heat the olive oil. Add the andouille and cook over high heat, stirring occasionally, until lightly browned, about 3 minutes. Transfer to a bowl.

2. Add the onion, bell pepper, celery and garlic to the casserole. Cover and cook over high heat, stirring occasionally, until the vegetables are softened, about 3 minutes. Add the Old Bay, rice and andouille and cook, stirring occasionally, until the rice is opaque, about 2 minutes. Add the chicken stock, water and thyme, season lightly with salt and black pepper and bring to a boil. Cover and cook over very low heat until the rice is tender and the liquid is absorbed, about 15 minutes. Fluff the rice with a fork and stir in the crab meat and scallions. Cover and let stand for 2 to 3 minutes, just until the crab is hot; discard the thyme sprig. Serve the jambalaya in bowls, passing hot sauce at the table.

—*Grace Parisi*

PISTACHIO-APRICOT BIRYANI

CRAB-AND-ANDOUILLE JAMBALAYA

Jasmine Rice with Carrot Relish

 TOTAL: 25 MIN
4 SERVINGS ● ●

⅔ cup jasmine rice, rinsed
1⅓ cups water
2 tablespoons fresh lime juice
1 tablespoon vegetable oil
1 tablespoon Asian fish sauce
1½ teaspoons honey
1 tablespoon chopped mint
1 garlic clove, minced
½ Thai chile, minced
4 medium carrots, peeled and coarsely shredded

1. In a small saucepan, combine the rice and water and bring to a boil. Cover and cook over low heat for 12 minutes. Quickly remove the lid and wipe off any water that clings to it. Cover the rice again immediately and let stand off the heat for 5 minutes. Fluff the rice with a fork and cover.

2. In a bowl, combine the lime juice with the oil, fish sauce, honey, mint, garlic and chile. Add the carrots and toss to coat with the sauce. Serve the carrot relish on the rice. —*Marcia Kiesel*

Jamaican Rice and Peas

 ACTIVE: 15 MIN; TOTAL: 40 MIN
6 SERVINGS ● ● ●

This spicy side is great alongside jerk or curry dishes. "Peas" in Jamaica refers to beans—in this case, kidney beans.

2 tablespoons canola oil
1 small onion, finely chopped
1½ tablespoons finely grated fresh ginger
2 cups long-grain white rice, such as jasmine
One 15-ounce can kidney beans, drained and rinsed
½ Scotch bonnet or habanero chile, seeded

One 14-ounce can unsweetened coconut milk
1½ cups water
Salt and freshly ground pepper
4 scallions, thinly sliced

1. In a large saucepan, heat the oil. Add the onion and ginger and cook over moderate heat, stirring, until softened, about 5 minutes. Add the rice and cook, stirring, until coated with the oil. Stir in the kidney beans and Scotch bonnet, then stir in the coconut milk and water. Season with salt and pepper and bring to a boil. Cover and cook over low heat until the rice is tender and the liquid is absorbed, 18 minutes.

2. Remove the rice from the heat and let stand, covered, for 5 minutes. Fluff with a fork. Stir in the scallions and season with salt and pepper. Discard the Scotch bonnet and serve. —*Bradford Thompson*

MAKE AHEAD The Jamaican Rice and Peas can be refrigerated overnight.

potatoes, grains & beans

Green-Chile Rice with Beans

 **TOTAL: 30 MIN**
6 SERVINGS

For an elegant version of everyday rice and beans, F&W's Melissa Rubel starts with fragrant basmati rice, then cooks it with wonderfully aromatic flavorings like onion, garlic and cumin. She mixes in vibrant green chiles and pinto beans, then serves the dish in the traditional Latin manner— with a bracing dash of hot sauce.

- 1 tablespoon unsalted butter
- 2 tablespoons extra-virgin olive oil
- 1 medium onion, cut into ¼-inch dice
- 2 medium garlic cloves, very finely chopped
- 1 teaspoon ground cumin
- 2 cups basmati rice

Two 4-ounce cans green chiles, drained

Two 15-ounce cans pinto beans, drained and rinsed

- 3½ cups water
- 1 tablespoon kosher salt

Hot sauce, for serving

In a large saucepan, melt the butter in the olive oil. Add the diced onion and chopped garlic and cook over moderately high heat, stirring occasionally, until the onion is softened, about 3 minutes. Add the ground cumin and cook, stirring, until fragrant. Add the basmati rice and stir until the grains of rice are evenly coated with fat, about 30 seconds. Gently stir in the drained green chiles and pinto beans. Add the water and kosher salt and bring to a simmer. Cover and cook the rice and beans over low heat until the water is absorbed, about 15 minutes. Remove the saucepan from the heat and let stand, covered, until the rice is tender, about 5 minutes. Gently fluff the rice with a fork, being careful not to break up the beans, and serve with hot sauce. —*Melissa Rubel*

SERVE WITH Roasted chicken or fish.

Rice with Chorizo, Shrimp and Green Olives

TOTAL: 45 MIN
4 SERVINGS

This recipe relies on excellent chorizo, the Spanish pork sausage. First the chorizo is cooked in a casserole dish so that it crisps in its own deliciously spiced fat; then the rice is prepared in the same dish so it absorbs any fat left in the pan.

- ¾ pound dry chorizo, sliced on the bias ¼ inch thick
- ¾ pound shelled and deveined large shrimp
- 1 onion, cut into ¼-inch dice
- 1 large garlic clove, minced
- 3¼ cups water
- 2 cups basmati rice

Kosher salt and freshly ground pepper

- 12 large pimiento-stuffed green olives, thinly sliced
- 2 tablespoons chopped flat-leaf parsley

Lemon wedges and hot sauce, for serving

1. Heat a medium enameled cast-iron casserole. Add the chorizo and cook over moderately high heat until it starts to crisp, about 3 minutes. Add the shrimp and cook, stirring occasionally, until white throughout, about 3 minutes. Using a slotted spoon, transfer the chorizo and shrimp to a plate. Drain off all but 2 tablespoons of the fat in the casserole.

2. Add the onion and garlic to the casserole and cook over moderate heat until tender, about 3 minutes. Add the water and rice and bring to a boil. Season with salt and pepper. Cover and cook over low heat until the rice is just tender, about 18 minutes. Remove from the heat and let stand, covered, until all of the water is absorbed, about 5 minutes. Gently fold in the chorizo, shrimp, olives and parsley and season with salt and pepper. Spoon the rice into shallow bowls and serve with lemon wedges and hot sauce. —*Melissa Rubel*

Seafood-and-Chicken Paella with Chorizo

TOTAL: 1 HR
6 SERVINGS

Chef Tamara Murphy makes her own chorizo for the paella served at her Seattle restaurant, Brasa. As for the seafood in the dish, Murphy breaks with Spanish tradition by sautéing the shrimp and steaming the mussels and clams before adding them to the paella during the last few minutes of cooking; this keeps the seafood moist and delicious.

- 4 ounces fresh chorizo, casings removed
- 1 small onion, thinly sliced
- 1 garlic clove, thinly sliced
- ½ cup canned diced tomatoes
- 1 cup arborio rice

Pinch of saffron threads dissolved in 2 tablespoons of water

- 1½ cups water

Salt and freshly ground pepper

- ¼ cup plus 1 tablespoon extra-virgin olive oil
- 1 pound large shrimp, shelled and deveined
- ¼ cup dry white wine
- 1 tablespoon fresh lemon juice
- ½ pound mussels, scrubbed and debearded
- ½ pound cockles, scrubbed and rinsed
- 1½ cups cooked chicken, preferably dark meat (8 ounces)
- 2 tablespoons chopped flat-leaf parsley
- 1 scallion, thinly sliced

1. Preheat the oven to 350°. In a 10-inch paella pan or ovenproof skillet, cook the chorizo over moderate heat, breaking it up with a spoon, until some of the fat is rendered and the chorizo is browned, 4 minutes. Add the onion and garlic and cook over low heat, stirring, until softened and just beginning to brown, 8 minutes. Stir in the tomatoes, rice, saffron with its liquid

and the 1½ cups of water. Season with salt and pepper and bring to a boil. Cover and simmer over low heat, without stirring, until the rice is al dente and the liquid is absorbed, 15 minutes.

2. In a large skillet, heat the ¼ cup of olive oil until shimmering. Season the shrimp with salt and pepper, add them to the skillet and cook over high heat, turning once, until pink and cooked through, about 3 minutes. Using a slotted spoon, transfer the shrimp to the rice. Discard the oil.

3. Wipe out the skillet. Pour in the wine and lemon juice. Add the mussels and cockles, cover and cook, shaking the skillet, until the shellfish open, about 3 minutes. Discard any shellfish that do not open. Pour the mussels and cockles and their cooking liquid over the rice.

4. Stir the cooked chicken into the rice. Cover and cook in the oven for about 5 minutes, until the paella is just heated through. Garnish with the parsley and scallion, drizzle with the remaining 1 tablespoon of olive oil and serve.
—*Tamara Murphy*

Quick Three-Bean Chili

TOTAL: 30 MIN
4 SERVINGS ● ●

Some chilis need to simmer for a long time to help the flavors develop. Here, though, a little bit of bacon instantly adds meatiness and a nice smoky flavor.

- 2 tablespoons vegetable oil
- 3 slices of bacon, cut crosswise into ¼-inch strips
- 1 onion, cut into ¼-inch dice
- 2 jalapeños, seeded and cut into ¼-inch dice
- 2 garlic cloves, very finely chopped
- ¼ cup chili powder
- One 15-ounce can Great Northern beans, drained and rinsed
- One 15-ounce can pinto beans, drained and rinsed
- One 15-ounce can black beans, drained and rinsed
- One 28-ounce can diced tomatoes
- 2 cups chicken stock or low-sodium broth
- Kosher salt and freshly ground black pepper
- Chopped cilantro and sour cream, for serving

In a medium soup pot, heat the vegetable oil until hot. Add the bacon strips, diced onion and jalapeños and chopped garlic and cook over moderately high heat until the onion is softened and the bacon fat has been rendered, about 5 minutes. Add the chili powder and cook over moderate heat until fragrant, about 1 minute. Stir in the beans, tomatoes and stock and bring to a simmer. Simmer the chili over moderately low heat until thickened, about 15 minutes. Season with salt and pepper and serve with cilantro and sour cream.
—*Melissa Rubel*

Cassoulet with Duck Confit

ACTIVE: 50 MIN; TOTAL: 3 HR PLUS 2 HR SOAKING AND OVERNIGHT RESTING
8 SERVINGS ●

Chef Laurence Jossel of San Francisco's Nopa restaurant created this stripped-down version of the classic French stew, with creamy white beans, store-bought duck confit, smoky French garlic sausage and slab bacon. Letting the beans rest overnight develops their flavors.

- 5 tablespoons extra-virgin olive oil
- Two ½-inch-thick slices of pancetta (4 ounces), cut into ½-inch dice
- 1 medium onion, cut into ½-inch dice
- 1 pound dried flageolets or Great Northern beans, rinsed and picked over, then soaked for 2 hours and drained
- 4 thyme sprigs
- 2 quarts water
- 1 quart chicken stock
- 1 large head of garlic, separated into cloves and peeled
- Kosher salt
- 4 pieces of duck leg confit, trimmed of excess fat
- ¾ pound French garlic sausage, sliced crosswise ½ inch thick
- 4 ounces lean slab bacon, cut into 1-inch cubes
- 2 cups coarse fresh bread crumbs
- 2 tablespoons chopped parsley

1. In a large saucepan, heat 3 tablespoons of the olive oil. Add the pancetta and cook over moderate heat until the fat has been rendered, about 5 minutes. Add the onion and cook, stirring occasionally, until softened, about 7 minutes. Add the beans, thyme sprigs, water and stock and bring to a boil. Simmer over low heat, stirring and skimming occasionally, until the beans are al dente, about 1 hour.

2. Add the garlic cloves to the beans and simmer until the garlic and beans are tender, about 15 minutes. Discard the thyme sprigs. Season the beans with salt and let cool to room temperature. Cover and refrigerate the saucepan overnight.

3. Preheat the oven to 350°. Rewarm the beans over moderate heat. Transfer the beans to a large, deep baking dish. Nestle the duck legs, garlic sausage and bacon into the beans. Bake for about 40 minutes, until the cassoulet is bubbling and all of the meats are hot. Remove from the oven and let rest for 15 minutes.

4. In a skillet, heat the remaining 2 tablespoons of olive oil. Add the bread crumbs and cook over moderately high heat, stirring, until browned and crisp, about 3 minutes. Sprinkle the bread crumbs and the parsley over the cassoulet and serve.
—*Laurence Jossel*

MAKE AHEAD The cassoulet can be prepared through Step 3 and refrigerated for up to 2 days. Rewarm before proceeding.

MAPLE-GLAZED BEANS

Maple-Glazed Beans

ACTIVE: 20 MIN; TOTAL: 7 HR 45 MIN
PLUS OVERNIGHT SOAKING
6 SERVINGS ● ●

- 1 pound dried yellow eye or navy beans, rinsed and picked over, then soaked overnight and drained
- 2 cloves
- 1 small onion, sliced ½ inch thick
- 2 bay leaves
- ½ pound meaty bacon, fat side scored
- ½ cup pure maple syrup
- 3 tablespoons Worcestershire sauce
- 2 teaspoons dry mustard
- ¼ cup plus 1 tablespoon ketchup
- 2 teaspoons kosher salt
- 1 tablespoon Dijon mustard

1. Preheat the oven to 325°. In a large pot, cover the beans with 2 inches of water and bring to a boil. Reduce the heat to low and simmer, skimming occasionally, until the skins peel back when you blow on them, about 1 hour. Reserve 4 cups of the cooking liquid and drain the beans.

2. Transfer the drained beans to a 10-by-13-inch baking dish. Stick the cloves in a slice of onion; nestle the onion slices, bay leaves and bacon, fat side up, among the beans.

3. In a bowl, whisk 2 cups of the reserved cooking liquid with the maple syrup, Worcestershire, dry mustard, ¼ cup of the ketchup and 1 teaspoon of the salt; pour over the beans and bake for 3 hours.

4. Stir the remaining 1 teaspoon of salt into 1 cup of the cooking liquid; pour over the beans and bake for 1½ hours longer.

5. Whisk the remaining cooking liquid and ketchup with the Dijon mustard; pour over the beans. Bake for 1½ hours longer, until the beans are richly browned. Let stand for 15 minutes. Discard the cloves and bay leaves, and serve. —*Marcia Kiesel*

Baked Beans with Maple-Glazed Bacon

ACTIVE: 35 MIN; TOTAL: 4 HR PLUS
2 HR SOAKING
8 SERVINGS ●

- 3½ cups dried yellow eye or cannellini beans, rinsed and picked over, then soaked for 2 hours and drained
- Kosher salt
- 9 thick slices of bacon, 1 slice cut crosswise into ¼-inch strips
- 1 large onion, cut into ½-inch dice
- 1 cup apple cider vinegar
- ¼ cup dark brown sugar
- ¼ cup dark unsulfured molasses
- 1 teaspoon crushed red pepper
- ½ teaspoon freshly ground black pepper
- ¼ cup pure maple syrup
- 1 tablespoon red wine vinegar
- 1½ teaspoons Dijon mustard

1. In a large pot, cover the beans with 2 inches of water and bring to a boil. Simmer over low heat, stirring occasionally, until just tender, about 2 hours; add water as needed to keep the beans covered by 2 inches. Season with salt and let stand for 5 minutes. Drain the beans, reserving 4 cups of the cooking liquid. Transfer the beans to a large, deep baking dish.

2. Preheat the oven to 350°. In a skillet, cook the bacon strips over moderate heat until the fat has rendered, 5 minutes. Add the onion and cook over moderately low heat until softened, 10 minutes. Stir in the vinegar, brown sugar, molasses, red pepper, black pepper and 1½ tablespoons of salt and simmer for 1 minute. Pour the bacon-onion mixture over the beans and stir in the reserved bean cooking liquid. Cover with foil and bake for 45 minutes.

3. Meanwhile, in a small bowl, mix the maple syrup with the red wine vinegar and mustard. Arrange the remaining 8 bacon slices on a rimmed baking sheet; generously brush them with the maple syrup

mixture. Bake the bacon in the same oven as the beans for about 15 minutes, basting 3 times and turning the bacon twice, until richly glazed. Transfer the bacon to a plate.

4. Carefully pour ⅓ cup of water onto the baking sheet and return it to the oven for 3 minutes to dissolve the caramelized syrup. Uncover the beans; stir in the syrup. Bake the beans, uncovered, for 20 minutes, until the liquid has reduced by one-fourth.

5. Increase the oven temperature to 400°. Top the beans with the bacon; bake until browned, 15 minutes. Let rest for 10 minutes before serving. —*Laurence Jossel*

Refried Beans with Spicy Pickled Nopales

ACTIVE: 45 MIN; TOTAL: 3 HR 45 MIN
PLUS 2 HR SOAKING
8 SERVINGS ● ● ●

- 2 cups dried pinto beans, rinsed and picked over, then soaked for 2 hours and drained
- Kosher salt
- 3 tablespoons lard or bacon fat
- ½ medium red onion, finely diced
- 1½ teaspoons dried Mexican oregano
- Warm tortillas, crumbled *queso fresco,* and Spicy Pickled Nopales (p. 378)

1. In a saucepan, cover the beans with 2 inches of water and simmer over low heat, stirring occasionally, until tender, about 3 hours. Add water as necessary to keep the beans covered by 2 inches. Season the beans with salt and let stand for 5 minutes; drain, reserving 1 cup of the cooking liquid.

2. In a large skillet, heat the lard. Add the onion and cook over moderately low heat, stirring, until softened, 7 minutes. Add the beans, oregano and ½ cup of the reserved cooking liquid. Using a potato masher, coarsely mash the beans. Add more of the reserved bean liquid until the mixture is thick but not soupy. Season with salt. Transfer the beans to a bowl and serve with the tortillas, *queso fresco* and Spicy Pickled Nopales. —*Laurence Jossel*

potatoes, grains & beans

New Year's Day Black-Eyed Peas

ACTIVE: 30 MIN; TOTAL: 2 HR 30 MIN PLUS OVERNIGHT SOAKING

10 SERVINGS ● ●

Many Southerners believe that eating black-eyed peas on New Year's Day brings good luck. Chef Ryan Hardy, who grew up in the South, has childhood memories of black-eyed peas simmering on the stove.

- 6 tablespoons extra-virgin olive oil, plus more for brushing
- 1 very large onion, finely chopped
- 1 very large carrot, finely chopped
- 5 garlic cloves—4 minced, 1 whole
- 1 pound dried black-eyed peas (about 2¼ cups), soaked overnight and drained
- Two 1-pound smoked ham hocks
- 2 quarts chicken stock
- 2 bay leaves
- Salt and freshly ground pepper
- 1 small baguette, sliced diagonally ¾ inch thick
- Freshly grated Parmigiano-Reggiano cheese, for serving

1. In a large enameled cast-iron casserole, heat 2 tablespoons of the olive oil. Add the onion, carrot and minced garlic and cook over moderate heat, stirring occasionally, until softened, 6 minutes. Add the drained black-eyed peas, smoked ham hocks, stock and bay leaves and bring to a boil. Reduce the heat to very low, cover partially and cook until the beans are tender, about 1½ hours. Season the beans generously with salt and pepper and let stand for 30 minutes.

2. Meanwhile, preheat the oven to 350°. Toast the bread slices in the oven for about 8 minutes, until golden. Brush with olive oil and rub lightly with the garlic clove.

3. Drain the black-eyed peas; discard the ham hocks and bay leaves. Transfer the black-eyed peas to a serving bowl. Stir in the remaining ¼ cup of oil and season with salt and pepper. Serve with the toasts, passing grated cheese at the table. —*Ryan Hardy*

Spiced Pinto Beans with Chorizo

 TOTAL: 20 MIN

4 SERVINGS ●

- 1 tablespoon extra-virgin olive oil
- 1 small onion, finely diced
- 1 garlic clove, minced
- ½ teaspoon ground cumin
- ¼ teaspoon chipotle powder
- 8 ounces fresh chorizo or hot Italian sausage, casings removed
- One 15-ounce can pinto beans, with their liquid
- 2 tablespoons water
- Salt and freshly ground pepper
- 1 cup fried pork rinds, coarsely chopped, for garnish

In a medium saucepan, heat the oil until shimmering. Add the onion, garlic, cumin and chipotle and cook over moderate heat until softened, 5 minutes. Add the chorizo and cook, breaking up the meat into small lumps with a spoon, until lightly browned, about 5 minutes. Add the beans and their liquid along with the water and simmer until slightly thickened, about 5 minutes. Season with salt and pepper. Spoon the beans into bowls, sprinkle pork rinds on top and serve at once. —*Dionicio Jimenez*

Bean-and-Leek Cassoulet

ACTIVE: 45 MIN; TOTAL: 2 HR 35 MIN

6 SERVINGS ● ● ●

- 2¼ pounds fresh cranberry beans, shelled (3 cups)
- Kosher salt
- 12 thyme sprigs, tied together with butcher's string, plus 1 tablespoon chopped thyme
- 2 bay leaves
- ½ ounce dried porcini mushrooms
- 3 large leeks, white and light green parts only, halved lengthwise and sliced crosswise ½ inch thick
- 2 tablespoons unsalted butter
- ½ cup crème fraîche
- 1 tablespoon chopped marjoram
- Freshly ground black pepper
- 1 cup *panko* (Japanese bread crumbs)
- 2 tablespoons extra-virgin olive oil

1. In a large soup pot, cover the cranberry beans with 3 quarts of cold water. Add 1 tablespoon of kosher salt, the bundle of thyme sprigs and the bay leaves. Bring to a simmer and cook over moderate heat until the beans are tender, about 40 minutes. Drain the beans and discard the thyme sprigs and bay leaves.

2. Meanwhile, in a large bowl, pour 4 cups of boiling water over the dried porcini and let stand until the mushrooms are soft, about 15 minutes. Remove the mushrooms and squeeze them dry over the bowl; reserve the soaking liquid. Coarsely chop the mushrooms.

3. Preheat the oven to 375°. Position a rack in the top third of the oven. Slowly pour the mushroom soaking liquid into a large saucepan, discarding the last bit of gritty liquid. Add the porcini, leeks, butter and 2 teaspoons of salt. Bring to a simmer and cook over moderate heat until the leeks are very tender and the liquid has thickened slightly, about 35 minutes. Remove from the heat. Stir in the crème fraîche, 2 teaspoons of the chopped thyme, 2 teaspoons of the chopped marjoram and the reserved beans. Season with salt and pepper. Transfer the bean mixture to a 9-by-13-inch baking dish.

4. In a small bowl, toss the *panko* with the olive oil and the remaining 1 teaspoon each of chopped thyme and marjoram; season with salt and pepper. Sprinkle the *panko* over the beans. Bake for about 40 minutes, until the beans are bubbling and the *panko* is browned. Remove the cassoulet from the oven and let stand for 5 minutes. Spoon into warm bowls and serve.

—*Jerry Traunfeld*

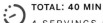

Chickpea Tagine

ACTIVE: 30 MIN; TOTAL: 1 HR 40 MIN
PLUS OVERNIGHT SOAKING

6 SERVINGS ● ●

This hearty and fragrant chickpea stew was inspired by a trip to Morocco's High Atlas Mountains.

- 1 cup dried chickpeas, soaked overnight and drained
- ¼ teaspoon saffron threads
- 1 quart plus 2 tablespoons water
- 1 large onion, finely diced
- 2 garlic cloves, thinly sliced
- 1 tablespoon unsalted butter
- 2 tablespoons extra-virgin olive oil
- 2 teaspoons ground cumin

One 3-inch cinnamon stick
- ¼ teaspoon crushed red pepper
- ½ pound butternut squash, peeled and cut into 1-inch dice
- 2 medium red potatoes, peeled and cut into 1-inch dice

One 14.5-ounce can whole tomatoes, drained and chopped

Salt
- 2 small zucchini, diced
- 1 tablespoon minced preserved lemon rind

Freshly ground black pepper
- 3 tablespoons chopped cilantro

Yogurt and *harissa,* for serving

1. In a saucepan, cover the chickpeas with 2 inches of water and bring to a boil. Reduce the heat to low and simmer until tender, about 45 minutes. Drain.

2. In a bowl, crumble the saffron in the 2 tablespoons of water; steep for 10 minutes.

3. In a deep skillet, cook the onion and garlic in the butter and oil over moderate heat until golden, 8 minutes. Add the cumin, cinnamon stick and crushed red pepper and cook for 2 minutes. Add the saffron water, chickpeas, squash, potatoes, tomatoes, the quart of water and a large pinch of salt; bring to a boil, then simmer until the squash and potatoes are tender, 30 minutes.

4. Add the zucchini and the preserved lemon; simmer until the zucchini is tender, 5 minutes. Discard the cinnamon stick. Season the tagine with salt and pepper and stir in the cilantro. Serve in bowls with yogurt and *harissa.* —*Christine Manfield*

MAKE AHEAD The Chickpea Tagine can be refrigerated for up to 2 days. Reheat before serving.

Indian Spiced Chickpea Salad with Yogurt and Herbs

 TOTAL: 20 MIN

6 SERVINGS ● ● ○ ○

At Poppy, his new Seattle restaurant, Jerry Traunfeld serves each guest an assortment of small plates. He flavors this creamy chickpea salad with aromatic herbs and Indian spices, among them mustard, cumin and fennel seeds.

Two 15-ounce cans chickpeas—rinsed, drained and patted dry
- 2 tablespoons peanut oil
- 1 teaspoon mustard seeds
- ¾ teaspoon cumin seeds
- ¾ teaspoon fennel seeds
- ¼ teaspoon crushed red pepper
- ¾ cup plain whole-milk yogurt
- 1½ tablespoons fresh lemon juice
- 2 scallions, thinly sliced
- ¼ cup chopped cilantro
- ¼ cup chopped mint
- 1 teaspoon kosher salt

Pour the chickpeas into a large bowl. In a small skillet, heat the peanut oil until shimmering. Add the mustard seeds, partially cover the skillet and cook over moderately high heat until the mustard seeds stop popping, about 1 minute. Add the cumin and fennel seeds and the crushed red pepper and cook until the mixture is fragrant, about 30 seconds. Pour the hot oil and spices over the chickpeas. Stir in the yogurt, lemon juice, sliced scallions, chopped cilantro and mint and salt. Serve the chickpea salad at room temperature. —*Jerry Traunfeld*

Oven-Braised Chickpeas and Merguez with Yogurt and Mint

TOTAL: 40 MIN

4 SERVINGS ●

This dish was inspired by the Middle Eastern combination of spiced lamb and yogurt. Using merguez (a hot North African sausage made with lamb, or sometimes beef) is a quick way to get that spiced-meat flavor.

- 2 tablespoons extra-virgin olive oil
- 1 pound merguez sausage or andouille, cut into 5-inch lengths
- 1 red onion, cut into ¼-inch dice
- 1 large garlic clove, minced
- ½ teaspoon ground cumin

Two 15-ounce cans chickpeas, drained and rinsed

Kosher salt and freshly ground black pepper
- ⅓ cup chicken stock or low-sodium broth
- ½ cup plain yogurt
- 2 tablespoons finely shredded mint leaves

1. Preheat the oven to 400°. In a large ovenproof skillet, heat the olive oil. Add the merguez and cook over moderately high heat, turning occasionally, until browned all over, about 5 minutes. Transfer the merguez to a plate.

2. Add the red onion, garlic and cumin to the skillet and cook over moderate heat until the onion is softened, about 3 minutes. Stir in the drained chickpeas and season with salt and pepper. Return the merguez and any juices to the skillet. Add the chicken stock. Transfer the skillet to the oven and bake for 15 minutes, until the merguez is cooked through.

3. Spoon the chickpeas into wide, shallow bowls and top with the browned merguez sausage. Spoon the plain yogurt over the top, sprinkle with the shredded mint leaves and serve immediately. —*Melissa Rubel*

potatoes, grains & beans

Chickpea-and-Spinach Stew

TOTAL: 35 MIN

4 SERVINGS ● ● ● ●

Spanish cookbook author Janet Mendel uses tomato, golden raisins and saffron to transform canned chickpeas in this sweet and savory specialty of Seville.

- 1 cup water
- 10 ounces baby spinach
- 2 large garlic cloves, crushed

Kosher salt

Pinch of saffron threads

- 2 teaspoons sweet paprika
- ¼ teaspoon ground cumin

Pinch of ground cloves

Pinch of freshly ground
    black pepper

Two 15-ounce cans chickpeas,
    with their liquid

- ¼ cup extra-virgin olive oil
- 1 small onion, finely chopped
- 1 large tomato—peeled, seeded
    and coarsely chopped
- ¼ cup golden raisins

1. In a large, deep skillet, bring the water to a boil. Add the spinach and toss over high heat until wilted, about 2 minutes. Drain the spinach, pressing on the leaves to extract the liquid. Coarsely chop the spinach.
2. Using the flat side of a large knife, mash the garlic to a paste with ½ teaspoon of salt and the saffron. Transfer the paste to a small bowl. Stir in the paprika, cumin, cloves and pepper and ¼ cup of the chickpea liquid.
3. Wipe out the skillet. Add 2 tablespoons of the olive oil and heat until shimmering. Add the chopped onion and tomato and cook over moderately high heat until softened, about 3 minutes. Add the spiced garlic sauce and cook for 1 minute. Add the chickpeas and their remaining liquid along with the raisins and bring to a boil. Add the chopped spinach and simmer over moderate heat for 10 minutes. Transfer the chickpea stew to 4 deep bowls, drizzle with the remaining 2 tablespoons of olive oil and serve. —*Janet Mendel*

Charred Fava Bean Salad with Lemon and Tarragon

TOTAL: 1 HR 15 MIN

8 TO 10 SERVINGS ● ● ●

It's impossible to grill tiny favas, but the sweet-starchy beans get a similar smoky flavor when they're charred quickly in a hot skillet. Master chef and contributing editor Jean-Georges Vongerichten tosses the charred beans with garlic, jalapeño, tarragon and cubes of cheese for a warm salad.

- 3 pounds fresh fava beans,
    shelled (2½ cups)
- 2 tablespoons extra-virgin
    olive oil
- 1 large garlic clove, thinly sliced
- 1 small jalapeño, seeded
    and minced

Salt

- 2 tablespoons unsalted butter
- 1 medium shallot, very finely
    chopped
- ½ tablespoon fresh lemon juice
- 1 tablespoon finely diced
    Parmigiano-Reggiano cheese
- 1 tablespoon chopped tarragon

1. Fill a large bowl with ice water. In a large saucepan of boiling salted water, blanch the fava beans for 1 minute. Transfer to the ice water, drain, then peel them.
2. In a small saucepan, heat 1 tablespoon of the olive oil. Add the garlic and cook over low heat until golden, about 2 minutes. Add the jalapeño and cook for 1 minute longer. Season with salt.
3. In a large skillet, heat the remaining 1 tablespoon of olive oil until shimmering. Add the fava beans and cook over moderately high heat, without stirring, until blackened in spots, 1 minute. Transfer to a serving bowl and season with salt.
4. Add the butter to the skillet and cook over moderately high heat until it just starts to brown, about 30 seconds. Add the shallot and cook over low heat until softened, about 3 minutes. Stir in the lemon juice and remove from the heat.

5. Add the garlic-jalapeño mixture and the warm shallot vinaigrette to the beans along with the cheese and tarragon and toss well to coat. Season the fava bean salad with salt and serve.
—*Jean-Georges Vongerichten*

MAKE AHEAD The blanched and peeled fava beans can be refrigerated overnight.

Giant Lima Beans with Stewed Tomatoes and Oregano Pesto

**ACTIVE: 40 MIN; TOTAL: 5 HR PLUS
4 HR SOAKING**

8 SERVINGS ● ●

Tangy feta cheese, a bright herbal pesto and a crisp bread crumb topping all elevate this tomato-bean stew. It's sensational made with heirloom giant limas, but gigantes or large lima beans from the grocery store are also terrific.

LIMA BEANS

- 3 cups dried giant lima beans
    or gigantes, rinsed and picked
    over, then soaked for 4 hours
    and drained (see Note)

Kosher salt

- 5 tablespoons extra-virgin
    olive oil
- 1 medium onion, finely diced
- 1 garlic clove, minced

One 16-ounce can whole tomatoes—
    juices reserved, tomatoes
    coarsely chopped

- 2 tablespoons chopped oregano
- 1 cup coarsely crumbled
    feta cheese (6½ ounces),
    for sprinkling
- 2 cups coarse fresh
    bread crumbs

PESTO

- ¼ cup plus 2 tablespoons
    extra-virgin olive oil
- 2 tablespoons chopped oregano
- 2 tablespoons chopped parsley
- 1 small garlic clove, very
    finely chopped

Kosher salt

1. **PREPARE THE LIMA BEANS:** In a large saucepan, cover the soaked lima beans with 2 inches of water and bring to a boil. Simmer over low heat, stirring occasionally, until the lima beans are just tender but still al dente, about 2½ hours; add water as needed to keep the beans covered by 2 inches. Season the lima beans with salt and let stand at room temperature for about 5 minutes. Drain the limas, reserving 1½ cups of the cooking liquid.

2. In a medium saucepan, heat 3 tablespoons of the olive oil. Add the onion and garlic and cook over moderately low heat until softened, about 8 minutes. Add the tomatoes and their juices, the oregano and the reserved bean cooking liquid and simmer over low heat, stirring occasionally, until reduced to 1½ cups, about 1 hour. Season the tomato sauce with salt.

3. **MEANWHILE, MAKE THE PESTO:** In a mini food processor, combine the olive oil with the oregano, parsley and garlic and pulse to a coarse puree. Season the oregano pesto with salt.

4. Preheat the oven to 425°. In a 9-by-13-inch baking dish, mix the limas with the tomato sauce and sprinkle the feta on top. Bake in the upper third of the oven for about 40 minutes, until the beans are bubbling and the cheese is browned. Remove from the oven and let stand for 10 minutes.

5. Meanwhile, in a large skillet, heat the remaining 2 tablespoons of olive oil. Add the bread crumbs and cook over moderately high heat, stirring constantly, until toasted, 3 minutes. Season with salt.

6. Top the beans with the bread crumbs, dollop with the oregano pesto and serve.
—*Laurence Jossel*

NOTE Heirloom beans are available from ranchogordo.com.

MAKE AHEAD The cooked and cooled limas, tomato sauce and pesto can be covered and refrigerated separately overnight. Bring the ingredients back to room temperature before proceeding.

CHICKPEA-AND-SPINACH STEW

CHARRED FAVA BEAN SALAD WITH LEMON AND TARRAGON

potatoes, grains & beans

Green-Lentil Salad with Hazelnut Vinaigrette

ACTIVE: 25 MIN; TOTAL: 1 HR

6 SERVINGS ● ●

15 black peppercorns
6 parsley sprigs
5 thyme sprigs
2 whole cloves
1 bay leaf
3 thick slices of bacon,
    cut crosswise into
    ⅓-inch-thick sticks
1 medium carrot,
    cut into ¼-inch dice
1 medium onion,
    cut into ¼-inch dice
1 garlic clove, minced
4 cups chicken stock
1½ cups French green lentils
    (10 ounces)
¼ cup hazelnut oil
2 tablespoons sherry vinegar
Kosher salt and freshly ground pepper
1 medium shallot, thinly sliced

1. Wrap the peppercorns, parsley sprigs, thyme sprigs, cloves and bay leaf in a piece of cheesecloth. Tie securely with string.
2. In a large saucepan, cook the bacon over moderate heat, stirring occasionally, until crisp, about 8 minutes. Drain off all but 3 tablespoons of the bacon fat. Add the diced carrot and onion and the minced garlic and cook, stirring occasionally, until softened, about 5 minutes. Add the herb bundle, chicken stock and green lentils and bring to a simmer. Cover and cook over moderate heat until the lentils are tender, about 30 minutes. Drain the lentils, transfer them to a large bowl and discard the herb bundle; keep warm.
3. Meanwhile, in a small bowl, whisk the hazelnut oil with the sherry vinegar and season with salt and pepper. Pour the hazelnut vinaigrette over the lentils and add the shallot. Toss the salad until the lentils are evenly coated and serve warm. —*William Abitbol*

MAKE AHEAD The green-lentil salad can be refrigerated, covered, for up to 1 day. Let the salad return to room temperature, or rewarm gently before serving.

Phyllo-Crusted Goat Cheese and Lentil Pie

ACTIVE: 40 MIN; TOTAL: 3 HR 15 MIN

8 SERVINGS ● ○

"It's remarkable how the combination of goat cheese and lentils tastes like lamb," says Seattle chef Jerry Traunfeld about this vegetarian pie. The secret to achieving a perfect phyllo crust, he adds, is letting the dough defrost gradually in the refrigerator before assembling the pie, then slicing through the top layer of the crust before it bakes, so it won't crumble when you serve it.

2 tablespoons extra-virgin
    olive oil
1 medium onion, cut into
    ⅓-inch dice
1 fennel bulb, cut into
    ⅓-inch dice
1 red bell pepper, cut into
    ⅓-inch dice
2 garlic cloves, minced
1 cup French green lentils
2 teaspoons fennel seeds
Kosher salt
2 cups water
¼ cup chopped mint
1 tablespoon chopped
    thyme leaves
1 tablespoon red wine vinegar
8 ounces soft goat cheese
Freshly ground pepper
1 stick unsalted butter, melted
Fourteen 9-by-14-inch sheets
    of phyllo dough

1. In a large saucepan, heat the olive oil. Add the onion, fennel, red pepper and garlic and cook over moderately high heat until softened, about 5 minutes. Stir in the lentils, fennel seeds and a pinch of salt. Add the water and bring to a simmer. Cover and cook over low heat until the lentils are just tender, about 35 minutes. Drain the lentils in a strainer and let cool for 15 minutes.
2. Preheat the oven to 375°. In a large bowl, mix the lentils with the mint, thyme and vinegar. Crumble in the goat cheese, season with salt and pepper and mix well.
3. Brush a 10-inch glass pie plate with melted butter. Lay 1 sheet of phyllo over the pan; tuck it into the pan and let the ends hang over the side. Brush the phyllo generously with butter. Repeat with 6 more phyllo sheets, rotating each one 45 degrees to create a circle of overhanging phyllo. Spread the lentil filling in the pan and top with the remaining 7 sheets of phyllo, buttering between each one, to make a top crust. Loosely roll up all of the overhanging phyllo to create a 1-inch-wide border. Brush the border with butter.
4. Using a sharp knife, cut the pie into 8 wedges, cutting through the top layer of phyllo only. Bake the pie for about 1 hour and 40 minutes, until the top is golden brown. Transfer to a rack and let stand until cooled slightly, about 15 minutes. Cut the pie into wedges and serve hot, warm or at room temperature. —*Jerry Traunfeld*

MAKE AHEAD The pie can be baked up to 6 hours in advance.

Black Bean Burgers

ACTIVE: 40 MIN; TOTAL: 2 HR 10 MIN

PLUS 4 HR SOAKING

8 SERVINGS ● ○

1¼ cups dried black beans, rinsed
    and picked over, then soaked
    for 4 hours and drained
Kosher salt
3½ tablespoons extra-virgin
    olive oil
⅓ cup farro
1 small onion, finely diced
¼ teaspoon crushed red pepper
1 garlic clove, minced
2 large eggs, lightly beaten
1 cup coarse fresh bread crumbs

¼ cup chopped basil

¼ cup chopped cilantro

¼ teaspoon freshly ground pepper

Vegetable oil, for sautéing

8 toasted buns

Smoky Red Pepper Spread (p. 379)
and thickly sliced red onions,
for serving

1. In a saucepan, cover the beans with 2 inches of water. Simmer over moderately low heat, stirring occasionally, until tender, about 1 hour; add water as needed to keep the beans covered by 2 inches. When the beans are tender, season them with salt and let stand for 5 minutes; drain.

2. Meanwhile, in a saucepan, heat ½ tablespoon of the olive oil. Add the farro and cook over moderately high heat, stirring, 2 minutes. Add 1½ cups of water and a pinch of salt and bring to a boil. Cover and simmer until the grains are al dente, about 30 minutes.

3. In a small skillet, heat the remaining 3 tablespoons of olive oil. Add the diced onion and cook over moderate heat until softened, about 3 minutes. Add the crushed red pepper and garlic and cook until fragrant, about 2 minutes.

4. In a food processor, pulse all but ½ cup of the beans to a chunky puree; transfer to a bowl. Fold in the remaining ½ cup of beans, the farro, the onion mixture, eggs, bread crumbs, basil, cilantro, pepper and 1 teaspoon of salt. Form the mixture into 8 patties. Cover and refrigerate for 30 minutes.

5. In a large nonstick skillet, heat ⅛ inch of vegetable oil. Add the patties and cook over moderate heat, turning once, until browned and heated through, about 6 minutes. Transfer to the buns. Top with the Smoky Red Pepper Spread and onion slices, close the burgers and serve.
—*Laurence Jossel*

MAKE AHEAD The bean burgers can be prepared through Step 4 and refrigerated overnight.

Crispy Black Bean Cakes with Sour Cream and Avocado

 **TOTAL: 30 MIN**
4 SERVINGS ● ● ○

These pan-fried cakes are crispy on the outside (thanks to a thin coating of bread crumbs) and creamy in the center. They make an excellent vegetarian meal, especially alongside a green salad.

2 tablespoons vegetable oil,
plus more for frying

1 small onion, cut into
¼-inch dice

1 large garlic clove, very
finely chopped

¾ teaspoon ground cumin

¼ teaspoon cayenne pepper

Two 15-ounce cans black beans,
drained

1¼ cups plain dry bread crumbs

Kosher salt and freshly ground
black pepper

⅓ cup all-purpose flour

2 large eggs, beaten

Sour cream, avocado, scallions
and lime wedges, for serving

1. In a medium skillet, heat the 2 tablespoons of vegetable oil. Add the onion and garlic and cook over moderate heat just until softened, about 3 minutes. Add the cumin and cayenne and cook until fragrant, about 1 minute. Scrape the onion mixture into the bowl of a food processor. Add 1½ cups of the beans and pulse until the mixture is finely chopped but not smooth. Scrape the mixture into a medium bowl. Mix in the remaining whole beans and ½ cup of the bread crumbs and season with salt and pepper. Form the mixture into twelve ¼-cup patties about ½ inch thick.

2. Put the flour, beaten eggs and the remaining ¾ cup of bread crumbs into 3 shallow bowls. Dust each black bean cake with the flour, tapping off the excess. Dip the cakes in the egg and then in the bread crumbs, pressing so that the bread crumbs adhere.

3. In a very large skillet, heat ⅛ inch of oil until shimmering. Add the cakes and fry over moderate heat until golden brown, about 2 minutes per side. Drain on paper towels. Serve the black bean cakes with sour cream, avocado, scallions and lime wedges. —*Melissa Rubel*

Fresh Shell Bean Stew

ACTIVE: 45 MIN; TOTAL: 1 HR 15 MIN
10 SERVINGS ● ● ○

¼ cup extra-virgin olive oil

½ small onion, finely diced

1 small carrot, finely diced

3 garlic cloves, minced

1 Anaheim chile pepper or
other mild green chile pepper,
seeded and minced

3 pounds fresh cranberry beans,
shelled (about 3 cups)

2 bay leaves, 3 thyme sprigs,
1 rosemary sprig, 1 teaspoon
black peppercorns, ½ teaspoon
allspice berries and 4 cloves,
tied in cheesecloth

4 cups water

Salt

1 pound small romano beans or
larger beans, cut into 2-inch
lengths

1. In a large saucepan, heat the olive oil. Add the onion, carrot, garlic and chile and cook over low heat, stirring occasionally, until the vegetables are softened but not browned, about 8 minutes. Add the fresh cranberry beans, the spice-herb bundle and the water and bring to a boil over high heat. Reduce the heat and simmer until the beans are tender, about 30 minutes. Discard the spice bundle and season the stew with salt.

2. Meanwhile, bring a large saucepan of water to a boil. Add salt and the romano beans and cook until tender, about 5 minutes. Drain the beans and keep warm. Just before serving, stir the romano beans into the fresh cranberry bean stew. Season with salt and serve hot. —*Peter Hoffman*

ROSEMARY FLATBREAD WITH BLUE
CHEESE, GRAPES AND HONEY (P. 277)

breads, pizzas & sandwiches

> **66** *It's a tradition for winemakers to bake bread with grapes to celebrate the harvest.* **99**
> —**DAVID PAGE,** WINEMAKER, SHINN ESTATE VINEYARDS, MATTITUCK, NEW YORK

IRISH BROWN BREAD

POTATO-LEEK FOCACCIA

Irish Brown Bread

ACTIVE: 10 MIN; TOTAL: 1 HR

MAKES ONE 8-BY-5-INCH LOAF ● ○ ○

Dense, hearty and complex-tasting, this bread requires no yeast and therefore no rising time.

- 3 cups whole wheat flour
- 1 cup all-purpose flour
- 1 teaspoon baking soda
- 1 teaspoon salt
- 1¼ cups buttermilk
- 1 large egg, lightly beaten

1. Preheat the oven to 375°. Butter an 8-by-5-inch metal loaf pan.

2. In a large bowl, whisk the whole wheat and all-purpose flours with the baking soda and salt. In a small bowl, whisk the buttermilk with the egg; stir the wet ingredients into the dry ingredients with a wooden spoon until a rough dough forms.

3. Transfer the dough to a lightly floured work surface and knead until smooth.

Form the dough into a loaf shape and put it in the prepared pan. Bake for about 50 minutes, until the bread has risen about ½ inch above the rim of the pan. Once unmolded, the loaf should sound hollow when it is gently tapped on the bottom. Let the brown bread cool to warm or room temperature, then slice and serve.
—*Cathal Armstrong*

SERVE WITH Irish farmhouse cheeses.

Potato-Leek Focaccia

ACTIVE: 50 MIN; TOTAL: 4 HR

12 SERVINGS ● ● ○ ○

DOUGH

- 2 large baking potatoes, peeled

Salt

- 2 teaspoons active dry yeast
- 1 cup warm water
- 3½ cups all-purpose flour
- 3 tablespoons extra-virgin olive oil, plus more for oiling

TOPPINGS

- 6 large leeks, halved lengthwise and sliced crosswise ⅛ inch thick (3 cups)
- 1½ teaspoons thyme leaves
- ¼ teaspoon salt
- ¼ teaspoon sugar
- 2 tablespoons extra-virgin olive oil, plus more for brushing
- 4 ounces Emmentaler cheese, cut into ½-inch dice

Coarse sea salt

- 2 tablespoons white truffle oil (optional)

1. MAKE THE DOUGH: In a saucepan, boil the potatoes in salted water until tender, about 25 minutes; drain. Rice or finely mash. Measure out 1⅓ cups of potatoes.

2. Meanwhile, in a bowl, combine the yeast with the warm water and ½ cup of the flour. Cover tightly with plastic wrap and let stand for about 25 minutes, until frothy.

3. In the bowl of a standing electric mixer fitted with the paddle, combine the yeast mixture, the mashed potatoes, the 3 tablespoons of olive oil, 2 teaspoons of salt and the remaining 3 cups of flour. Beat at medium speed for 2 minutes. Switch to a dough hook and knead until a soft, slightly sticky dough forms, 5 minutes. Transfer the dough to a lightly oiled bowl; turn to coat. Let stand, covered, in a warm, draft-free spot until doubled in bulk, about 1 hour.

4. MEANWHILE, PREPARE THE TOPPINGS: In a skillet, cook the leeks, thyme, salt and sugar in the olive oil over moderate heat, stirring, until the leeks are caramelized, 15 minutes.

5. Lightly oil an 11-by-17-inch baking sheet. Transfer the dough to the baking sheet and gently press to form an 11-by-17-inch rectangle. Lightly brush the dough with olive oil; let stand, loosely covered, in a warm, draft-free spot until puffy, about 35 minutes.

6. Preheat the oven to 425°. Using your fingers, make indentations all over the top of the dough. Top with the leeks, cheese, sea salt and 1 tablespoon of the truffle oil.

7. Bake on the middle rack for 20 minutes, until the cheese is bubbling and the crust is golden brown. Transfer to a rack and brush with the remaining 1 tablespoon of truffle oil. Let stand for 30 minutes before serving. —*Marco Flavio Marinucci*

Shrimp-and-Chorizo Pizzas with Escarole and Manchego

ACTIVE: 45 MIN; TOTAL: 2 HR

4 SERVINGS ●

DOUGH

- ½ teaspoon honey
- ½ cup warm water
- 1¼ teaspoons active dry yeast
- 1½ cups bread flour
- 1½ teaspoons extra-virgin olive oil, plus more for oiling
- ½ teaspoon kosher salt

TOPPINGS

- 2 tablespoons extra-virgin olive oil, plus more for brushing

- 1 large garlic clove, minced
- ½ head of escarole, cut into 1-inch pieces (4 cups)

Salt and freshly ground pepper

- 6 ounces Manchego cheese, shredded (2 cups)
- ½ pound medium shrimp—shelled, deveined and halved lengthwise
- 1½ ounces dry chorizo, thinly sliced

1. MAKE THE DOUGH: In a large bowl, dissolve the honey in 2 tablespoons of the warm water. Sprinkle the yeast on top and let stand until foamy, about 10 minutes.

2. Add the remaining 6 tablespoons of water, then stir in the bread flour, the 1½ teaspoons of olive oil and the salt; stir until a lumpy mass forms. On a floured work surface, knead the dough until smooth. Transfer to a lightly oiled bowl, cover with plastic and let stand in a warm place until doubled in bulk, about 1 hour.

3. Preheat the oven to 500° and set a pizza stone on the bottom of the oven to heat for at least 30 minutes. On a floured work surface, divide the dough in half and roll each half into a ball. Flatten each ball into a 6-inch disk and transfer to a large, floured baking sheet. Cover with plastic wrap and let stand until puffed, about 15 minutes.

4. MEANWHILE, PREPARE THE TOPPINGS: In a skillet, heat the 2 tablespoons of olive oil. Add the garlic; cook over moderate heat until golden, about 1 minute. Add the escarole and cook, tossing, until wilted, about 2 minutes. Season with salt and pepper.

5. On a floured surface, roll out 1 disk of dough to an 11-inch round. Transfer to a floured pizza peel and lightly brush the edge with oil. Scatter half of the cheese on top, leaving a ½-inch border. Top with half of the shrimp, chorizo and escarole. Slide onto the hot stone and bake for 5 minutes, until the crust is browned on the bottom, the shrimp are cooked through and the toppings are sizzling. Cut into wedges and serve. Repeat with the remaining dough and toppings. —*Michael Schwartz*

White Cheese Pizza with Ramps

ACTIVE: 30 MIN; TOTAL: 2 HR

MAKES ONE 12-INCH PIZZA ● ●

DOUGH

- 1 cup all-purpose flour
- 1½ teaspoons active dry yeast
- ½ teaspoon salt
- ¼ teaspoon sugar
- ¼ cup plus 2 tablespoons warm water

TOPPINGS

- 10 ramps or medium scallions

Extra-virgin olive oil, for brushing

- 1 cup coarsely grated fresh mozzarella cheese (4 ounces)

Salt and freshly ground pepper

- ¼ cup freshly grated Parmigiano-Reggiano cheese

1. MAKE THE DOUGH: Whisk the flour together with the yeast, salt and sugar. Pour in the water and stir to form a dough. Scrape onto a lightly floured work surface and knead for a few minutes until smooth. Transfer to a lightly oiled bowl. Cover with plastic wrap or a damp towel and let stand in a warm place until doubled in bulk, 1½ hours.

2. Set a pizza stone on the bottom or on the bottom shelf of the oven and preheat to 500° for at least 30 minutes.

3. PREPARE THE TOPPINGS: Blanch the ramps in boiling salted water until they are bright green but still al dente, 1 minute. Drain, pat dry and cut into 1-inch lengths.

4. Punch down the dough and transfer to a lightly floured work surface. Roll out to a 12-inch round about ⅛ inch thick. Transfer to a floured pizza peel or inverted baking sheet. Brush with oil and sprinkle on the mozzarella. Scatter the ramps over the mozzarella and season lightly with salt and pepper. Top with the Parmigiano-Reggiano.

5. Slide the pizza onto the hot stone. Bake for about 8 minutes, until the cheese has melted and the crust is browned and crisp on the bottom. Cut into wedges and serve. —*Tony Mantuano*

Pizza with Charred Cherry Tomatoes and Pesto

TOTAL: 2 HR PLUS OVERNIGHT RESTING

6 SERVINGS

- ¾ pound cherry tomatoes
- ¼ cup *panko* (Japanese bread crumbs)
- 2 garlic cloves, thinly sliced
- 1 shallot, thinly sliced
- 5 basil leaves, torn
- 2 tablespoons extra-virgin olive oil

Salt and freshly ground pepper

Pizza Dough (recipe follows)

- ¾ cup coarsely grated aged Gouda (3 ounces)
- 6 tablespoons freshly grated Parmigiano-Reggiano cheese

Basil Pesto (recipe follows)

1. Preheat the broiler. In a medium baking dish, toss the cherry tomatoes with the *panko,* garlic, shallot, basil and olive oil and season with salt and pepper. Broil 6 inches from the heat for about 5 minutes, or until the tomatoes pop and brown lightly.

2. Preheat the oven to 500°. Set a pizza stone on the bottom of the oven and heat for at least 30 minutes.

3. On a lightly floured work surface, roll out each ball of dough to a 7-inch round. Transfer 2 rounds to a lightly floured pizza peel. Spoon one-sixth of the cherry tomatoes onto each round. Slide the pizzas onto the heated stone and bake for about 5 minutes, or until sizzling and just set. Remove from the oven and sprinkle each with 2 tablespoons of the Gouda and 1 tablespoon of the Parmigiano. Return to the oven and bake for 5 minutes, until the cheeses are melted and the crust is lightly browned. Drizzle with a little pesto. Repeat twice more to make 6 pizzas.
—*Shea Gallante*

PIZZA DOUGH

TOTAL: 25 MIN PLUS OVERNIGHT RESTING

MAKES ENOUGH DOUGH FOR SIX 7-INCH PIZZAS ● ○

- 1 envelope active dry yeast
- ¾ cup warm water
- 1 tablespoon canola oil, plus more for brushing
- 2 cups "00" pizza flour or all-purpose flour, plus more for dusting

Pinch of sugar

Pinch of salt

In a large bowl, mix the yeast with the water and let stand until foamy, about 5 minutes. Using a wooden spoon, stir in the 1 tablespoon of oil, followed by the 2 cups of flour and the sugar and salt. Continue stirring until a soft dough forms. Transfer the dough to a lightly floured work surface and knead until smooth and silky, about 5 minutes. Let the dough stand uncovered for 10 minutes, then divide it into 6 equal pieces. Roll each piece into a ball and transfer to a lightly oiled baking sheet. Brush the tops with oil and cover loosely with plastic wrap. Refrigerate overnight until slightly risen. Return to room temperature before using. —*SG*

BASIL PESTO

TOTAL: 20 MIN

MAKES ¾ CUP ● ● ○

- 1 tablespoon pine nuts
- 2 cups basil leaves (1 bunch)
- 2 garlic cloves, smashed
- 6 tablespoons freshly grated Parmigiano-Reggiano cheese
- 6 tablespoons extra-virgin olive oil

Salt

1. In a small skillet, toast the pine nuts over moderate heat, stirring, until golden, 5 minutes. Transfer to a plate to cool.

2. In a blender or food processor, pulse the pine nuts with the basil, garlic and cheese until finely chopped. While the machine is on, drizzle in the olive oil and puree until smooth. Season with salt. —*SG*

MAKE AHEAD The pesto can be refrigerated overnight or frozen for up to 1 month.

Montasio-Chickpea Flatbreads

TOTAL: 20 MIN

8 SERVINGS ● ● ●

For this ingenious flatbread, F&W's Grace Parisi tops store-bought naan with a tasty mixture of chickpeas, Montasio (a nutty Italian cheese), scallion and cayenne pepper.

One 15-ounce can chickpeas, drained

- 1 scallion, finely chopped
- ¼ teaspoon cayenne pepper
- 1 tablespoon extra-virgin olive oil, plus more for brushing

Coarse salt

- 1½ cups shredded Montasio, young pecorino or Fontina cheese

Four 12-inch round flatbreads, such as naan or pocketless pita

1. Preheat the oven to 450° and preheat a griddle. In a bowl, toss the chickpeas with the scallion, cayenne and 1 tablespoon of olive oil; season with salt. Using a fork, coarsely mash the chickpeas. Stir in the cheese. Spread the mixture over the flatbreads, leaving a 1-inch border.

2. Brush the griddle with olive oil and cook the flatbreads, in batches, over high heat until the bottoms are lightly browned, about 2 minutes. Transfer to baking sheets and bake for 3 minutes, until the crust is golden and the cheese is melted. Transfer the flatbreads to a work surface, cut into wedges and serve hot or warm. —*Grace Parisi*

SUPERFAST SUPERFAST

fresh-baked breadsticks

Use the pizza dough recipe on this page to make breadsticks. Instead of forming rounds, roll the dough into a ½-inch-thick rectangle. Cut it into strips, brush with oil and sprinkle with salt or cheese. Bake at 450° for about 10 minutes.

PIZZA WITH CHARRED CHERRY
TOMATOES AND PESTO

breads, pizzas & sandwiches

Chickpea-Chile Flatbreads

TOTAL: 1 HR 20 MIN

MAKES 10 FLATBREADS ● ●

New York City chef Suvir Saran rolls this savory flatbread dough into a cone shape before flattening it to create extra-flaky layers. In India, griddled flatbreads like these are often slathered with butter or served with yogurt, but Saran also likes them with chutney and pickles.

- ½ cup whole wheat flour
- ½ cup unbleached all-purpose flour
- ½ cup *besan* (chickpea flour)
- 1½ teaspoons salt
- ⅛ teaspoon garam masala
- 1 tablespoon melted unsalted butter, plus softened butter for serving
- 2 jalapeños, seeded and very finely chopped
- ½ cup very finely chopped red onion
- ½ cup chopped cilantro
- ¼ cup water
- 1 tablespoon vegetable oil, plus more for frying

1. In a bowl, whisk the whole wheat, all-purpose and chickpea flours with the salt and garam masala. Add the melted butter and rub the flours between your fingers until the butter is completely incorporated and the mixture resembles fine cornmeal. Add the jalapeños, onion, cilantro, water and the 1 tablespoon of oil and mix with your hands to form a soft, slightly sticky dough; transfer to a clean bowl, cover with plastic wrap and let rest for 20 minutes.

2. Break off a golf-ball-size piece of dough. On a lightly floured work surface, roll the dough into a tight ball, then flatten it into a 5-inch disk. Using a paring knife, make a cut from the center of the disk to the edge. Starting with one side of the slit, roll the dough onto itself to form a cone. Set the cone pointy side down in the palm of your hand and flatten it into a disk. On the lightly floured work surface, roll out the disk into a 5- to 6-inch round about ⅛ inch thick; transfer to a lightly floured baking sheet and cover with plastic wrap. Repeat with the remaining dough.

3. Heat a cast-iron griddle or large skillet. Add the flatbreads in batches and cook over moderately high heat until bubbles form on the bottom and the dough starts to brown, about 1 minute. Turn the flatbreads and cook until bubbles form again, 30 seconds to 1 minute. Spoon a small amount of oil over the flatbreads. Using the back of a spoon, rub the oil into the flatbreads and cook, pressing, until evenly browned on the bottom, about 1 minute. Flip the flatbreads and repeat with more oil; serve hot, with softened butter. —*Suvir Saran*

Yemenite Flatbreads

ACTIVE: 45 MIN; TOTAL: 2 HR

MAKES 8 FLATBREADS ●

To create the layered flatbread called *mahlouach,* Philadelphia chef Michael Solomonov relies on a technique similar to one used to make puff pastry: He repeatedly brushes the dough with butter and folds it before rolling it out. To bolster the flavor, he sears the dough in the superhot *taboon* (wood-burning oven) of his restaurant Zahav. The bread is also delicious grilled.

- 3 cups all-purpose flour, plus more for dusting
- 1½ teaspoons salt
- 1 cup plus 2 tablespoons water
- 1 tablespoon fresh lemon juice
- Oil, for greasing
- 6 tablespoons unsalted butter, melted

1. In a large bowl, combine the 3 cups flour with the salt. Add the water and lemon juice and stir well with a wooden spoon until a sticky dough forms. Turn the dough out onto a lightly floured work surface and knead until smooth. Transfer the dough to a clean, oiled bowl. Cover with plastic wrap; refrigerate for 30 minutes.

2. Oil a large, rimmed baking sheet. Turn the dough out onto the sheet and divide it into 8 equal pieces. Press each piece into a 6-inch round that's ¼ inch thick. Brush the rounds with 2 tablespoons of the melted butter and roll them up into cylinders. Cover the cylinders with plastic wrap and refrigerate for 15 minutes.

3. Unwrap the dough cylinders and flatten them into rounds again. Brush the rounds with 2 tablespoons of the melted butter; roll them up into cylinders. Wrap the cylinders in plastic wrap and refrigerate for 15 minutes. Repeat the flattening, brushing, rolling and chilling one last time.

4. Light a grill. Working with one cylinder at a time, unwrap and roll it out as thinly as possible between two sheets of waxed paper to form a ¹⁄₁₆-inch-thick round.

5. Carefully transfer 2 or 3 rounds of the flatbread at a time to the grill. Grill over high heat, carefully turning the breads once with tongs, until they are lightly charred and starting to puff, about 4 minutes. Transfer the grilled flatbreads to foil and keep hot while you grill the remaining flatbreads. Serve the breads hot. —*Michael Solomonov*

MAKE AHEAD The flatbread dough can be prepared through Step 2 and refrigerated overnight.

infused olive oil

Transform store-bought flatbreads like naan or pita with flavored olive oil. For a quick infusion, gently heat olive oil with herbs, garlic, chiles or peppercorns for 8 minutes. Warm the breads, brush with the oil and season with salt.

Rosemary Flatbread with Blue Cheese, Grapes and Honey

ACTIVE: 30 MIN; TOTAL: 1 HR 45 MIN

MAKES ONE 13-INCH FLATBREAD ● ● ●

"It's a tradition for winemakers to bake bread with grapes to celebrate the harvest," says Long Island chef-turned-winemaker David Page. Each fall, he uses his wood-burning oven to make this crusty flatbread studded with creamy crumbled blue cheese and sweet table grapes.

- 1 envelope active dry yeast
- 2 tablespoons sugar
- 2 cups bread flour, plus more for rolling
- ¾ cup warm water
- 2 teaspoons chopped fresh rosemary
- ½ teaspoon fine salt
- ¼ teaspoon freshly ground black pepper
- ½ pound red grapes (1½ cups)

Coarse sea salt

- 3 ounces blue cheese, crumbled (½ cup)
- 1 tablespoon honey
- 1 tablespoon snipped chives

1. In a large bowl, whisk the yeast and sugar with ¼ cup of the flour. Stir in ¼ cup of the warm water and let stand until slightly foamy, about 5 minutes. Add the rosemary, fine salt, pepper and the remaining 1¾ cups of flour and ½ cup of water; stir until a dough forms. Turn the dough out onto a lightly floured work surface and knead until smooth, about 5 minutes. Transfer the dough to an oiled bowl, cover and let rise in a draft-free spot until billowy and doubled in bulk, about 1 hour.

2. Meanwhile, preheat the oven to 450°. Place a pizza stone in the bottom of the oven, and preheat for at least 30 minutes.

3. Turn the dough out onto a lightly floured work surface. Press and stretch the dough into a 13-inch round, then transfer to a lightly floured pizza peel. Press the grapes into the dough and sprinkle with sea salt.

4. Slide the flatbread onto the hot stone and bake for about 12 minutes, until the crust is golden and the grapes have begun to release some of their juices. Sprinkle the blue cheese on top and bake for about 2 minutes longer, until the cheese melts. Slide the flatbread onto a work surface and drizzle with the honey and sprinkle with the chives. Cut into wedges and serve. —David Page

MAKE AHEAD The dough can be left to rise in the refrigerator overnight. Let stand at room temperature for at least 15 minutes before using.

Greek Hand Pies with Greens, Dill, Mint and Feta

ACTIVE: 1 HR; TOTAL: 2 HR

MAKES 4 HAND PIES ● ●

- 2¼ cups all-purpose flour, plus more for dusting

Salt

- ¾ cup water
- ¼ cup plus 2 tablespoons extra-virgin olive oil
- 1 tablespoon red wine vinegar
- 6 medium scallions, sliced ¼ inch thick
- 1½ pounds greens, such as Swiss chard, spinach and dandelion greens, stemmed and coarsely chopped
- ½ cup coarsely chopped dill
- ½ cup coarsely chopped mint
- ¼ cup coarsely chopped fresh oregano
- ½ cup crumbled feta (2 ounces)
- 2 tablespoons freshly grated Parmigiano-Reggiano cheese
- 1 large egg, lightly beaten

Freshly ground pepper

Vegetable oil, for frying

1. In a large bowl, mix the 2¼ cups flour with ¾ teaspoon of salt. Make a well in the center and add the water, ¼ cup of the olive oil and the vinegar. Mix until the dough comes together; it will be sticky.

2. Transfer the dough to a floured work surface and knead until it is smooth and no longer tacky, using a pastry scraper to free it from the work surface. Wrap the dough in plastic wrap and refrigerate it for 1 hour.

3. In a large skillet, heat the remaining 2 tablespoons of olive oil. Add the scallions and cook over moderate heat, stirring occasionally, until softened, about 3 minutes. Add the chopped greens and cook over high heat, stirring, until they are wilted, about 2 minutes. Stir in the chopped dill, mint and oregano and cook until the herbs are wilted, about 1 minute. Transfer the contents of the skillet to a colander and let cool. When the greens are cool enough to handle, use your hands to squeeze out any excess liquid.

4. In a large bowl, combine the cooked and drained greens with the crumbled feta, grated Parmigiano-Reggiano cheese and the beaten egg. Season with ¼ teaspoon each of salt and pepper.

5. Lightly flour a large rimmed baking sheet. Turn the dough out onto a lightly floured work surface; cut into 4 equal pieces. Roll each piece out to a 9-inch round ⅟₁₆ inch thick. Using an 8-inch plate as a template, cut an 8-inch disk from each round. Mound one-fourth of the filling on the lower half of each disk of dough. Fold the dough over to make a half-moon; press the edge of the dough to seal. Using a lightly floured fork, crimp the edges. Transfer the formed hand pies to the prepared baking sheet.

6. In a large skillet, heat ¼ inch of vegetable oil over moderately high heat until shimmering. Add 2 pies at a time and fry, turning once, until deep golden brown, about 6 minutes. Drain the pies on paper towels. Serve hot. —Jacques Pépin

MAKE AHEAD The dough and filling can each be refrigerated, separately, overnight. Bring the filling to room temperature before assembling.

GRILLED GRUYÈRE AND
SWEET ONION SANDWICH

perfecting the panini

*F&W's **Grace Parisi** reinvents the classic grilled cheese by experimenting with four fantastic hot-sandwich breads and fillings.*

Grilled Gruyère and Sweet Onion Sandwiches

ACTIVE: 30 MIN; TOTAL: 1 HR

MAKES 4 SANDWICHES ● ●

- 3 tablespoons unsalted butter, softened
- 1 tablespoon extra-virgin olive oil
- 1 large onion, halved and thinly sliced crosswise (4 cups)

Salt and freshly ground pepper

Eight ½-inch-thick slices of whole-grain bread

Dijon mustard

- 8 ounces imported Gruyère cheese, thinly sliced
- 2 half-sour pickles, thinly sliced lengthwise

1. In a deep skillet, melt 1 tablespoon of the butter in the oil. Add the onion, cover and cook over high heat, stirring once or twice, until softened, about 5 minutes. Uncover and cook over moderate heat, stirring occasionally, until the onion is very tender and caramelized, about 25 minutes longer. Add water to the skillet as necessary, ¼ cup at a time, to prevent the onion from scorching. Season the caramelized onion with salt and pepper.

2. Spread the bread with the remaining 2 tablespoons of butter and arrange, buttered side down, on a work surface. Spread a thin layer of mustard on each slice. Top half of the slices with the onion, Gruyère and pickles and close the sandwiches.

3. Preheat a skillet or panini press. Grill the sandwiches over low heat until the bread is toasted and the cheese is melted, 10 minutes. If using a skillet, press the sandwiches with a spatula and flip them halfway through. Cut in half and serve right away.

Three Great Variations

1 Grilled Cheddar and Ham with Apple and Chutney

Grace likes the sweetness of the mango chutney in this sandwich.

Using pumpernickel bread, spread each slice with mango chutney and fill the sandwiches with half of a shredded Granny Smith apple, thinly sliced sharp cheddar cheese and Virginia ham. Close the sandwiches and grill as directed.

2 Grilled Pepper Jack and Roast Beef *Buttered pita makes this a deliciously crispy version of a Philly cheesesteak.*

Split 4 thick pocketless pitas and spread the cut sides with a thin layer of mayonnaise. Fill the sandwiches with thinly sliced red onion, pepper Jack cheese and rare roast beef. Butter the outside of the sandwich and grill as directed.

3 Grilled Fontina and Vegetable Antipasti *For an extra-savory sandwich, add a touch of grated Parmesan cheese.*

Using peasant bread, brush the slices with extra-virgin olive oil instead of butter. Fill the sandwiches with thinly sliced imported Fontina, roasted red peppers, drained marinated artichokes and pickled jalapeños. Grill as directed.

FIG-AND-PROSCIUTTO FLATBREAD

OPEN-FACED GRILLED EGGPLANT SANDWICHES

Fig-and-Prosciutto Flatbreads

ACTIVE: 20 MIN; TOTAL: 1 HR 15 MIN
MAKES TWO 13-INCH ROUND
FLATBREADS

Chef Todd English's much-lauded house-made flatbread, topped with sticky-sweet fig jam, pungent Gorgonzola cheese and salty prosciutto, is a staple at his Olives restaurants. For a simpler preparation, this recipe uses store-bought pizza dough instead of homemade.

Two 12-ounce balls of pizza dough,
    at room temperature
All-purpose flour
¼ **cup extra-virgin olive oil**
1 **garlic clove, minced**
1 **teaspoon minced fresh**
    rosemary leaves
Salt and freshly ground pepper
½ **cup fig jam (from a 6-ounce jar)**
¼ **pound Gorgonzola cheese,**
    crumbled (1 cup)
3 **ounces sliced prosciutto**
1 **scallion, thinly sliced**

1. Place a pizza stone in the bottom of the oven and preheat the oven to 500°. Allow at least 45 minutes for the pizza stone to heat thoroughly.

2. Meanwhile, on a lightly floured surface, roll out one piece of the pizza dough to a 13-inch round. Dust a pizza peel with flour and slide the dough onto it. Drizzle with about 2 tablespoons of the olive oil and sprinkle with half of the garlic and rosemary. Season with salt and pepper. Dollop ¼ cup of the fig jam all over the crust, being sure to leave a 1-inch border of dough all around. Scatter half of the cheese and prosciutto over the dough.

3. Slide the flatbread onto the stone and bake for about 15 minutes, until puffed and golden. Transfer the flatbread to a cutting board and let cool for 10 minutes before slicing. Repeat with the remaining ingredients to make the second flatbread. Garnish with the sliced scallion and serve.
—*Todd English*

Open-Faced Grilled Eggplant Sandwiches

TOTAL: 25 MIN
4 SERVINGS

Eight ½-inch-thick slices of
peasant bread
Extra-virgin olive oil, for
brushing
One 1¼-pound eggplant, sliced
crosswise 1 inch thick
Salt and freshly ground
black pepper
4 plum tomatoes, sliced
crosswise ¼ inch thick
½ pound buffalo mozzarella,
sliced ¼ inch thick
8 large basil leaves, torn
Coarse sea salt

1. Light a grill. Brush the bread slices on both sides with olive oil and grill them over high heat until they are crisp on the outside but still soft inside, about 30 seconds per side. Transfer the grilled bread slices to a serving platter.
2. Brush the eggplant slices with olive oil and season them generously with salt and black pepper. Grill the eggplant over moderate heat until the slices are charred on the bottom, about 5 minutes. Turn and grill until the eggplant is tender, about 3 minutes longer.
3. Top the grilled eggplant with the plum tomato slices, buffalo mozzarella and torn basil leaves. Cover the grill and cook until the mozzarella cheese melts, about 2 minutes. Transfer the eggplant to the bread, sprinkle with sea salt and serve the open-faced sandwiches right away.
—Kristin Donnelly

Cheesy Eggplant Sandwiches

TOTAL: 40 MIN
8 FIRST-COURSE SERVINGS
Chef Brenda Langton of Spoonriver restaurant and Cafe Brenda in Minneapolis drizzles pomegranate molasses on these crispy eggplant sandwiches for tartness.

1 tablespoon extra-virgin
olive oil
1 medium onion,
very finely chopped
3 garlic cloves,
very finely chopped
½ cup crumbled feta cheese
2 ounces semi-aged provolone
cheese, coarsely shredded
(about ½ cup)
2 tablespoons chopped
flat-leaf parsley
2 tablespoons coarsely
chopped basil leaves
Freshly ground pepper
1 large egg
¼ cup milk
½ cup all-purpose flour
1 cup fine, dry bread crumbs
Salt
2 medium eggplants (about
12 ounces each), sliced
crosswise ½ inch thick
1½ cups vegetable oil
Pomegranate molasses,
for drizzling

1. Preheat the oven to 375°. In a small skillet, heat the olive oil. Add the chopped onion and garlic and cook over moderate heat, stirring occasionally, until soft. Transfer to a bowl; let cool. Stir in the crumbled feta, the shredded provolone and the chopped parsley and basil; season with pepper.
2. In a shallow bowl, beat the egg. Whisk in the milk. Spread the flour and bread crumbs in separate shallow bowls. Season the bread crumbs with salt and pepper. Select 8 pairs of uniform eggplant slices; reserve the rest for another use. Dip the eggplant slices in the flour, then in the egg and finally in the bread crumbs, pressing to help the crumbs adhere. Transfer the coated eggplant slices to a wax paper–lined baking sheet.
3. In a large skillet, heat the vegetable oil. Line a baking sheet with several layers of paper towel. Add the coated eggplant

slices to the skillet in batches and fry over moderately high heat, gently turning once, until the eggplant is crisp and deeply browned, about 5 minutes. Drain on the paper towels.
4. Top 8 eggplant slices with the cheese and herb mixture and cover with the remaining fried eggplant slices. Transfer the sandwiches to a baking sheet and bake for 10 minutes, until the cheese is melted. Drizzle the sandwiches lightly with pomegranate molasses and serve.
—Brenda Langton

Cubano Sandwiches

ACTIVE: 30 MIN; TOTAL: 1 HR
MAKES 4 SANDWICHES
These *cubano* sandwiches from food and travel writer Anya von Bremzen get their character from a classic Cuban *mojo*, which can be either a marinade or, as here, a sauce. Like most Cuban *mojos*, this one starts with fresh orange juice. Cumin, garlic, oregano, cilantro and quick-pickled red onions add complexity and kick.

½ cup fresh orange juice
¼ cup fresh lime juice
2 tablespoons olive oil
2 garlic cloves, mashed
1 tablespoon dried oregano,
crumbled
1 teaspoon ground cumin
¼ cup chopped cilantro
¼ cup thinly sliced red onion
Salt and freshly ground pepper
¾ pound boneless roast pork,
very coarsely shredded
4 soft hero rolls, split but still
attached at one side
6 ounces Black Forest ham
4 ounces sliced Genoa salami
6 ounces sliced Swiss cheese
2 large dill pickles, thinly sliced
lengthwise
Yellow mustard and hot sauce,
for serving
Melted unsalted butter, for brushing

SWEET AND SPICY CATFISH SANDWICH

CREAM BISCUITS WITH DILL

1. In a bowl, whisk the orange juice with the lime juice, olive oil, garlic, oregano, cumin, cilantro and onion and season with salt and pepper. Stir in the shredded pork and let stand for 30 minutes.

2. Using a slotted spoon, mound the pork on the bottom of each roll. Spoon a little of the marinade over the pork and top with the ham, salami, Swiss cheese and dill pickles. Spread mustard and hot sauce on the top half of each roll and press the sandwiches closed. Brush the rolls on top and bottom with butter.

3. Preheat a panini press. Working with one or two sandwiches at a time, press the *cubanos* until the rolls are toasted and the Swiss cheese is melted. Cut the sandwiches in half and serve immediately.
—*Anya von Bremzen*

MAKE AHEAD The sandwiches can be assembled up to 8 hours ahead and grilled just before serving.

Sweet and Spicy Catfish Sandwiches

TOTAL: 45 MIN
MAKES 4 SANDWICHES ●

These fantastic sandwiches are filled with moist, sweetly glazed catfish, a spicy *sambal* mayonnaise, crunchy cucumbers and fragrant cilantro.

- 4 soft baguette rolls (about 7 inches long), split lengthwise
- 2 tablespoons unsalted butter, softened
- ½ cup plus ¼ teaspoon honey
- 2 tablespoons soy sauce
- 1 tablespoon very finely chopped fresh ginger
- 1 scallion, white and green parts, chopped
- 3 garlic cloves, 2 very finely chopped

Salt and freshly ground black pepper

- ¼ cup cider vinegar
- ½ cup shredded carrots
- ¼ cup mayonnaise
- 1 tablespoon *sambal oelek* or other Asian red chile sauce (see Note)
- 2 large, thick, skinless catfish fillets (about 10 ounces each), halved lengthwise

Vegetable oil, for brushing

Thinly sliced cucumber and cilantro sprigs, for serving

1. Preheat the broiler and position a rack 6 inches from the heat. Brush the cut sides of the rolls with the softened butter.

2. In a small bowl, whisk ¼ cup of the honey with the soy sauce, ginger, scallion and chopped garlic. Season the honey glaze lightly with salt and black pepper. In another small bowl, whisk ¼ cup of the honey with the cider vinegar and 1 teaspoon of salt. Add the shredded carrots and toss to combine. In a third small bowl, whisk the mayonnaise with the *sambal oelek* and the remaining ¼ teaspoon of honey; season the *sambal* mayonnaise with salt.

3. Arrange the fish fillets on a baking sheet; brush with vegetable oil and season lightly with salt and black pepper. Broil for about 6 minutes, until the fish is just beginning to turn opaque. Brush the fillets very liberally with the honey glaze and broil for 8 minutes longer, until the catfish is browned and cooked through.

4. Broil the buttered rolls for 1 minute, until they are toasted. Cut the whole garlic clove in half; rub the cut sides of the garlic all over the toasted sides of the rolls. Spread the rolls with the *sambal* mayonnaise. Using a slotted spoon, lift the carrots from the pickling liquid and spread them on the toasted rolls. Top with the glazed fish fillets, cucumber slices and cilantro sprigs and close the sandwiches. Cut the sandwiches in half and serve right away.

—*Ratha Chau*

NOTE *Sambal oelek* is a spicy, bright red Southeast Asian chile sauce typically served as a condiment. It is available at Asian markets.

MAKE AHEAD The honey glaze, *sambal* mayonnaise and shredded carrots in their pickling liquid can be refrigerated separately overnight.

Cream Biscuits with Dill

ACTIVE: 10 MIN; TOTAL: 35 MIN
MAKES 12 BISCUITS ● ● ○

"Biscuits are like pie crusts in that we assign magical powers to people who can make really good ones," says Amber Huffman, the personal chef to vintner Jess Jackson on his Kentucky horse farm. Huffman's grandmother Mimi got her hooked on cream biscuits, which substitute cream for butter, eliminating the tricky step of cutting fat into flour. "They're less fussy, and you can make them in two seconds," Huffman says. "I wish there were a pie crust equivalent."

- **2 cups all-purpose flour, plus more for dusting**
- **1½ tablespoons chopped fresh dill**
- **2 teaspoons baking powder**
- **1 teaspoon salt**
- **1 teaspoon sugar**
- **1¼ cups plus 2 tablespoons heavy cream**

1. Preheat the oven to 400°. Line a large baking sheet with parchment paper. In a large bowl, whisk the 2 cups of flour with the dill, baking powder, salt and sugar. Add the cream and mix with a wooden spoon just until a dough forms.

2. On a lightly floured work surface, gently knead the biscuit dough just until it comes together and pat it into a ¾-inch-thick disk. Using a floured 2¼-inch round cookie cutter, stamp out as many biscuits as possible. Combine the scraps and repeat to make more biscuits.

3. Transfer the biscuits to the parchment paper–lined baking sheet and bake them for about 22 minutes, rotating the pan halfway through baking, until the biscuits are lightly golden on top. Serve the cream biscuits hot or warm.

—*Amber Huffman*

Grilled Chicken, Tomato and Onion Sandwiches

TOTAL: 30 MIN
MAKES 4 SANDWICHES ●

Except for the olive-oregano relish, all the components of this chicken sandwich are grilled—the chicken, tomatoes, sweet onion and even the bread—making for the ultimate grilled sandwich.

- **3 ounces pitted mixed olives (1 cup)**
- **1 garlic clove, crushed**
- **2 teaspoons fresh oregano leaves**
- **¼ cup plus 2 tablespoons extra-virgin olive oil, plus more for brushing**
- **Freshly ground pepper**
- **2 large tomatoes, sliced ⅓ inch thick**
- **1 Vidalia onion (or any sweet onion), sliced crosswise ¼ inch thick**
- **4 crusty rolls, such as ciabatta, sourdough or hero, split horizontally**
- **Salt**
- **1¾ pounds thin chicken cutlets**

1. Light a grill. In a mini food processor, pulse the pitted olives with the crushed garlic and fresh oregano until chopped. Add the ¼ cup plus 2 tablespoons of olive oil and pulse until finely chopped. Season the relish with pepper.

2. Brush the tomato and Vidalia onion slices and the cut sides of the rolls with olive oil. Grill the tomato and onion slices over high heat until they are softened and lightly charred, about 2 minutes for the tomatoes and 6 minutes for the onion. Transfer the grilled vegetables to a plate and season with salt and pepper. Grill the rolls cut side down until lightly toasted, about 2 minutes.

3. Season the chicken cutlets with salt and pepper and grill them over high heat, turning occasionally, until they are lightly browned in spots and cooked through, 5 to 6 minutes. Cut the grilled chicken cutlets so that they will fit on the toasted rolls and layer them on the sandwiches. Top the chicken with the grilled tomato and onion slices and the olive-oregano relish. Close the grilled chicken sandwiches, cut them in half and serve right away.

—*Grace Parisi*

MAKE AHEAD The olive-oregano relish can be refrigerated for up to a week. Bring the relish to room temperature before spreading it on the warm sandwiches.

Baby Brioches with Chicken Salad and Bacon

TOTAL: 25 MIN
8 SERVINGS

This classic chicken salad can be bolstered with any number of seasonings, from curry powder or mustard to *harissa*. To turn these two-bite snacks into mini sandwiches, cut the brioche rolls in half, mound the chicken salad, tomato and bacon inside and secure with a toothpick.

- 4 slices of applewood-smoked bacon
- 16 mini brioche rolls (about 2 inches)
- ⅓ cup mayonnaise
- 1 celery rib, minced
- ½ small shallot, minced
- 2 teaspoons minced flat-leaf parsley, plus 32 large flat-leaf parsley leaves
- 1 teaspoon fresh lemon juice
- 2 chicken breasts from a rotisserie chicken—skin and bones discarded, chicken cut into ⅓-inch dice

Kosher salt and freshly ground black pepper

- 2 small plum tomatoes, cut into ¼-inch slices (16 slices)

1. Preheat the oven to 325°. In a large skillet, cook the bacon over moderate heat until browned and crisp all over, about 5 minutes.

Transfer the bacon to paper towels to drain, then cut each slice into 4 pieces.

2. Using a paring knife, cut a 1-inch round plug out of the top of each brioche roll. Carefully hollow out the rolls. Set the rolls on a baking sheet and warm them in the oven to refresh them, about 5 minutes.

3. In a medium bowl, combine the mayonnaise with the celery, shallot, minced parsley and lemon juice. Stir in the diced chicken and season the chicken salad with salt and black pepper.

4. Spoon 1 tablespoon of the chicken salad into each brioche roll, garnish with parsley leaves and cover with a tomato slice. Top each roll with 1 teaspoon of chicken salad, garnish with the bacon and serve.
—*Melissa Rubel*

MAKE AHEAD The chicken salad can be prepared up to 2 days in advance. Cover and refrigerate.

Radish, Parsley and Lemon-Butter Tea Sandwiches

TOTAL: 30 MIN
MAKES ABOUT 32 SANDWICHES ● ○

These open-faced sandwiches created by F&W's Marcia Kiesel can be cut into whimsical shapes. Look for radishes of varying colors and sizes.

- 4 tablespoons unsalted butter, softened
- ½ teaspoon finely grated lemon zest
- 1 teaspoon fresh lemon juice

Salt

- 7 slices of sandwich bread, crusts removed
- ½ cup flat-leaf parsley leaves
- 6 ounces red radishes, very thinly sliced on a mandoline

1. In a small bowl, blend the softened butter with the lemon zest and lemon juice and season with salt.

2. Spread the bread slices with the lemon butter. Using a 1½-inch round biscuit cutter, cut 16 rounds from 4 slices. Cut the

remaining slices into 2½-by-1-inch rectangles. Top with the parsley leaves and radish slices. Serve at once, or cover the sandwiches with plastic wrap and let stand at room temperature for up to 2 hours.
—*Marcia Kiesel*

Tuna-and-Gruyère Panini

TOTAL: 30 MIN
MAKES 4 SANDWICHES

- 6 tablespoons mayonnaise

Two 8-ounce jars tuna packed in olive oil, drained, plus 1 tablespoon of the oil

- 1 tablespoon fresh lemon juice
- 1 teaspoon Dijon mustard
- ¼ cup finely diced celery
- 6 cloves mashed roasted garlic (see Note)
- 2 tablespoons chopped flat-leaf parsley
- 1 tablespoon drained capers
- ¼ teaspoon celery seeds

Kosher salt and freshly ground black pepper

- 8 slices of multigrain sandwich bread
- 4 ounces thinly sliced Gruyère cheese

In a medium bowl, mix the mayonnaise with the 1 tablespoon of olive oil from the tuna, the lemon juice, Dijon mustard, celery, garlic, parsley, capers and celery seeds. Mix in the tuna. Season with salt and pepper. Spoon the tuna mixture onto 4 slices of multigrain bread, then top each one with 1 ounce of Gruyère and another slice of bread. Toast the sandwiches in a panini press until they're golden and the cheese is melted. —*Rob Evans*

NOTE To roast the garlic, place the unpeeled cloves on a sheet of aluminum foil and drizzle with olive oil. Seal the foil and roast the cloves at 300° for about 1 hour, until completely tender. Let the cloves cool, then squeeze them out of their skins and mash them.

crisping radishes

To make radishes snappy and supercrispy (as for the tea sandwich recipe at right), submerge them in a bowl of ice water and refrigerate for about 1 hour before eating or slicing.

RADISH, PARSLEY AND LEMON-
BUTTER TEA SANDWICHES

breads, pizzas & sandwiches

Ham-and-Cheddar Sourdough Stuffing

ACTIVE: 30 MIN; TOTAL: 1 HR 45 MIN

12 SERVINGS ● ●

This rich stuffing wittily combines all the ingredients of a classic ham-and-cheese sandwich. To prevent the stuffing from scorching as it cooks on the grill, F&W's Grace Parisi places it in an aluminum pan nested in two other pans, keeping the stuffing as far from the flames as possible.

1½ pounds sourdough bread,
       sliced ¾ inch thick
  4 tablespoons unsalted butter,
       plus more for greasing the pan
  ¼ cup extra-virgin olive oil
  1 onion, thinly sliced
  4 inner celery ribs, thinly sliced
  3 small leeks (1 pound), white and
       light green parts only, thinly sliced
Salt and freshly ground pepper
1¼ pounds roasted ham, sliced
       ½ inch thick and cut into
       ½-inch cubes
  1 tablespoon chopped sage
  1 tablespoon chopped thyme
  ½ pound extra-sharp cheddar
       cheese, coarsely shredded
3½ cups turkey stock

1. Toast the bread in a toaster oven until golden. Cut into 1½-inch pieces and transfer to a large bowl. In a large, deep skillet, melt the 4 tablespoons of butter in the olive oil. Add the onion, celery and leeks and season with salt and pepper. Cook over moderate heat, stirring occasionally, until the vegetables are softened, about 10 minutes. Stir in the ham, sage and thyme. Add the mixture to the pieces of toast along with the cheese and toss well. Add the stock, season with salt and pepper and stir until the stock is absorbed.

2. Light a gas grill and set the burners to moderate (about 375°). Stack three 9-by-12-by-3-inch disposable foil pans and butter the inside of the top one. Spoon the dressing into the pan. Cover with foil and

grill with the lid closed for 30 minutes, just until heated through. Remove the foil and continue to grill with the lid closed for 45 minutes longer, until the stuffing is sizzling around the edges and the top is very crisp. Alternatively, bake the dressing in the oven in a 9-by-13-inch glass or ceramic baking dish. Serve hot. —*Grace Parisi*

MAKE AHEAD The assembled dressing can be refrigerated overnight. Bring to room temperature before cooking.

Fennel, Red Onion and Focaccia Stuffing

ACTIVE: 25 MIN; TOTAL: 1 HR 40 MIN

12 SERVINGS ● ●

With its excellent crust, focaccia is a terrific base for stuffing, especially in this recipe with fennel, fennel seed and red onion. As the stuffing bakes, the center becomes creamy and soft while the edges and top turn crunchy and chewy.

  2 pounds plain or onion
       focaccia, cut into 1-inch
       dice (16 cups)
  4 tablespoons unsalted butter
  2 tablespoons extra-virgin olive oil
  3 medium fennel bulbs—halved
       lengthwise, cored and sliced
       lengthwise ¼ inch thick
  2 red onions, halved and sliced
       lengthwise ¼ inch thick
  3 medium garlic cloves, very
       finely chopped
1½ teaspoons chopped thyme
  1 teaspoon fennel seeds
3½ cups chicken stock or
       low-sodium broth
Kosher salt and freshly ground
       black pepper

1. Preheat the oven to 375°. Spread the focaccia on a large rimmed baking sheet. Toast for about 30 minutes, stirring halfway through, until dry and golden around the edges. Transfer to a large bowl.

2. In a large skillet, melt 2 tablespoons of the butter in the olive oil. Add the fennel

and onions and cook over moderate heat, stirring occasionally, until very tender, about 15 minutes. Add the garlic, thyme and fennel seeds and cook until fragrant, about 1 minute. Scrape the fennel mixture into the bowl with the focaccia. Add the chicken stock and toss until evenly moistened. Season with salt and pepper.

3. Increase the oven temperature to 400°. Butter a 9-by-13-inch baking dish with 1 tablespoon of the butter. Scrape the stuffing into the baking dish and dot the top with the remaining 1 tablespoon of butter. Cover with foil. Bake for about 20 minutes, until heated through. Remove the foil and bake for about 20 minutes longer, until the top is golden and crisp. Serve hot. —*Melissa Rubel*

MAKE AHEAD The assembled stuffing can be refrigerated overnight. Bring to room temperature before baking.

Chorizo Corn Bread Stuffing with Herbs

ACTIVE: 1 HR; TOTAL: 2 HR 15 MIN

12 SERVINGS ●

CORN BREAD

  2 tablespoons vegetable oil
  1 cup plus 2 tablespoons
       all-purpose flour
4½ tablespoons sugar
1½ tablespoons baking powder
1½ teaspoons salt
1¾ cups plus 2 tablespoons
       yellow cornmeal
1½ cups whole milk
  3 eggs, lightly beaten
4½ tablespoons unsalted
       butter, melted

STUFFING

  ½ pound dry chorizo, cut into
       ¼-inch dice
  4 tablespoons unsalted butter
  2 onions, cut into ¼-inch dice
  2 celery ribs, cut into ¼-inch dice
  1 carrot, cut into ¼-inch dice
  3 large garlic cloves, minced

1 tablespoon chopped thyme
1 tablespoon chopped sage
2 teaspoons chopped rosemary
2 cups chicken stock or
     low-sodium broth
2 large eggs, beaten
1 tablespoon kosher salt
¼ teaspoon freshly ground pepper

1. MAKE THE CORN BREAD: Preheat the oven to 425°. Warm a 10-inch cast-iron skillet over moderate heat. Add the oil and heat.

2. Meanwhile, in a bowl, sift the flour with the sugar, baking powder and salt. Stir in the cornmeal. Add the milk and eggs and stir lightly. Add the melted butter and stir just until blended.

3. Scrape the batter into the hot skillet; the oil should sizzle. Transfer the skillet to the oven and bake the corn bread for about 25 minutes, or until the center springs back when gently pressed. Turn the corn bread out onto a rack to cool. (This will yield 3 pounds of corn bread.)

4. MEANWHILE, PREPARE THE STUFFING: Reduce the oven temperature to 375°. In a large saucepan, cook the chorizo over moderate heat until the edges are crisp, about 6 minutes. Add the butter and let it melt. Add the onions, celery and carrot and cook until the onions are translucent, about 12 minutes. Add the garlic, thyme, sage and rosemary and cook until fragrant, about 1 minute. Transfer the chorizo mixture to a large bowl.

5. Cut the corn bread into 1-inch pieces. Spread it on a rimmed baking dish and toast for about 20 minutes, stirring once, until golden in spots. Add the corn bread to the chorizo. Add the chicken stock, eggs, salt and pepper and toss gently until evenly coated. Transfer the stuffing to a 10-by-14-inch baking dish. Bake in the top third of the oven for about 40 minutes, until golden on top. Serve warm. —*Jose Garces*

MAKE AHEAD The baked stuffing can be refrigerated overnight. Bring to room temperature before reheating.

Corn Bread Dressing with Brussels Sprouts

ACTIVE: 1 HR 15 MIN;

TOTAL: 2 HR 30 MIN

12 SERVINGS ● ●

This prosciutto-studded corn bread dressing includes plenty of brussels sprouts, so it's like two classic Thanksgiving side dishes in one.

CORN BREAD

2 tablespoons vegetable oil
2½ cups stone-ground
     yellow cornmeal
2½ cups all-purpose flour
¼ cup sugar
1 tablespoon plus 1 teaspoon
     baking powder
1 teaspoon salt
¾ teaspoon baking soda
3 cups buttermilk
2 large eggs
1½ sticks unsalted butter, melted

DRESSING

4 tablespoons unsalted butter,
     plus more for greasing the pans
2 tablespoons extra-virgin
     olive oil
3 celery ribs, finely diced
1 carrot, finely diced
1 small onion, finely chopped
½ pound thinly sliced prosciutto,
     finely chopped
1 tablespoon chopped sage
1 cup dry white wine
3 large eggs
2 cups chicken stock,
     turkey stock or canned
     low-sodium broth
Kosher salt and freshly ground
     black pepper
2 pounds brussels sprouts,
     halved lengthwise

1. MAKE THE CORN BREAD: Preheat the oven to 425°. Pour the vegetable oil onto an 11-by-17-inch rimmed baking sheet and heat in the oven. In a large bowl, whisk the cornmeal with the flour, sugar, baking powder, salt and baking soda. In another bowl, whisk the buttermilk with the eggs. Pour the buttermilk mixture into the dry ingredients, add the melted butter and stir just until blended.

2. Remove the baking sheet from the oven and swirl to coat with the oil. Scrape the batter onto the baking sheet and bake for 25 minutes, until the corn bread is springy. Transfer to a rack and let cool. Lower the oven temperature to 375°.

3. PREPARE THE DRESSING: Generously butter two 9-by-13-inch metal baking pans. In a large skillet, melt 2 tablespoons of the butter in 1 tablespoon of the olive oil. Add the celery, carrot and onion and cook over moderate heat, stirring occasionally, until the vegetables have softened, about 10 minutes. Add the prosciutto and sage and cook until the prosciutto starts to crisp, about 8 minutes. Stir in ½ cup of the white wine and let cool slightly.

4. Crumble the cooled corn bread into a large bowl in small chunks. In a bowl, whisk the eggs with the stock, then pour over the corn bread. Add the prosciutto mixture, season with salt and pepper and toss to combine. Spread the corn bread dressing in the prepared baking pans.

5. Wipe out the skillet and melt the remaining 2 tablespoons of butter in the remaining 1 tablespoon of olive oil. Add the brussels sprouts and cook over moderate heat, stirring occasionally, until they begin to brown, 10 minutes. Add the remaining ½ cup of white wine and cook for 5 minutes. Season with salt and pepper.

6. Tuck the brussels sprouts into the dressing. Cover and bake for 20 minutes, until heated through. Uncover and bake for 10 minutes longer, until crisp on top. Serve hot. —*Rachel Soszynski*

MAKE AHEAD The baked and cooled corn bread can be frozen for up to 1 month. The unbaked dressing can be refrigerated overnight. Bring the dressing to room temperature before baking.

POACHED EGGS WITH BAKED
FETA AND OLIVES (P. 292)

breakfast & brunch

" I think there's lots of potential for creativity at breakfast that hasn't been tapped. "

—NEAL FRASER, CHEF AND CO-OWNER, BLD RESTAURANT, LOS ANGELES

SCRAMBLED EGGS WITH HERBED CROUTONS

TORTILLA ESPAÑOLA

Scrambled Eggs with Herbed Croutons

 TOTAL: 25 MIN
4 SERVINGS ●

In this witty take on a classic breakfast staple, crisp herbed croutons are stirred right into soft, creamy scrambled eggs—eliminating the need for a side of toast.

- **4 slices of multigrain bread (about 5 ounces), crusts removed and bread cut into ½-inch cubes**
- **¼ cup extra-virgin olive oil**
- **2 garlic cloves, lightly smashed**
- **2 thyme sprigs**
- **One 2-inch rosemary sprig**
- **Salt and freshly ground black pepper**
- **1 tablespoon unsalted butter**
- **10 large eggs, beaten**
- **2 tablespoons snipped chives**

1. In a medium bowl, toss the bread cubes with the olive oil, garlic cloves and thyme and rosemary sprigs. Transfer to a large nonstick skillet and cook over moderate heat, stirring constantly, until the bread cubes are crisp and browned and the herb sprigs are frizzled, about 10 minutes. Transfer the croutons to a plate and discard the garlic cloves. Finely chop the herbs and add them to the croutons. Season with salt and pepper and toss well.

2. Wipe out the skillet and melt the butter in it. Season the eggs with salt and pepper and pour them into the skillet. Cook over moderate heat, stirring gently with a rubber spatula, until the eggs are partially set, about 2 minutes. Add the herbed croutons and snipped chives and gently fold them in, cooking the eggs to soft curds, about 1 minute longer. Transfer the scrambled eggs to plates and serve right away.
—*Grace Parisi*

Tortilla Española

 TOTAL: 45 MIN
6 SERVINGS ● ● ●

Tortilla española exists in almost every corner of Spain: as a tapa in fancy city restaurants; as a filling for *bocadillos* (sandwiches) at gas-station cafés; and as a main course served on worn metal plates in home kitchens. Star chef Mario Batali's version, based on one he tasted in the Ribera del Duero wine region, is baked until golden brown and offers an especially high ratio of potatoes to eggs.

- **¼ cup plus 2 tablespoons extra-virgin olive oil**
- **1¼ pounds red bliss potatoes, peeled and sliced ⅛ inch thick**
- **1 onion, halved and very thinly sliced**
- **Kosher salt and freshly ground black pepper**
- **8 large eggs**

1. Preheat the broiler. Heat ¼ cup of the olive oil in a large cast-iron skillet. Add the potato and onion slices, season with salt and pepper and cook over moderate heat, stirring frequently, until the potatoes and onion are tender but not browned, about 15 minutes.

2. In a large bowl, lightly beat the eggs and season with salt and pepper. Scrape the potato mixture into the bowl, being sure not to leave any in the skillet.

3. Return the skillet to the heat and add the remaining 2 tablespoons of oil. Add the egg mixture, spreading it out in an even layer. Cover and cook over low heat until the *tortilla* is set on the bottom and the edge, about 10 minutes. Transfer the skillet to the oven and broil 8 inches from the heat just until the top is set, about 1 minute longer. Set a large plate over the skillet and carefully invert the *tortilla* onto the plate. Let stand for 5 minutes. Cut into wedges and serve warm or at room temperature.
—Mario Batali

MAKE AHEAD The *tortilla* can stand at room temperature for 3 hours before serving.

Spanish-Style Scrambled Eggs

 TOTAL: 40 MIN
6 SERVINGS ●

At BLD Restaurant in Los Angeles, chef Neal Fraser serves lots of charcuterie. For this dish, he uses spicy chorizo and Spanish *lomo* (cured pork loin) in scrambled eggs along with potatoes, piquillo peppers and smoky paprika. *Lomo* can be hard to find; serrano ham is a good, readily available substitute.

½ **pound fingerling potatoes, scrubbed**
2 **tablespoons extra-virgin olive oil**
Salt and freshly ground pepper
4 **ounces dry chorizo, quartered lengthwise and thinly sliced**
4 **ounces thinly sliced *lomo* or serrano ham, cut into wide ribbons**

¼ **cup piquillo peppers from a jar, drained and thinly sliced**
1 **dozen large eggs, beaten lightly**
4 **ounces Manchego cheese, coarsely shredded (1 cup)**
Pinch of smoked paprika

1. Bring a saucepan of water to a boil. Add the potatoes and cook over moderately high heat until tender, about 10 minutes. Drain; slice the potatoes crosswise ¾ inch thick.

2. In a large nonstick skillet, heat the oil until shimmering. Add the potato slices and cook over moderately high heat, turning occasionally, until lightly browned, about 5 minutes. Season with salt and pepper. Add the chorizo and ham and cook over moderately high heat, stirring occasionally, until the ham is crisp, about 2 minutes. Stir in the piquillo peppers and cook for 1 minute.

3. In a medium bowl, beat the eggs with a generous pinch of salt and pepper. Add them to the skillet and use a rubber spatula to scrape and stir until large, soft curds form, about 5 minutes. Stir in the Manchego and cook, stirring, just until melted, about 30 seconds. Transfer the eggs to a platter, sprinkle with smoked paprika and serve right away.
—Neal Fraser

White Bean Huevos Rancheros

TOTAL: 1 HR
6 SERVINGS

7 **tablespoons extra-virgin olive oil**
1 **large garlic clove, minced**
1 **large onion, finely chopped**
3 **large tomatoes, cored and coarsely chopped**
½ **canned chipotle chile in adobo, minced (about 1 teaspoon), plus 1 teaspoon of the adobo sauce from the can**
1 **tablespoon freshly squeezed lime juice**
2 **tablespoons minced cilantro**

Salt and freshly ground pepper
4 **ounces thickly sliced ham, coarsely chopped**
Two 15-ounce cans white beans, drained
½ **cup water**
12 **corn tortillas, warmed**
1 **dozen large eggs**
½ **cup crumbled *queso fresco***
Sour cream, for serving

1. In a medium saucepan, heat 2 tablespoons of the oil. Add the garlic and half of the onion and cook over moderately high heat, stirring, until softened, about 5 minutes. Add the tomatoes, chipotle and adobo sauce and cook over low heat, stirring, until the tomatoes have broken down but are still slightly chunky, about 20 minutes. Stir in the lime juice and cilantro and season with salt and pepper; keep warm.

2. Meanwhile, in a medium skillet, heat 2 tablespoons of the oil until shimmering. Add the remaining onion and cook over moderately high heat, stirring, until softened, about 5 minutes. Add the ham and cook, stirring, until browned, about 5 minutes. Add the beans and water, season with salt and pepper and cook over moderately low heat, mashing, about 10 minutes.

3. Preheat the broiler. Spoon the bean mixture into 6 ovenproof shallow bowls and top with 2 folded tortillas. Set the bowls on a sturdy baking sheet.

4. In a large nonstick skillet, heat 1 tablespoon of the oil. Crack 4 eggs into the skillet and cook over moderate heat until the bottoms are just set, about 2 minutes. Transfer 2 eggs to each bowl. Repeat 2 more times with the remaining oil and eggs.

5. Sprinkle the *queso fresco* over the eggs. Broil the eggs 6 inches from the heat for about 1 minute, until the cheese is lightly browned and the egg yolks are just set. Spoon the warm tomato salsa on top and serve immediately, with sour cream.
—Neal Fraser

SERVE WITH Guacamole.

Poached Eggs with Baked Feta and Olives

⏱ TOTAL: 30 MIN
6 SERVINGS ● ●

Six 3-inch squares of rosemary
    focaccia, halved horizontally
  2 tablespoons extra-virgin olive
    oil, plus more for brushing
 10 ounces feta cheese,
    cut into 6 slabs
Aleppo pepper or ancho chile
    powder, for sprinkling
  6 large eggs
Salt
 18 pitted kalamata olives
  1 tablespoon chopped sage

1. Preheat the broiler and position a rack 6 inches from the heat. Bring a large, deep skillet of water to a simmer. Brush the focaccia with oil and broil until lightly toasted. Put a slab of feta into each of 6 individual gratin dishes. Drizzle each slab with 1 teaspoon of the oil. Sprinkle lightly with Aleppo pepper and broil until lightly browned and sizzling.
2. Meanwhile, crack the eggs one at a time into a small bowl, then slide them into the simmering water. Poach until the whites are set but the yolks are still runny, about 4 minutes. Using a slotted spoon, transfer the eggs to the gratin dishes and season with salt. Sprinkle with Aleppo pepper, the olives and sage. Serve with the focaccia.
—*Defne Koryürek*

soft-cooked eggs

Set large eggs in a single layer in a saucepan. Cover with 1 inch of cold water; bring to a boil. Immediately place the lid on the pan and remove from the heat. Let stand for 3 minutes, then cool the eggs in cold water.

Tomato-Pepper Stew with Poached Eggs and Harissa

ACTIVE: 30 MIN; TOTAL: 1 HR
6 SERVINGS ● ●

Called *shakshuka,* this Israeli dish of eggs poached in a hearty paprika-scented sauce is deliciously messy. To give his stew an exotic kick, chef Michael Solomonov adds *harissa,* a Tunisian red-chile-pepper paste.

  ¼ cup extra-virgin olive oil
  1 large onion, cut into ½-inch dice
  1 green bell pepper, cut into
    ½-inch dice
Salt
  1 teaspoon sweet smoked paprika
  1 teaspoon ground coriander
  1 tablespoon *harissa*
  1 tablespoon tomato paste
One 28-ounce can diced tomatoes
  ¼ cup chopped parsley
  ¼ cup chopped cilantro
  6 large eggs
Pitas or crusty bread, for serving

1. In a large skillet, heat the olive oil. Add the onion and bell pepper, season with salt and cook over moderate heat, stirring occasionally, until softened, about 7 minutes. Stir in the paprika and coriander and cook until fragrant, about 1 minute. Stir in the *harissa* and tomato paste and cook over low heat for 3 minutes. Add the tomatoes and their juices and simmer over low heat until the sauce has thickened, about 20 minutes. Stir in the parsley and cilantro and season with salt.
2. Raise the heat to moderate. One by one, break the eggs into a cup and add them to the simmering sauce. Poach the eggs until the whites are firm but the yolks are still runny, about 5 minutes. Season the eggs with salt. Transfer the eggs to bowls along with some of the sauce. Serve with warmed pitas or crusty bread.
—*Michael Solomonov*

MAKE AHEAD The recipe can be prepared through Step 1 and refrigerated for up to 3 days. Reheat before proceeding.

Poached Eggs with Cubanelle Pepper Puree

TOTAL: 1 HR
4 SERVINGS ● ●

Cubanelles are long sweet peppers that are usually light green (you can occasionally find red ones as well) and sometimes have a slight kick. Tony Maws (an F&W Best New Chef 2005) of Craigie on Main in Cambridge, Massachusetts, chars the peppers, then blends them with green hot sauce. He serves the puree with meaty mushrooms and runny poached eggs.

  4 Cubanelles or Italian
    frying peppers
  ¼ cup plus 1 tablespoon extra-virgin
    olive oil, plus more for brushing
  ½ pound mixed wild mushrooms,
    thickly sliced
  1 shallot, minced
  1 garlic clove, minced
  1 tablespoon minced marjoram
Salt and freshly ground pepper
  1 teaspoon jalapeño hot sauce
  4 large eggs

1. Preheat the oven to 400°. On a baking sheet, brush the peppers with olive oil and roast for 20 minutes, turning once, until lightly browned and softened. Transfer the peppers to a bowl, cover with plastic wrap and let cool for 10 minutes.
2. Meanwhile, in a medium skillet, heat 2 tablespoons of the olive oil. Add the mushrooms and cook over moderately high heat, stirring, until lightly browned, 4 minutes. Stir in the shallot, garlic and marjoram and cook until fragrant, 2 minutes. Season with salt and pepper and keep warm.
3. Peel, core and seed the peppers. Transfer the peppers to a blender and puree. With the machine on, add the remaining 3 tablespoons of oil and the hot sauce and puree. Season with salt and pepper.
4. Bring a large saucepan filled with 3 inches of water to a simmer. Crack each egg into a cup, then slide it into the water. Poach the eggs over low heat until the

whites are set and the yolks are runny, 4 minutes. Using a slotted spoon, lift the eggs out of the water and blot them dry.

5. Spoon the pepper puree onto plates and top with the mushrooms. Set the eggs on the mushrooms, season lightly with salt and pepper and serve immediately. —*Tony Maws*

SERVE WITH Toasted peasant bread.

Salmon Hash with Poached Eggs

 TOTAL: 45 MIN
4 SERVINGS

Hash is a great way to use leftovers like the cooked salmon called for here. Any other cooked or smoked fish—or diced ham—could be used in place of the salmon.

- 1 **pound small Yukon Gold potatoes**
- 4 **slices of bacon**
- 2 **tablespoons unsalted butter**
- 1 **small red onion, finely chopped**
- ¾ **pound cooked skinless salmon fillet, flaked**
- 2 **tablespoons snipped chives**

Salt and freshly ground black pepper

- 4 **eggs**

Hot sauce, for serving

1. Put the potatoes in a pot of water and bring to a boil. Cook until tender, about 20 minutes. Drain and peel the potatoes, then cut them into 1-inch chunks.

2. Meanwhile, in a large nonstick skillet, cook the bacon over moderately high heat until browned and crisp, about 6 minutes. Transfer the bacon to paper towels to drain, then crumble.

3. Melt the butter in the bacon fat in the skillet. Add the onion and potatoes and cook over moderate heat, stirring occasionally and gently mashing the potatoes, until browned in spots, about 8 minutes. Add the bacon, salmon and chives; season with salt and pepper. Cook just until the salmon is heated through.

4. Meanwhile, bring a large, deep skillet of water to a simmer. Crack the eggs into individual bowls, then carefully add them to the simmering water. Poach the eggs over moderate heat until the whites are set but the yolks are still slightly runny, about 5 minutes.

5. Using a slotted spoon, carefully lift the eggs out of the water; blot dry with paper towels. Spoon the hash onto plates, top with the eggs and serve. Pass hot sauce at the table. —*Grace Parisi*

Steak and Eggs Benedict with Red Wine Hollandaise

TOTAL: 1 HR
6 SERVINGS

- ¼ **cup Cabernet Sauvignon**
- ¼ **cup ruby port**
- 2 **large egg yolks**
- 1½ **sticks unsalted butter, melted**
- 1 **tablespoon fresh lemon juice**

Salt and freshly ground pepper

Three 1-inch-thick beef tenderloin steaks (6 ounces each)

Olive oil, for brushing

- 1 **dozen large eggs**
- 6 **English muffins, split and toasted**

1. In a small saucepan, combine the Cabernet and port and bring to a boil. Simmer over moderate heat until reduced to 2 tablespoons, 15 minutes. Let cool slightly.

2. Set a medium metal bowl over a pot of simmering water. Put the egg yolks in the bowl and whisk over low heat until thick, about 2 minutes. Very gradually whisk in the melted butter and whisk constantly until thick and creamy, 4 to 5 minutes. Whisk in the wine reduction and lemon juice in a thin stream and season with salt and pepper. Keep the hollandaise sauce warm over very low heat, stirring occasionally.

3. Heat a grill pan. Brush the steaks lightly with olive oil and season with salt and pepper. Grill the steaks over high heat, turning once or twice, until medium-rare, about 8 minutes; let rest for 10 minutes.

4. Meanwhile, bring 2 large, deep skillets of water to a simmer. Crack 6 eggs into each skillet and simmer over moderately low heat until the whites are set and the yolks are runny, about 4 minutes. Using a slotted spoon, transfer the poached eggs to a plate; blot dry with paper towels.

5. Arrange 2 English muffin halves on each plate. Thinly slice the steaks, arrange the meat on the muffins and season lightly with salt and pepper. Top with the poached eggs. Spoon the hollandaise on top and serve. —*Neal Fraser*

Mustard Green–and–Sweet Onion Frittata

 TOTAL: 45 MIN
8 SERVINGS ●●

- 3 **tablespoons extra-virgin olive oil**
- 1 **large sweet onion, diced**
- 1½ **pounds mustard greens, stems discarded, leaves chopped**
- 16 **large eggs, beaten**

Kosher salt and freshly ground pepper

- ⅓ **cup freshly grated Parmigiano-Reggiano cheese**

1. Preheat the oven to 350°. In a large ovenproof nonstick skillet, heat 1 tablespoon of the oil. Add the onion and cook over moderately high heat until golden brown, about 10 minutes. Add the mustard greens and cook until wilted, 5 minutes.

2. Season the eggs with salt and pepper and whisk in the remaining 2 tablespoons of oil. Pour the eggs into the skillet and cook over moderate heat until the bottom and side begin to set. Lift the side of the frittata to allow the uncooked eggs to seep under. Continue cooking until the bottom is set and the top is still runny, 3 minutes. Sprinkle the cheese on top of the frittata.

3. Transfer the skillet to the oven and bake for about 8 minutes, until the center of the frittata is set. Slide the frittata onto a cutting board. Cut into 1½-inch squares and serve hot, warm or at room temperature. —*Gabe Thompson*

WILD MUSHROOM AND GOAT CHEESE OMELET

OMELET WITH PRESSED CAVIAR AND SOUR CREAM

Wild Mushroom and Goat Cheese Omelets

 **TOTAL: 45 MIN**
6 SERVINGS ● ●

- 6 tablespoons unsalted butter
- ¾ pound shiitake mushrooms, stems discarded and caps thickly sliced
- 3 medium shallots, very finely chopped
- 6 ounces pea shoots
- Salt and freshly ground black pepper
- 1½ dozen large eggs
- 8 ounces fresh goat cheese, crumbled

1. Preheat the oven to 225°. In a large skillet, melt 3 tablespoons of the butter. Add the shiitake and cook over moderately high heat, stirring occasionally, until golden, about 7 minutes. Add the shallots and cook, stirring, until softened, about 3 minutes. Add the pea shoots, season with salt and pepper and cook just until wilted, about 1 minute. Keep the filling warm.

2. Crack 6 eggs into a medium bowl, season with salt and pepper and beat with a whisk. In a 10-inch nonstick skillet, melt 1 tablespoon of the butter. Whisk the eggs again and add them to the skillet. Cook over moderately high heat, lifting the edge with a spatula to allow the uncooked eggs to seep underneath, until the bottom of the omelet is golden and the top is nearly set, about 4 minutes.

3. Spoon one-third of the filling down the center of the omelet and sprinkle with one-third of the goat cheese. Using a rubber spatula, fold the sides over the filling to enclose it completely. Slide the omelet onto a large heatproof plate and cut it in half; serve immediately or transfer it to the oven to keep warm. Repeat with the remaining butter, eggs and filling to make 2 more omelets. Serve at once.
—*Neal Fraser*

SERVE WITH Crusty bread.

Omelet with Pressed Caviar and Sour Cream

TOTAL: 10 MIN
1 SERVING ●

In a superlative combination of fish eggs and chicken eggs, master chef Jacques Pépin stuffs a classic French omelet with sour cream, chives and diced pressed caviar, the paste made from fish eggs that break during the packing of traditional caviar. For an extra indulgence, he drapes the finished omelet with strips of pressed caviar.

- 3 tablespoons pressed caviar (3 ounces; see Note)
- 2 tablespoons sour cream
- 1 tablespoon very finely chopped chives
- 2 large eggs

Salt and freshly ground black pepper

- 1 tablespoon unsalted butter

1. Roll out the caviar between 2 sheets of plastic wrap to a 5-by-8-inch rectangle about ⅛ inch thick. Cut half of it into ½-inch strips. Finely dice the remaining caviar and transfer it to a bowl. Add the sour cream and all but a pinch of the chives and stir to combine.

2. In a small bowl, beat the eggs until frothy and season with salt and black pepper. In a 6-inch nonstick skillet, melt the butter over high heat until the foam subsides. Add the beaten eggs and stir constantly with a heat-proof rubber spatula, while shaking the skillet, until the eggs are set but still moist.

3. Remove the skillet from the heat and dollop the sour cream and caviar mixture across the center of the eggs. Shake the skillet gently to loosen the omelet, then fold one-third of the eggs over the sour cream filling. Tilt the skillet and turn the omelet out onto a plate, folding it over itself as you tilt. Garnish the omelet with the reserved pressed caviar strips, sprinkle with the remaining chopped chives and serve right away. —*Jacques Pépin*

NOTE Pressed caviar is available from californiacaviar.com.

Serrano Ham and Potato Frittata with Watercress Salad

TOTAL: 45 MIN
4 SERVINGS ●

Yukon Gold potatoes give this Spanish-style egg dish a nice creaminess.

- ¼ cup plus 1 tablespoon extra-virgin olive oil
- 2 medium Yukon Gold potatoes, peeled and thinly sliced
- 1 medium white onion, very thinly sliced
- 4 thin slices of serrano ham (1 ounce), torn

Salt and freshly ground black pepper

- 8 large eggs, beaten
- 2 teaspoons red wine vinegar
- 1 bunch of watercress, thick stems discarded

1. Preheat the oven to 350°. In a medium nonstick ovenproof skillet, heat 3 tablespoons of the olive oil. Add the potatoes and cook over moderate heat, turning and stirring occasionally, until the slices are tender and beginning to brown, about 7 minutes. Add the onion and cook, stirring occasionally, until softened, about 3 minutes. Stir in the pieces of serrano ham and season with salt and pepper.

2. Season the eggs with salt and pepper and gently stir them into the skillet. Cook over moderate heat until the eggs are just beginning to set at the edge, about 3 minutes. Transfer the skillet to the oven and bake the frittata for about 12 minutes, until the eggs are completely set.

3. Meanwhile, in a large bowl, whisk the vinegar with the remaining 2 tablespoons of olive oil. Add the watercress, season with salt and pepper and toss.

4. Cut the frittata into wedges and serve with the watercress salad on the side.
—*Mike Price*

SERVE WITH Crusty bread.

MAKE AHEAD The frittata can be kept at room temperature for up to 6 hours.

Prosciutto-and-Fresh-Mozzarella Frittata

TOTAL: 1 HR
6 SERVINGS ●

Frittatas are among the easiest breakfasts to make for a group: Simply warm the fillings in a skillet, add the eggs, cook for 3 or 4 minutes on the stove to set, then pop the pan in the oven. Best of all, unlike most other egg dishes, frittatas are as good—if not better—at room temperature.

- 10 large eggs
- ¼ cup milk
- 2 tablespoons freshly grated Parmigiano-Reggiano cheese
- 2 tablespoons chopped parsley
- 2 tablespoons chopped basil
- ¾ teaspoon salt
- ½ teaspoon freshly ground pepper
- 3 tablespoons extra-virgin olive oil
- 2 medium shallots, thinly sliced
- 1 tomato, cut into ½-inch dice
- 4 thin slices of prosciutto, cut into ¼-inch strips
- 4 ounces fresh mozzarella, cut into 1-inch cubes

1. Preheat the oven to 350°. In a large bowl, beat the eggs. Beat in the milk, grated Parmigiano-Reggiano cheese, parsley and basil. Season with the salt and pepper.

2. In an 8-inch nonstick ovenproof skillet, heat the olive oil. Add the shallots and cook over moderate heat until softened, about 7 minutes. Add the tomato and prosciutto and cook, stirring, until warm, about 2 minutes. Pour in the eggs and cook until beginning to set on the bottom, about 3 minutes. Poke the mozzarella cubes into the eggs. Transfer the skillet to the oven and bake the frittata for about 20 minutes, until just firm when lightly pressed.

3. Set the skillet over high heat and shake the frittata until it releases, about 10 seconds. Place a large, flat plate over the skillet and carefully invert the frittata onto it. Let cool for 5 minutes, then cut into wedges and serve. —*Marcia Kiesel*

●HEALTHY ●MAKE AHEAD ●VEGETARIAN ●STAFF FAVORITE

Mushroom and Fried-Egg BLT Clubs

TOTAL: 35 MIN
4 SERVINGS ●

These knife-and-fork club sandwiches rearrange all the elements of a traditional hearty breakfast—runny fried over-easy eggs, crisp toast and strips of lean bacon.

- 8 **thick slices of lean bacon**
- 2 **tablespoons unsalted butter**
- 1 **tablespoon extra-virgin olive oil, plus more for frying**
- 1 **pound white mushrooms, thinly sliced**

Salt and freshly ground pepper

- 4 **large eggs**

Twelve ¼-inch thick slices of whole wheat sandwich bread, toasted

Mayonnaise

- 4 **romaine lettuce leaves**
- 8 **thin tomato slices**

1. In a large nonstick skillet, cook the bacon over moderate heat, turning once, until crisp, about 4 minutes per side. Drain on paper towels. Wipe out the skillet.

2. In the skillet, melt the butter in the 1 tablespoon of oil. Add the mushrooms and season with salt and pepper. Cover and cook over moderate heat until the mushrooms soften and release their liquid, about 7 minutes. Uncover and cook, stirring often, until richly browned, about 8 minutes longer. Transfer to a bowl.

3. Wipe out the skillet and coat it with a thin film of olive oil. Carefully crack the eggs into the skillet and fry them over-easy over moderate heat, about 3 minutes on one side and about 30 seconds on the other side. Season the fried eggs with salt and pepper.

4. On a work surface, spread 8 slices of the whole wheat toast with mayonnaise. Top 4 of these with the lettuce, tomato slices and bacon; top the other 4 with the mushrooms and fried eggs. Stack the sandwiches and cover with the remaining 4 slices of toast. Cut the sandwiches in half and serve immediately.
—*Marcia Kiesel*

Ham and Cheese on Rye Bread Salad

TOTAL: 30 MIN
4 SERVINGS ●

In this fun version of the sandwich classic, F&W's Grace Parisi creates a delectable ham salad mixed with crunchy rye bread croutons and bits of Gruyère cheese, then tosses it in a mustardy dressing with celery and chives. She likes to wrap the salad in Bibb lettuce leaves for an inside-out sandwich.

- 4 **slices of seeded rye bread, cut into 1-by-½-inch batons**
- ¼ **cup plus 1 tablespoon canola oil**
- 3 **tablespoons grainy mustard**
- 3 **tablespoons mayonnaise**
- 2 **tablespoons cider vinegar**

Freshly ground pepper

- 1 **cup chopped celery (3 ribs)**
- 1 **pound thickly sliced smoked ham, cut into 1-by-½-inch batons**
- 6 **ounces Gruyère cheese, coarsely shredded (2 cups)**
- ¼ **cup snipped chives**

1. Preheat the oven to 350°. On a rimmed baking sheet, toss the rye bread batons with 2 tablespoons of the canola oil. Bake for 15 minutes, stirring once, until the batons are lightly toasted. Let cool.

2. In a large bowl, whisk the mustard with the mayonnaise and vinegar. Gradually whisk in the remaining 3 tablespoons of canola oil and season with pepper. Add the chopped celery, ham, Gruyère, snipped chives and the rye bread croutons, toss well and serve immediately.
—*Grace Parisi*

MAKE AHEAD The rye bread croutons can be stored in an airtight container at room temperature for up to 1 day.

Bread Salad with Prosciutto

TOTAL: 30 MIN
4 SERVINGS ●

Two ½-inch-thick slices of white country bread, crusts removed

- 1 **tablespoon unsalted butter, melted**

Salt

- 1½ **tablespoons extra-virgin olive oil**
- 4 **thin slices of prosciutto (1 ounce), torn into strips**
- 1 **large garlic clove, minced**
- 1½ **teaspoons tomato paste**
- 1½ **teaspoons Pernod**
- 1½ **tablespoons water**

One 1-ounce piece of firm sheep's-milk cheese, such as Pyrenees brebis or Manchego, cut into 1½-by-¼-inch matchsticks

- 2 **tablespoons coarsely chopped roasted almonds**
- ¼ **cup coarsely chopped parsley leaves**

1. Preheat the oven to 350°. Brush the bread on both sides with the melted butter. Using a serrated knife, cut the bread into 1-inch dice. Transfer the bread to a baking sheet and sprinkle lightly with salt. Bake for about 8 minutes, until crisp.

clotted cream

Slightly tangy and superrich, clotted cream is the thick, buttery layer that forms when raw milk is heated and cooled. It's delicious spread on scones and bread or spooned over fresh fruit (*$6 for 6 oz; englishteastore.com*).

2. Meanwhile, in a large skillet, heat the olive oil. Add the prosciutto and cook over moderately high heat until sizzling, about 30 seconds. Using tongs, transfer the prosciutto to a plate, shaking any excess oil back into the skillet.

3. Add the garlic to the skillet and cook over moderate heat until fragrant, about 1 minute. Stir in the tomato paste and cook for 30 seconds. Stir in the Pernod and water and simmer for 20 seconds. Remove the skillet from the heat and stir in the prosciutto strips and a pinch of salt. Fold in the toasted bread cubes.

4. Transfer the bread salad to plates. Garnish with the sheep's-milk cheese, the chopped almonds and parsley and serve right away. —Marcia Kiesel

Toasted Cornmeal Corn Bread

ACTIVE: 15 MIN; TOTAL: 1 HR
MAKES ONE 9-BY-13-INCH
CORN BREAD ●
Toasting the cornmeal before mixing it into the batter gives this sweet and moist corn bread a heartier flavor.

- 2 **cups coarse yellow cornmeal**
- 2 **cups all-purpose flour**
- 1 **tablespoon baking powder**
- 1 **tablespoon kosher salt**
- 1½ **cups whole milk**
- ⅔ **cup honey, warmed**
- 2 **large eggs, beaten**
- 1 **stick unsalted butter, melted**

1. Preheat the oven to 350°. Oil a 9-by-13-inch metal baking pan.

2. In a medium skillet, toast the cornmeal over moderately high heat, stirring constantly, until lightly browned, about 5 minutes. Transfer to a large bowl and whisk in the flour, baking powder and kosher salt. In a separate bowl, whisk the milk with the warmed honey and beaten eggs. Add the liquid to the dry ingredients and whisk until moistened. Add the melted butter and whisk until smooth.

3. Pour the batter into the prepared pan and bake in the center of the oven for 30 minutes, until the top is golden and a toothpick inserted in the center comes out clean. Let cool on a rack for 15 minutes. Cut into squares and serve warm or at room temperature. —Michael Symon

Old-Fashioned Banana Bread

ACTIVE: 20 MIN; TOTAL: 1 HR 30 MIN
MAKES ONE 9-BY-5-INCH LOAF ●
This extraordinarily simple and tasty banana bread has a moist center and crispy crust.

Unsalted butter
- 1¼ **cups all-purpose flour, plus more for dusting**
- 1 **teaspoon baking soda**

Pinch of salt
- 2 **large eggs, beaten**
- ½ **cup canola oil**
- 1 **cup sugar**
- 2 **large, very ripe bananas, mashed**

Confectioners' sugar, for dusting

1. Preheat the oven to 350°. Butter and flour a 9-by-5-inch metal loaf pan. In a medium bowl, whisk the 1¼ cups of flour with the baking soda and salt. In another bowl, whisk the eggs with the canola oil, sugar and mashed bananas. Stir the banana mixture into the dry ingredients until combined.

2. Scrape the batter into the prepared pan and bake in the center of the oven for about 50 minutes, until the banana bread is golden and a toothpick inserted in the center of the loaf comes out clean. Transfer the pan to a rack and let cool for 15 minutes, then turn the bread out onto the rack and let cool completely. Dust the top with confectioners' sugar, cut into slices and serve the bread warm.
—Lisa Ritter

MAKE AHEAD The banana bread can be wrapped in plastic and refrigerated for up to 1 week.

Lemony Cornmeal–Cherry Scones

ACTIVE: 20 MIN; TOTAL: 1 HR
MAKES 12 SCONES ● ●
Because the dough for these slightly crunchy cornmeal scones isn't rolled, it's less likely to be overworked, resulting in a more delicate crumb. For extra flavor, you can soak the cherries (or other dried fruit) in hot tea or apple juice.

- 5 **ounces dried sour cherries (1 cup)**
- 1½ **cups all-purpose flour**
- ½ **cup yellow cornmeal**
- 1 **tablespoon baking powder**
- ¼ **teaspoon baking soda**
- ½ **teaspoon kosher salt**

Finely grated zest of 2 lemons
- 6 **tablespoons unsalted butter, cut into ½-inch cubes and chilled**
- ½ **cup whole milk**
- ¼ **cup pure maple syrup**
- 1 **teaspoon pure vanilla extract**
- 1 **egg yolk mixed with 1 tablespoon of water**

Coarse sugar, for sprinkling

1. Preheat the oven to 350°. Line a large baking sheet with parchment paper. In a heatproof measuring cup, cover the dried sour cherries with hot water and let stand for 15 minutes. Drain and pat dry.

2. In a medium bowl, mix the flour with the cornmeal, baking powder, baking soda, salt and lemon zest. Using a pastry blender or 2 knives, cut in the butter until it is the size of small peas. Add the cherries. In the measuring cup, combine the milk, maple syrup and vanilla. Add the liquid to the bowl and stir with a wooden spoon until the dough is evenly moistened; it will be a little wet.

3. Scoop ¼ cup mounds of dough 2 inches apart on the baking sheet. Brush the tops with the egg wash and sprinkle lightly with coarse sugar. Bake for about 30 minutes, until golden. Transfer the scones to a rack to cool slightly. Serve warm or at room temperature. —Mariah Swan

● HEALTHY ● MAKE AHEAD ● VEGETARIAN ● STAFF FAVORITE

Lemon-Currant-Cream Scones

ACTIVE: 20 MIN; TOTAL: 45 MIN
MAKES 12 SCONES ●

You can make these light scones in traditional triangles rather than in rounds, as they are here. To do so, in Step 2, pat the dough into two smaller rounds and use a sharp knife or pizza wheel to cut the rounds into wedges. Bake as directed.

- 2 cups all-purpose flour
- 3 tablespoons sugar, plus more for sprinkling
- 1 tablespoon baking powder
- ¼ teaspoon salt
- 1 stick cold unsalted butter, cut into ½-inch cubes
- ¼ cup dried currants
- 1 teaspoon finely grated lemon zest
- 1 cup heavy cream

1. Preheat the oven to 375°. In a large bowl, whisk the flour with the 3 tablespoons of sugar, the baking powder and the salt until the ingredients are combined. Using a pastry blender or 2 knives, cut the butter into the dry ingredients until it is the size of small peas. Stir in the dried currants and grated lemon zest. Add ¾ cup plus 2 tablespoons of the heavy cream and stir just until the dough is evenly moistened. Gather the dough into a ball and gently knead it a few times.

2. On a lightly floured surface, pat the dough into a ½-inch-thick round. Using a 2½-inch round biscuit cutter, stamp out as many scones as you can. Gently gather the scraps, press them together and cut several more scones. Transfer the scones to a baking sheet.

3. Brush the scones with the remaining 2 tablespoons of cream and sprinkle the tops generously with sugar. Bake the scones in the lower third of the oven for about 25 minutes, or until they are golden. Transfer the baking sheet to a cooling rack and let the scones cool slightly before serving. —*Grace Parisi*

Spiced Yogurt Muffins

ACTIVE: 20 MIN; TOTAL: 45 MIN
MAKES 18 MUFFINS ● ●

These ingeniously moist muffins are from baker Jennifer Musty of Fraîche, a yogurt shop in Palo Alto, California. They're rich in calcium and low in fat.

- 2 cups all-purpose flour
- 1 cup light brown sugar
- 1 tablespoon baking powder
- ½ teaspoon baking soda
- ½ teaspoon salt
- 1 teaspoon cinnamon
- ½ teaspoon ground allspice
- ½ teaspoon ground cloves
- ¾ teaspoon freshly grated nutmeg
- 2 large eggs, at room temperature
- 1¼ cups plain low-fat yogurt
- 4 tablespoons unsalted butter, melted
- ¼ cup unsweetened applesauce
- 1 teaspoon pure vanilla extract
- 1 tablespoon granulated sugar

1. Preheat the oven to 375°. Line 18 muffin cups with paper or foil liners. Lightly spray the liners with vegetable oil spray.

2. In a food processor, combine the flour, brown sugar, baking powder, baking soda, salt, cinnamon, allspice, cloves and ½ teaspoon of the nutmeg and pulse to blend; transfer to a large bowl. In a medium bowl, whisk the eggs, yogurt, butter, applesauce and vanilla. Fold the yogurt mixture into the dry ingredients until just blended.

3. Spoon the batter into the prepared muffin cups. Sprinkle the granulated sugar and remaining ¼ teaspoon nutmeg over the muffins. Bake for 18 minutes, until the muffins are springy; let cool in the pans for 5 minutes, then transfer to a wire rack. Serve warm or at room temperature.
—*Jennifer Musty*

MAKE AHEAD The Spiced Yogurt Muffins can be kept at room temperature for up to 2 hours.

Grill-Roasted Bacon-and-Scallion Corn Muffins

ACTIVE: 20 MIN; TOTAL: 45 MIN
MAKES 12 MUFFINS ●

When cooking these bacon-and-scallion-flecked corn muffins—a great accompaniment to all kinds of barbecue—F&W's Nick Fauchald prefers the grill to a conventional oven for two reasons: The muffins absorb great smoky flavors, and this style of cooking means that he can spend more time outside.

- 5 slices of bacon
- 1 cup all-purpose flour
- 1 cup yellow cornmeal
- ¼ cup sugar
- 2 teaspoons baking powder
- 2 teaspoons salt
- ½ teaspoon baking soda
- ½ teaspoon freshly ground black pepper
- Pinch of cayenne pepper
- 1½ cups frozen corn kernels, thawed
- 4 large scallions, white and light green parts, finely chopped
- 2 large eggs
- 1 cup sour cream
- 4 tablespoons unsalted butter, melted

1. Set up a grill for indirect grilling, with the coals on one side, and heat to 425°. Meanwhile, in a medium skillet set on the grill or the stove, cook the bacon over moderate heat, turning once, until crisp, about 6 minutes. Drain the slices on paper towels and crumble.

2. Line a 12-cup muffin tin with paper liners. In a large bowl, whisk the flour, cornmeal, sugar, baking powder, salt, baking soda, black pepper and cayenne. Stir in the corn, scallions and crumbled bacon.

3. In a medium bowl, whisk the eggs with the sour cream and melted butter. Fold the wet ingredients into the dry until just blended. Pour the batter into the lined muffin cups.

4. Place the muffins on the grate opposite the coals, cover and grill for 20 minutes, or until a toothpick inserted in the center comes out with only a few crumbs. Serve slightly cooled. —*Nick Fauchald*

MAKE AHEAD The muffins can be kept in an airtight container overnight. Reheat in a 350° oven.

Brioche French Toast with Fresh Berry Compote

TOTAL: 30 MIN
6 SERVINGS

At L.A.'s BLD Restaurant, pastry chef Mariah Swan tops French toast with a compote that comes together in less than 10 minutes but tastes surprisingly complex.

- 1 **pound mixed fresh berries, such as strawberries and raspberries, sliced (4 cups)**
- ¼ **cup plus 3 tablespoons sugar**
- 2 **tablespoons water**

- 6 **large eggs, beaten**
- ½ **cup heavy cream**
- ¼ **teaspoon cinnamon**
- ¼ **teaspoon ground ginger**
- ⅛ **teaspoon ground allspice**

Unsalted butter, for the griddle

Twelve ¾-inch-thick slices of brioche (from 2 small loaves)

Crème fraîche, for serving

1. Preheat the oven to 225°. In a medium saucepan, combine the fresh berries with ¼ cup of the sugar and the water and bring the mixture to a simmer. Cook over moderate heat, stirring occasionally, until the berries have softened and released their juices and the sugar has dissolved completely, about 8 minutes.

2. In a large bowl, whisk the eggs with the heavy cream, the remaining 3 tablespoons of sugar and the cinnamon, ginger and allspice. Transfer the cream and egg mixture to a 9-by-13-inch baking dish.

3. Heat a large cast-iron griddle over moderate heat and lightly butter it. Working in batches, dip half of the brioche slices in the cream and egg mixture, turning them once, until the slices are moistened but not soggy. Transfer the soaked brioche slices to the griddle and cook them over moderate heat, turning once, until they are golden on both sides and cooked through, about 4 minutes. Transfer the finished French toast to a baking sheet, cover loosely with foil and keep warm in the oven while you soak and cook the remaining brioche slices. Transfer the French toast to plates and serve right away, accompanied by the warm berry compote and crème fraîche.
—*Mariah Swan*

MAKE AHEAD The warm berry compote can be cooled, covered and refrigerated overnight. Reheat the compote gently before serving.

●**HEALTHY** ●**MAKE AHEAD** ●**VEGETARIAN** ●**STAFF FAVORITE**

Cornmeal Pancakes with Maple-Cranberry Butter

TOTAL: 30 MIN
4 SERVINGS

Instead of pouring maple syrup at the table, F&W's Melissa Rubel tops her crispy-edged cornmeal pancakes with a fabulous cranberry butter sweetened with maple syrup.

- 1 stick unsalted butter, softened, plus 3 tablespoons melted butter, and more for brushing
- ¼ cup fresh cranberries
- 3 tablespoons pure maple syrup
- 1½ teaspoons kosher salt
- ⅔ cup all-purpose flour
- ⅔ cup yellow cornmeal
- 2 tablespoons sugar
- 1½ teaspoons baking powder
- 1 cup whole milk
- 1 large egg

1. In a mini food processor, pulse the stick of softened butter with the cranberries, maple syrup and ½ teaspoon of the salt until the cranberries are incorporated but still chunky; scrape into a bowl.

2. In a large bowl, whisk the flour, cornmeal, sugar, baking powder and the remaining 1 teaspoon of salt. Whisk in the milk, egg and the 3 tablespoons of melted butter until just combined.

3. Heat a cast-iron skillet over moderate heat and lightly brush with butter. Ladle in 2 tablespoons of batter for each pancake and cook until until golden on the bottom and just beginning to set, about 2 minutes. Flip the pancakes and cook until just cooked through, about 2 more minutes. Transfer the pancakes to plates, spread with the cranberry butter and serve.
—*Melissa Rubel*

MAKE AHEAD The maple-cranberry butter can be wrapped well in plastic and refrigerated for up to 4 days or frozen for up to 1 month. Bring the butter to room temperature before serving.

Ricotta Pancakes with Blueberries

TOTAL: 30 MIN
6 SERVINGS

Adding fresh ricotta to the batter makes these pancakes incredibly moist and light.

- 1½ cups all-purpose flour
- 1 teaspoon baking powder
- 1½ teaspoons kosher salt
- 3 large eggs, separated
- 1¾ cups plus 2 tablespoons milk
- 6 ounces ricotta cheese (½ cup plus 2 tablespoons)
- ¼ cup sugar
- 1 tablespoon pure vanilla extract
- Unsalted butter, for the griddle
- 1 pint fresh blueberries or 2 cups frozen blueberries, thawed
- Pure maple syrup, for serving

1. In a small bowl, whisk the flour, baking powder and salt. In a large bowl, whisk the egg yolks with the milk, ricotta, sugar and vanilla. Add the dry ingredients and whisk until the batter is smooth.

2. In a large bowl, using an electric mixer, beat the egg whites at medium speed until frothy. Beat at high speed until soft peaks form. Fold the egg whites into the batter until no streaks remain.

3. Preheat the oven to 225°. Heat a griddle, then lightly butter it. For each pancake, ladle a scant ¼ cup of the batter onto the griddle; be sure to leave enough space between the pancakes. Cook over moderately low heat until the bottoms are golden and the pancakes are just beginning to set, 1 to 2 minutes. Sprinkle each pancake with a few blueberries and press lightly. Flip the pancakes and cook until golden on the bottom and cooked through, 1 minute. Transfer the pancakes to plates and keep warm in the oven while you make the rest. Serve with maple syrup. —*Neal Fraser*

MAKE AHEAD The batter can be refrigerated overnight. Bring to room temperature and whisk briefly before cooking.

French Toast Stuffed with Ricotta and Strawberry Jam

TOTAL: 30 MIN
4 SERVINGS

Many stuffed French toast recipes call for cutting a pocket into each slice of bread. This one, however, simplifies the technique by sandwiching the creamy, fruity fillings between two slices.

- Eight ¾-inch-thick slices of firm white bread
- ½ cup fresh ricotta cheese
- ¼ cup plus 2 tablespoons strawberry jam
- 2 large eggs
- ½ cup milk
- ½ teaspoon pure vanilla extract
- Pinch of cinnamon
- Pinch of salt
- 4 tablespoons unsalted butter
- Confectioners' sugar, for dusting

1. Spread 4 slices of the bread with the ricotta cheese. Spread the remaining 4 slices of bread with the strawberry jam. Close the sandwiches, pressing gently so they stay closed.

2. In a shallow bowl or pie plate, whisk the eggs with the milk, vanilla, cinnamon and salt. Dip both sides of each sandwich into the egg mixture until well coated.

3. In a large skillet, melt 2 tablespoons of the butter. Add 2 of the sandwiches and cook until golden, about 4 minutes per side. Repeat with the remaining butter and sandwiches. Cut the stuffed French toast sandwiches in half on the diagonal and transfer to plates. Dust them with confectioners' sugar and serve immediately.
—*Melissa Rubel*

Classic Belgian Waffles

ACTIVE: 30 MIN; TOTAL: 1 HR
MAKES 4 WAFFLES

- 1½ teaspoons active dry yeast
- 1 cup warm water
- 3 cups all-purpose flour

½ teaspoon salt

1 cup whole milk

1 stick unsalted butter, melted

2 large eggs, separated

½ teaspoon pure vanilla extract

Confectioners' sugar,
  for dusting

Belgian Chocolate-Fudge Sauce
  (recipe follows), for serving

1. In a small bowl, dissolve the yeast in the water. In a large bowl, stir together the flour and the salt. Whisk in the yeast mixture, the milk, melted butter, egg yolks and vanilla extract. Continue whisking until the waffle batter is smooth.

2. In a medium bowl, beat the egg whites until soft peaks form. Fold them into the waffle batter and let stand for about 20 minutes.

3. Preheat the oven to 225°. Heat and grease a waffle iron. Pour 1¼ cups of the batter into the iron and cook until the waffles are golden, 6 minutes. Transfer the waffles to the oven. Repeat with the remaining batter. Dust the waffles with confectioners' sugar, drizzle with the Belgian Chocolate-Fudge Sauce and serve. —*Thomas DeGeest*

BELGIAN CHOCOLATE-FUDGE SAUCE

TOTAL: 15 MIN

MAKES 2 CUPS ● ● ●

1 cup heavy cream

10 ounces bittersweet
  chocolate, chopped

2 tablespoons confectioners'
  sugar

In a saucepan, bring the cream to a boil. Remove from the heat and add the chopped chocolate. Let stand for 2 minutes, then stir until the chocolate is melted. Add the confectioners' sugar and whisk until smooth. —*TD*

MAKE AHEAD The sauce can be refrigerated for up to 4 days. Reheat gently, stirring frequently, before serving.

Crêpes with Sweet Yogurt and Raspberry-Apricot Sauce

TOTAL: 45 MIN

MAKES 8 CRÊPES ●

3 large eggs

1¼ cups milk

Pinch of salt

1 cup all-purpose flour

3 tablespoons unsalted butter,
  melted

¼ cup apricot preserves

½ cup frozen raspberries

1 tablespoon fresh lemon juice

1½ cups plain Greek-style yogurt

3 tablespoons light brown sugar

½ teaspoon pure vanilla extract

1. In a medium bowl, whisk the eggs with ¼ cup of the milk and the salt until blended. Whisk in the flour until the batter is smooth, then whisk in the remaining 1 cup of milk and 1 tablespoon of the melted butter. Let the crêpe batter stand at room temperature for about 20 minutes.

2. In a saucepan, combine the apricot preserves with the raspberries and lemon juice and cook over moderate heat until jammy, about 5 minutes. Cover and keep warm.

3. In a bowl, mix the yogurt with the brown sugar and vanilla.

4. Heat a 10-inch crêpe pan or nonstick skillet over moderate heat. Brush the pan with some of the melted butter. Pour in a scant ⅓ cup of the crêpe batter and immediately rotate the pan to evenly coat the bottom. Cook the crêpe until lightly browned on the bottom, about 45 seconds. Flip the crêpe and cook until brown dots appear on the other side, about 15 seconds longer. Transfer the crêpe to a large plate covered with parchment paper. Continue making crêpes with the remaining batter, brushing the pan with the remaining melted butter as needed.

5. Spoon 3 tablespoons of the yogurt onto each crêpe and roll them up. Transfer to plates. Spoon the raspberry-apricot sauce on top and serve. —*Rachel Soszynski*

Smoked Salmon and Cream Cheese Crêpes

ACTIVE: 45 MIN; TOTAL: 1 HR 45 MIN

8 SERVINGS

1½ cups whole milk

½ cup water

6 tablespoons butter, melted

3 large eggs

1½ cups all-purpose flour

¾ teaspoon salt

8 ounces cream cheese, softened

2 tablespoons butter, softened

2 tablespoons lemon zest

1 medium shallot, minced

¼ cup capers, rinsed and chopped

1 tablespoon minced dill

¼ teaspoon Asian fish sauce

Freshly ground pepper

3 cups baby spinach (3 ounces)

1 teaspoon extra-virgin olive oil

1 teaspoon balsamic vinegar

½ pound sliced smoked salmon

2 plum tomatoes, thinly sliced

1. In a bowl, whisk the milk with the water, melted butter and eggs. Mix the flour and salt in another bowl. Whisk the milk mixture into the flour. Strain the batter into a measuring cup and refrigerate for 1 hour.

2. In a bowl, blend the cream cheese with the butter, lemon zest, shallot, capers, dill and fish sauce and season with pepper.

3. Spray a 12-inch nonstick skillet with cooking spray. Heat the skillet over moderate heat. Pour ⅓ cup of the batter into the skillet and swirl the pan to coat it evenly. Cook the crêpe until lightly golden on the bottom, 1 minute. Flip and cook for about 30 seconds longer. Transfer to a plate and repeat with the remaining batter.

4. In a bowl, toss the spinach with the oil and vinegar. Fold each crêpe in half. Spread 2 tablespoons of the cream cheese vertically down the center of each crêpe and lay the salmon over it. Top with the spinach and tomatoes and season with pepper. Fold one side of the crêpe over the filling, roll to close and serve. —*Andrea Day-Boykin*

Cinnamon-Pecan Buns

ACTIVE: 35 MIN; TOTAL: 1 HR 5 MIN

MAKES ABOUT 15 BUNS ● ● ●

- 4 tablespoons unsalted butter, melted and cooled
- ¾ cup pecans
- ½ cup light brown sugar
- 1 teaspoon cinnamon
- ¼ teaspoon kosher salt
- 1 cup cottage cheese
- ½ cup buttermilk
- 1 egg yolk
- ⅓ cup granulated sugar
- 1 teaspoon pure vanilla extract
- 2 teaspoons finely grated orange zest (optional)
- 2¼ cups all-purpose flour, plus more for dusting
- 1 tablespoon baking powder
- ¼ teaspoon baking soda
- ½ teaspoon fine salt

1. Preheat the oven to 350°. Brush the bottom and side of a 10-inch springform pan with half of the melted butter.

2. In a food processor, combine the pecans with the brown sugar, cinnamon and kosher salt; pulse until the nuts are almost finely ground (avoid overprocessing, as they can become pasty). Transfer the mixture to a bowl and sprinkle a scant ¾ cup over the bottom of the prepared pan. Wipe out the food processor.

3. Add the cottage cheese, buttermilk, egg yolk, granulated sugar, vanilla and orange zest to the processor and puree until smooth. In a medium bowl, combine the 2¼ cups of flour with the baking powder, baking soda and fine salt; whisk to mix. Add the flour mixture to the processor and pulse just until the dough comes together; it will be quite soft and sticky.

4. Turn the dough out onto a lightly floured work surface and use your hands to gather it into a smooth ball. With a lightly floured rolling pin, roll out the dough to an 11-by-16-inch rectangle, flouring the work surface as necessary. Brush the dough with the remaining melted butter, leaving a ½-inch border all around. Sprinkle on the remaining pecan-sugar mixture.

5. Working from a long side, roll the dough into a tight cylinder and cut it into 1-inch slices. Arrange the slices cut side up in the prepared pan. Bake the buns in the middle of the oven for about 25 minutes, until lightly browned on top and slightly firm to the touch. Transfer the pan to a rack and let cool for 5 minutes. Run a knife around the inside of the pan to loosen the buns. Remove the springform ring. Invert the buns onto a plate and carefully remove the bottom of the pan. If any of the pecan mixture sticks to the pan, simply scrape it onto the buns. Serve warm.
—*Rachel Soszynski*

MAKE AHEAD The Cinnamon-Pecan Buns can be made up to 2 days ahead and rewarmed in a 350° oven.

Pecan-Honey Buns

ACTIVE: 35 MIN; TOTAL: 3 HR 15 MIN

MAKES 12 BUNS ● ● ●

The honeyed glaze on these sticky, nutty breakfast rolls is luscious and soft when warm, then turns nicely chewy when cool.

DOUGH

- 2¼ teaspoons active dry yeast
- 2 tablespoons granulated sugar
- 1 cup milk, warmed
- 4 tablespoons unsalted butter, melted, plus more for brushing
- 3 large egg yolks
- 2 tablespoons honey, preferably orange blossom or clover
- 1 teaspoon pure vanilla extract
- 3½ cups plus 3 tablespoons all-purpose flour, plus more for dusting
- 1 teaspoon kosher salt

TOPPING

- ½ cup honey, preferably orange blossom or clover
- ½ cup packed light brown sugar
- 4 tablespoons unsalted butter, plus more for brushing
- 1½ cups pecans (6 ounces), coarsely chopped

FILLING

- ¾ cup packed light brown sugar
- 1 tablespoon cinnamon
- 6 tablespoons unsalted butter, softened

1. MAKE THE DOUGH: In the bowl of an electric mixer fitted with the paddle, combine the yeast with a pinch of granulated sugar and the milk and let stand until foamy, 5 minutes. Add the remaining sugar, the 4 tablespoons of melted butter and the egg yolks, honey and vanilla; mix until blended. Mix in the flour and salt. Switch to the dough hook and knead at medium speed until the dough forms a smooth ball, about 4 minutes.

2. Brush a large bowl with butter. Add the dough and brush the top with butter. Cover and let stand in a warm place until doubled in volume, about 1 hour.

3. MEANWHILE, MAKE THE TOPPING: Butter a 9-by-13-inch glass baking dish. In a medium saucepan, melt the honey with the brown sugar and the 4 tablespoons of butter over moderate heat, stirring, until the sugar is dissolved, about 1 minute. Pour the hot honey mixture into the buttered baking dish and sprinkle evenly with the chopped pecans.

artisanal honey

Single-varietal honeys have distinct colors and flavors. Tupelo honey, which is bright yellow and has complex herbal and floral notes, is delicious simply stirred into Greek-style yogurt (*$8 for 16 oz; floridatupelohoney.com*).

PECAN-HONEY BUNS

CINNAMON-RAISIN BREAD CUSTARD WITH FRESH BERRIES

4. MAKE THE FILLING: In a small bowl, mix the sugar with the cinnamon. On a lightly floured work surface, roll out the raised dough to a 12-by-18-inch rectangle. Spread the softened butter over the dough, leaving a 1-inch border all around. Sprinkle the dough with the cinnamon sugar. Starting at a long side of the rectangle, roll the dough into a log and turn it seam side down. Cut the dough into 12 slices. Arrange the slices cut side up in the baking dish. Cover and let stand in a warm place until the buns double in volume, about 1 hour.

5. Preheat the oven to 350°. Bake the honey buns for about 35 minutes, until golden brown. Remove from the oven and let stand for 5 minutes. Invert the buns onto a baking sheet and let cool slightly. Serve the honey buns warm.

—*Susan Spungen*

MAKE AHEAD The honey buns can be made a day ahead. Rewarm before serving.

Cinnamon-Raisin Bread Custard with Fresh Berries

ACTIVE: 15 MIN; TOTAL: 40 MIN PLUS COOLING

6 TO 8 SERVINGS ● ●

This ultrarich bread pudding is perfect for brunch or dessert. It can be made with store-bought cinnamon-raisin bread, but a fresh bakery loaf cut into ½-inch-thick slices is best.

- **16** slices of cinnamon-raisin bread
- **6** tablespoons unsalted butter, melted and cooled slightly
- **4** large eggs
- **2** large egg yolks
- **¾** cup granulated sugar
- **3** cups milk
- **1** cup heavy cream
- **1** tablespoon pure vanilla extract

Confectioners' sugar

Fresh berries, for serving

1. Preheat the oven to 350°. Butter a 9-by-13-inch glass or ceramic baking dish. Brush both sides of each bread slice with melted butter. Arrange the bread in the prepared dish in two even rows.

2. In a large bowl, whisk the whole eggs with the egg yolks until blended. Whisk in the granulated sugar, milk, heavy cream and vanilla. Strain the milk mixture over the bread, pressing on the slices to make sure they're evenly moistened.

3. Place the baking dish in a larger roasting pan and pour enough warm water into the pan to reach halfway up the sides of the dish. Bake in the upper third of the oven for about 25 minutes, or until the top is lightly browned and the custard is set. Transfer the baking dish to a rack and let the custard rest for 15 minutes. Sift confectioners' sugar over the custard and cut into squares. Serve with berries.

—*Bradley Ogden*

Strawberry-Pecan Quick Bread

ACTIVE: 20 MIN; TOTAL: 1 HR 45 MIN
8 SERVINGS ● ○

As this loaf bakes in the oven, the texture of the chewy dried strawberries softens slightly. Buy your dried strawberries at a specialty food shop or health food store that rotates its stock frequently to make sure that the fruit is plump and moist.

1½ cups all-purpose flour
1½ teaspoons baking powder
½ teaspoon salt
1 stick unsalted butter, softened
1 cup plus 2 tablespoons sugar
2 eggs
1 teaspoon pure vanilla extract
½ cup milk
¾ cup dried strawberries, coarsely chopped
½ cup pecans, coarsely chopped
1 teaspoon cinnamon

1. Preheat the oven to 350°. Spray a 9-by-5-inch loaf pan with vegetable oil. In a medium bowl, whisk the flour with the baking powder and salt. In a large bowl, beat the softened butter with 1 cup of the sugar until pale and fluffy. Using a handheld mixer at medium speed, beat in the eggs one at a time, beating until fully incorporated between additions. Add the vanilla. At low speed, working in 2 batches, alternately beat in the dry ingredients and the milk. Using a spatula, fold in the dried strawberries and chopped pecans until evenly incorporated.
2. Scrape the batter into the prepared pan. Mix the remaining 2 tablespoons of sugar with the cinnamon and sprinkle on top. Bake for about 1 hour and 5 minutes, or until a cake tester inserted in the center of the loaf comes out clean. Let the bread cool in the pan for 15 minutes, then turn it out onto a rack and let cool completely before slicing. —*Melissa Rubel*
MAKE AHEAD The bread can be wrapped in plastic and kept for up to 2 days.

Almond Toasted Brioche

 TOTAL: 40 MIN
6 SERVINGS ● ● ○

F&W's Grace Parisi simplifies almond brioche (brioche filled with almond paste), a Parisian breakfast favorite, by soaking store-bought brioche in almond-infused custard—almost as if she were making French toast—and baking it until crisp. The brioche is lovely sprinkled with confectioners' sugar and topped with berries.

1¼ cups sliced blanched almonds
½ cup granulated sugar
2 large eggs, at room temperature
4 tablespoons unsalted butter, softened
¼ teaspoon pure almond extract (optional)
¼ cup plus 2 tablespoons whole milk
Six 1-inch-thick slices of brioche, cut from a 1-pound loaf
Confectioners' sugar, for sprinkling
Berries, for serving

1. Preheat the oven to 375°. In a food processor, combine 1 cup of the almonds with the granulated sugar and process until powdery, about 2 minutes. Add the eggs, 2 tablespoons of the butter and the almond extract and process until creamy, about 2 minutes. With the food processor on, add the milk and process until blended. Transfer the custard mixture to a shallow baking dish.
2. Spread the remaining 2 tablespoons of butter evenly on one side of each slice of brioche. Dip the unbuttered sides of the brioche into the custard and transfer to a baking sheet, custard side up. Spoon any remaining custard over the bread and sprinkle with the remaining ¼ cup of sliced almonds. Bake the almond brioche for about 20 minutes, until the bottom is golden and crisp and the almonds are lightly browned. Transfer the brioche to plates and dust lightly with confectioners' sugar. Top with fresh berries and serve. —*Grace Parisi*

Apple Rye Turnovers with Celery Seeds

ACTIVE: 35 MIN; TOTAL: 2 HR 15 MIN
MAKES 8 TURNOVERS ● ● ●

1¾ cups plus 1 tablespoon all-purpose flour, plus more for dusting
1 cup dark rye flour
Salt
2 sticks cold unsalted butter (8 ounces), cut into ½-inch pieces
¾ cup ice water
2 Golden Delicious apples, peeled and cut into ½-inch dice
¼ cup plus 2 tablespoons granulated sugar
¼ teaspoon cinnamon
⅛ teaspoon freshly grated nutmeg
1 egg white, lightly beaten with 2 teaspoons of water
¼ cup turbinado sugar mixed with 2 teaspoons of celery seeds

1. In a food processor, combine 1¾ cups of the all-purpose flour with the rye flour and ¾ teaspoon of salt. Add the butter and pulse until it is the size of raisins. Add the ice water and pulse until the dough is evenly moistened. Divide the dough into 2 pieces and press into disks. Wrap the disks in plastic and refrigerate for 1 hour.
2. Preheat the oven to 375°. In a bowl, toss the apples with the granulated sugar, cinnamon, nutmeg, ⅛ teaspoon of salt and the remaining 1 tablespoon of flour.
3. On a lightly floured surface, roll out one disk of dough into an 11½-inch square about ¼ inch thick. Trim off a ¼-inch border to even the edges. Cut the dough into four 5½-inch squares. Spoon half of the apple filling onto the squares of dough. Fold over the corners of the dough to form triangles. Using a fork, crimp the edges to seal them. Transfer the turnovers to a parchment paper–lined baking sheet. Repeat with the remaining dough and filling for a total of 8 turnovers.

4. Brush the tops of the turnovers with the egg white wash and sprinkle generously with the celery-seed sugar. Make two small slits in the top of each turnover. Bake for about 35 minutes, until golden all over. Let cool on the pan for 15 minutes. Serve warm.
—*Jerry Traunfeld*

Scrambled Tofu with Potatoes, Mushrooms and Peppers

TOTAL: 40 MIN
6 SERVINGS ● ●

½ pound fingerling potatoes, scrubbed
3 tablespoons extra-virgin olive oil
5 ounces oyster mushrooms, thickly sliced
Salt and freshly ground pepper
1 pound firm tofu—drained, patted dry and cut into ½-inch cubes
One 12-ounce jar roasted red bell peppers, drained and thinly sliced
3 ounces mozzarella-style soy cheese, coarsely shredded (½ cup)
2 tablespoons prepared pesto

1. Boil the potatoes in salted water until tender, about 10 minutes. Drain and slice the potatoes crosswise ¾ inch thick.
2. In a large nonstick skillet, heat the oil until shimmering. Add the potato slices and cook over moderately high heat, turning occasionally, until lightly browned, about 5 minutes. Add the mushrooms, season with salt and pepper and cook, stirring occasionally, until browned, about 6 minutes. Add the tofu and roasted red peppers and season lightly with salt and pepper. Cook, stirring and lightly mashing the tofu, until the ingredients are combined and heated through, about 5 minutes. Add the soy cheese and 1 tablespoon of the pesto and stir to melt the cheese. Transfer the scramble to a platter, drizzle with the remaining 1 tablespoon of pesto and serve right away. —*Neal Fraser*

Fruit-and-Nut-Packed Granola

ACTIVE: 20 MIN; TOTAL: 1 HR 30 MIN
MAKES 13 CUPS ● ●

1 stick unsalted butter
½ cup light brown sugar
¼ cup honey
1 teaspoon cinnamon
1 teaspoon pure vanilla extract
½ teaspoon kosher salt
3¾ cups rolled oats (12 ounces)
3 ounces finely grated unsweetened coconut (1 cup)
3 ounces raw cashews (½ cup)
3 ounces pecans (½ cup)
3 ounces shelled raw pistachios (½ cup)
3 ounces slivered almonds (½ cup)
1 cup fresh orange juice
10 ounces mixed dried fruit, such as cranberries, golden raisins, cherries and chopped apple slices (2 cups)

1. Preheat the oven to 275°. Line a large rimmed baking sheet with parchment paper. In a medium saucepan, combine the butter, brown sugar, honey, cinnamon, vanilla and salt and bring to a simmer, stirring until the brown sugar is dissolved, about 2 minutes. Let cool slightly.
2. In a very large bowl, toss the oats with the coconut, cashews, pecans, pistachios and almonds. Add the warm brown sugar mixture and stir to coat thoroughly. Spread the granola on the baking sheet and bake for 1 hour and 15 minutes, stirring once or twice, until golden.
3. Meanwhile, in a medium bowl, pour the orange juice over the dried fruit and let stand until plumped, about 1 hour.
4. Drain the dried fruit, pressing to extract the liquid; discard the liquid. Stir the fruit into the granola and bake for 5 minutes. Let cool; the granola will crisp as it cools.
—*Neal Fraser*

MAKE AHEAD The granola can be stored in an airtight container for up to 2 weeks. Recrisp in a 275° oven for 15 minutes.

Apple-Nut Breakfast Porridge

TOTAL: 15 MIN PLUS OVERNIGHT SOAKING
1 SERVING ● ● ●

2 tablespoons coarsely chopped raw nuts, such as almonds, hazelnuts or Brazil nuts, soaked overnight and drained
1 Granny Smith apple—peeled, cored and coarsely chopped
2 dried white figs, coarsely chopped
¼ teaspoon chopped fresh ginger
1 teaspoon dried goji berries
½ teaspoon ground flax seeds

In a food processor, grind the nuts. Add the apple, figs and ginger; pulse until chunky. Transfer the porridge to a bowl. Top with the goji berries and ground flax.
—*Adina Niemerow*

Overnight Oatmeal with Almonds and Dried Cranberries

TOTAL: 15 MIN PLUS OVERNIGHT SOAKING
6 SERVINGS ● ●

1½ cups steel-cut oats
6 cups water
¼ cup chopped salted roasted almonds
¼ cup dried cranberries
Brown sugar or pure maple syrup, for serving

1. In a large saucepan, boil the oats in the water for 1 minute. Cover and let stand overnight at room temperature.
2. The next day, uncover the oats and bring to a boil over high heat. Reduce the heat to low and simmer, stirring frequently, until the oatmeal is cooked and creamy but still a little chewy, about 10 minutes. Spoon the oatmeal into bowls, top with the almonds and cranberries and sweeten to taste with brown sugar or maple syrup.
—*Grace Parisi*

MAKE AHEAD The oatmeal can be refrigerated for up to 1 week. Rewarm in a microwave and thin with water if necessary.

CRANBERRY AND ORANGE
PAVLOVA (P. 331)

pies & fruit desserts

> **66** *I finished my portion and began eyeing my mother's plate; she, no fool, shut me down completely.* **99**

—**RAY ISLE**, DEPUTY WINE EDITOR, FOOD & WINE MAGAZINE

APPLE PIE BARS

BAKED APPLES WITH CURRANTS AND SAUTERNES

Apple Pie Bars

ACTIVE: 1 HR; TOTAL: 2 HR

MAKES 4 DOZEN BARS ● ○ ○

These bars have a nutty, streusel-like topping and a crisp shortbread crust. They're incredibly portable and can be made well in advance and frozen.

CRUST

- 3 sticks (12 ounces) unsalted butter, softened
- ¾ cup granulated sugar
- 3 cups all-purpose flour
- ½ teaspoon kosher salt

FILLING

- 6 tablespoons unsalted butter
- ½ cup light brown sugar
- 12 Granny Smith apples (about 6 pounds)—peeled, cored and thinly sliced
- 1 tablespoon cinnamon
- ¼ teaspoon freshly grated nutmeg
- 1 cup water, as necessary

TOPPING

- ¾ cup walnuts
- 3 cups quick-cooking oats
- 2 cups all-purpose flour
- 1½ cups light brown sugar
- 1¼ teaspoons cinnamon
- ½ teaspoon baking soda
- ½ teaspoon kosher salt
- 3 sticks (12 ounces) unsalted butter, cut into ½-inch cubes and chilled

1. MAKE THE CRUST: Preheat the oven to 375°. Line a 15-by-17-inch rimmed baking sheet with parchment paper. In an electric mixer fitted with a paddle, beat the butter with the granulated sugar at medium speed until light and fluffy, about 2 minutes. At low speed, beat in the flour and salt until a soft dough forms. Press the dough over the bottom of the prepared pan and ½ inch up the sides in an even layer. Bake in the center of the oven for about 20 minutes, until golden and set. Let cool on a rack.

2. MEANWHILE, MAKE THE FILLING: In each of 2 large skillets, melt 3 tablespoons of the butter with ¼ cup of the brown sugar. Add the apples to the skillets and cook over high heat, stirring occasionally, until softened, about 10 minutes. Stir half of the cinnamon and nutmeg into each skillet. Cook until the apples are caramelized and very tender and the liquid is evaporated, about 10 minutes longer; scrape up any bits stuck to the bottom of the skillets and add up to ½ cup of water to each pan to prevent scorching. Let cool.

3. MAKE THE TOPPING: Spread the walnuts in a pie plate and toast until golden and fragrant, 8 minutes. Let cool; coarsely chop. In a large bowl, mix the oats with the flour, brown sugar, cinnamon, baking soda and salt. Using a pastry blender or two knives, cut in the butter until the mixture resembles coarse meal. Stir in the walnuts and press the mixture into clumps.

4. Spread the apple filling over the crust. Scatter the crumbs on top, pressing them lightly into an even layer. Bake in the center of the oven for 1 hour, until the topping is golden; rotate the pan halfway through baking. Let cool completely on a rack before cutting into 2-inch bars.

—*Mary Odson*

MAKE AHEAD The bars can be stored in an airtight container at room temperature for 4 days or frozen for up to a month.

Baked Apples with Currants and Sauternes

ACTIVE: 15 MIN; TOTAL: 1 HR

4 SERVINGS ● ● ○

- 4 small Cortland or Rome apples (6 ounces each), cored
- ½ cup dried currants
- ½ cup light brown sugar
- ¼ cup plus 2 tablespoons Sauternes or other late-harvest wine
- 1 small thyme sprig, plus 4 sprigs for garnish

Plain low-fat yogurt, for serving

1. Preheat the oven to 350°. Arrange the apples in an 8-by-10-inch baking dish, leaving space between them. Fill each apple cavity with 2 tablespoons of currants. Sprinkle the brown sugar over the apples and into the dish. Drizzle the Sauternes over and around the apples and add the thyme sprig to the dish.

2. Cover with foil and bake for 45 minutes, or until the apples are tender but still holding their shape. Transfer to plates and drizzle with the pan juices. Garnish with the thyme sprigs and serve with yogurt.

—*Clark Frasier and Mark Gaier*

Raisin-Studded Apple Bread Pudding

ACTIVE: 30 MIN; TOTAL: 1 HR 30 MIN

6 SERVINGS ● ○

New York chef-turned-winemaker David Page tosses golden raisins into his apple bread pudding, a recipe he developed years ago with Melissa Murphy of Brooklyn, New York's Sweet Melissa's Pâtisserie. Whipping the egg whites before folding them into the custard makes the pudding exceptionally light.

- 1 pound bakery white bread, crusts removed, cut into 1-inch cubes
- 1 Granny Smith apple, peeled and cut into ½-inch pieces
- 1 cup golden raisins (6 ounces)
- 3 large eggs, separated
- ¾ cup sugar
- ¼ teaspoon cinnamon
- ⅛ teaspoon freshly grated nutmeg
- ⅛ teaspoon ground ginger
- ¼ teaspoon pure vanilla extract
- ¼ teaspoon salt
- 3 cups whole milk
- 2 tablespoons unsulfured molasses
- ¼ cup sliced almonds

1. Preheat the oven to 350°. Spread the bread cubes on a baking sheet and toast in the oven for 6 minutes, until crisp. Transfer to a bowl and add the apple and raisins.

2. Generously butter six 8-ounce ramekins and set them on the baking sheet.

3. In a medium bowl, using a handheld electric mixer, beat the egg yolks with the sugar until pale, about 3 minutes. Beat in the ground spices, vanilla and salt.

4. In a medium saucepan, heat the milk with the molasses until warm to the touch. Gradually beat the warm milk into the egg yolk mixture, scraping the bottom and side of the bowl. In another bowl, using clean beaters, beat the egg whites at high speed until stiff. Fold the whites into the custard.

5. Pour the custard over the bread mixture and stir until moistened. Let stand for 5 minutes. Spoon the mixture into the prepared ramekins, distributing the raisins and custard evenly. Sprinkle the almonds on top. Bake in the center of the oven for about 40 minutes, until puffed and set, with the tops lightly browned. Let the bread puddings rest for at least 15 minutes before serving. —*David Page*

Puff Pastry Apple Pie

ACTIVE: 30 MIN; TOTAL: 2 HR 45 MIN

MAKES ONE 9½-INCH

DEEP-DISH PIE ●

Cathal Armstrong (an F&W Best New Chef 2006) tells of how a family friend came over for lunch one day and marveled at his mother Angela's apple pie. When his father, Gerry, asserted that it must have been the apples he grew that made the pie taste so good, the friend said, "Angela, you tell him pastry like that doesn't grow on trees." Since puff pastry can be tricky to prepare, this version of Angela's apple pie uses a high-quality, store-bought puff pastry.

- 3 pounds Granny Smith apples— peeled, cored and sliced into ¼-inch wedges
- ½ cup granulated sugar
- 3 tablespoons all-purpose flour, plus more for dusting

Two 14-ounce packages all-butter puff pastry, chilled

1. In a large bowl, toss the apples wedges with the sugar and the 3 tablespoons of flour until coated.

2. On a lightly floured work surface, roll out each piece of puff pastry to a 14-inch square. Ease one pastry square into a 9½-inch-deep glass pie plate. Scrape the apples and their juices into the shell. Lay the second layer of puff pastry on top. Press the edges of the pastry sheets together to seal and trim the overhang to 1 inch. Crimp the edge decoratively and cut a few slits on top of the pie for venting. Freeze the pie for 1 hour.

3. Preheat the oven to 400°. Place the apple pie on a baking sheet and transfer it to the oven. Bake the pie for 30 minutes, until the crust is lightly golden. Reduce the oven temperature to 375° and bake for 40 minutes longer, until the top is deep golden brown. Transfer the pie to a wire rack to cool slightly before serving.

—*Cathal Armstrong*

pies & fruit desserts

Skillet Apple Charlotte

ACTIVE: 25 MIN; TOTAL: 50 MIN

4 SERVINGS ○ ●

A classic apple charlotte has a crust of buttered bread slices filled with caramelized apples. In this quick version, apple wedges are sautéed with honey and maple syrup, topped with buttered toast and turned out of the pan like a tarte Tatin.

- 3 Granny Smith apples (about 1½ pounds)—peeled, cored and cut into sixths
- 2 tablespoons pure maple syrup
- 1 tablespoon honey
- 3 tablespoons unsalted butter
- 4 slices of white sandwich bread, crusts removed
- 1 teaspoon sugar
- 3 tablespoons apricot preserves

Sour cream, for serving

1. Preheat the oven to 400°. In a 7- or 8-inch ovenproof nonstick skillet, arrange the apples snugly, cored side up. Add the maple syrup, honey and 2 tablespoons of the butter and bring to a boil over high heat. Reduce the heat to low, cover and cook, gently shaking the pan occasionally, until the apples are tender, 5 minutes. Uncover and cook over high heat, shaking the pan a few times, until the liquid is evaporated and the apples are caramelized, about 7 minutes.

2. Arrange the bread slices in a square on a work surface. Trim the corners of the slices to form a round the size of the skillet. Spread the bread with the remaining 1 tablespoon of butter and sprinkle with the sugar. Arrange the bread over the apples, sugared side up. Bake for 20 minutes, until the bread is toasted. Invert the charlotte onto a plate.

3. In a heatproof bowl, melt the apricot preserves in a microwave oven for 30 seconds, then spread them over the apples. Cut the apple charlotte into wedges and serve warm with a dollop of sour cream.
—*Jacques Pépin*

Apple Tart with Almond Cream

ACTIVE: 1 HR 15 MIN; TOTAL: 3 HR

MAKES ONE 9-INCH TART ● ○ ○

This delicious dessert is a large version of the individual tartlets served at Racines, a popular wine bar in Paris. The thin, crisp pastry shell is filled with a layer of almond cream made from both finely ground and coarsely chopped nuts that give the tart layers of texture. The thinly sliced apples on top caramelize as the tart bakes.

- 1 cup slivered almonds (about 4 ounces)
- ½ cup granulated sugar
- ¼ cup all-purpose flour
- ¼ teaspoon salt
- 4 tablespoons unsalted butter, softened, plus 1 tablespoon melted butter, for brushing
- 2 large eggs
- 1 tablespoon dark rum

Baked Pastry Shell (recipe follows)
- 3 large Golden Delicious apples—peeled, halved, cored and sliced ⅛ inch thick
- ¼ cup light brown sugar

1. Preheat the oven to 400°. In a mini processor, pulse ¾ cup of the slivered almonds until they are finely ground. Transfer to a medium bowl. Pulse the remaining ¼ cup of almonds until coarsely chopped. Transfer to the bowl and add the granulated sugar, flour and salt. Toss the almond mixture gently to combine.

2. In another bowl, using a handheld mixer, beat the 4 tablespoons of softened butter until creamy. Add the almond mixture and beat until blended. Add the eggs one at a time, beating well after each addition. Beat in the rum.

3. Spread the almond filling in the Baked Pastry Shell. Arrange the apple slices on top in concentric circles. Brush the apple slices with the melted butter and sprinkle with the brown sugar.

4. Bake the tart for 1 hour, until the filling is set and the apples are browned and tender. Transfer the tart to a rack and let cool slightly. Remove the ring and serve the tart warm or at room temperature.
—*Pierre Jancou*

MAKE AHEAD The apple tart can be baked 1 day ahead. Wrap well and keep at room temperature.

BAKED PASTRY SHELL

ACTIVE: 15 MIN; TOTAL: 1 HR 45 MIN

MAKES ONE 9-INCH SHELL ● ○

- 1¼ cups all-purpose flour, plus more for dusting
- ¼ teaspoon salt
- 5 tablespoons cold unsalted butter, cut into small pieces
- 1 large egg yolk

2 to 3 tablespoons ice water

1. Preheat the oven to 400°. In a food processor, pulse the 1¼ cups of flour and the salt. Add the butter pieces and pulse until the mixture resembles small peas. Add the egg yolk and 2 tablespoons of ice water and pulse just until the dough holds together when pinched; if necessary, add the remaining 1 tablespoon of ice water. Transfer the dough to a lightly floured surface and knead until smooth. Flatten into a disk, wrap in plastic and chill the dough until firm, about 1 hour.

2. On a lightly floured surface, use a rolling pin to roll out the chilled dough to a 12-inch round about ⅛ inch thick. Transfer to a 9-inch fluted tart pan with a removable bottom. Push a rolling pin over the top to trim away any overhang. Prick the bottom in several places with a fork.

3. Line the tart shell with foil and fill with pie weights. Bake for 25 minutes, until the shell is lightly colored around the edge. Remove the foil and weights and bake for 10 minutes more, or until the shell is golden. Let cool completely before filling. —*PJ*

MAKE AHEAD The pastry shell can be baked 1 day ahead. Wrap well.

Pear Tart with Pecan Crust

ACTIVE: 45 MIN; TOTAL: 3 HR

MAKES ONE 11½-INCH TART ● ● ●

This tart combines sweet fall pears and a rich, nutty crust full of buttery pecans. Dollops of honey-sweetened whipped cream speckled with toasted pecans push the dessert over the top.

TART

1½ cups pecans (6 ounces)
 ¼ cup plus 2 tablespoons granulated sugar
2¼ cups all-purpose flour, plus more for dusting
 ¾ teaspoon salt
  1 stick plus 6 tablespoons cold unsalted butter, cut into ½-inch dice
  6 tablespoons ice water
  8 firm ripe Bartlett pears, peeled and cut into 1-inch dice
  2 tablespoons light brown sugar
  2 teaspoons fresh lemon juice
 ½ vanilla bean, split, seeds scraped

WHIPPED CREAM

 ¾ cup pecans
1½ cups heavy cream
  3 tablespoons honey

1. MAKE THE TART: In a food processor, pulse the pecans with ¼ cup of the granulated sugar until finely ground. Add 2 cups of the flour and the salt and pulse to mix. Add the butter and pulse just until the dough is the size of small peas. Add the ice water and pulse just until evenly moistened. Transfer the dough to a work surface and pat into a disk. Wrap in plastic and refrigerate until chilled, at least 30 minutes.

2. On a lightly floured work surface, roll out the dough to a 16-inch round about ¼ inch thick. Fit the dough into an 11½-inch tart pan with a removable bottom and trim the overhang. Pat the scraps into a disk and roll out to a 12-inch round. Cut ten ¾-inch-wide strips. Transfer the strips to a baking sheet. Refrigerate the dough strips and tart shell until chilled, about 30 minutes.

3. Preheat the oven to 400°. In a medium bowl, toss the pears with the light brown sugar, lemon juice, vanilla seeds and the remaining ¼ cup of flour and 2 tablespoons of granulated sugar.

4. Set the tart shell on a large rimmed baking sheet. Scrape the filling into the shell. Lay 5 evenly spaced strips of dough over the tart; lay the remaining 5 strips of dough perpendicular to the others to form a cross-hatch pattern. Trim the strips as necessary and press the ends against the tart rim to adhere. Bake the tart for about 1 hour and 10 minutes, until the crust is golden brown and the filling is bubbly. Transfer to a rack and let cool for at least 30 minutes.

5. MEANWHILE, MAKE THE WHIPPED CREAM: Spread the pecans in a pie plate and toast in the oven for about 6 minutes, until fragrant. Let the nuts cool, then coarsely chop them. In a bowl, using an electric mixer, whip the cream with the honey. Fold in the chopped pecans.

6. Remove the tart from the pan and transfer to a platter. Cut into wedges and serve each with a dollop of the honey-pecan whipped cream. —*Melissa Rubel*

MAKE AHEAD The unbaked tart can be refrigerated for up to 4 hours. The baked tart can be kept at room temperature overnight.

Marilyn Batali's Blackberry Pie

ACTIVE: 30 MIN; TOTAL: 3 HR
PLUS 4 HR COOLING

MAKES ONE 9-INCH PIE ●

While walking in Spain, star chef Mario Batali spotted a bush full of ripe blackberries, his "favorite fruit in life," and recalled filling the back of his parents' station wagon with buckets of blackberries when he was growing up in Seattle. After getting his mother, Marilyn, to e-mail him her recipe, Batali prepared this luscious pie.

CRUST

2½ cups all-purpose flour, plus more for dusting
  3 tablespoons sugar
 ¼ teaspoon salt
  1 cup solid vegetable shortening, chilled
  5 tablespoons ice water

FILLING

  2 pints blackberries (1½ pounds)
 ½ cup sugar
  3 tablespoons all-purpose flour
  1 tablespoon fresh lemon juice
  1 tablespoon cold unsalted butter, cut into cubes

1. MAKE THE CRUST: In a large bowl, whisk the 2½ cups of flour, the sugar and salt. Add the shortening; using a pastry blender or two knives, cut it into the flour until the mixture resembles coarse meal. Add the ice water and stir with a fork until the dough is moistened. Turn the dough out onto a lightly floured surface and gather it into a ball. Knead the dough two or three times, just until it comes together. Divide in half; flatten each piece into a disk. Wrap each disk in plastic and refrigerate until chilled, at least 1 hour.

2. Preheat the oven to 375°. Let the dough stand at room temperature for 10 minutes. Working on a lightly floured surface, roll out one disk of dough to a 12-inch round. Transfer to a 9-inch glass pie plate. Roll out the remaining dough to an 11-inch round.

3. MAKE THE FILLING: Meanwhile, in a bowl, stir the blackberries with the sugar, flour and lemon juice, lightly mashing a few berries; scrape into the prepared pie crust and sprinkle the butter cubes on top.

4. Brush the overhanging pastry with water and carefully set the top crust over the berry filling. Press the edges of the dough together and trim the overhang to 1 inch. Fold the edge under itself and crimp decoratively. Cut 4 slits in the top crust.

5. Bake the pie in the center of the oven for 1 hour and 15 minutes, until the bottom crust is golden and the fruit is bubbling. If necessary, cover the edge with foil for the last few minutes. Let cool for at least 4 hours before serving. —*Marilyn Batali*

DOUBLE-CRUST APPLE PIE

perfecting apple pie

Using a mix of Granny Smith, Pink Lady and Golden Delicious apples, F&W's **Grace Parisi** *transforms one iconic pie into a trio of desserts.*

Double-Crust Apple Pie

ACTIVE: 40 MIN; TOTAL: 2 HR 40 MIN PLUS 4 HR COOLING

8 SERVINGS ● ●

- 2¾ cups all-purpose flour, plus more for dusting
- ½ teaspoon salt
- 2 sticks plus 1 tablespoon cold unsalted butter, cubed
- ½ cup ice water
- 6 large apples—peeled, cored and cut into 1-inch chunks or thinly sliced
- 2 tablespoons fresh lemon juice
- 1 cup sugar
- ¼ teaspoon cinnamon

1. In a food processor, pulse 2½ cups of the flour and the salt. Add 2 sticks of the butter and pulse until it is the size of peas. Drizzle on the ice water and pulse until evenly moistened crumbs form; turn out onto a surface and form into a ball. Divide the dough in half. Flatten into disks, wrap in plastic and refrigerate until firm.

2. Preheat the oven to 375°. Set a baking sheet on the bottom rack. In a bowl, toss the apples, lemon juice, sugar, the remaining ¼ cup of flour and the cinnamon.

3. On a floured surface, roll a disk of the dough to a 13-inch round; fit it into a deep 10-inch glass pie plate and brush the overhang with water. Spoon in the apples and top with the remaining 1 tablespoon of cubed butter. Roll out the second disk of dough to a 12-inch round and center it over the filling. Press the edges of dough together and trim the overhang to a scant 1 inch; fold the overlay under itself and crimp. Cut a few slits in the top crust for steam to escape.

4. Bake the pie in the center of the oven for 1 hour and 10 minutes, until the crust is golden. Cover the edge of the pie if it begins to darken. Let the pie cool for at least 4 hours before serving.

Three Great Variations

1 **Apple Crostatas** Add 1 cup shredded cheddar to the dough with the water. Roll both dough disks to 13-inch rounds; transfer to parchment-lined baking sheets. Arrange the apples on top of each, leaving a 2-inch border, and pour the liquid in the bowl over. Fold the edges over the apples. Bake as directed. Brush with warm apricot preserves.

2 **Dutch Apple Pie** Assemble the pie with bottom crust only; crimp the dough. Whisk 1 cup flour, ½ cup light brown sugar, ½ teaspoon baking soda and ¼ teaspoon salt. Add 6 tablespoons softened butter and rub the mixture until sandy. Add ½ cup chopped walnuts. Press the mixture into clumps and sprinkle over the pie. Bake as directed.

3 **Apple Pandowdy** Prepare half of the dough. Spread the apple filling in an 8-by-11-inch baking dish. Roll out the dough ⅛ inch thick and cut it into 2-inch squares. Arrange the squares of dough in a patchwork pattern over the apples, pressing them onto the edge of the baking dish; leave a few openings for steam to escape. Bake as directed.

pies & fruit desserts

Fig-and-Raspberry Tart with Chestnut Honey

ACTIVE: 40 MIN; TOTAL: 4 HR

MAKES ONE 12-INCH TART ● ○ ○

This fruit tart gets its spicy kick from a Tuscan classic, chestnut honey, or *miele di castagno,* which has an unusually potent, savory flavor.

DOUGH

- 2½ cups all-purpose flour, plus more for dusting
- 2 teaspoons sugar
- ½ teaspoon salt
- Finely grated zest of 1 lemon
- 1 stick plus 6 tablespoons cold unsalted butter, cubed
- 3 tablespoons heavy cream
- ¼ cup ice water

TART

- 30 fresh figs (1½ pounds), stemmed and sliced lengthwise ⅓ inch thick
- 24 fresh raspberries
- 2 tablespoons sugar
- 1 tablespoon chestnut honey
- 11 small fresh bay leaves
- 13 small, tender rosemary sprigs
- Sweet Red Wine Ice Cream (recipe follows), for serving

1. PREPARE THE DOUGH: In a food processor, combine the 2½ cups of flour with the sugar, salt and lemon zest and pulse to blend. Add the butter and cream and pulse until the mixture resembles small peas. Sprinkle the ice water over the mixture and pulse until it starts to come together. Scrape the dough out onto a work surface and knead gently a few times. Pat the dough into a flat disk, cover with plastic wrap and refrigerate until chilled, about 1 hour.

2. On a lightly floured surface, roll the dough out into a 14-inch round about ¼ inch thick. Transfer the round to a 12-inch tart pan with a removable bottom, gently pressing it on the bottom and up the side without stretching. Trim off any excess dough and patch any cracks with the scraps. Refrigerate until firm, about 30 minutes.

3. Preheat the oven to 350°. Line the tart shell with foil and fill with pie weights or dried beans. Bake for about 40 minutes, until the tart shell is set. Carefully remove the foil and weights and bake the shell until golden brown all over, about 25 minutes longer. Transfer to a rack and let cool.

4. MAKE THE TART: Increase the oven temperature to 425°. Arrange the figs standing up in concentric circles in the tart shell; dot with the raspberries. Sprinkle with the sugar and drizzle with the honey. Insert the bay leaves among the fig slices. Scatter the rosemary on top and bake for 30 minutes, until the fruits have begun to release their juices. Serve warm or at room temperature, cut into wedges and topped with Sweet Red Wine Ice Cream. —*Peter Pastan*

SWEET RED WINE ICE CREAM

ACTIVE: 20 MIN; TOTAL: 1 HR 50 MIN

MAKES ABOUT 5 CUPS ● ○ ○

- 6 large egg yolks
- 2 cups heavy cream
- 1 cup milk
- ½ cup sugar
- ½ cup sweet red wine, such as Moscato Rosa, Sagrantino Passito or Recioto di Valpolicella

1. In a heatproof bowl, mix the egg yolks. In a saucepan, combine the cream, milk and sugar and bring to a simmer over moderate heat, stirring to dissolve the sugar, about 4 minutes. Gradually whisk the hot cream into the eggs yolks; return the mixture to the saucepan. Cook over moderate heat, stirring constantly, until the custard is thick enough to coat the back of a spoon, about 5 minutes; do not let the custard boil or it will curdle.

2. Strain the custard into a bowl. Stir in the red wine. Cover and refrigerate until thoroughly chilled, about 1 hour. Freeze in an ice cream freezer according to the manufacturer's instructions. Cover and store in the freezer until serving time. —*PP*

Berry-Brioche Bread Pudding

ACTIVE: 20 MIN; TOTAL: 1 HR 30 MIN PLUS 30 MIN COOLING

8 SERVINGS ○

- Unsalted butter, for greasing the dish
- ¼ cup turbinado sugar
- 2 cups heavy cream
- 2 cups whole milk
- ⅔ cup plus ¼ cup granulated sugar
- 1 teaspoon kosher salt
- 4 large eggs
- 4 large egg yolks
- 1½ teaspoons pure vanilla extract
- 2 cups blueberries and raspberries, plus more for serving
- One 1-pound loaf of brioche, cut into ½-inch dice
- Whipped cream, for serving

1. Preheat the oven to 350°. Butter an 8-by-11-inch baking dish and coat the dish with the turbinado sugar.

2. In a large saucepan, bring the cream, milk, ⅔ cup of the granulated sugar and the salt to a simmer over moderately high heat, then remove from the heat.

3. In a bowl, whisk the whole eggs, egg yolks and vanilla. Gradually whisk in the hot cream until blended. Strain the custard through a fine strainer into a large bowl.

4. In a small bowl, toss the 2 cups of berries with 2 tablespoons of the granulated sugar. Using a fork, coarsely mash the berries. Let stand until juicy, 5 minutes.

5. Mix the brioche into the custard. Fold in the berries. Transfer to the baking dish and sprinkle with the remaining 2 tablespoons of granulated sugar. Cover with foil and bake for 45 minutes, until set in the center. Uncover and bake in the top third of the oven for 20 minutes, until lightly golden.

6. Preheat the broiler. Broil the pudding for 1 minute, until golden brown. Transfer to a rack and let stand for 30 minutes, until cooled slightly. Cut the bread pudding into squares and serve with blueberries, raspberries and whipped cream.

—*Karen DeMasco*

FIG-AND-RASPBERRY TART WITH CHESTNUT HONEY

BERRY-BRIOCHE BREAD PUDDING

Olive Oil–Thyme Cake with Figs and Black Pepper

ACTIVE: 45 MIN; TOTAL: 2 HR 15 MIN

12 SERVINGS ● ●

CAKE

- ¾ cup plus 1½ teaspoons pastry flour
- ¼ cup plus 1½ tablespoons bread flour
- 1 teaspoon baking powder
- 3 large egg yolks
- ¼ cup plus 1 tablespoon extra-virgin olive oil
- ½ cup water
- 1½ teaspoons chopped fresh thyme
- ¾ teaspoon salt
- ½ teaspoon pure vanilla extract
- 1 cup plus 2 tablespoons sugar
- 5 large egg whites

FIGS

- 1 pound fresh figs, quartered or sliced
- ¼ cup sugar
- 1 tablespoon extra-virgin olive oil
- 1 teaspoon chopped fresh thyme, plus 12 thyme sprigs for garnish
- ¼ teaspoon freshly ground black pepper

Pinch of salt

- ½ cup crème fraîche

1. MAKE THE CAKE: Preheat the oven to 375°. Line a 9-by-13-inch baking pan with parchment paper and coat lightly with nonstick vegetable oil spray. In a medium bowl, stir the pastry flour and bread flour with the baking powder. In a large bowl, mix the egg yolks with the olive oil, water, thyme, salt, vanilla and ¾ cup plus 1 tablespoon of the sugar. With a handheld electric mixer, beat the egg yolk mixture at medium speed until very frothy, about 3 minutes. Add the flour mixture and mix at low speed until fully incorporated.

2. In a clean bowl, using clean beaters, beat the egg whites at medium-high speed until foamy. Gradually add the remaining ¼ cup plus 1 tablespoon of sugar and beat until thick and glossy, about 4 minutes. Scoop a cup of the egg whites into the batter and stir until combined. Fold the remaining egg whites into the batter until no streaks remain. Scrape into the pan and bake for 35 minutes, until the cake is golden and starts to pull away from the side. Set the pan on a rack and let cool, about 1 hour.

3. MEANWHILE, PREPARE THE FIGS: In a bowl, toss the figs with the sugar, olive oil, chopped thyme, pepper and salt. Let stand for 1 hour, until the figs begin to soften.

4. Cut the cake into 12 rectangles. Spoon the figs and their juices over the cake, top each slice with crème fraîche and a thyme sprig and serve. —*Elizabeth Dahl*

MAKE AHEAD The cake can be kept at room temperature for up to 1 day.

● HEALTHY ● MAKE AHEAD ○ VEGETARIAN ● STAFF FAVORITE

315

Lime Cream–Blackberry Pie

ACTIVE: 55 MIN; TOTAL: 1 HR 35 MIN
PLUS 4 HR CHILLING
12 SERVINGS ●

Blackberries are transformed into a zippy jam, then topped with a lime cream for this pie's filling. Jarred preserves are also good.

baking essentials

Mix-and-Pour Batter Bowl
Thanks to a large spout and a locking cover, Food Network's bowl makes pouring easy and keeps batter fresh (*$30; kohls.com*).

Wet-Dry Scale The add-and-weigh function on Salter's digital scale lets you weigh ingredients in the same bowl by simply pushing a button in between each addition, eliminating multiple-bowl measuring (*$60; williams-sonoma.com*).

Heatproof Bowls Oxo's heat-resistant mixing bowls protect hands from extreme temperatures and have nonskid bottoms for stable stirring (*$45 for a set of three; oxo.com*).

Precut Parchment Circles
Sized for nine-inch cake pans, these one-use parchment paper circles create a perfect nonstick surface for baking (*$18 for 250; bakedeco.com*).

Reversible Measuring Cups
Flipper cups by Trudeau take up half the space with their reversible rubber scoops: A gentle push turns 1 cup into ½ cup (*$16 for a three-piece set; laprimashops.com*).

CRUST
- 1 cup graham cracker crumbs
- 1 tablespoon sugar
- 6 tablespoons unsalted butter, melted

FILLING
- 2 cups blackberries
- 1 cup sugar
- 1 teaspoon powdered gelatin
- 2 tablespoons hot water
- One 14-ounce can sweetened condensed milk
- 1 cup heavy cream
- 3 tablespoons lime zest
- ¾ cup fresh lime juice

1. MAKE THE CRUST: Preheat the oven to 350°. In a bowl, combine the crumbs, sugar and butter; press the mixture over the bottom and up the side of a 9-inch glass pie plate. Bake the crust for 15 minutes; let cool.

2. MAKE THE FILLING: In a saucepan, simmer the blackberries over moderate heat, stirring, 10 minutes. Stir in the sugar and cook until the mixture is thick and jammy, 40 minutes. Transfer to a bowl and let cool.

3. In a heatproof bowl, sprinkle the gelatin over the hot water; let stand until softened, 10 minutes. Using an electric mixer, beat the condensed milk, cream, lime zest, lime juice and gelatin until soft peaks form. Spread the jam over the crust, top with the lime cream and refrigerate for at least 4 hours, until firm. Serve. *—Colleen Hubbard*

Blackberries with Lemon Cream and Toasted Brioche

ACTIVE: 45 MIN; TOTAL: 3 HR
8 SERVINGS ● ●
- ½ cup water
- 1½ cups plus 1 tablespoon sugar
- One 2-inch rosemary sprig
- ¼ vanilla bean, split, seeds scraped
- ¼ cup finely grated lemon zest
- 4 large eggs
- ¾ cup fresh lemon juice
- 1 stick plus 2 tablespoons unsalted butter, cut into tablespoons

- Eight ½-inch-thick slices of brioche, crust removed
- 1 cup heavy cream
- 3 cups blackberries (12 ounces)

1. In a saucepan, simmer the water with ½ cup of the sugar until the sugar is dissolved. Add the rosemary and the vanilla bean and seeds and let stand for 2 hours.

2. Meanwhile, in a heatproof bowl, rub the lemon zest into 1 cup of the sugar. Whisk in the eggs and lemon juice. Set the bowl over a saucepan of simmering water and cook over moderate heat, whisking, until thickened, about 6 minutes. Strain the custard into a food processor; let cool slightly.

3. With the processor on, add the butter 1 piece at a time and process until fully incorporated before adding more. Process the cream until doubled in volume, about 3 minutes. Scrape the lemon cream into a bowl, press a piece of plastic wrap directly onto the surface and refrigerate until chilled, about 2 hours.

4. Discard the rosemary and vanilla bean from the syrup. Simmer the syrup over moderately low heat until slightly thickened, about 15 minutes; let cool.

5. Preheat the broiler. Arrange the brioche slices on a baking sheet and broil for 1 minute, turning once, until golden.

6. In a bowl, beat the heavy cream with the remaining 1 tablespoon of sugar until softly whipped. Add the blackberries to the sugar syrup and toss gently. Spoon the lemon cream onto 8 plates, top with the brioche and a dollop of the whipped cream. Scatter the blackberries on top; serve at once. *—Molly Hawks-Fagnoni*

Red Fruit Compote

TOTAL: 45 MIN PLUS 3 HR CHILLING
8 TO 10 SERVINGS ● ● ● ●
This chilled compote of quick-stewed plums, Bing cherries and berries in a light wine–and–black currant syrup is a refreshing summertime alternative to fruit pie.

1 cup dry white wine

1 cup black currant syrup
or crème de cassis

⅓ cup fresh orange juice

¼ cup good-quality seedless
strawberry jam

1 tablespoon finely grated
orange zest

1 pound red plums, such as
Santa Rosa—halved,
pitted and cut into wedges

1 pound Bing cherries, pitted

1 large fresh basil sprig

1 pound seedless red grapes,
stemmed

1 pound blueberries

1 pound strawberries,
hulled and quartered

1 cup sour cream or crème fraîche

2 tablespoons sugar

Fresh mint sprigs, for garnish

1. In a medium nonreactive saucepan, combine the white wine with the black currant syrup, orange juice, strawberry jam and orange zest. Bring to a boil over moderate heat and boil for 1 minute, stirring to dissolve the jam.

2. Add the plum wedges, cherries and basil sprig to the saucepan and bring to a rolling boil over high heat; boil for 1 minute. With a slotted spoon, transfer the plums and cherries to a large glass or ceramic bowl. Add the grapes to the saucepan and boil for 30 seconds; transfer the grapes to the bowl of fruit. Finally, add the blueberries and strawberries to the saucepan and bring just to a boil. Transfer the berries to the bowl with the slotted spoon.

3. Drain all of the accumulated juices from the fruit back into the saucepan. Bring the syrup to a boil and simmer over moderate heat until reduced to 2 cups, about 10 minutes. Pour the reduced syrup over the fruit and let cool. Cover with plastic and refrigerate for a few hours or overnight.

4. In a small bowl, blend the sour cream with the sugar and 2 tablespoons of water.

Remove the basil sprig from the fruit. Spoon 2 to 3 tablespoons of the black currant syrup onto each serving plate and spoon the fruit in the center. Garnish each serving with a mint sprig and a dollop of the sweetened sour cream.

—Jacques Pépin

Strawberry–Red Wine Sorbet with Crushed Meringue

ACTIVE: 45 MIN; TOTAL: 3 HR 30 MIN

10 SERVINGS ● ●

Superchef Jean-Georges Vongerichten uses the first strawberries of summer to make this perfect alfresco dessert.

MERINGUE

5 large egg whites

Pinch of salt

1¼ cups sugar

SORBET

2 pounds strawberries, hulled
and quartered, plus 30
medium strawberries, hulled,
for garnish

¼ cup fresh lemon juice

1 cup dry red wine

2 cups sugar

1 vanilla bean, split

Vanilla ice cream, aged balsamic
vinegar and sweetened
whipped cream, for serving

1. MAKE THE MERINGUE: Preheat the oven to 200°. Line a large baking sheet with parchment paper. In a large bowl, using an electric mixer, beat the egg whites with the salt at high speed until soft peaks form. With the machine on, slowly pour in the sugar and continue beating until stiff, glossy peaks form.

2. Using a spatula, spread the meringue on the prepared baking sheet in a 1-inch layer. Bake for 2 hours. Turn the oven off and leave the meringue in with the door closed for 1 hour. The meringue should be crisp and snowy white on the outside and slightly chewy within. Break the meringue into bite-size pieces.

3. MEANWHILE, MAKE THE SORBET: In a large bowl, toss the 2 pounds of quartered strawberries with the lemon juice. In a medium saucepan, stir the red wine with the sugar. Scrape the seeds from the vanilla bean into the saucepan; save the bean for another use. Warm the wine syrup over moderate heat, stirring to dissolve the sugar. Pour the syrup over the strawberries. Let cool to room temperature, then refrigerate the strawberries and syrup until chilled, about 25 minutes.

4. Transfer the strawberries and syrup to a food processor and puree. Transfer the strawberry puree to an ice cream maker and freeze according to the manufacturer's instructions.

5. Place a scoop each of the sorbet and vanilla ice cream into bowls. Drizzle with the balsamic vinegar. Top with the whole strawberries, whipped cream and a few meringue pieces and serve.

—Jean-Georges Vongerichten

MAKE AHEAD The baked meringue can be kept overnight in an airtight container. The sorbet can be frozen for up to 3 days.

Melon Sorbet

ACTIVE: 15 MIN; TOTAL: 45 MIN

PLUS 4 HR FREEZING

MAKES 3½ CUPS ● ●

2½ pounds cantaloupe or honeydew
melon—peeled, seeded and cut
into 1-inch dice (about 4 cups)

¾ cup Sugar Syrup (p. 323)

1. In a blender, puree the cantaloupe until smooth. You should have 2½ cups of melon puree; reserve any extra for another use. Stir in the Sugar Syrup. Pour the sorbet base into an ice cream maker and freeze according to the manufacturer's instructions.

2. Pack the melon sorbet into an airtight plastic container. Press a sheet of plastic wrap directly onto the surface of the sorbet, cover and freeze until firm, about 4 hours. Scoop into bowls and serve.

—Jeni Britton

pies & fruit desserts

Lemon-Blueberry Frozen Yogurt

ACTIVE: 30 MIN; TOTAL: 1 HR 30 MIN
PLUS 4 HR FREEZING
MAKES 5 CUPS ●●

- ½ cup fresh lemon juice, plus 1 tablespoon finely grated lemon zest
- One ¼-ounce package unflavored powdered gelatin
- ⅔ cup plus 6 tablespoons sugar
- ¼ cup light corn syrup
- 2 cups plain whole-milk yogurt
- ½ cup heavy cream
- ¾ cup blueberries
- 2 teaspoons water

1. Fill a large bowl with ice water. Pour 2 tablespoons of the lemon juice into a small bowl. Sprinkle the powdered gelatin over the lemon juice and let the mixture stand for 5 minutes.

2. Meanwhile, in a small saucepan, whisk the remaining 6 tablespoons of lemon juice with ⅔ cup of the sugar and the corn syrup. Bring to a boil and cook over moderate heat until the sugar dissolves, 1 minute. Remove from the heat and stir in the lemon gelatin.

3. In a medium bowl, mix the yogurt with the grated lemon zest. Stir in the lemon juice mixture, then whisk in the heavy cream. Set the yogurt base in the ice water bath and let stand, stirring occasionally, until cold, 20 minutes.

4. Meanwhile, in a saucepan, mix the blueberries with the remaining 6 tablespoons of sugar and the water. Simmer over moderate heat until saucy, 4 minutes. Let cool.

5. Pour the lemon yogurt into an ice cream maker and freeze according to the manufacturer's instructions.

6. Scoop alternating spoonfuls of the yogurt and blueberry sauce into a plastic container. Press a sheet of plastic wrap directly onto the surface and close with an airtight lid. Freeze until firm, about 4 hours.
—Jeni Britton

MAKE AHEAD The yogurt can be frozen for up to 1 week.

Strawberry Frozen Yogurt

ACTIVE: 20 MIN; TOTAL: 1 HR 20 MIN
PLUS 4 HR FREEZING
MAKES 5 CUPS ●

- 2 tablespoons fresh lemon juice, plus 1 teaspoon finely grated lemon zest
- One ¼-ounce package unflavored powdered gelatin
- 12 ounces strawberries, hulled and halved
- ¾ cup sugar
- ¼ cup light corn syrup
- 2 cups plain whole-milk yogurt
- ½ cup heavy cream

1. Fill a large bowl with ice water. Pour the lemon juice into a small bowl. Sprinkle the powdered gelatin over the lemon juice and let stand for 5 minutes.

2. Meanwhile, in a blender, puree the strawberries until smooth; you should have about 1 cup of strawberry puree.

3. In a small saucepan, combine the strawberry puree with the sugar and corn syrup and bring to a boil. Cook the puree over moderately high heat, stirring, until the sugar dissolves completely, about 1 minute. Remove the strawberry mixture from the heat and stir in the lemon juice and gelatin mixture until it melts.

4. In a medium bowl, mix the yogurt with the lemon zest and the hot strawberry puree. Stir in the heavy cream. Set the bowl in the ice water bath and let stand, stirring occasionally, until the strawberry yogurt is cold, about 20 minutes.

5. Pour the strawberry yogurt into an ice cream maker and freeze according to the manufacturer's instructions.

6. Pack the frozen yogurt into a plastic container. Press a sheet of plastic wrap directly onto the surface of the frozen yogurt and close with an airtight lid. Freeze until the yogurt is firm, about 4 hours.
—Jeni Britton

MAKE AHEAD The yogurt can be frozen for up to 1 week.

Watermelon Granita with Cardamom Syrup

ACTIVE: 30 MIN; TOTAL: 3 HR 15 MIN
6 SERVINGS ●●○

- ¾ cup water
- 1¼ cups sugar
- 3 pounds seedless watermelon, rind removed, flesh cut into 1½-inch pieces (6 cups)
- 1 tablespoon fresh lemon juice
- 1½ teaspoons cardamom pods, crushed

1. In a saucepan, combine ½ cup of the water with ¾ cup of the sugar and stir over moderate heat until the sugar has dissolved, 2 minutes.

2. In a blender, working in batches, puree the watermelon with the sugar syrup and lemon juice until smooth. Pour the mixture into a 9-by-13-inch baking pan and freeze for 30 minutes. Using a fork, stir the granita; continue stirring every 30 minutes until frozen and fluffy, about 3 hours.

3. Meanwhile, in a saucepan, combine the remaining ¼ cup of water and ½ cup of sugar with the cardamom pods and bring to a boil. Simmer over moderate heat until the sugar is dissolved, 2 minutes. Remove from the heat and let stand for 5 minutes. Strain the syrup and refrigerate.

4. Fluff the granita with a fork. Scoop into bowls, drizzle with the cardamom syrup and serve. *—Marisa Churchill*

Cornmeal Crêpes with Peaches and Caramel

ACTIVE: 45 MIN; TOTAL: 1 HR 15 MIN
6 SERVINGS ●○

Pastry chef Nicole Krasinski uses sherry vinegar in her tangy caramel sauce, which she drizzles, warm, over sweet ripe peaches and buttery-crisp crêpes. Apricots would also work nicely here.

CRÊPES

- 8 tablespoons unsalted butter, 5 tablespoons melted
- 1¼ cups whole milk

LEMON-BLUEBERRY AND STRAWBERRY FROZEN YOGURT   WATERMELON GRANITA WITH CARDAMOM SYRUP

½   cup plus 2 tablespoons
     all-purpose flour
¼   cup plus 2 tablespoons
     cornmeal
1   teaspoon kosher salt
2   large eggs, at room temperature
CARAMEL
8   tablespoons unsalted butter
¼   cup honey
¼   cup light brown sugar
1   tablespoon granulated sugar
Pinch of kosher salt
3   tablespoons heavy cream
1   tablespoon sherry vinegar
3   ripe peaches—halved, pitted and
     cut into ½-inch dice

1. MAKE THE CRÊPES: In a small skillet, cook the 3 tablespoons of unmelted butter over moderate heat until golden brown and fragrant, about 4 minutes.
2. In a blender, combine the milk with half of the flour and blend. Add the cornmeal,

salt and the remaining flour and blend until smooth. With the machine on, add the eggs one at a time, then add the browned butter in a thin stream. Transfer the batter to a bowl, cover with plastic wrap and refrigerate for 30 minutes.
3. MEANWHILE, MAKE THE CARAMEL: In a medium saucepan, melt the butter over moderate heat. Add the honey, sugars and salt, whisking to dissolve the sugars. Bring to a boil and cook without whisking for about 30 seconds, until the caramel bubbles vigorously. Remove the saucepan from the heat and whisk in the cream and vinegar. Strain the caramel and keep warm.
4. Line a plate with wax paper. Heat an 8-inch nonstick crêpe pan or skillet. Lightly brush the pan with some of the 5 tablespoons of melted butter. Add 3 tablespoons of the batter and immediately swirl the pan to coat the bottom. Cook the crêpe over moderate heat until the edge is

golden and the batter is set, about 30 seconds. Flip the crêpe over and cook until the bottom is lightly browned in spots, about 20 seconds. Transfer the crêpe to the prepared plate. Repeat with the remaining batter to make 12 crêpes, adding more melted butter as needed.
5. Shortly before serving, preheat the oven to 400°. Arrange the crêpes on a work surface. Lightly brush both sides with the remaining melted butter. Fold the crêpes into quarters and arrange them on a baking sheet. Bake the crêpes until sizzling and lightly browned, about 4 minutes.
6. Spoon the peaches into shallow bowls and cover them with 2 crêpes each. Drizzle the warm caramel sauce on top and serve right away. —Nicole Krasinski
MAKE AHEAD The crêpes can be kept at room temperature for up to 4 hours. The caramel sauce can be refrigerated for up to 3 days. Rewarm before serving.

●HEALTHY ●MAKE AHEAD ●VEGETARIAN ●STAFF FAVORITE

perfecting fruit desserts

*F&W's **Grace Parisi** loves to bake big fruit desserts for summer parties. Here, she creates easy mix-and-match fillings and toppings.*

Mixed-Berry Spoon Cake

ACTIVE: 20 MIN; TOTAL: 2 HR 20 MIN

8 TO 10 SERVINGS ● ● ○

To vary the filling here, or in any of the variations below, use 4 pounds of peaches, nectarines and/or apricots, cut into large wedges; or 4 pounds of plums, cut into 1-inch cubes; or 6 pints of blueberries plus 2 tablespoons of fresh lemon juice.

FILLING

- 4 pints strawberries (2 pounds), hulled and quartered
- 2 pints blackberries (12 ounces)
- 2 pints raspberries (12 ounces)
- ¾ cup sugar
- 2 tablespoons cornstarch

BATTER

- 1½ cups all-purpose flour
- 1 cup sugar
- 2 teaspoons finely grated lemon zest
- 1½ teaspoons baking powder
- 1 teaspoon kosher salt
- 2 eggs
- ½ cup milk
- 1 teaspoon pure vanilla extract
- 1½ sticks unsalted butter, melted

1. MAKE THE FILLING: In a bowl, toss the berries with the sugar and cornstarch and let stand for 10 minutes.

2. MEANWHILE, MAKE THE BATTER: Preheat the oven to 375°. In a medium bowl, whisk the flour with the sugar, lemon zest, baking powder and salt. In a small bowl, whisk the eggs with the milk and vanilla. Whisk the liquid into the dry ingredients until evenly moistened, then whisk in the melted butter until smooth.

3. Spread the filling in a 9-by-13-inch baking dish. Spoon the batter on top, leaving small gaps. Bake in the center of the oven for 1 hour, until the fruit is bubbling and a toothpick inserted into the topping comes out clean. Let cool for 1 hour before serving.

Three Great Topping Variations

1 Cobbler In a food processor, pulse 2 cups flour with ½ cup cornmeal, ¾ cup sugar, 2 tablespoons minced candied ginger, 1 tablespoon baking powder and 1 teaspoon salt. Add 2 sticks cubed cold butter and pulse until crumbly. Add ¾ cup milk and pulse until moistened. Scoop 15 mounds of dough over the filling. Bake for 1 hour and 15 minutes.

2 Crumble In a processor, pulse 1⅓ cups all-purpose flour with ⅔ cup light brown sugar, 1 teaspoon baking soda and 1 teaspoon salt. Add 1 stick plus 2 tablespoons cubed cold butter and pulse until crumbly. Add 1 cup thick-cut rolled oats and pulse. In a bowl, press the topping into clumps and scatter over the filling. Bake for 1 hour.

3 Pound Cake Crisp Slice about 12 ounces plain pound cake into 1-inch cubes and spread on a baking sheet. Toast in a 375° oven for 10 minutes. Let cool, toss with 6 tablespoons melted butter, ¼ cup sugar and 1 teaspoon finely grated lemon zest. Arrange the cubes over the filling and bake for 50 minutes, covering with foil for the first 30 minutes.

Peach Crisps

ACTIVE: 30 MIN; TOTAL: 1 HR 40 MIN

12 SERVINGS ● ● ●

Paul Virant (an F&W Best New Chef 2007) bakes his simple peach crisps in individual ramekins, but the sweet summer fruit and crunchy topping could be prepared in a single baking dish as well.

TOPPING

- 1 cup all-purpose flour
- ¼ cup plus 2 tablespoons granulated sugar
- ¼ cup plus 2 tablespoons light brown sugar
- ½ cup rolled oats
- 7 tablespoons cold unsalted butter, cut into small pieces
- ¼ teaspoon salt

FILLING

- 3 pounds peaches
- ¼ cup cornstarch

Ice cream, for serving (optional)

1. MAKE THE TOPPING: In a food processor, combine the flour, sugars, oats, butter and salt and process until the mixture resembles coarse meal.

2. MAKE THE FILLING: Blanch the peaches in a large pot of boiling water for 1 minute to loosen their skins. Transfer the peaches to a large rimmed baking sheet. When cool enough to handle, peel off the skins and cut the peaches into ½-inch dice. Transfer the peaches to a large bowl and sprinkle with the cornstarch. Toss well to coat and let stand for a few minutes.

3. Preheat the oven to 325°. Butter and sugar twelve 5-ounce ramekins and arrange them on a large rimmed baking sheet. Spoon the peaches into the ramekins and sprinkle with the topping.

4. Bake the crisps for about 1 hour, until the filling is bubbling. Remove from the oven and increase the temperature to 400°. Bake the crisps on the upper rack for 8 minutes, until the topping is browned. Serve warm or at room temperature with ice cream, if desired. —*Paul Virant*

Peach-Lavender Cobbler

ACTIVE: 30 MIN; TOTAL: 1 HR 30 MIN

8 SERVINGS ●

Pastry chef Nicole Krasinski loves the combination of peaches and lavender because the dried blossoms amplify the floral flavor of the fresh fruit.

FILLING

- 4½ pounds freestone peaches— peeled, pitted and diced (10 cups)
- 2½ tablespoons instant tapioca
- ⅓ cup sugar
- ½ teaspoon kosher salt
- ½ teaspoon fresh lemon juice

TOPPING

- 1 teaspoon dried lavender blossoms
- 1 cup all-purpose flour
- ½ cup plus 2 tablespoons rolled oats
- ¼ cup granulated sugar
- 1 tablespoon baking powder
- 1¼ teaspoons kosher salt

Finely grated zest of 1 lemon

- 5 tablespoons unsalted butter, diced
- ½ cup heavy cream, plus more for brushing
- ¼ cup buttermilk
- 2 tablespoons turbinado sugar

1. MAKE THE FILLING: Preheat the oven to 400°. In a bowl, mix the peaches, tapioca, sugar, salt and lemon juice. Transfer the filling to a 9-by-13-inch baking dish.

2. MAKE THE TOPPING: Using a spice grinder or a mortar and pestle, grind the lavender to a powder. In a bowl, combine the lavender, flour, oats, granulated sugar, baking powder, salt and lemon zest. Cut in the butter using a pastry blender or two knives, until the mixture resembles coarse meal. Add the ½ cup of cream and the buttermilk; stir until the dough is just moistened.

3. Using two spoons, form 3-tablespoon mounds of the topping and arrange them over the peaches. Brush with cream and sprinkle with the turbinado sugar. Bake for 50 minutes, until the topping is golden brown and the fruit is bubbling. Let cool slightly before serving. —*Nicole Krasinski*

Port-Mulled Cherries with Ricotta

TOTAL: 25 MIN

4 SERVINGS ● ●

"The cherries absorb the natural sweetness of the port," explains pastry chef Gale Gand (an F&W Best New Chef 1994) about one of her favorite desserts.

- 2 cups ruby port
- 1½ cups pitted fresh cherries or one 10-ounce bag frozen cherries, thawed and drained
- 2 cups fresh ricotta cheese

In a medium saucepan, simmer the port over moderately high heat until a thick syrup forms, about 10 minutes. Stir in the cherries. Scoop ½ cup fresh ricotta into each bowl, spoon the cherries and syrup on top and serve. —*Gale Gand*

Cherry-Almond Clafoutis

ACTIVE: 20 MIN; TOTAL: 1 HR 15 MIN

12 SERVINGS ●

Unsalted butter, for greasing the dish

- ½ cup sugar, plus more for sprinkling
- 2 cups heavy cream
- 6 large eggs
- 1½ cups almond flour (6 ounces)
- ½ cup all-purpose flour
- 2 vanilla beans, split, seeds scraped
- 1 pound sweet cherries, pitted and halved

1. Preheat the oven to 325°. Butter a 10-by-15-inch baking dish and sprinkle it with sugar. In a large bowl, using an electric mixer at low speed, beat the ½ cup of sugar with the heavy cream, eggs, almond flour, all-purpose flour and vanilla seeds until the batter is blended.

2. Scatter the cherries in the prepared baking dish; pour the batter on top. Bake for about 45 minutes, until a toothpick inserted in the center comes out clean. Let the clafoutis cool slightly before serving. —*Paul Virant*

Sour Cherry–Lambic Sorbet

ACTIVE: 15 MIN; TOTAL: 45 MIN
PLUS 4 HR FREEZING
MAKES 5 CUPS ●●○

- 3 cups pitted sour cherries (18 ounces)
- ¾ cup Sugar Syrup (recipe follows)
- 1 cup cherry lambic beer

1. In a blender, puree the cherries until smooth. Stir in the Sugar Syrup and the cherry lambic beer. Pour the sorbet base into an ice cream maker and freeze according to the manufacturer's instructions.

2. Pack the Sour Cherry–Lambic Sorbet into a plastic container. Press a sheet of plastic wrap directly onto the surface of the sorbet and close the container with an airtight lid. Freeze until firm, 4 hours. —*Jeni Britton*

SUGAR SYRUP

ACTIVE: 5 MIN; TOTAL: 35 MIN
MAKES ¾ CUP ●○

- ½ cup sugar
- ¼ cup light corn syrup
- ¼ cup water

In a small saucepan, combine the sugar, corn syrup and water and bring to a boil. Cook over moderate heat until the sugar dissolves, about 2 minutes. Remove from the heat. Let stand until cool, 30 minutes. —*JB*

Dried Cherry Compote with Shortbread and Mascarpone

ACTIVE: 20 MIN; TOTAL: 1 HR 15 MIN
4 SERVINGS ●○

SHORTBREAD
- 1 cup all-purpose flour
- 3 tablespoons sugar
- ¼ teaspoon salt
- Rounded ¼ teaspoon anise seeds
- 1 stick chilled unsalted butter, diced
- 1 large egg yolk

COMPOTE
- ¾ cup dry red wine
- ⅓ cup sugar
- ¾ cup dried sour cherries (3 ounces)
- ⅓ cup mascarpone

1. **MAKE THE SHORTBREAD:** Preheat the oven to 350°. In a medium bowl, whisk the flour with the sugar, salt and anise seeds. Using a pastry cutter or two knives, cut in the butter until it resembles coarse meal. Using a fork, blend in the egg yolk. Gather the dough together and transfer it to a baking sheet. Press it to form a 6-inch round that's 1 inch thick. Using the blunt edge of a knife, mark 8 wedges.

2. Bake the shortbread for about 35 minutes, until the dough is pale brown around the edge. While the shortbread is still warm, using a serrated knife, cut it into 8 wedges. Let cool to room temperature.

3. **MAKE THE COMPOTE:** In a small saucepan, simmer the wine with the sugar until the sugar is dissolved. Add the dried sour cherries, cover and simmer until they're plump, about 4 minutes. Let cool.

4. Dollop the mascarpone into bowls. Spoon the cherry compote on top and serve with the shortbread. —*Marcia Kiesel*

Stone-Fruit Panzanella with Zabaglione

TOTAL: 1 HR 15 MIN
10 SERVINGS ●○

A classic Italian *panzanella* (bread salad) combines juicy tomatoes and bread cubes. Here, San Francisco chef Chris Cosentino swaps in stone fruits like apricots and peaches for the tomatoes, then dollops the "salad" with an airy zabaglione, a frothy sauce of egg yolks whipped with sweet dessert wine.

- ¼ cup plus 1 tablespoon sugar
- 1 tablespoon hot water
- 3 tablespoons extra-virgin olive oil
- One ¾-pound loaf sourdough bread, crusts removed and bread cut into 1-inch cubes (about 10 cups)
- 4 pounds mixed stone fruits, such as peaches, apricots and plums, each pitted and cut into 8 wedges
- 2 tablespoons fresh orange juice
- ¾ cup plus 2 tablespoons Moscato d'Asti
- 8 large egg yolks
- 1 tablespoon finely chopped mint

1. Preheat the oven to 350°. In a bowl, mix 1 tablespoon of the sugar with the hot water, stirring to dissolve the sugar. Add 2 tablespoons of the oil and stir to combine.

2. Arrange the bread cubes on a large rimmed baking sheet. Drizzle the bread cubes with the sugar-syrup-and-olive-oil mixture and toss to coat. Bake until the bread cubes are crisp and golden brown, about 10 minutes.

3. In a large bowl, toss the fruit slices with the fresh orange juice and 2 tablespoons of the Moscato d'Asti and let stand at room temperature for 10 minutes.

4. Meanwhile, in a medium stainless steel bowl, whisk the egg yolks with the remaining ¼ cup of sugar and ¾ cup of Moscato. Fill a large bowl with ice water. Set the bowl with the eggs over a medium saucepan filled with 1 inch of barely simmering water (you can also use a double boiler).

5. Using a whisk or a handheld electric mixer on low speed, beat the egg yolk mixture until it is hot and foamy and forms a ribbon when the beaters are lifted, about 8 minutes. Don't cook the zabaglione for too long, or it will curdle.

6. Remove the zabaglione from the heat and whisk in the remaining 1 tablespoon of oil. Carefully set the bowl in the ice bath and whisk until chilled, about 5 minutes.

7. To serve, add the bread cubes and mint to the fruit in the bowl and toss well. Transfer the *panzanella* to shallow bowls, top each one with a large dollop of zabaglione and serve right away. —*Chris Cosentino*

MAKE AHEAD The zabaglione can be refrigerated, covered, overnight. Whisk well before serving.

Plum-and-Honey Sabayon Gratins

TOTAL: 30 MIN
4 SERVINGS ● ●

This stunning sabayon—an airy custard with honey and Moscato—is summer's answer to crème brûlée. If you don't have Moscato, any honey-inflected dessert wine will do, such as a late-harvest Riesling.

- 2 tablespoons unsalted butter
- 6 tablespoons clover honey
- 5 large plums (1½ pounds), quartered and pitted
- 3 large egg yolks
- ⅓ cup Moscato d'Asti or other dessert wine

honey buzzwords

Colony Collapse Disorder A sudden abandonment of beehives by the adult population. CCD affected roughly one-third of U.S. beehives in 2007. So far, no cause is known.

Single-Varietal Honey Also called monofloral, this honey is predominantly made from the nectar of one species of flower grown in one place, yielding a distinct flavor and color.

Raw Honey Honey that hasn't been pasteurized, processed or filtered retains the pollen, enzymes and nutrients believed to provide health benefits.

Apitherapy An age-old health practice that uses honey, pollen and other bee-derived products to alleviate allergies and promote well-being. For information, go to *apitherapy.org*.

1. Preheat the broiler. In a large skillet, melt the butter with 2 tablespoons of the honey over moderately high heat until foaming. Add the quartered and pitted plums and cook, turning occasionally, until the fruit has softened and the honey has thickened slightly, 6 minutes. Scrape the plums and their juices onto a plate.

2. In a medium heatproof bowl set over a saucepan of simmering water, whisk the egg yolks, Moscato and the remaining ¼ cup of honey until the mixture is thick and pale yellow, about 8 minutes. Remove from the heat and whisk the sabayon until cooled slightly, about 1 minute.

3. Scrape the sabayon into four 8-ounce gratin dishes. Top with the plums and their juices. Transfer to a baking sheet. Broil 3 inches from the heat for about 1 minute, until the sabayon is golden, and serve.
—*Susan Spungen*

Almond-Plum Tart

ACTIVE: 45 MIN; TOTAL: 3 HR
6 SERVINGS ● ●

ALMOND CRUNCH
- 1 cup slivered almonds, chopped
- 3 tablespoons granulated sugar
- 2 teaspoons water

TART
- 3 tablespoons unsalted butter, softened
- 5 packed tablespoons light brown sugar
- ¼ cup Chambord
- 5 ripe plums (1 pound)—halved, pitted and cut into ½-inch wedges
- ½ cup slivered almonds
- 1½ tablespoons all-purpose flour, plus more for dusting
- 2 large eggs
- 1 tablespoon pure vanilla extract
- 14 ounces all-butter puff pastry, thawed in the refrigerator

1. MAKE THE ALMOND CRUNCH: Preheat the oven to 350°. In a bowl, toss the almonds, sugar and water until coated, then spread on a parchment paper–lined baking sheet. Bake for about 11 minutes, stirring once and rotating the baking sheet, until golden; let cool. Break up any large pieces.

2. MAKE THE TART: In a large skillet, melt 1 tablespoon of the butter with 3 tablespoons of the brown sugar over moderately high heat for 1 minute. Add the Chambord and bring to a simmer. Add the plums and cook, stirring occasionally, until the edges begin to soften, about 2 minutes. Using a slotted spoon, transfer the plums to a baking sheet to cool. Reserve the juices in the skillet.

3. In a food processor, grind the almonds until very fine. In a medium bowl, combine the remaining 2 tablespoons each of butter and brown sugar. Stir in the ½ cup of ground almonds and the 1½ tablespoons of flour. Add 1 egg and the vanilla and stir until fully incorporated.

4. On a lightly floured surface, roll out the pastry to a rough 13-by-11-inch rectangle. Cut the pastry in half lengthwise and transfer one piece to a parchment paper–lined baking sheet. In a small bowl, beat the remaining egg. Lightly brush the beaten egg over the pastry on the baking sheet.

5. Cut out the center of the remaining piece of pastry, leaving a 1-inch-wide rectangular border; reserve the center for another use. Neatly lay the pastry frame on the rectangle on the baking sheet. Lightly brush the border with the beaten egg. Spread the almond mixture over the base of the pastry. Arrange the plums on the almond filling and refrigerate for at least 30 minutes, until chilled.

6. Preheat the oven to 375°. Bake the tart for 1 hour, until the pastry is golden brown and cooked through. Let stand for 15 minutes, or until cooled slightly. Brush the plums with the Chambord juices. Cut the tart crosswise into slices and garnish with the almond crunch (or sliced almonds). Serve the tart warm or at room temperature.
—*Mitchelle Dy*

PLUM-AND-HONEY SABAYON GRATIN

ALMOND-PLUM TART

Homemade Yogurt with Plum Compote

ACTIVE: 25 MIN; TOTAL: 45 MIN
PLUS OVERNIGHT RESTING
4 SERVINGS ● ● ○

1 quart 1 percent milk
½ cup nonfat yogurt
1 pound plums, pitted and
   sliced ½ inch thick
½ cup water
3 tablespoons sugar

1. Preheat the oven to 175°. In an 8-by-11-inch glass or ceramic baking dish, mix the milk with the yogurt. Press a sheet of wax paper directly onto the milk mixture, followed by a sheet of foil. Put the baking dish in the oven and turn off the heat. Let stand in the oven overnight. In the morning, refrigerate the yogurt until chilled, 30 minutes. **2.** Meanwhile, in a medium saucepan, combine the plums with the water and sugar and bring to a simmer. Cook over moderate heat until the plums are tender, about 10 minutes. Transfer the plums and their juices to a food processor and pulse until coarsely chopped. Transfer to a bowl and refrigerate, stirring occasionally, until chilled, about 20 minutes. Serve the compote with the yogurt in bowls.
—*Stéphane Vivier*

MAKE AHEAD The yogurt can be refrigerated for up to 1 week. The compote can be refrigerated for up to 3 days.

Brandied Prunes Jubilee

ACTIVE: 15 MIN; TOTAL: 1 HR 30 MIN
4 SERVINGS ● ○

When Queen Victoria celebrated the 50th year of her reign, the eminent chef Auguste Escoffier created a dish in her honor called Cerises Jubilee: cherries poached in sugar syrup and kirsch, then flambéed. This modern version uses prunes, Asian spices and brandy. It's delectable on buttered toast.

1 cup water
½ cup sugar
½ cinnamon stick
½ star anise pod
2 tablespoons brandy
1 cup pitted prunes
Crème fraîche or vanilla ice cream,
   for serving

1. In a small saucepan, combine the water, sugar, cinnamon stick and star anise and bring to a boil. Simmer the spiced sugar syrup over moderate heat for 15 minutes. **2.** Discard the cinnamon stick and star anise. Off the heat, stir in the brandy and prunes. Let the brandied prunes stand at room temperature until they plump, at least 1 hour, but preferably overnight. **3.** Just before serving, rewarm the prunes. Serve in bowls over spoonfuls of crème fraîche or ice cream. —*Barbara Lynch*
MAKE AHEAD The prunes can be refrigerated in their syrup for up to 1 week.

pies & fruit desserts

Plum Cake with Hazelnut Brittle and Honey Mascarpone

ACTIVE: 1 HR; TOTAL: 2 HR

10 SERVINGS ● ●

New York City chef Peter Hoffman likes using purple plums, a.k.a. Italian prune plums, in this lightly spiced cake; as the batter cooks, the flavor of the plums intensifies, but the fruit doesn't become mushy. He tops the dessert with honey-spiked mascarpone cream and a sprinkling of chopped nut brittle.

CAKE

- 2 pounds plums—halved, pitted and cut into 1-inch pieces
- ½ cup plus 2 tablespoons turbinado sugar
- 1 tablespoon fresh lemon juice
- 2 cups all-purpose flour
- 2 teaspoons baking powder
- ½ teaspoon salt
- ½ teaspoon cinnamon
- ¼ teaspoon ground cardamom
- 6 tablespoons cold unsalted butter, cut into cubes
- 2 large eggs, lightly beaten
- 1 teaspoon pure vanilla extract
- ¾ cup milk

HONEY MASCARPONE

- 1 cup heavy cream
- ¼ cup honey
- 1 cup mascarpone (8 ounces)

Hazelnut Brittle (recipe follows)

1. MAKE THE CAKE: Preheat the oven to 325°; butter a 10-inch cast-iron skillet. In a bowl, toss the plums with 2 tablespoons of the sugar and the lemon juice.

2. In a food processor, pulse the flour with the baking powder, salt, cinnamon, cardamom and the remaining ½ cup of sugar. Add the butter and process until finely chopped. Add the eggs and vanilla and process until incorporated. With the processor on, gradually add the milk in a thin stream and process until the batter is smooth. Add the batter to the plums, gently folding them in.

3. Transfer the batter to the prepared skillet and smooth the surface. Bake the cake for about 1 hour, until the top is golden and a toothpick inserted in the center comes out clean. Let cool in the pan.

4. MAKE THE HONEY MASCARPONE: In a medium bowl, beat the heavy cream with the honey at medium-high speed until softly whipped. Beat in the mascarpone at medium-low speed.

5. In a food processor, pulse the Hazelnut Brittle until coarsely chopped.

6. Cut the cake into wedges and transfer to plates. Spoon a dollop of the honey mascarpone on top, sprinkle with the chopped nut brittle and serve.
—*Peter Hoffman*

HAZELNUT BRITTLE

TOTAL: 25 MIN

MAKES ABOUT 2 CUPS ● ●

- ½ cup sugar
- 2 tablespoons water
- 2 tablespoons light corn syrup
- 1 tablespoon unsalted butter
- 1¼ cups skinned roasted hazelnuts, coarsely chopped (about 6 ounces)
- ¼ teaspoon salt
- ¼ teaspoon baking soda
- ¼ teaspoon pure vanilla extract

Line a baking sheet with buttered parchment paper. In a medium saucepan, combine the sugar, water, corn syrup and butter and bring to a boil, stirring until the sugar is melted. Cook over moderate heat without stirring until the syrup reaches 270° on a candy thermometer, about 10 minutes. Stir in the chopped hazelnuts, salt, baking soda and vanilla and cook until the mixture is golden, about 3 minutes longer. Immediately pour onto the parchment and spread in a thin layer using a spatula. Let the brittle cool completely, then break into pieces. —*PH*

MAKE AHEAD The brittle can be stored in an airtight container at room temperature for up to 3 days.

Sweet Semolina and Dried-Apricot Pilaf

ACTIVE: 20 MIN; TOTAL: 45 MIN

6 SERVINGS ●

This lovely dessert or late-breakfast dish is made by toasting semolina and almonds in butter, then simmering them with sweetened milk and dried apricots. The result is crumbly, aromatic and pilaf-like.

- 2 cups whole milk
- ¾ cup sugar
- 1 stick unsalted butter
- 1 cup coarse semolina (6 ounces; see Note)
- ½ cup slivered almonds
- ½ cup dried apricots, finely diced
- ¼ teaspoon pure almond extract

Pinch of salt

Crème fraîche or orange sorbet, for serving

1. In a small saucepan, bring the whole milk to a boil with the sugar. Simmer over low heat for 5 minutes.

2. In a large saucepan, melt the butter. Add the semolina and almonds and cook over moderate heat, stirring constantly, until golden and fragrant, about 8 minutes. Remove from the heat and gradually stir in the milk mixture, apricots, almond extract and salt. Cover and let stand until the liquid is completely absorbed, about 20 minutes. Fluff with a fork and serve with crème fraîche or sorbet.
—*Defne Koryürek*

NOTE Coarse-ground semolina is available at Middle Eastern groceries and from Kalustyan's (800-352-3451 or kalustyans.com).

Yogurt and Apricot Pie with Crunchy Granola Crust

ACTIVE: 25 MIN; TOTAL: 1 HR 10 MIN

PLUS 2 HR CHILLING

MAKES ONE 9-INCH PIE ● ● ●

CRUST

- 1 cup all-purpose flour
- ⅓ cup sugar
- ¼ cup sliced almonds, crushed

¼ cup rolled oats

Pinch of salt

2 tablespoons unsalted butter

¼ cup canola oil

FILLING

1 cup low-fat plain Greek yogurt

2 large eggs, lightly beaten

¼ cup sugar

3 tablespoons fresh
   lemon juice

1 teaspoon pure vanilla extract

½ cup warmed apricot preserves

1. MAKE THE CRUST: Preheat the oven to 350°. In a large bowl, combine the flour, sugar, almonds, oats and salt. In a large skillet, melt the butter in the canola oil. Add the granola mixture and cook over moderate heat, stirring constantly, until golden, 5 minutes; transfer the mixture to a 9-inch glass pie plate and let cool slightly.

2. Using a flat-bottomed glass, gently press the granola evenly over the bottom and side of the pie plate to form a ½-inch-thick crust. Freeze the crust for about 10 minutes, until completely cooled.

3. MEANWHILE, MAKE THE FILLING: In a bowl, whisk the yogurt with the eggs, sugar, lemon juice and vanilla until smooth. Pour into the pie shell and bake for 25 minutes, until the filling is set but still slightly jiggly in the center. Let stand at room temperature for 5 minutes. Pour the warm apricot preserves on top and gently spread in an even layer. Refrigerate until the pie is chilled, at least 2 hours. Cut into wedges and serve.
—*Jessica Gilmartin and Patama Roj*

Caramel Cream Pie with Crispy Rice Topping

ACTIVE: 1 HR 15 MIN; TOTAL: 2 HR PLUS OVERNIGHT CHILLING

MAKES ONE 10-INCH PIE ● ●

Humble ingredients like puffed rice cereal (transformed into a brilliant topping) and graham crackers (crushed with hazelnuts to yield a tender crust) are the core of this surprisingly luxe dessert.

CRUST

3 ounces blanched hazelnuts
   (¾ cup)

1 cup graham cracker crumbs

2 tablespoons sugar

6 tablespoons unsalted butter,
   melted

CARAMEL PUDDING

1 cup sugar

¼ cup water

4 cups whole milk

1 teaspoon pure vanilla extract

1 teaspoon unflavored gelatin

½ cup cornstarch

1 teaspoon kosher salt

4 large egg yolks

CRISPY RICE

½ cup sugar

1 tablespoon water

1 teaspoon light corn syrup

½ teaspoon kosher salt

1½ cups puffed rice cereal

**Lightly sweetened whipped
   cream, for serving**

1. MAKE THE CRUST: Preheat the oven to 350°. Spread the hazelnuts in a glass pie plate and toast for about 8 minutes, until lightly golden and fragrant; let cool. Transfer the nuts to a mini food processor and coarsely grind. Pour the ground nuts into a medium bowl and add the graham cracker crumbs, sugar and butter; mix until evenly moistened. Press the crumbs over the bottom and up the side of the pie plate in an even layer. Bake the crust for 8 minutes, until barely set. Transfer the pie plate to a rack to cool.

2. MEANWHILE, MAKE THE CARAMEL PUDDING: In a large, heavy saucepan, combine the sugar and water and bring to a boil over moderately high heat, gently swirling the pan until the sugar dissolves. Cook over moderate heat, undisturbed, until a deep-amber caramel forms, about 8 minutes. Remove the saucepan from the heat. Carefully pour in 1 cup of the milk, then cook over moderately low heat,

whisking gently, until the caramel is smooth, about 5 minutes.

3. In a small glass bowl, combine ¼ cup of the milk with the vanilla; sprinkle the gelatin on top and let stand until softened. In a large glass measuring cup, whisk the remaining 2¾ cups of milk with the cornstarch and kosher salt. Pour the milk mixture into the caramel and bring to a boil over moderately high heat, whisking constantly until thickened, about 10 minutes. Remove from the heat and whisk in the egg yolks, one at a time. Return the mixture to a boil and cook until thickened once again, about 5 minutes. Whisk in the gelatin mixture.

4. With a rubber spatula, gently spread the caramel pudding in the cooled crust. Tap the pie plate gently on a work surface to settle the pudding. Press a piece of plastic wrap directly on the surface of the pie and refrigerate overnight.

5. MAKE THE RICE TOPPING: Line a rimmed baking sheet with parchment paper and coat with vegetable spray. In a small, heavy saucepan, bring the sugar, water and corn syrup to a boil over moderately high heat. Lower the heat to moderate and simmer undisturbed until a deep-amber caramel forms, about 5 minutes. Remove the caramel from the heat and stir in the salt and rice cereal. Scrape the caramelized cereal onto the prepared baking sheet and let cool for 30 minutes, until it is hardened.

6. Break the crispy rice into shards; transfer to a sturdy plastic bag. Using a rolling pin, crush the topping into small pieces.

7. Spread the whipped cream on top of the chilled pie, making deep swirls. Top the pie with the crispy rice and serve.
—*Rachel Soszynski*

MAKE AHEAD The crispy rice topping can be stored in an airtight container at room temperature for up to 3 days. The pie can be refrigerated for up to 6 hours. Top with the crispy rice just before serving.

Chocolate Cream Pie

TOTAL: 30 MIN PLUS 3 HR CHILLING

MAKES ONE 9-INCH PIE ● ● ●

This dreamy, creamy dessert started as a simple chocolate pudding made with workaday cocoa. F&W's Melissa Rubel turned it into a homey, silky pie by adding a quick chocolate crust and vanilla whipped cream. "But you could still serve just the filling as a pudding," she says.

CRUST

6 ounces chocolate wafer cookies, finely ground

4½ tablespoons unsalted butter, melted

2 tablespoons granulated sugar

Pinch of fine sea salt

FILLING

2 cups whole milk

½ cup plus 2 tablespoons granulated sugar

3 egg yolks

¼ cup cornstarch

¼ teaspoon fine sea salt

4 ounces semisweet chocolate, chopped

1 ounce unsweetened chocolate, chopped

¾ cup heavy cream

1 teaspoon pure vanilla extract

Chocolate shavings, for garnish

1. MAKE THE CRUST: Preheat the oven to 350°. In a medium bowl, mix the cookie crumbs with the butter, sugar and salt until the crumbs are evenly moistened. Pour the mixture into a 9-inch glass pie dish and press evenly over the bottom and up the side of the dish to form a crust. Bake for 8 minutes, until the crust is fragrant. Remove from the oven and, using the bottom of a drinking glass, immediately press the crumbs again to compact the crust. Let cool completely.

2. MAKE THE FILLING: In a medium saucepan, heat the milk with ¼ cup of the sugar until bubbles form around the edge. In a large bowl, whisk the egg yolks with ¼ cup of the sugar, the cornstarch and salt. Gradually whisk in the hot milk mixture. Pour the mixture into the saucepan and cook over moderate heat, whisking constantly, until very thick, about 3 minutes. Remove from the heat and whisk in the semisweet and unsweetened chocolate until smooth. Strain the chocolate filling into the pie crust through a coarse sieve and smooth the surface with a rubber spatula. Press a piece of plastic wrap directly on the surface of the pie filling and refrigerate for 3 hours, until chilled.

3. Let the pie stand at room temperature for 10 minutes. Meanwhile, in a medium bowl, beat the cream with the remaining 2 tablespoons of sugar and the vanilla until firm. Spread the whipped cream over the pie, cut into wedges and serve, garnished with chocolate shavings. —*Melissa Rubel*

MAKE AHEAD The pie can be made up to 1 day in advance and refrigerated.

Tropical Fruit Cobbler with Coconut Macaroon Topping

ACTIVE: 1 HR; TOTAL: 2 HR PLUS 3 HR COOLING

10 SERVINGS ● ●

New York City chef Adam Perry Lang wanted to play on the idea of a macaroon in this clever dessert, so he turned the cookie into a fluffy meringue with toasted coconut and ground almonds, then used it to top a juicy mixture of fresh pineapple and mango.

7 large ripe mangoes (about 1 pound each), peeled and thinly sliced (16 cups)

3 cups fresh pineapple chunks (¾ pound), cut into ½-inch cubes

1¼ cups sugar

One 14-ounce bag shredded sweetened coconut (about 5 cups)

2 tablespoons canola oil

¼ cup thick coconut cream from the top of a can of full-fat coconut milk (see Note)

9 large egg whites

½ cup roasted almonds, finely ground

1. In a large bowl, toss the mangoes and pineapple with ½ cup of the sugar and let stand for 30 minutes.

2. Meanwhile, preheat the oven to 325°. Spread the coconut on a baking sheet and toast for about 8 minutes, stirring occasionally, until golden and fragrant. Let cool.

3. In each of 2 large skillets, heat 1 tablespoon of the canola oil until shimmering. Divide the mangoes and pineapple between the skillets and cook over high heat, stirring and shaking the skillets, until the fruit is slightly softened, about 5 minutes. Add 2 tablespoons of the thick coconut cream to each skillet and stir until melted. Transfer all of the fruit to a 3½- to 4-quart shallow baking dish.

4. In the bowl of a standing electric mixer, beat the egg whites at medium-high speed until soft peaks form. With the machine on, gradually beat in the remaining ¾ cup of sugar until the whites are firm and glossy, about 3 minutes. Using a large rubber spatula, fold in the toasted coconut and ground almonds.

5. Spoon ¼-cup mounds of the macaroon mixture over the mangoes and pineapple, leaving little gaps here and there. Bake the fruit cobbler for about 45 minutes, until the fruit is bubbling and the macaroon topping is browned and firm. Transfer to a rack and let cool completely before serving, about 3 hours. —*Adam Perry Lang*

NOTE Don't shake the can of coconut milk before opening it; let the can settle so you can scoop the thick cream off the top. Reserve the milk for another use.

MAKE AHEAD The tropical fruit cobbler can be made early in the day and kept at room temperature.

Flaky Blood Orange Tart

ACTIVE: 45 MIN; TOTAL: 3 HR PLUS
4 HR FREEZING

6 SERVINGS ● ○ ○

- 1 cup all-purpose flour,
  plus more for dusting
- ¼ cup plus 2 tablespoons
  granulated sugar
- ¼ teaspoon baking powder
- ¼ teaspoon salt
- 1 stick plus 1 tablespoon
  unsalted butter, the stick
  cut into ½-inch pieces
  and chilled
- 3 tablespoons ice water
- 8 to 10 blood oranges
  (about 5 ounces each)
- 1 large egg yolk mixed with
  2 tablespoons of water
- Salted Caramel Sauce (recipe follows),
  for serving

1. In a food processor, pulse the 1 cup of flour with 2 tablespoons of the sugar and the baking powder and salt. Add the stick of cold butter and pulse several times, just until the lumps of butter are the size of peas. Sprinkle the dough with the ice water and pulse just until moistened crumbs form. Turn the crumbs out onto a work surface, knead once or twice to bring the dough together and pat the pastry into a disk. Wrap the pastry in plastic and chill for 30 minutes.

salted caramel

The Salted Caramel Sauce in the tart recipe above is so versatile—and delicious—you'll want to make extra. Use it as a dip for apple slices, drizzled over ice cream or sandwiched between two wafer cookies.

2. On a floured work surface, roll out the chilled pastry to an 11-inch round about ¼ inch thick. Transfer the rolled pastry to a parchment paper–lined flat cookie sheet and refrigerate for about 15 minutes, or until chilled.

3. Meanwhile, peel the blood oranges, removing all of the bitter white pith. Thinly slice 2 of the oranges crosswise; remove the pits. Transfer the orange slices to a plate. Working over a sieve set over a bowl, cut in between the membranes of the remaining oranges, releasing the sections into the sieve. Remove the pits and gently shake out as much juice as possible without mashing the sections; you will need 1 cup of sections. Reserve the orange juice for another use.

4. Arrange the orange sections on the pastry, leaving a 2-inch border all around. Sprinkle 2 tablespoons of the sugar over the oranges. Using a paring knife, thinly slice the remaining 1 tablespoon of butter over the oranges. Fold up the pastry over the oranges, leaving most of the oranges uncovered. Brush the pastry with the egg wash and sprinkle lightly with 1 tablespoon of the sugar. Arrange the orange slices on top, leaving a 1-inch border of pastry all around. Sprinkle the remaining 1 tablespoon of sugar on top. Freeze the tart until solid, at least 4 hours or preferably overnight.

5. Preheat the oven to 375° and position a rack in the center. Place a baking sheet on the rack below to catch any drips. Bake the tart directly from the freezer for 1 hour and 15 minutes, until the fruit is bubbling and the pastry is deeply browned. Transfer the cookie sheet to a rack and let the tart cool for 30 minutes. Carefully slide the parchment paper onto the rack and let the tart cool completely. Serve with the Salted Caramel Sauce. —Zoe Nathan

MAKE AHEAD The unbaked tart can be tightly wrapped in plastic and frozen for up to 2 weeks.

SALTED CARAMEL SAUCE

TOTAL: 10 MIN PLUS 1 HR COOLING

MAKES ABOUT 1½ CUPS ● ○

- 1 cup sugar
- ¼ cup water
- 2 tablespoons light corn syrup
- ¾ cup heavy cream
- 4 tablespoons unsalted butter
- 1½ teaspoons gray sea salt,
  crushed

In a medium saucepan, combine the sugar, water and corn syrup and bring to a boil. Using a wet pastry brush, wash down any crystals on the side of the pan. Boil over high heat until a deep amber caramel forms, about 6 minutes. Remove the saucepan from the heat and carefully whisk in the cream, butter and salt. Let the caramel cool to room temperature, about 1 hour. —ZN

MAKE AHEAD The Salted Caramel Sauce can be refrigerated for up to 2 weeks. Rewarm before serving.

White Chocolate–Coated Grapes with Orange Curd

ACTIVE: 35 MIN; TOTAL: 1 HR

4 SERVINGS ● ○ ○

A fine layer of white chocolate gives both green and red grapes a creamy crunch. The orange curd dipping sauce could not be simpler; it's hard to imagine a more elegant use of the microwave.

CURD

- 2 cups fresh orange juice
- 4 large egg yolks
- ¼ cup granulated sugar
- 3 tablespoons unsalted butter,
  cut into 1-inch pieces

GRAPES

- 4 ounces white chocolate,
  chopped
- 1 tablespoon vegetable oil
- 1 pound green or red grapes,
  stemmed and chilled
- 2 tablespoons confectioners'
  sugar

1. **MAKE THE CURD:** In a saucepan, boil the orange juice until it's reduced to ⅓ cup, about 12 minutes. Let cool.

2. In a microwave-safe bowl, whisk the egg yolks with the granulated sugar. Whisk in the reduced orange juice and stir in the butter. Microwave the mixture on high power for 1 minute, until thickened. Whisk until smooth. Press a piece of plastic wrap directly onto the surface of the orange curd and refrigerate for 1 hour, or until chilled.

3. **MAKE THE GRAPES:** Line a rimmed baking sheet with parchment paper. In a microwave-safe bowl, combine the white chocolate with the oil. Microwave on high power for 1 minute, until the chocolate is just melted; whisk until smooth. Let cool.

4. Dry the grapes with a towel and set them in a large bowl. Pour the white chocolate mixture over the grapes and, using a rubber spatula, fold the grapes into the chocolate until they are coated. Sift the confectioners' sugar on top of the chocolate-coated grapes and stir until the grapes separate; transfer the grapes to the baking sheet and refrigerate for 10 minutes, until the chocolate sets. Serve the chocolate-coated grapes in glasses with the orange curd in ramekins alongside.
—*Michel Richard*

Gingered Orange Gratin

TOTAL: 30 MIN
4 SERVINGS

- 4 navel and/or blood oranges
- 2 tablespoons orange marmalade
- 4 teaspoons light brown sugar
- 8 ounces crème fraîche
- 2 tablespoons minced crystallized ginger
- 2 teaspoons shredded mint

1. Preheat the broiler and position a rack 6 inches from the heat. Using a sharp knife, peel the oranges, removing all of the bitter white pith. Cut each orange crosswise into six ⅓-inch-thick slices. Arrange the orange slices in 4 gratin dishes, overlapping them

slightly, and spread with the marmalade. Sprinkle the brown sugar on top and broil for about 10 minutes, shifting the dishes for even browning, until bubbling and lightly caramelized in spots. Transfer to a rack and let cool for 10 minutes.

2. Meanwhile, using an electric mixer, beat the crème fraîche until lightly whipped. Fold in the crystallized ginger. Spoon the ginger crème fraîche over the orange slices, sprinkle with the shredded mint and serve immediately. —*Grace Parisi*

Cranberry and Orange Pavlovas

ACTIVE: 1 HR; TOTAL: 3 HR
12 SERVINGS
MERINGUES

- 6 large egg whites, at room temperature
- 1 teaspoon cream of tartar
- ¼ teaspoon salt
- 1¼ cups granulated sugar

TOPPING

- 2 cups granulated sugar
- 1 cup water
- 1 vanilla bean, split, seeds scraped
- 2 large navel oranges
- 1½ pounds cranberries (6 cups)
- 2 cups heavy cream
- 2 tablespoons confectioners' sugar

Mint sprigs, for garnish

1. **MAKE THE MERINGUES:** Preheat the oven to 250°. Line 2 large baking sheets with parchment paper. Arrange racks in the lower and middle thirds of the oven.

2. In the bowl of a standing electric mixer fitted with the whisk attachment, beat the egg whites with the cream of tartar and salt at medium speed until soft peaks form. Increase the speed to medium-high and gradually beat in the sugar, 2 tablespoons at a time, until the meringue is stiff and glossy, about 6 minutes.

3. Using a large spoon, dollop 6 mounds of meringue onto each baking sheet. Using the back of the spoon, spread the mounds into 5-inch squares and make an impression in the center of each one. Bake the meringues for 1 hour and 45 minutes, until the outsides are firm but the insides are still slightly soft; shift the pans from top to bottom and front to back halfway through. Transfer the baking sheets to racks and let the meringues cool completely.

4. **MEANWHILE, MAKE THE TOPPING:** In a large saucepan, combine the granulated sugar and water. Scrape the vanilla seeds onto a plate and add the pod to the saucepan. Using a vegetable peeler, remove 2 long strips of zest from one of the oranges and add them to the pan. Halve the orange and squeeze the juice into the saucepan. Bring to a simmer, stirring until the sugar is dissolved. Add the cranberries and cook over low heat just until the berries are softened, 8 minutes. Let cool completely. Discard the vanilla bean and orange zest and refrigerate the cranberries until chilled.

5. Finely grate the zest of the remaining orange and transfer it to a food processor. Using a knife, peel the orange, removing all of the white pith. Working over the food processor, cut in between the membranes to release the orange sections into the food processor. Pulse until chopped.

6. In a clean bowl, using clean beaters, whip the cream with the confectioners' sugar and vanilla seeds until firm. Add the chopped orange and its juice and beat just until combined.

7. Arrange the meringues on plates and spoon a mound of orange whipped cream into each one. Using a slotted spoon, top with the cranberries. Drizzle with some of the juices, garnish with mint and serve right away. —*Wendy Boys*

MAKE AHEAD The cooked cranberries can be refrigerated overnight. The meringues can be made up to 8 hours ahead (on a dry day) and kept at room temperature.

NOT YOUR USUAL LEMON MERINGUE PIE

SPICED RHUBARB SOUP WITH VANILLA ICE CREAM

Not Your Usual Lemon Meringue Pie

TOTAL: 1 HR

6 SERVINGS

In her version of lemon meringue pie, pastry chef Gale Gand forgoes a traditional crust for quick-baked sheets of sugared phyllo dough, which she layers with house-made lemon curd and a brown-sugar meringue. The recipe appears in Gand's book *Butter Sugar Flour Eggs* (Clarkson Potter). Here, good-quality store-bought phyllo dough and lemon curd speed things up.

- 3 **sheets of phyllo dough, plus more in case of tearing**
- 4 **tablespoons unsalted butter, melted**
- 2 **tablespoons granulated sugar**
- 1 **cup light brown sugar**
- 5 **large egg whites**

One 12-ounce jar lemon curd

Raspberries, for garnish

1. Preheat the oven to 350°. Cut 2 sheets of parchment paper to fit a large baking sheet. Place 1 sheet of the parchment on a work surface. Top with a sheet of phyllo and brush with the melted butter. Sprinkle 2 teaspoons of the granulated sugar over the phyllo dough. Repeat with 2 more sheets of phyllo and the remaining granulated sugar so that you have a stack of 3 sugared sheets. Using a ruler, trim the phyllo to a 12-by-16-inch rectangle, then cut it into twelve 4-inch squares. Slide the parchment onto a baking sheet and top with the second sheet of parchment paper. Bake for 18 minutes, until the phyllo squares are golden and crisp. Let the squares cool completely.

2. Preheat the broiler. Put the brown sugar in a food processor; pulse to break up any lumps. In the bowl of a standing electric mixer fitted with a whisk, beat the egg whites at medium-high speed until soft peaks form. Beat in the brown sugar at high speed, a few tablespoons at a time, until the whites are glossy, 2 to 3 minutes. Transfer the meringue to a pastry bag with a plain tip.

3. Spoon a dollop of the lemon curd onto each phyllo square. Pipe a layer of the brown sugar meringue over the lemon curd (alternatively, you can spoon the meringue over the curd). Broil the squares 6 inches from the heat, watching them carefully, for 1 minute, or until the tops of the meringues are lightly toasted. Set 6 phyllo squares on each of 6 dessert plates and top them with the remaining 6 squares of meringue-topped phyllo. Garnish the top layer of meringue with fresh raspberries and serve the lemon meringue pies right away. —*Gale Gand*

Spiced Rhubarb Soup with Vanilla Ice Cream

ACTIVE: 15 MIN; TOTAL: 25 MIN
PLUS 2 HR CHILLING

4 SERVINGS ●●

This silky fruit dessert is delicious on its own or topped with vanilla ice cream. Just be sure to only barely cook the rhubarb so that it retains its crispness and tangy flavor.

1 cup crème de cassis
1 cup dry red wine
¼ cup light brown sugar
2 cloves
1 star anise pod
1 cinnamon stick, halved
One 3-inch strip of lemon zest
½ vanilla bean, split
1½ pounds rhubarb, stalks peeled and sliced crosswise ½ inch thick
Vanilla ice cream, for serving

1. In a large saucepan, bring the crème de cassis, red wine, brown sugar, cloves, star anise, cinnamon, lemon zest and vanilla bean to a boil over high heat, stirring to dissolve the sugar. Reduce the heat and remove and discard the flavorings. Stir in the sliced rhubarb and return the liquid to a simmer. Remove the saucepan from the heat and let the soup stand for 10 minutes. Transfer to a large bowl; refrigerate the soup until chilled, about 2 hours.

2. Spoon the rhubarb soup into 4 bowls. Top each with a scoop of vanilla ice cream and serve the rhubarb soup right away.
—Michel Richard

Coconut Pavlovas with Tropical Fruit

ACTIVE: 20 MIN; TOTAL: 1 HR 45 MIN

6 SERVINGS ●○○

4 large egg whites
⅛ teaspoon cream of tartar
1 cup granulated sugar
1 teaspoon pure vanilla extract
⅓ cup unsweetened shredded coconut
4 large ripe passion fruits, halved (see Note)
2 kiwis—peeled, halved lengthwise and sliced ¼ inch thick
1 small mango, peeled and thinly sliced

1. Preheat the oven to 275°. Line a baking sheet with parchment paper and lightly spray it with cooking spray. In a large bowl, using an electric mixer, beat the egg whites with the cream of tartar at medium speed until frothy. Beat in the sugar, 1 tablespoon at a time, until the meringue is thick and glossy. Beat in the vanilla extract, then fold in the shredded coconut.

2. Scoop the meringue into six 3½-inch mounds on the prepared baking sheet. Using the back of a spoon, make a 1½-inch well in the center of each meringue.

3. Bake the coconut meringues in the center of the oven for about 1 hour, until they are crisp and lightly golden but still chewy on the inside. Remove from the oven and let the meringues cool completely on the baking sheet.

4. Scoop the pulp and seeds from the passion fruits into a bowl. Set the meringues on 6 dessert plates. Mound the kiwi and mango slices into the center of the meringues, spoon the passion fruit on top and serve the pavlovas right away.
—Marisa Churchill

NOTE Passion fruits are oval fruits slightly larger than lemons. When the fruit is ripe, the deep purple skin becomes slightly wrinkled and the orange flesh has an intensely tart, tropical fruit flavor. Look for passion fruit wherever specialty or tropical produce is sold.

MAKE AHEAD The baked and cooled coconut meringues can be stored overnight in an airtight container at room temperature. The sliced mango and kiwi can be refrigerated for up to 4 hours.

Caramelized Pineapple Sundaes with Coconut

 TOTAL: 30 MIN

10 SERVINGS ●●

Chef Kerry Simon tops creamy frozen yogurt with chunks of caramelized pineapple and slivers of fresh coconut (toasted, shredded coconut is just as delicious). For a variation, swap out the pineapple for bananas and garnish with the Japanese herb shiso.

One 2-pound pineapple—peeled, cored and sliced into ½-inch-thick rings (see Note)
2 teaspoons vegetable oil
½ cup sweetened shredded coconut
2½ pints fat-free vanilla frozen yogurt
Mint sprigs, for garnish

1. Light a grill. Brush the pineapple rings with the vegetable oil. Grill over moderately high heat, turning occasionally, until the pineapple rings are lightly charred and softened, about 8 minutes. Transfer the rings to a work surface and cut them into bite-size pieces.

2. In a medium skillet, toast the shredded coconut over moderate heat until golden, about 2 minutes. Transfer the toasted coconut to a plate to cool.

3. Scoop the frozen yogurt into sundae glasses or bowls. Top with the grilled pineapple, sprinkle with the toasted coconut, garnish with the mint sprigs and serve right away. —Kerry Simon

NOTE Some fruit markets sell fresh cored, sliced pineapple. To core a whole pineapple, you'll need a pineapple corer (available at kitchen stores). Alternatively, you can slice and grill the pineapple, then cut out the core as you cut the rings into pieces.

MAKE AHEAD The pineapple can be grilled up to 4 hours ahead. Rewarm in the oven before serving. The coconut can be toasted up to 4 hours ahead.

●HEALTHY ●MAKE AHEAD ○VEGETARIAN ●STAFF FAVORITE

CHOCOLATE-CARAMEL
SANDWICH COOKIES (P. 348)

cakes, cookies & more

" I'm part witch when it comes to baking. I bake late, late in the night. The grandkids are asleep, the phones don't ring and there are no interruptions . . . it's just me in the kitchen. "

—FLO BRAKER, COOKBOOK AUTHOR AND TEACHER, SAN FRANCISCO

ALMOND CAKE WITH PEARS

LEMON-RICOTTA SOUFFLÉS

Almond Cake with Pears and Crème Anglaise

ACTIVE: 45 MIN; TOTAL: 1 HR 30 MIN

8 SERVINGS ● ◐

For this simple but elegant dessert, a basic sponge cake baked with fragrant almond flour is split and filled with a layer of tender pears. Cooked in butter in a covered pan, the pears steam in their own juices, releasing a syrupy sauce all their own.

CAKE

1½ cups almond flour (see Note)

¼ cup all-purpose flour

1 teaspoon finely grated orange zest

Salt

1 cup granulated sugar

2 large eggs, beaten

6 large egg whites

PEARS

3 tablespoons unsalted butter

3 tablespoons granulated sugar

4 ripe but firm Bartlett pears—peeled, cored and cut into ½-inch wedges

Confectioners' sugar, for dusting

Crème Anglaise (recipe follows), for serving

1. MAKE THE CAKE: Preheat the oven to 350°. Butter and flour a 10-inch springform pan. In a large bowl, whisk the almond flour with the all-purpose flour, grated orange zest, a pinch of salt and ½ cup of the granulated sugar. Add the whole eggs and whisk well.

2. In a large bowl, using a handheld mixer, beat the egg whites with a pinch of salt until soft peaks form. Gradually beat in the remaining ½ cup of granulated sugar and beat until the egg whites are firm and glossy, about 2 minutes. Fold one-third of the beaten egg whites into the almond-flour mixture. Fold in the remaining egg whites until just incorporated.

3. Scrape the batter into the prepared pan and bake for 30 minutes, until the cake is puffed and golden brown and a toothpick inserted in the center comes out with a few moist crumbs attached. Let the cake cool in the pan for 15 minutes, then turn it out onto a wire rack to cool completely.

4. MEANWHILE, PREPARE THE PEARS: In a large skillet, melt the butter with the granulated sugar over moderate heat, stirring to dissolve the sugar. Arrange the pear wedges in the skillet in an even layer. Cover the skillet and cook over low heat until the pears are tender and a syrupy sauce forms, about 7 minutes.

5. Using a large serrated knife, cut the cake into two layers. Spoon the pears and their sauce over the bottom layer of cake and cover with the top layer. Lightly dust the cake with confectioners' sugar and serve, passing the Crème Anglaise at the table.

—*Florence Daniel Marzotto*

NOTE Almond flour is available at specialty food stores and large supermarkets like Whole Foods. To make your own, finely grind blanched almonds.

MAKE AHEAD The cake can be prepared through Step 4 and kept covered at room temperature overnight before proceeding. The poached pears can be refrigerated overnight; rewarm gently before assembling.

CRÈME ANGLAISE

TOTAL: 30 MIN
MAKES ABOUT 2 CUPS ● ●

- 3 large egg yolks
- ¼ cup sugar
- 2 teaspoons cornstarch
- 1¼ cups milk
- ½ teaspoon pure vanilla extract

1. In a medium bowl, whisk the egg yolks with the sugar and cornstarch. In a saucepan, heat the milk. Gradually add the milk to the egg mixture in a thin stream, whisking constantly, until the mixture is smooth.
2. Return the mixture to the saucepan and cook over moderate heat, stirring constantly with a wooden spoon, until the sauce is thick enough to coat the back of the spoon, about 6 minutes. Stir in the vanilla extract and transfer to a medium bowl set in a large bowl filled with ice water. Stir occasionally until chilled, 10 minutes, then serve with the cake. *—FDM*

MAKE AHEAD The Crème Anglaise can be refrigerated for up to 3 days.

Lemon-Ricotta Soufflés

ACTIVE: 50 MIN; TOTAL: 2 HR
4 SERVINGS ● ●

To firm up these individual soufflés, Maria Helm Sinskey (an F&W Best New Chef 1996) uses choux pastry (the dough for gougères and profiteroles) mixed with airy meringue and ricotta. While the insides of the soufflés are nicely custardy, the edges and sides are deliciously crisp. The soufflés can be served hot, warm or cool, when they become like mini citrus cakes.

- 6 tablespoons unsalted butter, softened, plus more for buttering the ramekins
- 1 cup granulated sugar, plus more for dusting
- ¾ cup water

Kosher salt

- ¾ cup all-purpose flour
- 4 large egg yolks
- 1 tablespoon finely grated lemon zest
- 3 tablespoons fresh lemon juice
- 1¾ cups Creamy Ricotta (p. 11)
- 6 large egg whites
- ½ teaspoon cream of tartar

Confectioners' sugar, for dusting

1. Preheat the oven to 425°. Butter four 10-ounce ramekins and dust generously with granulated sugar.
2. In a medium saucepan, bring the 6 tablespoons of butter, the water and ½ teaspoon of salt to a boil. Remove from the heat and stir in the flour all at once. Cook over moderate heat, stirring with a wooden spoon, until the dough comes together, 2 minutes. Transfer the dough to the bowl of a standing mixer fitted with the paddle. Beat at medium speed for 10 seconds. Add the egg yolks one at a time; beat well between additions. Add the lemon zest and juice and Creamy Ricotta and beat at high speed until very smooth and creamy, scraping down the bowl occasionally. Transfer to a large bowl.
3. Wash and dry the mixer bowl. Add the egg whites, the cream of tartar and a pinch of salt. Using the whisk, beat the egg whites at medium-high speed until soft peaks form. Add the 1 cup of granulated sugar in a thin stream and beat at high speed until stiff, glossy peaks form, about 2 minutes. Gently fold the whites into the ricotta dough just until no streaks remain.
4. Spoon the soufflé mixture into the prepared ramekins. Run the blade of a knife over the top of each soufflé so it's level, then run your thumb around the inside

rim to help the soufflés rise evenly. Bake the soufflés in the center of the oven for 35 to 40 minutes, or until firm, risen and deep golden on top. Let cool for 15 minutes. Dust the tops with confectioners' sugar and serve the soufflés hot, at room temperature or cool. *—Maria Helm Sinskey*

Lemon-Glazed Mini Pound Cakes

ACTIVE: 30 MIN; TOTAL: 1 HR 30 MIN
MAKES 18 MINI POUND CAKES
● ● ●

These buttery individual pound cakes get their intense citrus flavor from a double glazing of lemon syrup.

- 3 large eggs
- 4 cups confectioners' sugar
- 2½ sticks (10 ounces) unsalted butter, melted
- 2½ cups all-purpose flour
- 1 teaspoon baking powder
- ¼ teaspoon salt
- ¾ cup milk
- ⅓ cup fresh lemon juice

1. Preheat the oven to 350°. Spray 18 muffin cups with cooking spray. In a large bowl, using a handheld mixer, beat the eggs at low speed until blended. Add 3 cups of the sugar, the melted butter, flour, baking powder and salt. Beat at medium speed until smooth, about 1 minute. Beat in the milk.
2. Spoon ¼ cup of the batter into each prepared muffin cup. Bake for 25 minutes, until the pound cakes are golden and a toothpick inserted in the center comes out clean. Let cool for 5 minutes, then turn the cakes out onto a rack to cool, 30 minutes.
3. In a saucepan, whisk the remaining 1 cup of sugar with the lemon juice and bring to a simmer over moderate heat, stirring, until thickened to a syrup, 8 minutes. Let cool.
4. Brush the tops of the pound cakes with the lemon syrup. Let stand until the glaze has set, 10 minutes. Brush again with the remaining syrup, let set, then serve.
—Magdalena Niementowski

Pistachio-Topped Lemon–Olive Oil Cake

ACTIVE: 25 MIN; TOTAL: 1 HR 30 MIN PLUS 1 HR STANDING

10 SERVINGS ● ●

Colorado chef Ryan Hardy's citrusy, nutty and dense olive-oil cake was inspired by an all-butter cake from London's River Café. Hardy substitutes extra-virgin olive oil for some of the butter and insists that the cake be served with tangy crème fraîche and an espresso.

CAKE

- ¾ cup whole blanched almonds
- ⅔ cup plus ½ cup unsalted raw pistachios (about 7 ounces)
- 6 tablespoons unsalted butter, softened, plus more for buttering
- 1¼ cups sugar
- 4 large eggs
- 1 tablespoon finely grated lemon zest
- 1 tablespoon fresh lemon juice
- 1 vanilla bean, halved lengthwise and seeds scraped
- ¼ cup plus 2 tablespoons extra-virgin olive oil
- ⅔ cup all-purpose flour
- ¼ teaspoon salt

SYRUP

Finely grated zest of 1 lemon

Juice of 2 lemons

- ¼ cup sugar
- 2 tablespoons water

Crème fraîche, for serving

1. MAKE THE CAKE: Preheat the oven to 350°. Butter a 10-inch round cake pan, line the bottom with parchment paper and butter the paper. In a food processor, pulse the almonds with ⅔ cup of the pistachios until finely ground.

2. In a large bowl, using a handheld electric mixer, beat the butter with the sugar at medium speed until it's the texture of moist sand. Add the eggs one at a time, beating well between additions. Add the lemon zest, lemon juice and vanilla seeds and beat until smooth. Gradually beat in the olive oil in a thin stream. Using a rubber spatula, fold in the ground nuts, the flour and salt. Scrape the lemon cake batter into the prepared pan.

3. Bake the cake for about 55 minutes, or until a toothpick inserted in the center comes out clean. Transfer the pan to a rack and let the cake cool for 15 minutes. Invert the cake onto the rack and peel off the parchment paper. Invert the cake again onto a serving plate.

4. Meanwhile, toast the remaining ½ cup of pistachios in a pie plate for 8 minutes, or until fragrant.

5. MAKE THE SYRUP: In a small saucepan, combine the lemon zest, lemon juice, sugar and water and bring to a simmer over moderate heat, stirring until the sugar is dissolved. Pour the lemon syrup over the warm cake and scatter the toasted pistachios all over the top. Let the cake stand for 1 hour, then cut into wedges and serve with crème fraîche. —*Ryan Hardy*

MAKE AHEAD The cake can be kept in an airtight container at room temperature for up to 2 days.

Honey Tea Cake

ACTIVE: 30 MIN; TOTAL: 2 HR

MAKES ONE 9-BY-5-INCH LOAF ● ●

This deeply flavored cake is made with buckwheat honey, which has a spicy molasses character. The cake is wonderful served warm, but its flavors intensify overnight.

- 4 tablespoons unsalted butter, melted, plus more for buttering
- 2¼ cups all-purpose flour
- ¾ cup sugar
- 1 tablespoon plus 1 teaspoon finely grated orange zest
- 2 teaspoons baking powder
- ½ teaspoon baking soda
- 2 teaspoons anise seeds
- ½ teaspoon ground ginger
- ½ teaspoon cinnamon
- ½ teaspoon kosher salt
- ⅛ teaspoon freshly ground black pepper
- ¾ cup plus 2 tablespoons buckwheat honey
- ¾ cup hot water
- 3 tablespoons Cognac

1. Preheat the oven to 350°. Butter a 9-by-5-inch loaf pan. In a medium bowl, whisk the flour with the sugar, orange zest, baking powder, baking soda, anise seeds, ginger, cinnamon, salt and pepper.

2. In the bowl of an electric standing mixer fitted with the paddle, combine ¾ cup of the honey with the water, Cognac and 4 tablespoons of melted butter; mix until blended. Add the flour mixture and mix at medium-low speed until incorporated.

3. Scrape the batter into the prepared pan and bake for about 1 hour, until a cake tester inserted into the center comes out clean. Let the cake cool in the pan for about 5 minutes.

4. In a small bowl, microwave the remaining 2 tablespoons of honey until fluid, 20 seconds. Turn the cake out onto a rack, then right side up. Brush the top and sides with the honey. Let the cake cool for about 30 minutes before serving.

—*Susan Spungen*

MAKE AHEAD The cake can be made up to 2 days in advance and stored at room temperature, wrapped tightly in plastic.

Polenta Cake with Grilled-Rhubarb Jam and Mascarpone

ACTIVE: 45 MIN; TOTAL: 1 HR 30 MIN

MAKES ONE 9-INCH CAKE ● ●

CAKE

- 1¼ cups cake flour
- ½ cup yellow cornmeal
- 2 teaspoons baking powder
- ¼ teaspoon salt
- 1½ sticks (6 ounces) unsalted butter, softened
- ¾ cup sugar
- 3 large eggs

Finely grated zest of 1 orange

1 tablespoon fresh
  orange juice
3 tablespoons orange blossom
  honey or other floral honey,
  preferably Bee Raw (see Note)
1 tablespoon water

JAM

1¼ pounds rhubarb stalks,
  halved crosswise
Vegetable oil, for rubbing
¾ cup sugar
1 tablespoon fresh
  lemon juice

MASCARPONE CREAM

1 cup heavy cream
1 teaspoon pure vanilla extract
2 tablespoons sugar
½ cup mascarpone

1. MAKE THE CAKE: Preheat the oven to 350°. Butter a deep 9-inch cake pan. Line the bottom of the pan with parchment paper and butter the paper. In a medium bowl, whisk the cake flour with the cornmeal, baking powder and salt.

2. In a large bowl, using a handheld electric mixer, beat the butter with the sugar at high speed until light and fluffy, about 3 minutes. Beat in the eggs one at a time, beating well between additions. Beat in the orange zest and juice, then gradually beat in the dry ingredients at low speed until almost blended. Using a rubber spatula, gently fold the batter until smooth.

3. Scrape the cake batter into the prepared pan and bake for about 30 minutes, until the cake springs back when lightly pressed in the center. Transfer the pan to a wire rack and let cool. While the cake is still slightly warm, invert it onto a plate. Peel off the paper, then invert the cake onto the rack. Whisk the honey with the water and brush over the cake until evenly glazed. Let the cake cool completely.

4. MEANWHILE, MAKE THE JAM: Light a grill or heat a grill pan. Rub the rhubarb with oil and grill over high heat until lightly charred, 2 minutes per side; chop coarsely.

5. In a large saucepan, combine the sugar with the lemon juice and bring to a simmer over moderate heat, stirring, until the sugar starts to melt, about 3 minutes. Add the chopped rhubarb and simmer, stirring often, until the rhubarb releases its juices and cooks down to a thick jam, about 10 minutes longer.

6. MAKE THE MASCARPONE CREAM: In a large, chilled bowl, using a handheld electric mixer, beat the heavy cream with the vanilla at medium speed until softly whipped. Add the sugar and beat until firm. Beat in the mascarpone until smooth.

7. Cut the polenta cake into wedges and top with the mascarpone cream. Spoon the grilled-rhubarb jam alongside.
—*Steve Corry*

NOTE Orange blossom honey is a versatile medium-amber honey. Bee Raw honey is available from beeraw.com.

MAKE AHEAD The polenta cake can be kept covered at room temperature overnight. The grilled-rhubarb jam and mascarpone cream can be covered separately and refrigerated overnight. Bring the rhubarb jam to room temperature before spooning it over the cake.

Tres Leches Cake with Dulce de Leche

ACTIVE: 1 HR; TOTAL: 3 HR PLUS OVERNIGHT SOAKING

9 SERVINGS ●●

Tres leches—"three milks" in Spanish—is an immensely popular dessert throughout Latin America. The cake, soaked in condensed milk, evaporated milk and cream, is one of Manhattan chef Sue Torres's favorites. Although the cake can be served right away, it is even better the next day. "Just be careful to cover it well before putting it in the refrigerator," Torres says. Her rich, cinnamon-flavored dulce de leche caramel is worth the effort, but jarred dulce de leche, available in many supermarkets, is fine, too.

1 cup all-purpose flour
1 tablespoon baking powder
6 large eggs, separated
1 cup sugar
One 14-ounce can sweetened
  condensed milk
One 12-ounce can whole
  evaporated milk
1½ cups heavy cream
½ cup light rum
Dulce de Leche (recipe follows)

1. Preheat the oven to 325°. Butter a 9-inch square baking pan. In a medium bowl, whisk the flour with the baking powder. In a large bowl, using a handheld electric mixer, beat the egg whites at medium-high speed until stiff peaks form. In another large bowl, beat the egg yolks with the sugar at medium speed until pale and thick, about 3 minutes. Beat the egg whites and the dry ingredients into the egg yolk mixture until smooth.

2. Scrape the batter into the prepared pan and bake in the center of the oven for 30 minutes, until the batter is golden and a toothpick inserted in the center comes out clean. Let the cake cool in the pan for 15 minutes, then invert onto a wire rack to cool completely.

3. In a 9-by-13-inch baking dish, whisk the condensed milk with the evaporated milk, heavy cream and rum. Cut the cake into 3-inch squares and add them to the baking dish, turning gently once or twice to coat them with the milk mixture. Tilt the baking dish and spoon the liquid over the squares until the cake is well soaked, about 5 minutes. Pour off all but a thin layer of the liquid and reserve it for another use. Cover and refrigerate the cake squares in the pan overnight.

4. Carefully transfer the cake squares to plates. Drizzle them with the Dulce de Leche and serve. —*Sue Torres*

MAKE AHEAD The *tres leches* cake can be prepared up to 1 day ahead. Keep it well covered in the refrigerator.

DULCE DE LECHE

TOTAL: 1 HR
MAKES 2 CUPS ●●○

- 1 quart whole milk
- 1 cup sugar
- 1 tablespoon dark corn syrup
- ½ small cinnamon stick

1. In a large, heavy pot, combine the milk, sugar, corn syrup and cinnamon stick and bring the liquid to a boil, stirring with a wooden spoon until the sugar is thoroughly dissolved. Reduce the heat and simmer over moderate heat, stirring frequently, until the mixture is reduced to 2 cups and becomes the consistency of warm caramel, about 40 minutes. Discard the cinnamon stick and let the Dulce de Leche cool to room temperature.

2. Transfer the dulce de leche to a blender and puree until smooth. Skim off the foam and transfer to a pitcher. —*ST*

MAKE AHEAD The Dulce de Leche can be refrigerated for up to 3 days. Warm gently over low heat to loosen to drizzling consistency before serving.

Chocolate Soufflés with Crème Anglaise

ACTIVE: 1 HR; TOTAL: 1 HR 20 MIN
PLUS CHILLING
8 SERVINGS ○

"I love the simple elegance of chocolate soufflés," says F&W's Grace Parisi. She uses top-quality chocolate from brands like Valrhona or Callebaut, which lends a deep, almost smoky flavor to the airy dessert. Tahitian vanilla beans—some of the world's best—add a floral sweetness to the crème anglaise served with the soufflés.

- 3 ounces chocolate wafer cookies, finely crushed (⅔ cup)
- ½ cup plus 2 tablespoons granulated sugar
- 3 tablespoons unsalted butter, softened, plus more for brushing
- 6 ounces bittersweet chocolate, coarsely chopped
- 2 ounces unsweetened chocolate, coarsely chopped
- 4 large egg yolks
- 6 large egg whites

Pinch of salt

Vanilla Bean Crème Anglaise (recipe follows)

1. Preheat the oven to 400°. In a medium bowl, combine the crushed chocolate wafer cookies with 2 tablespoons of the granulated sugar. Brush eight 4-ounce ramekins with softened butter and coat them with the cookie and sugar mixture, pouring out and reserving the excess. Place the cookie-dusted ramekins on a baking sheet and refrigerate.

2. In a double boiler over medium heat, melt the 3 tablespoons of softened butter with the coarsely chopped bittersweet and unsweetened chocolates, stirring frequently, until the mixture is smooth. Remove the top of the double boiler from the heat and let the melted chocolate mixture cool completely.

3. In a large bowl, using a handheld electric mixer, beat the egg yolks with 6 tablespoons of the granulated sugar at medium speed until pale yellow and thickened, about 4 minutes. Gradually beat in the cooled chocolate mixture.

4. In another large bowl, using clean beaters, beat the egg whites with the pinch of salt until the whites form soft peaks. Gradually beat in the remaining 2 tablespoons of granulated sugar until the beaten whites are glossy. Beat one-fourth of the egg whites into the chocolate mixture, then gently fold in the remaining whites with a rubber spatula just until no streaks remain. Carefully spoon the soufflé batter into the prepared ramekins, filling them almost to the top. Sprinkle each soufflé with ½ teaspoon of the remaining cookie and sugar mixture. Run your thumb inside the rim of each ramekin to smooth the sides of the soufflés and help them rise evenly.

5. Bake the chocolate soufflés in the center of the oven for 15 minutes, or until they are risen and set around the edges but still soft in the centers. Carefully transfer the hot ramekins to heatproof dessert plates and serve the soufflés right away, with the Vanilla Bean Crème Anglaise.
—*Grace Parisi*

MAKE AHEAD The soufflés can be made through Step 4 and refrigerated for up to 4 hours. Bake them straight out of the refrigerator, adding a few minutes to the baking time as needed.

VANILLA BEAN CRÈME ANGLAISE

TOTAL: 30 MIN
MAKES ABOUT 2 CUPS ●○

- 2 cups half-and-half
- ½ cup sugar
- 1 vanilla bean, preferably Tahitian, split and seeds scraped
- 4 large egg yolks

1. In a medium saucepan, combine the half-and-half, sugar and scraped vanilla bean and seeds and bring to a simmer over moderate heat, whisking until the sugar is completely dissolved.

2. Set a medium bowl inside a larger bowl of ice water. In another medium bowl, whisk the egg yolks until smooth. Whisking the yolks constantly, gradually pour in the hot half-and-half mixture until smoothly combined. Discard the split vanilla bean. Return the mixture to the saucepan and cook over moderate heat, stirring constantly with a wooden spoon, until the crème anglaise is thick enough to coat the back of the spoon, about 6 minutes (avoid overheating this mixture to ensure that the eggs do not curdle). Scrape the crème anglaise into the medium bowl in the ice bath. Stir until the crème anglaise is completely cooled, about 10 minutes. —*GP*

MAKE AHEAD The cooled Vanilla Bean Crème Anglaise can be covered and refrigerated for up to 5 days.

CHOCOLATE SOUFFLÉ
WITH CRÈME ANGLAISE

oozy chocolate cake

What's more decadent than molten chocolate cake? F&W's Grace Parisi's *molten chocolate cake filled with warm peanut butter, caramel, raspberry or marshmallow.*

Molten Chocolate Cakes with Peanut Butter Filling

⏱ **ACTIVE: 15 MIN; TOTAL: 40 MIN**
   4 SERVINGS ◦ ●

- 1 **stick plus 1 tablespoon unsalted butter, plus melted butter for brushing**
- 1 **tablespoon unsweetened cocoa powder**
- ¼ **cup plus 1 tablespoon all-purpose flour**
- 6 **ounces dark chocolate (70 percent cacao), chopped**
- 3 **tablespoons creamy peanut butter**
- 1 **tablespoon confectioners' sugar, plus more for sprinkling**
- ½ **cup granulated sugar**
- 3 **large eggs, at room temperature**

Pinch of salt

1. Preheat the oven to 425°. Brush four 6-ounce ramekins with melted butter. In a bowl, whisk the cocoa with 1 tablespoon of the flour; dust the ramekins with the cocoa mixture, tapping out the excess. Transfer the ramekins to a sturdy baking sheet.

2. In a medium saucepan, melt 1 stick of butter with the chocolate over very low heat, stirring occasionally. Let cool slightly.

3. In a bowl, blend the peanut butter with the 1 tablespoon of confectioners' sugar and the remaining 1 tablespoon of butter.

4. In a bowl, using an electric mixer, beat the granulated sugar with the eggs and salt at medium-high speed until thick and pale yellow, 3 minutes. Using a rubber spatula, fold in the melted chocolate until no streaks remain. Fold in the ¼ cup of flour.

5. Spoon two-thirds of the batter into the prepared ramekins, then spoon the peanut butter mixture on top. Cover with the remaining chocolate batter. Bake in the center of the oven for 16 minutes, until the tops are cracked but the centers are still slightly jiggly. Transfer the ramekins to a rack and let cool for 5 to 8 minutes.

6. Run the tip of a knife around each cake. Invert a small plate over each cake and, using pot holders, invert again. Carefully lift off the ramekins. Dust the cakes with confectioners' sugar and serve.

Three Great Variations

1 Molten Chocolate Cakes with Caramel Filling

Replace the peanut butter filling in each cake with 1 heaping teaspoon of cold store-bought caramel sauce and a sprinkling of flaky Maldon sea salt.

2 Molten Chocolate Cakes with Raspberry Filling

In a small bowl, coarsely mash 16 raspberries with 4 teaspoons of seedless raspberry preserves. Replace the peanut butter filling with the raspberry filling.

3 Molten Chocolate Cakes with Marshmallow Filling

Replace the peanut butter filling in each cake with 1 tablespoon of Marshmallow Fluff—use a slightly moistened spoon to prevent the Fluff from sticking.

Chocolate-Buttermilk Cake

ACTIVE: 20 MIN; TOTAL: 2 HR 45 MIN

8 SERVINGS ● ● ○

Bay Area pastry chef Marisa Churchill uses shredded beet to sweeten this cake. The recipe is one she devised for a healthy-cooking challenge on *Top Chef* Season 2.

CAKE

1¾ cups all-purpose flour
1½ cups granulated sugar
1 teaspoon baking powder
1 teaspoon baking soda
½ teaspoon salt
1 cup unsweetened cocoa powder
1¼ cups low-fat buttermilk
1 cup fat-free plain yogurt
1 medium red beet (5 ounces), peeled and finely shredded
4 egg whites

GLAZE

½ cup confectioners' sugar
2 tablespoons unsweetened cocoa powder
2 tablespoons water

Raspberries, for serving

1. MAKE THE CAKE: Preheat the oven to 350°. Spray a 10-by-2-inch cake pan with cooking spray. In a bowl, whisk the flour with the granulated sugar, baking powder, baking soda, salt and cocoa powder. In another bowl, whisk the buttermilk with the yogurt and beet. Mix the beet mixture into the dry ingredients. In another bowl, beat the egg whites until soft peaks form. Fold the egg whites into the cake batter.

2. Scrape the batter into the baking pan. Bake for 55 minutes, until a toothpick inserted in the center comes out clean. Cool the cake on a rack for 20 minutes, then turn it out and let cool completely.

3. MAKE THE GLAZE: Sift the confectioners' sugar and cocoa powder into a bowl. Whisk in the water until smooth.

4. Cut the cake into wedges and transfer to plates. Spoon 1 tablespoon of the glaze over each slice. Serve with the raspberries.

—Marisa Churchill

Chocolate S'mores Cake

ACTIVE: 1 HR; TOTAL: 1 HR 45 MIN

16 SERVINGS

San Francisco chocolatier Michael Recchiuti decorates the gooey marshmallow topping for this exquisite chocolate cake with shards of his own graham crackers, but store-bought ones work just fine.

CAKE

2 cups all-purpose flour, plus more for dusting
2 cups sugar
⅔ cup unsweetened cocoa powder
1 teaspoon baking powder
1 teaspoon baking soda
1 teaspoon kosher salt
1½ cups milk
½ cup vegetable oil
2 extra-large eggs
2 tablespoons pure vanilla extract

TOPPING

1½ teaspoons unflavored gelatin
2 tablespoons cold water
1 cup sugar
¾ cup light corn syrup
3 large egg whites
½ vanilla bean, split and seeds scraped
6 whole graham crackers, broken
2 ounces bittersweet chocolate, melted

1. MAKE THE CAKE: Preheat the oven to 325°. Butter two 8-inch square baking pans and line the bottoms with parchment paper. Butter the paper and dust the pans with flour, tapping out the excess.

2. In a large bowl, whisk the 2 cups of flour with the sugar, cocoa powder, baking powder, baking soda and salt. In a medium bowl, whisk the milk with the vegetable oil, eggs and vanilla. Add the liquid to the dry ingredients and whisk just until smooth.

3. Scrape the batter into the prepared pans. Bake for about 40 minutes, until a toothpick inserted in the center of the cakes comes out with a few crumbs attached. Let cool in the pans on a wire rack, then turn out to cool completely. Peel off the parchment. Turn the cakes right side up onto 2 baking sheets.

4. MAKE THE TOPPING: In a small bowl, sprinkle the gelatin over the cold water and let stand until softened, about 5 minutes.

5. In a saucepan, combine ½ cup of the sugar with the corn syrup and stir over moderate heat until the sugar is thoroughly dissolved. Bring the corn syrup mixture to a boil, wiping down any sugar crystals that may form on the side of the pan with a moistened pastry brush. Cook over moderate heat, without stirring, until the corn syrup mixture reaches 250° on a candy thermometer, about 10 minutes. Remove from the heat and stir in the softened gelatin; the mixture will foam up.

6. Meanwhile, in the bowl of a standing electric mixer fitted with a whisk, beat the egg whites and vanilla seeds at medium speed until soft peaks form. Add the remaining ½ cup of sugar 1 tablespoon at a time, beating well between additions. Beat until stiff and glossy, 5 minutes.

7. With the mixer at medium speed, carefully pour the hot corn syrup mixture in a thin stream into the egg whites, aiming for the area between the whisk and side of the bowl. Beat the topping until very thick and opaque, about 8 minutes.

8. Preheat the broiler and position a rack 8 inches from the heat. Using an offset spatula, spread the marshmallow topping over the tops of the cakes. Let stand for about 1 minute, until slightly set. Broil the cakes one at a time, shifting the pan as necessary for even browning, about 5 minutes. Insert the graham crackers into the marshmallow and drizzle with the melted chocolate. Serve the cakes while the marshmallow topping is still warm.

—Michael Recchiuti

MAKE AHEAD The cakes can be prepared through Step 3 and kept refrigerated for up to 4 days. Bring to room temperature before proceeding.

Cinnamon Cake with Chile-Chocolate Buttercream

ACTIVE: 1 HR; TOTAL: 2 HR

12 SERVINGS ● ● ●

CAKE

- 1½ sticks (6 ounces) unsalted butter, softened, plus more for buttering the paper
- 1½ cups all-purpose flour, plus more for dusting
- 1 cup cake flour
- 1 teaspoon baking soda
- 1 teaspoon baking powder
- ¾ teaspoon cinnamon
- ½ teaspoon salt
- 1½ cups granulated sugar
- 3 large eggs, at room temperature
- 2 teaspoons pure vanilla extract
- 1 cup sour cream

making perfect layer cakes

To create a perfectly flat cake top, either invert the top layer so the flat side faces up, or shave off the rounded portion with a serrated knife before frosting the cake.

To make a finished cake easy to move, set it on a cardboard round of the same size before frosting.

To evenly frost a cake, set the layers on a rotating cake stand or lazy Susan.

To garnish a frosted cake, decorate with bittersweet chocolate shavings, shredded dried coconut or finely chopped walnuts.

FROSTING

- 5 sticks unsalted butter, softened
- 1 pound confectioners' sugar, sifted
- ¼ cup heavy cream
- 1 teaspoon pure vanilla extract
- 1 teaspoon cinnamon
- 1 teaspoon ancho chile powder
- ½ teaspoon cayenne pepper
- 5 ounces bittersweet chocolate, melted and cooled
- 5 ounces white chocolate, melted and cooled

1. MAKE THE CAKE: Preheat the oven to 350°. Butter two 9-inch round cake pans. Line the bottoms with parchment paper and butter the paper. Dust the pans with flour, tapping out the excess.

2. In a medium bowl, whisk the 1½ cups of all-purpose flour with the cake flour, baking soda, baking powder, cinnamon and salt. In a standing mixer fitted with a paddle, beat the butter with the sugar at medium speed until fluffy, about 3 minutes. Beat in the eggs and vanilla until incorporated. In 3 alternating additions, add the dry ingredients and sour cream, scraping down the side of the bowl between additions.

3. Scrape the batter evenly into the prepared pans. Bake the cakes on the lower and middle racks of the oven for about 30 minutes, until the tops are golden and springy and the edges begin to pull away from the sides of the pans. Transfer the pans to racks and let cool for 15 minutes, then turn the cakes out and let them cool completely. Remove the parchment paper.

4. MEANWHILE, MAKE THE FROSTING: In a standing mixer fitted with a paddle, beat the butter until creamy. At low speed, beat in the confectioners' sugar. Increase the speed to high and beat until fluffy, scraping down the side of the bowl, about 2 minutes longer. At low speed, beat in the cream, vanilla, cinnamon, ancho chile powder and cayenne, then gradually beat in the bittersweet and white chocolate. Scrape down the bowl and paddle, increase the speed to

medium-high and beat until light, 3 minutes. Using a wooden spoon, vigorously beat the buttercream for 30 seconds to deflate any air bubbles.

5. Place one cake layer on a plate and spread with 1 cup of frosting. Top with the second layer and spread the remaining frosting over the top and side. Refrigerate for at least 30 minutes. Bring to room temperature before serving. —*Lisa Ritter*

MAKE AHEAD The cake can be refrigerated for up to 3 days. The buttercream can be refrigerated for up to 5 days. Return to room temperature before using.

Pumpkin Cheesecake with Pecan-Praline Topping

ACTIVE: 45 MIN; TOTAL: 6 HR PLUS OVERNIGHT CHILLING

12 SERVINGS ● ● ●

One 15-ounce can pumpkin puree

- 8 whole graham crackers, broken
- ½ cup pecans (2 ounces)
- 1 tablespoon light brown sugar
- 5 tablespoons unsalted butter, melted, plus more for buttering the pan
- 1½ cups cream cheese (14 ounces), at room temperature
- 1½ cups granulated sugar
- 1 teaspoon salt
- 1 teaspoon cinnamon
- ¼ teaspoon freshly ground nutmeg
- ¼ teaspoon ground cloves
- ¼ teaspoon ground allspice
- 5 large eggs, at room temperature
- 1 cup heavy cream, at room temperature
- 1 tablespoon fresh lemon juice
- 2 teaspoons pure vanilla extract

Pecan Praline Topping (recipe follows) and whipped cream, for serving

1. Set a rack over a baking sheet and line the rack with 2 layers of paper towels. Spread the pumpkin puree over the paper towels and let drain for 2 hours, until the puree is fairly dry.

CINNAMON CAKE WITH CHILE-CHOCOLATE BUTTERCREAM

PUMPKIN CHEESECAKE WITH PECAN-PRALINE TOPPING

2. Preheat the oven to 500°. Butter the bottom and side of a 9-inch springform pan. In a food processor, pulse the graham crackers until finely ground. Add the pecans and brown sugar and pulse until finely ground. Add the 5 tablespoons of melted butter and pulse just until incorporated. Press the crumbs onto the bottom of the prepared pan. Bake the crust for about 8 minutes, just until it is fragrant and lightly browned. Let the crust cool completely.

3. In the bowl of a standing electric mixer fitted with the paddle, beat the cream cheese until it is very smooth. In a small bowl, whisk the granulated sugar with the salt, cinnamon, nutmeg, cloves and allspice. With the machine on, add the spiced sugar to the cream cheese and beat until creamy, scraping the bottom and side of the bowl. Carefully add the drained pumpkin puree and beat until smooth. Add the eggs one at a time, beating well and

scraping down the bowl between each addition. Beat in the cream, lemon juice and vanilla until the mixture is smooth.

4. Pour the cheesecake mixture over the cooled crust and bake for 12 minutes. Lower the oven temperature to 225° and bake the cheesecake for about 3 hours, until an instant-read thermometer inserted in the center registers 150°; the center will be very jiggly but not liquidy. Let the cheesecake cool on a rack, then cover with plastic wrap and refrigerate overnight.

5. Run a hot knife around the cheesecake and loosen the springform ring. Carefully remove the ring and transfer the cake to a plate. Using a warm knife, cut the cake into wedges and serve with the Pecan Praline Topping and whipped cream.
—*Katherine Beto*

MAKE AHEAD The cooled pumpkin cheesecake can be covered and refrigerated for up to 3 days.

PECAN-PRALINE TOPPING
ACTIVE: 15 MIN; TOTAL: 1 HR
MAKES 3 CUPS ● ●

- 1½ **sticks unsalted butter**
- ¾ **cup dark brown sugar**
- ½ **cup heavy cream**
- ¼ **teaspoon salt**
- 2 **cups pecans (8 ounces)**

1. Preheat the oven to 350°. In a large saucepan, combine the butter and brown sugar and cook over moderate heat, stirring, until smooth. Stir in the heavy cream and salt and bring to a boil. Simmer just until slightly thickened, about 3 minutes. Let the caramel cool.

2. Spread the pecans on a rimmed baking sheet and toast for about 8 minutes, until they are lightly browned and fragrant. Transfer the pecans to a work surface and let them cool. Coarsely chop the nuts, stir them into the cooled caramel and serve.
—*KB*

● HEALTHY ● MAKE AHEAD ● VEGETARIAN ● STAFF FAVORITE

MINI BLACK-BOTTOM CHEESECAKES WITH JAM

PEANUT BUTTER—POUND CAKE S'MORES

Mini Black-Bottom Cheesecakes with Jam

TOTAL: 45 MIN
MAKES 12 CHEESECAKES ● ○ ○

Vegetable oil spray

24 plain chocolate wafer cookies, preferably Nabisco's Famous Chocolate Wafers, broken

3 tablespoons unsalted butter, melted

8 ounces cream cheese, at room temperature

¼ cup sugar

⅔ cup *fromage blanc* or crème fraîche, at room temperature

2 large eggs

2 teaspoons pure vanilla extract

¼ cup seedless raspberry jam or apricot preserves, warmed

1. Preheat the oven to 350°. Line a standard 12-cup muffin tin with foil baking cups and lightly spray the cups with vegetable oil spray.

2. In a food processor, finely crush the chocolate wafer cookies. Add the butter and process until fine crumbs form. Spoon the cookie crumbs into the prepared foil baking cups and press with the bottom of a glass to compact the crumbs. Bake for 5 minutes, or until the crusts are almost set. Leave the oven on.

3. Meanwhile, in a medium bowl, using a handheld electric mixer, beat the cream cheese with the sugar at medium speed until smooth. Beat in the *fromage blanc* until incorporated, then add the eggs and vanilla and beat until smooth.

4. Pour the cheesecake batter into the baking cups, filling them three-quarters full. Bake the cheesecakes for about 15 minutes, or until the centers are slightly jiggly. Remove from the oven and spoon 1 teaspoon of the warmed fruit jam or preserves on top of each cheesecake.

5. Transfer the muffin tin to the freezer and chill the cheesecakes until cooled, about 15 minutes. (If you're not in a hurry,

you can let the cheesecakes cool to room temperature and then refrigerate them.)
6. Carefully remove the cheesecakes from the muffin tin and peel off the foil baking cups. Transfer the cheesecakes to a platter or plates and serve. —*Grace Parisi*
MAKE AHEAD The cheesecakes can be refrigerated for up to 4 days.

Peanut Butter–Pound Cake S'mores

TOTAL: 25 MIN
4 SERVINGS ● ●

In this take on the campfire classic, Marshmallow Fluff and peanut butter are sandwiched in buttery store-bought pound cake and served alongside a cup of warm melted chocolate for dipping.

- 2 ounces semisweet chocolate, chopped
- ½ cup heavy cream

One 1-pound frozen pound cake, preferably Sara Lee, thawed
- ¼ cup creamy or chunky peanut butter (not natural)
- ⅓ cup Marshmallow Fluff
- 1 tablespoon unsalted butter, softened

1. Put the chocolate in a small heatproof bowl. In a small saucepan, heat the cream until hot to the touch. Pour the cream over the chocolate and let stand until melted. Whisk the chocolate sauce until smooth.
2. Preheat a griddle or skillet. Trim off the top and bottom of the pound cake so that the cake is about 1¼ inches thick. Carefully split the pound cake in half horizontally. Spread the peanut butter on one half and the marshmallow on the other, leaving a ½-inch border. Sandwich the halves together and spread the top and bottom with the butter. Place on the griddle and cook over high heat, turning once, until golden and nearly warmed through, 2 minutes. Transfer to a work surface and cut the cake into twelve ¾-inch-wide strips. Serve at once, with the chocolate sauce. —*Grace Parisi*

Pecan-Praline Cheesecake with Caramel Sauce

ACTIVE: 45 MIN; TOTAL: 1 HR 45 MIN
PLUS OVERNIGHT CHILLING
16 SERVINGS ● ● ●

You can use store-bought pralines to make the crust for this fluffy cheesecake, but the quick praline recipe here is worth the bit of extra effort, as is the buttery caramel sauce that pools on top of the cake slices.

CRUST
- ½ cup pecan halves
- 1 stick plus ½ teaspoon unsalted butter, melted
- ⅓ cup plus ½ tablespoon granulated sugar
- 2 tablespoons light brown sugar
- 1½ tablespoons heavy cream
- Pinch of salt
- 2 packets graham crackers (about 10 ounces), crushed

FILLING
- 1 pound full-fat cream cheese, softened
- 1 cup granulated sugar
- 3 large eggs
- 1 teaspoon pure vanilla extract
- 24 ounces full-fat sour cream
- Caramel Sauce (recipe follows), for serving

1. **MAKE THE CRUST:** Preheat the oven to 375°. Line a baking sheet with parchment paper. Wrap the outside of a 10-inch round springform pan with foil.
2. In a medium bowl, toss the pecans with ½ teaspoon of the butter, ½ tablespoon of the granulated sugar, the brown sugar, cream and salt. Spread the nuts on the prepared baking sheet and arrange them right side up in a single layer. Bake for about 18 minutes, until the sugar is caramelized and the pecans are toasted. Let cool.
3. Transfer all but 12 of the toasted pecans to a food processor. Add the crushed graham crackers and pulse until finely ground. Add the remaining stick of melted butter and ⅓ cup of granulated sugar and pulse

until the crumbs are moistened. Press the crumbs over the bottom and two-thirds of the way up the side of the prepared springform pan.
4. **MAKE THE FILLING:** In a clean food processor, pulse the cream cheese with the sugar until smooth. Add the eggs one at a time and pulse until incorporated. Scrape down the side of the bowl. Pulse in the vanilla and sour cream. Scrape the filling into the pan and bake in the center of the oven for about 1 hour, until the top of the cheesecake is lightly golden in spots and the center is slightly jiggly. Transfer the cheesecake to a rack and let cool completely. Wrap in plastic and refrigerate overnight.
5. Unwrap the cheesecake and discard the foil. Remove the ring and transfer the cake to a plate. Arrange the 12 reserved pecans on top. Using a warm, slightly moistened knife, cut the cake into wedges, wiping and rewetting the blade between slices. Transfer the slices to plates and pour some of the Caramel Sauce on top. Serve with the remaining Caramel Sauce. —*Lisa Ritter*
MAKE AHEAD The cheesecake can be refrigerated for up to 5 days.

CARAMEL SAUCE

TOTAL: 15 MIN PLUS 2 HR CHILLING
MAKES 1¼ CUPS ●
- 4 tablespoons unsalted butter, softened
- 2 tablespoons granulated sugar
- 2 tablespoons light brown sugar
- ⅓ cup dark brown sugar
- ½ cup heavy cream
- ¼ teaspoon pure vanilla extract
- ¼ teaspoon salt

In a medium saucepan, combine the butter with all three sugars and bring to a boil, stirring constantly. Cook over moderately high heat for 2 minutes, stirring constantly. Add the cream and boil for 2 minutes. Transfer to a pitcher. Stir in the vanilla and salt and refrigerate the Caramel Sauce until cold, at least 2 hours. —*LR*

cakes, cookies & more

Mini Chocolate-Hazelnut Cheesecakes

ACTIVE: 10 MIN; TOTAL: 40 MIN
MAKES 12 CHEESECAKES ● ○ ○

Cream-filled chocolate sandwich cookies ground with hazelnuts and butter create a supercrunchy crust for these delectable mini cheesecakes. The cream filling in the chocolate sandwich cookies sweetens the crust while also preventing it from becoming too crumbly.

- 15 cream-filled chocolate sandwich cookies
- 2 tablespoons raw or roasted hazelnuts, skinned
- 2 tablespoons unsalted butter, softened
- 8 ounces cream cheese
- ¾ cup hazelnut-chocolate spread, preferably Nutella
- ½ cup sour cream
- 2 large eggs
- 2 tablespoons sugar
- 2 tablespoons mini chocolate chips

1. Preheat the oven to 350°. Line a 12-cup muffin tin with paper liners. Spray the liners with vegetable oil spray.

2. In a food processor, combine the chocolate sandwich cookies, hazelnuts and softened butter and process to very fine crumbs. Divide the crumbs among the cups; using a flat-bottomed glass, press on the crumbs to compact them. Bake the crumb crusts for 5 minutes.

3. Meanwhile, wipe out the food processor bowl. Add the cream cheese, Nutella, sour cream, eggs and sugar and puree until smooth. Spoon the filling into the cups until it nearly reaches the top; there may be a few tablespoons of leftover batter. Sprinkle the chocolate chips on top and bake for about 20 minutes, until the cheesecakes have risen and the surfaces are lightly cracked. Let the cheesecakes cool slightly, then transfer the muffin tin to a rack and freeze for about 10 minutes, until the cheesecakes are slightly cooled. Serve the mini cheesecakes chilled or at room temperature.
—*Grace Parisi*

MAKE AHEAD The mini cheesecakes can be refrigerated for up to 3 days.

Chocolate-Caramel Sandwich Cookies

ACTIVE: 1 HR 10 MIN; TOTAL: 3 HR
MAKES 42 SANDWICH COOKIES ● ○ ○

Rachel Thebault, owner of Tribeca Treats in New York City, has reimagined the humble Oreo as an indulgence that is spectacular as an afternoon snack or as the end of an elegant meal.

COOKIE DOUGH

- 1½ sticks unsalted butter, softened
- 1 cup sugar
- 1 large egg, at room temperature
- 1½ cups plus 2 tablespoons all-purpose flour
- ½ cup unsweetened cocoa powder

Pinch of salt

CARAMEL FILLING

- 2¼ cups sugar
- 1¾ cups heavy cream
- ⅓ cup honey
- 1 tablespoon light corn syrup
- 1 vanilla bean, split, seeds scraped
- 4 tablespoons unsalted butter, softened

CHOCOLATE GLAZE

- 12 ounces bittersweet chocolate, coarsely chopped
- 3 tablespoons unsalted butter

1. MAKE THE COOKIE DOUGH: In a standing electric mixer fitted with the paddle attachment, beat the softened butter and sugar at medium speed until fluffy. Beat in the egg. Sift the flour, cocoa and salt into the bowl and beat at low speed until the dough comes together, 2 minutes. Turn the dough out onto a lightly floured surface and knead 2 or 3 times. Flatten the dough into 2 disks, wrap in plastic and chill until firm, about 30 minutes.

2. Preheat the oven to 350°. Line 2 large baking sheets with parchment paper. Roll out each disk of dough between 2 sheets of plastic wrap to a scant ¼-inch thickness. Using a floured 1¾-inch round cookie cutter, stamp out as many rounds as possible; transfer to the baking sheets. Gather the scraps, reroll and stamp out as many cookies as possible. Bake the cookies for about 20 minutes, until puffed and set, shifting the baking sheets for even baking. Let the cookies cool on the baking sheets.

3. MEANWHILE, MAKE THE CARAMEL: Oil the bottom and sides of a 9-inch-square cake pan and line the bottom with a sheet of wax paper long enough to reach 2 inches up 2 sides of the pan. In a medium saucepan, stir together the sugar, cream, honey, corn syrup and vanilla seeds and bring to a boil. (Reserve the vanilla pod for another use.) Set a candy thermometer in the saucepan and cook the caramel over moderately high heat, stirring occasionally, until the temperature reaches 250°. Remove from the heat. Remove the thermometer and stir in the butter. Pour the caramel into the prepared pan and let cool for 45 minutes.

4. Lift the caramel out of the pan and transfer to a cutting board. Using a 1¼-inch round cookie cutter, stamp out rounds of caramel and sandwich them between the cookies, pressing gently to flatten slightly. Wrap any remaining caramel bits individually in wax paper and save for another use.

5. MAKE THE GLAZE: Melt the chocolate with the butter in a double boiler. Line a baking sheet with wax paper. Dip the cookies halfway into the chocolate glaze, allowing any excess to drip back into the pot. Set the cookies on the wax paper and refrigerate for about 20 minutes, until just set. Transfer the cookies to a plate and serve.
—*Rachel Thebault*

MAKE AHEAD The sandwich cookies can be stored in an airtight container at room temperature for up to 4 days.

Hazelnut Sandwich Cookies

ACTIVE: 45 MIN; TOTAL: 3 HR 30 MIN
MAKES 40 SANDWICH COOKIES ●●

Many traditional holiday flavors come together in this little treat, with its layer of chocolate sandwiched between cookies spiced with cinnamon, allspice and cloves. A sprinkle of chopped hazelnuts gives additional crunch.

- ¾ cup raw hazelnuts
- ¾ cup sugar
- 2¼ cups all-purpose flour
- ½ teaspoon cinnamon
- ⅛ teaspoon ground allspice
- Pinch of ground cloves
- ⅛ teaspoon salt
- 2 sticks plus 6 tablespoons unsalted butter, softened
- 3 ounces milk chocolate, finely chopped
- 3 ounces semisweet chocolate, finely chopped

1. Preheat the oven to 325° and position a rack in the center. Spread ¼ cup of the hazelnuts in a pie plate and toast for about 15 minutes, until the skins blister. Transfer the hazelnuts to a clean kitchen towel and rub vigorously to remove the skins. Finely chop the hazelnuts.

2. In a food processor, finely grind the remaining ½ cup of hazelnuts with 2 tablespoons of the sugar. Add the flour, cinnamon, allspice, cloves, salt and the remaining ½ cup plus 2 tablespoons of sugar and pulse to combine. Add 2 sticks of the butter and pulse until a dough forms. Transfer the dough to a work surface and knead 2 or 3 times. Pat the dough into two 8-inch disks, wrap in plastic and chill until firm, at least 30 minutes.

3. Line 2 large baking sheets with parchment paper. On a lightly floured surface, working with one disk at a time, roll out the dough to a 10-inch round, ¼ inch thick. Using a 1½-inch round cookie cutter, stamp out rounds as closely together as possible. Arrange the cookies on a baking sheet about ½ inch apart. Repeat with the second disk of dough. Gather the scraps from both batches and pat into a disk. Chill for about 15 minutes, then cut out a few more cookies. Don't use the dough scraps again.

4. Bake the cookies one sheet at a time for about 20 minutes, until the bottoms are lightly colored but the tops are still pale. Transfer the baking sheet to a rack to let the cookies cool.

5. In a medium saucepan, melt the milk and semisweet chocolates with the remaining 6 tablespoons of butter over very low heat, whisking until smooth. Transfer the chocolate sauce to a medium bowl and let it cool for 10 minutes.

6. Turn half of the cooled cookies bottom side up. Spoon a small dollop of the chocolate in the center of each cookie. Dip the remaining cookies halfway into the chocolate and sandwich over the bottoms, pressing to seal. Sprinkle the chopped toasted hazelnuts on the chocolate and let the sandwich cookies stand for about 30 minutes, until the chocolate is set. —*Flo Braker*

MAKE AHEAD The sandwich cookies can be stored in an airtight container between sheets of wax paper for up to 1 week.

Ginger Sandwich Cookies

ACTIVE: 40 MIN; TOTAL: 1 HR 50 MIN
MAKES 20 SANDWICH COOKIES ●

Despite their name, gingersnaps don't usually have a lot of snap; rather, the molasses in the recipe makes them a bit chewy. New York City baking guru Nick Malgieri adds a puckery note to his gingersnap cookies by sandwiching them with a fresh lemon cream.

COOKIES

- 1½ cups all-purpose flour
- 1½ teaspoons baking soda
- 2 teaspoons ground ginger
- 1 teaspoon cinnamon
- ¼ teaspoon salt
- 1 stick plus 2 tablespoons unsalted butter, softened
- ¾ cup sugar
- 1 large egg, at room temperature
- ¼ cup unsulfured molasses

FILLING

- 6 tablespoons unsalted butter, softened
- 2 cups confectioners' sugar
- 1½ tablespoons fresh lemon juice

1. Preheat the oven to 350° and position racks in the upper and lower thirds. Line 2 baking sheets with parchment paper.

2. MAKE THE COOKIES: In a bowl, whisk the flour, baking soda, ginger, cinnamon and salt. In the bowl of a standing electric mixer fitted with the paddle, beat the butter and sugar at medium speed until light and fluffy, about 3 minutes. Beat in the egg and molasses. Add the dry ingredients and beat at low speed until incorporated, scraping down the side of the bowl.

3. Working in 2 batches, drop scant tablespoons of the dough onto the baking sheets 3 inches apart. Bake the cookies for 20 minutes, until risen and fallen and slightly firm; shift the sheets from top to bottom and front to back halfway through for even baking. Let cool slightly, then transfer the parchment paper to racks and let the cookies cool completely. Bake the remaining cookies.

4. MAKE THE FILLING: In the bowl of a standing electric mixer fitted with the paddle, beat the butter with the confectioners' sugar at medium speed until light and fluffy, about 3 minutes. Beat in the lemon juice.

5. Arrange the cookies in pairs on a large work surface. Spoon or pipe 1 rounded tablespoon of the lemon filling onto the flat side of half of the cookies. Sandwich with the remaining cookies, pressing them together so the filling spreads to the edge. —*Nick Malgieri*

MAKE AHEAD The sandwich cookies can be stored in an airtight container between sheets of wax paper for up to 1 week.

Cinnamon Spritz Sandwich Cookies

ACTIVE: 30 MIN; TOTAL: 1 HR 30 MIN

MAKES 16 SANDWICH COOKIES ● ●

Spritz cookies are buttery Scandinavian sweets made by forcing ("spritzing") dough through a press, creating fun shapes. This cakey version—piped with a pastry bag, then sandwiched with fluffy meringue—resembles a little whoopie pie.

COOKIES

- 2 cups all-purpose flour
- 1 teaspoon cinnamon
- ¼ teaspoon ground cardamom
- ¼ teaspoon salt
- 2 sticks unsalted butter, at room temperature
- ¾ cup sugar
- 1 large egg

FILLING

- 1 large egg white
- ½ cup granulated sugar
- 2 tablespoons water
- 2 teaspoons corn syrup
- ½ teaspoon pure vanilla extract

Confectioners' sugar, for dusting

1. Preheat the oven to 350° and position racks in the upper and lower thirds. Line 2 large baking sheets with parchment paper.
2. MAKE THE COOKIES: In a medium bowl, mix the flour with the cinnamon, cardamom and salt. In the bowl of a standing electric mixer fitted with the paddle, beat the butter with the sugar at medium-high speed until fluffy, 2 minutes. Scrape down the side of the bowl. Add the egg and beat at medium speed until incorporated. Add half of the dry ingredients and beat at low speed until just incorporated. Beat in the remaining dry ingredients. Scrape the dough into a pastry bag fitted with a ½-inch star tip. Pipe the dough onto the baking sheets in 1¾-inch rosettes; you should have about 32. Refrigerate until chilled, 20 minutes.
3. For cakey cookies, bake the cookies for 14 minutes, until the tops are dry; for crispier cookies, bake for about 16 minutes, until the edges are golden. Shift the baking sheets from top to bottom and front to back halfway through for even baking. Let the cookies cool on the baking sheets for 5 minutes, then transfer them to a wire rack to cool completely.
4. MEANWHILE, MAKE THE FILLING: In a saucepan, bring 2 inches of water to a simmer. In the bowl of a standing electric mixer, combine the egg white with the sugar, water, corn syrup and vanilla. Set the bowl over (but not in) the pan of simmering water and stir constantly until the sugar is dissolved, about 4 minutes. Transfer the bowl to the mixer and whip the mixture at high speed until firm, glossy peaks form, about 5 minutes.
5. Scrape the meringue into a piping bag fitted with a ¼-inch star tip. Arrange half of the cookies flat side up. Pipe the meringue filling on top and close the sandwiches. Dust the cookies with confectioners' sugar. —Matt Lewis and Renato Poliafito

MAKE AHEAD The sandwich cookies can be stored in an airtight container at room temperature for up to 3 days.

Reverse Chocolate Chip Cookies

ACTIVE: 20 MIN; TOTAL: 1 HR

MAKES 28 LARGE COOKIES ● ●

- 2 cups all-purpose flour
- 1 cup unsweetened Dutch-process cocoa, sifted
- 1 teaspoon baking soda
- 1 teaspoon kosher salt
- 2 sticks (8 ounces) unsalted butter, softened
- 1 cup granulated sugar
- 1 cup light brown sugar
- 2 large eggs
- 2 teaspoons pure vanilla extract
- 12 ounces bittersweet chocolate, coarsely chopped into chunks
- 12 ounces white chocolate, coarsely chopped into chunks

1. Preheat the oven to 350°. Line 2 large cookie sheets with parchment paper. In a medium bowl, sift the flour with the cocoa, baking soda and salt.
2. In a standing electric mixer fitted with the paddle, beat the butter with the granulated and light brown sugars at medium speed until light and fluffy, about 3 minutes. Beat in the eggs and vanilla. Add the dry ingredients and beat at low speed until incorporated. At low speed, beat in the bittersweet- and white-chocolate chunks until they are evenly distributed.
3. Scoop eight ¼-cup mounds of batter onto each of the prepared cookie sheets, leaving 3 inches between them. Flatten the mounds into 2-inch rounds. Bake on the lower and middle racks of the oven for 20 minutes, until the cookies rise and then flatten slightly; switch the cookie sheets halfway through baking. Let the cookies cool for 10 minutes, then slide the parchment paper onto racks and let the cookies cool completely. Line the cookie sheets with fresh parchment and repeat to make the remaining cookies. —Lisa Ritter

Chocolate-Mint Thumbprints

ACTIVE: 1 HR; TOTAL: 2 HR 30 MIN

MAKES 44 COOKIES ● ● ●

- 2 ounces bittersweet chocolate, chopped
- 2 ounces mint chocolate, chopped
- 1½ cups all-purpose flour
- ½ cup unsweetened Dutch-process cocoa
- ¾ teaspoon salt
- 2 sticks unsalted butter, softened
- ⅓ cup granulated sugar
- 2 tablespoons dark brown sugar
- 2 large egg yolks
- 1 teaspoon pure vanilla extract
- 1 cup coarse sugar such as Turbinado, for rolling
- 3 ounces white chocolate, chopped
- 3 tablespoons heavy cream
- ½ teaspoon pure peppermint extract

1. In a microwave-safe bowl, melt the bittersweet and mint chocolates in 30-second intervals until nearly melted. Whisk until smooth, then let cool. In a medium bowl, whisk the flour with the cocoa and salt.

2. In the bowl of a standing electric mixer fitted with the paddle, beat the butter until creamy. Add the granulated sugar and brown sugar and beat at medium-high speed until light and fluffy, about 3 minutes. Beat in the egg yolks and vanilla. Scrape the chocolate into the mixer and beat just until incorporated. Add the dry ingredients and beat at low speed, scraping the side of the bowl occasionally, until smooth. Transfer the dough to a sheet of plastic wrap and pat it into a 7-inch disk; wrap it up and refrigerate until chilled and firm, at least 1 hour.

3. Preheat the oven to 350° and position racks in the upper and lower thirds. Line 2 cookie sheets with parchment paper. Spread the coarse sugar in a shallow bowl. Scoop up tablespoons of the dough and roll them into balls, then roll in the coarse sugar; transfer to the baking sheets. Using your thumb or a melon baller, make an indentation in the center of each cookie. Bake the cookies for 10 minutes, until slightly firm. Remove the cookie sheets from the oven. Using the melon baller, press into the cookies again. Return the cookies to the oven, shifting the cookie sheets, and bake for 5 minutes longer, just until dry but not hard. Transfer the cookie sheets to racks to cool completely.

4. Put the white chocolate in a heatproof cup. Put the cream into a microwave-safe bowl and microwave at high power until boiling, about 30 seconds. Pour the hot cream over the white chocolate and let stand until melted, then whisk until smooth. Stir in the peppermint extract. Fill the thumbprints with the white-chocolate ganache and refrigerate just until set, about 30 minutes.

—*Matt Lewis and Renato Poliafito*

MAKE AHEAD The cookies can be stored in an airtight container for up to 1 week.

Fudgy Chocolate-Walnut Cookies

ACTIVE: 25 MIN; TOTAL: 45 MIN
MAKES 12 LARGE COOKIES ● ● ○ ○

These nutty flourless chocolate cookies from star pastry chef François Payard are divinely gooey—and healthy!

2¾ cups walnut halves
  (9 ounces)
3 cups confectioners' sugar
½ cup plus 3 tablespoons unsweetened Dutch-process cocoa powder
¼ teaspoon salt
4 large egg whites, at room temperature
1 tablespoon pure vanilla extract

1. Preheat the oven to 350°. Position 2 racks in the upper and lower thirds of the oven. Line 2 large rimmed baking sheets with parchment paper.

2. Spread the walnut halves on a large rimmed baking sheet and toast in the oven for about 9 minutes, until they are golden and fragrant. Let cool slightly, then transfer the walnut halves to a work surface and finely chop them.

3. In a large bowl, whisk the confectioners' sugar with the cocoa powder and salt. Whisk in the chopped toasted walnuts. Add the egg whites and vanilla extract and beat just until the batter is moistened (be careful not to overbeat or the batter will stiffen). Spoon the cookie batter onto the prepared baking sheets in 12 evenly spaced mounds.

4. Bake the cookies for about 20 minutes, until the tops are glossy and lightly cracked and feel firm to the touch; shift the baking sheets from front to back and top to bottom halfway through.

5. Slide the parchment paper (with the cookies) onto 2 wire racks to cool completely before serving.

—*François Payard*

MAKE AHEAD The cookies can be stored in an airtight container for up to 3 days.

Sugar-Crusted Chocolate Cookies

ACTIVE: 30 MIN; TOTAL: 1 HR 30 MIN
PLUS 4 HR CHILLING
MAKES ABOUT 40 COOKIES ●

These chocolate cookies are pastry chef Jacques Torres's version of *sablés*, a classic French butter cookie with a sandy, crumbly texture (*sablé* means "sandy").

1¾ cups all-purpose flour
½ cup unsweetened cocoa
Pinch of salt
1 stick plus 2 tablespoons unsalted butter, cut into tablespoons
¾ cup plus 2 tablespoons confectioners' sugar
2 tablespoons cold milk
1 teaspoon pure vanilla extract
1 large egg white
½ cup granulated sugar

1. In a food processor, pulse the flour, cocoa and salt. Add the butter and process until sandy, about 3 minutes. Add the confectioners' sugar, milk and vanilla extract and process until a firm dough forms. Transfer the dough to 2 sheets of plastic wrap and form into two 7-inch logs about 1½ inches thick. Wrap in plastic and refrigerate until very firm, at least 4 hours or overnight.

2. Preheat the oven to 350° and position racks in the upper and lower thirds. Line 2 large baking sheets with parchment paper. Beat the egg white in a small bowl. Sprinkle the granulated sugar in a 7-inch square on a sheet of wax paper. Brush the logs with the egg white and roll in the sugar, pressing to help it adhere. Cut the logs into ¼-inch slices and transfer to the prepared baking sheets about ½ inch apart. Bake the cookies for about 20 minutes, until they are just firm to the touch; shift the sheets from top to bottom and front to back halfway through for even baking. Transfer the baking sheets to racks to cool.

—*Jacques Torres*

Cherry-Nut Mudslides

ACTIVE: 30 MIN; TOTAL: 1 HR 45 MIN

MAKES 5 DOZEN COOKIES ● ● ○

- ½ cup hazelnuts
- 2 pounds bittersweet chocolate, finely chopped
- 6 ounces unsweetened chocolate, finely chopped
- ½ cup plus 3 tablespoons flour
- 2¾ teaspoons baking powder
- 1¼ teaspoons salt
- 6 tablespoons unsalted butter, at room temperature
- 2¼ cups sugar
- 5 large eggs, at room temperature
- ½ cup salted pistachios, chopped
- ½ cup chopped dried cherries

1. Preheat the oven to 350°. Toast the hazelnuts in a pie plate for 12 minutes, until the skins blister. Transfer to a clean kitchen towel and rub to remove the skins. Coarsely chop the nuts.

2. In a large bowl set over a pan of simmering water, melt 1 pound of the bittersweet chocolate with all of the unsweetened chocolate. Let cool completely.

3. In a small bowl, whisk the flour, baking powder and salt. In the bowl of a standing electric mixer fitted with the paddle, beat the butter at medium speed until creamy. Beat in the sugar until sandy. Beat in the eggs, then beat in the melted chocolate. At low speed, beat in the dry ingredients. Fold in the pistachios, cherries, hazelnuts and the remaining bittersweet chocolate.

4. For each cookie, scoop 2 tablespoons of dough onto a parchment-lined baking sheet and roll into a ball; space them about 1½ inches apart. Bake in batches for 15 minutes, just until the tops are lightly cracked; shift the sheets from top to bottom and front to back halfway through for even baking. Transfer the sheets to racks to cool slightly, then transfer the cookies to a rack. Serve warm or at room temperature.
—*Jacques Torres*

Roll-and-Cut Sugar Cookies

ACTIVE: 1 HR; TOTAL: 3 HR

MAKES ABOUT 4 DOZEN 3- TO 4-INCH COOKIES, OR 2 DOZEN SANDWICH COOKIES ● ● ●

"Roll-and-cut" sugar cookies are made by flattening dough with a rolling pin, then cutting out shapes. The dough recipe here is ideal: durable enough to withstand rolling and rerolling, yet tender enough to cut neatly. The cookies themselves are extremely versatile. They can be simply sprinkled with sugar and baked; or, after they're baked, they can be decorated with icing or sandwiched with jam and sprinkled with confectioners' sugar.

- 2¼ cups all-purpose flour
- ¾ cup sugar
- ¼ teaspoon salt
- 2 sticks cold unsalted butter, cut into ½-inch pieces
- 2 large egg yolks
- 2 teaspoons pure vanilla extract
- ¾ cup seedless raspberry or apricot jam (for jam-filled cookies)
- Royal Icing (recipe follows), sprinkles, sparkles and dragées, for decorating

1. In the bowl of a standing electric mixer fitted with the paddle, mix the flour with the sugar and salt. Add the butter and mix at low speed until the butter is broken up into small pieces, about 2 minutes. Increase the speed to medium and mix until the flour and butter form small clumps, about 1 minute. Add the egg yolks and vanilla and mix at low speed until the dough comes together in a few large clumps. Pat the cookie dough into two ½-inch-thick disks, wrap them in plastic and refrigerate until chilled but not firm, about 30 minutes.

2. Preheat the oven to 375°. Line 2 large rimmed baking sheets with parchment paper. Working with one disk at a time, on a lightly floured surface, roll out the dough ⅛ inch thick. Using 3- to 4-inch cookie cutters, cut the dough into shapes and transfer to the prepared baking sheets. Reroll the scraps and cut out more cookies. (Alternatively, cut the dough into 3- to 4-inch shapes and, using a smaller cutter, stamp out the center of half of the cookies.) Refrigerate the cookies until chilled, about 30 minutes.

3. Bake the cookies for about 13 minutes, until they are lightly golden around the edges; shift the baking sheets from top to bottom and front to back halfway through for even baking. Let the sugar cookies cool on the baking sheets for about 5 minutes, then, using a metal spatula, carefully transfer them to a rack to cool completely, about 20 minutes.

4. For sandwich cookies, spread a thin layer of raspberry or apricot jam on the solid cookies and top with the corresponding cutout cookies to expose the jam. Otherwise, decorate as desired with the Royal Icing, sprinkles, sparkles and dragées.
—*Cindy Mushet*

MAKE AHEAD The decorated and/or jam-filled cookies can be stored in an airtight container for up to 1 week.

ROYAL ICING

TOTAL: 10 MIN

MAKES ABOUT 1¼ CUPS ○

- 1 egg white
- ½ pound confectioners' sugar (2¼ cups)
- 1 tablespoon water

1. In a medium bowl, beat the egg white at medium speed until foamy. Add the confectioners' sugar 1 cup at a time, beating between additions until the sugar is completely incorporated. Add the water and beat at high speed until the icing holds its shape, about 5 minutes.

2. Spoon the icing into a piping bag fitted with a plain tip and use at once; thin with water if necessary. —*CM*

CHERRY-NUT MUDSLIDES

ROLL-AND-CUT SUGAR COOKIES WITH ROYAL ICING

Almond Cookies with Caramel Dipping Sauce

ACTIVE: 30 MIN; TOTAL: 2 HR 30 MIN
MAKES 5 DOZEN COOKIES ●●

This is New York City chef Fabio Trabocchi's all-butter version of a crumbly Spanish almond cookie called *polvorone* that is traditionally made with pork fat.

COOKIES

- 2 sticks (8 ounces) unsalted butter, softened
- 1 cup sugar
- 2 cups almond flour, store-bought or homemade (see Note)
- 1½ cups all-purpose flour
- ½ tablespoon finely grated lemon zest
- ½ teaspoon cinnamon
- ¼ teaspoon pure almond extract

Pinch of salt

- 5 dozen whole blanched almonds, for garnish

CARAMEL

- 1 cup sugar
- ¼ cup water
- ½ cup heavy cream

Pinch of salt

1. MAKE THE COOKIES: In the bowl of a standing electric mixer fitted with the paddle, combine the butter with the sugar, almond flour, all-purpose flour, lemon zest, cinnamon, almond extract and salt. Beat at low speed until evenly combined. Increase the speed to medium and beat until smooth. Transfer the dough to a work surface and divide it into thirds. Form each piece into a log and wrap the logs separately in plastic wrap. Refrigerate for at least 1 hour, until slightly firm.

2. Preheat the oven to 300°. Line 3 large rimmed baking sheets with parchment paper. Cut each log crosswise into 20 pieces and roll into balls. Arrange the balls about 2 inches apart on the baking sheets.

Press an almond into each cookie. Bake for about 45 minutes, rotating the pans twice, until golden. Let the cookies cool for 10 minutes, then slide the parchment onto racks and let the cookies cool.

3. MEANWHILE, MAKE THE CARAMEL: In a saucepan, cook the sugar in the water over moderate heat, stirring, until the sugar is dissolved. Raise the heat to moderately high and cook without stirring until a medium-amber caramel forms. Off the heat, carefully pour in the cream and stir until smooth. Add the salt and transfer to a heatproof pitcher. Serve with the cookies. —*Fabio Trabocchi*

NOTE Almond flour is available at specialty shops. To make your own, finely grind blanched almonds.

MAKE AHEAD The cookies can be kept in an airtight container for up to 3 days. The caramel can be refrigerated for up to 1 week; rewarm before serving.

●HEALTHY ●MAKE AHEAD ●VEGETARIAN ●STAFF FAVORITE

353

Coconut-Pistachio Meringues

ACTIVE: 20 MIN; TOTAL 2 HR

MAKES ABOUT 4 DOZEN

COOKIES ● ○ ○

Delicate and substantial at the same time, these meringues are chewy on the inside and crisp on the outside. For the best results, bake them on a dry day: Humidity can make meringues disappointingly soft.

- 2 **cups sweetened shredded coconut (7 ounces)**
- 1 **cup sugar**
- 2 **teaspoons cornstarch**
- 4 **large egg whites**

Pinch of salt

- ½ **cup salted roasted pistachios, coarsely chopped and sifted to remove dust**

1. Preheat the oven to 300° and position racks in the middle and lower thirds. Line 2 large baking sheets with parchment paper.

making better butter cookies

Simple butter cookies like the Baby Buttons on this page contain very few ingredients, so the quality of each counts.

To improve the dough, use the best unsalted butter you can find.

To add flavor to baked butter cookies, toss them as soon as they come out of the oven (while they're still warm) in confectioners' sugar spiced with ground cinnamon, cardamom or ginger.

To make mini cookie sandwiches, flatten the dough before baking. After baking and cooling the cookies, layer two of them with jam, melted chocolate or peanut butter.

2. In a food processor, pulse the coconut, ⅓ cup of the sugar and the cornstarch until finely ground. In the bowl of a standing electric mixer fitted with the whisk, beat the egg whites and salt at medium-high speed until firm peaks form. Add the remaining ⅔ cup of sugar 1 tablespoon at a time and beat until stiff. Fold in the coconut mixture.

3. Transfer the meringue to a pastry bag fitted with a ½-inch star tip. Pipe 1½-inch mounds of meringue onto the baking sheets about 1 inch apart. Sprinkle with the pistachios and bake for 25 minutes, until the meringues are very slightly browned and set but not dry; shift the sheets from top to bottom and front to back halfway through for even baking. Turn the oven off, prop the door open about 8 inches and let the meringues dry for 1 hour. Transfer the baking sheets to racks and let the cookies cool completely. —*Nick Malgieri*

Coconut-Almond Balls with Dried Fruit

TOTAL: 15 MIN

MAKES 20 BALLS ● ● ○

- 1 **cup raw almonds (5 ounces)**
- ⅛ **teaspoon kosher salt**
- ¼ **vanilla bean, split and seeds scraped**
- 1 **cup dried pineapple (4 ounces), coarsely chopped**
- 1 **cup soft Medjool dates, pitted (4½ ounces)**
- 2 **tablespoons dried cranberries**
- ¼ **cup shredded unsweetened coconut**

In a food processor, pulse the almonds with the salt and vanilla seeds until very finely ground. Add the pineapple and dates and process until the mixture holds together. Transfer the mixture to a bowl and stir in the cranberries. Roll into 1-inch balls. Roll the balls in the coconut until coated. —*Ani Phyo*

MAKE AHEAD The coconut-almond balls can be refrigerated for up to 3 days.

Baby Buttons

ACTIVE: 30 MIN; TOTAL: 1 HR

MAKES 4 DOZEN COOKIES ● ○

These tiny butter cookies are easy to customize: Add food coloring to the dough or brush on a light citrus-flavored glaze. See Making Better Butter Cookies, below left, for more ideas.

- 2 **sticks (8 ounces) unsalted butter, softened**
- 1½ **cups confectioners' sugar**
- ½ **cup cornstarch**
- ½ **teaspoon pure vanilla extract**
- 1½ **cups all-purpose flour, plus more for dusting**

1. Preheat the oven to 350°. Line a large baking sheet with parchment paper. In a food processor, pulse the softened butter with ½ cup of the confectioners' sugar until smoothly combined. Add the cornstarch, vanilla and 1½ cups of flour to the processor and pulse until a soft dough forms. Transfer the dough to a work surface and divide it into 4 equal pieces.

2. On a lightly floured work surface, roll each piece of dough into a 12-inch rope. Cut each rope into 12 pieces and roll each piece into a ball. Transfer the balls to the baking sheet; they won't spread much. Bake the cookies on the center rack of the oven for about 22 minutes, until the bottoms of the cookies are golden but the tops are still pale.

3. Immediately sift the remaining 1 cup of confectioners' sugar into a medium bowl. Add 12 warm cookies to the bowl at a time and toss to coat them well with sugar. Transfer the sugar-dusted cookies to a clean baking sheet. While the cookies are still warm, poke 4 shallow holes into each one with a toothpick or skewer to make a buttonhole pattern. Let the cookies cool completely before serving or storing. —*Lisa Ritter*

MAKE AHEAD The cookies can be stored in an airtight container at room temperature for up to 1 week.

Vanilla Crescents

ACTIVE: 30 MIN; TOTAL: 1 HR

MAKES ABOUT 3 DOZEN COOKIES ●

Incredibly, these light, crispy and fragrant crescent cookies require only five ingredients.

    2 sticks unsalted butter,
       softened
    ½ cup confectioners' sugar,
       plus more for dusting
 1½ tablespoons pure vanilla extract
 2¼ cups all-purpose flour
 Pinch of salt

1. Preheat the oven to 350° and position one rack in the upper third and one in the lower third. Line 2 large baking sheets with parchment paper.

2. In the bowl of a standing electric mixer fitted with the paddle, beat the butter with the ½ cup of confectioners' sugar until pale white, about 5 minutes. Beat in the vanilla. Add the flour and salt and beat at low speed just until combined.

3. On a lightly floured surface, roll level tablespoons of the dough into 3-inch ropes. Taper the ends slightly and form the ropes into crescents. Carefully transfer the crescents to the baking sheets about ½ inch apart.

4. Bake the crescents for about 22 to 24 minutes, until the bottoms are golden and the tops are pale blond; shift the baking sheets from top to bottom and front to back halfway through for even baking. Transfer the baking sheets to racks and let the cookies cool for 10 minutes.

5. Fill a small bowl with confectioners' sugar. While the cookies are still warm, coat them in the sugar and transfer to a clean sheet of parchment paper to cool slightly. Roll the cooled cookies in the sugar again and let cool completely. *—Cindy Mushet*

MAKE AHEAD The crescent cookies can be stored in an airtight container between sheets of wax paper for up to 1 week. Dust the cookies very lightly with confectioners' sugar before serving.

Peanut Butter Cookies

TOTAL: 25 MIN

MAKES 2 DOZEN COOKIES ● ● ●

Peanut butter binds these supernutty flourless cookies from Southern cook Elizabeth Woodson, a former art director at F&W.

    1 cup smooth peanut butter
    1 cup sugar
    1 teaspoon baking soda
    1 extra-large egg,
       lightly beaten
    2 tablespoons very finely
       chopped peanuts
    ¼ cup mini chocolate chips
       (optional)

1. Preheat the oven to 350°. In a medium bowl, mix the peanut butter with the sugar, baking soda and beaten egg until smoothly blended. Add the chopped peanuts and mini chocolate chips and stir until they are evenly distributed.

2. Using your hands, roll tablespoons of the dough into 24 balls. Arrange 12 of the balls on each of 2 large ungreased baking sheets, spacing the cookies evenly. Using the back of a fork, press a crosshatch pattern onto the top of each ball of dough. Bake the cookies for about 15 minutes, shifting the baking sheets from front to back and top to bottom halfway through for even baking, until the cookies are lightly browned all over. Transfer the cookies to a wire rack and let cool completely. *—Elizabeth Woodson*

Crispy Sesame Tuiles

ACTIVE: 40 MIN; TOTAL: 2 HR 10 MIN

MAKES ABOUT 32 TUILES ● ●

Kyotofu, a sleek New York City dessert bar, uses Japanese ingredients like green tea and sesame seeds in updated versions of Japanese classics. It recently began collaborating with the renowned Japanese tea company Tafu, whose top-tier teas pair beautifully with sweets like these tuiles, developed by Kyotofu founder Nicole Bermensolo and her chef, Ritsuko Yamaguchi.

    ¾ cup sesame seeds (3 ounces)
 1¼ cups sugar
    ½ cup all-purpose flour
    4 tablespoons unsalted butter,
       melted
    1 tablespoon Japanese
       sesame paste or tahini,
       at room temperature
    ½ cup fresh orange juice
    2 teaspoons fresh lemon juice
 Black sesame seeds, for sprinkling
       (see Note)

1. In a food processor, finely grind the sesame seeds. In a medium bowl, whisk the ground sesame seeds with the sugar and flour. In a small bowl, whisk the butter with the sesame paste until smooth. Stir the orange and lemon juices into the flour mixture, then stir in the sesame butter until the batter is smooth. Cover and let stand at room temperature for 1 hour.

2. Preheat the oven to 350°. Line 2 large cookie sheets with parchment paper. Scoop tablespoons of batter onto the prepared sheets, spacing them 2 inches apart. Using an offset spatula, lightly spread the batter into 3-inch rounds of even thickness. Sprinkle a pinch of black sesame seeds on each tuile.

3. Bake the sesame tuiles for about 10 minutes, until they are evenly golden. Remove from the oven and let the tuiles stand until firm, about 3 minutes. Using a metal spatula, transfer the tuiles to a rack to cool completely; if the tuiles stick to the pan and become too brittle to transfer, simply reheat them in the oven for a minute or two until they are pliable. Repeat with the remaining batter and black sesame seeds.

—Nicole Bermensolo and Ritsuko Yamaguchi

NOTE Black sesame seeds are available at Asian markets.

MAKE AHEAD The sesame tuiles can be kept in an airtight container at room temperature for up to 3 days.

Coconut Brownie Bars

TOTAL: 1 HR 30 MIN PLUS 5 HR COOLING
MAKES 40 BARS ● ●

BROWNIES

- 14 ounces bittersweet chocolate, chopped
- 1 cup granulated sugar
- 1 stick plus 1 tablespoon unsalted butter, cut into tablespoons
- ¼ cup light corn syrup
- ¼ cup water
- ¾ cup all-purpose flour
- ¼ teaspoon salt
- 2 large eggs
- 1 tablespoon pure vanilla extract

COCONUT TOPPING

- 7 large egg whites
- 1⅓ cups granulated sugar
- 1 pound finely shredded unsweetened coconut (6½ cups)
- ¼ cup sour cream
- 1 vanilla bean, split, seeds scraped
- 1 teaspoon finely grated orange zest (optional)

GLAZE AND GARNISH

- 1 pound 2 ounces bittersweet chocolate, chopped
- 4½ tablespoons unsalted butter, cut into tablespoons
- 4½ tablespoons light corn syrup
- 2¼ cups heavy cream
- 40 unsalted roasted almonds

1. MAKE THE BROWNIES: Preheat the oven to 350°. Line an 11-by-17-inch baking sheet with parchment and spray with cooking spray. Put the chocolate in a bowl.

2. In a medium saucepan, combine the sugar, butter, corn syrup and water and bring to a boil. Pour the mixture over the chopped chocolate and let stand for about 1 minute, then whisk until smooth. Whisk in the flour and salt, then whisk in the eggs and vanilla until fully incorporated.

3. Scrape the brownie batter onto the prepared baking sheet and spread it to the edge. Bake for about 15 minutes, until the top of the brownie looks dry and crackly.

Transfer the baking sheet to a rack to cool, then transfer the baking sheet to the freezer to chill for 30 minutes, until the brownie base is completely firm.

4. MEANWHILE, MAKE THE COCONUT TOPPING: In a large heatproof bowl, combine the egg whites with the sugar. Set the bowl over a large saucepan of boiling water and whisk the mixture over moderate heat until it is warm to the touch and the sugar is dissolved, about 2 minutes. Remove from the heat.

5. Using an electric mixer, beat the egg whites at medium-high speed until stiff, glossy peaks form, about 8 minutes. Fold in the shredded coconut, sour cream, vanilla seeds and grated orange zest, if using. Spread the coconut topping evenly over the brownie base. Bake for 30 minutes, until the coconut topping is lightly golden and set. Transfer to a rack to cool, then cover and refrigerate until firm, at least 4 hours or overnight.

6. MAKE THE GLAZE: Combine the chopped bittersweet chocolate, butter and corn syrup in a large bowl. In a medium saucepan, bring the heavy cream to a boil. Pour the hot cream over the chocolate and let stand for 1 minute, then whisk until the chocolate is melted and the glaze is smooth. Let stand until warm to the touch, about 10 minutes.

7. Meanwhile, using a sharp knife, trim the border of the chilled brownie base to make it neat. Cut the base into 2-inch squares and transfer them to 2 wire racks set over baking sheets. Top each square with an almond. Using a small ladle, pour a thick coating of the chocolate glaze over each brownie bar. Using a small offset spatula, spread the glaze to coat the top and sides completely. (Rewarm the glaze over a pot of simmering water if it gets too thick.) Refrigerate until the glaze sets up, 1 hour. Serve chilled. —*Cheryl Burr*

MAKE AHEAD The brownie bars can be refrigerated for up to 3 days.

Seven-Layer Bars

ACTIVE: 30 MIN; TOTAL: 1 HR PLUS 4 HR COOLING
MAKES 3 DOZEN BARS ● ●

- 1 cup walnuts
- 2 sticks (8 ounces) unsalted butter, melted
- 3½ cups graham cracker crumbs (from one 14.4-ounce box)
- 4 cups semisweet chocolate chips (1 pound 5 ounces)
- One 11-ounce bag butterscotch chips (1¼ cups)
- ¾ cup white-chocolate chips
- One 14-ounce bag sweetened shredded coconut
- One 14-ounce can sweetened condensed milk (1½ cups)

1. Preheat the oven to 350°. Spread the walnuts in a pie plate and toast until golden and fragrant, about 8 minutes. Let cool, then coarsely chop.

2. In a large bowl, mix the melted butter with the graham cracker crumbs until evenly moistened. Press the crumbs evenly over the bottom of a 15-by-17-inch baking pan. Scatter the semisweet chocolate chips on top, followed by the butterscotch chips, white-chocolate chips, chopped toasted walnuts and shredded coconut. Scrape the condensed milk into a microwave-safe container and heat it at high power for about 30 seconds, until just fluid. Drizzle the condensed milk evenly over the shredded coconut.

3. Bake the bars in the center of the oven for about 30 minutes, until the coconut is toasted; rotate the pan once for even cooking. Transfer the pan to a rack and let the bars cool completely, at least 4 hours. Cut the bars lengthwise into 6 strips and crosswise into 6 strips to make 36 bars. —*Mary Odson*

MAKE AHEAD The bars can be kept in an airtight container at room temperature for up to 5 days, refrigerated for up to 1 week or frozen for up to 1 month.

Butterscotch-Glazed Coffee Shortbread Bars

ACTIVE: 40 MIN; TOTAL: 1 HR 30 MIN
MAKES 40 BARS ● ○ ○

Baking master Flo Braker flavors her ethereally light shortbread with finely ground espresso beans. Perhaps the best part is the golden, gooey butterscotch glaze, which becomes deliciously fudgy as the bars sit in the cookie jar.

SHORTBREAD

- 2 sticks unsalted butter, softened
- ½ cup plus 1 tablespoon sugar
- 1 teaspoon pure vanilla extract
- ¼ teaspoon salt
- 2¼ cups plus 2 tablespoons all-purpose flour
- 1 tablespoon finely ground espresso beans

GLAZE

- 4 tablespoons unsalted butter, softened
- ⅓ packed cup light brown sugar
- 1 tablespoon strong-brewed espresso
- 1 tablespoon light corn syrup

Pinch of salt

- 40 chocolate-covered espresso beans

1. Preheat the oven to 300° and position a rack in the center of the oven. Line the bottom of a 9-by-13-inch baking pan with parchment paper.

2. MAKE THE SHORTBREAD: In the bowl of a standing electric mixer fitted with the paddle attachment, beat the softened butter with the sugar at medium speed until fluffy and very pale, about 5 minutes. Beat in the vanilla extract and salt. In a small bowl, whisk the flour with the ground espresso beans. Add the dry ingredients to the mixer in 3 batches, scraping down the side of the bowl and beating just until the dough is combined.

3. Press the dough into the baking pan. Spread a sheet of plastic wrap directly onto the dough and, using a flat-bottomed glass, smooth the dough into an even layer. Remove the plastic wrap and bake the shortbread for about 50 minutes, until very lightly browned on top and firm but not solid to the touch. Transfer the pan to a rack to cool slightly, about 10 minutes.

4. Using a ruler, cut the warm shortbread lengthwise into 8 strips, then cut crosswise into 5 rows. Let the shortbread bars cool completely.

5. MAKE THE GLAZE: In a small, heavy saucepan, combine the butter, brown sugar, espresso, corn syrup and salt and bring to a boil over moderate heat, swirling the pan. Boil just until slightly thickened, 1½ to 2 minutes; remove from the heat. When the bubbling subsides, immediately pour the hot glaze over the shortbread. Working quickly with a small offset spatula, spread the glaze in an even layer. Using the tip of a lightly oiled paring knife, score the glaze between the cuts, without dragging. Press an espresso bean in the center of each bar. Let cool slightly, then carefully lift out the bars and transfer to a plate.
—*Flo Braker*

MAKE AHEAD The bars can be stored in an airtight container for up to 1 week.

Orange-Cardamom Date Bars with a Nutty Crust

ACTIVE: 30 MIN; TOTAL: 2 HR 30 MIN
MAKES 18 BARS ● ● ○

CRUST

Vegetable oil

- ½ medium orange
- ½ cup soft pitted Medjool dates
- ¼ cup water
- ¾ cup raw almonds (4 ounces)
- 2 cups raw pecan halves (8 ounces)
- 1 teaspoon cinnamon
- ½ teaspoon ground cardamom

FILLING

- 1 large orange
- 2 cups soft pitted Medjool dates
- 3 tablespoons water

1. MAKE THE CRUST: Lightly oil an 8-inch-square baking pan. Using a sharp knife, peel the orange half, removing all of the bitter white pith. Working over the bowl of a food processor, cut in between the orange membranes to release the sections into the bowl. Squeeze the juice from the orange membranes into the bowl; discard the membranes. Add the dates and water to the processor and puree until the mixture is very smooth, scraping down the side of the bowl as needed, about 1 minute. Scrape the date puree into a bowl. Rinse and dry the processor bowl.

2. In the food processor, process the almonds until very finely ground. Add the pecans, cinnamon and cardamom and pulse until the pecans are coarsely chopped. Add ¼ cup of the date puree; reserve any extra for another use. Pulse until the mixture holds together. Using oiled fingers, press half of the nut crust into the prepared baking pan in an even layer. Transfer the remaining nut crust to a bowl. Rinse the processor bowl again and pat dry.

3. MAKE THE FILLING: Using a vegetable peeler, remove the orange zest in strips, then thinly slice the zest and set it aside. Using a sharp knife, peel the orange, removing all of the bitter white pith. Working over the bowl of the processor, cut in between the membranes to release the sections into the bowl. Squeeze the juice from the membranes into the bowl. Add the dates and water; puree until the filling is smooth.

4. Spread the filling over the crust. Crumble the reserved nut crust evenly over the filling; press down to compact it. Refrigerate the bars for at least 2 hours, until firm enough to cut.

5. Cut the bars into 18 triangles, garnish with the reserved orange zest and serve.
—*Ani Phyo*

MAKE AHEAD The orange-cardamom date bars can be refrigerated in an airtight container for up to 3 days.

perfecting the cupcake

F&W's Grace Parisi *plays with two sensational batters, three fabulous frostings and loads of toppings (from granola to crushed Oreos) to create ten cupcakes.*

Two Sensational Cake Batters

Golden Cupcakes

ACTIVE: 20 MIN; TOTAL: 45 MIN
MAKES 12 CUPCAKES ● ○ ○

- 1 cup plus 2 tablespoons all-purpose flour
- 2 tablespoons cornstarch
- 1¼ teaspoons baking powder
- ⅛ teaspoon salt
- ¾ cup granulated sugar
- 2 large eggs, at room temperature
- 1¼ teaspoons pure vanilla extract
- 4 tablespoons unsalted butter, melted
- ¼ cup vegetable oil
- ½ cup milk, at room temperature

1. Preheat the oven to 350°. Line a 12-cup muffin tin with paper or foil liners.

2. In a medium bowl, whisk the flour with the cornstarch, baking powder and salt.

3. In a large bowl, using a handheld electric mixer, beat the sugar with the eggs and vanilla extract at medium-high speed until smooth and thickened slightly, about 3 minutes. Add the butter and oil and beat until incorporated, scraping the bottom and side of the bowl. Add the dry ingredients and milk in 3 alternating batches, beating well between additions. Carefully pour the batter into the lined muffin tins, filling them about two-thirds full.

4. Bake the cupcakes in the center of the oven for 20 to 23 minutes, until the tops are springy and a toothpick or cake tester inserted in the center comes out clean. Let the cupcakes cool slightly in the muffin tin, then transfer them to a wire rack to cool completely. Frost and top the cupcakes as desired (see the variations on the next page).

MAKE AHEAD The unfrosted cupcakes can be wrapped in plastic and stored at room temperature for up to 2 days or frozen for up to 1 month.

Chocolate Cupcakes

ACTIVE: 20 MIN; TOTAL: 45 MIN
MAKES 12 CUPCAKES ● ○ ○

- 4 tablespoons unsalted butter
- ¼ cup vegetable oil
- ½ cup water
- 1 cup all-purpose flour
- 1 cup granulated sugar
- ¼ cup plus 2 tablespoons unsweetened cocoa powder (not Dutch-process)
- ¾ teaspoon baking soda
- ⅛ teaspoon salt
- 1 large egg
- ¼ cup buttermilk
- 1 teaspoon pure vanilla extract

1. Preheat the oven to 350°. Line a 12-cup muffin tin with paper or foil liners.

2. In a medium saucepan, melt the butter with the vegetable oil and water over low heat.

3. In a large bowl, sift the flour with the sugar, cocoa, baking soda and salt. Add the melted butter mixture; beat with a handheld mixer at low speed until smooth. Add the egg and beat until incorporated. Add the buttermilk and vanilla and beat until smooth, scraping the bottom and side of the bowl. Pour the batter into the lined muffin tins, filling them about three-fourths full.

4. Bake the cupcakes in the center of the oven for about 25 minutes, until the tops are springy and a toothpick inserted in the center comes out clean. Let the cupcakes cool slightly, then transfer them to a rack to cool completely. Frost and top the cupcakes as desired (see the variations on the next page).

MAKE AHEAD The unfrosted cupcakes can be wrapped in plastic and stored at room temperature for up to 2 days or frozen for up to 1 month.

White Buttercream Frosting

TOTAL: 15 MIN

MAKES 1¼ CUPS (ENOUGH TO FROST 12 CUPCAKES) ● ●

6 tablespoons unsalted butter, softened

2 cups confectioners' sugar, sifted

½ teaspoon pure vanilla extract

Pinch of salt

2 tablespoons milk or heavy cream

In a medium bowl, using a handheld electric mixer, beat the softened butter at medium speed until smooth. Add the confectioners' sugar, vanilla extract and salt and beat the mixture at low speed just until combined. Increase the mixer speed to medium and beat until smooth. Add the milk or heavy cream and beat until light and fluffy, about 2 minutes. Spread the frosting on the cupcakes and top as desired.

MAKE AHEAD The White Buttercream Frosting can be refrigerated in an airtight plastic container for up to 2 days. Return to room temperature before using.

Chocolate Frosting

TOTAL: 1 HR 45 MIN

MAKES ABOUT 1 CUP (ENOUGH TO FROST 12 CUPCAKES) ● ●

4 ounces bittersweet chocolate, finely chopped

½ cup heavy cream

3 tablespoons unsalted butter

1 tablespoon light corn syrup

Pinch of salt

Put the chopped chocolate in a heatproof medium bowl. In a small saucepan, heat the heavy cream with the butter, corn syrup and salt until hot but not boiling. Immediately pour the mixture over the chocolate. Let stand for 5 minutes, then whisk until smooth. Let the frosting cool, whisking occasionally, until thick enough for dipping and glazing the cupcakes, about 30 minutes. For a frosting firm enough to spread, let stand for about 1 hour.

MAKE AHEAD The Chocolate Frosting can be refrigerated in an airtight container for up to 3 days. Return to room temperature before using.

Marshmallow Frosting

TOTAL: 20 MIN

MAKES ABOUT 4 CUPS (ENOUGH TO FROST 12 CUPCAKES) ● ●

1 cup granulated sugar

3 tablespoons water

2 large egg whites, at room temperature

Pinch of cream of tartar

Pinch of salt

1. In a small saucepan, combine the granulated sugar with the water and bring to a boil over moderately high heat, stirring constantly until the sugar has dissolved, 2 to 3 minutes.

2. In a large bowl of a standing electric mixer, beat the egg whites with the cream of tartar and salt until soft peaks form.

3. With the mixer at medium speed, carefully pour the hot sugar syrup into the egg whites. Continue beating the frosting until cool and billowy, about 5 minutes. Immediately spread the frosting on the cupcakes and top as desired.

Ten Mix-and-Match Cupcake Ideas

Caramel-Pretzel Spread Chocolate Frosting on Golden Cupcakes; top with crushed pretzels and caramel sauce.

Chocolate-Coconut Spread Chocolate Frosting on Golden Cupcakes and top with sweetened shredded coconut and mini nonpareil candies.

Cookies & Cream Mix white Buttercream Frosting with crushed Oreos and spread on Chocolate Cupcakes.

Fluffernutter Mix Marshmallow Frosting with creamy peanut butter and chopped chocolate-covered peanuts and spread on Golden Cupcakes.

Granola Bar Spread White Buttercream Frosting on Chocolate Cupcakes and top with crunchy granola and finely chopped dried fruit.

Lemon Meringue Mix Marshmallow Frosting with lemon zest and juice; spread on Golden Cupcakes and broil.

Piña Colada Mix Marshmallow Frosting with shredded coconut, chopped macadamia nuts and chopped candied pineapple and spread on Golden Cupcakes.

Rocky Road Mix Chocolate Frosting with chopped salted peanuts, mini chocolate chips and mini marshmallows and spread on Chocolate Cupcakes.

S'mores Mix Marshmallow Frosting with finely crumbled chocolate-covered graham crackers and mini marshmallows. Spread on Chocolate Cupcakes and broil.

Strawberry Shortcake Mix White Buttercream Frosting with strawberry jam and spread on Golden Cupcakes.

Apricot Blondies

ACTIVE: 25 MIN; TOTAL: 1 HR 15 MIN
MAKES 16 BARS ● ●

Daniel Orr, chef and owner of Farm Bloomington market-restaurant in Bloomington, Indiana, folds nuts and dried fruit into these bars along with white-chocolate chips.

- 1½ **cups all-purpose flour**
- 1½ **teaspoons baking powder**
- ½ **teaspoon baking soda**
- ¼ **teaspoon salt**
- **Freshly ground pepper**
- 1 **stick unsalted butter, softened**
- ¾ **cup plus 2 tablespoons light brown sugar**
- 2 **teaspoons pure vanilla extract**
- 1 **large egg**
- ½ **cup dried apricot halves, chopped**
- ½ **cup white-chocolate chips**
- ½ **cup salted roasted almonds, chopped**

1. Preheat the oven to 325°. Butter an 8-inch square metal baking pan. In a small bowl, whisk the flour with the baking powder, baking soda, salt and pepper to combine thoroughly.

2. In a large bowl, using a handheld electric mixer, beat the softened butter with the brown sugar and vanilla extract at medium speed until the mixture is smooth and creamy. Beat in the egg until smoothly combined. Mixing at low speed, beat in the chopped apricots, white-chocolate chips and chopped almonds, then beat in the dry ingredients.

3. Using a rubber spatula, scrape the blondie dough into the prepared baking pan, pressing it into an even layer. Bake in the lower third of the oven for about 45 minutes, until the top is golden and a toothpick inserted in the center comes out with a few moist crumbs attached. Let the blondies cool completely in the pan. Cut into 2-inch bars to serve.
—*Daniel Orr*

MAKE AHEAD The blondies can be kept in an airtight container for up to 3 days.

Chocolate-Almond Bars

ACTIVE: 10 MIN; TOTAL: 45 MIN
MAKES 16 BARS ● ●

Almonds and chocolate are a winning combination. Here, roasted almonds and chocolate chips are mixed into an almond butter–rich dough for crisp, chewy bars.

- 1 **cup salted almond butter**
- 2 **cups confectioners' sugar**
- 4 **tablespoons unsalted butter, softened**
- ½ **teaspoon baking soda**
- 1 **large egg**
- ¾ **cup semisweet chocolate chips**
- ½ **cup salted roasted almonds, coarsely chopped**

Preheat the oven to 375°. Line a 9-by-13-inch metal baking pan with aluminum foil. In a food processor, combine the almond butter with the confectioners' sugar, butter, baking soda and egg and pulse just until creamy; don't overmix or the fat will separate. Transfer the dough to a bowl and stir in the chocolate chips and roasted almonds. Press the dough evenly into the prepared pan and bake for about 18 to 20 minutes, until the top is shiny and lightly browned and the center is a bit soft. Transfer the pan to a rack and let the bar cool for about 10 minutes. Slide the bar with the foil onto a work surface. Discard the foil, cut into 16 bars and serve.
—*Grace Parisi*

MAKE AHEAD The Chocolate-Almond Bars can be kept in an airtight container for up to 3 days.

Bittersweet-Chocolate Bark with Candied Orange Peels

ACTIVE: 45 MIN; TOTAL: 2 HR
MAKES 1½ POUNDS ● ● ●

In this resourceful recipe, orange peels are boiled in water, simmered in syrup and coated in sugar. Then they're tossed with roasted pistachios and scattered over melted bittersweet chocolate to create a divine dessert.

- **Peels from 2 navel oranges, washed**
- 3½ **cups sugar**
- ¼ **cup light corn syrup**
- 1 **pound bittersweet chocolate (preferably 66 percent), chopped**
- ½ **cup unsalted roasted pistachios**

1. Using a sharp knife, remove the bitter white pith from the orange peels so they are about ⅛ inch thick; cut the peels into ¼-inch-wide strips. Transfer the peels to a saucepan filled with cold water; bring to a boil and boil the peels for 7 minutes. Drain. Repeat with fresh water, until the orange peels are tender, 15 minutes total. Drain.

2. Rinse out the saucepan. Add 2½ cups of the sugar, the corn syrup and 2 cups of water and bring to a boil, stirring until the sugar is dissolved. Add the orange peels and simmer over low heat until slightly translucent, about 30 minutes.

3. Spread the remaining 1 cup of sugar in a pie plate. Using a slotted spoon, lift the candied peels from the syrup, letting the syrup drip back into the saucepan; transfer the peels to the pie plate. Toss the warm peels in the sugar to coat thoroughly. Let the peels cool completely in the sugar, tossing occasionally, about 30 minutes.

4. Line a cookie sheet with parchment paper. In a double boiler set over a pot of simmering water, heat the bittersweet chocolate until two-thirds melted. Remove from the heat. Stir the chocolate with a rubber spatula until it is completely melted and registers about 90° on an instant-read thermometer.

5. Spread the chocolate on the parchment to a rough 9-by-13-inch rectangle. Working quickly, so the chocolate doesn't set, pick out the orange peels, reserving the sugar for another use. Scatter the orange peels and pistachios evenly over the chocolate; gently tap the cookie sheet on the work surface to flatten the chocolate and allow the toppings to sink in slightly. Refrigerate for 15 minutes, just until firm. Break into 2-inch pieces to serve. —*Grace Parisi*

Chocolate-Macadamia Tart

ACTIVE: 10 MIN; TOTAL: 50 MIN
PLUS COOLING
MAKES ONE 9-INCH TART ●

Buttery macadamia nuts dot this custardy crustless tart, while maple syrup unexpectedly lightens the chocolate flavor.

- 1 cup heavy cream
- ½ cup chopped bittersweet chocolate (3 ounces)
- 3 large eggs
- ½ cup pure maple syrup
- ¼ cup sugar
- ½ teaspoon kosher salt
- 2 cups macadamia nuts (10 ounces)

1. Preheat the oven to 325°. Butter a 9-inch pie plate. In a heatproof bowl, microwave the cream and chocolate for 25 seconds, until melted. Whisk until smooth, then let cool to warm. Whisk in the eggs, maple syrup, sugar and salt.

2. Pour the mixture into the pie plate. Insert the macadamias in an even layer. Bake the tart for 40 minutes, until the custard is just set. Let cool, cut into wedges and serve.
—*Michel Richard*

Gâteau Basque

ACTIVE: 1 HR; TOTAL: 2 HR 15 MIN
PLUS 4 HR CHILLING
MAKES ONE 9-INCH TART ●

There are many versions of this exquisite tart from the Pays Basque region of France. In this one, a flaky crust surrounds pastry cream strewn with brandied cherries. The excess dough from this recipe can be made into cookies: Roll the dough out to a ¼-inch thickness. Using a sharp knife, cut the dough into 3-inch squares. Brush the squares with egg wash, score them with a fork and bake in a 350° oven for 20 minutes, until golden.

DOUGH

- 3¼ cups all-purpose flour
- 1½ tablespoons baking powder
- 1½ teaspoons salt
- 2 sticks plus 2 tablespoons unsalted butter, softened
- 2 cups sugar
- 3 large egg yolks
- 2 large eggs
- ½ teaspoon pure lemon oil (see Note)
- ½ teaspoon almond oil
- 1 cup almond flour (see Note on p. 337)

FILLING

- 2¼ cups milk
- 1 vanilla bean, split and seeds scraped
- ½ cup cornstarch
- ½ cup plus 2 tablespoons granulated sugar
- 3 tablespoons all-purpose flour
- 6 large egg yolks
- 2 large eggs
- 1 cup brandied cherries, drained
- 1 egg mixed with 1 tablespoon of milk, for brushing

1. MAKE THE DOUGH: In a medium bowl, whisk the flour with the baking powder and salt. In a standing mixer fitted with the paddle, beat the butter with the sugar at medium speed until light and fluffy, about 3 minutes. Add the egg yolks to the mixing bowl along with the whole eggs, lemon oil and almond oil. Beat until they are thoroughly incorporated. At low speed, gradually beat in the flour mixture and the almond flour.

2. Scrape the pastry dough out onto a work surface and form it into 3 disks. Wrap each disk in plastic wrap and refrigerate until very firm, at least 4 hours or overnight.

3. MAKE THE FILLING: In a medium saucepan, bring the milk to a simmer over moderate heat with the vanilla seeds. In a medium heatproof bowl, whisk the cornstarch with the sugar and flour. Whisk the hot milk into the cornstarch mixture, then pour the mixture into the saucepan and cook over moderate heat, whisking constantly, until the mixture is bubbling and very thick, about 5 minutes. Add the egg yolks and the whole eggs and simmer, whisking, for 3 minutes longer. Scrape the pastry cream into a large heatproof bowl and press a piece of plastic wrap directly onto the surface. Let the pastry cream cool to room temperature, about 30 minutes.

4. Preheat the oven to 350°. On a lightly floured work surface, roll out the first disk of dough to a ¼-inch thickness and cut out a 12-inch round. Slide the round onto a lightly floured baking sheet and refrigerate until firm, about 10 minutes.

5. Meanwhile, roll the second disk out to a ¼-inch thickness and cut out a second 12-inch round. Transfer it to a 9-inch fluted tart pan with a removable bottom. Lightly press the dough onto the bottom and up the side of the pan. Trim off the excess and refrigerate the tart shell until firm, about 10 minutes. Reserve the third disk and dough scraps for cookies, if desired.

6. Spread the pastry cream in the tart shell in an even layer and dot with the brandied cherries. Cover the tart with the first round of dough and press gently to seal the edge. Trim off any excess. Brush the tart with the egg wash. Using a fork or skewer, lightly score the top of the tart in a diamond pattern.

7. Set the tart on a baking sheet and bake on the bottom shelf of the oven for 20 minutes. Rotate the tart and transfer it to the upper third of the oven. Bake the tart for about 40 minutes longer, until golden brown on top. Transfer the tart to a large wire rack to cool. Serve warm or at room temperature, cut into wedges.
—*Daniel Boulud*

NOTE Pure lemon oil, cold-pressed from lemon rinds, is available at specialty food shops and from boyajianinc.com.

MAKE AHEAD The tart dough can be frozen for up to 1 month. The pastry cream can be refrigerated, covered, overnight. Bring the dough and pastry cream to room temperature before using.

Honeyed Goat Cheese Tart with Pistachio Crust

ACTIVE: 30 MIN; TOTAL: 4 HR

MAKES ONE 9-INCH TART ● ●

Like sugar, honey caramelizes as it cooks. Here, warm honey is drizzled over a mixture of goat cheese and Greek yogurt, where it cools to a caramel-like consistency. For a crunchier topping, heat the honey until it reaches 250° on a candy thermometer.

- ½ cup unsalted shelled pistachios
- 1 stick (4 ounces) unsalted butter, softened
- ½ cup granulated sugar
- ½ teaspoon pure almond extract
- ½ teaspoon salt
- 1¼ cups all-purpose flour
- 11 ounces soft goat cheese
- 2 cups full-fat Greek-style yogurt
- 2 tablespoons fresh lime juice
- 2 teaspoons finely grated lime zest
- ½ cup confectioners' sugar
- ⅓ cup clover honey

1. In a food processor, pulse the shelled pistachios just until finely ground. In the bowl of a standing electric mixer fitted with the paddle attachment, beat the softened butter with the granulated sugar at medium speed until pale, about 1 minute. Add the ground pistachios, the almond extract and the salt and beat until combined. Add the flour and beat at low speed until the flour is incorporated and the dough is crumbly.

2. Scrape the dough into a 9-inch fluted tart pan with a removable bottom. Using the bottom of a glass, press the dough over the bottom and up the side of the tart pan. Refrigerate until the dough is chilled, about 30 minutes.

3. Preheat the oven to 300°. Prick the dough all over with a fork. Bake the crust for about 45 minutes, until lightly golden. Transfer to a rack and let cool completely.

4. In the bowl of the mixer, beat the goat cheese, yogurt, lime juice and lime zest until combined. Add the confectioners' sugar and beat until smooth. Scrape the filling into the crust and refrigerate for 2 hours.

5. Just before serving, in a small saucepan, cook the honey over moderately high heat until it reaches 236° on a candy thermometer, about 2 minutes. Remove from the heat and stir until slightly cooled, about 2 minutes. Drizzle the honey over the tart and let stand until the honey firms up, about 5 minutes. Cut into wedges and serve.
—*Susan Spungen*

MAKE AHEAD The tart can be prepared through Step 4 and refrigerated overnight.

Vanilla-Orange Flan

ACTIVE: 45 MIN; TOTAL: 2 HR 30 MIN PLUS OVERNIGHT CHILLING

MAKES TWO 10-INCH FLANS ● ●

Following his mother's recipe, Philadelphia chef Jose Garces gives thick, creamy flan a hit of vanilla and orange. He likes to serve the flan alongside a refreshing salad of melon and citrus.

- 1½ cups sugar
- ½ cup water
- 5 large eggs
- 1 vanilla bean, split, seeds scraped
- 2 teaspoons finely grated orange zest
- 2 teaspoons Cointreau or other orange liqueur

Two 14-ounce cans sweetened condensed milk

Two 12-ounce cans evaporated milk

- 3 navel oranges
- 3 limes
- ¾ pound Galia, cantaloupe or honeydew melon, diced
- 1 tablespoon finely shredded basil
- 1½ teaspoons extra-virgin olive oil

Pinch of salt

1. Preheat the oven to 300°. Set two 10-inch deep-dish glass pie plates in 2 medium roasting pans.

2. In a saucepan, cook the sugar and water over moderately high heat, stirring just until the sugar dissolves. Using a wet pastry brush, wash down any crystals from the side of the pan. Cook the syrup undisturbed until a medium-amber caramel forms, 6 minutes. Immediately pour the caramel into the pie plates, tilting them to coat the bottoms. Let the caramel cool completely.

3. In a large bowl, whisk the eggs with the vanilla seeds, orange zest and liqueur. Whisk in both milks until evenly combined. Pour the custard into the pie plates. Set the roasting pans in the upper and lower third of the oven. Carefully pour enough hot water into each roasting pan until it reaches halfway up the side of the pie plate. Cover the roasting pans with foil and bake for 1½ hours to 1 hour and 50 minutes (depending on oven placement), until the flans are firm and set but still slightly jiggly in the centers. Transfer the roasting pans to racks and let the flans cool slightly in the water. Transfer the pie plates to racks and let the flans cool, then cover and refrigerate overnight.

4. Using a sharp knife, peel the oranges and limes, removing all of the bitter white pith. Working over a bowl to catch the juices, cut in between the membranes to release the sections. Cut each section in thirds and return them to the bowl. Add the melon, basil, olive oil and salt.

5. To unmold each flan, run a knife around the rim of the pie plate, being sure to reach the caramel on the bottom; tilt the plate slightly to allow a bit of the caramel into the gap. Invert a rimmed round platter over the pie plate. Grabbing both the pie plate and the platter, carefully invert the flan onto the platter; if it doesn't release immediately, lift one side of the pie plate about an inch and slip the tip of the knife between the glass and the flan to release the seal. Lift off the pie plate. Pour and scrape the caramel onto the flan. Cut into wedges and serve with the fruit salad. —*Jose Garces*

HONEYED GOAT CHEESE TART WITH PISTACHIO CRUST

VANILLA-ORANGE FLAN

Goat Cheese Mousse with Red-Wine Caramel

ACTIVE: 30 MIN; TOTAL: 1 HR 30 MIN

4 SERVINGS ● ●

- 2 cups dry red wine
- ½ cup ruby port
- 1 teaspoon whole black peppercorns
- 1 shallot, minced
- 2 thyme sprigs plus ½ teaspoon chopped thyme
- 1½ cups sugar
- 4 cups strawberries, hulled (2 pints)
- 2 teaspoons finely grated orange zest
- 2 tablespoons water
- One 11-ounce log of fresh goat cheese, softened
- 2 tablespoons heavy cream

Pinch of freshly ground pepper

Crostini and toasted walnuts, for serving

1. In a saucepan, bring the wine, port, black peppercorns, shallot, thyme sprigs and 1 cup of the sugar to a boil, stirring until the sugar dissolves. Using a moistened pastry brush, wash down any sugar crystals on the side of the pan. Cook over moderate heat, without stirring, until syrupy and reduced to 1 cup, about 35 minutes. Strain and discard the solids. Let the caramel cool slightly.

2. Meanwhile, in a medium saucepan, toss the strawberries, orange zest, water and the remaining ½ cup of sugar and let stand until juicy, about 30 minutes.

3. Bring the strawberries to a boil and simmer over moderate heat until slightly thickened and jammy, about 15 minutes. Transfer the compote to a bowl and let cool.

4. In a bowl, using an electric mixer, beat the goat cheese, cream, ground pepper and chopped thyme until creamy. Spoon into a bowl and serve with the compote, caramel, crostini and walnuts. —*Karen Small*

Mascarpone-Stuffed Dates

 **TOTAL: 20 MIN**

8 SERVINGS ●

A dusting of unsweetened cocoa adds an appealing bitter note to this simple one-bite dessert.

- 16 Medjool dates
- ½ cup mascarpone cheese
- 2 tablespoons confectioners' sugar

Unsweetened cocoa powder, for dusting

Make a lengthwise slit in each date and remove the pits (without halving the dates). In a bowl, whisk the mascarpone with the sugar. Spoon the mascarpone into the dates, close them loosely and arrange on a plate, split side up. Sift the cocoa over the dates and serve. —*Maurizio Quaranta*

MAKE AHEAD The stuffed dates can be refrigerated overnight. Bring to room temperature before sprinkling with cocoa.

Lemon-Cherry Yogurt Parfaits

ACTIVE: 25 MIN; TOTAL: 45 MIN
4 SERVINGS ●

Thick and creamy Greek-style yogurt is a fast and healthy base for rich, tangy parfaits. Here, F&W's Grace Parisi folds some of the yogurt with lemon juice and zest, combines some more with chunky cherry preserves, then spoons the mixtures into glasses in alternating layers.

- 1 cup heavy cream, chilled
- 1 cup 2 percent plain Greek-style yogurt
- ¼ cup cherry preserves
- ¼ teaspoon unflavored powdered gelatin
- 1 teaspoon water
- 1 tablespoon fresh lemon juice
- 1 teaspoon finely grated lemon zest
- 3 tablespoons confectioners' sugar

1. In a medium bowl, using an electric mixer, beat the heavy cream at high speed until firm. Add the Greek yogurt and beat just until combined. Transfer half of the mixture to another bowl and fold in the cherry preserves.

2. In a small microwave-safe bowl, sprinkle the gelatin over the water and let stand until softened, about 1 minute. Microwave the gelatin at high power for about 5 seconds, just until melted. Add the gelatin to the plain whipped cream and yogurt mixture along with the lemon juice, grated lemon zest and confectioners' sugar and beat at medium speed just until the ingredients are combined.

3. Spoon half of the lemon yogurt cream into 4 wineglasses and top with half of the cherry yogurt cream. Top with the remaining lemon and cherry yogurt creams and refrigerate for 20 minutes before serving.
—*Grace Parisi*

MAKE AHEAD The parfaits can be refrigerated overnight.

Creamy Rice Pudding with the Quickest Strawberry Jam

ACTIVE: 25 MIN; TOTAL: 1 HR 10 MIN
6 SERVINGS ● ●

In this amazing dessert, British star chef Jamie Oliver turns strawberries into a quick jam, which he then stirs into a lush but low-fat rice pudding.

- 2 pounds strawberries, hulled, plus 6 strawberries hulled and thinly sliced
- ½ cup plus 2 tablespoons granulated sugar
- 5 cups 1 percent milk
- 1 cup medium-grain or basmati rice
- ½ vanilla bean, split and seeds scraped
- 6 small store-bought meringue cookies, coarsely crushed

1. In a large skillet, combine the whole strawberries with ½ cup of the sugar. Using your hands, squeeze the berries with the sugar until they become coarse chunks. Let stand until the sugar has dissolved into the juices, about 10 minutes.

2. Bring the strawberry mixture to a simmer and cook over moderately low heat, skimming off any foam from the top, until slightly thickened, about 25 minutes.

3. Meanwhile, in a large saucepan, combine the milk with the rice, the vanilla bean and seeds and the remaining 2 tablespoons of sugar. Bring to a simmer. Cover the saucepan and cook over low heat, stirring occasionally, until the rice pudding is thick and creamy, about 30 minutes. Remove the vanilla bean.

4. Spoon the rice pudding into bowls and top with the strawberry jam. Using a spoon, swirl the jam into the rice pudding. Sprinkle with the sliced strawberries and crushed meringues and serve.
—*Jamie Oliver*

MAKE AHEAD The strawberry jam can be refrigerated for up to 2 days. Rewarm the jam gently in the microwave before stirring it into the rice pudding.

Double-Chocolate Pudding

TOTAL: 20 MIN PLUS CHILLING
6 SERVINGS ● ● ●

This recipe from the late, great cookbook author Richard Sax has everything you could ask for in a chocolate pudding—an intense flavor and a texture that's silky yet firm enough to stand a spoon in. For the best possible pudding, use top-quality cocoa powder and chocolate.

- 2¼ cups whole milk
- ½ cup sugar
- Pinch of salt
- 2 tablespoons cornstarch
- 3 tablespoons unsweetened cocoa powder
- 1 large egg
- 2 large egg yolks
- 5 ounces semisweet or bittersweet chocolate, finely chopped
- 2 tablespoons unsalted butter, cut into pieces
- 1 teaspoon pure vanilla extract
- Lightly whipped cream, for serving

1. In a medium saucepan, combine 2 cups of the milk with ¼ cup of the sugar and the salt and bring to a boil over moderate heat, stirring to dissolve the sugar. Remove from the heat.

2. In a medium bowl, whisk the cornstarch with the unsweetened cocoa powder and the remaining ¼ cup of sugar until blended. Add the remaining ¼ cup of milk and whisk until smooth. Whisk this mixture into the hot milk in the saucepan and bring to a boil over moderate heat, whisking constantly. Reduce the heat to moderately low and simmer, whisking constantly, until the pudding is thick enough to coat the back of a spoon, about 2 minutes.

3. In a medium bowl, whisk the whole egg with the egg yolks. Gradually whisk about 1 cup of the hot cocoa pudding into the eggs until thoroughly incorporated, then scrape the pudding back into the saucepan. Cook the pudding over moderate heat, whisking constantly, until it just comes to boil, about 2 minutes.

4. Strain the pudding into a medium heatproof bowl. Add the chopped chocolate, butter and vanilla and whisk until the chocolate and butter are melted and incorporated and the pudding is smooth, about 2 minutes. Press a piece of plastic wrap directly onto the surface of the pudding in the bowl and refrigerate until chilled. Alternatively, transfer the pudding to six 6-ounce ramekins, cover and refrigerate. Serve with lightly whipped cream.
—*Richard Sax*

MAKE AHEAD The chocolate pudding can be covered with plastic wrap and refrigerated for up to 4 days.

Chocolate Bread Pudding with Bourbon Caramel Sauce
ACTIVE: 20 MIN; TOTAL: 1 HR 50 MIN
6 SERVINGS ● ● ●
10 ounces bittersweet
    chocolate, chopped
1½ cups whole milk
1 cup heavy cream
3 large eggs
3 large egg yolks
½ cup plus 2 tablespoons
    granulated sugar
1 teaspoon pure
    vanilla extract
½ teaspoon salt
One 1-pound loaf challah,
    crusts removed and bread
    cut into 1-inch dice (12 cups)
Bourbon Caramel Sauce
    (recipe follows)
Unsweetened whipped cream,
    for serving

1. Butter an 8-by-11-inch glass or ceramic baking dish. In a medium glass bowl, microwave the chopped bittersweet chocolate at high power in 30-second intervals until completely melted, stirring between intervals.

2. In a medium saucepan, bring the milk and cream to a simmer over moderately high heat. In a large bowl, whisk the whole eggs and yolks with ½ cup of the sugar, the vanilla and salt. Slowly whisk the hot milk mixture into the egg mixture, then whisk in the melted chocolate.

3. Spread the challah cubes in the prepared baking dish and pour the chocolate custard over the top. Press the challah into the custard until evenly soaked, then let stand for 20 minutes.

4. Preheat the oven to 325°. Sprinkle the remaining 2 tablespoons of sugar over the bread pudding. Set the baking dish in a roasting pan and fill the pan halfway with hot water. Bake the bread pudding for 50 minutes, until a knife inserted into the center comes out clean. Remove the dish from the water bath and let stand for 20 minutes. Serve the bread pudding warm or at room temperature with the Bourbon Caramel Sauce and whipped cream.
—*Amber Huffman*

BOURBON CARAMEL SAUCE
TOTAL: 15 MIN
MAKES 2 CUPS ● ●
2 cups sugar
½ cup water
1 tablespoon light corn syrup
1 cup heavy cream
½ cup bourbon

In a medium saucepan, bring the sugar, water and corn syrup to a boil over high heat. Cook until the sugar is dissolved, washing down the side of the pan with a wet pastry brush. Continue cooking, without stirring, until an amber caramel forms, about 6 minutes. Remove the saucepan from the heat and carefully stir in the cream. Let cool for 1 minute, then stir in the bourbon. Bring the mixture to a boil over moderate heat and cook, stirring, for 1 minute. Let the caramel sauce cool slightly and serve it warm or at room temperature. —*AH*

Pumpkin-Gingersnap Tiramisù
TOTAL: 45 MIN PLUS OVERNIGHT CHILLING AND 6 HR THAWING
12 SERVINGS ●
3½ teaspoons unflavored gelatin
2 tablespoons water
6 large egg yolks
¼ cup plus 2 tablespoons cornstarch
¼ teaspoon salt
1½ cups plus 1 tablespoon sugar
1 quart whole milk
One 15-ounce can pumpkin puree
1 tablespoon pure vanilla extract
¾ teaspoon cinnamon
1 pound mascarpone (2 cups)
3 tablespoons Calvados or
    other apple brandy
1¼ pounds gingersnaps, ¼ pound
    finely crushed

1. In a bowl, sprinkle the gelatin over the water and let stand for 5 minutes. In a large bowl, whisk the yolks, cornstarch, salt and 1½ cups of the sugar until is moistened. In a large saucepan, heat the milk just until steaming. Whisk 1 cup of the hot milk into the yolk mixture. Pour the mixture into the milk in the saucepan and cook over moderate heat, whisking, until boiling and thick, about 5 minutes. Whisk in the pumpkin puree and cook, whisking, for 1 minute. Off the heat, whisk in the gelatin, vanilla and cinnamon. Whisk in the mascarpone.

2. In a small microwave-safe bowl, microwave the Calvados with the remaining 1 tablespoon of sugar at high power for 10 seconds, just until the sugar is dissolved.

3. Arrange one-third of the whole gingersnaps in a 9-by-13-by-2½-inch dish. Lightly brush them with Calvados and top with one-third of the custard. Repeat the layering twice more to use all the whole gingersnaps, Calvados and custard. Sprinkle half the crushed gingersnaps on top and press plastic wrap directly on the surface. Freeze overnight.

4. Let thaw at room temperature for about 6 hours. Sprinkle with the remaining gingersnaps and serve. —*Grace Parisi*

BROWN-SUGAR CUSTARD WITH ORANGE ZEST

YOGURT PANNA COTTAS WITH HONEY

Brown-Sugar Custards with Orange Zest

ACTIVE: 20 MIN; TOTAL: 1 HR 30 MIN PLUS 3 HR CHILLING

4 SERVINGS ● ● ○

Cookbook author Pam Anderson uses low-fat evaporated milk to give sauces and desserts creaminess without using cream. "I put it in pasta sauces, panna cotta, quiche, tea—you can't tell the difference," she says.

1¾ cups 2 percent evaporated milk
¾ cup dark brown sugar
2 large eggs
1 large egg yolk
1 teaspoon pure vanilla extract
½ teaspoon grated orange zest
Candied orange zest, for garnish (optional)

1. Preheat the oven to 325°. Place four 4-ounce ramekins in a small baking dish or roasting pan.

2. In a medium saucepan, bring the evaporated milk to a simmer with the brown sugar. Cook over moderate heat, stirring constantly until the brown sugar dissolves. In a large bowl, whisk together the whole eggs, egg yolk, vanilla extract and grated orange zest. Slowly whisk the hot milk and brown-sugar mixture into the beaten egg mixture. Strain the brown-sugar custard through a fine-mesh sieve into a large heat-proof glass measuring cup.

3. Pour the custard into the ramekins. Add enough hot water to the baking dish to reach halfway up the sides of the ramekins. Bake for about 1 hour and 10 minutes, until the custards are just set. Transfer the ramekins to a rack and let cool. Cover the custards with plastic wrap and refrigerate until firm, at least 3 hours. Garnish with the candied orange zest.
—Pam Anderson

MAKE AHEAD The custards can be refrigerated for up to 2 days. Garnish with the candied orange zest just before serving.

Yogurt Panna Cottas with Honey

ACTIVE: 10 MIN; TOTAL: 3 HR 10 MIN

6 SERVINGS ● ●

1½ teaspoons unflavored gelatin
1 tablespoon water
1 cup fat-free milk
⅓ cup sugar
1 cup low-fat buttermilk
1 cup fat-free plain
   Greek yogurt
2 tablespoons honey
Red grapes, for serving

1. In a small bowl, mix the gelatin with the water and let stand until softened, about 5 minutes. In a small saucepan, bring the milk to a simmer with the sugar and cook until the sugar is dissolved, about 1 minute. Remove from the heat and stir in the softened gelatin until dissolved.

2. In a medium bowl, whisk the buttermilk with the yogurt. Whisk in the warm milk until smooth. Pour the panna cotta mixture into six 4-ounce ramekins and refrigerate until set, about 3 hours.

3. To serve, drizzle the panna cottas with the honey and garnish with the grapes.
—*Marisa Churchill*

MAKE AHEAD The yogurt panna cottas can be covered and refrigerated for up to 1 day before serving.

Italian Trifle with Marsala Syrup

ACTIVE: 1 HR 15 MIN; TOTAL: 4 HR 30 MIN PLUS 6 HR CHILLING

10 SERVINGS ● ○

When he's in Italy, Manhattan chef Fabio Trabocchi (an F&W Best New Chef 2002) makes this special-occasion dessert with Alchermes, a bright red cinnamon-scented liqueur rarely seen in the United States. The Sicilian fortified wine Marsala is a good substitute: It has a subtler color but a similarly spiced flavor, perfect for drenching squares of soft sponge cake layered with vanilla-infused pastry cream.

PASTRY CREAM
1 quart milk
1 plump vanilla bean, split
   and seeds scraped
1¾ cups sugar
1 dozen large egg yolks
¼ cup cornstarch
SPONGE CAKE
6 large eggs
¾ cup sugar
Finely grated zest of 1 orange
½ cup plus 2 tablespoons
   cake flour
½ cup cornstarch
¼ teaspoon salt
MARSALA SYRUP
1 cup sweet Marsala
⅓ cup sugar
Whipped cream and fresh
   berries, such as whole
   raspberries or sliced
   strawberries, for garnish

1. MAKE THE PASTRY CREAM: In a large saucepan, combine the milk with the scraped vanilla bean and seeds and ¾ cup of the sugar. Bring the milk to a simmer, stirring to dissolve the sugar. Remove the saucepan from the heat, cover and let stand at room temperature for 1 hour. Discard the vanilla bean.

2. In a large bowl, whisk the egg yolks with the cornstarch and the remaining 1 cup of sugar until smooth. Whisk in 1 cup of the vanilla-infused milk. Whisk the egg mixture into the milk remaining in the saucepan and cook over moderately high heat, stirring constantly with a rubber spatula, until the custard just begins to thicken and coat the spatula, about 4 minutes. Switch back to a whisk and cook, whisking constantly, until the custard is very thick and bubbling, about 4 minutes longer. Transfer the vanilla custard to a large heatproof bowl. Let cool completely, then press a sheet of plastic wrap directly onto the surface of the custard. Refrigerate until chilled, at least 3 hours or overnight.

3. MEANWHILE, MAKE THE SPONGE CAKE: Preheat the oven to 350°. Butter a 12-by-17-inch rimmed baking sheet and line with parchment paper. Butter the parchment and dust it lightly with flour. In the bowl of a standing electric mixer fitted with the whisk attachment, beat the eggs with the sugar at medium-high speed until the mixture is mousse-like and pale yellow, about 7 minutes. Reduce the speed and beat in the grated orange zest.

4. In a small bowl, whisk the cake flour with the cornstarch and salt until well combined. Working in 2 batches, sift the flour mixture over the beaten eggs and fold it in with a rubber spatula or whisk. Pour the batter onto the parchment-lined baking sheet and smooth the surface of the batter with a rubber spatula. Bake the sponge cake in the center of the oven for about 20 minutes, until the cake is golden and springs back when touched. Let cool in the pan on a rack.

5. MAKE THE MARSALA SYRUP: In a small saucepan, combine the Marsala with the sugar and bring to a simmer, stirring to dissolve the sugar. Let cool.

6. Run the blade of a paring knife along the sides of the cake and invert the cake onto a work surface. Peel off the parchment. Cut the cake into 3-inch squares. Reserve any scraps to patch holes. In a large glass trifle bowl, arrange a layer of sponge cake squares. Using a pastry brush, soak the cake squares with some of the Marsala syrup. Top with a 1-inch layer of the vanilla pastry cream. Repeat with the remaining cake squares, Marsala syrup and pastry cream, ending with a layer of cake. Cover the trifle loosely with plastic wrap and refrigerate for at least 6 hours or overnight. Top the trifle with the whipped cream and berries and serve.
—*Fabio Trabocchi*

MAKE AHEAD The trifle can be refrigerated for up to 2 days.

● HEALTHY ● MAKE AHEAD ● VEGETARIAN ● STAFF FAVORITE

Caramelized-Pineapple Baked Alaskas

 TOTAL: 30 MIN
4 SERVINGS •

- 1 pint coconut or vanilla ice cream
- 1 tablespoon unsalted butter
- 2 cups fresh pineapple chunks (12 ounces), cut into ½-inch dice
- 3 tablespoons dulce de leche
- 1 large egg white

Pinch of salt

- ¼ cup superfine sugar

1. Peel the carton off the ice cream and slice the ice cream into 4 rounds. Pack the slices into four 6-ounce ramekins, place on a baking sheet and freeze.

2. In a large nonstick skillet, melt the butter. Add the pineapple and cook over high heat, stirring occasionally, until lightly browned, 2 minutes. Add 2 tablespoons of the dulce de leche and cook, stirring, until lightly caramelized, 3 minutes. Add the remaining 1 tablespoon of dulce de leche and transfer the pineapple to a plate. Place the plate in the freezer to cool.

3. Preheat the broiler and position the rack nearest the heat. Put the egg white and salt in a clean mixing bowl set over a saucepan of boiling water. Using an electric mixer with clean beaters, beat at high speed to firm peaks. Add the sugar 1 tablespoon at a time and beat until stiff and glossy.

4. Spoon the cooled pineapple over the ice cream along with any juices. Dollop the meringue over the pineapple and broil just until lightly toasted, about 45 seconds. Serve right away. —*Grace Parisi*

Zebra Icebox Cake

TOTAL: 2 HR PLUS 24 HR CHILLING
8 TO 10 SERVINGS •

WAFERS

- 1½ sticks unsalted butter, softened
- 1 cup light brown sugar
- ¾ cup granulated sugar
- 1 tablespoon honey
- ¼ cup milk

- 1 tablespoon pure vanilla extract
- 1¼ cups all-purpose flour
- ¾ cup whole wheat flour
- 1 cup plus 2 tablespoons unsweetened cocoa powder (not Dutch-process)
- ½ teaspoon baking soda
- ½ teaspoon kosher salt

FILLING

- 1 teaspoon unflavored gelatin
- 1½ tablespoons cold water
- 6 large egg yolks
- ½ cup confectioners' sugar
- ¼ cup Marsala

Pinch of salt

- 8 ounces mascarpone cheese
- 1 cup heavy cream, chilled

MERINGUE

- 6 large egg whites
- 1 cup sugar
- 1½ teaspoons unflavored gelatin
- 2 tablespoons cold water
- 1½ teaspoons finely ground espresso

1. **MAKE THE WAFERS:** Preheat the oven to 350°. In a standing mixer fitted with the paddle, beat the butter, sugars and honey at medium speed until smooth. Beat in the milk and vanilla. Add both flours, the cocoa, baking soda and salt and beat at low until combined. Flatten the dough into 2 disks, wrap in plastic and chill for 30 minutes.

2. Line 2 large baking sheets with parchment paper. Roll out each piece of dough between 2 sheets of plastic wrap to an 11-inch square. Trim to form 2 neat 10-inch squares. Transfer the squares to the baking sheets. Bake for about 20 minutes, shifting the pans, until the dough is slightly springy. Let the dough cool on the baking sheets for 5 minutes, then slide the parchment onto a work surface. While the squares are still warm, cut each one into 4 strips about 2½ inches wide. Trim the edges; you should have eight 9-by-2½-inch wafers. Let cool.

3. **MEANWHILE, MAKE THE FILLING:** In a bowl, sprinkle the gelatin over the cold water; let stand until softened, 2 minutes.

In a large metal bowl set over a pan of simmering water, whisk the egg yolks, confectioners' sugar, Marsala and salt until tripled in volume, about 4 minutes. Whisk in the gelatin until melted. Scrape the mixture into a standing mixer fitted with a whisk and beat at medium-high until cool, 5 minutes. Add the mascarpone and beat just until combined; transfer to another bowl.

4. Wipe out the mixer. Add the cream and whip until soft peaks form. Fold the cream into the Marsala-mascarpone filling.

5. Line a 9-by-5-inch loaf pan with enough plastic wrap to hang over on all sides. Tip the loaf pan on its side. Arrange the wafers on a work surface. Spread the filling thickly on all but 1 of the wafers. Stack the cream-topped wafers and top with the plain wafer. Slide the stack into the tilted loaf pan. Return the pan to its upright position so the wafers stand vertically. Fold the plastic tightly over the cake. Refrigerate for 24 hours.

6. **MAKE THE MERINGUE:** In the bowl of a standing mixer fitted with a whisk, combine the egg whites and sugar. Set the bowl over a pan of simmering water and whisk until warm to the touch and the sugar is dissolved. Meanwhile, in a small bowl, sprinkle the gelatin over the cold water and let stand until softened, 2 to 3 minutes. Whisk the softened gelatin into the egg whites along with the espresso and beat at high speed until thick and fluffy, about 5 minutes.

7. Unwrap the cake and invert it onto a plate. Remove the plastic. Spread the filling to fill any gaps. Spread about one-third of the meringue all over the cake and refrigerate until firm, 10 minutes. Spoon the remaining meringue into a large pastry bag fitted with a star tip. Pipe lengthwise stripes of meringue along the top and long sides of the cake, starting from the bottom and working up as you go. Refrigerate until firm, about 15 minutes.

8. Using a blow torch, toast the meringue until golden, then serve.
—*Kim Schwenke*

ZEBRA ICEBOX CAKE

cakes, cookies & more

Torrone Semifreddo

TOTAL: 15 MIN PLUS 6 HR FREEZING

8 SERVINGS ● ○ ○

Torrone is an Italian nougat made with honey, egg whites, sugar and nuts. It can be soft and chewy or hard and crunchy. The recipe here calls for folding crunchy store-bought nougat into whipped cream and honey, then freezing the mixture. The result is an utterly delicious, wonderfully simple ice cream–like dessert.

- 2 cups heavy cream
- ¼ cup acacia honey
- ½ pound hard hazelnut or almond *torrone*, finely chopped

Warm hot fudge sauce, for serving

1. In a large bowl, whip the cream with the honey until firm. Fold in the chopped *torrone*. Transfer the mixture to a large, deep plastic container and press a piece of plastic wrap directly on the surface. Freeze until firm, at least 6 hours.

2. Spoon the semifreddo into bowls, drizzle with hot fudge sauce and serve.
—*Maurizio Quaranta*

MAKE AHEAD The semifreddo can be frozen for up to 2 days. Let soften for 15 minutes in the refrigerator before serving.

Semifreddo S'mores

ACTIVE: 50 MIN; TOTAL: 4 HR 25 MIN

8 SERVINGS ● ○ ○

Mathew Rice, pastry chef at Niche in St. Louis, always has a semifreddo on the menu. His favorite is toasted marshmallow, which he serves with salted milk-chocolate sauce and graham crackers.

SEMIFREDDO

- 2 cups Marshmallow Fluff
- 2 cups heavy cream
- 8 large egg yolks
- ¼ cup granulated sugar
- ¼ cup water

GRAHAM CRACKERS

- 2 sticks unsalted butter, at room temperature
- ½ packed cup light brown sugar
- ¼ cup honey
- 2 cups whole wheat flour
- ½ cup all-purpose flour, plus more for dusting
- 1 teaspoon salt

MILK-CHOCOLATE SAUCE

- ½ packed cup light brown sugar
- ½ cup light corn syrup
- ⅓ cup heavy cream
- 1 tablespoon unsweetened cocoa powder
- 1 cup milk-chocolate chips
- ¼ teaspoon pure vanilla extract
- 1 teaspoon coarse sea salt, such as Maldon

1. MAKE THE SEMIFREDDO: Preheat the broiler. Line a large baking sheet with parchment paper and lightly spray the parchment with vegetable oil spray. Spread the Marshmallow Fluff on the parchment in an even ½-inch-thick layer. Broil the Fluff for 1 minute, until golden brown all over. Let stand until cool, then fold the Fluff a few times to slightly incorporate the browned top.

2. In a large bowl, using an electric mixer, beat the heavy cream at medium-high speed until it holds firm peaks. Refrigerate the whipped cream until ready to use. In a standing mixer fitted with the whisk attachment, beat the egg yolks at medium-high speed until they are pale yellow, about 3 minutes. Meanwhile, in a small saucepan, combine the granulated sugar with the water and bring to a boil, stirring until the sugar dissolves. Boil over moderately high heat until the syrup reaches 235° on a candy thermometer, about 5 minutes. Remove the saucepan from the heat immediately.

3. With the mixer running at medium speed, gradually pour the hot sugar syrup into the egg yolks (avoiding the whisk), then beat at medium-high speed until tripled in volume, about 8 minutes. Gently fold in the chilled whipped cream until no streaks remain.

4. Using a spatula or fork, pull off 1-inch chunks of the toasted Fluff and fold into the whipped cream mixture. Scrape the semifreddo into an 8-by-11½-inch glass dish, cover with plastic wrap and freeze for 4 hours, until frozen.

5. MAKE THE GRAHAM CRACKERS: Preheat the oven to 325°. Line an 11-by-17-inch rimmed baking sheet with parchment paper. In a standing mixer, beat the butter with the brown sugar and honey at medium speed until pale and fluffy, about 2 minutes. Add the whole wheat flour, ½ cup all-purpose flour and the salt and mix at low speed until just combined.

6. Turn the dough out onto the prepared baking sheet and pat it into a disk. Lightly dust the dough with flour and roll it out to a ¼-inch thickness. Bake for 30 minutes, until golden; turn the baking sheet halfway through for even browning. Let the graham cracker stand until completely cool, about 1 hour, then break the cracker into 3-inch shards.

7. MAKE THE MILK-CHOCOLATE SAUCE: In a small saucepan, bring the brown sugar, corn syrup, heavy cream and cocoa powder to a simmer. Cook over moderately high heat until the sugar is dissolved, about 1 minute. Remove from the heat. Stir in the chocolate chips and vanilla until smooth. Pour the sauce into a small pitcher and let stand until cooled slightly, about 30 minutes. Stir in the salt just before serving.

8. Let the semifreddo stand at room temperature for 10 minutes. Scoop the semifreddo into bowls and top with the warm chocolate sauce. Garnish with the graham cracker shards and serve right away.
—*Mathew Rice*

MAKE AHEAD The semifreddo can be frozen for up to 1 week. The graham crackers can be stored in an airtight container for up to 3 days. The milk-chocolate sauce can be cooled, covered and refrigerated for up to 5 days. Gently rewarm it and stir in the salt just before serving.

Milk-Chocolate Cremoso with Espresso Parfait

TOTAL: 1 HR 15 MIN PLUS 4 HR CHILLING

10 SERVINGS ● ● ●

Although Miamians are assumed to be too bathing-suit conscious to indulge in dessert, this decadent milk-chocolate *cremoso* (a silky, pudding-like dish) with olive oil is one of the best-sellers at Michael's Genuine Food & Drink in Miami's Design District. "Some people are like, 'Whoa . . . olive oil and chocolate?'" says chef-owner Michael Schwartz. "But the olive oil reinforces the richness of the *cremoso*. As if you need any more richness."

CREMOSO

- 2 **cups heavy cream**
- ⅓ **cup granulated sugar**
- 5 **large egg yolks**
- 1 **pound good-quality milk chocolate, chopped**

ESPRESSO PARFAIT

- 2 **cups heavy cream**
- ½ **cup confectioners' sugar**
- 1 **tablespoon strong-brewed espresso, cooled**
- 1 **teaspoon pure vanilla extract**
- 2 **tablespoons unsalted butter, softened**
- 5 **thin slices of white sandwich bread, halved diagonally and crusts trimmed**
- ½ **cup roasted hazelnuts, chopped**

Extra-virgin olive oil, for drizzling

1. MAKE THE CREMOSO: In a saucepan, heat the cream with the granulated sugar until hot to the touch. In a medium bowl, whisk the egg yolks. Gradually whisk in 1 cup of the hot cream. Scrape the mixture into the saucepan and cook over moderate heat, whisking constantly, until slightly thickened, 3 minutes. Remove from the heat. Add the chocolate and let stand until melted, 5 minutes. Whisk until smooth. Transfer to a shallow bowl and refrigerate until very cold, at least 4 hours.

2. MEANWHILE, MAKE THE ESPRESSO PARFAIT: In a large bowl, using a hand-held electric mixer, beat the heavy cream with the confectioners' sugar, espresso and vanilla extract until firm. Spoon the cream into ten ½-cup ramekins and freeze until firm.

3. Preheat the oven to 350°. Butter the bread on both sides and arrange the slices on a baking sheet. Bake for about 10 minutes, or until lightly toasted.

4. Spoon the milk-chocolate *cremoso* onto plates, sprinkle with the hazelnuts and drizzle lightly with olive oil. Serve the espresso parfait and toast on the side.
—*Michael Schwartz*

MAKE AHEAD The *cremoso* can be refrigerated for up to 3 days; the espresso parfait can be frozen for up to 1 week.

Chocolate–Peanut Butter Brownie Banana Splits

TOTAL: 1 HR PLUS 2 HR CHILLING

8 SERVINGS, PLUS 10 BROWNIES
● ●

Hedy Goldsmith, the pastry chef at Michael's Genuine Food & Drink in Miami, created this stupendous dessert in which fudgy peanut butter brownies are topped with bananas caramelized in dulce de leche. They're then served with scoops of vanilla ice cream, whipped cream and Goldsmith's house-made peanut brittle.

BROWNIES

- 1½ **cups sugar**
- ½ **cup all-purpose flour**
- 1½ **teaspoons baking powder**
- 1½ **teaspoons kosher salt**
- 1 **pound bittersweet chocolate, coarsely chopped**
- 2 **sticks unsalted butter**
- 4 **large eggs**
- ½ **cup sour cream**
- 2 **teaspoons pure vanilla extract**
- 1 **cup natural peanut butter (8 ounces)**

BANANA SPLITS

- 1 **cup dulce de leche**
- 4 **firm but ripe bananas, split lengthwise and halved crosswise**

Vanilla ice cream, lightly sweetened whipped cream and crushed peanut brittle, for serving

1. MAKE THE BROWNIES: Preheat the oven to 325°. Line the bottom of a 9-by-13-inch metal baking pan with parchment paper. In a small bowl, whisk the sugar with the flour, baking powder and salt.

2. In a medium saucepan, combine the chocolate and butter and cook over very low heat, stirring, just until melted; let cool slightly. In a large bowl, whisk the eggs with the sour cream and vanilla. Whisk in the dry ingredients followed by the melted chocolate mixture. Transfer 2 tablespoons of the batter to a small bowl and stir in the peanut butter.

3. Scrape the batter into the prepared baking pan and dollop the peanut butter mixture all over the top. Swirl in the peanut butter mixture, but don't overmix. Bake in the center of the oven for about 45 minutes, or until the brownies have risen and the top is lightly cracked and glossy; the brownies will still be jiggly. Transfer the pan to a rack to cool, then refrigerate until the brownies are chilled, at least 2 hours. Cut the brownies into 18 rectangles.

4. MAKE THE BANANA SPLITS: In a large skillet, melt the dulce de leche over moderate heat. Add the bananas and cook, turning occasionally, until heated through, about 3 minutes. Set 8 brownies on individual plates and top with the bananas and dulce de leche. Spoon the ice cream and whipped cream alongside, top with the crushed peanut brittle and serve.
—*Hedy Goldsmith*

MAKE AHEAD The brownies can be tightly wrapped in plastic and refrigerated for up to 1 week or frozen for up to 3 months.

Peanut Butter and Milk-Chocolate Mousse Parfaits

ACTIVE: 45 MIN; TOTAL: 3 HR 20 MIN

6 SERVINGS ●

PEANUT BUTTER MOUSSE

- ½ teaspoon powdered gelatin
- 2 tablespoons cold water
- 1 cup heavy cream
- 2 large egg yolks
- 1½ tablespoons sugar
- 3 tablespoons salted smooth peanut butter

MILK-CHOCOLATE MOUSSE

- ½ cup half-and-half
- 2 large egg yolks
- 1 teaspoon granulated sugar
- 3 ounces milk chocolate, chopped
- 2 ounces bittersweet chocolate, chopped
- ⅔ cup heavy cream

CARAMEL SAUCE

- 1 cup sugar
- ½ cup plus 2 tablespoons water

Caramel corn, for serving

1. MAKE THE PEANUT BUTTER MOUSSE: In a bowl, dissolve the gelatin in the water and let stand for 5 minutes. In a saucepan, cook the cream over moderately high heat until it bubbles around the edge. In a medium bowl, whisk the egg yolks with the sugar. Gradually whisk the hot cream into the egg yolks. Pour the mixture into the saucepan and cook over moderately low heat, stirring constantly, until thickened, 3 minutes. Remove from the heat and whisk in the peanut butter, then the gelatin. Scrape the peanut butter mixture into the bottom of six 12-ounce jars or parfait glasses and refrigerate for 1 hour, until set.

2. MAKE THE MILK-CHOCOLATE MOUSSE: In a small saucepan, heat the half-and-half until it bubbles around the edge. In a medium bowl, whisk the egg yolks with the sugar. Gradually whisk the hot half-and-half into the egg yolks. Pour the mixture into the saucepan and cook over low heat, stirring, until thickened, about 2 minutes.

Place both chocolates in a medium bowl. Pour the half-and-half mixture over the chocolate and let stand for 1 minute, then whisk until completely melted.

3. In another medium bowl, beat the heavy cream until softly whipped. Stir one-fourth of the whipped cream into the chocolate mixture, then gently fold in the remaining whipped cream. Pour the chocolate mousse over the peanut butter mousse and refrigerate for 1 hour, until set.

4. MAKE THE CARAMEL SAUCE: In a medium saucepan, cook the sugar with ¼ cup of the water over moderately high heat until the sugar is dissolved, washing down the side of the pan with a wet pastry brush. Continue cooking, without stirring, until a honey-colored caramel forms, 7 minutes. Remove from the heat and stir in the remaining ¼ cup plus 2 tablespoons of water. Let cool for 1 hour.

5. To serve, pour a thick layer of the caramel sauce over the chocolate mousse. Top with the caramel corn and serve.
—*Jerome Chang*

Guinness Ice Cream with Chocolate-Covered Pretzels

ACTIVE: 30 MIN; TOTAL: 5 HR

MAKES 10 CUPS ●●

This ice cream has a strong, malty Guinness flavor that goes supremely well with salty, milk-chocolate-covered pretzels. If you would rather not make the chocolate-covered pretzels, the store-bought kind is good, too.

- 2 cups Guinness (16 ounces)
- 2 cups heavy cream
- 1¾ cups whole milk
- 15 large egg yolks
- 1 cup granulated sugar

Chocolate-Covered Pretzels (recipe follows), for serving

1. In a large saucepan, combine the Guinness with the cream and milk and bring to a simmer over moderately high heat. In a large bowl, whisk the egg yolks with the sugar. Gradually add the hot Guinness cream to the yolks, whisking constantly until well blended.

2. Pour the mixture into the saucepan and cook over moderate heat, stirring constantly until it coats the back of a spoon, about 6 minutes; do not let it boil. Pour the custard into a medium bowl set in a large bowl filled with ice water. Let stand until the custard is cold, stirring occasionally, about 30 minutes.

3. Pour the custard into an ice cream maker and freeze according to the manufacturer's instructions (this may have to be done in 2 batches). Pack the ice cream into an airtight container and store in the freezer until firm, about 4 hours.

4. Spoon the ice cream into bowls and top with some Chocolate-Covered Pretzels. Serve at once. —*Cory Barrett*

CHOCOLATE-COVERED PRETZELS

ACTIVE: 10 MIN; TOTAL: 30 MIN

10 SERVINGS ●●

- 6 ounces milk chocolate, chopped
- 2 cups thin pretzel sticks

Line a baking sheet with wax paper. Melt the chocolate in a heatproof bowl set over a saucepan of simmering water. Let cool for 10 minutes, stirring occasionally. Add the pretzels and stir gently until coated. Using a fork and letting the excess chocolate drip back into the bowl, transfer the pretzels to the paper. Refrigerate the pretzels until the chocolate is set, 20 minutes.
—*CB*

Vanilla Bean Ice Cream

ACTIVE: 20 MIN; TOTAL: 1 HR 20 MIN PLUS 4 HR FREEZING

MAKES 3½ CUPS ●●

- 2 cups whole milk
- 1 tablespoon plus 1 teaspoon cornstarch
- 1½ ounces cream cheese, softened (3 tablespoons)
- 1¼ cups heavy cream

⅔ cup sugar

1½ tablespoons light corn syrup

1 vanilla bean, split and
   seeds scraped

⅛ teaspoon kosher salt

1. Fill a large bowl with ice water. In a small bowl, mix 2 tablespoons of the milk with the cornstarch. In another large bowl, whisk the cream cheese until smooth.

2. In a large saucepan, combine the remaining milk with the heavy cream, sugar, corn syrup and vanilla bean and seeds. Bring the milk mixture to a boil and cook over moderate heat until the sugar dissolves and the vanilla flavors the milk, about 4 minutes. Off the heat, gradually whisk in the cornstarch mixture. Return to a boil and cook over moderately high heat until the mixture is slightly thickened, about 1 minute.

3. Gradually whisk the hot milk mixture into the cream cheese until smooth. Whisk in the salt. Set the bowl in the ice water bath and let stand, stirring occasionally, until cold, about 20 minutes.

4. Strain the ice cream base into an ice cream maker and freeze according to the manufacturer's instructions. Pack the ice cream into a plastic container.

5. Press a sheet of plastic wrap directly onto the surface of the ice cream and close with an airtight lid. Freeze the vanilla ice cream until firm, about 4 hours.
—*Jeni Britton*

PISTACHIO VARIATION Omit the vanilla bean and seeds. Add ½ cup toasted and very finely ground pistachios, ¼ teaspoon pure almond extract and an additional ⅛ teaspoon kosher salt to the cream cheese. When straining the ice cream base in Step 4, press the ground pistachios with the back of a spoon to extract all of the flavor.

MINT VARIATION Omit the vanilla bean and seeds. Add 1 cup of coarsely chopped mint leaves to the cream cheese. When straining, press the mint leaves with the back of a spoon to extract all of the flavor.

Nutella Fondue

 TOTAL: 5 MIN
   8 SERVINGS ●

1 cup Nutella

1 cup heavy cream

Biscotti, for dipping

Spoon the Nutella into a heatproof bowl. In a microwave-safe cup, heat the cream at high power for 45 seconds, or until very hot. Slowly whisk the cream into the Nutella until smooth. Transfer to 8 small espresso cups and serve with biscotti.
—*Grace Parisi*

Chocolate Fondue with Fruit and Grilled Pound Cake

 TOTAL: 25 MIN
   6 SERVINGS ●

A grill works just as well as a stovetop for melting this bourbon-kissed chocolate fondue, served here with fresh apricots and grilled pound cake and pineapple.

1 pineapple—peeled, cored
   and sliced 1 inch thick

One 1½ pound pound cake,
   sliced 1½ inches thick

2 tablespoons unsalted
   butter, melted

4 apricots, pitted and
   quartered

1 cup heavy cream

2 tablespoons bourbon

10 ounces semisweet chocolate,
   coarsely chopped (2¼ cups)

10 ounces bittersweet chocolate,
   coarsely chopped (2¼ cups)

Pinch of salt

1. Light a grill. Grill the pineapple slices over moderate heat until charred on both sides, about 8 minutes. Brush the pound cake slices with the melted butter and grill over moderate heat until toasted, about 4 minutes.

2. Cut the pound cake into 1-inch cubes and transfer to a plate. Cut the pineapple into 1-inch cubes and transfer to a separate plate along with the apricots.

3. In a saucepan set on the grill, bring the cream and bourbon to a simmer. Add both chocolates and the salt and remove from the grill. Let stand for 5 minutes, then whisk until smooth. Serve with the grilled pound cake and fruit. —*Nick Fauchald*

Brown-Butter Crêpes with Nutella and Jam

 TOTAL: 40 MIN
   4 SERVINGS ●

2 tablespoons unsalted butter,
   plus more for the pan

1 large egg

1 large egg yolk

1 cup half-and-half

¾ cup all-purpose flour

Salt and freshly ground pepper

½ cup strawberry or peach jam

½ cup Nutella

1. Preheat the oven to 225°. In an 8-inch nonstick skillet, brown the 2 tablespoons of butter over moderately high heat, about 4 minutes. Transfer to a bowl and let cool.

2. In a bowl, whisk the egg and yolk with the half-and-half. Whisk in the flour and browned butter. Season with salt and pepper.

3. Set the skillet over high heat. When it is hot, add a scant ¼ cup of batter, swirling to coat the bottom of the pan. Cook until the crêpe is browned around the edge and the top is set, about 45 seconds. Flip the crêpe and cook until the underside is lightly browned, about 30 seconds longer. Transfer the crêpe to a plate. Repeat with the remaining batter, buttering the pan as needed. You should have about 8 crêpes.

4. Spread each crêpe with 1 tablespoon of the jam and fold into quarters. Transfer the crêpes to a small baking dish, overlapping slightly. Bake for 10 minutes, until the crêpes are just heated through.

5. Meanwhile, in a small microwave-safe bowl, heat the Nutella in a microwave oven on high power in 20-second bursts just until runny. Drizzle the Nutella over the warm crêpes and serve. —*Mike Price*

FOUR-CITRUS
SALSA (P. 379)

INDIAN SPICED
TOMATO SALSA
(P. 378)

DRIED-FRUIT
CHOW CHOW
(P. 382)

SWEET-AND-SOUR
PINEAPPLE CHUTNEY
(P. 382)

sauces & condiments

66 I prefer lighter sauces with bright flavors—like relishes and chutneys—over creamy ones, especially at home. 99

—**CLARK FRASIER,** CO-CHEF AND CO-OWNER, ARROWS RESTAURANT, OGUNQUIT, MAINE, AND SUMMER WINTER, BURLINGTON, MASSACHUSETTS

PICKLED RED ONIONS (LEFT) AND SPICY TOMATO SAUCE

SALSA VERDE

Pickled Red Onions

TOTAL: 10 MIN PLUS OVERNIGHT
PICKLING

MAKES 1 CUP ● ● ○

  1 medium red onion,
     very thinly sliced

  ½ cup fresh lime juice

  ¼ habanero chile with
     seeds, minced

Kosher salt

In a jar with a tight-fitting lid, combine the red onion slices with the lime juice, minced habanero chile and a pinch of salt. Cover and shake gently to combine the ingredients and coat the onion slices. Refrigerate overnight, gently shaking the jar occasionally. Drain the pickled onions and season them with salt before serving.
—*Sue Torres*

MAKE AHEAD The pickled onions can be refrigerated in the jar with their pickling liquid for up to 3 days.

Spicy Tomato Sauce

 TOTAL: 30 MIN

MAKES 1 CUP ● ● ○

  2 large ripe tomatoes (¾ pound),
     coarsely chopped

  3 large garlic cloves, halved

  ½ small onion, minced

  1 canned chipotle in
     adobo sauce, with seeds

  1 tablespoon vegetable oil

Salt and freshly ground pepper

1. In a blender or mini food processor, combine the tomatoes, garlic, onion and chipotle and puree until smooth.

2. In a medium saucepan, heat the oil. Add the tomato puree and season with salt and pepper. Cook over high heat, stirring frequently, until the sauce is thick, about 15 minutes, stirring frequently.
—*Sue Torres*

MAKE AHEAD The sauce can be refrigerated for up to 3 days.

Salsa Verde

TOTAL: 25 MIN

MAKES 2½ CUPS ● ● ○

 10 tomatillos (about 1¼ pounds)—
     husked, rinsed and quartered

  1 lightly packed cup
     cilantro sprigs

  1 serrano chile, quartered

  ½ medium white onion, chopped

  2 garlic cloves, smashed

  1 tablespoon vegetable oil

Salt and freshly ground pepper

In a blender, combine the tomatillos, cilantro, serrano, onion and garlic and puree until smooth. In a medium saucepan, heat the vegetable oil. Add the salsa, season with salt and pepper and bring to a boil. Simmer over moderate heat until reduced to 2½ cups, about 10 minutes. Let cool.
—*Sue Torres*

MAKE AHEAD The Salsa Verde can be refrigerated for up to 5 days.

Pico de Gallo

ACTIVE: 15 MIN; TOTAL: 1 HR 15 MIN
MAKES 2½ CUPS ● ● ○

    4 large plum tomatoes,
       seeded and finely diced
    ½ medium white onion, finely diced
    1 serrano chile, finely diced
    2 tablespoons fresh lime juice
    2 tablespoons chopped cilantro
Pinch of salt

Toss all of the ingredients together in a large bowl and let stand at room temperature for at least 1 hour. —*Sue Torres*
MAKE AHEAD The Pico de Gallo can be refrigerated overnight.

Grilled-Tomatillo Salsa Verde

TOTAL: 25 MIN
MAKES 2 CUPS ● ● ○

Salsa verde means "green sauce" in both Italian and Spanish. In this version, lightly charred vegetables impart an alluring smokiness; fresh cilantro and tart lime juice make all the flavors pop.

    1 pound tomatillos, husked
       and halved
    2 jalapeños, halved and seeded
    1 small onion, sliced ½ inch thick
    2 garlic cloves, unpeeled
    ¼ cup vegetable oil
    ¼ cup cilantro leaves
    2 tablespoons fresh lime juice
Salt and freshly ground
       black pepper

Preheat a grill pan. In a large bowl, toss the tomatillos, jalapeños, onion and garlic with 2 tablespoons of the vegetable oil. Grill over high heat, turning occasionally, until the vegetables are slightly softened and charred in spots, about 5 minutes. Let cool slightly, then transfer to a food processor. Pulse until coarsely chopped. Add the cilantro, lime juice and the remaining 2 tablespoons of vegetable oil and pulse until chunky. Season with salt and pepper and serve warm or at room temperature.
—*Grace Parisi*

Salsa Verde with Tarragon and Chervil

ACTIVE: 30 MIN; TOTAL: 1 HR 30 MIN
MAKES 2 CUPS ● ● ○

Fresh tarragon gives this lemony salsa verde a nice summery quality. Serve it with grilled fish like swordfish or tuna steaks, as a spread in sandwiches or swirled into soups. If fresh chervil proves difficult to find, a mixture of extra tarragon and parsley is a fine substitute.

    1 medium red onion,
       finely chopped
    2 tablespoons red wine
       vinegar
Salt
    2 tablespoons salted capers
    ¾ cup extra-virgin olive oil
    4 tablespoons fresh
       lemon juice
    1 teaspoon finely grated
       lemon zest
    3 garlic cloves, very
       finely chopped
    ½ cup coarsely chopped
       flat-leaf parsley
    ½ cup coarsely chopped chervil
    ¼ cup coarsely chopped
       tarragon
    ¼ cup very finely
       chopped chives
Freshly ground pepper

1. In a small nonreactive bowl, combine the chopped red onion with the red wine vinegar and a pinch of salt. Let stand for about 10 minutes.
2. Meanwhile, in a small bowl, cover the capers with warm water and let stand for about 10 minutes. Using a slotted spoon, transfer the capers to a work surface and finely chop them.
3. In a medium bowl, combine the olive oil with the lemon juice, lemon zest and chopped garlic, parsley, chervil, tarragon and chives. Drain the chopped onion, squeezing out any excess vinegar, and add to the bowl along with the capers. Mix well and season with

salt and pepper. Let the salsa verde stand for at least 1 hour before serving.
—*Chris Cosentino*
MAKE AHEAD The salsa verde can be refrigerated, covered, overnight. Bring the salsa to room temperature before serving, or serve lightly chilled.

Salsa Picante

ACTIVE: 30 MIN; TOTAL: 1 HR 30 MIN
MAKES 2½ CUPS ● ● ○

This piquant, bright red blend of dried and fresh chiles has a bracing kick, making it ideal for rich meats like grilled pork chops and beef rib eyes.

    8 dried New Mexico chiles
    3 *guajillo* chiles
    3 dried cayenne chiles or
       chiles *de arbol*
    2 fresh serrano chiles, seeded
       and minced
    ¾ cup extra-virgin olive oil
    1 medium red onion, very
       finely chopped
    4 fresh red Fresno chiles or
       jalapeños, seeded and
       finely chopped
    2 tablespoons fresh lemon juice
    1 tablespoon finely grated
       lemon zest
    1 cup finely chopped
       flat-leaf parsley
Kosher salt and freshly ground
       black pepper

1. In a large, heatproof bowl, cover the New Mexico, *guajillo* and cayenne chiles with hot water. Let stand until the chiles soften, about 15 minutes. Drain, seed and coarsely chop the chiles and transfer to a blender. Add the serranos and the olive oil and puree until smooth.
2. Transfer the chile puree to a medium bowl. Stir in the onion, Fresno chiles, lemon juice, lemon zest and parsley and season with salt and black pepper. Let the salsa stand for at least 1 hour before serving.
—*Chris Cosentino*

sauces & condiments

Indian Spiced Tomato Salsa

TOTAL: 20 MIN

MAKES 2 CUPS ● ● ○ ○

½ cup canola oil

1 serrano chile with seeds, sliced

1 cup thinly sliced white onion

1 teaspoon garam masala, store-bought or homemade (see below)

1 pint grape tomatoes, coarsely chopped

2 tablespoons fresh lime juice

Salt and freshly ground pepper

½ cup coarsely chopped cilantro

In a large skillet, heat the canola oil until smoky. Add the sliced chile and white onion and stir-fry over high heat for 30 seconds. Add the garam masala and stir-fry until the onion is crisp-tender, 2 minutes. Toss in the chopped tomatoes and lime juice. Transfer the ingredients to a small bowl; season with salt and pepper. Stir in the chopped cilantro. Serve hot or at room temperature. —*Grace Parisi*

SERVE WITH Fish, shellfish, chicken, lamb, beef, pork.

MAKE AHEAD The salsa can be refrigerated for up to 3 days.

garam masala

This Indian spice blend (used in the recipe above) is more vibrant when you make it yourself.

Grind ½ cup cumin seeds, ¼ cup coriander seeds, ¼ cup cardamom pods, 1 bay leaf, 2 cinnamon sticks and 1½ tablespoons whole cloves. Sift into a bowl and blend with 2½ tablespoons ground ginger, ⅛ teaspoon freshly grated nutmeg, and ⅛ teaspoon ground mace.

Spicy Pickled Nopales

ACTIVE: 25 MIN; TOTAL: 1 HR 10 MIN PLUS 2 DAYS PICKLING

MAKES 2 CUPS ● ● ○ ○

1 pound *nopales* (fresh cactus paddles)—thorns removed, paddles peeled and sliced ¼ inch thick (see Note)

2 jalapeños, sliced crosswise ¼ inch thick

¼ cup kosher salt

2 cups water

1 cup apple cider vinegar

¾ cup sugar

1 teaspoon sweet pimentón de la Vera (smoked Spanish paprika)

1. In a large bowl, toss the cactus paddles and jalapeños with the salt and let stand for 45 minutes. Drain well. Transfer the cactus and jalapeños to a heatproof bowl.
2. In a medium saucepan, combine the water with the vinegar, sugar and paprika and bring to a boil. Pour the brine over the cactus and jalapeños and stir well. Let cool to room temperature, then cover and refrigerate for 2 days before serving. —*Laurence Jossel*

NOTE Most *nopales* are sold with the spikes removed; any stray spikes can be removed with a sharp paring knife.

MAKE AHEAD The pickled cactus and jalapeños can be refrigerated in their brine for up to 1 week.

Pickled Farm-Stand Tomatoes with Jalapeños

TOTAL: 30 MIN PLUS 4 HR PICKLING

6 TO 8 SERVINGS ● ● ○ ○

At Blue Duck Tavern in Washington, D.C., chef Brian McBride serves side dishes separately from entrées so diners can mix and match. These pickled tomatoes are terrific with a simple grilled steak, but they're also delicious with plenty of crusty bread to sop up the ginger-and-cumin-scented tomato juices.

1 cup rice vinegar

¼ cup light brown sugar

1 teaspoon salt

1 cup extra-virgin olive oil

1 garlic clove, very finely chopped

1½ teaspoons finely grated fresh ginger

1 teaspoon mustard seeds

1 teaspoon coarsely ground black pepper

1 teaspoon ground turmeric

1 teaspoon ground cumin

Pinch of cayenne pepper

6 medium tomatoes (1½ pounds), each cut into 6 wedges

4 scallions, white and tender green parts only, thinly sliced

2 jalapeños, thinly sliced into rings and seeded

1. In a medium saucepan, bring the rice vinegar, brown sugar and salt to a boil over moderate heat, stirring constantly to dissolve the sugar and salt. Remove the saucepan from the heat.
2. In a medium skillet, heat the olive oil. Add the chopped garlic, grated ginger, mustard seeds, black pepper, turmeric, cumin and cayenne pepper and cook over low heat, gently swirling the pan a few times, until the spices are fragrant, about 2 minutes. Carefully pour the hot oil and seasonings into the vinegar, brown sugar and salt mixture.
3. In a large heatproof nonreactive bowl, combine the tomato wedges, scallion slices and jalapeño rings. Stir in the hot pickling liquid and let stand at room temperature for 4 hours, or let cool and refrigerate for 8 hours, then serve. —*Brian McBride*

SERVE WITH Grilled steak or fish.

MAKE AHEAD The pickled tomatoes and jalapeños can be refrigerated in their liquid for up to 3 days.

Roasted Red Pepper Tartar Sauce

TOTAL: 15 MIN

MAKES 1½ CUPS ●

Roasted bell peppers and cornichons provide hits of sweet and salty flavors to this creamy, lemony tartar sauce. For added smokiness, use jarred piquillo peppers in place of the bell peppers.

- 1 cup roasted red bell peppers (8 ounces)
- ¼ cup finely chopped cornichons
- 2 tablespoons salted capers, rinsed and finely chopped
- 2 teaspoons finely chopped tarragon
- ½ teaspoon finely grated lemon zest
- 1 tablespoon fresh lemon juice
- ½ cup mayonnaise

Salt and freshly ground pepper

Pat the roasted peppers dry and finely chop them. Transfer the peppers to a medium bowl and stir in the cornichons, capers, tarragon, lemon zest and juice and mayonnaise. Season with salt and pepper and serve. —*Grace Parisi*

SERVE WITH Fish, shellfish, chicken, lamb, steak, burgers.

MAKE AHEAD The sauce can be refrigerated for up to 3 days.

Smoky Red Pepper Spread

TOTAL: 10 MIN

MAKES ABOUT 1¼ CUPS ●

- 1 small red bell pepper
- 1 cup feta cheese, crumbled
- ½ teaspoon hot pimentón de la Vera (smoked Spanish paprika)

Roast the pepper over a gas flame until charred and softened. Let the pepper cool; peel, seed and chop. In a food processor, puree the pepper with the feta and pimentón; transfer to a bowl and serve.
—*Laurence Jossel*

Burrata Salsa

TOTAL: 15 MIN

MAKES 1¼ CUPS ● ●

Chris Cosentino, chef at Incanto in San Francisco, serves this puree of burrata (cream-filled mozzarella) with bison strip loin, a combination he calls "Italian cheesesteak." Buffalo mozzarella can also be substituted for the burrata. The sauce is a luxe match for any grilled meat.

- 4 ounces burrata cheese, coarsely chopped
- 1 tablespoon whole milk
- 2 tablespoons fresh lemon juice
- 2 tablespoons extra-virgin olive oil

Salt and freshly ground pepper

In a blender or food processor, combine the burrata with the milk and lemon juice and blend until smooth. With the machine on, add the olive oil in a thin stream. Season with salt and pepper and serve.
—*Chris Cosentino*

Hazelnut–and– Green Olive Pesto

TOTAL: 30 MIN

MAKES 1½ CUPS ● ● ●

This isn't a typical pesto, since it has no cheese; instead, it's made with an irresistible blend of crunchy toasted hazelnuts, fresh parsley, green olives and garlic.

- 1 cup hazelnuts (5 ounces)
- ½ cup flat-leaf parsley leaves
- 1 garlic clove, crushed
- ¼ cup pitted green olives
- ¼ teaspoon crushed red pepper
- 1 cup extra-virgin olive oil

Salt and freshly ground black pepper

1. Preheat the oven to 350°. Spread the hazelnuts in a pie plate and toast for 15 minutes, until the skins blister; transfer to a kitchen towel and let cool slightly. Rub the nuts in the towel to remove the skins, then transfer to a food processor and let cool completely.

2. Add the parsley leaves and crushed garlic to the food processor and pulse until coarsely chopped. Add the green olives and crushed red pepper and pulse until all the ingredients are finely chopped. Transfer the pesto to a bowl, stir in the olive oil and season with salt and pepper.
—*Grace Parisi*

SERVE WITH Fish, chicken, pork, steak.

MAKE AHEAD The pesto can be refrigerated for up to 3 days.

Four-Citrus Salsa

TOTAL: 30 MIN

MAKES 2 CUPS ● ●

Juicy bits of orange, grapefruit, lemon and lime form the base of this vibrant salsa; green olive tapenade and sliced red onion add extra zestiness, which makes the salsa so good on everything from fish to avocado slices.

- 1 navel orange
- 1 ruby red grapefruit
- 1 lemon
- 1 lime
- ¼ cup extra-virgin olive oil
- 1 teaspoon green olive tapenade
- ½ cup thinly sliced red onion
- 2 tablespoons chopped flat-leaf parsley

Salt and freshly ground pepper

Using a sharp knife, peel the orange, grapefruit, lemon and lime, removing all of the white pith. Working over a strainer set over a bowl, cut in between the membranes and release the citrus sections into the strainer. Squeeze the membranes over the bowl to extract as much of the juice as possible. Whisk the olive oil and tapenade into the juice. Cut the citrus sections into ½-inch pieces and add them to the dressing along with the red onion and parsley. Season with salt and pepper. —*Grace Parisi*

SERVE WITH Fish, shellfish, chicken, pork, sliced avocado.

MAKE AHEAD The salsa can be refrigerated overnight.

ASIAN-STYLE KEBABS

kebab party

*F&W's **Tina Ujlaki** has a sneaky summer party strategy: She sets out chunks of meat, poultry, fish and vegetables, then asks guests to make and grill their own kebabs.*

Mediterranean

START WITH
- swordfish + lemon + bay leaves
- tuna + cherry tomatoes + bread cubes
- lamb + halloumi cubes + zucchini
- shrimp + fennel + orange + red onions
- pork + red peppers + yellow squash
- beef + fennel + tomatoes + onions

BRUSH WITH Four-Herb Oil
In a processor, pulse ½ cup olive oil, 2 garlic cloves, 10 sage leaves and 1 teaspoon each of fresh oregano, thyme and rosemary until herbs are chopped. Season with salt, black pepper and hot pepper flakes.

SERVE WITH Herb and Sun-Dried Tomato Pesto Make another batch of the Herb Oil. Add 1 cup Italian parsley leaves and ½ cup sliced sun-dried tomatoes to the processor; pulse to chop. Season with salt, black pepper and hot pepper flakes.

Mexican

START WITH
- shrimp + chorizo + zucchini
- pork + pineapple + pickled jalapeños
- chicken + yellow squash + poblanos
- tuna + okra + cherry tomatoes
- beef + red onions + red peppers
- scallops + okra + tomatoes

BRUSH WITH Cumin-Adobo Oil
In a bowl, combine ½ cup olive oil with 1½ teaspoons ground cumin, 1½ teaspoons minced fresh oregano, 1 minced garlic clove and 2 teaspoons adobo sauce (from a can of chipotles). Season the oil with salt.

SERVE WITH Chipotle Mayo
Mix ½ cup mayonnaise, 3 finely chopped chipotles in adobo, 1 tablespoon orange juice, 1 teaspoon lime juice, ¾ teaspoon minced fresh oregano and 1 tablespoon each of minced red onion and cilantro. Season with salt.

Asian

START WITH
- beef + scallions + mushrooms
- tofu + zucchini + red peppers
- shrimp + sugar snap peas + zucchini
- chicken + asparagus + mushrooms
- scallops + Chinese sausage + peppers
- salmon + asparagus + green beans

BRUSH WITH Ginger-Sesame Oil
Mix ½ cup vegetable oil, 2 tablespoons low-sodium soy sauce, 2 teaspoons each of minced ginger and garlic and 4 teaspoons Asian sesame oil. Season with ½ teaspoon five-spice powder and a big pinch of white pepper.

SERVE WITH Hoisin Glaze and Sauce
Mix ½ cup hoisin sauce with ¼ cup each of Shaoxing wine, low-sodium soy sauce and finely chopped scallions. Add 4 teaspoons each of Asian sesame oil and finely grated fresh ginger; season the sauce with white pepper.

sauces & condiments

Chipotle-Citrus Barbecue Sauce

TOTAL: 50 MIN

MAKES 2 CUPS ● ●

Inspired by a recent trip to Mexico City, Jean-Georges Vongerichten added ancho and chipotle chiles to his arsenal of Asian flavors, creating this tangy sauce to spoon over luscious spit-roasted pork.

- 1 ancho chile, stemmed and seeded
- 1 dried chipotle chile, stemmed and seeded
- 1 cup sugar
- ½ cup water
- 10 garlic cloves, very finely chopped
- 1 cup fresh lemon juice
- 1 cup fresh orange juice
- ¾ cup fresh lime juice
- ⅓ cup Asian fish sauce

1. Heat a small skillet. Add the ancho and chipotle chiles and toast over moderate heat until fragrant, about 3 minutes. Transfer to a work surface and let cool completely, about 10 minutes. Crumble the toasted chiles into ¼-inch pieces.

2. Meanwhile, in a medium saucepan, combine the sugar with the water and bring to a simmer over moderately high heat, stirring until the sugar is dissolved. Reduce the heat to moderate and cook without stirring until a richly browned caramel forms, about 16 minutes. Add the crumbled toasted chiles and the chopped garlic and simmer until fragrant, about 30 seconds. Carefully stir in the lemon, orange and lime juices and boil over high heat until the sauce is reduced to a syrupy glaze, about 12 minutes. Remove the saucepan from the heat. Stir in the fish sauce and let the barbecue sauce cool to room temperature before serving.

—*Jean-Georges Vongerichten*

MAKE AHEAD The barbecue sauce can be refrigerated for up to 5 days. Bring to room temperature before serving.

Sweet-and-Sour Pineapple Chutney

 TOTAL: 40 MIN

MAKES 1½ CUPS ● ● ●

Mixing sweet pineapple, onion and vinegar with a quick, light caramel sauce results in a fabulous sweet-and-sour chutney.

- ¼ cup sugar
- ¾ cup plus 2 tablespoons water
- 2 cups diced fresh pineapple (12 ounces)
- 1 small red onion, finely diced

Pinch of crushed red pepper

- ¼ cup plus 2 tablespoons distilled white vinegar

Salt

- 2 tablespoons slivered mint leaves

In a saucepan, combine the sugar with 2 tablespoons of the water; cook over high heat until the sugar is dissolved. Cook without stirring until the sugar begins to caramelize around the edge, 2 minutes. Remove from the heat, add the pineapple, onion, crushed red pepper, vinegar and the remaining ¾ cup of water; season lightly with salt. Bring to a simmer and cook, stirring occasionally, until jamlike, 15 minutes. Stir in the mint. Serve warm or at room temperature. —*Grace Parisi*

SERVE WITH Fish, chicken, pork, steak.

MAKE AHEAD The chutney can be refrigerated for up to 3 days.

Tropical Fruit Chutney

ACTIVE: 30 MIN; TOTAL: 1 HR

MAKES ABOUT 3 CUPS ● ●

- ¼ cup red wine vinegar
- 2 tablespoons honey
- 2 tablespoons light brown sugar
- ¼ teaspoon ground coriander

One 2-inch cinnamon stick

Pinch of ground cloves

- 1 small bay leaf
- 1½ cups finely diced pineapple (½-inch dice)
- 1½ cups finely diced mango (½-inch dice)

- 1 cup finely diced papaya (½-inch dice)
- 1 small garlic clove, very finely chopped
- ½ teaspoon finely grated fresh ginger
- ½ small Scotch bonnet or habanero chile, very finely chopped

Salt and freshly ground white pepper

In a large saucepan, combine the vinegar, honey, brown sugar, coriander, cinnamon stick, cloves and bay leaf and bring to a simmer. Add the pineapple, mango, papaya, garlic, ginger and Scotch bonnet and season lightly with salt and white pepper. Simmer over low heat for 30 minutes. Let cool. Discard the cinnamon and bay leaf. Serve at room temperature or chilled.

—*Bradford Thompson*

MAKE AHEAD The chutney can be refrigerated for up to 2 weeks.

Dried-Fruit Chow Chow

TOTAL: 20 MIN

MAKES 1 CUP ● ●

Chow chow is a mustard-based vegetable relish. In this sensational sweet-spicy variation, F&W's Grace Parisi substitutes dried apricots and cherries for the vegetables and adds apricot jam and grainy mustard.

- 1 cup coarsely chopped mixed dried fruit, such as cherries, golden raisins and apricots (4 ounces)
- ¼ cup cider vinegar
- ½ cup water
- 1 tablespoon unsalted butter
- 1 medium onion, finely chopped
- ¼ cup apricot jam
- 2 tablespoons grainy mustard

Salt and freshly ground pepper

1. In a microwave-safe bowl, combine the chopped dried fruit with the cider vinegar and water. Cover and microwave at high power for 1 minute, until the dried fruit is softened and plump.

2. In a saucepan, melt the butter. Add the onion and cook over moderately high heat, stirring, until softened, 4 minutes. Add the jam; cook until melted and sizzling. Add the dried fruit and its liquid; bring to a boil. Simmer over moderately low heat, stirring, until thickened, 5 minutes. Remove from the heat and stir in the mustard. Season with salt and pepper. Serve warm or at room temperature. —*Grace Parisi*

SERVE WITH Chicken, pork, duck, steak, sausages.

MAKE AHEAD The chow chow can be refrigerated for 1 week.

Spiced Fall Fruit Jam with Hazelnuts and Red Wine

ACTIVE: 30 MIN; TOTAL: 2 HR 10 MIN
MAKES 1 QUART ● ● ○ ○ ○

A Piedmontese specialty that's served with a cheese like Castelmagno, this robust compote, known as *côgnà* in Italian, is also terrific with a pan-seared pork chop or on a turkey sandwich.

- 3 cups fresh red wine must or young fruity red wine, such as Beaujolais or Zinfandel
- 1 pound fresh figs, stemmed and halved
- 2 Bartlett pears—peeled, cored and coarsely chopped
- 2 Granny Smith apples—peeled, cored and coarsely chopped
- 1 quince—peeled, cored and coarsely chopped
- ½ cup sugar, plus more to taste
- Three 3-by-½-inch strips of orange zest
- 1 bay leaf, preferably fresh
- One 2-inch cinnamon stick
- ½ cup roasted hazelnuts, coarsely chopped

1. In a large nonreactive saucepan, combine the red wine must with the figs, pears, apples, quince, ½ cup of sugar, orange zest, bay leaf and cinnamon stick. Bring to a boil over moderately high heat, stirring to dissolve the sugar.

2. Reduce the heat to moderate and simmer the *côgnà*, stirring often, until very thick and reduced to 4 cups, about 1 hour and 10 minutes. If the *côgnà* is not sweet enough, you can add up to another ½ cup of sugar. Discard the orange zest, bay leaf and cinnamon stick. Stir in the hazelnuts and simmer for 10 minutes longer. Let the *côgnà* cool to room temperature before serving. —*Peter Pastan*

Cranberry-Pomegranate Sauce

ACTIVE: 15 MIN; TOTAL: 2 HR 15 MIN
MAKES 6 CUPS ● ●

- 1½ pounds fresh or frozen cranberries (6 cups)
- 2 cups sugar
- 1 cup pomegranate juice
- 2 cups fresh pomegranate seeds

In a medium saucepan, combine the cranberries with the sugar and pomegranate juice. Bring to a simmer and cook over moderate heat, stirring occasionally, until most of the cranberries have burst, about 10 minutes. Scrape the cranberry sauce into a medium bowl and let stand until cool, about 2 hours. Fold in the pomegranate seeds and serve the sauce chilled or at room temperature. —*Melissa Rubel*

Pink Applesauce

TOTAL: 30 MIN PLUS 1 HR CHILLING
MAKES 1 QUART ● ●

- 3 McIntosh apples (1½ pounds), quartered and cored
- 3 Paula Red, Northern Spy or Empire apples (1½ pounds), quartered and cored
- 3 black plums or large Italian prune plums (10 ounces), halved and pitted
- 6 cups water
- ⅓ cup sugar
- 1 tablespoon fresh lemon juice
- ½ teaspoon cinnamon
- Pinch of freshly grated nutmeg

1. In a saucepan, cover the apples and plums with the water and bring to a simmer. Cover and cook over low heat until the fruit breaks down, 5 minutes. Drain in a fine sieve set over a bowl and reserve 2 tablespoons of the cooking liquid. Using a wooden spoon, press the fruit through the sieve into the bowl to make a puree. Discard the skins.

2. In a saucepan, combine the apple-plum puree with the sugar, lemon juice and spices. Simmer over moderately low heat, stirring frequently, until the sugar dissolves, 3 minutes. Stir in the reserved 2 tablespoons of cooking liquid. Scrape the applesauce into a bowl, cover and refrigerate until chilled, at least 1 hour. —*Ivor Simmons*

Dukka

TOTAL: 25 MIN
MAKES 2 CUPS ● ○ ○

An intensely flavored Egyptian blend of toasted nuts and seeds, dukka is traditionally eaten on bread dipped in olive oil.

- ¼ cup each of raw pistachios, raw cashews, blanched almonds and blanched hazelnuts
- ¼ cup coriander seeds
- ¼ cup unsweetened shredded coconut
- 1½ tablespoons cumin seeds
- ¼ cup sesame seeds
- ¼ teaspoon kosher salt
- ⅛ teaspoon freshly ground pepper

In a 350° oven, toast the nuts for 8 minutes, until golden, then coarsely chop them. In a skillet, toast the coriander over moderate heat until fragrant, 2 minutes. Transfer to a food processor and pulse until chopped. Toast the coconut and cumin seeds in the skillet, stirring, until the coconut is golden, 2 minutes; add to the food processor along with the chopped nuts and pulse until coarsely ground. Transfer to a bowl. Toast the sesame seeds in the skillet until golden, 4 minutes. Stir into the nut mixture and season with the kosher salt and ground pepper. —*Jody Adams*

ZEN SANGRIA (P. 392)

drinks

" Parties here always start with people hanging around the bar. Then they peel off into the kitchen to cook. Then they come back for more cocktails. "

—SCOTT MORRISON, CREATOR, PAPER DENIM & CLOTH
AND EARNEST SEWN, NEW YORK CITY

SOUR-CHERRY GIN SLINGS

ZOMBIE

Sour-Cherry Gin Slings

ACTIVE: 20 MIN; TOTAL: 1 HR 30 MIN

MAKES 12 DRINKS

Like Paul Virant, chef at Vie in Western Springs, Illinois, bar manager Mike Page and pastry chef Todd Feitl think hyper-seasonally. They based this sweet-tart concoction on the classic Singapore sling, replacing the traditional cherry brandy with an intensely vibrant homemade sour-cherry syrup. With a squirt of sparkling water, the syrup also makes a great kid-friendly cherry soda.

SOUR-CHERRY SYRUP

- 1 **pound sour cherries, stemmed**
- ¾ **cup sugar**
- 1 **cup water**

Strips of zest from ½ lemon

Strips of zest from ½ orange

GIN SLINGS

- 2 **cups gin**
- ⅔ **cup Cointreau**
- ⅔ **cup fresh lime juice**

Angostura bitters

Ice

Sparkling water

Lime wheels and fresh cherries,
  for garnish

1. MAKE THE SOUR-CHERRY SYRUP: In a large saucepan, combine the sour cherries with the sugar, water and citrus zests and bring to a boil. Cover and simmer over low heat for 40 minutes. Pass the mixture through a fine strainer, pressing on the solids; you should have 2½ cups of sour-cherry syrup. Let cool.

2. MAKE THE GIN SLINGS: In a pitcher, combine the gin with the Cointreau, lime juice, 2¼ cups of the sour-cherry syrup and a few dashes of bitters and stir well. Pour the slings into ice-filled glasses and top each drink with sparkling water. Garnish with the lime wheels and fresh cherries and serve. —*Mike Page*

Zombie

 TOTAL: 5 MIN

 MAKES 1 DRINK

This lower-proof version of the high-octane classic is made with Velvet Falernum, an almond-and-lime-flavored liqueur that's a key ingredient in many tiki drinks.

Ice

- 1½ **ounces amber rum**
- ½ **ounce dark rum**
- ½ **ounce 151-proof rum**
- ¾ **ounce fresh pineapple juice**
- ¾ **ounce fresh lime juice**
- ½ **ounce Velvet Falernum**
- ½ **ounce brown sugar simple syrup**
  (brown sugar dissolved in equal
  part simmering water and cooled)

Mint sprig, for garnish

Fill a cocktail shaker with ice. Add the remaining ingredients and stir well. Strain into an ice-filled tiki mug or collins glass. Garnish with the mint. —*Nick Fauchald*

Gin Blossom

TOTAL: 5 MIN
MAKES 1 DRINK

"Eau-de-vie can be a challenging spirit to work with," says Julie Reiner, co-owner of Manhattan's Flatiron Lounge and Clover Club in Brooklyn. "It can add a lot of depth to cocktails, but it's also very intense, so I like to pair it with other aromatic spirits." In this fragrant, crystal-clear cocktail, Reiner matches apricot eau-de-vie with juniper-scented gin.

Ice
1½ ounces Plymouth gin
¾ ounce apricot eau-de-vie
¾ ounce Martini Bianco vermouth (see Note)
2 dashes of orange bitters
1 lemon twist, for garnish

Fill a pint glass with ice. Add the gin, eau-de-vie, vermouth and bitters and stir well. Strain into a chilled coupe and garnish with the lemon twist. —*Julie Reiner*
NOTE Martini Bianco is a slightly sweet, vanilla-flavored vermouth.

Mai Tai

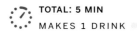

TOTAL: 5 MIN
MAKES 1 DRINK

The origin of this classic rum-based cocktail is one of the great debates in tikidom. Both Donn Beach (a.k.a. "Don the Beachcomber," the father of tiki culture) and Trader Vic founder Victor Bergeron lay claim to its invention. This version includes Pernod and Angostura bitters for complexity.

Ice cubes
1½ ounces dark rum, such as Myers's Plantation
1 ounce white rum
¾ ounce fresh lime juice
½ ounce orange curaçao
2 dashes of Angostura bitters
1 dash of Pernod
1 cup cracked ice
Pineapple wedge, cherry and mint sprig, for garnish

Fill a shaker with ice cubes. Add 1 ounce of the dark rum and the white rum, lime juice, curaçao, bitters and Pernod and shake well. Fill a rocks glass with cracked ice. Strain the drink into the glass and float the remaining ½ ounce of dark rum on top. Garnish with a pineapple wedge, a cherry and a mint sprig. —*Nick Fauchald*

Rhum Swizzle

TOTAL: 10 MIN
MAKES 1 DRINK

Popular in the Caribbean (and tiki bars around the world), a swizzle is an icy concoction named for the bar tool used to mix it, traditionally fashioned out of a woody stem and branches of a tropical plant. The base for this grapefruit-flavored swizzle is *rhum agricole,* a rum made from fresh sugarcane juice in French-speaking Caribbean islands, notably Martinique.

7 large mint leaves
Crushed ice
3 ounces amber *rhum agricole*
2 ounces fresh grapefruit juice
½ ounce brown sugar simple syrup (brown sugar dissolved in equal part simmering water and cooled)
⅛ ounce grenadine

In a collins glass, gently muddle the mint leaves. Fill the glass with crushed ice. Add the *rhum agricole,* grapefruit juice, brown sugar simple syrup and grenadine. Using a swizzler or bar spoon, mix the drink by spinning the handle of the spoon between your palms while moving the spoon up and down. Top the drink with more crushed ice and serve. —*Nick Fauchald*

Amberjack

TOTAL: 5 MIN
MAKES 1 DRINK

Mixologists are adding beer to their arsenal of ingredients. Jacqueline Patterson stirs Belgian apple lambic into apple vodka and Calvados for her fruity Amberjack.

Ice
1 ounce apple vodka
½ ounce Macallan amber liqueur
½ ounce Calvados
½ ounce fresh lime juice
1½ ounces apple lambic
1 thin apple slice, for garnish

Fill a shaker with ice. Add the apple vodka, Macallan, Calvados and lime juice and shake well. Strain into a chilled martini glass, stir in the lambic and garnish with the apple slice. —*Jacqueline Patterson*

Mojito Jell-O Shots with White Rum and Fresh Mint

ACTIVE: 20 MIN; TOTAL: 3 HR 30 MIN
10 SERVINGS ●●

Michael Symon (an F&W Best New Chef 1998) stirs unflavored gelatin into a mojito to create a fun, sophisticated version of the lowbrow Jell-O shot.

1 cup water
1 cup sugar
2 tablespoons plus ¾ teaspoon powdered unflavored gelatin (from 3 envelopes)
1 cup fresh lime juice
1 lightly packed cup mint leaves
1 cup white rum

1. In a small saucepan, heat the water with the sugar over moderate heat, stirring, until the water is simmering and the sugar dissolves, 4 minutes. Sprinkle the gelatin over the syrup and whisk over low heat until the gelatin has dissolved, 1 minute.
2. Put the lime juice and mint in a heat-proof bowl and pour in the sugar syrup. Let steep for 15 minutes. Stir in the rum. Strain the mixture into a large measuring cup, pressing on the mint with a spoon to extract as much liquid as possible.
3. Arrange 30 small paper cups on a rimmed baking sheet. Carefully pour the mojito Jell-O mixture into the cups and refrigerate until the shots are chilled, about 3 hours. Serve cold. —*Michael Symon*

drinks

Puente Punch

TOTAL: 5 MIN
MAKES 1 DRINK

A fantastic dessert drink, this creamy cocktail is named after the famous timbale-banging bandleader Tito Puente, who helped popularize Latin music worldwide. Manhattan mixologist Cyrus Kehyari uses aged Dominican rum to give depth to what he calls "a grown-up Orange Julius."

- 1 lime wedge
- ½ teaspoon granulated sugar, plus more for coating

Ice

- ¼ cup fresh orange juice
- 2 tablespoons sweetened condensed milk, at room temperature
- ⅛ teaspoon pure vanilla extract
- ¼ cup amber rum, preferably Brugal Añejo Dominican rum

Moisten the outer rim of a highball glass with the lime wedge and coat with granulated sugar. Fill the glass and a cocktail shaker with ice. To the shaker, add the ½ teaspoon of sugar, the orange juice, condensed milk, vanilla and rum; shake well. Strain into the prepared glass.
—*Cyrus Kehyari*

simple syrup

This syrup is one of the most universal mixers.

MAKES ABOUT 12 OUNCES

In a small saucepan, combine 1 cup water and 1 cup sugar and bring to a boil, stirring to dissolve the sugar. Remove from the heat and let cool completely.
MAKE AHEAD The syrup can be refrigerated for up to 1 month.

Sour Cherry–Yuzu Bellinis

TOTAL: 40 MIN
MAKES 10 DRINKS

- ½ pound pitted fresh or frozen sour cherries (2 cups)
- ½ cup sugar
- 4 tablespoons fresh yuzu juice or 2 tablespoons each of fresh tangerine and fresh lime juice

One 750-milliliter bottle plus 2 cups chilled brut Champagne

Ice

1. Puree the cherries in a food processor. Pass the puree through a fine strainer set over a small saucepan, pressing on the solids; you should have ½ cup of juice. Stir in the sugar and bring to a simmer over moderate heat, stirring to dissolve the sugar. Transfer to a small bowl and refrigerate until chilled, about 15 minutes.

2. In a large pitcher, combine the cherry juice with the yuzu juice. Slowly pour in the Champagne. Serve the bellinis over ice. —*Jean-Georges Vongerichten*

MAKE AHEAD The sweetened cherry-and-yuzu juice can be refrigerated, covered, for up to 2 days.

Peach–and–Lemon Verbena Bellinis

TOTAL: 20 MIN
MAKES 10 DRINKS

- 1 pound very ripe white peaches, peeled and quartered
- ½ cup fresh lemon verbena leaves
- 1 cup ice
- 2 bottles Prosecco, chilled

1. In a blender, puree the peaches until smooth. Strain the puree into a glass measuring cup; you should have 1½ cups.

2. In a cocktail shaker, muddle the lemon verbena leaves with the ice. Add the peach puree and shake well. Strain the puree into the measuring cup. Pour the peach puree into Champagne flutes, top with the Prosecco and serve right away.
—*Chris Cosentino*

Kumquat Mojitos

TOTAL: 10 MIN
MAKES 10 DRINKS

Classic mojitos are made with rum and muddled mint and limes; star chef Jean-Georges Vongerichten keeps things interesting by swapping the limes for tart kumquats and *kalamansi* concentrate, the frozen juice of the sour Asian citrus fruit. If *kalamansi* isn't available, use regular orange juice concentrate.

- 20 kumquats (½ pound), halved lengthwise
- 1 cup mint leaves

One 10-ounce can frozen *kalamansi* or orange juice concentrate, thawed

- 1¾ cups white rum
- 1 quart club soda
- 1 large lime, cut into 10 thin wedges

Ice

In a large pitcher, combine the halved kumquats and mint leaves. Using a large wooden spoon, vigorously muddle the mixture. Pour in the *kalamansi* juice concentrate, white rum and club soda and squeeze in the lime juice before adding the wedges. Fill the pitcher with ice and serve.
—*Jean-Georges Vongerichten*

Classic Caipirinha

TOTAL: 10 MIN
MAKES 1 DRINK

This delicious, deceptively potent cachaça-based cocktail is traditionally flavored with lime. In Brazil, however, guava and passion fruit are commonly used too, as is *caju,* the vanilla-scented fruit of the cashew tree.

- ½ lime, cut into 4 wedges
- 1 to 2 teaspoons sugar or Simple Syrup (see recipe at left)
- 1 cup ice
- 2 ounces cachaça

Gently muddle the lime and sugar in a cocktail shaker. Add the ice and cachaça, shake and pour the drink with ice into a large rocks glass. —*Olie Berlic*

KUMQUAT MOJITOS (LEFT) AND
SOUR CHERRY–YUZU BELLINIS

drinks

Brazilian Honeybee

ACTIVE: 10 MIN; TOTAL: 1 HR 15 MIN
MAKES 10 DRINKS ○

New York City chef Peter Hoffman keeps beehives on the roof of his apartment building in downtown Manhattan. He uses his superior honey to sweeten this excellent South American–inspired cocktail; the only additional ingredients are muddled limes, cachaça and water.

- ¾ cup honey
- ½ cup hot water
- 5 limes, cut into 8 wedges each
- 2½ cups cachaça (20 ounces), chilled

Ice

1. In a large pitcher, stir the honey and hot water until blended. Let cool, then add the lime wedges and muddle them. Refrigerate the mixture until completely chilled, about 1 hour.

2. Add the cachaça and ice to the pitcher, stir well and let stand for 30 seconds. Strain into chilled martini glasses and serve.

—*Peter Hoffman*

Fields of Gold

 TOTAL: 5 MIN
MAKES 1 DRINK ○

This version of a whiskey sour is based on one that New York City mixologist Cyrus Kehyari encountered at Manhattan's Milk & Honey bar. A citrus-based drink that pairs well with Latin food, it's designed for bourbon-lovers.

- 1 tablespoon honey
- 1½ teaspoons warm water
- 3 orange slices, quartered, plus 1 orange wheel for garnish

Ice

- 1½ tablespoons fresh lemon juice
- ¼ cup bourbon

In a cocktail shaker, stir the honey and water until the honey is dissolved. Add the orange slices and muddle. Fill the shaker with ice and add the lemon juice and bourbon. Shake well and strain into an ice-filled rocks glass. Garnish with the orange wheel.

—*Cyrus Kehyari*

Filibuster Cocktail

 TOTAL: 5 MIN
MAKES 1 DRINK ○ ●

Erik Adkins codesigned the bar list at Flora, a cocktail-minded spot in Oakland, California, where Adkins emphasizes regional spirits and clever combinations like the maple syrup and rye in his Filibuster. He's also bar manager of San Francisco's ultra-popular Vietnamese restaurant Slanted Door, where he makes his own mixers, including eight different bitters.

- 1½ ounces rye whiskey
- ¾ ounce fresh lemon juice
- ¼ ounce pure maple syrup

Dash of Angostura bitters

- 1 large egg white

Ice

- 1 lemon twist, for garnish

Fill a cocktail shaker with the rye, lemon juice, maple syrup, Angostura bitters and egg white and shake well. Add ice and shake again. Strain the drink into a chilled coupe and garnish with the lemon twist.

—*Erik Adkins*

essentials for the home bar

Just as chefs love exotic spices and rare produce, mixologists seek out obscure spirits and mixers. A bar stocked with these unusual spirits allows the amateur bartender to create ambitious cocktails at home.

Barolo Chinato This spicy wine-based digestif contains quinine, which is what gives tonic water its bitterness.

Carpano Antica Formula This sweet Italian vermouth is a more robust, full-bodied alternative to standard vermouth like Martini & Rossi.

Chartreuse V.E.P. A complex French liqueur that's aged much longer than regular Chartreuse, giving it a mellower, more integrated flavor.

Fernet-Branca Amaro Mixologists like to add this intensely flavored Italian herbal digestif to drinks in small doses, in place of bitters.

Laird's Bonded Applejack Bartenders love the intense appley flavor of this pure, 100-proof brandy.

Lucid Absinthe Now that the U.S. ban on absinthe has been relaxed, this sweet American brand will be key to a resurgence in anise-flavored cocktails.

Rhum Clémont Créole Shrubb A rum-based orange liqueur that is a more complex substitute for triple sec.

St-Germain This elderflower-based liqueur smells like spring and tastes like summer, adding a floral bouquet and tropical flavors to cocktails.

Velvet Falernum A low-alcohol sugarcane-based liqueur from Barbados flavored with lime and spices, it's great in tropical drinks like the mojito.

The Red and the Black

TOTAL: 30 MIN PLUS 4 HR CHILLING
MAKES 10 DRINKS ● ●

This strawberry and tequila cocktail is bar manager Michael Cecconi's brainchild. It's the top-selling drink during strawberry season at both of Peter Hoffman's New York City restaurants, Savoy and Back Forty. A clever black pepper–infused syrup makes it more sophisticated than most fruity cocktails.

2¼ cups sugar
2 cups warm water
½ cup coarsely cracked black pepper, plus 1 tablespoon finely ground black pepper
2 quarts strawberries, hulled and halved
2½ cups blanco tequila (20 ounces)
1¼ cups fresh lime juice (10 ounces)
1 teaspoon salt
1 lemon wedge
Ice

1. In a medium saucepan, combine 2 cups of the sugar with the warm water and bring to a boil, stirring to dissolve the sugar. Remove the saucepan from the heat, stir in the ½ cup of coarsely cracked black pepper and let cool. Cover with plastic and refrigerate for 3 hours. Pour the black pepper syrup through a fine-mesh strainer into a large measuring cup.
2. In a large pitcher, muddle the halved strawberries. Add 2¼ cups of the black pepper syrup, the tequila and fresh lime juice (reserve the remaining black pepper syrup for another cocktail). Refrigerate until chilled, about 1 hour.
3. On a small plate, mix the remaining ¼ cup of sugar with the finely ground pepper and the salt. Moisten half of the outer rims of 10 rocks glasses with the lemon wedge and coat lightly with the pepper and salt mixture. Fill the rocks glasses with ice. Stir the drink well, then pour or strain into the prepared rocks glasses and serve at once. —*Michael Cecconi*

Punto Pomelo

TOTAL: 30 MIN
MAKES 1 DRINK ●

Mixologist Cyrus Kehyari created this recipe for Socialista, a trendy Havana-themed restaurant and nightclub in Manhattan's West Village. The name of this margarita-like cocktail means "the point of grapefruit," referring to Kehyari's belief that citrus-based cocktails have an affinity for spicy food.

½ cup sugar
½ cup water
½ cinnamon stick, broken
3 whole cloves
Pinch of freshly grated nutmeg
Ice
2 tablespoons fresh lime juice
2 tablespoons fresh grapefruit juice
¼ cup silver tequila
1 cherry, for garnish (optional)

1. In a small saucepan, combine the sugar, water, cinnamon stick, cloves and nutmeg. Bring to a simmer, stirring, until the sugar is dissolved. Let cool, then strain.
2. Fill a cocktail shaker with ice. Add the lime and grapefruit juices, tequila and 2 tablespoons of the spiced simple syrup. Shake well and strain into an ice-filled collins glass. Garnish with a cherry, if desired. —*Cyrus Kehyari*

Mango-Mezcal Paloma

TOTAL: 5 MIN
MAKES 1 DRINK ●

Mixologists like Sean Beck at Houston's Backstreet Café are enamored with small-batch mezcals for the alluring smokiness they add to cocktails, as in Beck's riff on the paloma, a popular Mexican refresher.

Ice
1½ ounces mezcal
½ ounce fresh lime juice
6 ounces mango soda, preferably R.W. Knudsen (available at Whole Foods)
Small pinch of pure chile powder
1 teaspoon coarsely chopped cilantro (optional)

Fill a shaker halfway with ice. Add the mezcal, lime juice, mango soda and chile powder. Stir and strain into an ice-filled collins glass. Stir in the cilantro. —*Sean Beck*

Rosé Sangria with Cranberries and Apples

ACTIVE: 20 MIN; TOTAL: 1 HR 30 MIN
PLUS OVERNIGHT MACERATING
12 SERVINGS ● ●

This strong but not overly sweet sangria is nicely spiced with cinnamon, anise and cloves and has just enough crushed red pepper to give it a tiny kick.

1 cup water
1 cup sugar
¼ teaspoon crushed red pepper
1 large cinnamon stick
4 allspice berries
3 whole cloves
1 star anise pod
2 cups cranberries
2 Granny Smith apples, cut into ½-inch dice
One 750-milliliter bottle Spanish rosé, such as Tempranillo
⅓ cup ruby port
⅓ cup Cointreau
⅓ cup cranberry juice
Ice cubes

1. In a medium saucepan, mix the water with the sugar, crushed red pepper, cinnamon, allspice, cloves and star anise. Simmer over moderately low heat for 15 minutes. Strain the syrup into a large bowl and add the cranberries and apples. Cover and refrigerate overnight.
2. Strain the fruit, reserving the spiced syrup. In a large pitcher, mix the rosé with the port, Cointreau, cranberry juice, fruit and ¾ cup of the spiced syrup. Refrigerate until chilled, about 1 hour. Serve over ice. —*Jose Garces*

drinks

Zen Sangria

⏱ **TOTAL: 25 MIN**
4 SERVINGS ● ●

Chef Kerry Simon's Asian-style sangria combines Sauvignon Blanc with green tea–flavored vodka, but it can be made with plain or citrus vodka as well.

One 750-ml bottle dry white wine,
    such as Sauvignon Blanc
2½ cups pomegranate juice,
    chilled
2½ cups pear nectar, chilled
2½ cups apricot nectar, chilled
  1 cup green-tea vodka
    (see Note)
Ice
  1 Anjou or Bartlett pear,
    thinly sliced, for garnish

In a pitcher, combine the wine with the pomegranate juice, pear and apricot nectars and vodka; refrigerate until chilled, 20 minutes. Pour into glasses over ice, garnish with the pear slices and serve. —*Kerry Simon*

NOTE Charbay brand green-tea vodka is available at large liquor stores.

Grape Sparklers

TOTAL: 30 MIN PLUS CHILLING
MAKES 8 DRINKS ● ●

In this delightfully fizzy cocktail, New York chef-turned-winemaker David Page showcases the fruitiness of just-pressed grape juice, blending it with dry sparkling wine to keep it from tasting too sweet.

  4 pounds red grapes, stemmed
One 750-milliliter bottle dry
    sparkling wine, such as
    Prosecco, chilled
  8 mint sprigs, for garnish

1. Thinly slice 1 cup of the grapes and refrigerate. In a food processor, working in batches, pulse the remaining grapes until coarsely chopped. Transfer the chopped grapes to a saucepan and bring to a simmer. Cook until the grapes have released most of their juice, 5 minutes.

2. Working in batches, strain the grape juice into a bowl, pressing hard on the solids with the back of a spoon. You should have about 3½ cups of fresh-pressed grape juice; refrigerate the juice until it is well chilled.

3. To serve, divide the chilled sliced grapes equally among 8 Champagne flutes. Pour the chilled fresh grape juice into the flutes and top with the sparkling wine. Garnish each drink with a mint sprig and serve the Grape Sparklers immediately. —*David Page*

MAKE AHEAD The grape juice can be refrigerated for up to 2 days.

Kill-Devil Punch

TOTAL: 20 MIN PLUS 6 HR FREEZING
AND CHILLING
6 SERVINGS ● ●

Even more than most East Coast bartenders, Philip Ward is obsessed with traditional recipes, which he learns by heart, then tweaks. At New York City's Death & Co., one of the first places in the country to offer old-fashioned punch-bowl service, Ward cools his Kill-Devil Punch with a block of raspberry ice that releases berries into the bowl as it melts.

RASPBERRY ICE
 12 ounces water
 18 raspberries
PUNCH
  9 ounces amber rum
  6 ounces pineapple juice
  5 ounces Simple Syrup (p. 388)
  4 ounces fresh lime juice
  5 ounces chilled Champagne
 12 raspberries, for garnish
 12 lime wheels, for garnish

1. MAKE THE RASPBERRY ICE: Pour the water into a plastic container and arrange 18 raspberries in the container. Freeze for at least 6 hours.

2. MAKE THE PUNCH: In a pitcher, combine the rum, pineapple juice, Simple Syrup and lime juice and refrigerate until chilled, at least 1 hour.

3. Stir the chilled punch and strain it through a sieve into a medium punch bowl. Unmold the raspberry-studded ice and add it to the punch. Pour in the chilled Champagne and stir the punch once. Garnish the bowl with the fresh raspberries and lime wheels. Ladle the Kill-Devil Punch into teacups or small rocks glasses to serve. —*Philip Ward*

MAKE AHEAD The raspberry ice can be frozen for up to 1 week. The punch can be prepared through Step 2 and refrigerated overnight.

Mother's Ruin Punch

ACTIVE: 20 MIN; TOTAL: 1 HR 20 MIN
8 SERVINGS ● ●

Classicist bartenders have resurrected the centuries-old ritual of the formal punch service. Here, mixologist Philip Ward makes a potent concoction named after the old British slang for gin.

 24 sugar cubes or ½ cup
    granulated sugar
  ¾ cup chilled club soda
1½ cups gin
1½ cups fresh grapefruit juice,
    plus 3 thinly sliced grapefruit
    wheels for garnish
  ¾ cup fresh lemon juice
  ¾ cup sweet vermouth
2¼ cups chilled Champagne
    or sparkling wine
Ice

1. In a large pitcher, stir the sugar with the chilled club soda until the sugar has dissolved. Stir in the gin, grapefruit and lemon juices and sweet vermouth and refrigerate the mixture until chilled, about 1 hour.

2. Transfer the punch to a large serving bowl. Gently stir in the Champagne and float the grapefruit wheels on top. Serve right away in punch glasses over ice. —*Philip Ward*

MAKE AHEAD Mother's Ruin Punch can be prepared through Step 1 and refrigerated overnight.

KILL-DEVIL PUNCH

SHERRY COCKTAIL

STRAWBERRY-ALMOND SMOOTHIES

Brasserie Lebbe

 **TOTAL: 5 MIN**
MAKES 1 DRINK

"My mother was a pastry chef," says bar manager Neyah White of San Francisco's Nopa restaurant, "so I take a lot of cues from that part of the kitchen." This festive sparkling cocktail combines intense pear and vanilla aromas with the yeasty, bready flavors of Champagne. "It has all the elements of a pear tart," he says.

Ice

- ¾ ounce pear eau-de-vie
- ¾ Navan (see Note) or Licor 43
- ½ ounce fresh lemon juice
- 3 ounces dry Champagne

Fill a cocktail shaker with ice. Add the eau-de-vie, Navan and lemon juice. Shake vigorously for 20 seconds and strain into a flute. Top with the Champagne.
—Neyah White

NOTE Navan is a vanilla-flavored Cognac.

Thai Boxer

TOTAL: 10 MIN
MAKES 1 DRINK

Scott Beattie, a third-generation San Franciscan, maintains a 40-page, meticulously annotated cocktail and spirits list at Cyrus, a renowned restaurant in Sonoma County. His drinks rely heavily on local, sustainable ingredients, many of which are grown specifically for him by local farmers, then delivered to his door. Some of his favorite drink ingredients are herbs, like the Thai basil, mint and cilantro he muddles into his sweet and spicy Thai Boxer.

- 10 Thai basil leaves,
  plus 1 Thai basil sprig for garnish
- 10 mint leaves
- 10 cilantro leaves
- ½ ounce Simple Syrup
  (p. 388)

Ice

- 1½ ounces vanilla-spiced rum

- ½ ounce unsweetened coconut milk
- ½ ounce fresh lime juice
- 1 ounce chilled ginger beer

In a cocktail shaker, muddle the basil leaves with the mint and cilantro leaves and Simple Syrup. Add ice and the vanilla-spiced rum, coconut milk and lime juice and shake well. Strain the drink into an ice-filled highball glass and stir in the ginger beer. Garnish with the basil sprig.
—Scott Beattie

The Chancellor

TOTAL: 5 MIN
MAKES 1 DRINK

The Australian-born, fauxhawk-coiffed Sam Ross is a rock star in Manhattan mixology circles. A brilliant interpreter of venerable cocktails, he's made a signature of unsung classics like the Chancellor, a nicely dry variation on the Manhattan that combines Scotch, port and vermouth.

Ice

2 ounces single-malt Scotch

½ ounce ruby port

½ ounce dry vermouth

Dash of Peychaud's bitters

Fill a pint glass with ice. Add the remaining ingredients and stir well. Strain the drink into a chilled coupe. —*Sam Ross*

Sherry Cocktail

TOTAL: 10 MIN
MAKES 1 DRINK ●

Ice

1 ounce palo cortado or amontillado sherry

1 ounce brandy, preferably Spanish

½ ounce grenadine

¼ ounce fresh lemon juice

¼ ounce Cherry Heering or other cherry liqueur

1 orange twist, for garnish

1 brandied cherry, for garnish

Fill a cocktail shaker with ice. Add the sherry, brandy, grenadine, lemon juice and Cherry Heering and shake well. Strain into an ice-filled rocks glass. Flame the twist: Holding the twist skin side down over the drink, pinch the edges while holding a lit match underneath. Garnish the drink with the flamed twist and the cherry.
—*Junior Merino*

Babylon Sister

TOTAL: 10 MIN
MAKES 1 DRINK ●

1 lemon wedge

Unsweetened cocoa powder

Ice

1 ounce kirsch (cherry eau-de-vie)

½ ounce maraschino liqueur

¼ ounce white crème de cacao

½ ounce heavy cream

¼ ounce Simple Syrup (p. 388)

3 brandied cherries skewered on a pick, for garnish

Moisten half of the outer rim of a martini glass with the lemon wedge and coat lightly with cocoa powder. Fill a cocktail shaker with ice. Add the kirsch, maraschino liqueur, crème de cacao, heavy cream and Simple Syrup and shake well. Strain the drink into the prepared martini glass and garnish with the skewered brandied cherries. —*Jonny Raglin*

Cherry Blossom

TOTAL: 5 MIN
MAKES 1 DRINK ●

Ice

1¼ ounces rye whiskey

¾ ounce kirsch (cherry eau-de-vie)

¼ ounce crème de cacao

Dash of Angostura bitters

2 *griottine* cherries, skewered on a pick (see Note)

Fill a pint glass with ice. Add the rye, kirsch, crème de cacao and bitters and stir well. Strain into a chilled coupe and garnish with the skewered cherries.
—*Jamie Boudreau*

NOTE *Griottine* cherries are sour cherries in kirsch or syrup. They are available in supermarkets or from zingermans.com.

Strawberry-Almond Smoothie

TOTAL: 25 MIN PLUS OVERNIGHT SOAKING

1 SERVING ● ●

Although coconut water is low in sugar, it imparts a lovely sweetness to this dairy-free smoothie.

2 tablespoons raw almonds, soaked overnight and drained

1 cup coconut water

Pinch of salt

1 cup frozen strawberries

2 dried white figs, such as Calimyrna, coarsely chopped

½ teaspoon agave nectar

Pinch of cinnamon

In a blender, puree the almonds with the coconut water and salt until smooth. Strain the almond milk through a fine sieve. Rinse out the blender. Add the strawberries to the blender with the figs, agave nectar, cinnamon and the almond milk and puree. Pour into a tall glass and serve.
—*Adina Niemerow*

MAKE AHEAD The almond milk can be refrigerated for up to 3 days.

Lemonade Slushies with Mint and Lemon Verbena

ACTIVE: 10 MIN; TOTAL: 40 MIN
4 SERVINGS ● ●

Philadelphia chef Michael Solomonov was born in Ganei Yehuda, Israel, where this lemon *nana* flavored with mint and lemon verbena is a popular cooler. You don't have to serve it as a slushie; just froth the herb-infused lemonade in the blender before pouring it over ice.

1¼ cups water

½ cup plus 2 teaspoons sugar

¼ cup dried lemon verbena leaves

Zest of 2 lemons, cut into 3-inch-long strips, plus ¾ cup fresh lemon juice

½ cup mint leaves

2 cups ice

1. In a small saucepan, combine the water with the sugar and bring to a simmer over low heat, stirring until the sugar dissolves. Add the dried lemon verbena leaves and the strips of lemon zest and simmer for about 10 minutes.

2. Remove the saucepan from the heat. Stir in the lemon juice and mint and let stand at room temperature until cool. Refrigerate the lemon mixture until thoroughly chilled, about 20 minutes.

3. Strain the lemon mixture into a blender along with the ice. Blend on high speed until smooth and frothy. Pour into tall glasses and serve right away.
—*Michael Solomonov*

MAKE AHEAD The strained lemon mixture can be refrigerated for up to 3 days.

wine pairings

*F&W's deputy wine editor, **Ray Isle**, has created the ultimate user-friendly guide to pairing wine and food. The glossary here, with descriptions of key wine varieties and advice on pairing specific bottles with specific recipes, is both flexible and focused.*

champagne & sparkling wines

Champagne, which is produced only in the Champagne region of France, is the greatest sparkling wine in the world—it's effervescent and lively, at the same time offering tremendous complexity and finesse. Champagnes are usually a blend of grapes, typically Pinot Noir and Chardonnay, often with a touch of Pinot Meunier as well. They range from dry (brut) to mildly sweet (demisec) to very sweet (doux). Different producers, or "houses," have different styles, too, ranging from light and delicate to rich and full-flavored. Many other countries also make sparkling wines. Those from North America tend to be more fruit-forward than most Champagnes. Cava, an inexpensive sparkler from Spain, often has an earthy character. Italy's Prosecco is also affordable, and popular for its engaging foaminess and hint of sweetness on the finish. Sparkling wines make great aperitifs, but they're also good throughout the meal, especially with shellfish and salty or spicy dishes.

DRY, LIGHT CHAMPAGNE
Nicolas Feuillatte Brut (France)
Pierre Peters Blanc de Blancs Brut (France)
Taittinger Brut La Française (France)

PAIRINGS
- Fettuccine with Tomatoes and Crispy Capers, p. 74
- Pork with Arugula, Prosciutto and Tomatoes, p. 134
- Ginger-and-Lemon-Steamed Striped Bass, p. 183

DRY, RICH CHAMPAGNE
Bollinger Brut Special Cuvée (France)
Veuve Clicquot Brut Yellow Label (France)
Vilmart et Cie Grand Cellier (France)

PAIRINGS
- Chicken in Vinegar Sauce, p. 112
- Pork Rib Roast with Balsamic Onion Marmalade, p. 126
- Pork Braised in Champagne Vinegar, p. 131

DRY, FRUITY SPARKLING WINE
Domaine Chandon Blanc de Noirs (California)
Gloria Ferrer Sonoma Brut (California)
Mionetto Prosecco Brut (Italy)

PAIRINGS
- Triple-Tomato Penne, p. 78
- Green Jalapeño Hot Wings, p. 99
- Jerk Cornish Game Hens, p. 116
- Roasted Pork Tenderloin with Raisin-Ginger Pan Sauce, p. 134
- Pan-Roasted Salmon with Tomato Vinaigrette, p. 176
- Grappa-Cured Striped Bass, p. 185

DRY, EARTHY SPARKLING WINE
Gramona Gran Cuvee (Spain)
Jaume Serra Cristalino Brut NV (Spain)
Segura Viudas Brut Reserva (Spain)

PAIRINGS
- Shrimp and Noodle Salad with Ginger Dressing, p. 88
- Pop-Open Clams with Horseradish-Tabasco Sauce, p. 209
- Lager-Steamed Mussels with Mustard, Kielbasa and Dill, p. 211

whites

ALBARIÑO & VINHO VERDE

The Albariño grape produces Spain's best white wines, fresh, lively bottlings that pair especially well with seafood—no surprise, as Albariño is grown in Galicia, where the fishing industry drives the economy. Mostly made in

wine pairings

stainless steel tanks without oak, Albariño has crisp flavors that suggest grapefruit and other citrus fruits, with a light mineral edge. Vinho Verde, or "green wine," from northern Portugal, often blends the Albariño grape (called Alvarinho there) with local varieties Loureiro and Trajadura. Bottled so young that it often has a lightly spritzy quality, Vinho Verde has a razor-sharp acidity and ocean freshness; it too is an ideal match for raw shellfish.

ZESTY, FRESH ALBARIÑO/VINHO VERDE

Casal Garcia Vinho Verde (Portugal)
Do Ferreiro Albariño (Spain)
Vionta Albariño (Spain)

PAIRINGS

- Halibut with Grilled Ratatouille, p. 179
- Pan-Seared Cod with Preserved-Lemon Aioli, p. 187
- Ginger-Garlic Shrimp with Tangy Tomato Sauce, p. 199
- Gwyneth's Clams, p. 209
- Thai Seafood Noodle Salad, p. 212

WHITE BURGUNDY & CHARDONNAY

Chardonnay is grown in almost every wine-producing country in the world, and it's used to create wines in a wide range of styles. It is originally from France's Burgundy region, where the best white Burgundies are powerful and rich, with complex fruit flavors and notes of earth and minerals. More affordable Chardonnays from Burgundy—for instance, those simply labeled Bourgogne Blanc—are crisp and lively, with apple and lemon flavors. Chardonnays from America, Australia and Chile tend to be ripe and full-bodied, even buttery, with higher alcohol levels and vanilla notes from oak aging. Recently, however, more and more wine regions have been experimenting with fruity, fresh Chardonnays produced with very little or even no oak aging. Pair Chardonnays in the leaner Burgundian style with roasted chicken or seafood; the more voluptuous New World Chardonnays pair well with pasta dishes made with cream or cheese, with lobster or other rich seafood and with Asian dishes that include coconut milk.

LIGHT, CRISP WHITE BURGUNDY

Domaine Laroche Petit Chablis (France)
Louis Latour Mâcon-Lugny (France)
Olivier Leflaive Bourgogne Blanc Les Sétilles (France)

PAIRINGS

- Herb-and-Lemon-Roasted Chicken, p. 97
- Chicken with White Wine and Crème Fraîche, p. 114
- Apricot-Glazed Turkey with Fresh Herb Gravy, p. 117
- Octopus Salad with Potatoes and Green Beans, p. 213

RICH, COMPLEX WHITE BURGUNDY

Domaine Bouchard Père & Fils Beaune du Château Premier Cru (France)
Joseph Drouhin Beaune Clos des Mouches Blanc Premier Cru (France)
Lucien Le Moine Bourgogne Blanc (France)

PAIRINGS

- Veal Chops with Cognac Sauce, p. 140
- Swordfish Sicilian-Style, p. 180
- Seared Cod with Spicy Mussel Aioli, p. 186
- Skate with Mushrooms and Hazelnuts, p. 190
- Vineyard Sea Grill, p. 216

FRUITY, LOW-OAK CHARDONNAY

Foxglove Edna Valley (California)
Kim Crawford Marlborough Unoaked (New Zealand)
Morgan Metallico (California)

PAIRINGS

- Quick-Roasted Chicken with Mustard and Garlic, p. 92
- Chicken Hot Pot with Mushrooms and Tofu, p. 112
- Pan-Fried Salmon with Citrus Vinaigrette, p. 176
- Barramundi with Tomato-Basil Salsa, p. 192
- Cornmeal-Fried Trout with Grapefruit and Fried Sage, p. 192
- Stir-Fried Shrimp with Bacon, Mint and Chiles, p. 200
- Roasted Lobsters with Verjus and Tarragon, p. 203
- Fusilli with Shrimp and Grated Pressed Caviar, p. 217

RIPE, LUXURIOUS CHARDONNAY

Beringer Napa Valley (California)
Hess Monterey (California)
Rosemount Estate Show Reserve Hunter Valley (Australia)

PAIRINGS

- Pasta with Cauliflower, Peppers and Walnut Pesto, p. 77
- Marja's Mac and Cheese, p. 87
- Spicy Roast Chicken, p. 92
- Roasted Chicken Legs with Potatoes and Kale, p. 100
- Chicken Goulash with Biscuit Dumplings, p. 111
- Chicken-and-Sausage Gumbo, p. 114

- Fish Tacos with Creamy Lime Guacamole and Cabbage Slaw, p. 186
- Chile-Lime Crab Salad with Tomato and Avocado, p. 204
- Grilled Scallops with Mexican Corn Salad, p. 206

CHENIN BLANC

Chenin Blanc is the star of France's Loire region, where it's used for complex Vouvrays and Savennières. Chenin has also proved to be at home in parts of California (particularly the little-known Clarksburg region), in Washington State and in South Africa, which produces some of the best-value white wines around—tart, medium-bodied whites with flavors of apple and peach. The more affordable South African, Californian and Washington versions are good with light fish or simple poultry dishes.

FRUITY, SOFT CHENIN BLANC
Hogue (Washington State)
Indaba (South Africa)
Man Vintners (South Africa)

PAIRINGS
- Moroccan Roasted Chicken, p. 97
- Clams with Black Bean Sauce, p. 208
- Mussels with Crème Fraîche and Jalapeños, p. 211

COMPLEX, AROMATIC CHENIN BLANC
Champalou Vouvray (France)
Domaine des Baumard Clos du Papillon (France)

PAIRINGS
- Cumin-Scented Duck with Peach Succotash, p. 120
- Pan-Seared Sausages with Apples, p. 137

GEWÜRZTRAMINER

One of the most easily identifiable grapes—the flamboy-ant aroma recalls roses, lychee nuts and spices such as clove and allspice—Gewürztraminer reaches its peak in France's Alsace region, producing full-bodied wines ranging from dry to quite sweet, with flavors of apricot, apple and baking spices. Gewürztraminer pairs well with Alsace cuisine—a tarte flambée made with ham and Gruyère, for instance. American Gewürztraminers tend to be less dense and unctuous, though they typi-cally have a touch of sweetness on the finish and a delicate spiciness. Pair them with Asian food.

RICH ALSACE GEWÜRZTRAMINER
Hugel (France)
Trimbach (France)

PAIRINGS
- Duck with Miso-Almond Butter, p. 121
- Halibut with Pork-and-Peanut Ragù, p. 179
- Black Cod with Miso, p. 189
- Grilled Sour Cream–Marinated Shrimp, p. 196

SPICY AMERICAN GEWÜRZTRAMINER
Navarro Vineyards (California)
Thomas Fogarty Monterey (California)

PAIRINGS
- Green Chicken Masala, p. 111
- Indian Coconut Fish Curry, p. 176
- Seared Scallops with Bacon-Braised Chard, p. 206

GRÜNER VELTLINER

Grüner Veltliner, from Austria, has become a darling of American sommeliers, after decades of near obscurity in the United States. A refreshing, medium-bodied, pep-pery white wine with stone fruit flavors, it goes with everything from green salads to cold poached salmon to roasted chicken. The best Grüners can be expensive and have enormous aging potential.

PEPPERY, REFRESHING GRÜNER VELTLINER
Bründlmayer Kamptaler Terassen (Austria)
Domäne Wachau (Austria)

PAIRINGS
- Tangy Roasted Chicken with Artichoke Panzanella, p. 94
- Coconut-Rice Crêpes Filled with Pork, p. 136
- Crispy Shrimp with Noodle and Bean Sprout Salad, p. 200

PINOT BIANCO & PINOT BLANC

These are two names for the same grape; the first one is Italian and the second French. The French versions, from Alsace, are musky and creamy-textured; those from Italy have zippier acidity, with pear or soft citrus flavors. American Pinot Blancs are usually made in the French style. Pour Pinot Blancs with cheese-based dishes; Pinot Biancos go nicely with light foods like chicken breasts or flaky white fish.

ZIPPY, FRESH PINOT BIANCO
Abbazia di Novacella (Italy)
St. Michael-Eppan (Italy)

wine pairings

PAIRINGS
- Farfalle with Tomatoes and Green Vegetables, p. 76
- Pasta with Sausage, Basil and Mustard, p. 81
- Pasta with Artichokes and Rouget, p. 82

CREAMY, SUPPLE PINOT BLANC

Chalone Vineyard (California)

Hugel & Fils (France)

PAIRINGS
- Crunchy Fish Sticks with Tartar Sauce, p. 189
- Shrimp-and-Poblano Salad with Tortillas, p. 197

PINOT GRIGIO & PINOT GRIS

Pinot Grigio (from Italy) and Pinot Gris (from France's Alsace) are the same grape variety. Italian Pinots (and others modeled on them) tend to be light, simple wines with suggestions of peach and melon. These crisp, fresh whites are ideal as an aperitif or with light seafood or chicken breast dishes. Bottlings from Alsace are richer, with strong notes of almonds, spice and sometimes honey. American versions, mainly from Oregon, often tend more toward the Alsace style, and thus are mostly labeled Pinot Gris. They go well with creamy pastas or smoked foods.

LIGHT, FRESH PINOT GRIGIO

Marco Felluga (Italy)

Meridian (California)

Tiefenbrunner (Italy)

PAIRINGS
- Linguine with Littleneck Clams and Genoa Salami, p. 82
- Pan-Fried Smoked-Trout Cakes with Lemony Salad, p. 193
- Creole Shrimp with Garlic and Lemon, p. 200

FULL-BODIED, RICH PINOT GRIS

Domaines Schlumberger Les Princes Abbés (France)

Domaine Weinbach (France)

King Estate (Oregon)

MacMurray Ranch (California)

PAIRINGS
- Mexican Chicken Pozole Verde, p. 108
- Grilled Shrimp with Mangoes and Chile, p. 197
- Curry Crab Rundown, p. 204

RIESLING

Riesling is one of the great white grape varieties, and the style of the wines it produces varies dramatically by region. German Rieslings balance impressive acidity with apple and citrus fruit flavors, and range from dry and refreshing to sweet and unctuous. Alsace and Austrian Rieslings are higher in alcohol, which makes them more full-bodied, but they are quite dry, full of mineral notes. Australia's Rieslings (the best are from the Clare Valley) are zippy and full of lime and other citrus flavors. Those from Washington State tend to split the difference, offering juicy, appley fruit and lively acidity, with a hint of sweetness. Rieslings are extraordinarily versatile with food. As a general rule, pair lighter, crisper Rieslings with delicate (or raw) fish; more substantial Rieslings are good with Asian food, chicken, salmon and tuna.

TART, CITRUSY RIESLING

Banrock Station (Australia)

Leasingham Magnus (Australia)

Penfolds Eden Valley Reserve (Australia)

PAIRINGS
- Asian Chicken Salad with Wasabi Dressing, p. 104
- Cider-Brined Double-Cut Pork Chops, p. 128
- Lemongrass-Marinated Pompano, p. 189

VIVID, LIGHTLY SWEET RIESLING

Columbia Winery Cellarmaster's (Washington State)

J. Lohr Estates Bay Mist (California)

Weingut Selbach-Oster Estate (Germany)

PAIRINGS
- Ginger-Roasted Chicken, p. 97
- Red Curry Chicken Kebabs with Minty Yogurt Sauce, p. 101
- Smoky-Hot Ginger Chicken Stir-Fry, p. 104
- Caramelized Black Pepper Chicken, p. 111
- Smoked Ham with Apple-Riesling Sauce, p. 133
- Lemongrass Pork with Pickled Carrots, p. 135
- Fish Fry with Ramp Aioli, p. 182
- Spiced Catfish with Avocado, p. 185
- Grilled Trout with Grilled Romaine Salad, p. 193
- Sake-Steamed Mussels with Ginger, Miso and Spinach, p. 211

FULL-BODIED, MINERALLY RIESLING

Domaine Marc Kreydenweiss Andlau (France)

Dr. Konstantin Frank (New York State)

Hiedler Heiligenstein (Austria)

- Vietnamese Glazed Skinny Pork Chops, p. 128
- Sautéed Trout with Citrus-Olive Relish, p. 192
- Lobster BLTs, p. 204

SAUVIGNON BLANC

Sauvignon's herbal scent and tart, citrus-driven flavors make it instantly identifiable. The best regions for Sauvignon are the Loire Valley in France, where it takes on a firm, minerally depth; New Zealand, where it recalls the tartness of gooseberries and, sometimes, an almost green, jalapeño-like note; California, where it pairs crisp grassiness and a melon-like flavor; and South Africa, particularly the Cape region, where it combines the minerality of France with the rounder fruit of California. Sauvignon Blanc teams well with light fish, shellfish, salads and green vegetables, and it's a perfect aperitif, too.

LIVELY, TART SAUVIGNON BLANC
Franciscan (California)
Geyser Peak Winery (California)
Honig (California)

PAIRINGS
- Spaghetti with Spinach, Tomatoes and Goat Cheese, p. 75
- Sea Bass Fillets with Parsley Sauce, p. 181
- Steamed Sea Bass with Caper Bread Crumbs, p. 182
- Shrimp-and-Avocado Salad with Mango Dressing, p. 196
- Jumbo Shrimp with Mushrooms and Garlic, p. 198
- Sauvignon Blanc–Steamed Mussels with Garlic Toasts, p. 211

MINERALLY, COMPLEX SAUVIGNON BLANC
Château de Sancerre Sancerre (France)
Concha y Toro Terrunyo (Chile)
Craggy Range Winery (New Zealand)

PAIRINGS
- Angel Hair Pasta with Red Pepper Pesto and Basil, p. 78
- White Bean and Chicken Soup, p. 115
- Halibut with Parsley-Lemon Sauce, p. 179
- Roasted Sea Bass with Potatoes, Olives and Tomatoes, p. 180
- Mussels with Speck, Lemon and Oregano, p. 208

SOAVE, VERDICCHIO & GAVI

These three light, usually inexpensive wines from Italy all match well with a wide range of foods. Soave, mostly made from the Garganega grape, is a fruity white that often has an almond note. Verdicchio, made from the grape of the same name, has a lemony zestiness. Gavi, made from a grape called Cortese, is typically tart, with an aroma that suggests fresh limes. All three wines pair well with herby pasta sauces like pesto, white fish or fresh vegetable dishes.

FRESH, LIVELY SOAVE OR SIMILAR ITALIAN WHITE
Banfi Principessa Gavi (Italy)
Pieropan Soave Classico (Italy)
Villa Bucci Verdicchio (Italy)

PAIRINGS
- Farfalle with Zucchini and Parsley-Almond Pesto, p. 74
- Pasta Salad with Tomatoes, Arugula, Pine Nuts and Herb Dressing, p. 76
- Chicken with Garlicky Crumbs and Snap Peas, p. 98
- Grilled Mackerel with Cauliflower "Tabbouleh," p. 190
- Lobster and Fennel Salad, p. 203
- Ligurian Seafood Soup, p. 212

VERMENTINO

An up-and-coming white grape from the coastal regions of Italy, Vermentino marries vivacious acidity with stony minerality. The best Vermentinos come from very different parts of Italy—from Liguria in the north and from the island of Sardinia, off the central west coast. Drink Vermentino with seafood dishes of all kinds.

FRESH, MINERALLY VERMENTINO
Antinori (Italy)
Argiolas Costamolino (Italy)
Sella & Mosca La Cala (Italy)

PAIRINGS
- Farfalle with Yogurt and Zucchini, p. 76
- Steamed Red Snapper Packets, p. 183
- Roasted Branzino with Caper Butter, p. 190
- Mango Shrimp, p. 199
- Scallops with Roasted Cauliflower and Raisins, p. 206
- Warm Seafood Salad with Pistachios and Capers, p. 213

wine pairings

VIOGNIER

Viogniers are seductive white wines, lush with peach and honeysuckle scents, a round, mouth-filling texture and little acidity. The Condrieu region in France's Rhône Valley produces the world's greatest Viogniers, and they can often be quite expensive; California and occasionally Australia have also had success with this grape. Viognier pairs well with grilled seafood; it's also a good match for most foods flavored with fruit salsas.

LUSH, FRAGRANT VIOGNIER
Alban Vineyards (California)
Cave Yves Cuilleron Condrieu (France)
Cono Sur (Chile)

PAIRINGS
- Chicken Breasts with Apricot-Onion Pan Sauce, p. 94
- Creamy Indian Spiced Halibut Curry, p. 178
- Garlic Shrimp with Polenta, p. 198
- Bouillabaisse, p. 214

rosés

Rosé—that is, dry rosé—may be the world's most under-rated wine. Combining the light, lively freshness of white wines with the fruit and depth of reds, good rosés pair well with a remarkable range of foods, from delicate fish like sole to meats such as pork and veal. They also complement a range of ethnic cuisines—Chinese, Thai, Mexican and Greek. The best rosés, from southern France, are typically blends of grapes such as Syrah, Grenache, Cinsaut and Mourvèdre. Italy, Greece and Spain also produce terrific, refreshing rosés. American and Australian rosés, which tend to be fruitier and heavier, can also be very good.

FRESH, FRUITY ROSÉ
Crios de Susana Balbo (Argentina)
La Bargemone (France)
Muga (Spain)

PAIRINGS
- Chinese Noodles with Cockles and Pork, p. 89
- Red Curry Peanut Noodles, p. 89
- Curry-Roasted Chicken, p. 97
- Herb-Grilled Chicken with Goat Cheese Ravioli, p. 99
- Chicken with Piquillos, p. 101
- Olive-Brined Chicken with Grilled Onions and Paprika Oil, p. 102

- Skillet Chicken-and-Mushroom Potpie, p. 114
- Pan-Seared Skirt Steaks with Anchovies and Lime, p. 149
- Grilled Tuna with Tomato-Cilantro Salsa, p. 174
- Salmon with Oyster Mushrooms and Peppers, p. 174
- Red Snapper with Zucchini and Black Olive Tapenade, p. 185
- Chipotle Shrimp Tostadas, p. 198
- Baja Fried-Shrimp Tacos, p. 203
- Seared Scallops with Beet Salad and Horseradish Cream, p. 209
- Shrimp-and-Crab Gumbo, p. 216

reds

BARBERA

Barbera, which grows primarily in Italy's Piedmont region, mostly produces medium-bodied wines with firm acidity and flavors suggesting red cherries with a touch of spice. (Barrel-aged versions tend to be more full-bodied, and more expensive.) A great wine for pastas with meat- or tomato-based sauces, Barbera is also good with game and hard cheeses.

BRIGHT, TART BARBERA
Coppo Camp du Rouss Barbera d'Asti (Italy)
Michele Chiarlo Barbera d'Asti (Italy)
Renwood Barbera Sierra Series (California)

PAIRINGS
- Creamy Pasta with Tomato Confit and Goat Cheese, p. 75
- Pappardelle with Porcini and Pistachios, p. 81
- Grilled-Chicken Banh Mi, p. 106
- Roast Squabs with Bacon and Grapes, p. 117
- Fontina-Stuffed Veal Meatballs, p. 138
- Osso Buco with Citrus Gremolata, p. 141
- Crosshatch Hot Dogs on Grilled Croissants, p. 168
- Pan-Seared Tuna Steaks with Capers and Oregano, p. 175

BEAUJOLAIS & GAMAY

Gamay, the grape of France's Beaujolais region, makes wines that embody everything that region is known for: light, fruity, easy-to-drink reds, ideal for a party or a picnic. Typically they are not aged in oak barrels and are released early (Beaujolais Nouveau, which appears on shelves little more than a month after the grapes are harvested, is the extreme example). Little Gamay is grown outside of Beaujolais, but what has been planted pairs well with the same foods as Beaujolais: light chicken dishes, salads, cheeses and charcuterie.

FRUITY, LIGHT-BODIED BEAUJOLAIS/GAMAY
Georges Duboeuf Beaujolais-Villages (France)
Jean-Paul Brun Terres Dorees (France)
Marcel Lapierre Morgon (France)

PAIRINGS
- Mushroom-and-Goat-Cheese-Stuffed Chicken Thighs, p. 98
- Circassian Chicken Salad, p. 105
- Veal Scallopine with Charred Cherry Tomato Salad, p. 140
- Cambozola Cheeseburgers with Herbed Fries, p. 171
- Grilled Salmon with Dill Pickle Butter, p. 175

CABERNET SAUVIGNON
Arguably the most significant red wine grape, Cabernet Sauvignon has traveled far beyond its origins in France's Bordeaux—it's now widely planted in almost every wine-producing country. Depending on climate, Cabernet can make either firm, tannic wines that recall red currants with a touch of tobacco or green bell pepper (colder climates) or softer wines that recall ripe black currants or black cherries (warmer climates). It almost always has substantial tannins, which help great Cabernets age for many years. The classic pairing with Cabernet is lamb, but it goes well with almost any meat—beef, pork, venison, even rabbit.

FIRM, COMPLEX CABERNET SAUVIGNON
Château de Pez (France)
St. Clement Napa Valley (California)
Wynns Coonawarra (Australia)

PAIRINGS
- Roast Duck with Citrus Pan Sauce, p. 120
- Beef Tenderloin Steaks with Celery Root Gratin, p. 144
- Hanger Steaks with Bourbon and Green Peppercorn Sauce, p. 149
- Oven-Roasted Lamb Chops with Mint Chimichurri, p. 159

RICH, RIPE CABERNET SAUVIGNON
Justin Vineyards & Winery (California)
Layer Cake Napa Valley (California)
Paringa (Australia)

PAIRINGS
- Meat Loaf with Red Wine Glaze, p. 138
- Curry-Glazed Beef Tenderloins, p. 145
- Grilled Skirt Steak with Fregola-Orange Salad, p. 147
- Classic Pot Roast, p. 157
- Moroccan Spiced Lamb with Date Barbecue Sauce, p. 163

DOLCETTO
Though Dolcetto means "little sweet one," wines from this Italian grape are dry, grapey, tart, simple reds distinguished by their vibrant purple color and ebullient berry juiciness. Dolcettos should be drunk young, with antipasti, pastas with meat sauces or roasted poultry of any kind.

JUICY, FRESH DOLCETTO
Massolino Dolcetto d'Alba (Italy)
Parusso Dolcetto d'Alba Piani Noce (Italy)
Vietti Dolcetto d'Alba Tre Vigne (Italy)

PAIRINGS
- Smoky Pork Pappardelle, p. 84
- Celery Root and Mushroom Lasagna, p. 87
- Pretzel-Crusted Chicken, p. 98
- Steak, Chicken and Vegetable Tacos, p. 146
- Sweet Onions Stuffed with Spiced Lamb, p. 166

GRENACHE
When made well, Grenache produces full-bodied, high-alcohol red wines that tend to be low in acidity and full of black cherry and raspberry flavors. Grenache is often blended with other grapes to make dark, powerful reds in regions such as France's Châteauneuf-du-Pape or Spain's Rioja and Priorato. On its own in Australia and the United States, it can produce deeply fruity, juicy wines that go perfectly with grilled meats, sausages and highly spiced dishes.

JUICY, SPICY GRENACHE
Beckmen Vineyards Estate (California)
Bodegas Zabrin Garnacha de Fuego (Spain)
Yalumba Bush Vine (Australia)

PAIRINGS
- Smoky Bacon-Roasted Chicken, p. 93
- Garlic-and-Spice-Rubbed Pork Loin Roast, p. 124
- Honey-Tamarind Baby Back Ribs, p. 129
- Flank Steak with Tamarind Glaze and Orange Gremolata, p. 150

global wine pairings

Classic Dish	Best Pairing	Perfect Wine

china

Clams with Black Bean Sauce (p. 208)	*Unoaked, fruity white blend*	2007 Tablas Creek Côtes de Tablas Blanc
Moo Shu Pork	*Lively, low-tannin Dolcetto d'Alba*	2007 Pio Cesare
Peking Duck	*Silky, cherry-inflected Pinot Noir*	2005 Truchard Napa Valley

cuba

Chicken with Rice	*Earthy, oaky Rioja*	2004 Ramón Bilbao Crianza
Cubano Sandwiches (p. 281)	*Smoky, ripe Malbec*	2006 Navarro Correas Colección Privada
Pernil (Slow-Roasted Pork)	*Spicy, curranty Carmenère*	2007 Calina Reserva

india

Coconut Fish Curry (p. 176)	*Spicy, full-bodied Gewürztraminer*	2007 Thomas Fogarty
Lamb Curry	*Ripe, berry-rich Zinfandel*	2005 Clos du Bois North Coast
Tandoori Chicken	*Medium-bodied, fruity French Grenache*	2004 Ey Vigne Las Collas

japan

Beef-and-Scallion Rolls (p. 22)	*Earthy, aromatic French white*	2006 Château d'Epiré Savennières Speciale
Sashimi	*Light, vibrant Torrontés*	2007 Michel Torino Don David
Sukiyaki	*Light-bodied, fragrant Pinot Noir*	2006 Vincent Girardin Bourgogne Rouge

mexico

Chicken Pozole Verde (p. 108)	*Rich, peach-inflected Pinot Gris*	2005 Gustave Lorentz Réserve
Pork in Adobo Sauce	*Dark-fruited, spicy Petite Sirah*	2004 Parducci
Ceviche	*Citrusy, unoaked Sauvignon Blanc*	2008 Babich

morocco

B'steeya (Shredded-Chicken Pie)	*Off-dry French Vouvray*	2007 François Pinon Cuvée Tradition
Lamb-and-Vegetable Couscous (p. 165)	*Plummy, spicy California Merlot*	2006 Blackstone
Lamb Tagine	*Spicy, powerful Syrah*	2007 Porcupine Ridge

russia

Caviar with Blinis	*Crisp, complex brut Champagne*	NV Pol Roger Brut Réserve
Chilled Borscht (p. 69)	*Berry-scented, crisp rosé*	2007 Mas de Gourgonnier
Shashlik (Marinated Lamb Kebabs)	*Soft, raspberry-rich Spanish Grenache*	2006 Las Rocas de San Alejandro

thailand

Chicken with Basil	*Light, crisply fruity Beaujolais*	2007 Clos de la Roilette Fleurie
Pad Thai	*Tart, lightly sweet German Riesling*	2006 Urban
Seafood Noodle Salad (p. 212)	*Crisp, minerally Spanish Albariño*	2007 Bodegas Fillaboa

- Braised Beef Short Ribs with Spices, p. 152
- Slow-Braised Short Ribs with Spinach, p. 152
- Herb-and-Spice Lamb Chops with Asparagus, p. 160
- Merguez-Spiced Lamb Shanks with Chickpeas, p. 160
- Lamb Sausage with Lentils and Sautéed Pears, p. 166
- Seared Cod with Provençal Vegetables, p. 186
- Seafood Paella, p. 214

MALBEC

Originally used as a blending grape in France's Bordeaux region, Malbec has found its true home in Argentina's Mendoza region. There, it produces darkly fruity wines with hints of black pepper and leather—like a traditional rustic country red, but with riper, fuller fruit. Malbecs are often very affordable, too, and go wonderfully with steaks and roasts, hearty stews and grilled sausages.

RUSTIC, PEPPERY MALBEC
Bodega Norton (Argentina)
Catena Zapata (Argentina)
Weinert (Argentina)

PAIRINGS
- Curry-and-Yogurt-Braised Chicken Thighs, p. 94
- Green Chile–Chicken and Pink Bean Stew, p. 116
- Asian Glazed Baby Back Ribs, p. 128
- Pork Cheek and Black-Eyed Pea Chili, p. 132
- Yucatán Pork Stew with Ancho Chiles and Lime Juice, p. 133
- Mexican Spice-Rubbed Rib Eyes with Lime Butter, p. 144
- Grilled Strip Steak with Warm Shallot Vinaigrette, p. 145
- Skirt Steak with Creamed Corn and Poblanos, p. 147
- Skirt Steak with Salsa Verde and Ricotta Salata, p. 148
- Skirt Steak with Salsa Verde, p. 149
- Japanese-Inspired Pot Roast, p. 157
- Beef-and-Lamb Cheddar Burgers with Caper Remoulade, p. 168

MERLOT

The most widely planted grape in France's Bordeaux region isn't Cabernet Sauvignon; it's Merlot. That's because Merlot blends so well with other grapes, and also because Merlot's gentle succulence and plummy flavors have gained favor as worldwide tastes have shifted toward fruitier, easier-drinking wines. Good Merlots are made in France, Italy, Chile, the United States and Australia, and all of them tend to share supple, velvety tannins and round black cherry or plum flavors. Merlot pairs beautifully with many foods—try it with pâtés or other charcuterie, pork or veal roasts, rich, cheesy gratins and even hamburgers.

LIVELY, FRUITY MERLOT
Columbia Crest Grand Estates (Washington State)
Francis Coppola Diamond Collection (California)
Hardys Stamp of Australia (Australia)

PAIRINGS
- Roast Chicken with Bread Salad, p. 93
- Chicken Salad with Blue Cheese and Grapes, p. 105
- Chipotle Chicken Burritos, p. 107
- Quick Chicken-and-Cheese Tamales, p. 107
- Red Chile–Chicken Enchiladas, p. 116
- Moroccan Lamb-and-Vegetable Couscous, p. 165

DEEP, VELVETY MERLOT
Avignonesi Desiderio (Italy)
L'Ecole No 41 (Washington State)
Paloma (California)

PAIRINGS
- Juniper-Brined Double-Cut Pork Chops, p. 126
- Grilled Beef Tenderloin with Ancho-Jalapeño Butter, p. 145
- Merlot-Braised Lamb Shoulder with Lemon Gremolata, p. 158
- Pot-Roasted Lamb Shanks with Cannellini Beans, p. 160

NEBBIOLO, BAROLO & BARBARESCO

Nebbiolo is the greatest grape of Italy's Piedmont. And if you ask a farmer, it is unquestionably one of the most difficult to grow. Certainly it is formidable, with fierce tannins and acidity, but it is also gloriously scented— "tar and roses" is the classic description—and has a supple, evocative flavor that lingers on the tongue. Those flavors are more substantial and emphatic in Barolos and more delicate and filigreed in Barbarescos, the two primary wines from Piedmont. Pour good Nebbiolo with foods such as braised short ribs, beef roasts, bollito misto and anything that involves truffles.

COMPLEX, AROMATIC NEBBIOLO
Pio Cesare Barolo (Italy)
Produttori del Barbaresco Barbaresco (Italy)
Prunotto Barolo (Italy)

wine pairings

PAIRINGS
- Baked Orecchiette with Pork Sugo, p. 86
- Citrus-Marinated Pork Rib Roast, p. 124
- Neapolitan Meat Loaf with Pine Nuts and Raisins, p. 167
- Seared Bison Strip Loin with Juniper and Fennel, p. 170

PINOT NOIR & RED BURGUNDY

Pinot Noir probably inspires more rhapsodies—and disappointments—among wine lovers than any other grape. When it's good, it's ethereally aromatic, with flavors ranging from ripe red berries to sweet black cherries, and tannins that are firm but never obtrusive. (When bad, unfortunately, the wine is acidic, raspy and bland.) The greatest Pinot Noirs come from France's Burgundy region, age-worthy wines that are usually quite expensive. More affordable and typically more fruit-forward Pinots can be found from California and Oregon as well as New Zealand, Chile and Australia. Pinot Noir pairs well with a wide range of foods—fruitier versions make a great match with salmon or other fatty fish, roasted chicken or pasta dishes; bigger, more tannic Pinot Noirs are ideal with duck and other game birds, casseroles or stews such as beef bourguignon.

RIPE, JUICY PINOT NOIR
A to Z (Oregon)
Au Bon Climat Santa Barbara County (California)
DeLoach Russian River Valley (California)

PAIRINGS
- Buttermilk Chicken with Crispy Cornflakes, p. 101
- Braised Chicken with Olives and Sweet Peppers, p. 110
- Honey-Glazed Duck with Savoy Cabbage, p. 121
- Stir-Fried Five-Spice Pork with Lettuce Cups, p. 134
- Skillet-Roasted Lamb Loins with Herbs, p. 158
- Salmon in Tomato-Olive Sauce, p. 178
- Sesame-and-Curry-Crusted Salmon, p. 178
- Striped Bass with Caramelized Brussels Sprouts, p. 182
- Barbecued Shrimp with Cheese Grits, p. 200

COMPLEX, ELEGANT PINOT NOIR
Faiveley Nuits-St-Georges (France)
Palliser Estate (New Zealand)
Scherrer (California)

PAIRINGS
- Chicken Tikka, p. 112
- Asian Pork, Mushroom and Noodle Stir-Fry, p. 136
- Smoky Tomato-Braised Veal Shoulder with Potatoes, p. 140

- Roasted Veal Chops with Grapes, p. 141
- Grilled Tuna with Smoked-Almond Romesco Sauce, p. 175
- Oven-Steamed Sea Bass with Wild Mushrooms, p. 180

RIOJA & TEMPRANILLO

Tempranillo, the top red grape of Spain, is best known as the main component in red Rioja, where it contributes earthy cherry flavors and firm structure. It is also used in almost every other region of Spain, and generally produces medium-bodied, firm reds suitable for meat dishes of all kinds, particularly lamb.

EARTHY, MEDIUM-BODIED TEMPRANILLO
Bodegas Montecillo Reserva (Spain)
Contino Reserva (Spain)
Marqués de Cáceres Crianza (Spain)

PAIRINGS
- Sautéed Chicken with Olives and Roasted Lemons, p. 109
- Citrus-Marinated Turkey, p. 119
- Fried Pork Rolls with Ham, p. 133
- Braised Short Ribs, p. 150
- Grilled Herbed Baby Lamb Chops, p. 159
- Lamb Chops with Harissa-Yogurt Sauce, p. 162

SANGIOVESE

Sangiovese is primarily known for the principal role it plays in Tuscan wines such as Chianti, Brunello and Carmignano, though these days it is also being grown in the United States and Australia. Italian Sangioveses have vibrant acidity and substantial tannins, along with fresh cherry fruit and herbal scents. New World versions tend toward softer acidity and fleshier fruit. Pair Sangioveses with rare steaks, game birds (or wild boar), rich chicken or mushroom dishes or anything with tomato sauce.

CHERRY-INFLECTED, EARTHY SANGIOVESE
Castello Banfi Col di Sasso (Italy)
Castello di Monsanto Chianti Classico Riserva (Italy)
Di Majo Norante (Italy)

PAIRINGS
- Crespelle with Ricotta and Marinara, p. 79
- Parmigiano-Crusted Rigatoni with Cauliflower, p. 81
- Pasta with Rosemary and Onion-Orange Marmalade, p. 82
- Spaghetti with Rich Meat Ragù, p. 86
- Spicy Chicken Cacciatore, p. 110
- Cream-and-Lemon-Braised Pork Shoulder, p. 129
- Goat Chili with Eye of the Goat Beans, p. 171

SYRAH & SHIRAZ

Probably no other grape scores higher on the intensity meter than Syrah. It's the marquee grape of France's Rhône Valley, where it makes full-bodied, smoky, powerful reds with hints of black pepper. It has also become the signature grape of Australia, where it's known as Shiraz, and typically produces fruitier, less tannic wines marked by sweet blackberry flavors and occasionally fresh espresso notes. American Syrahs lean more toward the Australian mold, thanks to California's similarly moderate weather; there are a few very good, earthy Syrahs coming from South Africa, too, particularly from the Stellenbosch subregion. Barbecued foods with a smoky char pair nicely with Syrah, as do lamb, venison and game birds.

INTENSE, SPICY SYRAH OR SHIRAZ

Delas Les Launes Crozes-Hermitage (France)
Dunham Cellars (Washington State)
M. Chapoutier La Sizeranne Hermitage (France)

PAIRINGS

- Chicken Stir-Fry with Asparagus and Cashews, p. 104
- Carne Asada with Black Beans, p. 146
- Red Wine–Braised Beef, p. 155
- Spicy Ancho Chile Pot Roast, p. 157
- Grilled Coconut-Curry Lamb Chops with Red Pepper Sauce, p. 163
- Mussel-and-Squid Pilaf with Sweet Spices and Dill, p. 216

ROUND, DEEP-FLAVORED SYRAH OR SHIRAZ

d'Arenberg The Footbolt (Australia)
Qupé Central Coast (California)
Torbreck Woodcutters (Australia)

PAIRINGS

- Slow-Cooked Pork Shoulder with Cherry Tomatoes, p. 131
- Spicy Pork Po'boys, p. 134
- Grilled Skirt Steak with Chimichurri Sauce, p. 147
- Roast Leg of Lamb with Red Wine Sauce, p. 158
- Lamb Rogan Josh, p. 162
- Lamb Tagine with Green Olives and Lemon, p. 165

FRUITY, LUSCIOUS SYRAH OR SHIRAZ

Oxford Landing (Australia)
Porcupine Ridge (South Africa)
Woop Woop (Australia)

PAIRINGS

- Baked Penne with Sausage and Creamy Ricotta, p. 84
- Moroccan Chicken with Apricot-and-Olive Relish, p. 102
- Carolina-Style Pulled Pork, p. 131
- Horseradish Brisket, p. 154
- Short Rib Stew, p. 154
- Lamb Chops with Spicy Thai Peanut Sauce, p. 162
- Grilled Beef-and-Lamb Köfte, p. 166

ZINFANDEL

Though Zinfandel is descended from the Croatian grape Crljenak, the wine it produces is entirely Californian in character. The California wine country's warm, easygoing weather gives Zinfandel a jammy, juicy fruitiness (except when it's made into dull, lightly sweet white Zinfandel). Typically high in both alcohol and flavor—boysenberries with a touch of brambly spiciness—Zinfandel is the perfect cookout wine, great with grilled burgers, sausages or chicken, or even chips and dip.

INTENSE, FRUITY ZINFANDEL

Bogle Vineyards Old Vine (California)
Plungerhead (California)
Ravenswood Lodi (California)

PAIRINGS

- Gemelli with Creamy Red Pepper Sauce and Fresh Mozzarella, p. 78
- Mexican-Style Chicken with Penne, p. 82
- Orzo Risotto with Sausage and Artichokes, p. 83
- Leek Mac and Cheese, p. 89
- Sticky Grilled Drumsticks with Plum Sauce, p. 99
- Braised Chicken and Greens with Gnocchi, p. 108
- Grilled Butterflied Turkey with Caraway-Ancho Gravy, p. 120
- Bacon-Crusted Pork Loin Roasts, p. 125
- Harissa-Crusted Pork Crown Roast, p. 125
- Spice-Roasted Ribs with Apricot Glaze, p. 126
- Sticky Marmalade-Glazed Baby Back Ribs, p. 129
- Simple Pork Posole, p. 132
- Mixed Grill with Rib Eyes, Sausages and Bacon Chops, p. 137
- Korean Grilled Beef, p. 150
- Slow-Roasted and Grilled Spiced Short Ribs, p. 153
- Horseradish-Crusted Roast Beef, p. 155
- Beer-Braised Pot Roast, p. 157
- Grilled Mini Meat Loaves, p. 167
- Juicy Texas Burgers, p. 169

recipe index

a

almonds

Almond Cake with Pears and Crème Anglaise, 336, **336**

Almond Cookies with Caramel Dipping Sauce, 353

Almond-Plum Tart, 324, **325**

Almond Toasted Brioche, 304

Apple Tart with Almond Cream, 310

Apricot Blondies, 360

Beet Salad with Candied Marcona Almonds, 46, **47**

Cherry-Almond Clafoutis, 322

Chocolate-Almond Bars, 360

Coconut-Almond Balls with Dried Fruit, 354

Duck with Miso-Almond Butter, 121

Dukka, 383

Farfalle with Zucchini and Parsley-Almond Pesto, 74, **74**

Fruit-and-Nut-Packed Granola, 305

Grilled Tuna with Smoked-Almond Romesco Sauce, 175

Orange-Cardamom Date Bars with a Nutty Crust, 357

Overnight Oatmeal with Almonds and Dried Cranberries, 305

Strawberry-Almond Smoothie, 395

Tropical Fruit Cobbler with Coconut Macaroon Topping, 329

Wine Bar Nut Mix, 34

Yogurt and Apricot Pie with Crunchy Granola Crust, 326

anchovies

Artichokes Stuffed with Anchovies, Garlic and Mint, 231

Green Olive Tapenade, 30

Pan-Seared Skirt Steaks with Anchovies and Lime, **148**, 149

Red Wine Bagna Cauda with Crudités, 33

Roasted Red Peppers with Tonnato Sauce, 228

Skirt Steak with Salsa Verde and Ricotta Salata, 148, **148**

Antipasto Salad with Green Olive Tapenade, 30, **31**

apples

Apple Crostatas, 313, **313**

Apple-Nut Breakfast Porridge, 305

Apple Pandowdy, 313, **313**

Apple Pie Bars, 308, **308**

Apple Rye Turnovers with Celery Seeds, 304

Apple Tart with Almond Cream, 310

Baked Apples with Currants and Sauternes, 308, 309

Double-Crust Apple Pie, **312**, 313

Dutch Apple Pie, 313, **313**

Grilled Cheddar and Ham with Apple and Chutney, 279, **279**

Pan-Seared Sausages with Apples, 137

Pink Applesauce, 383

Puff Pastry Apple Pie, 309

Raisin-Studded Apple Bread Pudding, 309

Rosé Sangria with Cranberries and Apples, 391

Skillet Apple Charlotte, 310

Smoked Ham with Apple-Riesling Sauce, 133

Spiced Fall Fruit Jam with Hazelnuts and Red Wine, 383

Sweet Potato, Chipotle and Apple Soup, 59, **59**

Applesauce, Pink, 383

apricots

Apricot Blondies, 360

Apricot-Glazed Turkey with Fresh Herb Gravy, 117

Chicken Breasts with Apricot-Onion Pan Sauce, 94, **95**

Chocolate Fondue with Fruit and Grilled Pound Cake, 373

Moroccan Chicken with Apricot-and-Olive Relish, 102, **103**

Moroccan Roasted Chicken, 97

Pistachio-Apricot Biryani, 258, **259**

Spice-Roasted Ribs with Apricot Glaze, 126, **127**

Sweet Semolina and Dried-Apricot Pilaf, 326

Yogurt and Apricot Pie with Crunchy Granola Crust, 326

artichokes

Artichokes Stuffed with Anchovies, Garlic and Mint, 231

August Chopped Salad, **38**, 44

Grilled Fontina and Vegetable Antipasti, 279, **279**

Herb-and-Lemon-Poached Baby Artichokes, 232, **233**

Orzo Risotto with Sausage and Artichokes, 83

Pasta with Artichokes and Rouget, 82

Seared Cod with Provençal Vegetables, 186

Tangy Roasted Chicken Thighs with Artichoke Panzanella, 94

Vegetable Stew with Crisp Ham and Garlic, 243

arugula

Arugula-and-Endive Salad with Honeyed Pine Nuts, 42

Arugula Salad with Olives, Feta and Dill, 42

Arugula Salad with Prosciutto and Oyster Mushrooms, 42

Circassian Chicken Salad, 105

Lobster and Fennel Salad, 203

Pan-Seared Tuna Steaks with Capers and Oregano, 175

Pasta Salad with Tomatoes, Arugula, Pine Nuts and Herb Dressing, 76

Pork with Arugula, Prosciutto and Tomatoes, 134

Sun-Dried Tomato Flans with Arugula Salad, 31

Veal Scallopine with Charred Cherry Tomato Salad, 140

Warm Fennel–and–Bitter Greens Salad, 43

Warm Potato Salad with Arugula, 250, **251**

asparagus

Asparagus and Grilled Shiitake with Soy Vinaigrette, 236

Chicken Stir-Fry with Asparagus and Cashews, 104

Creamy Asparagus Soup, 57

recipe index

recipe index

recipe index

recipe index

recipe index

h

recipe index

recipe index

recipe index

recipe index

q

r

recipe index

S

recipe index

recipe index

recipe index

PAGE NUMBERS IN BOLD INDICATE PHOTOGRAPHS

contributors

William Abitbol is the chef and owner of Alfred wine bar in Paris.

Jody Adams, an F&W Best New Chef 1993, is the chef and owner of Rialto in Cambridge, Massachusetts.

Erik Adkins is the bar manager at the Slanted Door in San Francisco.

Bruce Aidells is a chef, cookbook author and the founder of Aidells Sausage Company in San Leandro, California.

Engin Akin is a Turkish food writer, lecturer, cookbook author and media personality.

Ted Allen, author of *The Food You Want to Eat,* hosts Food Network's *Food Detectives.*

Pam Anderson has written five cookbooks, most recently *The Perfect Recipe for Losing Weight and Eating Great.*

Michael Anthony, an F&W Best New Chef 2002, is the executive chef at Gramercy Tavern in New York City.

Jessica Applestone and her husband, **Joshua Applestone,** co-own Fleisher's Meats, a purveyor of grass-fed and organic meats in Kingston, New York.

Cathal Armstrong, an F&W Best New Chef 2006, is the chef and co-owner of Restaurant Eve, Eamonn's and The Majestic, all in Alexandria, Virginia.

Cory Barrett is the executive pastry chef at Lola and Lolita, both in Cleveland, Ohio.

Lidia Bastianich is the chef and owner of six restaurants, including Del Posto and Becco in New York City. The author of several cookbooks, she also hosts the PBS series *Lidia's Family Table.*

Marilyn Batali, the mother of chef Mario Batali, co-founded Salumi in Seattle.

Mario Batali is the chef and co-owner of 14 restaurants in New York, Las Vegas and Los Angeles, as well as the co-owner of Manhattan's Italian Wine Merchants. He is the author of six cookbooks, his latest being *Spain . . . On the Road Again,* the companion book to the PBS series. He also stars on Food Network's *Iron Chef.*

Rick Bayless, an F&W Best New Chef 1988, is the chef and owner of Frontera Grill and Topolobampo in Chicago, the host of the PBS series *Mexico—One Plate at a Time,* the author of numerous cookbooks and the founder of Frontera Foods.

Scott Beattie is a consulting mixologist in Healdsburg, California, and the author of *Artisanal Cocktails.*

Sean Beck is the beverage director at Backstreet Café in Houston.

Olie Berlic, an author and award-winning sommelier, is the president and founder of Beleza Pura Cachaça and Caipirinha.

Nicole Bermensolo co-owns Kyotofu, a dessert bar in New York City.

John Besh, an F&W Best New Chef 1999, is the chef and owner of Restaurant August, Besh Steak and Lüke, all in New Orleans, and La Provence in Lacombe, Louisiana.

Katherine Beto is the beverage director and pastry chef at Braeburn in New York City.

Richard Betts is the wine director at Montagna restaurant in the Little Nell hotel in Aspen, Colorado.

Mark Bittman writes "The Minimalist" column for the *New York Times* and has authored several cookbooks, including *How to Cook Everything.*

Paul Bocuse, a master French chef and restaurateur, owns l'Auberge du Pont de Collonges near Lyon, France, and oversees a chain of brasseries in Lyon.

Jamie Boudreau is a traveling mixologist.

David Bouley, an F&W Best New Chef 1989, is the chef and owner of Bouley, Upstairs at Bouley, Bouley Bakery and Bouley Market, all in New York City. He co-authored *East of Paris: The New Cuisines of Austria and the Danube.*

Daniel Boulud, an F&W Best New Chef 1988, is the chef and owner of Daniel, Café Boulud, DB Bistro Moderne and Bar Boulud in New York City and spin-offs in Palm Beach, Florida, and Las Vegas. He has authored six cookbooks; his most recent is *Braise.*

Wendy Boys is a consulting pastry chef in Vancouver, Canada.

Arnaud Bradol owns Les Fines Gueules, a wine bar in Paris.

Flo Braker is a teacher and the author of four cookbooks, including *Baking for All Occasions.*

Terrance Brennan, an F&W Best New Chef 1995, is the chef and owner of Picholine and Artisanal Bistro in New York City and Artisanal in Chicago. He also founded Artisanal Premium Cheese in New York City.

Stuart Brioza, an F&W Best New Chef 2003, was the chef at Rubicon in San Francisco. He is planning a new restaurant with his wife, Nicole Krasinski.

Jeni Britton is co-owner and pastry chef of Jeni's Splendid Ice Creams based in Columbus, Ohio.

Jim Burke, an F&W Best New Chef 2008, is the chef and co-owner of James in Philadelphia.

Cheryl Burr is the pastry chef at Bacar in San Francisco.

Penelope Casas is a Spanish cookbook author and food writer in New York City.

Tanya Cauthen owns Belmont Butchery in Richmond, Virginia.

Michael Cecconi is the bar manager at Savoy and Back Forty in New York City.

Bob Chambers is a private chef in New York City.

Jerome Chang is the executive pastry chef and co-owner of Dessert Truck, a food truck in New York City.

Ratha Chau is the chef and owner of Kampuchea Restaurant in New York City.

Marisa Churchill, a contestant on *Top Chef* Season 2, is the pastry chef at Pampas in Palo Alto, California, and consulting pastry chef at Zare at Fly Trap in San Francisco.

Melissa Clark is a freelance food writer and columnist for the *New York Times.* She has written and co-authored 18 cookbooks; her most recent is *The Skinny: How to Fit into Your Little Black Dress Forever.*

Tom Colicchio, an F&W Best New Chef 1991, is a cookbook author and the chef and owner of several restaurants around the country, including Manhattan's Craft, Craftbar, Craftsteak and 'wichcraft. He also stars on Bravo's *Top Chef.*

Steve Corry, an F&W Best New Chef 2007, is the executive chef and co-owner of Five Fifty-Five in Portland, Maine.

Chris Cosentino is the executive chef at Incanto in San Francisco.

Gerard Craft, an F&W Best New Chef 2008, is the executive chef and owner of Niche and Veruca Bakeshop & Café in St. Louis.

Payton Curry is the executive chef at Digestif in Scottsdale, Arizona.

Tim Cushman, an F&W Best New Chef 2008, is the chef and co-owner of O Ya in Boston.

Elizabeth Dahl is the pastry chef at Boka in Chicago.

Andrea Day-Boykin is the savory chef and co-owner of Flip Happy Crepes, a trailer in Austin.

Thomas DeGeest is the chef and owner of Wafels & Dinges, a food truck in New York City.

Karen DeMasco, former pastry chef of Craft and Craftbar in New York City, is working on her forthcoming book, *The Craft of Baking,* due out in late 2009.

Semsa Denizsel is the chef and owner of Kantin restaurant in Istanbul.

Kristin Donnelly is an associate food editor at F&W.

Mitchelle Dy is the pastry chef at JiRaffe in Los Angeles.

Todd English, an F&W Best New Chef 1990, is a cookbook author, chef and restaurateur. His restaurants include Olives and Figs outposts throughout the U.S.; among his cookbooks are *The Olives Table* and *The Figs Table.*

Rob Evans, an F&W Best New Chef 2004, is the chef and co-owner of Duckfat and Hugo's in Portland, Maine.

Nick Fauchald, a former F&W food editor, is the editor of *Tasting Table,* an e-newsletter on eating and drinking.

Andrew Feinberg is the chef and co-owner of Franny's in Brooklyn, New York.

Bobby Flay is the chef and owner of five restaurants, including Mesa Grill, with outposts in New York City, Las Vegas and the Bahamas. He stars on Food Network's *Boy Meets Grill* and *Iron Chef.*

Jeremy Fox, an F&W Best New Chef 2008, is the chef and co-owner of Ubuntu in Napa.

Gabriel Frasca is the co-chef and co-owner of Nantucket's Straight Wharf Restaurant and Provisions, a bakery and sandwich shop.

Neal Fraser is the chef and co-owner of BLD Restaurant in Los Angeles.

Clark Frasier is the co-chef and co-owner of Arrows and MC Perkins Cove in Ogunquit, Maine, and Summer Winter in Burlington, Massachusetts.

Nobuo Fukuda, an F&W Best New Chef 2003, is the chef and co-owner of Sea Saw in Scottsdale, Arizona.

Mark Gaier is the co-chef and co-owner of Arrows and MC Perkins Cove in Ogunquit, Maine, and Summer Winter in Burlington, Massachusetts.

Shea Gallante, an F&W Best New Chef 2005, is the executive chef and partner of Cru in New York City.

Gale Gand, an F&W Best New Chef 1994, is the executive pastry chef and partner at Tru in Chicago and the author of several cookbooks, including *Chocolate and Vanilla* and *Gale Gand's Short and Sweet.*

Jose Garces is the executive chef and owner of Amada, Tinto and Distrito restaurants in Philadelphia and Mercat a la Planxa in Chicago.

George Germon is the co-owner and co-chef of Al Forno Restaurant in Providence.

Jessica Gilmartin co-owns Fraîche yogurt café in Palo Alto, California.

David Gingrass is the co-chef and co-owner of TWO in San Francisco.

Hedy Goldsmith is the executive pastry chef at Michael's Genuine Food & Drink in Miami.

Laurent Gras, an F&W Best New Chef 2002, is the chef and co-owner of L$_2$O Restaurant in Chicago.

Koren Grieveson, an F&W Best New Chef 2008, is the chef de cuisine at Avec in Chicago.

Ryan Hardy is the executive chef at the Little Nell hotel in Aspen, Colorado.

Tia Harrison is the head butcher and co-owner of Avedano's Holly Park Market butcher shop in San Francisco.

Chris Hastings is the chef and co-owner of Hot and Hot Fish Club in Birmingham, Alabama.

Molly Hawks-Fagnoni is the co-chef and co-owner of Hawks in Granite Bay, California.

Marcella Hazan is the author of six cookbooks, including *Marcella Says . . .* and *Essentials of Classic Italian Cooking.* Her latest book is *Amarcord: Marcella Remembers,* a memoir.

Maria Helm Sinskey, an F&W Best New Chef 1996, is a cookbook author and the culinary director of Robert Sinskey Vineyards in Napa.

contributors

Joshua Henderson co-owns Skillet, a food truck in Seattle.

Maria Hines, an F&W Best New Chef 2005, is the chef and owner of Tilth in Seattle.

Peter Hoffman is the chef and owner of Savoy and Back Forty in New York City.

Colleen Hubbard is a member of Cook Here and Now, a cooking club in San Francisco.

Amber Huffman is the personal chef for Jess and Barbara Jackson, owners of Kendall-Jackson Wine Estates.

Joseph Humphrey is the executive chef at Cavallo Point in Sausalito, California.

Hung Huynh, the winner of *Top Chef* Season 3, is the corporate chef at Solo in New York City.

Anna Imparato co-owns Montevetrano winery in Campania, Italy.

Raghavan Iyer is the author of *660 Curries.*

Stephanie Izard, the winner of *Top Chef* Season 4, is opening a restaurant in Chicago in 2009.

Pierre Jancou owns Racines, a wine bar in Paris.

Dionicio Jimenez is the executive chef and co-owner of Xochitl in Philadelphia.

Nicolás Jimenez is the chef at Restaurante Túbal in Tafalla, Spain.

Kimball Jones is the corporate chef for Wente Family Estates in Livermore, California, and co-author of *Sharing the Vineyard Table* and *The Casual Vineyard Table.*

Laurence Jossel is the co-owner and executive chef of Nopa in San Francisco.

David Joud is a member of Cook Here and Now, a cooking club in San Francisco.

Jonathan Justus is the executive chef and co-owner of Justus Drugstore in Smithville, Missouri.

Mini Kahlon is a member of Cook Here and Now, a cooking club in San Francisco.

Bernie Kantak is the executive chef at Cowboy Ciao, Kazimierz World Wine Bar and Mexican Standoff, all in Scottsdale Arizona.

Douglas Katz is the executive chef at Fire Food & Drink in Cleveland.

Cyrus Kehyari is the mixologist at 10AK in New York City.

Loretta Keller is the chef and owner of COCO500 in San Francisco and a chef at the Moss Room restaurant at the California Academy of Sciences.

Thomas Keller, an F&W Best New Chef 1988, is the executive chef and owner of eight restaurants, including the French Laundry and Bouchon in Napa Valley and Per Se in New York City. He is the author of several cookbooks, most recently *Under Pressure.*

Marcia Kiesel is the F&W Test Kitchen supervisor and co-author of *The Simple Art of Vietnamese Cooking.*

Johanne Killeen is the co-owner and co-chef of Al Forno Restaurant in Providence.

Defne Koryürek is a food blogger and co-owner of Dükkan butcher shop in Istanbul.

Nicole Krasinski, the former pastry chef at Rubicon in San Francisco, is planning a new restaurant with her husband, chef Stuart Brioza.

Kylie Kwong is the chef and owner of Billy Kwong in Sydney, a cookbook author and the host of *Kylie Kwong: Heart and Soul.*

Brenda Langton is the chef and owner of Cafe Brenda and Spoonriver in Minneapolis and the author of *The Cafe Brenda Cookbook.*

Matt Lewis co-owns Baked in Brooklyn, New York, and is the co-author of *Baked.*

Donald Link is the chef and owner of Herbsaint in New Orleans.

Amanda Lydon, an F&W Best New Chef 2000, is the co-chef and co-owner of Nantucket's Straight Wharf Restaurant and Provisions, a bakery and sandwich shop.

Barbara Lynch, an F&W Best New Chef 1996, is the executive chef and owner of No. 9 Park, B&G Oysters and Sportello restaurants, as well as the Butcher Shop, Drink, Stir, Plum Produce and 9 at Home catering company, all in Boston.

Lachlan Mackinnon-Patterson, an F&W Best New Chef 2005, is the chef and co-owner of Frasca Food and Wine in Boulder, Colorado.

Nick Malgieri is the director of baking at New York City's Institute of Culinary Education and a cookbook author. His latest book is *The Modern Baker.*

Christine Manfield is the chef and owner of Universal in Sydney.

Luke Mangan is the chef and owner of South Food + Wine Bar in San Francisco, Salt in Tokyo and Glass Brasserie in Sydney.

Tony Mantuano is the chef at Spiaggia in Chicago and co-author of *The Spiaggia Cookbook* and *Wine Bar Food.* He is opening a restaurant at the Art Institute of Chicago in May 2009.

Marco Flavio Marinucci is the founder of Cook Here and Now, a cooking club in San Francisco.

Florence Daniel Marzotto, a countess, lives at Villa Nievo in Vicenza, Italy.

Nobu Matsuhisa, an F&W Best New Chef 1989, is the chef and owner of Nobu, Ubon and Matsuhisa restaurants around the world and author of *NOBU: The Cookbook.*

Chris Mattera is the head charcutier at Belmont Butchery in Richmond, Virginia.

Tony Maws, an F&W Best New Chef 2005, is the chef and owner of Craigie On Main in Cambridge, Massachusetts.

Brian McBride is the executive chef at Blue Duck Tavern in Washington, D.C.

Tory McPhail is the executive chef at Commander's Palace in New Orleans.

Janet Mendel is the author of six Spanish cookbooks, most recently *Tapas: A Bite of Spain.*

Junior Merino is the mixologist at Rayuela in New York City.

Tamara Murphy, an F&W Best New Chef 1994, is the chef and co-owner of Brasa in Seattle.

Cindy Mushet is a pastry chef, culinary instructor for Sur La Table, food writer and cookbook author. Her latest release is *The Art & Soul of Baking.*

Jennifer Musty is a baker at Fraîche yogurt café in Palo Alto, California.

Zoe Nathan is the pastry chef at Rustic Canyon in Santa Monica, California.

Magdalena Niementowski is the chef at Cavestève in Paris.

Adina Niemerow is a private chef in San Francisco and the author of *Super Cleanse.*

Thomas Odermatt is the chef and owner of RoliRoti, a mobile rotisserie in San Francisco.

Mary Odson is a baker and co-owner of Big Sugar Bakeshop in Studio City, California.

Bradley Ogden is a San Francisco chef and restaurateur whose restaurants include the Lark Creek Inn in Larkspur, California, and Bradley Ogden in Las Vegas.

Jamie Oliver is a British food writer, cookbook author and host of Food Network's *Jamie at Home.* He oversees the social enterprise Fifteen Foundation and its restaurants around the world.

Daniel Orr is the chef and owner of Farm Bloomington in Bloomington, Indiana.

David Page is a winemaker and co-owner of Shinn Estate Vineyards in Mattituck, New York.

Mike Page is the bar manager at Vie in Western Springs, Illinois.

Gwyneth Paltrow is an Oscar-winning actress who recently starred in the PBS series *Spain . . . On the Road Again* with Mario Batali.

Grace Parisi is F&W's Test Kitchen senior recipe developer and the author of *Get Saucy.*

Peter Pastan is the chef and owner of Obelisk and the owner of 2Amys in Washington, D.C.

Jacqueline Patterson is the cocktail director at Zinnia in San Francisco.

François Payard is the owner of Payard Pâtisserie & Bistro in New York City, with locations in Las Vegas, Tokyo, Yokohama, Seoul and São Paulo. His most recent cookbook is *Chocolate Epiphany.*

Jacques Pépin is an F&W contributing editor, master chef, television personality, cookbook author and the dean of special programs for the French Culinary Institute in New York City.

Adam Perry Lang is the chef and owner of Daisy May's BBQ USA in New York City.

Charles Phan is the executive chef and owner of the Slanted Door in San Francisco and a chef at the Moss Room at the California Academy of Sciences.

Ani Phyo is the author of *Ani's Raw Food Kitchen* and host of *Ani's Raw Food Kitchen Show* on YouTube.

Renato Poliafito co-owns Baked in Brooklyn, New York, and is the co-author of *Baked.*

Monica Pope, an F&W Best New Chef 1996, is the chef and co-owner of T'afia in Houston.

Mike Price is the executive chef and owner of Market Table in New York City.

Michael Psilakis, an F&W Best New Chef 2008, is the executive chef and co-owner of Anthos, Kefi and Mia Dona, all in New York City.

Maurizo Quaranta is the chef at Locanda del Pilone in Alba, Italy.

Joanna Garnett Raeppold ran a food truck in Jersey City, New Jersey, and is now developing a food-studies curriculum for children and a line of baby food.

Jonny Raglin is the principal bartender at Absinthe in San Francisco.

Michael Recchiuti is the chocolatier and owner of Recchiuti Confections in San Francisco.

Julie Reiner is the beverage manager and co-owner of Flatiron Lounge in Manhattan and Clover Club in Brooklyn, New York.

Andrea Reusing is the chef and owner of Lantern in Chapel Hill, North Carolina.

Mathew Rice is the pastry chef at Niche in St. Louis.

Michel Richard is the chef and owner of Citronelle and Central in Washington, D.C., and the consulting chef of Citronelle in Carmel Valley, California, and Citrus at Social in Los Angeles. His cookbooks include *Happy in the Kitchen.*

Eric Ripert is executive chef and co-owner of Le Bernardin in New York City and co-author of three cookbooks, most recently *On the Line: Inside the World of Le Bernardin.*

Lisa Ritter is a baker and co-owner of Big Sugar Bakeshop in Studio City, California.

Patama Roj co-owns Fraîche yogurt café in Palo Alto, California.

Ilene Rosen is the chef at the City Bakery in New York City.

Sam Ross is a bartender at Little Branch in New York City.

Melissa Rubel is F&W's senior associate recipe developer and the associate food editor for F&W cookbooks.

Gabriel Rucker, an F&W Best New Chef 2007, is the chef at Le Pigeon in Portland, Oregon.

Frank Ruta, an F&W Best New Chef 2001, is the chef and owner of Palena in Washington, D.C.

Michael Rypka is executive chef and owner of Torchy's Tacos, a taco truck in Austin.

Suvir Saran is a cookbook author and co-chef and co-owner of Dévi in New York City. His most recent cookbook is *American Masala.*

Richard Sax, who died in 1995, authored eight cookbooks, including *Classic Home Desserts* and *Lighter, Quicker, Better.*

Michael Schlow, an F&W Best New Chef 1996, is a cookbook author and the executive chef and co-owner of five restaurants, including Radius and Great Bay in Boston.

contributors

Michael Schwartz is the chef and owner of Michael's Genuine Food & Drink in Miami.

Kim Schwenke was the pastry chef at Sepia in Chicago.

Barbara Shinn is a co-owner of Shinn Estate Vineyards in Mattituck, New York.

Jane Sigal, an F&W contributing editor, is a cookbook author in New York. She is researching a book on Paris wine bars.

Nancy Silverton, an F&W Best New Chef 1990, is the chef and co-owner of Osteria Mozza and Pizzeria Mozza in Los Angeles, a founder of La Brea Bakery in Los Angeles and the author of seven cookbooks.

Gail Simmons is F&W's special projects director and a judge on *Top Chef.*

Ivor Simmons, the father of F&W's Gail Simmons, is a retired chemical engineer living in Toronto.

Renée Simmons, the mother of F&W's Gail Simmons, is a retired food writer and music manager living in Toronto.

Kerry Simon is the chef and co-owner of Simon and CatHouse, both in Las Vegas, Simon LA in Los Angeles and Impala in San Francisco.

Nigel Slater is a British cook, cookbook author and food writer with a weekly food column in *The Observer.*

Karen Small is the chef and owner of the Flying Fig in Cleveland.

Michael Solomonov is the executive chef and co-owner of Zahav in Philadelphia.

Jeremy Sommer is a member of Cook Here and Now, a cooking club in San Francisco.

Rachel Soszynski is a recipe tester and regular contributor to F&W.

Champe Speidel is the chef and owner of Persimmon in Bristol, Rhode Island.

Susan Spungen is a food writer and cookbook author. Her most recent book is *Recipes: A Collection for the Modern Cook.*

Stu Stein was the chef and owner of Terroir in Portland, Oregon.

Ethan Stowell, an F&W Best New Chef 2008, is the chef and co-owner of Union, Tavolàta, Anchovies & Olives and How to Cook a Wolf, all in Seattle.

Vikram Sunderam is the chef at Rasika in Washington, D.C.

Johnathan Sundstrom, an F&W Best New Chef 2001, is the chef and co-owner of Lark in Seattle.

Allen Susser, an F&W Best New Chef 1991, is the chef and owner of Chef Allen's in Aventura, Florida. He is also a cookbook author and has his own packaged-food line.

Mariah Swan is the pastry chef at BLD Restaurant in Los Angeles.

Michael Symon, an F&W Best New Chef 1998, is the chef and owner of Lola and Lolita restaurants in Cleveland. He also stars on Food Network's *Iron Chef* and *Dinner Impossible.*

Giuseppe Tentori, an F&W Best New Chef 2008, is the executive chef at Boka and Perennial in Chicago.

Rachel Thebault is the confectioner and owner of Tribeca Treats in New York City.

Bradford Thompson, an F&W Best New Chef 2004, is the executive chef at Lever House in New York City.

Gabe Thompson is the chef and co-owner of Dell'anima in New York City.

Jacques Torres is the owner of Jacques Torres Chocolate in New York City, the dean of pastry arts at the French Culinary Institute and the author of several cookbooks, including *Dessert Circus.*

Sue Torres is the chef and owner of Sueños in New York City.

Fabio Trabocchi, an F&W Best New Chef 2002, is the chef and partner of Fiamma in New York City.

Suzanne Tracht, an F&W Best New Chef 2002, is the chef and owner of Jar and Tracht's, both in Los Angeles.

Jerry Traunfeld is the chef and owner of Poppy in Seattle.

Tina Ujlaki is F&W's executive food editor.

Parke Ulrich is the executive chef at Waterbar in San Francisco.

Nancy Verde Barr is a chef, author and teacher who served as executive chef to Julia Child. Her most recent book is *Backstage with Julia.*

Paul Virant, an F&W Best New Chef 2007, is the executive chef and owner of Vie in Western Springs, Illinois.

Stéphane Vivier is a winemaker at HdV Wines in Napa Valley.

Anya von Bremzen is a food and travel writer and the author of several cookbooks.

Jean-Georges Vongerichten, an F&W contributing editor, is the chef and co-owner of numerous restaurants around the world, including Jean Georges in New York City. He is the author of four cookbooks; the most recent is *Asian Flavors of Jean-Georges.*

Marja Vongerichten is the wife of Jean-Georges Vongerichten.

Philip Ward is the head bartender at Death & Co. in New York City.

Eric Warnstedt, an F&W Best New Chef 2008, is the executive chef and co-owner of Hen of the Wood in Waterbury, Vermont.

Carolyn Wente is the president of Wente Vineyards in Livermore, California, and co-author of *The Casual Vineyard Table* and *Sharing the Vineyard Table.*

Neyah White is the bar manager at Nopa in San Francisco.

Jason Wilson, an F&W Best New Chef 2006, is the chef and co-owner of Crush in Seattle.

Elizabeth Woodson is a former art director for F&W.

Joseph Wrede, an F&W Best New Chef 2000, is the chef and owner of Joseph's Table in Taos, New Mexico.

Ritsuko Yamaguchi is the chef at Kyotofu, a dessert bar in New York City.

Julia Yoon is the chef and owner of Seoul on Wheels, a food truck in San Francisco.

Sue Zemanick, an F&W Best New Chef 2008, is the chef at Gautreau's in New Orleans.

photographers

Achilleos, Antonis 51 (top), 96, 97, 248, 315 (right), 325 (right)

Angeles, Cedric 4 (top right), 127 (top), 144 (right), 161 (right), 170, 174 (left), 237, back cover (bison)

Bacon, Quentin 8, 21 (left), 26 (left), 38, 40 (left), 56 (left), 59 (top), 70 (top), 77 (top), 79 (right), 92 (left), 103, 122, 135 (left), 161 (left), 191 (bottom), 201 (right), 227 (left), 233 (right), 262, 280 (top), 290 (right), 303 (left), 308 (left), 325 (left), 332 (left), 345 (left), 353, 363 (left), 366 (top), front cover

Baigre, James 135 (right), 342

Cannon III, Brown 201 (left), 282 (right)

Carter, Earl 59 (bottom), 376, back cover (soup)

Foley, Stephanie 60 (left), 62, 63, 115 (right), 210, 211, 290 (left), 306, 308 (right), 345 (right), 346 (bottom)

French, Andrew flap photograph (Cowin), flap photograph (Heddings)

Gallagher, Dana 23, 109 (top), 130, 164, 177, 184, 202, 212 (left), 270

Geron, Amit 16 (top)

Halenda, Gregor 208

Howard, Rob 4 (lower left and lower right), 10 (left), 196 (left), 212 (right), 259 (left)

Hranek, Matthew 187 (left), 384

Janisch, Frances 26 (right), 29 (bottom), 31 (left), 51 (bottom), 72, 220 (left), 234 (bottom), 319, 366 (bottom)

Kernick, John 15, 47 (left), 48, 67, 124 (left), 148 (top), 169 (right), 191 (top), 196 (right), 205 (top), 246 (right), 251 (top), 272 (left), 294 (top), 299 (right), 386 (left)

Kim, Yunhee 259 (right), 278, 279, 299 (left)

Lagnese, Francesco 181 (right)

Linder, Lisa 115 (left), 144 (left), 233 (left), 396 (bottom right)

Miller, Ellie 36 (top), 294 (bottom), 394 (right)

Morrell, Martin 288

Ngo, Ngoc Minh 285

Nicolas, David 40 (right)

Nilsson, Marcus 52 (left), 56 (right), 275

Okada, Kana 47 (right), 69 (right), 74 (left), 80, 83 (right), 88, 113, 156, 157, 215 (top), 230, 244, 256 (right), 282 (left), 358, 359

Pearson, Victoria 6, 60 (right), 315 (left), 396 (bottom left)

Poulos, Con 124 (right), 127 (bottom), 139, 328, 334, 341, 369, back cover (cookies)

Prince, David 396 (top right),

Rupp, Tina 10 (right), 16 (bottom), 21 (right), 31 (right), 36 (bottom), 52 (right), 74 (right), 79 (left), 83 (left), 90, 95 (bottom), 100, 106, 109 (bottom), 142, 151, 169 (left), 172, 174 (right), 181 (left), 188, 207, 227 (right), 241 (right), 251 (bottom), 267 (top), 280 (bottom), 303 (right), 312, 313, 336 (right), 346 (top), 380, 381

Schaeffer, Lucy 18, 19, 29 (top), 69 (left), 92 (right), 95 (top), 148 (bottom), 187 (right), 215 (bottom), 220 (right), 234 (top), 238, 241 (left), 267 (bottom), 272 (right), 320, 321, 332 (right), 374, 386 (right), 389, 396 (top left)

Shroff, Zubin 225

Smart, Anson 4 (top left), 194

Tinslay, Petrina 54, 77 (bottom), 118, 218, 246 (left), 363 (right)

Watson, Simon 336 (left)

Webber, Wendell T. 78, 136, 240, 393, 394 (left)

Williams, Anna 32, 45, 70 (bottom), 85, 205 (bottom), 256 (left)

measurement guide

Basic Measurements

GALLON	QUART	PINT	CUP	OUNCE	TBSP	TSP	DROPS
1 gal	4 qt	8 pt	16 c	128 fl oz			
½ gal	2 qt	4 pt	8 c	64 fl oz			
¼ gal	1 qt	2 pt	4 c	32 fl oz			
	½ qt	1 pt	2 c	16 fl oz			
	¼ qt	½ pt	1 c	8 fl oz	16 tbsp		
			⅞ c	7 fl oz	14 tbsp		
			¾ c	6 fl oz	12 tbsp		
			⅔ c	5⅓ fl oz	10⅔ tbsp		
			⅝ c	5 fl oz	10 tbsp		
			½ c	4 fl oz	8 tbsp		
			⅜ c	3 fl oz	6 tbsp		
			⅓ c	2⅔ fl oz	5⅓ tbsp	16 tsp	
			¼ c	2 fl oz	4 tbsp	12 tsp	
			⅛ c	1 fl oz	2 tbsp	6 tsp	
				½ fl oz	1 tbsp	3 tsp	
					½ tbsp	1½ tsp	
						1 tsp	60 drops
						½ tsp	30 drops

U.S. to Metric Conversions

The conversions in the first three columns are approximations. For more precise conversions, use the formulas to the right.

VOLUME		WEIGHT		TEMPERATURE		CONVERSION FORMULAS
1 tsp	= 5 ml	1 oz	= 28 g	475°F	= 246°C	tsp x 4.929 = ml
1 tbsp	= 15 ml	¼ lb (4 oz)	= 113 g	450°F	= 232°C	tbsp x 14.787 = ml
1 fl oz	= 30 ml	½ lb (8 oz)	= 227 g	425°F	= 218°C	fl oz x 29.574 = ml
¼ c	= 59 ml	¾ lb (12 oz)	= 340 g	400°F	= 204°C	c x 236.588 = ml
½ c	= 118 ml	1 lb (16 oz)	= ½ kg	375°F	= 191°C	pt x .473 = L
¾ c	= 177 ml			350°F	= 179°C	qt x .946 = L
1 c	= 237 ml	LENGTH		325°F	= 163°C	oz x 28.35 = g
1 pt	= ½ L	1 in	= 2.5 cm	300°F	= 149°C	lb x .453 = kg
1 qt	= 1 L	5 in	= 12.7 cm	275°F	= 135°C	in x 2.54 = cm
1 gal	= 4 L	9 in	= 23 cm	250°F	= 121°C	(°F−32) x .556 = °C